Days Afield

Exploring Wetlands in the Chesapeake Bay Region

William S. Sipple

GATEWAY PRESS, INC.
Baltimore, MD   1999

Please direct all correspondence and book orders to:

William S. Sipple
512 Red Bluff Court
Millersville, MD 21108

Library of Congress Catalog Card Number 99-73329
ISBN 0-9673028-1-1

Published for the author by
Gateway Press, Inc.
1001 N. Calvert Street
Baltimore, MD 21202

Printed in the United States of America

Days Afield

To my wife Geri for her understanding, patient understanding, without which I could not have written this book.

And to pink lady's slippers and Virginia bluebells -- may they be with us forever; may their flowers never wilt.

Another Book By William S. Sipple

Through The Eyes Of A Young Naturalist

CONTENTS

FIGURES

*Nature is a language,
and every new fact that we learn is
a new word; but rightly seen, taken all together,
it is not merely a language, but the language
put together into a most significant and universal book.
I wish to learn the language, not that I may learn a new set of
nouns and verbs, but that I may read the great
book which is written in that tongue.*

RALPH WALDO EMERSON
1833

PREFACE

The years have a way of caring for things that do
not seek the safety of print.
- LOREN EISELEY, *The Unexpected Universe*

I suppose it was a normal day for most people in the spring of 1971 when I drove down the Delmarva Peninsula on Route 301 and crossed the William Preston Lane, Jr. Memorial Bridge (Chesapeake Bay Bridge). It was not for me, however, for I was traversing unfamiliar territory and heading for Annapolis, Maryland and my first job interview since finishing graduate school at the University of Pennsylvania. My anxiety grew with the miles. For sure, I could relate to the flat agricultural fields, the oldfields dotted with invading red cedars, the wood edges dense with young even-aged stands of sweet gum, the swampy floodplains, and the patchy oak-pine and oak-beech forests. The terrain and vegetation were not all that different from the Inner Coastal Plain in South Jersey where I grew up. Not so, however, when I crossed onto Kent Island. Large roadside marshes suddenly appeared, then the Chesapeake Bay with its far shore looming in the background. It was just so formidable I guess, especially knowing my interview was imminent. In fact, it was downright scary and my reaction was something like: "What the hell am I doing here?" I had never seen anything like it. The Maryland state map did not help matters either. It clearly showed that I was in a rather narrow part of the bay, and suggested that the Kent Island marshes were quite inconsequential compared to those of the lower Eastern Shore, an area I had heard so much about years before. Obviously, my anxiety to a large extent related to fear of the unknown -- the vast unfamiliar area, the pending interview, the uncertainty associated with potentially my first full-time professional job.

I was interviewed in Annapolis by Herbert M. Sachs, a man whom I would eventually learn befriended everyone and was well respected as a high level manager at the Maryland Department of Natural Resources. I felt quite comfortable being interviewed by Herb. I liked what I heard, and I guess Herb did too, for I started working for the Maryland Department of Natural Resources in its tidal wetland regulatory program on June 14, 1971.

Not long after moving to Maryland, I was ground-truthing the State's draft tidal wetland maps by foot and boat far down the Eastern Shore with my colleagues, Dick Wheeler, Harold Cassell, and Ray Schwartz. And with that, I experienced, for the first time, the vast Eastern Shore marshlands, not only those on the Chesapeake Bay proper, but also those along some of its major tributaries -- the Choptank, Nanticoke, Wicomico, and Pocomoke Rivers.

I worked for the Department of Natural Resources for about eight years, all the time building a keen interest in Maryland's wetlands, then moved on to a similar position with the U.S. Environmental Protection Agency in Washington, D.C. in 1979. Although I became involved nationally with wetlands in my new position, I remained active in the Chesapeake Bay Region, sometimes through the Agency, sometimes through other means. Many of these field experiences were associated with courses I taught for various educational institutions; others resulted from trips associated with an informal botanical group I organized years ago and from trips with my two sons.

These various field experiences served as fodder for this book. I could not have written it without them, and they are relied upon often in the chapters that follow. Similarly, I probably could not have written the book if I had not documented my outdoor and natural history observations and experiences since moving to Maryland in an extensive journal, the *Maryland Journal: Outdoor and Natural History Observations and Experiences*, which is now printed in six volumes totaling more than 1,200 pages covering 1971-1997 (1-6). My *Maryland Journal* for 1998 and 1999 will be printed in the year 2000 in either one or two volumes depending upon its total length.

Ever since my boyhood days in New Jersey, I have persistently maintained outdoor and natural history records and documented field observations. Moreover, I feel that such information is invaluable and that it should be published where appropriate, or otherwise archived in public institutions. My determination in this effort resulted in the printing of the

Jersey Journal: Outdoor and Natural History Observations and Experiences in 1992 (7), which covers a period between 1955 and 1971, and my first book, *Through the Eyes of a Young Naturalist*, in 1991 (8). By recording and archiving this technical material, I have preserved these observations and experiences and set some baselines against which future field workers can compare notes and document environmental and land-use changes.

My current book is a spin-off from the *Maryland Journal*. It represents considerable field work in the Chesapeake Bay Region -- somewhere in excess of 1,500 field trips spanning almost three decades. I have also incorporated considerable literature on the Region's wetlands. Being the bibliophile that I am, most of the material was readily available at home, from my extensive files and private library. Therefore, the technical information incorporated should be useful for professionals working in the field or otherwise interested in wetlands. In using considerable anecdotal material, I have also striven to produce a book readily understandable and interesting to the general public -- at least those people interested in natural history and the outdoors. Hopefully, I have met that goal.

Chapter One includes a running dialogue between an instructor (me) and his students as he takes the readers down the Delmarva Peninsula on one of the overnight field trips he annually led for the Graduate School, U.S. Department of Agriculture between 1972 and 1990. To some extent, this serves as an introduction to the chapters that follow. Chapter Two is on a sentimental favorite of mine -- freshwater marshes, both nontidal and tidal. Although substantially rewritten and supplemented, much of the material in this chapter was originally published in the *Atlantic Naturalist* in 1991, my first attempt at natural history writing for public consumption (9). Chapter Three is on the extensive brackish tidal marshes of Dorchester and Somerset Counties, which total about 135,000 acres and are so important to waterfowl and furbearers (10). To complete the range of tidal marshes in the Region, the low diversity but highly productive salt marshes of Maryland's coastal bays are discussed in Chapter Four. The Pocomoke River and Nanticoke River watersheds are treated separately in Chapters Five and Six. The extensive

Pocomoke Chapter is an updated version of an earlier natural history paper I wrote on the Pocomoke and printed in 1992; the shorter Nanticoke Chapter is new. The mysterious potholes of the Delmarva Peninsula, interesting nontidal depressional wetlands supporting numerous rare and endangered plants and animals, are addressed in Chapter Seven.

For a number of years, I have been very interested in the botanical finds of a turn-of-the-century botanist, Dr. Charles C. Plitt. Dr. Plitt regularly led field excursions into what he called the wilds of Anne Arundel, frequently coming into Anne Arundel County from Baltimore by train, particularly when he was visiting areas between Baltimore and Annapolis. Chapter Eight is devoted to his exploits. It also presents information on some botanically interesting sites in the County apparently unknown to Dr. Plitt and his followers.

Starting in 1987 and continuing well into the 1990s, I annually led a number of field excursions in the Chesapeake Bay Region with an informal group of botanical enthusiasts. These excursions involved ex-students of mine, friends, and other folks, assuming they had similar interests and were willing to really rough it, sometimes getting quite wet and muddy up to the waist. Eventually, my companions were mostly people from the Maryland or Delaware Natural Heritage Programs, who organized and led some of the trips. In Chapter Nine, I present verbatim accounts of some of these forays as documented in my *Maryland Journal*. The last chapter covers select examples of a group of small but interesting streams that I collectively call the Sleepers -- namely, Severn Run, Piscataway Creek, Mattawoman Creek, Zekiah Swamp Run, and the St. Mary's River -- that occur on the lower western shore of the Chesapeake Bay.

All of these chapters are interrelated and frequently cross-referenced. For example, some of the sites visited in the field trip down the Delmarva are also mentioned in the chapters on the brackish marshes of Dorchester and Somerset Counties, the salt marshes of Maryland's coastal bays, the Pocomoke River, and the Nanticoke River. Select trips with the informal botanical group also occur in the chapters on the Pocomoke River, the Nanticoke River, the wilds of Anne Arundel, and the Sleepers.

Having been personally and professionally involved in various capacities with wetlands in the Chesapeake Bay Region for almost thirty years, I have witnessed some rather dramatic and deploring man-induced changes -- some from lack of governmental regulation or policies at various levels, others through governmental regulation or policies. Many of these changes, like the extensive saltmarsh losses in the Ocean City area, are history, but represent pungent lessons that perhaps will not be readily forgotten. Others, like the drastic downcutting (incisement) of some of our streams, are ongoing today and more insidious. Hopefully, my views on the ongoing changes will be convincing to those potentially influential in correcting the problems, which, in the case of the stream degradation, will probably require major rethinking of our storm water management policies. Examples of these environmental insults are presented in Chapters One, Four, Five, Seven, and Eight. Given the nature of this book, I deemed it appropriate to state my views in this regard.

After considerable thought about moving all scientific names into an appendix, I chose not to. However, since the scientific names will be distractive to some readers, I have attempted to minimize their use by including them only for the first occurrence of a given species in each chapter. A major exception to this is for Chapters One, Eight, Nine, and Ten. These chapters include verbatim accounts taken from my *Maryland Journal* or otherwise quoted material, which, in some instances, have numerous scientific names, generally in lists. I have also included separate indices for plant and animal scientific names. These refer to the pages where a species is mentioned by either its scientific name or common name.

All of the scientific and common names used for rare plants and animals are, with few exceptions, consistent with applicable state Natural Heritage Program lists. Plant scientific names otherwise follow the nomencla-ture in the *National List of Scientific Plant Names* (11). Likewise, except for plants on the state Natural Heritage Program lists, plant common names generally follow those given in one or more of the derivative regional lists of the *National List of Plant Species that Occur in Wetlands: 1988 National Summary* (12); otherwise, they follow *Plants: Alphabetical Listing of Scientific Names* (13). However, I was not consistent in my use of common names for the following reasons: Quoted passages sometime contained common names other than those used in the references listed above; alternate common names for the same species were sometimes used in different quotations; the common names for the same species sometimes varied even between the Maryland and Delaware Heritage Programs; at times, I used a name that was in more common usage in the Chesapeake Bay Region or was of my own preference. For example, I see no utility to the name uptight sedge over the commonly used tussock sedge for *Carex stricta* in the Chesapeake Bay Region. Likewise, names like marsh elder for *Iva frutescens* and path rush for *Juncus tenuis* are certainly more appropriate for the Region than big-leaf sumpweed and poverty rush. All of this, of course, is indicative of the longtime problem, if not impossibility, of trying to standardize common names over large geographical areas. Few field people in the Chesapeake Bay Region, no doubt, would ever agree to call *Carex stricta* the uptight sedge no matter who suggested it.

For animals other than those on the Maryland or Delaware Heritage Program lists, I have used the scientific nomenclature that was prevalent at the time the data were recorded, or at least that which occurred in the field guides or technical books I generally use. Except for the rare species and a few other exceptions, I have not used scientific names for birds.

A number of species mentioned in this book are given rarity rankings based upon Natural Heritage Program lists from Maryland and Delaware. Unless otherwise indicated, I have used the most recent official state lists available to me (i.e., December 31, 1996 for Maryland plants; October 28, 1997 for Maryland animals; March 1998 for Delaware plants; August 1997 for Delaware animals). In this regard, the reader is forewarned that the status of what is considered rare, threatened, or endangered by state Natural Heritage Programs and individuals collecting distributional data may change due to new knowledge that results from herbarium research and particularly new field investigations.[1] Not uncommonly, soon after a rarity status is published, additional data surfaces, such as a new county or state record, or another study concludes differently. For the latest official rarity status of the species listed, one should always check with the appropriate state Natural Heritage Program. An explanation of the rarity statuses used by the States of Maryland and Delaware can be found in Tables I and II, respectively, in Chapter Two.

Verbatim accounts from my *Maryland Journal* sometimes include information in brackets, which is material that I added to my handwritten version when it was originally typed. The purpose of the bracketed material is to clarify points or expound on phenomena. Either the scientific names or common names are often also added in brackets.

All references are numbered chapter by chapter and have been placed in a literature cited section immediately following the last chapter. Because it is repeatedly referenced in the text, I have added my *Maryland Journal* only to the list of references cited in the preface, where it first appears. In each instance, however, reference to it in the text refers to one or more of the six volumes of the *Maryland Journal: Outdoor and Natural History Observations and Experiences* printed either in 1993 (Volumes I-II) or 1998 (Volumes III-VI). Generally, I simply refer to it as the *Maryland Journal* or just the *Journal* in the text.

One last point about writing this book -- it has been fun, I suppose to some extent because I enjoy reading this type of natural history material. I attribute most of my enjoyment, however, to the many memories it engendered, good memories. Memories of trips with my sons, with my students, with my friends, with my colleagues. What a wealth of memories. Perhaps some of you will also appreciate these memories since you experienced them with me. For those of you who did not, perhaps you will benefit

---

[1] Actually, the responsibility for rare, threatened, and endangered species in Maryland currently falls under the auspices of the Wildlife and Heritage Division of the Maryland Department of Natural Resources. In this book, however, I have maintained the use of the name Maryland Natural Heritage Program since it is used often in the quoted materials from my *Journal*.

vicariously, assuming I did a good job of conveying them. If I have, maybe someday you too will keep a journal, something I highly recommend.

ACKNOWLEDGEMENTS

I am very grateful to the following people for reviewing various chapters of this book: Carlo Brunori (Chapter Three), Frank Hirst (Chapter Seven), Randy Kerhin (Chapter Four), Haven Kolb (Chapter Eight), Bill McAvoy (Chapters Six and Seven), Brook Meanley (Chapter Three), Matt Perry (Chapter Three), Jan Reese (Chapter Three), Colby Rucker (Chapter Eight), Mark Stolt (Chapter Seven), Glenn Therres (Chapter Three), Ralph Tiner (Chapters One, Two, Four, and Five), John Paul Tolson (Chapter One), and Wayne Tyndall (Chapters Six, Seven, and Eight). In addition, a published, earlier version of Chapter Two on freshwater wetlands was reviewed by Dave Davis and Wayne Klockner. Similarly, an earlier version of Chapter Five on the Pocomoke watershed was reviewed by Gene Cooley, Joe DaVia, Glenn Eugster, Kathy Fisher, Frank Hirst, Wayne Klockner, Dave Lee, Arnold (Butch) Norden, and Ron Wilson. I certainly appreciate their comments, suggestions and encouragement. I would also like to thank Judy Broersma-Cole, Jeannie Colandrea, Joe DaVia, and Bob Franzen for their continuing support and help in proofreading the entire book. They caught many simple mistakes that I probably would have missed even if I read the final draft numerous times. The periodic guidance of Ann Hughes of Gateway Press, Inc. in formating the text was likewise very helpful.

Although the majority of the information used in writing this book came from either my *Maryland Journal* or my own library and files, this was not necessarily the case with the original version (1992) of what is now Chapter Five, on the Pocomoke watershed. For that effort, I had considerable help from a number of individuals and institutions. Much of the original information was gathered at libraries of the U.S. Geological Survey's Patuxent Wildlife Research Center in Laurel, Maryland and the Academy of Natural Sciences in Philadelphia. Lynda Garrett and Wanda Manning at the Center's library were particularly helpful in gaining access to its rich supply of journals, as was staff at the library of the Academy of

Natural Sciences. Ernie Schuyler at the latter institution also made available a complete set of *Bartonia*, a copy of Thomas Nuttall's 1818 flora, and Nuttall's voucher specimen of *Persea borbonia*. Art Tucker of Delaware State University sent me a copy of Charles S. Sargent's letter to H.M. Canby, which reference John Muir's trip to the Delmarva Peninsula. George Franchois of the Environmental Protection Agency's library in Washington, D.C. was helpful in obtaining through inter-library loan, a copy of John K. Small's "Peninsula Delmarva" and Roland M. Harper's "A forest reconnaissance of the Delmarva Peninsula." Sam Bennett sent me a packet of background information from his files on the Pocomoke State Forest and Park. Rick Ayella supplied me with copies of the State's tidal wetland maps for the lower Pocomoke River. This information was very helpful and I would like to thank all of these folks and their institutions for their invaluable aid.

Detailed information was also assembled by a number of individuals specifically for the original version of Chapter Five. Gene Cooley of the Maryland Natural Heritage Program contributed a printout of the rare, threatened and endangered species of the Pocomoke watershed; Wayne Klockner and Mary Droege of the Maryland Office of The Nature Conservancy did likewise for the Nassawango watershed. Gene also supplied herbarium records from the Maryland Natural Heritage Program files for a select number of rare fresh tidal aquatics. Glenn Therres made available very useful data from the Maryland and District of Columbia Breeding Bird Atlas Project. Linda Shaffer and Ralph Tiner of the U.S. Fish and Wildlife Service provided up-to-date wetland acreages for the Pocomoke watershed based upon the National Wetlands Inventory. Jim White of the Delaware Nature Society provided the information on the barking treefrog. To all of these people and their institutions, I am extremely grateful. I also appreciate the support and cooperation of my friends, Jack and Marion Spurling, who reside along the lower Pocomoke, and the cooperation of their neighbors, Chris and Maggie Rice, in obtaining access to some of its wetlands. Similarly, Elder Ghigiarelli provided a considerable amount of wetland inventory data on the Patuxent River's tidal wetlands for the original (1990) version of what is now Chapter Two.

I would also like to once again thank Glenn Eugster for his encouragement and for getting me involved in a workshop on the Pocomoke River in 1992. Had I not gotten involved and produced the original paper, as well as the earlier paper leading to Chapter Two, perhaps I would never have been written this book.

As was the case with the original version of Chapter Five, a number of individuals kindly supplied me with the material that I lacked, but felt essential, to complete this book. For Chapter Three, Glenn Therres provided up-to-date data on the bald eagle nesting in Maryland; Matt Perry supplied papers containing recent waterfowl data; Larry Hindman also provided some waterfowl data. For Chapter Five, Bill Grogan provided information and reprints on reptiles and amphibians occurring in the Pocomoke watershed. For Chapter Seven, Jim and Amy White submitted a list of reptiles and amphibians found in Delmarva potholes; Bill McAvoy provided a list of rare plants associated with these unique wetlands. For Chapter Eight, Wayne Tyndall forwarded site records and related material on the sweet pine sap; Lynn Davidson made a photocopy of Charles C. Plitt's journal available for review at the Maryland Department of Natural Resources; Jennifer Meininger supplied site data for the climbing fern on a Severn River tributary; Dennis Whigham conveyed soil chemistry data for a number of the Anne Arundel County bogs; Colby Rucker forwarded site data on wild lupine; Judy Broersma-Cole introduced me to Blackhole Creek Bog, supplied her floristic data for that site, and conveyed a list of introduced pitcher plants found at Round Bay Bog; Judy Broersma-Cole, Keith Underwood, and Phil Sheridan showed me Arden Bog and provided data on their southern white cedar survey in Anne Arundel County. For Chapter Nine, Chris Heckscher compiled a bird list from the Hickory Point Swamp based upon our trip to the Pocomoke River in 1997. For Chapter Ten, Arnold (Butch) Norden advised me on the taxonomic status of the Zekiah stone fly. The computerized prints of the aerial photographs in Chapters One, Two, Three, Four, Five, and Seven were kindly prepared by Rick Ayella of the Maryland Department of the Environment. Porter (Buck) Reed and Andrew Cruz of the U.S. Fish and Wildlife Service provided a computerized version of the Maryland flora that was very helpful in compiling my plant scientific name index. To all of these people and their institutions, I am deeply indebted. I have been utterly amazed at the cooperation I have received, which meant a great deal to me considering that I have been exploring Maryland's wetlands for almost thirty years and wanted so much to write this book.

Congratulations also go to my colleague, Tom Danielson, for his excellent illustrations, which add considerably to this book. Tom also aided in scanning the illustrations into the text. I especially want to thank Reed Pedlow for his wonderful caricature of me in Chapter One, something I will treasure forever. In addition, I used a number of photographs. Some of these were my own; others were sent to me over the years by students, friends, and colleagues. Unfortunately, except for a few instances, the sources of the photographs I received were not indicated. Where known, however, I have acknowledged the photographer in the caption.

Most importantly though, I thank all of my botanical friends, particularly the persistent regulars like Yvette Ogle, Dwight Fielder, Gene Cooley, and Wilbur Rittenhouse, for the numerous interesting adventures, generally quite wet and muddy adventures, we shared while exploring the Chesapeake Bay Region's wetlands. Many of our memories, of course, are incorporated into this book. In that regard too, I want to express my sincere appreciation to my two sons, Mike and Sean, whose names surface so often in my *Maryland Journal*, given the numerous field experiences we have had together. Mike, by the way, is the mud-splattered boy on the cover (then about age eight) holding a bullfrog that he caught while on one of our trips. And last, but most importantly, I thank my wife Geri for her patience and understanding during the preparation of this book. For both of us, but particularly her, sacrifices were made and opportunities were missed, as I labored persistently for many days and long nights in my basement sanctum seeing the book finally come to fruition.

ONE

A FIELD TRIP DOWN
THE DELMARVA

Tell me and I will forget;
Show me and I may remember;
Involve me and I will understand.
-- CHINESE PROVERB

IN 1972, only one year after I moved down from New Jersey to take my first full-time environmental job with the Maryland Department of Natural Resources, the opportunity surfaced to teach an aquatic and wetland ecology course at the Graduate School, U.S. Department of Agriculture in Washington, D.C.[1] This opportunity came about when a colleague of mine in the Department's tidal wetlands division, Dick Wheeler, signed up for that very course only to be told at the first meeting that the instructor was no longer available to teach it, and that it would be canceled if a replacement could not be immediately found. Dick's supervisor, who was also my supervisor, suggested that maybe I should inquire about teaching the course. I did, which soon found a man on a motorcycle arriving at my apartment complex in Glen Burnie to interview me. That man, Bob Lavell, had likewise signed up for the course and was also somewhat involved with the administration of the program under which it fell. We discussed the class content and the philosophy behind the overall natural history program, a program administered jointly with the Audubon Naturalist Society of the

---

[1]To quote from a program catalogue: "The Graduate School is a nonprofit organization and receives no appropriated funds. Its only source of income comes from tuition and fees. The school was established in 1921 by the Secretary of Agriculture to provide people with opportunities for career advancement. Since that time, the school has helped more than 400,000 people with their continuing education objectives. The school is open to all adults regardless of their place of employment or educational background."

Central Atlantic States.[2] Within a few days, Bob and I were in Frederick County, Maryland checking out field sites for the first class field trip. I suppose Bob was impressed by the interview for I promptly got the job -- on the spot as I recall. Perhaps he had no choice, considering that the course had already started without an instructor. So it was a mad scramble for me that first year, especially since the course, which was called Aquatic and Marsh Ecosystems, covered not only wetlands, but also estuaries, coastal marine environments, ponds, lakes, and streams. Evidently, the course was a success too, for I continued to teach it for eighteen years. A second course, Dune, Marsh, and Aquatic Plant Identification, soon followed when yet another instructor departed. Over that eighteen year period, I got to see a lot of the Coastal Plain in Maryland, as well as some areas around Frederick and Urbana and the Catoctins near Thurmont, while leading field trips for these courses.

I learned a lot from my involvement in the Graduate School courses, a lot about not only Maryland's wetlands, but also wetland ecology and management. In addition, I met many people with diverse educational, institutional, and technical backgrounds -- people from State and Federal agencies, conservation groups, environmental consulting firms, engineering firms, to name a few -- all of whom were very enthusiastic about wetlands. There were biologists, botanists, ecologists, wildlife specialists, and foresters; planners, consultants, engineers, and economists; housewives and retirees; at least one physicist and even a few attorneys. Although I doubt that my continuing education courses were a significant factor in this regard, many of these folks moved forward from either a technical or management perspective within their institutions; some even changed fields to become more involved environmentally, particularly with wetlands. I have interacted professionally

---

[2] To quote a 1985 Faculty Handbook, The Natural History Field Studies Program, which is co-sponsored by the Graduate School and the Audubon Naturalist Society of the Central Atlantic States, "...is designed to provide practical training in basic nature study techniques, a stimulating introduction to the natural history of the Central Atlantic Region, and a comprehensive, integrated approach to the study of ecology in order to give people the information they need to appreciate the natural world and to make informed choices regarding the effect of their actions on the environment."

with many of these people for many years now. And as fate would have it, one student, Dave Davis, would eventually hire me away from the Department of Natural Resources in 1979, which substantially catapulted my own career too. This is a good example of being in the right place at the right time. Dave took my course in the early years, five years or so later he still remembered me -- when I inquired, he hired. I remember a comment he made to me many years later, which was something like: "When we decided to go with you, John Crowder [my immediate supervisor after I was hired] and I figured that, if you didn't work out, we knew we would at least be obtaining a large library of technical materials." How true that was, and if they were to hire me today, I doubt that I could fit considering the collection of books and other technical materials I have now amassed! Thanks again Dave! And guess what -- Dave made out too, for he met JoAnn in the same class, who was soon to become his wife!

But what I liked the most about these people was their enthusiasm to learn about wetlands and their willingness, almost to the person, to follow me into some of the wettest and muddiest sites one could imagine. True, there were a few who held back, like the trimly attired lady that stood and watched us for a couple of hours from the edge of the neat Snug Harbor Marsh in Worcester County because she did not want to get her shoes muddy. Unknowingly perhaps, the majority understood my philosophy: To get a good feel for a wetland, you literally have to feel it. Needless to say, they got to feel it, for my trips generally found us quite messy by the end of the day -- boardwalk field lecturing was mostly out of the picture. Based upon the repeated positive feedback over the years from my students, the trips for both courses were a resounding success. I had a great tribute from one of my classes in 1988 when, Reed Pedlow, an illustrator taking the class, made an excellent caricature of "a mad man in the swamp" all dressed out in field gear, with plants in one hand and a soil probe in the other. The students all signed the illustration and it was presented to me at my last lecture that year (Figure 1). Quite frankly, I don't think anything could ever top that. It made me feel really good.

3

THE JOY OF LEARNING HAS NO EQUAL
WHEN SERVED UP BY A MADMAN IN THE SWAMP.

Figure 1. A caricature of the author presented to him by students
in his wetland ecology class in 1988.

You too can capitalize vicariously on these neat experiences that my students and I had in the 1970s and 1980s as you read this Chapter, which will take you down the Delmarva Peninsula on a fall overnight field trip in the mid-1970s. The trip, of course, is really a composite of what we saw and experienced over that eighteen year period; therefore, it is an expression of what could potentially be seen as opposed to what was seen on any given fall weekend. In other words, we experienced these phenomena on various trips as opposed to any one trip. So keep that in mind.

This Chapter also contains a running dialogue between the instructor and his students, which is given in the form of numerous quotes. This is not an attempt to present exactly what we said on those trips; that would be impossible, since my lectures in the field were not recorded. On the other hand, the information conveyed in the trip quotes is not exactly fabricated either. Remember, I led these same trips for eighteen years; my memory has not failed me yet. Therefore, the quotes are quite representative of what my students and I observed, and what I lectured about. They are also presented within the context of the time period involved, the mid-1970s, so keep that in mind as you read them. In addition, some of the material presented was derived from my *Maryland Journal* or my files for the course.

Another way that you can match these experiences, or perhaps even exceed them, is to take the trip yourself by following the directions given below and the accompanying map (Figure 2). There is nothing like first hand experience when it comes to natural history and the outdoors. But take a friend, colleague, or relative -- the shared experiences always seem more rewarding. If I did a good job of writing this Chapter, maybe you will do both, like I did when I read Brook Meanley's book, *Birds and Marshes of the Chesapeake Bay Country* (1). Years ago, after being with the Department of Natural Resources for a few years, I naively thought I was pretty knowledgeable about the Chesapeake Bay's wetlands -- knowledgeable that is, until I read Meanley's book. Boy, was I wrong. Make no doubt about it, Meanley's book stimulated me to get into the field to experience the sites and phenomena presented so well. I highly recommend it.

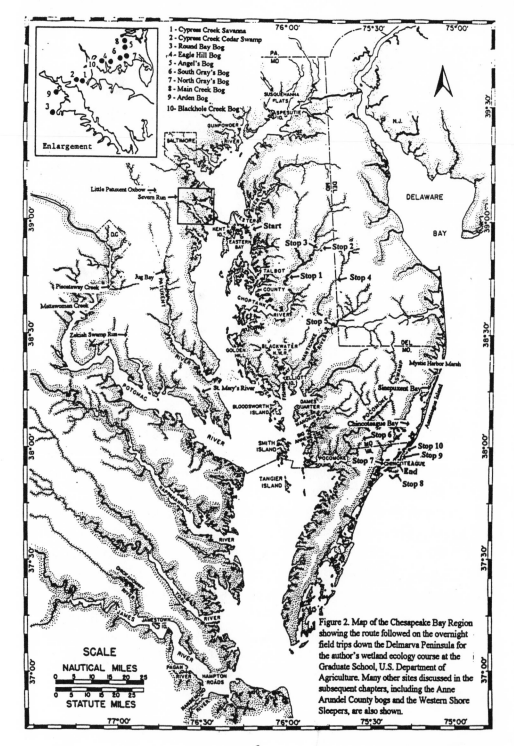

1 - Cypress Creek Savanna
2 - Cypress Creek Cedar Swamp
3 - Round Bay Bog
4 - Eagle Hill Bog
5 - Angel's Bog
6 - South Gray's Bog
7 - North Gray's Bog
8 - Main Creek Bog
9 - Arden Bog
10- Blackhole Creek Bog

Enlargement

Little Patuxent Oxbow →
Severn Run →

Start

Stop 3   Stop 2

Stop 1   Stop 4

Stop 5

Piscataway Creek

Mattawoman Creek

Zekiah Swamp Run →

St. Mary's River

Mystic Harbor Marsh

Sinepuxent Bay

Chincoteague Bay →
Stop 6

Stop 10
Stop 9
Stop 7   Chincoteague
End

Stop 8

DELAWARE

BAY

SCALE

NAUTICAL MILES
0   5   10   15   20   25

0   5   10   15   20   25
STATUTE MILES

Figure 2. Map of the Chesapeake Bay Region
showing the route followed on the overnight
field trips down the Delmarva Peninsula for
the author's wetland ecology course at the
Graduate School, U.S. Department of
Agriculture. Many other sites discussed in the
subsequent chapters, including the Anne
Arundel County bogs and the Western Shore
Sleepers, are also shown.

As usual on overnight field trips down the Delmarva Peninsula for my Aquatic and Marsh Ecosystems course, we met this brisk fall day at Holly's Restaurant on Route 50 just past the Kent Narrows Bridge at eight o'clock in the morning. By then everyone had eaten breakfast or gotten some freshly brewed coffee. When I walked into Holly's, the twenty or so students, including some of their spouses, were conversing about the trip and related outdoor experiences. Their excitement over the trip, given the good weather, was quite evident. Some of them no doubt had never experienced the wetlands of the Eastern Shore, and perhaps had traveled directly to Ocean City whenever they crossed the Bay Bridge in the past. Shortly, we moved outside to gather around my vehicle. I could see their enthusiasm grow as I dispersed a trip outline and briefly explained our stops for the morning. I answered a few logistical questions, as well as one on the identity of the tall grass, the common reed (*Phragmites australis*), growing along the highway near Kent Narrows. Before long we departed from Holly's in an eight vehicle caravan, heading east into the bright sun, all anticipating a great day on the Eastern Shore.

Stop 1 -- In the Tank: Freshwater marshes of the Choptank River.

From Holly's Restaurant, our automobile caravan proceeded to Easton, then east on Dover Road (Route 331) to where it crosses the Choptank River and our first stop. After crossing the small bridge that leads to a long earth fill causeway over the marsh, the visual experience was one of an expansive marshy area, a fresh to slightly brackish tidal marsh snuggled inside a huge meander in the river. The marsh bulged laterally from the uplands to the east in a large *D*-shaped protuberance (Figure 3). From the air, and as evidenced on high altitude aerial photographs that I had with me on this trip, it was clear that this protuberance, which was bounded by the river meander, and others alternately occurring both upstream and downstream from the bridge, are not unique. Rather, they are quite characteristic of the middle portions of most estuaries as their channels alternately swing (meander) from one side of the floodplain to the other. In the process, they run smack against the uplands on the outside bends of their meanders and accumulate substantial sediments, which support vast marshes (i.e., the *D-*

Figure 3. Computer-scanned printout of a 1985 aerial photograph showing the large *D*-shaped marsh on the inside bend of an estuarine meander of the Choptank River at Dover Bridge, Caroline County, Maryland. Similar areas of marsh also occur along the opposite shore just upstream and downstream from Dover Bridge.

shaped protuberances) on their inside bends. Consequently, from a few thousand feet in the air, the Choptank in this instance resembled a giant serpent with numerous repeatedly bifurcating legs (that is, tributaries commonly called tidal guts) slithering through a mosaic of greens, the very

8

marshes its estuarine waters have generated over hundreds of years.[3] In the Chesapeake Bay Region, the tide ebbs and flows twice daily over a vertical range of about two or three feet. The water slowly rises, spills over the smaller stream banks like an overflowing kitchen sink, and quickly spreads over the marsh surface in a shallow sheet-like flow. At slack tide, sediments are deposited, and about six hours later the water is gone from the marsh and even the more shallow guts. Each tidal cycle brings a new supply of sediments. On this particular day, we were approaching the slack end of the tidal cycle, yet we were destined to remain far from dry. Just across the bridge, we pulled off the shoulder of the road onto the accreting edge of this huge estuarine meander.

Most folks eagerly -- some perhaps rather anxiously -- exited their automobiles and donned their field gear, generally assorted boots, jackets or vests, and hats. Some sported binoculars; others toted sundry field guides hoping to see and identify what the wetland had to offer in the way of plants and wildlife. Immediately, when I made a loud clap with my hands a small flock of ducks, probably woodies given the time of the year, or perhaps mallards, flew up well out in the marsh, then some more. They were soon winging high overhead every which way. Large flocks of blackbirds were also on the move. Then someone noted what she thought at first was an osprey.

Student: "Bill, look, an osprey! No, an eagle, a bald eagle!"

Sure enough, it was a bald eagle with its white head beaming as brightly as a white picket fence. The eagle was very low and boldly arrowed right up the Choptank. The excitement of the students was quite apparent, for some were seeing an eagle for the very first time.

---

[3]As defined by Donald W. Pritchard (2), an estuary is "...a semi-enclosed coastal body of water which has a free connection with the open sea and within which sea water is measurably diluted with fresh water derived from land drainage." Therefore, as one travels up the tributaries of the Chesapeake Bay, areas under tidal influence but not brackish will eventually be encountered. These are fresh tidal waters, which commonly support fresh tidal wetlands, both marshes and swamps.

A brief roadside introductory lecture on the setting in relation to the Chesapeake Bay ensued, including a discussion of the wetland types present and the vegetation patterns in the marsh.

> Instructor: "By the way the Choptank meanders, we're about thirty miles up from its mouth at the Chesapeake Bay. The water is fresh to slightly brackish. Under a wetland classification by Shaw and Fredine, we have types 12 and 13 wetlands -- coastal shallow fresh marshes and coastal deep fresh marshes, respectively. I have to classify them this way, meaning fresh, under the system even though they may be slightly brackish at times. My other alternative would be to call them types 17 or 18, irregularly flooded saltmarshes and regularly flooded saltmarshes, which they definitely are not, since the marshes here are not that brackish. You see, this classification system doesn't treat estuarine areas well. There are other problems with the system too, some of which are applicable to our region, but I won't go over them just now. Instead, lets get down into the marsh, but first note the patchiness of the vegetation, all of that spatial heterogeneity. Very important from a wildlife perspective; allows more species to fit in."[4]

Off we trudged down a small dirt road paralleling the bridge, right down to the river. I pointed out the narrow intermittent band of smooth cordgrass (*Spartina alterniflora*), noting that the cordgrass is basically restricted to the riverbank this far up the river. Along the riverbank, there is less competition with the array of freshwater species typical of fresh tidal marshes, since most of them are found back in the marsh. Because the smooth cordgrass is also called the saltmarsh cordgrass, it seemed out of place in this

---

[4]This U.S. Fish and Wildlife Service classification system by Shaw and Fredine (3) was succeeded in 1979 by the *Classification of Wetlands and Deepwater Habitats of the United States* (4), which is the classification used by the Service in its National Wetland Inventory. The newer system, which I also taught in later years, is much more detailed, with many more types. Nevertheless, from my perspective, the old system, which has only twenty types, still has much merit when it comes to teaching about wetlands.

fresh to slightly brackish area. In fact, it is most abundant, and more characteristically found, in the more saline parts of the Chesapeake Bay and its tributaries, as well as in the Worcester County coastal bays (see Chapter Four). A band of bluish-green vegetation comprised of only one species, the common three-square (*Scirpus pungens*), protruded from the tidal waters that were rhythmically lapping the shore. I gestured towards the plants.[5]

> Instructor: "This bulrush, *Scirpus americanus*, which is usually called the common three-square, is typically found in places like this, where the waves have reworked and deposited sands, creating an ideal inorganic substrate for it. Make note of this species, and remember the substrate it's growing on. At some point on this trip, or at least when we travel to the vast Dorchester County marshes in November, we will see large stands of its relative, the Olney three-square, *Scirpus olneyi*, which prefers an organic substrate. This contrast between the soil preference of these two bulrushes was pointed out to me years ago by an old time Fish and Wildlife Service biologist, Fran Uhler. What a naturalist that Ulher was, quite an all around naturalist. He knew wetland and aquatic plants extremely well. Also their seeds and fruits -- and even aquatic invertebrates. He did stomach analyses for the Service over at the Patuxent Wildlife Research Center. Supposedly, just about everyone sent their samples to him for verification. When I first came to Maryland, I was fortunate enough to get in the field with him a few times. Learned a lot. You can't help but learn from those kind of people -- encyclopedic knowledge. Uhler and others like Brook Meanley are some of the last of the old time, all around naturalists. Now let's get into the marsh."

---

5 The scientific name for the Olney three-square was historically *Scirpus olneyi*; that for the common three-square was *Scirpus americanus*. The accepted scientific name for the Olney three-square is now *Scirpus americanus*; that for the common three-square is *Scirpus pungens*. Therefore, in the early 1970s I was still using the older names, as shown below. This is an excellent example of how confusing name changes can be despite their necessity.

As always, I led the way through the deceivingly flat terrain. After about seventy-five feet into the marsh, I stopped. A few students were right behind me, but as usual the last one was still back at the river bank. So my lecture in the field had a slight respite until they all caught up. This made for an awkward situation. Those already around me wanted to hear something; if I continued, those that had to catch up complained that they had missed something. I could not win either way. Past experience taught me to compromise -- talk slowly in sort of a stall, then repeat a little to keep the late comers happy.

It was a little tricky crossing the marsh, particularly for the uninitiated, since the terrain was deceptive -- it was not really flat at all, which was the principal reason for the strung out group. The main tidal gut and its primary branches were quite obvious and we circumvented them. On the other hand, crossing the smaller ones was relatively easy. This was not the case, however, with the muskrat (*Ondatra zibethicus macrodon*)tunnels. They were hidden -- hidden under the surface that generally caved in under the weight of humans, in this instance, surprised students. A subtle clue to their presence was the openings where tunnels emerged into the larger guts; these openings could be seen, however, only at low tide.

A more observant student, a biologist type, spotted some additional openings associated with the muskrat tunnels, vertical openings to the marsh surface back from the guts; then some muskrat runs on the surface leading away from them. She even noted muskrat feedbeds, droppings, and clipped cattails, then pointed to a bushel basket size pile of cattail stems and leaves plastered with mud -- a muskrat house (Figure 4). I explained that these holes led to the tunnels and that they were for access to the marsh surface; that the runs were simply trails through the marsh analogous to a well worn path left by humans through a field. Needless to say, a few students broke through, usually to about the knees, as the weak mud over the tunnels collapsed. Substantial laughter followed, although it was generally accepted by the good sports who broke through.

At a convenient, relatively firm spot, I remarked how the vegetative patterns vary across the marsh consistent with the expected frequency of tidal inundation. Certain species like arrow-arum (*Peltandra virginica*) and pickerelweed (*Pontederia cordata*) were found mostly in the more frequently

Figure 4. Muskrat house in fresh tidal marsh. (Photo by the author)

flooded areas along the tidal guts. Although we sometimes also found these two species in lower densities on the flat marsh surface just above the guts or in depressional areas at mini-basins where the guts terminated, much of this higher marsh supported a greater variety of plants, particularly halberd-leaf tearthumb (*Polygonum arifolium*), arrow-leaf tearthumb (*P. sagittatum*), dotted smartweed (*Polygonum puntatum*), rice cutgrass (*Leersia oryzoides*), saltmarsh loosestrife (*Lythrum lineare*), saltmarsh camphor-weed (*Pluchea purpurascens*), slender flatsedge (*Cyperus filicinus*), hair-like mock bishop-weed (*Ptilimnium capillaceum*), tidemarsh waterhemp (*Amaranthus cannabinus*), saltmeadow cordgrass (*Spartina patens*), saltgrass (*Distichlis spicata*), swamp rose mallow (*Hibiscus moscheutos*), saltmarsh mallow (*Kosteletskya virginica*), small spikerush (*Eleocharis parvula*), and Walter's millet (*Echinocloa walteri*). Larger patches of narrow-leaf cattail were also

13

noted, especially near the edge of the marsh; expansive golden-brown patches of switchgrass (*Panicum virgatum*) stood out in the background well into the marsh.

> Instructor: "A few years ago when I first visited the Choptank, I was quite surprised to see switchgrass growing in such wet areas. My experience with it in New Jersey suggested just the opposite -- it occurred in dry oldfields, or only at the edges of saltmarshes along the coast. Certainly, not in the intertidal zone."
>
> Student: "What's its scientific name?"
>
> Instructor: "*Panicum virgatum*. This genus contains a large number of species, many of which look very similar, especially the ones commonly referred to as panic grasses. Switchgrass and a few others, on the other hand, are much more robust than the typical panic grass type. This is something that I cover in much more detail in my wetland plant identification course, so I'll stop there."[6]

With all of these plant patches, the marsh was quite diverse vegetatively, a heterogeneous site indeed. And as with most fresh to slightly brackish tidal marshes, it also had a diverse vascular flora. For example, in 1987 I field tested the Environmental Protection Agency's wetland delineation manual in the marsh, but on the opposite side of Dover Road (5). My quadrats produced twenty-two species. Therefore, the setting was most appropriate for something that I always liked to cover with students, since they probably did not get it in their formal schooling -- an explanation of the difference between the terms vegetation and flora.

---

[6]At the time of these field trips, the genus *Panicum* had two subgenera, one of which included the more generally robust species like switchgrass, the other much finer species with shorter, generally stubbier leaves. They are now placed in two different genera: *Panicum* and *Dichanthelium*, respectively.

14

Instructor: "You'll soon notice on this trip that I refer to the terms vegetation and flora as if they were different. Well they are. Vegetation refers to the plant life on the ground, which has form and structure. It is the mosaic of plant communities across a landscape. The term flora on the other hand refers simply to a list of species or lower taxa that are present at a given site, such as the Hackensack Meadows in northern New Jersey, or in Bergen and Hudson Counties in which it occurs, or in the entire State of New Jersey, or for that matter the whole Northeast. Floras are sometime more elaborate books, which include taxonomic descriptions, habitat data, and distributional data, as well as diagnostic keys for identifying the taxa included. So the term vegetation is more of an ecological concept, whereas flora is more taxonomic in nature.[7] I'll frequently use these terms, so make sure you understand the difference."

While walking through the marsh, the students readily observed hundreds of green seeds about three-eighths of an inch in diameter -- the seeds of arrow-arum, which were all floating.

Instructor: "It's essentially impossible to step into a fresh to slightly brackish tidal marsh at this time of the year without seeing these seeds either floating in the tidal guts or lodged up in the marsh. This is a good example of seed dispersal by water. A number of marsh plants are spread this way; others, such as the cattail over there, are dispersed by the wind just like the dandelion in your yards. (That is, if you have yards that look like mine nowadays!) Some, like the various beggar-ticks, simply catch on to an animal's fur or feathers only to fall off later, perhaps many miles away. The jewelweed or touch-me-not (*Impatiens capensis*) manifests yet another approach to ensuring seed dispersal away from mother plants. Its fruits have a

---

[7] In this case of the Meadowlands, only nineteen vegetation types were described and most of the area was dominated by one species, the common reed. On the other hand, the Meadowland's flora included 151 species (6,7).

specialized trigger system, which when ripe in late summer, cause the fruiting capsule to actually explode when touched or when it touches something while swaying in the wind."

Student: "Does anything feed on all of these arrow-arum seeds?"

Instructor: "Yes, but as far as I know only the wood duck and king rail. You see, arrow-arum fruits contain calcium oxalate crystals. Like kidney stones in humans that tear up the tubes of the urinary system, these crystals can really do a job on the digestive tract of most animals. So from an evolutionary standpoint most critters appear to have learned to avoid them. Well, we're running a little behind already, so we better get out of here and on to the next stop."

On leaving the marsh, I took down a few notes: "Spotted one sora and flushed a number of snipe. Small flocks of bobolinks. Phragmites invasion along the edge." With my penknife I cut off some broad-leaf cattail (*Typha latifolia*), arrow-arum, and pickerelweed leaves and inserted them into a plastic bag stored in my vest.

Instructor: "We'll make use of these cattail, arrow-arum, and pickerelweed leaves later."

Stop 2 -- "Watts" that creek?

We were soon heading east again on Dover Road to the small town of Bethlehem, where we turned left onto Route 578. At Harmon, Route 578 merged with Route 16. Interestingly, as we traveled north on Route 16, I noticed strange names for two roads opposite each other -- Two Johns Road and American Corner Road.[8] We proceeded north to the junction of Route 16

---

[8]John Burroughs and John Muir? I doubt it, although I have seen them referred to in writing before as "the two Johns." American Corner is also a place location, but I have never been to it.

and Route 404 where we again turned left to head toward Denton.[9] Before going on to the next regular stop, Martinak State Park, we pulled into a roadside picnic area on the west side of Route 404 just over Watts Creek, a tidal tributary of the Choptank River. This found us soon on the east side of the bridge scanning the well-flooded fresh tidal marsh with its now browning wild rice (*Zizania aquatica*) and various broad-leaf aquatic plants. After a very brief discourse on the wild rice, including the merits of its grains as wildlife food, we started back, but evidence of an interesting upland critter soon caught my eye. (For more on the wild rice, see Chapter Two on freshwater marshes). I pointed to a series of tiny depressions in the sand -- merely small pits. Small pits indeed, for they were the sandy traps of the antlion (Family Myrmeleontidae), a flying insect that somewhat resembles a damselfly when mature, but whose larvae (sometimes called doodlebugs) are voracious predators with formidable sickle-like jaws, huge jaws relative to their three-eighths of an inch or so body size.

Instructor: "Is anyone familiar with these conical depressions? (no response) Look around. Does anyone see any ants?"

As I expected, someone soon spotted an ant, which I nabbed by stunning it slightly with a twig.

Instructor: "Keep still and watch."

I bent over one of the larger depressions, about an inch and a half in diameter at the top, then gently dropped the ant in. The ant quickly scampered up the slope of the depression only to promptly tumble partially down along with some sand grains. During its ascent, some sand seemed to kick up from the bottom of the pit in a couple of spurts. Up came the ant again and some more sand spurted. Down the ant partially slid, this time a little further; again

---

[9]Does 404 mean anything to you? It should if you are familiar with the Federal wetland regulatory program, which is governed by Section 404 of the Clean Water Act! How appropriate to be on a wetland field trip and traveling down Route 404.

it took some sand grains with it. Then the ant scrambled wildly up the slipping slope for a third time only to falter once more. This time, however, it tumbled to the bottom of the pit. More sand flew and the ant struggled madly but could go nowhere. In a short time, the critter would be in ant heaven, sent there by a rather small beast -- the ravenous antlion (Figure 5).

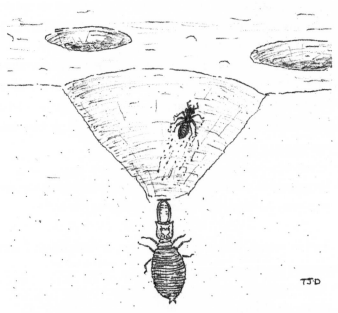

Figure 5. Predatory action in an ant lion pit.

Instructor: "Watch now. Look, the ant is slowly disappearing, sinking into the sand, deeper and deeper. It's almost gone. What you have seen is an antlion larva, the doodlebug, in action. It has two rather formidable jaws that suck the juices out of its victims. The ant will soon be nothing but a chitinous skeleton."

Students: "What a way to go!" "That was really neat. Obviously, where there's antlions, there will always be ants."

18

I demonstrated the action once more in another depression, then when I thought the doodlebug had a firm grip on the ant, quickly scooped out some sand, let it slowly filter through my fingers with most of it remaining in my palms, and located a little gray critter sporting impressive jaws. Everyone gathered around; their excitement was obvious. Anybody's would be if they had seen this phenomenon for the first time.

> Instructor: "Again, we need to get moving, but first let me show you what the critter does when I put it down."

Promptly, ever so promptly, the doodlebug buried into the sand; it also no doubt soon constructed another depression after we had left. One student was so fascinated that he periodically dropped back alone to feed some more doodlebugs, completely ignoring my subsequent discussion on the distribution of wild rice in Maryland.[10]

Stop 3 -- What's up spatterdock? Martinak State Park

Not far up Route 404, about two miles south of Denton, we turned left onto a small macadam road where a sign said Martinak State Park. The park entrance was on the left just down the road. We drove to the parking area near the boat ramp at the lower end of Watts Creek, parked, and were soon walking again. From the boat ramp, it was only about one-quarter of a mile (as the crow flies) to the Choptank River. We walked along the causeway (an obvious fill area behind a bulkhead) to what was apparently natural higher ground.[11] Heading southwest along the fill causeway, Watts Creek lay to our left with wetland along its opposite shore; to the right lay a green ash

---

[10]Incidentally, you do not need to be in the wild to see these interesting insects. They could occur in just about any sandy area, maybe even in your own yard. In 1997, for example, I found some antlion pits just four feet from my front door in a flower garden.

[11]For those unfamiliar with them, bulkheads are structures, generally wooden, placed along shorelines either to prevent erosion or to contain fill material when an open water area or wetland is obliterated to create upland.

(*Fraxinus pennsylvanica*) swamp that also supported some red maple (*Acer rubrum*) and black gum (*Nyssa sylvatica*). From the bulkhead looking southeast across Watts Creek, I pointed out the wetland types starting from the shoreline and working back: type 13 (coastal deep fresh marshes), followed by type 12 (coastal shallow fresh marshes), then by type 6 (shrub swamps), and finally by 7 (wooded swamps).

> Instructor: "Look at the type 13 wetland over there. Notice how the spatterdock (*Nuphar luteum*), the plant with the broad but rather brownish withering leaves, is the only species found in the deeper water. It has excellent adaptations for such areas, both morphological and physiological."

I went on to explain that many hydrophytes, such as water lilies, pondweeds, burreeds, cattails, pickerelweed, and spatterdock, have large air-filled tissues (lacunae) in their stems and leaves. These spongy tissues help some of these plants to stay afloat. They are also the means through which oxygen reaches the underground roots and rhizomes of many floating-leaf, as well as emergent, hydrophytes. To demonstrate, I retrieved the broad-leaf cattail and arrow-arum leaves from my plastic bag.

> Instructor: "So to better appreciate this, take one of these cattail or arrow-arum leaves and observe its petiole endways. Feel how light it is; then squash it between your fingers."

> Students: "Hey, neat!" "Interesting." "Sure -- I can see a bunch of tube-like holes at the end of this arrow-arum. And you're right, the stem is very spongy."

> Instructor: "Notice that the cattail is the same way."

I then addressed physiological adaptations.

20

Instructor: "Wetland plants also manifest various physiological adaptations for coping with the anaerobic conditions in wetland soils. A great example of this is the accumulation of the non-toxic metabolite, malate (in lieu of toxic ethanol) under anaerobic conditions in the roots and rhizomes of smooth cordgrass, reed meadowgrass, common reed, swamp tupelo, and possibly spatterdock; non-wetland species concentrate ethanol under anaerobic conditions, which is one reason why they don't do well in wetlands.[12] Another example..."

I was cut short on this explanation by a question.

Student: "Well, then why does the spatterdock look like it's dying?"

I explained that the above ground parts of spatterdock naturally die back each year even though it is a perennial, and that dieback had already set in. Furthermore, by late summer a similar dieback commonly occurs in populations of both the spatterdock and white waterlily (*Nymphaea odorata*); the leaves are usually riddled so badly by leaf-mining moth larvae and beetles and their larvae that they appear prematurely brown, which sometimes generates a new flush of growth.

The next zone of vegetation was a mixture of arrow-arum and pickerelweed, landward of which was a shrub swamp (type 6) followed by a wooded swamp (type 7). A brief discussion of the vegetation patterns followed, then I led them into the green ash swamp on the opposite side of the causeway. This swamp was very difficult to traverse. We had to stretch or jump from one small hummock to another while clinging to the shrubs or trees they supported. I tossed in a couple of dead logs as foot support for those that followed, but they (the logs, not the students!) substantially sank or snapped under the weight. Needless to say, many students waiting to proceed appeared

---

[12]Whereas I can not say for sure that spatterdock functions in this way, I strongly suspect that it does given the conditions under which it grows. One thing for sure thought, it has been known for some time that spatterdock can grow under anaerobic conditions (8,9,10).

a little nervous when I, in trying to reach a wild rice plant, sunk with one foot almost to the top of my hip boots. I persisted, however, since past experience told me that this site was floristically diverse and I was determined to penetrate the swamp at least far enough to obtain a rough count of the number of vascular plants. And despite the struggle, I did, as did most of the others. We tallied twenty-nine species within a thirty-foot radius from where I stood furthest in the swamp. I explained how I have found this species richness typical of most forested swamps, and how this is probably a reflection of the number of vegetative strata (i.e., canopy, subcanopy, shrub, and herbaceous layers).

> Instructor: "Are you starting to see the difference between vegetation and flora? In this instance, the vegetation is dominated by one species, the green ash (*Fraxinus pennsylvanica*). One might call this wetland a green ash swamp. On the other hand, the vascular flora of this green ash swamp is comprised of a least twenty-nine species." (Many heads nod affirmatively.)

I also indicated that the species diversity does not stop there; it is reflected in the animal life as well. I expounded on this point.

> Instructor: "A Virginia study conducted over five winters indicated that the number of resident bird species found in a forested swamp was about twice the number that occurred in an adjacent mixed pine and hardwood forest. A good example of summertime use is the various warblers alone, such as the yellowthroat, Louisiana water-thrush, parula warbler, prothonotary warbler, black and white warbler, and hooded warbler, to name a few."[13]

---

[13]To paraphrase from *Coastal Wetlands of Virginia* (11): Wintering birds that regularly used the Virginia swamp included the wood duck, woodcock, winter wren, swamp sparrow, hairy woodpecker. About forty additional species that are known to use other habitats as well were also reported. Even bluebirds and robins were often more commonly found in the swamp than in the upland forest. See Chapter Five on the Pocomoke River to better appreciate just how diverse the birdlife associated with swamps can be, particularly the warblers.

After concluding that discussion, we headed down the causeway, veered to our right at the forested upland, and proceeded northwest to the Choptank River. From a narrow fill intrusion into the marsh along the river, we had a great view of the river and its surrounding wetlands. With a loud clap of the hands, about ten wood ducks departed from the large area of spatterdock immediately upstream and to our right. Then a birder type noted a couple of great blue herons standing like statues on the far side of the river. And as we scanned the marsh for more herons, the birder also spotted an osprey swoop down and snatch a fish swimming too close to the surface. Soon, however, the wildlife action subsided and I dealt at length on the large spatterdock area and its substantial biomass, most of which lay hidden from view rooted in the mud, normally under a few feet of water at high tide.

Instructor: "There's more spatterdock biomass below the ground than there is above. Although the leaves of this broad-leaf aquatic die back each year, their horizontally oriented underground stems called rhizomes, remain, given that spatterdock is a perennial. See all those patches that seem to be overlapping? Well, they are -- for this plant continues to spread year after year to form large patches called clones that eventually coalesce into even bigger patches. Given how muddy it looks on this exceptionally low tide, you will all probably assume I'm a little nuts when I head into the spatterdock. Here I go. Do I look like I'm sinking? Well, I am -- but not much. Someone please hand me the shovel and lets see what we can dig up here."

With a few heavy-footed slices, the shovel blade momentarily cut through a thick rhizome in two places a couple of feet apart.

Instructor: "You can't see the rhizome, but I've severed it in two places, about two feet apart. Now here comes the messy part."

After thrusting my hands well into the mud, up the rhizome came with the broad leaves angling from the tip.

23

Students: "Impressive!" "Amazing!" "Wow!"

With little hesitation, I tossed the large, two-foot long by three-inch diameter, section of spatterdock rhizome towards the upland. It never quite made it and hit the mud a few feet short with a loud, mud slinging, *plop*; the effects of which a couple of students experienced in the way of flying mud. This rhizome quickly passed between various hands. When it got back to me, I broke it in half with an audible snap and showed them its white pulpy texture. Numerous large overlapping leaf scars running the entire length of the rhizomes were also readily evident, as were the many scattered vascular bundle scars on each leaf scar.

Next, I showed them one of my favorite plants, the square-stem spikerush, growing along the firmer shoreline, just downstream from the narrow fill area.

> Instructor: "And note how this spikerush, *Eleocharis quadrangulata*, can be easily overlooked in the presence of this other plant, the common three-square, *Scirpus americanus*. The three-square superficially resembles the spikerush; even grows on a similar substrate. Remember it? We saw this three-square species along the river at our first stop. Both of them have narrow sword-like stems that support only small or highly reduced leaves. However, true to its specific epithet, *quadrangulata*, the spikerush has a four-angle stem; the three-square's only three-angled. Thus, the name three-square is really a misnomer; if it has three angles, it can't be square!"

Although we were still running late, I was determined to discuss a relevant example of bad government in action -- in this instance, my own Department of Natural Resources. I explained, that back in 1971, the Department had proposed to dump spoil from a Choptank River maintenance dredging project onto a large spatterdock marsh and an adjacent shrub swamp and forested swamp at Martinak State Park, the very area we had been intently observing now for the last twenty minutes. The Department's proposal was to

24

dispose of the spoil, which ultimately would have resulted in the creation of upland for recreational use. Another staff person and I, who were in the tidal wetlands program, opposed it on ecological grounds. Consequently, there was considerable controversy surrounding the project, including at least one nasty editorial by a Denton newspaper editor attacking us and the Department. Fortunately, I was able to convey to my class a happy ending to the project. Although the dredging took place as planned, the spoil material went elsewhere, to an abandoned agricultural field as I recall. With that explanation over, and hunger pangs in our stomachs, we hiked back to a picnic area for lunch. By now, one-quarter of a two day trip had passed.

Stop 4 -- Any hope for the Marshyhope?

About 1:00 p.m saw us once again on Route 404, but this time heading in the opposite direction, southeast towards Delaware. Not long after entering Delaware, we crossed Marshyhope Creek and pulled off as carefully as possible along the narrow roadside shoulder protected by a robust metal guard rail. With the traffic zipping by, it was not easy or necessarily safe getting out of the cars.

> Instructor: "Please stay to the guard rail side of the road. Lots of traffic along here and it's tight. No need for field gear, although feel free to bring binoculars and field guides if you wish. Boots are not necessary. I'll be lecturing a bit right from the bridge if we can stand the noise."

> Student: "What this creek called?"

> Instructor: "The Marshyhope, which is a tributary of the Nanticoke River, a nifty system that even gets into Delaware as you can see. Let's take a look from the bridge."

Within a few minutes, I was standing on a slightly elevated concrete ledge leaning against the guard rail scanning downstream, then upstream. The downstream stretch of the creek was straight as an arrow as far as the eye could see; the upstream stretch made a fairly sharp bend to the left after a couple of hundred feet. There was absolutely no emergent vegetation at the toe of the steep stream banks and there was little floristic diversity on the higher ground astride the channel -- a few shrubs or saplings, some exotic looking grasses and legumes. Lateral to the arrow-like stream, however, were broad bands of trees -- swamp forests. Many of these trees were dead, simply grayish-brown skeletons, the remnants of ecologically better times. I purposely paused a bit to see how the students would react to the scene. Soon, some did.

Students: "Why are those trees dead? Why is the creek so straight? Wait a minute, you said the Nanticoke was a nifty system or something like that. Isn't this part of the Nanticoke? What was the impact of..."

Instructor: "Slow down, let me answer a few questions. First of all, the Nanticoke is a nifty system, no doubt about it. But some of its tributaries, particularly this one, which once was an attractive creek meandering through a contiguous hardwood swamp, have been severely impacted by man. In fact, a large portion of the Marshyhope, particularly above where we are now standing, has been gutted. What you are seeing today is the end result -- a severely channelized floodplain swamp. The creek channel you're now observing was designed to be straight in order to expedite the movement of upland runoff entering the floodplain from its watershed. And actually it's not uncommon, as in this case, to have some of the tributaries channelized as well. The higher, essentially unvegetated, areas astride the channel are the spoil banks, that is, the lineal areas where the excavated spoil from the channel was deposited, which is why they are on each side of the channel. The forested areas further out from

26

the channel are what remains of the floodplain swamp. I would also assume that..."

At that juncture, the bottom line question came in, the one I had cut off earlier.

Student: "Well, it looks pretty bad from here, but what exactly is the impact of all of this, ecologically?"

Instructor: "A good question; sorry I cut you off earlier. But let me answer with a question: If you were a fish, what would you prefer -- a nice meandering, shady, cool, well oxygenated, clear running stream replete with all kinds of coarse substrates, including fallen trees, logs, brush, and submerged aquatic vegetation, that provide ample cover and support sundry invertebrate prey? Or would you prefer a straight, unshaded, warm, poorly oxygenated, turbid stream having little in the way of coarse substrates available for cover and supporting little in the way of invertebrate prey? Actually, from the look on your faces, I think I know your answers, although I must admit that there are a few species that prefer, or at least survive under, the latter conditions. I would be flabbergasted if you preferred the channelized system.

"What you are observing here today, by the way, is formally called stream channelization, and it has plagued fish and wildlife biologists for way too many years. All too often, channelization is subsidized by certain government agencies in the name of flood control, which ironically commonly causes worse problems downstream, as the floodwaters from the various tributaries converge. The result is not just the additional flooding. Sediments and associated nutrients are also shunted downstream to be dumped into the receiving waters, where they cause, if too excessive, water quality problems due to sedimentation and nutrient enrichment. Normally, upon flooding, the sediments and nutrients are carried up

27

and over low natural stream banks and deposited on the floodplain. This is a benefit to the floodplain, or I should say the vegetation on the floodplain, which utilizes the nutrients in particular. In the process, the river and downstream waters also benefit, since it results in lower concentrations of sediments and nutrients downstream. This ecosystem level process is analogous to the function of mammalian kidneys in processing nitrogenous wastes. A number of studies have demonstrated this water quality abatement capacity of wetlands, particularly in relation to nitrogen. It has also been shown that when sediments and nutrients no longer replenish the floodplain, tree growth decreases.

"So to summarize, channelization shunts floodwaters downstream bypassing the watershed's kidneys -- its floodplain forests -- and frequently transfers the flooding problem to other people and property and ecosystems downstream. And that's only part of the problem. There are substantial impacts on fish and wildlife. I won't get into that now, but there's a big literature base documenting those impacts."

Student: "How the hell did they get away with this?"

Instructor: "Let's drop down to the stream bank where there's less noise and I'll explain."

We climbed over the guard rail and slipped down the embankment to the stream bank, which in reality, was simply one of the two lineal spoil piles from when they channelized (dredged) the stream.

Instructor: "Dwight, I really don't have a specific answer for you in this case -- for the Marshyhope that is. I didn't live in Maryland when it happened. But I'm sure all of you are aware of the kinds of pressures that can be put on agencies to deal with things like flooding, agricultural drainage, and mosquito control, all of which, by the way, can significantly impact wetland hydrology.[14] "Wetland hydrology is the driving force for all wetlands in relation to their natural functions, but it is also very important for their sustained viability as natural ecosystems. We just can't drain them and expect them to survive as wetlands. After all, wetlands are wetlands because they are wet -- at least periodically wet that is. Yes, if there's anything that all wetlands have in common, it is that they are at least periodically wet. I remember the first channelization that I encountered. It was at a New Jersey site that I visited while I was in graduate school. I was with a group of fellow graduate students from the University of Pennsylvania on an outing for the first Earth Day celebration. The small creek we visited, Parker's Creek, which ran through a great marsh/shrub swamp complex, had been recently gutted. Someone even found a dead bog turtle (a rare species) that was dug up, apparently during hibernation. I was appalled, for I had been to this neat site a few times before while leading organized birding trips.

"Then I moved to Maryland in 1971. One of my earlier field visits was to see the channelized Gilbert Run, a tributary of the Wicomico River in Charles County (Figure 6). Again straight as an arrow, and fairly recently done at the time. I've never forgotten the few saplings that were planted on the spoil banks as mitigation -- being small and with their support poles, they looked more like crosses signifying burials. Ironically, they were crosses, figuratively speaking, for the once wonderful Gilbert Run was wonderful no more. I was told by my colleague, that there was so much controversy over this project, that the District Conservationist for the Charles County Soil Conservation District indicated something to the effect that: 'Nixon has Vietnam, I have Gilbert Run.' This kind of thing is still going on. We'll discuss this more in class, but we really have to

---

[14]In Delaware, there is a tax ditch program that helps subsidize the construction and maintenance of drainage ditches. For example, 61% of the total Marshyhope watershed has been drained through this program; 37% has been petitioned for drainage (12).

29

move on now. My short stop has stretched out a little too much. Once I get started, there's just so much to say about these systems -- their ecology, as well as their management and regulation. Sometimes I just get carried away."

Stop 5 -- Deciduous swamps along the Nanticoke.

Continuing southeast on Route 404, we soon hit Bridgeville, made a left turn and passed on through the town, then turned right, still following Route 404, and headed southeast again until we came to Route 13. We traveled due south on Route 13 to Laurel, Delaware. After crossing Broad Creek, another tributary of the Nanticoke, we turned right onto Route 24 heading southwest and eventually back into Maryland. After about ten miles, we intersected Route 313 at Sharptown, Maryland, whereupon we crossed over the Nanticoke River and pulled off on the narrow grassy shoulder of the road to explore our fifth site, an extensive Nanticoke River deciduous swamp. I soon was out and in my field gear. With a Dorchester County map spread on the hood of my car and a high altitude aerial photograph in my hand, proceeded to explain our location and the environmental setting.

Instructor: "Of course, we're back in Maryland now, in Dorchester County; we left Wicomico County, Maryland when we crossed the Nanticoke. Dorchester County has the most wetlands in the State, somewhere around 121,000 acres based upon *Wetlands in Maryland*, a report that was done in 1973 (13). They are particularly significant in the lower part of the county, but we will get to that more on our November trip to the Blackwater area. As you can see from this blow-up of the nine by nine aerial photograph, this river meanders just like the Choptank. And similarly, that meandering has resulted in large wetlands on the Nanticoke's inside bends. You may have noticed that Sharptown was smack up against the Nanticoke, since it is located on the outside bend of the meander that swings into the upland. The large wetland that we are now observing is about one-

30

Figure 6. The channelized Gilbert Run, a tributary of the Wicomico River in Charles County, Maryland in 1971. Note the attempt to establish a few trees, which are shown in the right side of the photograph. (Photo by the author)

half mile wide. The system looks quite impressive as depicted in this aerial photo, which was taken at about 6000 feet. Any questions before we venture into the swamp?"

Student: "You mean that is all swamp depicted on the photo opposite of Sharptown?"

Instructor: "Yes, for the most part, but note that there are a few different color and texture patterns landward of the river. These represent the various vegetation types or zones in the wetland, and they show up quite well. The smooth greenish-gray color immediately adjacent to the river in places is from extensive stands of spatterdock, the same plant we saw so abundantly on the Choptank earlier. Note also that landward of it in places is a more coarse textured vegetation

31

signature on the aerial photo; this too is marsh, but it's situated a little higher in elevation and has a mix of hydrophytes. The last zone along the river is the major one, the forested swamp, which shows up quite coarse in the photo due to the tree crowns, and notice how it also contrasts with the larger tree crowns depicted in the adjacent upland to the northwest.[15] But we need to get into the swamp in order to get a good feel for it. Just up the road is a survey cut that I found last year; let's relocate it, which will give us easier access and we won't have to bother with a compass."

Students: "How wet will this site be?" "Do we need boots?"

Instructor: "Here's the scoop. As I indicated in class, you have three choices. You either wear boots and maybe stay dry, wear an old pair of sneakers and just get wet and muddy right off the bat, or stand on the roadside and pick up what you can, but soon you won't be able to hear the rest of us. It's your choice. Before we enter the swamp though, I want to show you some things along the shoulder over here."

So before entering the swamp, we walked the road shoulders where I pointed out the hydrophytes in the roadside ditches along both sides of Route 313. As expected, there was a nice variety of herbaceous plants, but also a few woody species. There were free floating plants like the lesser

---

[15]In the United States four generic types of wetlands are commonly acknowledged: marsh, swamp, bog, and fen. Sometimes there is a fifth – wet meadow. Marshes are wetlands dominated by herbaceous plants, like cattails, arrow-arum, pickerelweed, smartweeds, to name a few; swamps are dominated by woody plants, such as various shrubs like buttonbush (*Cephalanthus occidentalis*) and northern arrowwood (*Viburnum recognitum*) and trees like swamp tupelo (*Nyssa sylvatica* var. *biflora*) and sweetbay (*Magnolia virginiana*). They generally have inorganic soils. Bogs and fens are peatlands; thus they both have organic soils. They differ from each other in their hydrologies, nutrient levels, hydrogen ion concentrations, and their resultant floristic composition. All of the species mentioned above are hydrophytes – plants that grow either in open water or on soils that are at least periodically inundated or saturated with water.

duckweed (*Lemna minor*), greater duckweed (*Spirodela polyrrhiza*), and an aquatic liverwort (*Riccia fluitans*); emergents like common arrowhead (*Sagittaria latifolia*), arrow-arum, sweetflag (*Acorus calamus*), wild rice, and water hemlock (*Cicuta maculata*); shrubs like the buttonbush and water willow (*Decodon verticillatus*). I elaborated on a couple of these. I started with the arrowhead and arrow arum after I snipped a couple of leaves off to compare with the pickerelweed leaves that I had collected at Dover Bridge.

> Instructor: "Take a look at these two sets of leaves; I'll circulate one set each way. Notice that they are all arrowhead-shaped. I should explain that they are also from three different families of vascular plants: the arrowhead (*Sagittaria latifolia*) is in the Water-Plantain Family, the arrow-arum (*Peltandra virginica*) is in the Arum Family, and the pickerelweed (*Pontederia cordata*) is in its own family, the Pickerelweed Family. Other than for being all monocots, these plants are not related; yet they all have developed arrowhead-shaped leaves. From an evolutionary perspective, what do you think this may be an example of?"

> Student (a biologist type): "How about convergent evolution?"

> Instructor: "That would certainly be a good bet, and these are not the only plants that have this leaf form, even some dicots do, such as halberd-leaf tearthumb and arrow-leaf tearthumb. As I indicated already, the three plants I've been discussing are all monocots. A number of tropical plants, some of which are house plants, have similar leaf shapes. Good answer.
>
> "Now, why do you think they all evolved this way -- with broad, arrowhead-shaped leaves? Seems that it would have to be an adaptation for something. But what?"

> Student: "Here's my guess: Could it relate to light capture, given all of the surface area they have?"

Instructor: "Another good answer. It may even be correct! But I can't say for sure. I have a theory of my own on this, which I plan to discuss in class next week." (See Chapter Two for an elaboration of this, and an alternate explanation for the arrowhead-shaped leaves of these species.)

"Let's look at these two duckweeds over here -- the lesser duckweed, *Lemna minor,* and greater duckweed, *Spirodela polyrrhiza.* Both are free floating, but the lesser duckweed is green on both sides and only has one rootlet per thallus; the greater duckweed is usually maroonish underneath and has at least two rootlets per thallus, which is how it gets the specific epithet of *polyrrhiza*, meaning many-rooted.

"I'm going to digress a bit here. A scientific name is comprised of two words referred to as a binomial. It is generally given in italics or underlined. The first part of the binomial refers to the genus or generic name. The second part of the name is called the specific epithet (or sometimes the trivial name); it is often incorrectly referred to as the species name. The species name is actually the full binomial, in this instance, *Spirodela polyrrhiza*. Therefore, the genus is *Spirodela*; the specific epithet is *polyrrhiza.*

"Believe it or not, both of these duckweeds are angiosperms and thus have the capacity to produce flowers, although I've never seen any. The flowers are rather inconspicuous, and the plants spread mostly vegetatively by budding. This plant often covers entire ditches or small ponds during the summer. See this other floating plant? It's an aquatic liverwort, *Riccia fluitans*. Notice how this tiny non-vascular plant forks, producing small Y-shaped segments."

Student: "Does anything eat these floating plants?"

Instructor: "Yes, wood ducks, for example, consume duckweeds. Other puddle ducks probably do too. I've seen puddle ducks, like woodies and mallards, many times sifting through the shallow water along pond shorelines, or in marshes, seeking various aquatic invertebrates. In the process, they probably also inadvertently take in substantial duckweed too, since it's not uncommon to have, for example, pond snails and other invertebrates associated with the duckweed.

"Notice that plant with the multiple arching stems. Look close. It's the water willow. Not a true willow in Salicaceae, the Willow Family; rather, it's in Lythraceae, the Loosestrife Family -- the same family that the purple loosestrife, *Lythrum salicaria*, is in. The purple loosestrife, an invader from Europe, is becoming a nuisance in the Northeast and Midwest, since it forms essentially monotypic stands and displaces more desirable native species. See how the water willow seems to repeatedly arch again and again producing new stems were the tips have entered the water. This is also a means of vegetative reproduction. Now, pull up one of these arched branches to see how it is rooted at both ends."

Student: "They all seem to be attached; each of the arching stems goes to another plant. They're also swollen at the tips."

Instructor: "See this one? The swollen base will quickly shrink when I remove this pulpy tissue, which at first appears brown. See how white it is inside? This is what Sculthorpe in his book, *The Biology of Aquatic Vascular Plants*, called aerenchyma tissue (14). It's a great aid in keeping plants like the water willow afloat. Consequently, over time the water willow can cover a large part, or the entire surface, of a pond. We have some good examples of that in Anne Arundel County. As far as I know, however, this native plant is not a problem like the purple loosestrife."

Student: "The tissue pulls off quite easily; very pulpy. You're right, the stem is much more narrow at the base minus that pulpy stuff."

35

We moved across the road to the other ditch, where on past trips I had located some plants with long narrow leaves. Not far up the road I found them.

Instructor: "Anyone know this species?"

Students: "Cattail?" "Iris?" "Burreed?"

Instructor: "Neither. Here, smell this crushed leaf. It's the sweetflag. Those you have mentioned all look superficially alike. However, notice the cross section of the leaf I've sliced. It's more or less rhomboidal or diamond-shaped. The cattail is plano-convex or *D*-shaped in cross section; the burreed, generally triangular; the iris, rather flat or diamond-shaped. They are all monocots, but otherwise not related."

We continued down the road as I identified a number of other plants, eventually finding an umbelliferous plant.

Instructor: "One last plant before I test your mettle in the swamp. Here's an umbelliferous plant, the water hemlock. Note its smooth stems and compound leaves. It is poisonous. Not to touch; only to eat. Its scientific name is *Cicuta maculata*. A related plant, the classical hemlock of antiquity, the poison hemlock, *Conium maculatum*, is supposedly what killed Socrates. We may also find another close relative, the water parsnip, *Sium suave*, somewhere along this ditch. If so, you will readily tell it from the water hemlock by its deeply grooved stems. Its compound leaves also have a different shape."

Despite the straight survey cut, we did not exactly arrow into the swamp. Our route was a little circuitous as we stretched from hummock to hummock with the support of shrubs and saplings and utilized fallen logs for

36

foot support. Nevertheless, we penetrated well into the swamp despite its tricky terrain. For the most part, the swamp was dominated by green ash and red maple, but also had some black gums and sweetbays, as well as a few scattered southern white cedars. It was not easy going and a few people went in over their low boots. With hip boots I had no problem. After seeing the diversity in the swamp at Martinak State Park, the students quickly picked up on the plant richness here. There was quite a variety of shrubs, a few vines, and a number of forbs, such as the clearweed (*Pilea pumila*) and Virginia bugleweed (*Lycopus virginicus*). The most abundant fern was the royal fern (*Osmunda regalis*), which tended to grow on the small hummocks that supported trees or shrubs. Before leaving the swamp, I demonstrated the floating mat effect that we encountered in places by stomping on some hummocks and shaking a few saplings. I also gave them an indication of how deep the swamp sediments were by thrusting a dead branch about six feet into the soil with little resistance. Then we retraced our tracks to the road. Some folks were really messy by the time we got out, but I had forewarned them of that likelihood at our last class, so most people brought a change of clothes or at least a towel to clean up a bit. (For more on the Nanticoke River watershed, see Chapter Six.)

Stop 6 -- R & R for the night.

Three-thirty saw us heading for what was generally our last stop of the day on these overnighters, Shad Landing State Park.[16] Because it was a long ride to Worcester County and most folks wanted a chance to stop for gas or snacks, or to use restrooms, I explained the directions and informed them that they were on their own. Given the time, walking the nature trail at Shad Landing as planned was now out of the picture. Instead, our plan was to register for our campsites or hotel rooms, then meet for a seafood dinner. So some folks indicated that they would go straight to the campground; others to their hotel, the Quality Inn, just south of Pocomoke City.

---

[16]Shad Landing State Park is now called the Shad Landing Unit of the Pocomoke River State Park.

Instructor: "Here's my suggested route to Shad Landing State Park or the Quality Inn where some of you are staying. Take Route 313 south to Route 50, then Route 50 southeast to Salisbury. It's a little awkward, but you can pick up Route 12 at Salisbury, then head southeast towards Snow Hill. At Snow Hill turn right on Route 394, proceed through this quaint town and you will eventually merge with Route 113. Just southwest on Route 113, you will see the sign for Shad Landing on the right. To get to the Quality Inn, continue on Route 113 to Route 13 at Pocomoke City and turn left. Heading south on Route 13, the Quality Inn will be a few miles down the road on the right not far after The Upper Deck, a nice seafood restaurant. Those going directly to the Quality Inn can also take Route 13 out of Salisbury to and beyond Pocomoke City to the hotel. We'll have to skip the nature trail at Shad Landing; you can always do that some other time on your own anyway. By the way, how many would like to go out to dinner at a seafood place, say The Upper Deck, just south of Pocomoke City? [show of hands] Good, I'll make reservations for seven o'clock. See you then."

I made the reservations, the food was great, and we were out of the restaurant by about nine. We had some good discussions while eating, but it had been a long day. By now, everybody, including me, was ready for a good night's sleep.

Instructor: "Get a good rest. We'll have another long day tomorrow. We will meet at the Quality Inn at nine o'clock. Try to be on time and make sure you have already eaten. We will spend the entire day in Virginia, on Assateague and Chincoteague."

As I had anticipated, a few people arrived a little late Sunday morning. This was understandable, given that the latecomers had camped at Shad Landing, which is about eight miles northeast on Route 113. Before leaving, however, I briefed everyone on our upcoming adventure.

38

Instructor: "The vehicles should stick together for the rest of the trip. We will soon be in Virginia and shortly thereafter we'll make a left at Route 175; you'll see a big sign for Chincoteague. When you pass the NASA mainland setup, where you will see open grassy areas and large radar devices to the left, take note of how abruptly the upland you have been driving on drops down to the flat marshy area due east. You will have just driven off an old Pleistocene shoreline formed thousands of years ago, when sea level was much higher than it is today, and prior to the last glaciation. This ancient shoreline shows up very well on the satellite imagery that I'll show you in class next week. In fact, a rather straight line runs right down through southern New Jersey and the Delmarva Peninsula on the landward side of the expansive saltmarshes.

"The road you'll be on is the only one to Chincoteague and the southern end of Assateague Island. We will stop at the first pull-off out in the marsh. Make sure you pull up tight to the vehicle in front of you so we can all fit in. We'll examine the marsh on both sides of the road, then travel to Toms Cove to catch a low tide and visit an oyster bar and tidal flats. Then we eat lunch at the Chincoteague National Wildlife Refuge, which, by the way, is actually on Assateague Island. After lunch, we will take the drive around the shallow impoundments, where you should keep your eyes open for birds, particularly waterfowl. Next, we'll arrow north up Assateague to examine the Wash Flats area. Our last stop will be well beyond the Wash Flats where we will hike east across the barrier island to the ocean. On the way up the island, watch out for peregrine falcons, since they are migrating through by now. Okay, let's head out."

Stop 7 -- The marshes of Chincoteague.

At Route 175 in Virginia, we saw the big sign for Chincoteague and turned left. We soon passed the fenced off open fields of NASA, with all of the radar equipment. This was the mainland area associated with the Wallops Island facilities. After dropping off the Pleistocene shoreline, we pulled off at the first parking area, which was on the right just over a major tidal gut.

By the time we reached the parking area, many of the people had already noted large white birds out in the marsh, the snowy and great egrets, as well as a large grayish wading bird, a great blue heron. So as I assembled some equipment and got into my field gear, a number of students, particularly the birders were eagerly scanning the seemingly flat landscape with their binoculars. My equipment for this stop was a series of galvanized pipe sections with couplets, a four foot long corkscrew type soil auger, two large pipe wrenches, and a dip net, as well as a pack of matches, which I asked a student to hold.

Student: "What are the pipes for? And the matches?"

Instructor: "You'll see soon enough. Besides, I'd rather demonstrate than describe, other than to say the auger and pipes are to core into the marsh sediments. That way I will also get some of you involved. Before we go across the road with this equipment, however, let me show you a few things on this side along this major tidal gut.

"We're in luck, since the tide is almost out. See the cordgrass growing along the gut. It's *Spartina alterniflora*, the famous saltmarsh cordgrass or smooth cordgrass that people like Eugene Odum and the Teals studied at Sapelo Island, Georgia in the 1950s-1960s. Are you surprised? It's the same species we saw on the Choptank yesterday. Remember? It was growing there in essentially fresh water. [There was a nodding of a few heads in the affirmative.] I'm sure at least some of you have read the Teals' book -- *Life and Death of the Salt Marsh* (15). [There was a nodding of a few heads in the negative.] It's great; certainly got me interested. And it was

Figure 7. Gulf periwinkle (*Littorina irrorata*), a dominant invertebrate in saltmarsh cordgrass (*Spartina alterniflora*) marshes. (Photo by the author)

their work that documented how productive these coastal saltarshes are; it was instrumental in getting a lot of the early regulations into effect. In fact, they talked about the very creatures all about us right now -- marsh fiddlers (*Uca pugnax*), gulf periwinkles (*Littorina irrorata*), and ribbed mussels (*Modiolus demissus*), three of the four real obvious saltmarsh invertebrates on mid-Atlantic coast marshes. The saltmarshes abound in them, no doubt tens of thousands of them on big marshes like this. Oh, by the way, marshes dominated by the smooth cordgrass are considered type 18 wetlands, regularly flooded saltmarshes." (Figure 7)

By this time someone had a fiddler in their hand and remarked about its one large claw.

Student: "The large claw is longer than the body. What's its use?"

Instructor: "This particular fiddler is the marsh fiddler, *Uca pugnax*. Only the males have the one large claw, the other one is rather small; the female's claws are both small. The fiddler waves its large claw around as a defensive maneuver against other males, which is probably how it got the specific epithet of *pugnax*, referring to its pugnacity. It feeds at low tide by ingesting pieces of the muddy substrate and in so doing extracts the organic material. See those piles of small pellets; they are the indigestible material the fiddler leaves behind, which dissolve on the next high tide. These clumps of rejected material are different from the fiddler's smaller cylindrical fecal droppings.

"I don't see any but there is a slightly larger crab, the purple marsh crab, *Sesarme reticulata*, that eats the smooth cordgrass but also sometimes preys upon fiddlers. It has two large but stubby claws. All of these small holes are from the fiddler; in contrast, the purple marsh crabs holes are shielded partially by arching mud canopies." (Figures 8 and 9)

As I lectured, I also picked up a couple of gulf periwinkles and rooted out a ribbed mussel with my foot.

Instructor: "Here, I'll pass these around. The grayish-white univalve is the gulf periwinkle, *Littorina irrorata*; the dark elongated clam-like animal is the ribbed mussel, *Modiolus demissus*. The greenish tint to the periwinkle is from the epiphytic algae. This univalve is quite abundant in the well-flooded saltmarshes, such as along this tidal gut. Likewise for the ribbed mussel, which attaches itself to the base of the tall growth form of the smooth cordgrasses, exposed peat, or other shells. While sampling at the interesting Mystic Harbor

Figure 8. Purple marsh crab (*Sesarme reticulata*). This attractive crab with two large claws sometimes preys upon the marsh fiddler (*Uca pugnax*). (Photo by the author)

Marsh on Sinepuxent Bay in Maryland, I have encountered large numbers of the periwinkles, well over 100 per meter square in some quadrats. And you can readily see how abundant the fiddlers are."

Student: "What's the fourth invertebrate you mentioned? I only see three here."

Instructor: "That's the saltmarsh snail, *Melampus bidentatus*, but it occurs at a slightly higher elevation in the short growth form of the smooth cordgrass and in the salt meadows dominated by salt meadow cordgrass, *Spartina patens* and the saltgrass, *Distichlis spicata*.

"Maybe I should explain what I mean by the growth forms of the smooth cordgrass at this point. There are two main growth forms. The tall growth form grows along the tidal guts where it is,

43

Figure 9. Purple marsh crab (*Sesarme reticulata*) - marsh fiddler (*Uca pugnax*) comparison. The fiddler, a crab that abounds in the well-flooded saltmarshes, is smaller than the marsh crab. Its one large claw occurs only in the male. (Photo by the author)

on the average, flooded twice daily. In some areas, the smooth cordgrass marshes are entirely flooded on each tide, such as the Mystic Harbor Marsh near Ocean City and the marsh at Toms Cove, which we will soon see, so they are dominated by the tall growth form. These well-flooded marshes are young geologically. Most of the marshes we will see, such as that just across the road and the Snug Harbor Marsh on Sinepuxent Bay, are slightly higher in elevation beyond their tidal guts and therefore support the short growth form. Where both growth forms occur along a tidal gut, there is usually an intermediate growth form, which is simply transitional. With even more elevation, of course, the salt meadow cordgrass and saltgrass appear. Areas supporting stands of these two species are considered type 16 wetlands, coastal salt meadows. Anyone have any idea why the different growth forms of the smooth cordgrass exist?"[17]

Student: "You spoke a lot about the tidal flooding. Does it relate to that?"

Instructor: "Yes, but there's more to it than that. A number of theories have been suggested, most of which relate back in some way to the flooding. These involve nitrogen availability, iron toxicity, salinity, soil oxygenation resulting from the fiddler crab holes, and others. The one that seems to make a lot of sense to me is the nitrogen availability idea. Apparently, there is an ample supply of nitrogen in the estuarine waters bathing these marshes, but since only the lower marshes get a good dose of water, the smooth cordgrasses higher up don't receive enough nitrogen. Researchers have even tested this idea in experiments by applying nitrogen to various growth forms in the marsh. The short growth form, in situ on the higher marsh, responded by growing taller. There was little effect of nitrogen on the taller growth form. They've also done reciprocal field transplants, placing the tall growth form in the higher elevation, less frequently flooded marsh; the shorter growth form in the lower elevation, more frequently flooded marsh. Based upon these experiments, they concluded that the growth forms were not genetically fixed; rather they were environmentally controlled, since the short growth form grew taller in the presence of more tidal flooding, whereas the tall growth form became more stunted with less flooding on the higher marsh. So we call these forms ecophenes in-

---

[17]These growth forms all involve the same species, *Spartina alterniflora*. Rather than continually referring to the tall growth form of the smooth cordgrass and the short growth form of the smooth cordgrass, for readability I will, other than for in the dialogue, just call them tall smooth cordgrass and short smooth cordgrass, respectively.

stead of ecotypes. Ecophenes are not genetically fixed; ecotypes are. We'll see the short growth form across the road."

Student: "What about all of these invertebrates. What eats them?"

Instructor: "Clapper rails gorge on the fiddlers. They also take the periwinkles and saltmarsh snails, as do other marsh birds like the willets and glossy ibises. And diamondback terrapins (*Malaclemys terrapin terrapin*) even visit the marshes at times to chomp on the snails, periwinkles, and marsh fiddlers. I have found numerous ribbed mussel shells and droppings filled with fish scales and crab shell fragments on mosquito ditching spoil piles up at Sinepuxent Bay, no doubt the work of raccoons and otters. These invertebrates also fall prey to various herons and egrets. I heard at least two clappers since we've been here. Not far up the road, in fact, is where Robert Stewart, a U.S. Fish and Wildlife Service researcher, studied clapper populations back in 1951. Numerous clapper nests were found, as I recall, something like seventy. Most of these were located in the tall growth form of the smooth cordgrass, only about fifteen feet from the tidal guts.

"We better cross over to the other side of the road now, but first you should see how abundant these eastern mud nassas, *Nassarius obsoletus*, are in the shallow water and on the mudbank. Also see how they are more blunt-tipped than the periwinkle; the shells even appear to have been eroded somewhat at their tips. See how brown they are from the mud, yet there is an underlying purple tint. These univalves, along with the gulf periwinkle and saltmarsh snail, represent a good example of how related animals over evolutionary time have partitioned the resources to prevent interspecific competition, in this instance horizontal space across the marsh in response to an elevation change of less than a foot. The eastern mud nassa remains essentially in the tidal guts; the gulf periwinkle in the tall growth form of smooth cordgrass; the saltmarsh snail in the low growth form and in the salt meadow."

With that extended explanation, we climbed over the guard rail, divided up the equipment, and crossed the road. I immediately observed that some exceptionally high tides had sometime in the recent past rafted substantial tall smooth cordgrass flotsam up on the slightly sloping road shoulder. I turned over a batch, then another.

Student: "What are you looking for?"

Instructor: "A small mammal, the meadow vole, *Microtus pennsylvanicus*. See all of these runways, basically the voles roadways for getting around. Here's even a bedding area, this batch of clipped dried grasses. If we persist, we more than likely will roust one out of a runway or bedding area. Hand me that dip net."

Student: "I was wondering why we brought that along."

We continued to turn over the flotsam, and as I expected soon spotted a vole dart for cover; evading our pursuit, we immediately lost sight of it. We continued the procedure and before long another vole darted for cover. This time, however, a quick slap of the dip net had it pinned in some grasses. With a little maneuvering, I carefully slipped my hand under the netting and got the vole by the scruff of the neck. While it squirmed, I held firm.

Instructor: "This isn't your typical Mickey Mouse type rodent you're used to seeing in TV cartoons, like the deer mouse, *Peromyscus maniculatus*, in real life. As opposed to the deer mouse, which has long ears and a long tail, the meadow vole has short ears and a short tail and resembles lemmings somewhat. It is also much more aggressive than the peromyscid type mice. It is generally very abundant in upland fields; it is also common on saltmarshes,

47

particularly in the short growth form smooth cordgrass and in the salt meadows. To see what I mean, just kneel down in the marsh out there and separate some of the grass stems. You'll soon note numerous runs, droppings, feed beds of grass clipping, and even some bedding areas if you search long enough. I've been in marshes in Dorchester County that had just been burned; the numerous exposed meadow vole runs were quite evident and seemed to go everywhere, like roads on a map."

I released the vole and we circumvented a good size shallow open water area before getting about 150 feet into the marsh. The vegetation was mostly the short smooth cordgrass, but there were small muddy depressions that supported a succulent plant species. There were also some shallow depressions holding a foot or less of water. I lectured a little at this point.

Instructor: "See these succulent plants that have turned red. They are the slender glasswort, *Salicornia europaea*. They turn that color in the fall. Use your imagination for a minute. In miniature, don't they resemble dead trees in one of those deeply impounded areas along a river in the southeast or along the Mississippi, where all of the floodplain trees have died due to the permanent inundation? Their reflections even show on the still water. Makes for a great photo. [A couple of cameras soon snapped.] These small depressions, which sometimes have shallow water, are commonly called salt pans."

Student: "Why are they so succulent out here where it's so wet? I thought succulents occurred in dry areas like deserts."

Instructor: "Good question. Although the slender glasswort is a hydrophyte and therefore does very well under saturated soil conditions, it is also a halophyte and therefore does very well under high salinities too. In fact, some researchers consider the glassworts the only obligate halophytes, since most plants that occur under brackish or saline conditions also can do quite well, and sometimes even better, under fresh conditions. You see, non-halophytic plants would lose water by osmosis rather quickly if they were transplanted to saltmarshes. On the other hand, the glassworts are physiologically adapted to such conditions. They maintain a high concentration of salts in their tissues, which allows them to retain water. So you might say saltmarshes are physiologically dry, and only a handful of plants, like the glassworts and cordgrasses, are adapted to such conditions. As a matter of fact, the smooth cordgrass has specialized glands on the leaves for exuding excessive salts. Look closely at one of the leaves over there and you'll likely see the salt crystals. Notice too that there aren't many vascular plants in this marsh. This is another characteristic of saltmarshes -- they have low species richness, since only a handful of species can take the fluctuating salinity conditions, perhaps ten or so at the most on any one marsh."

In the open marsh near a small shallow pond, I stopped and explained that we were walking on a relatively thin mat of vegetation -- a six inch to one foot thick mat of roots and rhizomes from the saltmarsh cordgrass. I jumped up and down a couple of times to give them an effect they did not expect, a rather paradoxical effect. You see, on the one hand, the marsh peat seemed firm; on the other, everything started quaking when I started to jump up and down.

Instructor: "Don't worry. I guarantee you -- you won't break through and disappear into the muddy sediment below. No one ever sinks out of sight! The peat is really firm. Let me show you how thick it is."

With that comment, I took hold of the soil auger with both hands and thrust it into the peat; I screwed it in a little, then pushed and pushed. Soon it broke through and sank rather easily. I pulled out the auger and showed them some of the peat that was attached. I cleaned out the auger and pushed it readily this time through the two-inch diameter hole. All but two feet of it stuck out. With the aid of a student and the two pipe wrenches, I attached a five foot section of galvanized pipe to the auger. I easily pushed it down into the underlying silty substrate. I attached another section, then another and another, then two more, and finally my last section for an estimated total penetration exceeding thirty feet. Each section penetrated with ease, requiring only slight pressure with my arm as the underlying silt swallowed the pipes. Needless to say, this aroused the students interest, considering that we used all of the pipe sections and I promised them they (meaning the students!) would not disappear into the marsh.

Students: "How deep have we gone?" "You'll never get it back."

Instructor: "I've often thought about that, since I buy all of my own equipment and I would hate to lose the expensive auger on the end. We've gone down over thirty feet; we'll get an accurate depth when we extract the pipes. And we still haven't hit the old Pleistocene bottom.

"You see at one time the sea level was much lower along the coast; in fact, about 300-400 feet lower and many miles offshore. With the melting of the glaciers 15,000 or so years ago, the entire coastline was slowly inundated. At some point in the process, barrier islands like Chincoteague and Assateague were formed, as were the lagoons behind them and eventually the marshes. The rate of sea level rise had to be just right for this to occur; the sediment and organic accretion rates had to keep up with the rate of sea level rise or otherwise the incipient marshes would have been drowned out. Over thousands of years, the marshes continued to move, much like the barrier islands, upward and landward in time and space, eventually even transgressing over the low lying upland to the west. In the process, upland became wetland, a sort of retrogressive succession. Now then, lets see what this device looks like extended into the air."

A student and I attached the two pipe wrenches to the pipe for leverage and started pulling. Because of all of the suction I suppose, the extraction of the pipe sections was much more difficult -- and quite wet and muddy, an absolute mess. Up came one, then another, and another; soon we had this tall galvanized pole swaying from its own weight dangerously overhead. I knew from past experience that this was an unsafe situation, because one year a section snapped at the coupling and almost hit someone. Experience also taught me that lowering it to the side while all assembled would not work, for there had been another break. Yet I wanted them to see how impressive that height was, and they certainly were impressed (Figure 10).

> Students: "Man! Wow!" "Impressive! How deep is it to the Pleistocene?" (A couple of pictures were snapped.)

> Instructor: "Based upon past sampling, I'm surprised we didn't hit bottom today, since at least once in the past I did in this same general area. You can tell when you've hit bottom. It's firm at that point and you can hear the sand grinding as you twist the auger with the pipe wrenches. But first let's get this thing disassembled before someone gets hurt."

We pushed the pipes back down, then reversed the process, unscrewing each section piece by piece until we retrieved the auger. Then laid them out end to end in the short cordgrass to measure the total length. And we were a mess.

> Instructor: "Well, that totals thirty-five feet. And now you'll see why I chose this spot. We can somewhat clean up these pipes, auger, and wrenches in the shallow water. When you're done with the sections you have, put them in a pile over here. But wait; before we do that I have one other thing I would like to demonstrate."

Figure 10. The author with a small group of students probing the marsh peat and inorganic estuarine sediments under the Chincoteague Bay saltmarshes along Virginia Route 175. At times, depths of thirty-five feet were reached with this auger and its pipe extensions before encountering the basal Pleistocene sands.

With that said, I again slammed the auger into the peat and hooked the wrench to it; with a few twists and some pushing, the auger poked through. This time, however, I purposely didn't immediately extract auger.

> Instructor: "Now, who has my matches? Thanks. Let's see if we can tap some methane or hydrogen sulfide, both of which are flammable. To do this, we need to do a few things simultaneously -- slowly pull out the auger and watch for some bubbles coming up through the water in the bore hole, but at the same time light a match just above the bubbles and shield the flame from this breeze. Ready?"

I slowly pulled out the auger as someone lit a match and cupped their hands to block the moderate breeze. We all, of course, had our eyes fixed on the burning match flame when the few bubbles gushed up. And to all of our surprise, the flame clearly flared.[18] We then washed the equipment and I continued lecturing.

> Instructor: "I've done this marsh probing many times before, with and without students. But this time it has been more interesting, since we brought up some peaty material from the bottom. There's been a lot of work done in Delaware by Kraft and his students on similar wetlands. They've documented the stratigraphic sequence and have recovered buried, in situ, basal marsh peat at substantive depths. They radiocarbon dated it to determine its age. It's generally accepted that the smooth cordgrass always grew intertidally. Consequently, if you find in situ cordgrass basal peat say twenty feet down in these back bays and marshes, it probably was an intertidal marsh at that level when sea level was twenty feet lower. If you carbon date that basal peat at say 3000 years, then it's a good bet that sea level was twenty feet lower 3000 years ago (16,17).

---

[18]That was the first and only time, as I recall, in many of these trips that we were successful with this experiment. Generally, the breeze would not even allow the flame to last long enough to make contact with the gas leaving the bubbles.

"The basal peat we just found below the overlying estuarine sediments is from what has been called fringe marsh, since it formed along the leading edge of the system as the bays and marshes transgressed over the upland. So what we might have here is the older buried fringe marsh overtopped by estuarine sediments that formed as the bay filled in; these sediments then preserved the buried basal peat. When the shoals build upward enough to become intertidal, large expansive saltmarshes, such as what we are now standing on, developed out over them. These extensive saltmarshes then continued to transgress westward over the upland as sea level rose even more. I know it's hard for you to picture this process, but it will be much clearer in class next week when I discuss it with the aid of some excellent illustrations depicting the sedimentary sequence. We better move on now; we have to get across the marsh at Toms Cove and onto an oyster bar before the tide comes in." (See Chapter Four on the Maryland's coastal bays for more on the origin of the barrier islands, bays, and saltmarshes.)

Stop 8 -- Assateague Island and Toms Cove

Shortly thereafter, our caravan was heading due east again for Chincoteague. I thought to myself: These folks are observant; they will see all of these egrets, herons, gulls, and terns, and the exposed mud flats covered with shorebirds. As we eventually traveled up and over the short, hump-like bridge over Chincoteague Channel, I could not help but notice the berthed fishing fleet to my left. At the first traffic light we turned left onto Route 175 and passed through the business district, but soon turned right onto Maddox Boulevard, where a large sign proclaimed Assateague. At Piney Island, we went around the small circle and continued east. After crossing Assateague Channel, we proceeded past Chincoteague National Wildlife Refuge to Toms Cove on the right, within sight of the dunes at the Assateague Island National Seashore. We pulled off on the shoulder and donned our field gear.

Once again, we had substantial gear to lug with us, so I asked for volunteers. Two people took the 30-foot seine; someone took the brass standard sieve and a bulb planter for extracting benthic invertebrates; two people grabbed the two dip nets; a third took a plastic bucket. We dropped down the embankment and into the marsh. At the marsh edge, I pointed out a southern woody composite.

> Instructor: "See this plant. It's the sea ox-eye, *Borrichia frutescens*, a woody composite at or near the northern-most extent of its range. It's related to two more common composites found in or at the edge of saltmarshes in this area, the hightide bush, *Baccharis halimifolia* and the marsh elder, *Iva frutescens*. A question for you plant types: Why might you think this is odd for the East?"

> Student: "Aren't most composites herbs, like asters and goldenrods? I never heard of woody composites."

> Instructor: "That's what I'm getting at. In the East at least, you don't encounter many woody composites. As far as I know, the sea ox-eye, hightide bush, and marsh elder are the only three in our area. Here's some more glassworts, in this instance scattered in the short growth form of the smooth cordgrass. And look at this plant with its succulent leaves and withered inflorescence. Its inflorescence is shaped like a miniature elm tree, if you can relate to that. It's the sea lavender, *Limonium carolinianum*. But let's move on."

We moved through some exceptionally tall smooth cordgrass that was replete with gulf periwinkles. Being so well flooded, the substrate was understandably sinky, but before long we intersected a small tidal gut coming in from our right. I stepped into it since only a trickle of water remained and they followed, rather surprised at how firm the bottom was. This was a geologically young marsh and obviously well-flooded even on an average high tide. Ribbed mussels were abundant along the gut banks, particularly where

55

it emptied into the waters of Toms Cove. From the mouth of the gut looking southeast, only a short distance away sat a small oyster (*Crassostrea virginica*)bar. In the foreground lay the exposed sand and shell flats that were eagerly sought at times by recreational clammers seeking hardshell clams (*Mercenaria mercenaria*). All over the flats where small, somewhat hooked projections covered with bits of shells and macroscopic algae. Small gastropods were scattered over the shallows; schools of three to five-inch long fish darted helter-skelter with our advance.

> Instructor: "We will head straight across this shallow open water for the oyster bar; we'll check the sand flats later. Don't worry, it's only about two feet deep at the most since we are on a spring tide and the tide's still out."

At the oyster bar, I promptly unrolled the 30-foot seine from its two end poles and we went to work. I stationed a student holding one pole at a point where the water laps the shore. I then took the other pole and waded straight out as far as my hipboots would allow, only about fifteen feet due to the rather steep outer slopes of the oyster bar. I walked parallel to the shore with the seine dragging behind and bowing out as the student held firm to the other end. Because of the weights at the bottom of the seine and the floats at the top, it maintained its position throughout the shallow water column. I could envision many critters, especially fish, in it as I slipped along with the seine pole using it simultaneously to feel my way and not swamp my boots. As the seine tightened and bowed, it seemed to get heavier; I got excited. Next, I swung to my left to complete the ninety degree arc and hopefully trap the critters the seine had encircled. The two of us then carefully brought both ends together and walked quickly backwards up the oyster bar dragging the seine behind, all the time keeping it smack against the oyster bar to minimize the loss of the entrapped fish, particularly any larger ones, that might slip under the mesh. The general appearance of the seine at this juncture was an arching or bowing out towards the open water, sort of like the same effect produced by someone lying in a netted hammock. As we beached the seine and the water poured through the mesh, it seemed to come alive, alive with small fish. I dropped my pole and flipped back the top half of the seine exposing its contents. The anticipation and excitement of the students, which had been building as we pulled the seine up the beach, reached a crescendo, and understandably so. Hundreds of small fish, mostly Atlantic silversides were flipping around madly. Everyone gathered around. They had never seen a seining operation before; a group of fourth graders could not have been more excited. But I knew we had to move fast.

Instructor: "We need to move fast, or many of these fish, the ones with the stripe down their sides, the Atlantic silversides, *Menidia menidia*, will die; they can't stay long out of water. Let's make a quick sort to see what else we have. Look here's some striped killifish, *Fundulus majalis*. These have a more sleek body shape and more pointed nose than the common killifish or mummichog, *Fundulus heteroclitus*, which is found up in the tidal guts, mosquito ditches, and marsh pools. Look at..."

Student: "What are all these translucent shrimp-like critters?"

Instructor: "Grass or glass shrimp, the genus *Palaemonetes*. Look at them all, hundreds in this one seine haul. Excellent food for larger estuarine animals. They are related to the larger penaeid shrimp -- the brown shrimp, white shrimp, and pink shrimp -- that you all probably have eaten. Look, there's a few small blue crabs, also some sponges that are attached to oyster shells. But what's this fish? A new one for me I'm sure; strange.[19] Let's get these fish back into the water and make another run. Just turn the seine over into the water like this. See, some of the silversides are already floating belly up. We'll do our next run along the beach for thirty or forty feet before we pull it in."

---

[19]Upon checking up on this fish later, it turned out to be the mojarra, *Eucinostomus californiensis*, a new species for me.

A lady and I dragged the seine along the shallows of the shell beach for about forty feet, then she held fast at the shore and I looped in to her holding the other pole. Then we again dragged the seine up the beach. As I expected, we were substantially rewarded by our effort: Atlantic silversides and grass shrimp galore; more killifish and blue crabs (*Callinectes sapidus*) too; even another oddball, the puffer or toadfish (*Sphoeroides maculatus*). We promptly emptied the seine to minimize mortality, then I explained how small critters like the grass shrimp are so important in the detrital food web of the estuary, and the benefit of the silversides as forage fish for larger species like summer flounder (*Paralichthys dentatus*), black sea bass (*Centropristis striata*), spot (*Leiostomus xanthurus*), weakfish (*Cynoscion regalis*), silver perch (*Bairdiella chrysoura*), bluefish (*Pomatomus saltatrix*), and others. Also, how important the estuary is for the commercial fishing industry.

> Instructor: "The silversides and killifish are what's known as forage fish. They are preyed upon by larger fish, many of which have substantial recreational and commercial value. In fact, a large percentage of the total commercial fish catch is estuarine dependent. What I mean by that is that some part of the life cycles of many commercial fish is dependent upon estuaries. These fish are either born there or they spend a substantial part of their early years maturing in estuaries. The estuaries are the nursery areas. All of this leads to big bucks for the industry."

> Student: "So what I think you are saying is that we don't have to eat these animals, for example the killifish, silversides, and grass shrimp, to benefit by them. Is that correct?"

> Instructor: "Yes, and even if we didn't benefit indirectly like this, these critters have value in their own right. What I mean is that animals don't have to have economic value to man to be important. They were not put here just for our use. They have a right to exist

independent of any anthropomorphic values, if you follow my reasoning and I'm not getting too philosophical for some of you. But I suspect most if not all of you would agree with that statement. Now let's clean out the seine in the water and wind it up around the poles. Then we'll see what we can find in the benthos over on the exposed tide flat."

We stretched out the seine, flipped it over a few times in and out of the water, wound it up on the two poles, and waded with it dripping saltwater back to the flat. In transit, someone handed me an oyster shell that had an orange sponge attached. I dipped the shell in the water then took a close look. A couple of small reddish worm-like critters glided slowly across the shell. I pointed out these polychaete worms and mentioned how as a graduate student at the University of Maryland I had visited Toms Cove with my marine ecology class to sample these same tidal flats. The professor was particularly interested in the plumed worm (*Diopatra cuprea*), a large armored polychaete. So I spent substantial time collecting and subsequently identifying polychaetes and other estuarine invertebrates in the lab.

Instructor: "This red, worm-like critter is a worm. Not an earthworm type but a marine worm, a polychaete worm, perhaps a *Nereis* species. The orange glob is a sponge like the ones we just seined. The polychaetes are not all this small. See those hooked things sticking up, scattered generally in small bunches over the tide flat. They are the tubes of a large polychaete, the plumed worm, *Diopatra cuprea*. I've never seen the live worm itself. Every time I have dug for it, it retreated too deeply into its tube. Its presence is obvious, however, because of the debris attached to the tubes that protrude two or three inches out of the flat. See all of the shell pieces attached, and the bits of sea lettuce? This critter helps structure the community it lives in by providing additional substrate types for smaller critters to settle on. It's not uncommon to find more invertebrates in a sample that includes a couple of these tubes than in a sample in an open area devoid of tubes.

"This brings up another point. Oyster bars like the one we just sampled and those in deeper waters are probably the most diverse benthic communities in these coastal bays and the Chesapeake Bay, although disease and predation by oyster drills (*Urosalpinx cinerea*) have taken their toll on the oysters in these high salinity waters. A close second for invertebrate diversity goes to the beds of submerged aquatic vegetation, which are also replete with critters. The small animals, of course, attract bigger ones, so a large part of the estuarine food web is built around the oyster bars and submerged aquatic vegetation."

Student: "Look, that snail-like shell seems to be moving a bit, but it's not one of the ones you showed us earlier. Oh look, I think it's a hermit crab inside."

Instructor: "Right. The hermit crab has taken over an abandoned oyster drill shell. If we looked closely, a number of these shells should support hermit crabs, the genus *Pagurus*. As the crabs grow, they have to abandon their shells for more suitable ones, sort of like we do with shoe sizes, or some of us with belt sizes. By the way, did you notice how much the tide has already come in since we've been out here. It doesn't take long in such a flat area as this. Incidentally, I planned this trip purposely to catch an extra low tide, what's known as a spring tide.

"These tides have nothing to do with the spring of the year. You know, I once was at a public hearing where an expert witness for the other side implied that a spring tide occurred in the spring! How embarrassing for him when I tipped off our attorney and he nailed him on it. Actually, spring tides occur during full or new moons, when the sun, moon, and earth are all aligned, which is referred to as syzygy. As a result of this alignment, there is a greater gravitational pull than usual and the low tides are lower than normal, while the high tides are higher than normal. So, the tidal range is greater -- lower lows and higher highs. In a few hours this entire flat will be under three feet or so of water, and most of the marsh itself will have at least a foot of water over it.

"Let's head back to the vehicles now, even though we didn't use the dip nets yet. With the tide out, they wouldn't have been of much use anyway. We are quickly eating up our time. As I indicated this morning, from here we will drive back to the Refuge Visitor Center and eat a quick lunch in the parking lot, then circle the shallow man-made impoundments before traveling up Assateague Island to an area called the Wash Flats, then go on beyond to visit the dunes and beach."

Stop 9 -- Assateague's Impoundments and Wash Flats

During lunch I obtained the key and pass for access to the upper part of the Refuge, which is not usually open to vehicular traffic. We packed into one van and two other cars, then drove around the shallow impoundments designed to attract wildlife, particularly waterfowl. I informed the students that we would periodically stop along the dike to observe the wildlife, but that they should not leave their vehicles, since this would be just a quick pass through. They could always come back on their own if they were serious birders. We noted small flocks of greater snow geese, some black ducks, and a few herons and egrets. But it was at the end of the loop, just before we were to make a right after unlocking the gate to head north up the island, that we got a nice surprise -- a male peregrine falcon perched on the limb of a dead tree. A great view for everyone as I pointed with my hand out the window. Soon, however, we were heading north on the dirt road.

Our first stop was at another diked off area that, in this instance, was not flooded; rather, it supported numerous herbaceous species. Immediately upon exiting the vehicle, there was an inquiry about the nature of impoundments.

61

: "Just what are impoundments anyway? Are they natural or man-made?"

Instructor: "Well, impoundments are simply man-made water bodies, like lakes or reservoirs, or as in this case, former wetlands or low areas that are now enclosed by a peripheral dike system with water control structures. Because of the water control structures, water levels can be manipulated for various management purposes. Believe me though, they aren't without controversy, even the shallow waterfowl impoundments, especially if they are constructed in pre-existing wetlands." (See also the discussion on impoundments in Chapter Four.)

I explained how manipulating the water level, like they do back at the other impoundment we had just circled, allows the invasion of desirable plants which in turn attracts waterfowl. The idea is to drop the water level in the spring to allow the seeds to germinate. There seems to almost always be quite a seedbank available, dormant seeds just waiting for the right drawdown conditions for germination in the moist soil. Even a couple of inches of water prevents that. Then by fall, when these plants are mature and replete with seeds, a site is shallowly flooded. This coincides with the arrival of numerous waterfowl species from their breeding grounds in the north. The open water also allows waterfowl to readily land and forage in the shallows or move up into the emergent vegetation. Where we were standing was probably an example of a site that had not been flooded for a number of years, since it was so dense with vegetation some of which was perennial. I pointed out an excellent waterfowl food, the Walter's millet (*Echinochloa walteri*), and we moved on.

As we traveled down the road, I spotted a sika deer (*Cervus nippon*), a deer common on the island and introduced many years ago. We also jumped a few white-tailed deer (*Odocoileus virginianus*) in a diked area covered with herbaceous vegetation and scattered medium size black willows. Warblers, mostly myrtles (yellow-rumpted), flitted from bush to bush and by the numbers of flickers we passed, it was obvious that a major southern flight of that colorful woodpecker was on.

We pulled off at our next stop, the Wash Flats, and saw something of interest to everyone -- the legendary Assateague ponies. Their origin is unknown, but one legend has it that they originally arrived during a shipwreck; another, that they were put ashore by pirates to graze (Figure 11).

> Instructor: "Look over there at the salt meadow cordgrass growing on the road dike. See how cropped it is; and in this instance, it's growing in the upland. Look down in the marsh too. The tall growth form of the smooth cordgrass along the small gut had also been cropped. Both from the ponies over there. Isn't that a wonderful view against the backdrop of the marsh and bay?"

> Students: "What a view!" "Perfect!"

> Instructor: "Let's drop down over the other side and I'll explain just what these Wash Flats are."

From the Wash Flats looking north up the island, the flats were on our right, the saltmarsh to our left.[20] The Wash Flats were flat as a pancake, and essentially bare of vegetation. A 30-foot or so wide ditch was at the base of the road dike, so we could not actually get onto the flats. In the distance

---

[20]Some years later in 1987 while on my plant identification course field trip, I investigated this saltmarsh and found that a small area of it was rather diverse for a saltmarsh. I also found a plant, the seaside plantain, *Plantago maritima*, that has never been reported from Maryland. Steven Hill (18) did report it, however, from the Virginia part of Assateague via Harvill (19), and Larry Klotz (20) reported it from Wallops Island just to the south. My find was actually in Virginia, just south of the border, but considering that this species is of northern affinity, there's no doubt in my mind that it also occurs in Maryland. My voucher specimen (Sipple # 1943) is in the herbarium at Delaware State University.

63

Figure 11. Wild ponies grazing on an Assateague Island saltmarsh. (Photo by the author)

was a stationary jeep. Suddenly the jeep moved forward and someone got out and picked up a white object. As we stood at the dike base discussing two plants, the common three-square and small spikerush, the jeep suddenly arrived opposite us just across the ditch. Out jumped two people, one of which had a live peregrine falcon in his hand. It was Dr. Scott Ward, a researcher, and his assistant, who were investigating the migratory habits of prairie falcons. Dr. Ward gave us a brief overview of their investigations and how they trapped the falcon by the use of a tethered white pigeon (the white object) enclosed in netting. When the falcon struck, its feet got tangled which resulted in its capture. We thanked them for the overview as they departed, then I continued on the two plants.

Instructor: "That's the three-square, the same species that we saw yesterday on the Choptank, and again it's on inorganic soil. See these elongate reddish structures? They are three-square rhizomes that have been dug up by muskrats. Excellent muskrat food. Being underground stems, they have nodes and internodes; each node has the capacity to produce a new shoot, which is why these plants are interconnected underground and some are growing in a line. Look here's additional muskrat sign -- tracks and this line in between, which is the result of the muskrat's tail dragging behind. See this tiny, grass-like plant. It's actually a type of sedge, the small spikerush, *Eleocharis parvula*. The specific epithet means very small, a good characterization for this tiny plant.

"By the way, you may have noticed by now that I frequently point out what the specific epithets of plants and animals mean. Although they are not necessarily diagnostic -- and in some instance can be downright misleading -- they are usually instructive in describing something about the plant, at least those that are adjectival in nature. For example, in the saltgrass, *Distichlis spicata*, the specific epithet *spicata* means spiked -- in this instance, having a spike-like inflorescence; in the sea ox-eye, *Borrichia frutescens*, the specific epithet *frutescens* refers to the term frutescent-- meaning shrubby, which this species is. I like to point out these things, particularly in my plant identification course, since they can serve somewhat as mnemonic devices."

Student: "What about over on the Wash Flats? What plants occur there?"

Instructor: "Only a few will persist in this area. Examples would be the slender glasswort, *Salicornia europaea*, and sea purslane, *Sesuvium maritimum*."

Student: "My god, how do you remember all of those scientific names?"

Instructor: "You don't have to be bright for this. Just have a penchant for memorization and the zeal to do it. I've been doing it since about 1963. Initially started as a hobby of sorts, even prior to thoughts of college, which I didn't attend until I got my head straight about seven years after high school. I could tell you of my systematic attempt to memorize all of the scientific names in *Gray's Manual of Botany* back then, but we really should move on now."

Student: "But you haven't explained why they call this area the Wash Flats."

Instructor: "Sorry. You have to watch me. I get so engrossed in these things. I'll talk up a storm, but sometimes skip important points or have slips of the tongue. So feel free to check me if necessary. Look east towards the ocean, which is just over those low hills. The hills are the dunes, which are typical of most barrier islands. In this instance, however, they have been augmented by the use of sand fences that serve as baffles to the almost constantly blowing sand. In so doing, the fences trap sand and function in dune building.

"Many barrier island systems are generally moving upward and landward in time and space overtopping, or seemingly rolling over, the marshes and shallow lagoons on their back sides. Although we won't see it today, there's good evidence of this further up the island in the way of outcropped marsh peat and dead, in situ, pine stumps out on the eroding beach. This peat is from marshes that developed in protected shallow lagoons behind Assateague at much earlier times. The pines originated on the backside of the island, protected from ocean salt spray. This is clear evidence of the island's western migration. The Wash Flats are remnant overwash areas that were frequently flooded when storms passed through the area. Each overwash by the ocean brought in more sand, since the dunes were breached. Overwashes do not occur here anymore since they built up

66

the dune system you are now observing, although a major storm could break through someday."

We climbed back up the dike and I opened a map from a large government publication for discussion purposes (21).

Instructor: "Now that you've seen a lot of the Assateague-Chincoteague area, this is a good time to go over a little of its geologic history. The map in this publication on Assateague should help me explain all this [map is spread on hood of car]. As I indicated when we were augering this morning, sea level was substantially lower during the Pleistocene when so much water was tied up in the glaciers. As the glaciers began to melt 15,000 years or so ago, the coast was slowly inundated and eventually barrier islands formed, landward of which were shallow lagoons and eventually saltmarshes. Initially, Assateague Island was much further offshore, many miles in fact. Chincoteague was quite exposed to the ocean at the time, but as Assateague migrated west and extended by spit accretion south, it eventually captured Chincoteague in a geologic sense (22).

"See this recurved spit, Fishing Point, at the southern tip of Assateague? That's the latest spit that has formed and it is still quite active. Moving back, you can see a series of paleospits, including this -- Assateague Ridge, then this -- Lighthouse Ridge. Further back, between Assateague and Chincoteague is what remains of another spit, Piney Island, then the remains of a fifth spit, Morris Island. So you see Assateague moved southwest to ultimately capture Chincoteague, effectively cutting it off from the ocean. Therefore, Chincoteague is no longer an active barrier island migrating west in response to sea level rise. Assateague, on the other hand, still is quite active.

"We will discuss this more in class with the aid of some excellent slides." (See Chapter Four on saltmarshes of Maryland's coastal bays for more on the developmental history of this area.)

67

Student: "Fascinating, but how long did all of this take? I mean the capture?"

Instructor: "As I recall, it was suggested that Assateague Island had captured Chincoteague sometime during the last two thousand years. And there are historical records for this section from the northern end of Toms Cove down to Fishing Point, which has formed since around 1860. Now we better head further north to our last stop. It's already approaching three o'clock."

Stop 10 -- The dunes, beach, and ocean.

While motoring down the dirt road, we again saw many birds, mostly warblers flitting erratically in the bushes to our left. Then to our right out in a flooded section of the Wash Flats, a large flock of white birds, greater snow geese, stood out well against the grayish backdrop of the dunes. I decided to make a quick unplanned stop. When we stepped out of our cars, the whole flock was up in a roar, only to circle and land a couple of thousand feet further up the Wash Flats. A number of gulls were well out in the flats just beyond the open water, and a quick scan of the area produced a couple great blue herons. With the dunes and beach in mind, we climbed back into our vehicles and drove to a turn around area at the end of the dirt road and parked.

Two other roads continued on from here, but they were gated off. One of these roads headed east to the beach. We took the beach road carrying our equipment -- this time just the seine and an army surplus shovel. As we crossed the island, I discussed the various vegetation zones, but in this instance in reverse, starting from the back side of the island. We had already seen the saltmarsh, so the first zone we traversed was a forested area, which was dominated by loblolly pine (*Pinus taeda*). The loblolly is typical of Assateague's forested zone, although the large paleospit, Lighthouse Ridge,

68

near the Refuge Visitor Center has rather large deciduous trees too.[21] We next passed through the shrub zone. This was generally upland, but some low swales were very wet and at least one swale that we crossed had some shallow standing water. This large swale with shallow open water supported a number of wetland plants, including the square-stem spikerush (*Eleocharis quadrangulata*) and the coastal water-hyssop (*Bacopa monnieri*). Fox tracks were abundant along the sandy road and someone indicated that they had spotted a red fox (*Vulpes fulva*) along the edge of the large swale as we approached. The upland (xeric) thickets included mostly shrubs like bayberry (*Myrica pensylvanica*), wax myrtle (*M. cerifera*), and shadbush (*Ammelanchier canadensis*); the more mesic thickets in the swales had plants like highbush blueberry (*Vaccinium corymbosum*) and northern arrowwood (*Viburnum recognitum*). As we approached closer to the beach, secondary dunes were commonly vegetated also by large patches of the hudsonia (*Hudsonia tomentosa*), a low evergreen shrub, which in the spring sports colorful yellow flowers. Herbaceous species became more obvious -- plants like the seaside goldenrod (*Solidago sempervirens*), broom-sedge (*Androgon virginicus*), blue toadflax (*Linaria canadensis*), sand jointweed *Polygonella articulata*), beach pinweed (*Hypericum gentianoides*), and seaside threeawn (*Aristida tuberculosa*). At one point, the slithering trail of a medium size snake, probably a hognose snake (*Heterodon platyrhinos*), was noted. This is a fairly common snake on Assateague that feeds mostly on Fowler's toads (*Bufo woodhousei* var. *fowleri*). I mentioned how this snake, which manifests both a patterned (variously colored) phase and an unpatterned (melanistic) phase, feigns death through a physiological reaction to disturbance, and how a couple of years earlier my class and I observed a hognose perform this feat on a sandy spoil bank adjacent to the Snug Harbor Marsh at Sinepuxent Bay (Figure 12).

---

[21]We did not visit Lighthouse Ridge or the interesting large swale immediately northwest of it. I generally saved those areas for my Dune, Marsh, and Aquatic Plant Identification course field trips.

Figure 12. Hognose snake (*Heterodon platyrhinos*) that "played possum" for my wetland ecology class in the upland adjacent to the Snug Harbor marsh along Sinepuxent Bay, Worcester County, Maryland. (Photo by the author)

Not too far past the large swale, everyone felt substantially relieved as some breezes came in over the dunes. You see, we had been swatting numerous mosquitos and some pesky deerflies all along the dirt road. We climbed through a low wire fence erected to keep the ponies off the primary dunes and started towards the beach. On the way, I again showed them some plants.

> Instructor: "See this small plant -- it's a spurge, the seaside spurge, *Euphorbia polygonifolia*. Note how it spreads out over the surface of the sand, almost glued to it. One might wonder how in the world it gets water in this xeric environment. Let's dig this one up. See, it's easy to slip my fingers down into this loose sand. Now I'll sort of scoop the spurge out. Look, here's the dangling root and a couple of

branches; the tap root's really long compared to the spurge's height and even its spread on the surface."

Student: "So it taps deeply into the moist sand below."

Instructor: "Yes, and the plant's also somewhat succulent and therefore readily retains water. Look too at its milky juice where I snipped off a leaf. Let's scoop a little sand out here and replant it.

"Here's another species, the seabeach evening primrose, *Oenothera humifusa*. It too has a whorl of leaves at its base and somewhat sprawls along the sand. And here is a grass, the dune sandbur, *Cenchrus tribuloides*.

"Note that the common names of these three plants imply that they occur along the sea, which is true. They are good examples of how certain species within a genus occur on very specific habitats, in this instance the beaches and dunes along the coast. They all have congeners (that is, other species in the same genus) that occur in other habitats. Now I've been talking a lot these past two days. My voice is even starting to fail. Any questions?"

Student: "I have one. Where are the flowers on these plants?"

Instructor: "Well, sandbur is a grass, so it has a rather nondescript flower, generally only one flower in each spikelet and that has only a single style and three small anthers. Nothing showy at all. The most obvious thing on it are the burs. If you have ever walked in an old field in late summer or autumn you may have encountered one of its relatives, since the small burs catch hold on your socks, shoe laces, and pant legs quite easily.

"The spurge has a flower, but it is rather specialized and non-showy, and currently the plant is in fruit. On the other hand, the primrose has a showy yellow flower -- but its name, evening primrose, suggests its seeming absence right now. You see, the flower is closed, if it hasn't already gone to fruit; it's more commonly open in the evening, or on cloudy days at times."

Student: "What's that grass-like clump over there?"

Instructor: "That's the switchgrass, *Panicum virgatum*, the same species, believe it or not, that was in the well-flooded intertidal zone along the Choptank River yesterday. Remember it? I discussed the plant and mentioned how it generally grows more frequently in uplands or at the upland side of a wetland-upland border. Here it's growing under obvious xeric conditions. Given the variable habitats involved, this species might manifest ecotypic variation. That is, it might have populations that are genetically adapted to wetlands; others to uplands. I can see a related species over by the primary dunes. Let's check it out."

I showed them the other panic grass, the bitter panic grass (*Panicum amarum*), as well as the dominant dune grass in the northeast, the American beach grass (*Ammophila breviligulata*). Then someone else inquired about its role in beach stabilization; another about the identity of a goldenrod.

Student: "Is the beach grass the same one they use to stabilize the dunes?"

Instructor: "Yes, the American beach grass, *Ammophila breviligulata*, is what they use along the east coast down to about North Carolina. South of us they also utilize another native, the sea oats, *Uniola paniculata*, with large showy spikelets."[22]

Student: "What goldenrod is that over there that seems to be attracting the monarch butterflies?"

---

[22]The sea oats has not been reported from Maryland, but it has been found on Fisherman's Island at the tip of the Delmarva Peninsula (23).

Instructor: "The goldenrod is the seaside goldenrod, *Solidago sempervirens*. Break off a leaf and note how succulent it is, which makes it rather easy to tell from the sundry other goldenrods. And the monarchs do frequent it on their southward migration, as we are experiencing here today (Figure 13). This goldenrod also occurs in the saltmarshes. Let's move on to the beach now."

Student: "Bill, what about all of these holes? What are they from?"

Instructor: "Oh sure, I had intended to point those out. Anyone familiar with them? [no response] Well, these are from the ghost crabs, *Ocypode quadrata*, a sort of attractive decapod with a sand-colored body and two white claws. Let's dig one out. See there's their tracks leading from the holes. They come out mostly at night and are found also on the beach."

It took a while to dig one out, since care had to be taken to follow the hole deeper and deeper into the loose sand. My approach was to excavate slowly, extracting small increments of sand with each shovel slice so as to not lose sight of the hole as the sand collapsed. Experience taught me that if this was not done right, a crab would not be found. But in this instance, I took my time and succeeded. The students were impressed by the ghost crab's large white claws and long-stalked eyes (Figure 14).

Student: "Let me get a picture before you release it. It's very attractive."

Instructor: "Here, get one while it's in my hand. Then maybe another on the ground if it doesn't dart too fast. [a couple of camera shutters

73

Figure 13. Monarch butterfly (*Danaus plexippus*) on the seaside goldenrod (*Solidago sempervirens*) in the Assateague Island, Virginia dune fields. (Photo by the author)

Figure 14. Ghost crab (*Oxcypode quadrata*) at Assateague Island, VA. This crab occurs abundantly in the upper beach and foredune dune area. (Photo by the author)

snapped]. It occurs abundantly on the upper beach and the foredunes."

When I released the crab, it was off in a flash, scampering over the sand. At the first large hole it encountered, the crab promptly entered, whereupon we hiked on down to the beach.

On the beach, we again pulled the seine, this time in the rough surf. We got only one fish, an oddball known as the lookdown (*Selene volmer*) with a thin, laterally compressed body and, from a side view, a blocky bulldog-like head. The fish was strange looking and I did not know its identity at the time. We also got what I was really after -- numerous mole crabs (*Emerita talpoida*), as well as some small colorful bivalves, the Forida coquina (*Donax variabilis*). Both of these mobile species are well-adapted for the rough surf. And after the waves broke on the beach and the water retreated, we quickly nabbed some by scooping out the burrowing mole crabs wherever air bubbled out of the wet sand; similarly, we noted the bivalves hastily retreating with the aid of their muscular feet.

Instructor: "Look, no fish; I really didn't expect any. Wait, here's one -- an oddball. Never seen it before. Excuse me for a couple of minutes while I take down a few notes. I'll check on it at home. While I'm scribbling, check the seine."

Student (biologist type): "Wow! Look at all of these mole crabs -- hundreds. Here's a few small clams too, and some crab carapaces."

Instructor: "Okay, what else do we have. Well, the carapaces are from the lady crab, *Ovalipes ocellatus*. This is probably the crab that pinches while you're in the surf at Ocean City. And look up the beach. See that small group of birds running back and forth with the approach and retreat of the water from the breaking waves? They are sanderlings, and they are pursuing these mole crabs with fervor and perhaps also these small bivalves called coquinas. Let's get these

75

things back into the water. Watch how quickly the mole crabs and coquinas burrow into the sand.

"I'm going to give you a little free time at this point to walk up the beach, inspect the dunes, or just relax here. It's your choice, but be back by four o'clock, so we can head back to the Visitor Center where we left the other vehicles, then head for home. That's a good three and a half hours for some of you. Look -- see those dark birds skimming low over the water out there? They're a type of sea duck, a scoter, but without a better look I'm not sure which of the three species we're seeing."

As usual for this stop, a few people returned about fifteen minutes late. This was understandable given the setting and beautiful weather. Many of them had returned with an assortment of seashells, driftwood, and other oddities. We then made a direct hike back to the vehicles, once again through the mosquitoes and deerflies, and in a short time we were back at the Visitor Center. It was obvious to me that the long day had taken its toll. A few folks in the van even napped on the ride back. They all thanked me, even applauded, and we parted. I gave them some brief directions, as well as some last minute advice.

Instructor: "Okay, just take the road out of Chincoteague back to Route 13, turn right towards Maryland. Follow that to Salisbury and take Route 50 from there towards Cambridge. After passing Cambridge, you will hit Easton, then in about thirty-five minutes the Bay Bridge. From there you're on your own. An alternate route would be to take Route 13 further north into Delaware, where again outside of Bridgeville you catch our wetland friend, Route 404. Route 404 will take you back through Denton and on to Route 50, whereupon you should proceed northwest to the Bay Bridge. Remember, however, to go straight home; don't stop to examine any wetlands!" (Despite their weariness, substantial laughter ensued.)

*　　*　　*

Well now, I have taken you, patient readers, down the Eastern Shore, down the Delmarva on one of my many overnight field trips during the mid-1970s. I could have taken you on one of the field trips for my Dune, Marsh, and Aquatic Plant Identification course as well. Those trips were fun and informative too, although different things were discussed and some sites were different, like the interesting freshwater swale near the southern end of Assateague, which is replete with wildlife.

Similarly, not all of my trips for this wetland ecology course were always to the sites I have taken you on this weekend. There were some alternative sites, such as The Nature Conservancy's Kings Creek Preserve on the Choptank River a few miles upstream from Dover Bridge, instead of the Choptank at Dover Bridge. However, this site is difficult to locate. It is accessed through an easement for a private lane, which eventually winds around the periphery of a farm field before reaching a boardwalk that extends far into the marsh. An additional stop would be the Nassawango Creek at Route 364 (Nassawango Road) just prior to going into Snow Hill. This site has some fresh tidal marsh and a very diverse forested swamp that is extremely difficult to traverse, but can be examined readily from the road. Another option is to spend more time at Shad Landing, then travel to the northern end of Assateague and also visit the Snug Harbor Marsh on Sinepuxent Bay where the hognose snake played dead for us one year.

At various times, I have taken students to all of these areas while on field trips for one or the other of my courses. During the first few years, my trip agenda for the ecosystem course always listed one last site I had hoped to visit, a "Stop #11 (if time permits)." This would have been to "Either or both Fairmount Wildlife Management Area and Deal Island Wildlife Management Area (Somerset County)." It seems that time never permitted! Surely, you can imagine why by now. But you could always make stop #11 on your own and probably should, for it too has interesting wetlands to visit. The choices are yours, and there is plenty to see at all of these sites. My parting advice is to set aside a fall weekend and do it. Go see for yourself what my students and I

77

experienced and what kept me, and I suppose many of them, going, year after year, down the Delmarva. You won't be disappointed -- I'll stake the eighteen years on that.

TWO

A SENTIMENTAL FAVORITE: FRESHWATER MARSHES

As I write this a boy is going out to the marshes to watch with field glasses the mating of the red-winged blackbirds, rising up in airy swirls and clouds. Or perhaps he carries some manual to the field, and sits him down on an old log, to trace his way through Latin names, that seem at first so barbarous and stiff. There is no explaining why the boy has suddenly forsaken the ball and bat, or finds a kite less interesting in the spring skies than a bird. For a few weeks, or a few seasons, or perhaps for a lifetime, he will follow this bent with passion.
-- DONALD CULROSS PEATTIE, *An Almanac for Moderns*

MY first experience with wetlands came at the age of seven in Grassy Sounds, New Jersey, where my family lived in a small house over a saltmarsh. In the evening, I leisurely passed time catching slippery eels off the elevated walkway leading to our house. During the day, my older brother Gordon and I frequently collected milk bottles in the marsh. I gave most of the eels away, but each bottle meant a penny and the return of ten bought a lot at "Jipper Joe's" -- some candy, a small bag of marbles, or a few fish hooks.[1] Little did I realize that twenty-six years later, I would be working professionally with saltmarshes in Maryland and digging for old bottles as a hobby on weekends. My family stayed only two years in the house on stilts. Tropical storms meant evacuation to the mainland and our return meant finding seaweed almost in our kitchen. Consequently, most of my boyhood days were spent at Runnemede, a rural town in southern New Jersey where, at the age of eleven,

---

[1] "Jipper Joe's" was the name we gave to a small store that sold miscellaneous items like groceries, candy, and fishing supplies.

79

I discovered freshwater marshes. I spent most days rambling along the floodplain leading to a small man-made pond supporting a biologically interesting cattail marsh. A few years later I discovered a bigger, more interesting, natural history paradise -- the fresh tidal marshes of Big Timber Creek. I spent many of my teenage years at that creek trapping muskrats, hunting black ducks, fishing for carp, camping, and just plain enjoying nature. For the next decade or so, I continued to explore other natural places found in New Jersey's diverse landscapes in pursuit of natural history experiences. In retrospect, I suppose I was drawn mostly to the wetlands by their interesting plants and animals, and to some extent, by the excitement of just being near water -- the place were the critters were.

If you are a birder, think for a minute. Where have you seen most of your birds? I am sure that a number of aquatic and wetland sites will likely come to mind. For the novice, watch for sites on your next outdoor adventure or cross-country trip. You will be amazed at the number and diversity of aquatic and wetland areas you can see along a major highway. Visit some -- but be quiet and observant. You may get wet and muddy but every trip brings something new -- a new species, variety or growth form, a new seed, rhizome or leaf shape, a new track, skull or feather, a new adaptation, behavior or process. Imagine a world without wetlands!

In this Chapter, I briefly discuss the variety of freshwater wetland types occurring in the Chesapeake Bay Region. Next, I describe a range of fresh nontidal marsh types found in Delaware, Maryland, and Virginia. Finally, I present various physical, biological, and functional aspects of one type of wetland, the fresh tidal marsh, using the Patuxent River in Maryland as my primary example. With these descriptions and some field guides, hours of exploration await you in some of our Nation's richest wetland communities.

QUAGS, SPONGS, AND CRIPPLES!

Many types of wetlands occur in the Chesapeake Bay Region. Some are tidal; others nontidal. Some are fresh; others brackish or saline. There are permanently flooded, semi-permanently flooded, seasonally flooded, tempporarily flooded, intermittently flooded, regularly flooded, and irregularly flooded wetlands. In some, surface water is seldom present but the soils are seasonally saturated. They come in all shapes and sizes; both natural and man-made. A few have colorful names -- quags, spongs, and cripples. They all, however, fall under the general categories of bog, fen, swamp, or marsh. Bogs and fens are peatlands that are distinguished from swamps and marshes and from each other by soil-water chemistry and plant species composition. Marshes differ from swamps by the prevalence of herbaceous plants as opposed to trees and shrubs. Sometimes a fifth type, wet meadow, is differentiated from the marshes. Wet meadows support herbaceous vegetation, but are generally only seasonally saturated and seldom have standing water as do many marshes. Freshwater marshes are generally divided into nontidal and tidal.

The main differences between fresh nontidal marshes and fresh tidal marshes relates to their characteristic hydroperiods (the frequency, duration, and seasonality of flooding or soil saturation). Fresh nontidal marshes, which are either permanently, semi-permanently, or seasonally flooded, or have at least periodically saturated soils, have hydroperiods that are influenced principally by rainfall and runoff. On the other hand, fresh tidal marshes are permanently saturated and are flooded regularly or irregularly by tidal waters, with rainfall and runoff normally having a relatively minor effect on their hydroperiods. Fresh nontidal marshes are generally smaller than fresh tidal marshes, and in the Chesapeake Bay Region they are substantially less significant in total acreage.

Fresh tidal marshes occur above the estuarine waters of various coastal creeks and rivers where the salinity is less than 0.5 parts per thousand (that is, a concentration of one-half a part salt by weight for every 1,000 part water). These marshes are usually found along meandering creeks and rivers, like Maryland's Patuxent River (Figure 15) or on the alluvial deposits of river deltas, such as the Gunpowder River, also in Maryland. Examples of other major fresh tidal marshes in the Chesapeake Bay Region occur along the Elk, Sassafras, Chester, Choptank, Nanticoke, Pocomoke, and Wicomico Rivers in Maryland and the Rappahannock River and Mattaponi and Pamunkey

Figure 15. Computer-scanned printout of a 1971 aerial photograph showing the Patuxent River and Jug Bay area. The confluence of the Western Branch and the Patuxent River is near the center of the photograph, and the upper part of Jug Bay is at the lower right. The center of the photograph is about two miles south of Maryland Route 4. Three tracts of public land lie in the general area of Jug Bay: The Jug Bay Natural Area, which is part of the Maryland National Capital Park and Planning Commission's Patuxent River Park, the Jug Bay Wetlands Sanctuary owned by Anne Arundel County, and the Merkle Wildlife Sanctuary owned by the State of Maryland.

Creeks in Virginia. Others occur on some tributaries of the Potomac.

FRESH NONTIDAL MARSHES

The Chesapeake Bay Region contains a variety of fresh nontidal marshes. They usually occur either in areas of internal drainage such as lakes, ponds, and isolated depressions, or along streams. Although large, nearly uniform, stands of hydrophytes are often encountered, most fresh nontidal marshes are floristically diverse. They are dominated by broad-leaf emergents like arrow-arum (*Peltandra virginica*), arrowhead (*Sagittaria latifolia*), and pickerelweed (*Pontederia cordata*); narrow-leaf emergents such as broad-leaf cattail (*Typha latifolia*), American bur-reed (*Sparganum americanum*), and sweetflag (*Acorus calamus*); and various graminoid plants (grasses, sedges, and rushes). Numerous other species such as the St. John's-worts (*Hypericum* spp.), monkeyflowers (*Mimulus* spp.), and bedstraws (*Galium* spp.) are less obvious, but can be found with patient searching.

Although lakes generally do not spawn extensive wetlands, those receiving heavy sediment loads usually develop geomorphologically interesting delta marshes. The best delta marsh I have ever examined is at Lake Roland adjacent to Maryland Route 135 in Baltimore County, Maryland. If you are prepared to get wet, you can traverse this well-flooded cattail marsh and examine the leading edge of the active delta. Ironically, the delta's, sediment source originated from extensive residential and commercial development in the upstream watershed.

Ponds, on the other hand, being much more shallow than lakes, characteristically support wetlands. Many farm ponds, for instance, have lush broad-leaf cattail or bur-reed stands in their deeper emergent zones and a mixture of grasses, sedges, rushes, and other species closer to shore. These ponds generally teem with invertebrates, such as water measurers (*Hydrometra martini*), water striders (*Gerris* sp.), water scorpions (*Ranatra fusca*), and various diving beetles. They support muskrat (*Ondatra zibethicus*) populations, and frequently a pair of wood ducks or mallards. Drained mill ponds are ideal places to observe secondary succession involving wetland vegetation. There are a number of these sites on the Delmarva Peninsula. Mud Mill Pond adjacent to Mud Mill Road at Choptank Mills in Kent County, Delaware is a good example. These ponds have diverse floras with various sedges, rushes, grasses, and forbs, and they tend to have small streams running through them. Some on the Eastern Shore support rare vascular plants.

On the Delmarva Peninsula, particularly in Caroline, Queen Annes, and Kent Counties, Maryland and Kent County, Delaware, there are many wetland depressions variously referred to as Delmarva potholes, whale wallows, Carolina bays, Maryland basins, Delmarva bays, coastal plain ponds or vernal pools. Some of these are acidic glades, which are usually dominated by Walter's sedge (*Carex walteriana*), beardgrass (*Erianthus giganteus*), and nutrush (*Cladium mariscoides*). Consequently, they represent natural "grasslands" in the East (2). Maiden-cane (*Panicum hemitomon*) and Virginia chain fern (*Woodwardia virginica*) are also sometimes quite abundant. The rare carpenter frog (*Rana virgatipes*) and the prothonotary warbler occur in a number of them (3). A prime example is located about one mile north of Hollingsworth Crossroads near Jones Road in Caroline County. They also have a number of rare plants, such as Harper's fimbristylis (*Fimbristylis perpusilla*), Torrey's dropseed (*Muhlenbergia torreyana*), and Canby's dropwort (*Oxypolis canbyi*). (See Chapter Seven for a more detailed account of these interesting wetlands.)

A small but widely distributed fresh nontidal wetland type, which probably occurs in all of the physiographic provinces in the Chesapeake Bay Region, is the "pasture seep." Many of these wetlands are overgrazed and appear to be dominated by soft rush (*Juncus effusus*). Others are undisturbed and contain a variety of sedges, rushes, grasses, and forbs. Despite their small size, these wetlands serve as migration or wintering habitat for such birds as marsh wrens and swamp sparrows, and they provide critical breeding areas for local toads, spring peepers, newts, and many insects (Dave Davis, personal communication). A few pasture seeps can be observed along Route 50 between Annapolis and I-495 near Washington, DC.

Marshes sometimes develop where streams have been impeded because of beaver dams or earth fills associated with highway construction or undersized culverts that impound water. Scattered shrubs and both live and dead trees are also occasionally present. A characteristic example with a large variety of plant and wildlife species is found where Maryland Route 5 crosses the Zekiah Swamp in Charles County. Somewhat similar wetlands are associated with old stream or river oxbows. The quintessential example of this

84

in Maryland is the Little Patuxent Oxbow near Laurel. This oxbow, which has been called the crown jewel of natural areas in Anne Arundel County, is apparently the largest natural impoundment in the State. An exciting trip to this site is described in Chapter Nine.

Fresh nontidal marshes are also common in roadside ditches and sediment control ponds. Here they tend to be dominated by broad-leaf cattails or other emergent hydrophytes, and frequently support red-winged blackbirds and muskrats. The ditches and sediment control ponds are, of course, man-made structures, but the vegetation has generally invaded on its own. The marshes near the junction of Maryland Routes 2 and 100 and along the East-West Highway both in Anne Arundel County, Maryland are a good examples.

Baymouth barrier wetlands occur along estuarine shorelines land-ward of overwash berms resulting from sedimentation associated with littoral drift (4). (See Chapter Five for a geomorphological classification of Maryland's tidal wetlands.) These marshes and swamps are potentially good sites to find rare vascular plants. A prime example is found adjacent to the Chesapeake Bay at Cove Point in Calvert County, Maryland. Of the 397 vascular plants found at this site during a floristic survey by Brent Steury (5), an impressive forty-one species are considered rare, threatened, or endangered by the Maryland Natural Heritage Program. These included twelve species with a State endangered or endangered-extirpated status and two species with a State threatened status. An additional seven species found are State rare; nineteen others are considered uncommon; another species is under review for listing by the State. Thirty of the forty-one species, for example the southern wildrice (*Zizaniopsis miliacea*), American frog's-bit (*Limnobium spongia*), star duckweed (*Lemna trisulca*), and smooth fuirena (*Fuirena pumila*), were found in the wetland; five species, such as the clasping-leaved dogbane (*Apocynum sibiricum*) and large-seeded forget-me-not (*Myosotis macrosperma*), were found on an associated barrier dune; six species, including the yellow passionflower (*Passiflora lutea*) and glomerate sedge (*Carex aggregata*), were found fringing these habitats. Indubitably, this is quite an array of rarities. Steury also reported the State rare/watchlist red-bellied water snake (*Nerodia e. erythrogaster*) and the northeastern beach tiger beetle (*Cicindela d. dorsalis*), a Federally threatened species.

Another good example of this wetland type is Big Marsh, a huge marsh and swamp complex at Howell Point in Kent County, Maryland. In 1994, Gene Cooley of the Maryland Natural Heritage Program mentioned that tufted loosestrife (*Lysimachia thyrsiflora*), American frog's-bit (*Limnobium spongia*), flat-leaf bladderwort (*Utricularia intermedia*), and bulb-bearing water hemlock (*Cicuta bulbifera*) had recently been reported from the site, again by Brent Steury (who at the time was a naturalist at the Echo Hill School) and subsequently confirmed by Gene and Wayne Tyndall. Historically, the white water-crowfoot (*Ranunculus trichophyllus*), a State endangered species, was also reported from Big Marsh. In addition, Steury found clammyweed (*Polanisia dodecandra*, a State endangered-extirpated species) on the overwash berm that fronts Big Marsh on the Chesapeake Bay.

While working for the Maryland Department of Natural Resources in the early 1970s, I visited this site and was quite aware of its ecological significance back then, but I did not anticipate the rarities that have been subsequently reported. Consequently, when Gene Cooley informed me of these choice finds, I became rather excited and visited the area with Gene and Kathy McCarthy on October 14, 1994. We relocated all of the species mentioned above except for the clammyweed and white water-crowfoot, and also found a State watchlist species, the green spikerush (*Eleocharis olivacea*). A rather surprising upland species was the chinquapin oak (*Quercus muehlenbergii*), another watchlist species, which is uncommon on the Coastal Plain. (See Chapter Nine for a more detailed description of this site.)

Barrier islands have fresh nontidal wetlands in the swales between older dune ridges. I stumbled into one of these with a group of my students in 1980. The site, which was located adjacent to Toms Cove on Assateague Island in Accomack County, Virginia, had a dense mixed stand of marsh plants as well as monotypic patches of cattail. This small wetland waterhole surrounded by dense shrubby vegetation was teeming with wildlife. Muskrat

86

Figure 16. A live opossum (*Diadelphis marsupialis*) extracted from a trash can in the Jug Bay area of Patuxent River Park, Prince Georges County, Maryland by the author in 1991 while leading a field trip for Environmental Protection Agency personnel.

and raccoon tracks were abundant, and we saw a cottontail rabbit and two sika deer. I even managed to catch a raccoon by the tail in the dense marsh vegetation. Over the years (just for the heck of it I suppose), I have grabbed a number of critters by their tails, including this raccoon, an alligator (*Alligator mississipiensis*), a beaver, and an opossum to name a few. Granted, there is a certain excitement involved. And no doubt a little bit of the kid still left in me. On a field training session to the Patuxent River Park in 1992, I had an interesting experience in this regard. While waiting in the parking area for my group to arrive, a maintenance employee exclaimed, "There's a possum in there!" He was about to pick up a trash can to empty it, but an opossum had gotten in through the flap door and I suppose either could not, or chose not to, get out yet. I took a look and decided to nab it. Remembering my experiences with opossums from my boyhood fur trapping days, I picked up a paper cup to gently poked him in the face to see how feisty he might be. When he did not respond, I quickly grabbed him by the neck and back, then lifted him out. The beast hardly struggled until later when it squirmed a little after we photographed it (Figure 16). When I released the opossum, it moved quicker than I had anticipated, while heading for the cover of the woods almost forty feet away. Lest you think I am a bit crazy, I should point out that I am not alone in this curious habit. During his younger days for instance, Earnest Thompson Seton (6) in *Wild Animals at Home* described how he seized a badger by the tail at its den, which he and his companions soon disposed of, an event he subsequently lamented.

FRESH TIDAL MARSHES

In contrast to the surrounding, sometimes steeply-sloping, upland terrain, fresh tidal marshes are relatively flat. At least they appear to be until you hoof it through the dense, foot-tangling vegetation and mucky, gut-laced, substrate for a couple of hours under a burning summer sun. While working up a sweat, veteran swamp trompers will find the going fairly easy as they carefully avoid the soft spots and hidden muskrats runs, occasionally step from clump to clump of pickerelweed or arrow-arum, and willingly wade waist deep in the refreshing waters of tidal guts. For the uninitiated, however, it can be quite a different experience as a young U.S. Fish and Wildlife Service biologist discovered early one spring morning in 1974 at a fresh tidal marsh on Mattawoman Creek in Charles County, Maryland. At the time, I was employed by the Maryland Department of Natural Resources and was making a joint biological investigation with the young woman. As we hop-scotched across the clumps of arrow-arum, I had to hold her hand; otherwise, her investigation that day would have been strictly a windshield survey. Although the above-ground parts of arrow arum die back each winter, the subsurface biomass supports the weight of a human. She was amazed as I ably moved along. The young lady literally experienced the "feel" of the marsh that day, for she never quite made all the clumps. But that did not ruin her enthusiasm for the marsh, and she was soon on her way to learn more about tidal guts, sediments, and soils.

Actually, tidal guts are small streams tributary to tidal rivers and creeks. As they spread into the heartland of a marsh, they repeatedly bifurcate somewhat like the branches of a tree, and become progressively smaller. In the Chesapeake Bay Region, the tide ebbs and flows twice daily in these aquatic conduits over a vertical range of about two or three feet. The tidal water slowly rises, spills over the smaller stream banks like an overflowing kitchen sink, and quickly spreads over the marsh surface in a shallow sheet-like flow. At slack tide, sediments are deposited, and about six hours later the marsh is again "dry," even in the shallow guts. Each tidal cycle brings a new supply of sediments. As the tidal streams overflow their banks, the heavier sediments drop out of suspension before the lighter ones. This results in meandering streambank levees of slightly higher elevation and vegetation different from the surrounding marsh. Historically, these wetland soils have generally been mapped and labeled by the Soil Conservation Service (now called the Natural Resources Conservation Service) only as "tidal marshes," without recognition of the soil variation within the marsh. However, a close look reveals details in the substrate that are exciting for both the novice and scientist, and the Natural Resources Conservation Service currently maps hydric soils in much more detail.

The Patuxent River in Maryland is an excellent example of the tidal fresh marshes in the Chesapeake Bay Region. The tidal portion of the Patuxent is about forty-five miles long from its mouth at the Chesapeake Bay near Drum Point to the tidal limits near Queen Annes Bridge in Anne Arundel County. Based upon a Maryland Department of Natural Resources' wetland inventory involving very detailed vegetation classification and mapping (7), a total of 6,773 acres of fresh and brackish tidal wetlands occur along this stretch of the Patuxent and its tidal tributaries; 5,199 of these are fresh tidal marshes. The area of fresh tidal marsh vegetation on the Patuxent's mainstream begins in the vicinity of Ferry Landing in Calvert County, ends about nine miles upstream near Waysons Corner in Anne Arundel County, and comprises a total of 1,739 acres. Just downstream, between Ferry Point and Cocktown Creek, occurs a transition zone with a 440-acre mixture of both fresh and brackish vegetation types. The marsh is brackish south of Cocktown Creek except for local areas above the estuarine headwaters of some tributaries. I should point out that my description of the extent of fresh tidal marsh conflicts with that of Meanley (8), who considered it to be about five miles long lying between Upper Marlboro and the mouth of Lyons Creek, since I chose to make the fresh-brackish marsh cutoff where there is no overlap between fresh and brackish marsh vegetation types as shown by the Maryland Department of Natural Resources' inventory.

The Maryland Department of Natural Resources recognizes nine marsh vegetation types for the fresh tidal portion of the Patuxent River, all of which are dominated by hydrophytes, plants that grow either in open water or on soils that are at least periodically inundated or saturated with water (7). The 602-acre smartweed/rice cutgrass (*Polygonum* spp./*Leersia oryzoides*) type is the most prevalent. It occurs on the higher "plateaus" of the marshes and is not as frequently flooded as many of the other types, such as wildrice and spatterdock. Cattail is the next most abundant vegetation type, covering 379 acres. In the Chesapeake Bay region, there are four species of cattails (9); the most common are narrow-leaf and broad-leaf cattails (*Typha angustifolia* and *T. latifolia*). The narrow-leaf cattail is more abundant and is mostly an estuarine species; the broad-leaf is common in nontidal and fresh tidal

90

Figure 17. The common reed (*Phragmites australis*), a tall invasive grass that has displaced much of the wildrice along the Patuxent River. (Photo by the author)

marshes. As you might suspect, the Patuxent marshes support both species. Two other vegetation types occur extensively in the Patuxent's fresh tidal marshes -- the common reed (*Phragmites australis*, 255 acres) and wildrice

(*Zizania aquatica*, 240 acres). The common reed (Figure 17) is often considered the bane of the marshes because of its minimal wildlife value and aggressive vegetative displacement of more desirable species; whereas, the wildrice (Figure 18) is highly desirable from a wildlife perspective. Two of these vegetation types -- spatterdock (*Nuphar luteum*, 126 acres) and pickerelweed/arrow-arum (*Pontederia cordata/Peltandra virginica*, 52 acres) -- are dominated by broad-leaf hydrophytes. Frequently, these types occur as large monotypic stands, such as the spatterdock on the Pocomoke and Choptank Rivers in Maryland. At other times, they occur intermixed -- spatterdock, pickerelweed, and arrow arum moving progressively shoreward

Figure 18. Wildrice (*Zizania aquatica*), an important annual grass for wildlife along the fresh tidal portion of the Patuxent River.

-- usually in relation to water depth. Bulrush (*Scirpus* spp., 53 acres), swamp rose mallow (*Hibiscus moscheutos*, 18 acres), and sweet flag (*Acorus calamus*, 14 acres) are the remaining three types. The bulrush type usually contains other species and sweetflag is often monotypic. The swamp rose mallow type can be deceiving. Because of its clumping habit and large showy

92

flowers, it appears more abundant than it really is and, at times, is falsely assumed to be a dominant plant in a marsh.

Succession: Change Is Inevitable

According to classical successional theory, most habitats are destined to change their nature through time. Hydrarch succession is a classic example. Ponds fill in with sediment and are frequently invaded by emergent plants like cattails, bur-reeds, and bulrushes on the margins and floating-leaf waterlilies and pondweeds offshore. The kettle ponds of glacial terrain form floating vegetative mats that eventually cover the entire surface of the pond. Considering their depressed location and internal drainage, wetlands, however, will not likely become uplands. At most, a marsh or bog may become a swamp or might even return to open water. Estuaries are also filling in, sometimes at rapid rates. The Delaware, for instance, carries about one million tons of eroded soil from the New Jersey, New York, and Pennsylvania countryside to the sea annually (10). The Chesapeake Bay, with its 64,000 square mile watershed, likewise receives its share of sediment from eroded topsoil from farmlands and developing areas under construction (11). Ironically, many of its marshes, especially along its tidal tributaries, are the direct result of sedimentation, both natural and man-induced.

Although extensive fresh tidal marshes like those on the Patuxent River were probably hundreds if not thousands of years in the making, substantial changes have also occurred more recently. For example, the tobacco ports of Upper Marlboro on Western Branch (only a small stream today) and Queen Anne Town near the Patuxent's upstream tidal limit were both closed as a result of agricultural sedimentation in the 18th and 19th centuries. Research on pollen grains and seeds by Dr. Humaira Khan has documented that the Patuxent was much wider and deeper in the 1700s. Over time, open water areas became low marsh, which eventually succeeded to high marsh (12).

More contemporaneous changes in the Patuxent marshes have also been documented by Baxter (13), who examined sequential aerial photographs taken between 1938 and 1970 and concluded that the circular patches of the aggressive common reed were spreading radially at a rate of four feet per year into the surrounding marsh matrix near Mataponi Creek. Baxter ascribed these changes to heavy sedimentation. This was probably the correct explanation for the shift in vegetation, since minor changes in marsh elevation can result in major changes in species composition. Wildrice, for example, prefers the intertidal zone and is quickly outcompeted by the common reed at higher elevations. As of the early 1980s when the State conducted its inventory (7), there were only 240 acres of tidal marsh on the Patuxent in which wildrice occurred as a dominant, and 255 acres where the common reed dominated. As documented by C. S. Scofield in 1905, wildrice once grew extensively as far downstream as Whites Landing and was very abundant from Nottingham to Leon (14). The more recent Maryland wetland inventory maps showed wildrice to be dominant as far south as the Ferry Landing in the early 1980s, although it was most abundant between a point about one mile below Maryland Route 4 and the southern end of Jug Bay. The large, almost impenetrable, stands of common reed currently found in the Patuxent's fresh tidal marshes have displaced much of the wildrice for which the river is historically famous.

Given Scofield's description, the huge stands of common reed just north of Ferry Landing and near Mataponi Creek at the Merkle Wildlife Sanctuary were probably large wildrice marshes in the early 1900s, where at high tide in September, hunters in shallow draft boats eagerly sought soras. Unfortunately, successional changes that favor the common reed will continue, for with each tidal cycle a new deposit of silt accumulates on the marsh. With the continued spread of the common reed, the day may come when a loud clap of the hands on a September morning will no longer evoke vocal responses from a dozen or so soras stealthily slipping through the dense marsh vegetation. A long-term decline in use of the Patuxent marshes by soras has already been suggested (15).

Another predictable change for Maryland's fresh tidal marshes, is the spread of the purple loosestrife (*Lythrum salicaria*). This attractive European plant was brought to New England in the early 1800s probably as an ornamental and for the bee industry as a pollen source (16,17). Although it is currently most abundant and a threat to native flora in the Northeast and upper Midwest, it occurs in most states and in Canada. As pointed out by Daniel Q. Thompson, Ronald L. Stuckey and Edith B. Thompson (16) in the "Spread, Impact, and Control of Purple Loosestrife (*Lythrum salicaria*) in North American Wetlands," the impact of purple loosestrife on native vegetation has been disastrous, with more than 50% of the biomass of some wetland communities displaced. Although impacts on wildlife have not been well studied, they indicate serious reductions in waterfowl and aquatic furbearer productivity.

During the 1980s, I noticed this potential aggressive invader on the Eastern Shore, mostly as scattered individuals along a few roadside ditches and sometimes in fresh tidal marshes, one site being on the Choptank River at Dover Bridge on October 15, 1983. I first recorded it in my *Journal* for the Patuxent River on August 2, 1986, although I may have seen it there sooner. While searching for rare plants along the Patuxent with Wayne Tyndall and Mary Kilbourne on August 8, 1995, I recorded it again in my *Journal* for two tributaries, Mataponi and Lyon's Creeks, indicating that "...it appears to have spread somewhat along Mataponi Creek since I first noticed it there a few years ago, although it is still intermittent and not abundant." I noted that it seemed less frequent along Lyon's Creek (Figure 19). On a similar trip to the Patuxent River Park a few weeks later, Mary took me up Western Branch to point out some additional loosestrife. As I stood in the boat to scan the fresh tidal marsh, I was quite surprised. For the first time in Maryland, I had seen an actual stand of purple loosestrife in a tidal marsh. This does not bode well for the Patuxent and its fresh tidal marshes. Mary and I have decided to monitor this stand to determine the extent of its subsequent spread, which is undoubtedly a given.

An interesting and easily accessible place to explore the Patuxent's marshes is immediately south of Maryland Route 4. If you are energetic and examine it periodically, you will grow to appreciate its seasonal vegetative changes. Before visiting the marsh, I suggest that you first read a paper in *Chesapeake Science* by L.J. Shima, R.R. Anderson, and V. Carter (18). Using

95

Figure 19. The author on the Patuxent River confirming the identity of purple loosestrife (*Lythrum salicaria*) with his *Gray's Manual of Botany*. Because of its invasive nature, this loosestrife represents a potential threat to the native vegetation of the marshes. (Photo by Mary Kilbourne)

infrared aerial photographs taken at 6,000 feet, the authors delineated twelve vegetation units in the spring and fourteen in the fall. Spatterdock dominated one unit in the spring, but became obscured in some areas by taller plants such as pickerelweed and wildrice by the fall. Some large areas predominately covered by arrow-arum, a cattail, and a sedge in the spring had a mix of tearthumb, swamp rose mallow, jewelweed, and the sedge in September. Areas that in June were dominated by sweetflag had a combination of tearthumb and jewelweed as dominants in the fall. Seasonal changes were also documented at the Jug Bay Wetlands Sanctuary, where forty-five species were identified between 1988 and 1995. Perennial plants dominated early in the season; annuals later. Species richness increased between June and August, and also increased with increasing elevation (19). This seasonal turnover of plants is typical of fresh tidal marshes and stands in stark contrast to the situation in tidal saltmarshes (and many brackish marshes) which maintain a rather uniform vegetation throughout the growing season. This change in the dominants with the seasons in fresh tidal marshes is a function of the species' various growth rates and their flowering sequence, a phenomenon sometimes referred to as seasonal succession.

The Plant Life

One summer day in 1972, three other biologists and I launched two small boats at the Maryland Route 225 bridge in Charles County, Maryland and slowly drifted down Mattawoman Creek. Although our main purpose was to field check a number of draft wetland maps, I had an additional goal -- to find the premier of the broad-leaf aquatics for our region, the stately American lotus (*Nelumbo luteum*). I had been informed that this rare plant was there and was determined to not let it elude me again as it had over the years in New Jersey. Initially, the going was rough in the shallow gravel-bottomed creek, but before long the floodplain forest slowly merged downstream with the wetter swamp and tidal marsh. We started our motors and leisurely navigated along the well-flooded wetlands where the marsh sharply contrasted against the background of ash swamp. As we eagerly maneuvered our boats, we matched the apparent vegetation patterns on colored aerial photographs with the vegetation on the ground. The low growth of broad-leaf aquatics was easily distinguished from the taller cattails, as plant zonation was quite distinct. Coalescing clonal patches of spatterdock were in the deepest water. Arrow-arum and pickerelweed usually grew landward of the spatterdock, contrasting sharply with the taller dark-green stands of cattail on the "drier" portions of the marsh. It was a productive day for me since I was especially interested in the vascular plants. We noticed some areas with slightly different color patterns than the surrounding marsh. As we moved closer, some large umbrella-like leaves stood out amongst the smaller pickerelweed. At last, I had found the American lotus (Figure 20). A mile or so downstream we beached our boats for lunch on a small sandy spoil pile adjacent to the channel. A small pink flower near the edge of the marsh soon caught my eye. I immediately recognized it as something new to me, and later keyed it out to an invasive southern dayflower-like plant, the marsh dewflower (*Aneilema keisak*),which is currently common in Virginia, but still somewhat uncommon in Maryland (Figure 21).[2] Two years later, a colleague and I reported it for the first time on the Eastern Shore in a fresh tidal marsh on the Wicomico River near Salisbury, Maryland (20).

Despite having resided for only one year in Maryland, by 1972 I had already visited a number of highly brackish and saline tidal marshes on the Eastern Shore and in Worcester County. Therefore, the high plant diversity along Mattawoman Creek stood in sharp contrast with the low plant diversity associated with the brackish and saline marshes. Why? Well, it is a well estab-tablished fact that along estuaries the number of vascular plant species increases with decreasing salinity. For example, Maryland's highly productive but nearly monotypic saltmarshes, dominated by cordgrasses in Worcester, Somerset, and St. Mary's Counties, contrast sharply with its much richer brackish and freshwater marshes of the Nanticoke, Wicomico, and Choptank Rivers on the Eastern Shore. The composition of plant species changes along these Chesapeake Bay tributaries as the salt content gradually decreases in an upstream direction. The Patuxent is another good example of this shift in plant composition due to salinity changes (21,22). Vascular plant species

---

[2]The marsh dewflower is now called *Murdannia keisack*.

98

distribution data, which I collected at twenty-nine Patuxent River sites, showed that the average number of species shift for the brackish portion of the river between its mouth and Cocktown Creek was only thirteen. There was an average of twenty species found in the fresh-brackish transition zone between Cocktown Creek and Ferry Point. For the freshwater reach above

Figure 20. The premier of broad-leaf aquatics for the Chesapeake Bay Region, the American lotus (*Nelumbo lutea*). This rare plant grows abundantly in the fresh tidal marshes along the Mattawoman Creek in Charles County, Maryland. (Photo by the author)

Ferry Point extending north to the extent of the tidal marsh, I found an average of twenty-eight species. As reported by Marcy Damon (23), the low marsh at Jug Bay is dominated by spatterdock with a range of two to four other plant species; on the other hand, the high marsh supports sixteen to twenty-eight species. Therefore, if wetland plants meet your fancy, fresh tidal between marshes like those on Mattawoman Creek and the Patuxent River are your fortune. As far as wetlands go, they are second to none in our region in species richness, except possibly for some forested swamps and bogs. There

Figure 21. Marsh dewflower (*Murdannia keisak*) along Mattawoman Creek, Charles County, Maryland. This introduced plant has been expanding its range in the Chesapeake Bay Region. Its presence on the Maryland portion of the Eastern Shore was first reported in 1971, along the Wicomico River near Salisbury. (Photo by the author)

100

are many attractive vascular plants, such as cardinal flowers, swamp milkweeds, blue flag, pickerelweed, swampcandles, St. John's-worts, and jewelweed. Even the colorful stamens and feathery styles of the taxonomically difficult grasses, seen under a ten-power hand lens, will surprise you. On the Patuxent, watch for one spikerush in particular -- my favorite, the square-stem spikerush (*Eleocharis quadrangulata*). The second part of its scientific name means four-angled -- an appropriate name since the stem has a trapezoidal cross section. But look carefully for you could easily mistake it for another much more common sedge, Olney's three-square (*Scirpus americanus*). If you are exceptionally fortunate, you might chance upon some real freshwater marsh rarities in our region, such as mudwort (*Limosella subulata*), micranthemum (*Micranthemum micranthemoides*), waterwort (*Elatine americana* or *E. minima*), subulate arrowhead (*Sagittaria subulata*), water-hyssop (*Bacopa innominata*), or sensitive jointvetch (*Aeschynomene virginica*) (Figure 22). The highly State rare and endangered sensitive jointvetch, which was historically reported from the Patuxent River, was rediscovered along the Patuxent by Maryland Natural Heritage Program personnel in 1994 (24). (For more on Mattawoman Creek, see Chapter Ten.)

*   *   *

On August 25, 1995, while searching for rare plants with Mary Kilbourne along the Patuxent River, we found a waterwort (highly State rare and endangered) on Mataponi Creek and the subulate arrowhead (a watchlist species) on Lyon's Creek, the latter flowering. In addition, we identified the southern naiad (*Najas gracillima*), a species given an endangered-extirpated status by the Maryland Natural Heritage Program. (For an explanation of the ranking systems of the Maryland and Delaware Natural Heritage Programs, see Table I and Table II.) Earlier in the month, Mary, Wayne Tyndall, and I found the State rare New England bulrush (*Scirpus cylindricus*) and the State rare and threatened shoreline sedge (*Carex hyalinolepis*) along Lyon's Creek and the latter species along Mataponi Creek. We also located a rare vine, the spurred butterfly-pea (*Centrosema virginianum*), in the adjacent upland. I first found this attractive legume along the Patuxent River in 1972, two miles south of Deep Landing in Calvert County. I suspect that there are many more potential good finds along the Patuxent, especially in its fresh tidal marshes.

A list of over one hundred species of vascular plants that have been reported from fresh tidal marshes is given by Tiner and Burke (25), based upon their own observations and publications by McCormick and Somes (7)

Figure 22. Sensitive joint-vetch (*Aeschynomene virginica*), a rare plant rediscovered along the Patuxent River by Maryland Natural Heritage Program personnel in 1994.

and Shreve and his coauthors (26). Tiner and Burke indicate that this high plant diversity in freshwater marshes makes them vital habitats for the preservation of biodiversity.

*   *   *

The arrowhead-like marsh plants present another challenge. In the spirit of an old TV show, one might ask: Will the real arrowhead please stand

TABLE I. MARYLAND NATURAL HERITAGE PROGRAM SPECIES RANKS FOR RARE SPECIES.[1]	
STATE RANK	
Code	Description
S1	Highly State rare. Critically imperiled in Maryland because of extreme rarity (typically 5 or fewer estimated occurrences or very few remaining individuals or acres in the State) or because of some factor(s) making it especially vulnerable to extirpation. Species with this rank are actively tracked by the Maryland Natural Heritage Program (MNHP).
S2	State rare. Imperiled in Maryland because of rarity (typically 6 to 20 estimated occurrences or few remaining individuals or acres in the State) or because of some factor(s) making it vulnerable to becoming extirpated. Species with this rank are actively tracked by (MNHP)
S3	Watch List. Rare to uncommon with the number of occurrences typically in the range of 21 to 100 in Maryland. It may have fewer occurrences but with a large number of individuals in some populations, and it may be susceptible to large-scale disturbances. Species with this rank are not actively tracked by MNHP.
S3.1	A "Watch List" species that is actively tracked by MNHP because of the global significance of Maryland occurrences. For instance, a G3 S3 species is globally rare to uncommon, and although it may not be currently threatened with extirpation in Maryland, its occurrences in Maryland may be critical to the long term security of the species. Therefore, its status in the State is being monitored.[2]
S4	Apparently secure in Maryland with typically more than 100 occurrences in the State or may have fewer occurrences if they contain large numbers of individuals. It is apparently secure under present conditions, although it may be restricted to only a portion of the State.
S5	Demonstrably secure in Maryland under present conditions.
SA	Accidental or a vagrant in Maryland.
SE	Established, but not native to Maryland; it may be native elsewhere in North America.

SH	Historically known from Maryland, but not verified for an extended period (usually 20 or more years), with the expectation that it may be rediscovered.
SP	Potentially occurring in Maryland or likely to have occurred in Maryland (but without persuasive documentation).
SR	Reported from Maryland, but without persuasive documentation that would provide a basis for either accepting or rejecting the report (e.g., no voucher specimen exists).
SRF	Reported falsely (in error) from Maryland, and the error may persist in the literature.
SU	Possibly rare in Maryland, but of uncertain status for reasons including lack of historical records, low search effort, cryptic nature of the species, or concerns that the species may not be native to the State. Uncertainty spans a range of 4 or 5 ranks as defined above.
SX	Believed to be extirpated in Maryland with virtually no chance of rediscovery.
S?	The species has not yet been ranked.

STATE STATUS[3]	
Code	*Description*
E	Endangered; species whose continued existence as a viable component of the State's flora or fauna is determined to be in jeopardy.
I	In Need of Conservation; an animal species whose population is limited or declining in the State such that it may become threatened in the foreseeable future if current trends or conditions persist.
T	Threatened; a species of flora or fauna which appears likely, within the foreseeable future, to become endangered in the State.
X	Endangered Extirpated; a species that was once a viable component of the flora or fauna of the State, but for which no naturally occurring populations are known to exist in the State.
*	A qualifier denoting the species is listed in a limited geographic area only.

TABLE II. DELAWARE NATURAL HERITAGE PROGRAM STATE RANKS FOR RARE SPECIES [4]

Code	Description
S1	Extremely rare; typically 5 or fewer known occurrences in the State; or only a few remaining individuals; may be especially vulnerable to extirpation.
S2	Very rare; typically between 6 and 20 known occurrences; may be susceptible to becoming extirpated.
S3	Rare to uncommon; typically 21 to 50 known occurrences; S3 ranked species are not yet susceptible to becoming extirpated in the State but may be if additional populations are destroyed.
S4	Common; apparently secure under present conditions; typically 51 or more known occurrences, but may be fewer with many large populations; usually not susceptible to immediate threats.
S5	Very common; demonstrably more secure under present conditions.
SU	Status uncertain; a species thought to be uncommon in the State, but there is inadequate data to determine rarity. Also includes uncommon species of uncertain nativity in the State and of questionable taxonomic standing.
SH	Historically known from the State but not verified for an extended period (usually 15 years); there are expectations that the species may be rediscovered.
SX	Species has been determined or presumed to be extirpated. All historical occurrences have been searched, or all known sites have been destroyed, and a thorough search of potential habitat has been completed.
SE	Exotic or introduced in the State, not a part of the native flora; may be native elsewhere in North America (e.g., western United States).
SR	Reported from the State, but without persuasive documentation that would provide a basis for either accepting or rejecting the report.
SRF	Species reported falsely (in error) from the State, but this error persists in the literature.

.1	To date, only a single occurrence or populations of this species has been documented.

up? During the late 1960s and early 1970s, I had the good fortune to occasionally stomp the New Jersey and Pennsylvania outdoors with my good friend and mentor, the late Dr. Jack McCormick. It was on one of those outings that I discovered, much to my chagrin, that the real arrowhead, when sought, would not always stand up. Unfortunately for me, it was really arrow-arum that I was pointing to that hot summer day on the banks of Raccoon Creek. Jack, of course, quickly corrected me, and rightfully so. My identification had not been hasty -- for many years I had just assumed it was arrowhead. However, from that embarrassing moment on, I vowed to know the difference between the various "arrowheads." You can too with the following pointers. The name arrowhead refers to a number of plants in the genus *Sagittaria*. The most common species in our region is the broad-leaf arrowhead or duck-potato, *Sagittaria latifolia*. This broad-leaf aquatic plant has leaves superficially similar to two other hydrophytes (arrow-arum and pickerelweed) and is frequently confused with them, especially when it is not flowering. When looking at all three together, however, the vegetative differ-

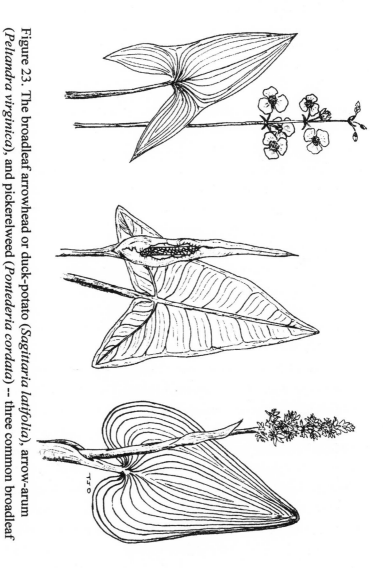

Figure 23. The broadleaf arrowhead or duck-potato (*Sagittaria latifolia*), arrow-arum (*Peltandra virginica*), and pickerelweed (*Pontederia cordata*) -- three common broadleaf aquatics with arrowhead-shaped leaves. These unrelated species as well as others (even some dicots like the halberdleaf tearthumb and arrowleaf tearthumb) have somewhat similar basal leaf lobes, an example of convergent evolution.

107

ences become quite apparent as shown in Figure 23. For example, arrow-arum leaves have two, usually divergent, basal lobes opposite their broadly-tapering tips. At the end of the leaf petiole, there are three large divergent veins -- one going to each basal lobe and the third to the leaf tip -- from which secondary veins emerge something like the teeth of a comb. Near the margins of the leaf, the secondary veins then merge with one or two veins occurring diagnostically parallel to the edge. Duck-potato leaves, on the other hand, while having somewhat similar basal lobes, have very different venation. The veins all curve out and upward from a point just above the junction of the leaf and its petiole, almost paralleling the leaf margins; below that point, the veins curve out and downward into the basal lobes. Pickerelweed leaves likewise have some veins originating from the distal end of the leaf petiole, but they are more obscure. However, those veins projecting downward arch concentrically into the basal lobes, then curve upward paralleling the leaf margins, and eventually end at the leaf tip. Pickerelweed also has exceptionally smooth leaves. As opposed to the duck-potato and arrow arum, which have only basal leaves, pickerelweed has petioled leaves arising from its stems. A fourth similar species, frequently found with the three "arrowheads" is the spatterdock, which has broader more roundish leaves with heart-shaped bases. Watch for it too.

In relation to these "arrowheads," I have often pondered the advantage, if any, of their arrowhead-shaped leaves. At first thought, one might assume that the substantial surface area associated with the broadleaves is an advantage for photosynthesis. Whereas this thought did come to mind (and may, in fact, be true), an alternative possibility soon surfaced when I recalled an old, seemingly paradoxical, gimmick my brother once made in a high school wood shop. It was a curved piece of wood, sort of pipe-shaped that curved down and then back up with a thicker rounded end. A groove above the thick part was used to insert a leather belt that, because of the angle of the groove, projected the bulk of the belt back towards the holder of the gimick as he balanced it on the tip of his finger (Figure 24). Without the belt slipped into the slot, the gimmick would immediately fall off the holder's finger, and most people would assume it would most certainly fall while

108

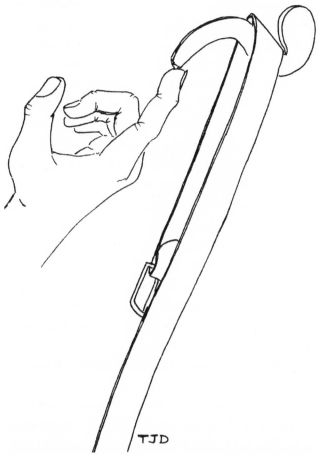

Figure 24. Device used by the author to demonstrate the counterbalance principal as it relates to the broad-leaf aquatics shown in Figure 23. The basal lobes of these broad-leaf aquatics might function similar to the device by balancing the leaves over their stems (petioles). This might prevent stem crimping during inclement weather or when birds land on the leaves, damage that would impede water and nutrient transfer.

supporting the belt. However, the belt, being slanted back towards the holder and under his hand, serves as a counterbalance, thus preventing the gimmick and belt from falling. Do you see the possible connection? As I see it, the two projecting lobes on arrowhead-like leaves might serve as a counterbalance for the generally long projecting leaf tip, thus preventing the stem from crimping or snapping when birds land on the leaves or during inclement weather.

My son Sean and I decided to test this hypothesis with a experiment at Severn Run in 1993. We clipped off the basal lobes of nine pairs of arrowhead and arrow-arum leaves as test specimens to compare with the undisturbed controls. Each pair was comprised of a cut specimen and a control and we apportioned the nine pairs of each species into three sample areas, each with three pairs of tests and corresponding controls.

As it turns out, this experiment did not go well. The arrow-arum plants died back naturally much quicker than the arrowheads, which could have affected our experiment on this species overall. Moreover, many plants of both species prematurely died due to a fungus. Perhaps conducting the experiment earlier in the year may have been more meaningful. However, some of the test arrowheads were still alive and still maintained their erect leaf blades despite the missing basal lobes; obviously, for them, the counter-balance was not necessary. I anticipate conducting a more elaborate repeat of the experiment some day, since I am fascinated by this relationship from an evolutionary perspective.

Here we have three monocots from three different families -- Water-Plantain Family (Alismataceae), Arum Family (Araceae), and Pickerelweed Family (Pontederiaceae) -- all having the same general leaf shape. Other monocots and even some dicots, the halberd-leaf and arrow-leaf tearthumbs (*Polygonum arifolium* and *P. sagittatum*) to name but two, have this shape, as does lizards tail (*Saururus cernuus*). What might that tell you? No doubt there is an advantage to the "arrowhead" leaf shape, and the similarities in leaf shapes in the three genera cited from three different families strongly suggests the possibility of convergent evolution.

As an aside, it is interesting to note that when I clipped the arrowheads, I noticed something that I had not observed before -- they all had a lactiferous juice. This was not the case with the arrow-arum, nor with a close relative of *Sagittaria*, the broad-leaf water plantain (*Alisma plantago-aquatica)*, which was growing nearby. Upon checking up on it later, I determined that the genus *Sagittaria* is known for its milky juice.

110

*   *   *

Marsh plants propagate both vegetatively (asexually) and by seed (sexually), and their seeds are generally dispersed by wind, water, or animals.

Figure 25. The author demonstrating the long rhizomes of the broad-leaf cattail (*Typha latifolia*).

Those producing many wind-dispersed seeds, such as cattails, have the capacity to quickly invade even temporarily wet sites where drainage has been impeded. Like many other marsh perennials, cattails quickly spread by rhizomes (underground stems) to form clones of genetically similar individuals (Figure 25). You can see these isolated populations around the

Figure 26. The author demonstrating the thick rhizomes of the spatterdock (*Nuphar luteum*).

periphery of small ponds. The dense stands of cattail on the Patuxent River are underlain by massive tangles of rhizomes. If you feel ambitious and do not mind getting muddy, dig a plant up and examine its stringy rhizomes. Spatterdock, in particular, produces thick (two to three inch diameter) starch-filled rhizomes that appear way out of proportion to the emergent leaves arising at their tips (Figure 26). Pickerelweed likewise produces rhizomes, but arrow-arum propagates vegetatively by bulbs (27). Some marsh perennials like arrow-arum, pickerelweed, and arrowhead have seeds that are usually dispersed by water, and it is difficult to set foot in a fresh tidal marsh in our region during October without quickly encountering numerous round greenish-black (three-eights inch or so in diameter) arrow-arum seeds (Figure 27).

Many of the seeds produced in freshwater marshes are dispersed by animals. For example, beggar-ticks or tickseed sunflowers have two-pronged spiny achenes (small, dry, and hard indehiscent fruits) that promptly attach to passing mammals (including humans unfortunately!) only to be dislodged later at some other spot. Interestingly, the two dominant grasses on the fresh tidal marshes of the Patuxent River, the common reed and wildrice, have opposite reproductive strategies. The common reed produces viable seeds only infrequently, but rapidly spreads vegetatively by rhizomes and stononiferous growth, whereas the annual wildrice must re-establish itself each spring from seeds lodged in the bare flats.

*   *   *

Given the short-term and long-term environmental variability associated with wetlands -- such as a superabundance of water, anaerobic soil conditions, heavy sedimentation, and salinity fluctuations -- the plants and animals living there are adapted in various ways. This allows them to exist (and even thrive) under the natural physical and chemical limitations present. Wetness, nevertheless, directly or indirectly, is probably the major environmental limitation affecting wetland biota, particularly the plants, for if there is one thing that all wetlands have in common, it is that they are at least periodically wet. Due to their waterlogged substrates, wetlands are frequently devoid of oxygen. To survive in this wet medium, wetland and aquatic plants have evolved an interesting variety of morphological adaptations. A few adaptations associated with herbaceous plants are discussed below. Buoyancy is an obvious requirement for floating-leaf species. Numerous hydrophytes, such as waterlilies and pondweeds, have large air-filled tissues (lacunae) in

113

their stems and leaves that keep them afloat. These spongy tissues are also the means through which oxygen reaches the underground organs, as in emergent cattails and bur-reeds. To view this, cut off a cattail or bur-reed leaf and observe it endways. Feel how light it is; then squash it between your fingers.

Figure 27. Seeds of arrow arum (*Peltandra virginica*) extracted from the capsule-like spathe that surrounds them. It is difficult to enter a fresh tidal marsh in the fall without encountering thousands of these buoyant seeds.

Water willow (*Decodon verticillatus*) has managed to survive the superabundance of water in another way. This shrub-like plant sends its arching stems in all directions. When one touches the surface of the water, the tip swells into a buoyant pulpy tissue (aerenchyma) that not only keeps the stem afloat but also results in a new stem. This process is repeated again and again; eventually, this dicot may cover a small pond. Wetlands dominated by water willow are very difficult to traverse and are the only kind in the Chesapeake Bay Region to ever turn me back. I have observed this aerenchyma tissue similarly at the stem bases of globe-fruit seedbox (*Ludwigia sphaerocarpa*) on the Eastern Shore and Drummond's rattle-bush

114

(*Sesbania drummondii*) in Mississippi. Again in all instances, it seemed to function in keeping the plant afloat, an idea that is supported by C. D. Sculthorpe in his book, *The Biology of Aquatic Vascular Plants* (28).

Freshwater marshes are also very productive. On large marshes like those along the Patuxent, literally tons of plant biomass are produced each year. One of the first attempts to quantify the amount of plant biomass produced on the fresh tidal marshes of the Patuxent River was during the 1969 and 1970 growing seasons at Maloy Marsh on Western Branch (29). The broad-leaf cattail community produced a maximum standing crop of 966 grams (dry weight) per square meter of marsh. This is equivalent to 4.3 tons for each acre. A mixed vegetation community dominated by dotted smartweed (*Polygonum punctatum*) and arrow-arum in the spring and dotted smartweed, beggarticks (probably *Bidens laevis*), and wildrice in the late summer produced 1,246 grams for each square meter of marsh or 5.6 tons per acre. Additional biomass studies were conducted at a few sites on the Patuxent in the summer of 1973 (30). Except for the high values for big cordgrass (*Spartina cynosuroides*) at Gott's Marsh in the fresh-brackish transitional area, the common reed usually had the highest living biomass, exceeding even wildrice and cattail at the freshwater sites. Based on an estimated total of 314 acres, Gotts Marsh alone produced a total of 3,900,000 pounds (dry weight) of plant biomass -- equivalent to the weight of 780 cars each weighing 5,000 pounds! One can also get an appreciation for this plant productivity by simply viewing the huge plants along the river. As I noted in my July 22, 1993 *Journal* entry, it never ceases to amaze me how big the Patuxent's marsh plants grow. At the Jug Bay Wetlands Sanctuary that day I measured eight to nine foot high narrow-leaf cattail and four foot high spatterdock, and noted that the arrow-arum, pickerelweed, and broad-leaf arrowhead (duck-potato) were almost as tall as the spatterdock. The broad-leaf arrowhead had about nine inch wide leaves! Over the years, I have likewise noted towering tidemarsh waterhemp (*Amaranthus cannabinus*) in the Patuxent's fresh tidal marshes, up to six feet high. The sediments in these marshes are obviously rich, but the marshes also receive effluent from a number of major sewage treatment plants in the watershed.

115

This plant biomass is very important for the herbivore-carnivore food web of the Patuxent's marshes. Muskrats, for example, consume marsh vegetation and are preyed upon by foxes and mink. Likewise, grasshoppers, which graze on marsh plants, are eaten by red-winged blackbirds which in turn are consumed by birds of prey, such as the Cooper's hawk. The dead vegetation also serves as a primary source of energy to detrital-based food webs. As the plant parts are carried to the river by ice scouring and tidal action, they become progressively smaller by physical abrasion and the feeding activity of an array of animals. Eventually, energy flowing through the detrital food web supports valuable recreational and commercial fisheries in the Patuxent as well as the Chesapeake Bay.

The Wildlife

Admittedly, when it comes to wetlands, I am a bit fickle. In the late 1960s, it was the savannas and cedar swamps of the New Jersey Pine Barrens that caught my fancy. However, I soon left New Jersey and by the early 1970s the large productive saltmarsh cordgrass marshes of Maryland's coastal embayments enticed me. Maybe it was the seemingly simplistic nature of the cordgrass ecosystem. One can feel a sense of oneness with it...a sort of confidence of understanding. After all, the vegetation lacks diversity. There are few mammals evident, and the birds are not difficult to identify -- clapper rails, willets, seaside sparrows and the like. And the obviously dominant macroinvertebrate species -- the marsh fiddler (*Uca pugnax*), gulf periwinkle (*Littorina irrorata*), saltmarsh snail (*Melampus bidentatus*), and ribbed mussel (*Modiolus demissus*) -- can be counted on one hand. Around 1973, my interests changed to deciduous swamps with their rich floral assemblages and exceptional winter bird species diversity. Swamps held my favor for about three years. Perhaps it was the latent boyhood nostalgia of the small New Jersey pond that eventually resulted in my switching to yet a fourth favorite wetland type in 1976. Or was it Brooke Meanley's exciting book, *Birds and Marshes of the Chesapeake Bay Country*? Either way, by late spring I was ripe for the field and heading for Kent County, Maryland to one of my favorite spots -- a marsh located about one mile north of Swan Point on the Chesapeake Bay near Rock Hall.

The trip to Swan Point was one of my better ones. You know the type -- not too warm, a slight yet comfortable breeze, the morning sun just over the marsh, and the site all to myself. The marsh was exemplary, a real gem -- a diverse, deeply-flooded freshwater community with occasional tidal influence. It was dominated by water willow, swamp rose mallow, swampdock (*Rumex verticillatus*), and broadleaf cattail manifesting a high interspersion of water and vegetation. An overwash berm with dune plants separated the marsh from the Chesapeake Bay. Wetland shrubs bordered much of its periphery, and at places, the marsh graded into wet switchgrass meadows. At the upper end of the marsh, a dense swamp rose mallow patch was separated from a small pond by a man-made earthen dike. I walked down a long dirt road and saw the pond to my left. By then I had already flushed a few blue-winged teal from a seasonally-flooded area impounded by the road, and instinctively sensed a good day in the field. As I waded chest deep through the clumps of switchgrass leading to the pond, the distant trill of a song sparrow reached my ear. Suddenly, two ducks ascended with an unmistakable rising whistle. I temporarily froze and watched the woodies as they circled once, then vanished into the upstream, bottomland hardwood forest. I continued along the pond in the direction of the marsh. Hardly troubled by my presence, a pair of Canada geese pushed off from shore and moved into deeper water. Almost everywhere along the bank, muskrat sign was abundant -- tracks, oblong droppings, and occasional den entrances in the bank below the water level. The entrances, which usually connect to snug abodes higher up in the bank, were recently used and still contained tell-tale murky water. One or more back entrances surfaced in the field beyond the top of the bank. From here, well-beaten trails led to favorite upland foraging areas where holes about the diameter of an orange had been dug in search of tender roots and rhizomes. I counted ten dens before I reached the earthen dike overlooking the swamp rose mallow patch.

From the dike, I could see and hear the red-winged blackbirds in the marsh; no doubt some of them were nesting in the swamp rose mallows. As

I listened to the various calls, a yellowthroat nervously maneuvered through the vegetation. Before long I noticed something move at the base of the mallows. It moved again and then again. On the third move, an elusive Virginia rail came within full view just thirty feet from me. It secretively stalked along and periodically pecked at the substrate, most likely for smartweed fruits (achenes) or small invertebrates. Perhaps I thought, it would soon be nesting on the marsh. [This rail nests in the Chesapeake Bay Region between late April and late August in the wetter portions of tidal marshes and in nontidal marshes (32,33).] It shortly disappeared into the marsh and I followed almost waist deep in water to see what else I could find. Within a few minutes, about twenty-five blue-winged teal took flight from the surface of one of the openings in the cattails. The wading was difficult and my progress slow, but I finally reached the opposite side. The going was much easier along the upland edge, and I was soon at the lower end of the marsh. I spotted a convenient duck blind, climbed in, and silently waited. As the teal alighted in the opening against the backdrop of the well-flooded cattail marsh, it was like a breathtaking scene out of Mutual of Omaha's *Wild Kingdom*. The trip was indeed a unique experience for me, and although I have never returned to that Kent County marsh, I have preferred to slake my natural history thirst since then with the taste of freshwater marshes.

*   *   *

Why are marshes like the one in Kent County, Maryland so diverse from a wildlife standpoint? Three factors -- spatial heterogeneity, standing water, and plant species diversity -- play an important role. The numerous interspersed vegetation types, along with the juxtaposed areas of open water and adjacent uplands, maximize the amount of edge and habitat diversity in freshwater marshes. The resultant spatial heterogeneity is readily seen on vegetation maps by L.J. Shima, R.R. Anderson, and V. Carter (18) and Flemer and his coauthors (30) for the Patuxent marshes. Since interfaces of vegetation types or cover-water edges are often key habitat features attractive to birds (34), freshwater marshes serve as ideal avian habitat. Even in uniform stands of cattail, the number of bird species increases with the number of open water areas. The maximum number of species may well be found in an area with 50-60 percent open water (35). W. J.Beecher demonstrated that nest-site selection by marsh birds is dominantly influenced by the structure of the plant community as opposed to the plant species as such (36). For example, a marsh with a given number of herbaceous species would be much less structurally diverse than one with the same number of species, but containing various-sized herbs as well as scattered shrubs and trees. This is very important for birds, given their species-specific nesting requirements.

The activities of animals often help maintain spatial heterogeneity. The muskrat is exemplary in this regard in marshes. By selectively feeding on plants like cattails, muskrats help reduce competition for space between the cattails and their competitors, allowing both the cattails and their competitors to co-exist. In this way, muskrats serve as biological community structuring agents by effecting greater plant species richness and vegetative spatial heterogeneity. I have observed this many times in Maryland marshes dominated by Olney's three-square or cattails, where other plants, pre-dominantly annuals, have colonized muskrat runs and the "eatouts" around muskrat houses. The muskrat houses further contribute to the environmental patchiness. At moderate muskrat densities, clearings around muskrat houses support a mosaic of plant communities. In contrast, the lack of muskrat activity typically leads to extensive, nearly monotypic, stands of cattails or Olney's three-square. As a result, variations in muskrat densities contribute to the dynamic landscape-wide patterns of marsh diversity. If muskrat populations become too dense, of course, extensive areas of marsh vegetation can be destroyed. Ed Garbisch observed this at a tidal marsh approximately nineteen miles north of Cambridge on the Choptank River (27). The site apparently had a solid root mat dominated almost exclusively by narrow-leaf cattail in 1981, but when Garbisch revisited the wetland in 1993 it had been converted almost exclusively to arrow arum. He further noted this muskrat "eatout" promoted the loss of peat structure, which in turn led to a lowering of the marsh surface by two to six inches. (See Chapter Three for more on the muskrat and its role in biological community structuring.)

Man too can be instrumental in increasing spatial heterogeneity as I witnessed in the summer of 1977 at the Merkle Wildlife Management Area (now called the Merkle Wildlife Sanctuary) along the Patuxent River near Nottingham. A group of State wildlife biologists met that morning to set off a large charge of ammonium nitrate-fuel oil mix in an extensive stand of common reed. Their goal was to open up this dense monotypic marsh area for wildlife by creating a pothole (a shallow circular open water area). Johnny Warren, an experienced old timer from the Maryland Wildlife Administration, put on an excellent demonstration of pothole blasting. He also showed how to make a lot of surprised people run for cover! As Johnny's crew elaborately laid the electrical line over 200-300 feet of marsh in an awkward-looking World War II amphibious vehicle, a few of us took in the abundant wildlife and chatted with the friendly Merkles for whom the Sanctuary is named. A few mallards, black ducks, and blue-winged teal occasionally rose from the marsh surface, and two female marsh hawks swooped low over the vegetation. Before long the monstrous swamp machine was back on upland, the charge was set, and we were all excitedly braced for action.

Johnny let it rip. As the loud bang rippled across the marsh, ducks frantically took flight every which way -- the pervasive peace of the marsh was temporarily suspended. No one moved. We just stood there in awe as the mud and thick peat sailed higher and higher and higher. But from our angle, the trajectory was deceiving, and almost everything that goes up must come down (Figure 28). When we finally sensed the oncoming thunderstorm of mud and peat, it was a mad scramble for cover. One brave soul dove partially under the amphibious hulk of steel; others hugged trees. I sort of fell to my knees and instinctively ducked my head. If you doubt that falling bodies accelerate at a rate of thirty-two feet per second, you would have seen evidence that day. Wads of peat literally dented the ground around us as we cringed. However, like a lightning bolt, it was over momentarily and our awkward experience quickly became an exciting novelty. Even the charming Mrs. Merkle, her face and attire slightly mud-splattered, took it rather jovially. Did Johnny inadvertently overshoot his mark that morning or was it just the breeze out of the east that laid the marsh on us? In all honesty, I do not recall.

Figure 28. View of a pothole blasting demonstration in a Patuxent River fresh tidal marsh dominated by the common reed (*Phragmites australis*) in 1977. (Photo by the author)

*   *   *

Fresh tidal marshes are not only spatially diverse; they also support numerous plant species. This is important to many marsh birds such as the king, Virginia, and sora rails, the wood duck, blue-winged teal and mallard, and the bobolink that feed on the fruits or seeds of wetland plants. Meanley (31) found some 50 different food items in 241 sora rail stomachs examined from birds collected on a fresh tidal marsh on the Patuxent River in the vicinity of House Creek. Four items -- halberd-leaf tearthumb, arrow-leaf tearthumb, dotted smartweed, and Walter's millet (*Echinochloa walteri*) -- comprised nearly eighty percent of the food by volume. The least bittern, wood duck, common gallinule or moorhen, and red-winged blackbird frequently use the extensive stands of spatterdock and pickerelweed on the fresh tidal portion of the Patuxent for feeding areas (37). Even the ruby-throated hummingbird seeks the nectar of the orange-flowered jewelweeds, *Impatiens capensis* (Wayne Klockner , personal communcation). In 1994 however, Andrew Dubill, an intern at the Jug Bay Wetlands Sanctuary, found only four species (the least bittern, long-billed marsh wren, common yellowthroat, and red-winged blackbird) breeding in the tidal wetlands at Jug Bay. He suggested that tidal flooding may be the main factor in limiting the number of nesting species on the marsh, since few species can build a safe nest that remains above the high tidal flooding (38).

Other bird species that are not characteristic of marshes may utilize them at times. On April 16, 1976, I was surprised to see a downy woodpecker feeding on the insect larvae within standing, but dead, broad-leaf cattail stems in a small marsh on Mattawoman Creek (39). It was feeding on grub-like larvae located within chambers in the pith of the cattail stems. Most of the cattail stems had been splintered open to the larval chambers and only a few larvae remained. The larvae and splintered stems were also found in other cattail clones on the marsh.

The floristic diversity of fresh tidal marshes is probably more significant for invertebrates than birds, but birds obviously benefit from the invertebrates as a food source. Crustaceans, a large group of almost exclusively aquatic invertebrates, are common inhabitants of fresh tidal marshes. Tiny copepods, cladocerans, and ostracods are hardly visible to the naked eye. Larger chimney crayfish (*Cambarus diogenes*) construct burrows two to three feet deep, topped by two to four inch high "chimneys" of excavated sediment. During the summer when wetland areas sometimes "dry" out, the crayfish retreat deeper into the moist ground below. Many other invertebrates also use these burrows, which serve as a refuge from desiccation analogous to the role played by alligator holes during droughts in the Florida Everglades. Medium-sized amphipods (scuds) and isopods (sowbugs) abound in the tangled marsh vegetation and tidal guts. Mollusks are also well represented. Univalves, such as the tadpole snail (*Physa* sp.) and pond snail (*Lemnaea* sp.), move slowly across the sediments and submerged vegetation, grazing on mud, algae, and detritus, while the larger snail, the amber marsh snail (*Oxyloma effusa*), more characteristically abounds in the tidal marsh vegetation, particularly the higher marsh. In the summer of 1991, this attractive snail was studied in the marshes of the Jug Bay Wetlands Sanctuary by Michelle Reynolds. She determined that most amber snails were found on arrow-arum (41%) and cattails (25%), with none was found in pure stands of spatterdock, wildrice, or common reed. Sampling produced a wide range of densities -- 0.8 to 63.5 snails per square meter (40). The snails fed readily on cattail detritus in laboratory experiments, and also accepted swamp rose mallow and arrowhead detritus. Bivalves, like the pill clam (*Pisidium* spp.), are relatively sedimentary and obtain their food by filtering the surface water. Other important invertebrates include various free-living flatworms (such as planaria), annelid worms (including leeches, aquatic earthworms, and tubificids), and nematodes. All of these animals, along with an assorted array of aquatic insects (beetles, true bugs, and the aquatic larvae of dragonflies, damselflies, mayflies, and midges), are washed into the tidal guts and river mainstreams, especially during the winter and early spring. The beneficiaries of this exported biomass, the foraging fishes, only have to lie in wait for the parade of passing critters.

The more terrestrial insects are especially abundant on marsh vegetation and forage on Olney's three-square, swamp rose mallow, and wildrice. By late summer, the leaves of both spatterdock and white waterlily are usually riddled so badly by leaf-mining moth larvae and beetles and their larvae that they appear prematurely brown. The diverse marsh vegetation has its share of invertebrate predators too -- assassin bugs (Family Reduviidae), longjawed spiders (*Tetragnatha* sp.), golden garden spiders (*Argiope aurantia*), and even an occasional praying mantis (Family Mantidae). After a heavy dew in late summer or early fall, the number of golden gardenspider webs on some marshes is amazing. Like observing for the first time an antlion feverishly grabbing for an ant from its sandy trap, my students are spellbound by the quickness (only a matter of seconds) with which a golden garden spider usually darts out from the edge of its web, injects its poisonous serum, and proceeds to embalm a grasshopper that wanders (or is conveniently tossed) into its sticky net.

Amphibians are abundant in fresh tidal and nontidal marshes. Permanent residents of the Patuxent River's marshes are the spring peeper (*Pseudacris c. crucifer*), upland chorus frog (*P. triseriata feriarum*), green treefrog (*Hyla cinerea*), gray tree frog (*Hyla chrysoscelis*), southern leopard frog (*Rana utricularia*), pickerel frog (*R. palustris*), green frog (*R. clamitans melanota*), and bullfrog (*R. catesbeiana*). In early spring, a chorus of hundreds of spring peepers can be heard from the marshes adjacent to the Maryland Route 4 bridge.

Other amphibians, such as salamanders and toads, use freshwater wetlands along the Patuxent, particularly small nontidal depressions, to breed in late winter or early spring. A good example of this can be found at the Jug Bay Wetlands Sanctuary, where a small wetland depression on the forested floodplain supports breeding spotted salamanders (*Ambystoma maculatum*), wood frogs (*R. sylvatica*), and American toads (*Bufo americanus*) in the late winter and early spring and breeding marbled salamanders (*A. opacum*) in the fall.

Reptiles are not as abundant as amphibians in the fresh tidal areas, but they are equally interesting. On the Patuxent, look for the northern water snake (*Nerodia s. sipedon*), a voracious predator on insects, amphibians, and small fish. This nonpoisonous reptile is frequently mistaken for the poisonous eastern cottonmouth or watermoccasin (much to the water snake's detriment), which many people erroneously assume occurs in Maryland and Delaware. Actually, the cottonmouth (*Agkistrodon p. piscivoris*) is found no farther north than southeastern Virginia on the East Coast. (As opposed to the water snakes, the cottonmouth and copperhead have vertically elliptical eye pupils; they also have pits, two sensory organs located a little below the midpoint of the eye and the nostril on each side of the head.) If you are lucky, you may also find a queen snake (*Regina septemvittata*), an uncommon and somewhat secretive reptile that has been reported from the Jug Bay Wetlands Sanctuary. Other snakes, like the black rat snake (*Elaphe o. obsoleta*) and eastern ribbon snake (*Thamnophis s. sauritus*), are more terrestrial but frequently venture into the marshes in search of small rodents, bird eggs, and insects, especially in the summer during low-water periods. I once saw an eastern ribbon snake swimming across the Patuxent near Jug Bay while I was on a canoe trip. The young snake was exhausted from its long trip and squirmed onto my companion's extended paddle. Fresh tidal marshes also harbor a number of turtles, such as the stinkpot (*Stenotherus odoratus*), eastern mud turtle (*Kinosternon s. subrubrum*), eastern painted turtle (*Chrysemys p. picta*), red-bellied turtle (*C. rubriventris*), spotted turtle (*Clemmys guttata*), and common snapping turtle (*Chelydra s. serpentina*). Watch especially for the abundant snapper, which according to Roger Conant, averages 10-35 pounds (41). This long-tailed turtle has a short temper and powerful jaws, so it may be best to observe rather than touch it! A list of reptiles and amphibians found at the Jug Bay Wetland Sanctuary, including its fresh tidal marshes, was published in *The Maryland Naturalist* in 1993 (42).

On June 4, 1994, my son Sean and I traveled to the Jug Bay Wetlands Sanctuary to participate in the Great Herp Search, an annual event held since 1989. Twenty-seven volunteers, young and old, under the guidance of resident naturalist, Shannon Smithberger, scoured designated sections of the Sanctuary, searching for a total of 70.5 cumulative hours. Upland as well as wetland habitats were examined. This intensive effort produced thirteen snakes, including the northern water snake, eastern kingsnake (*Lampropeltis g. getula*), rough green snake (*Opheodrys aestivus*), and eastern worm snake

125

(*Carphophis a. amoenus*); eleven lizards, including the eastern fence swift (*Sceloporus undulatus*), six-lined racerunner (*Cnemidophorus s.sexlineatus*), and five-lined skink (*Eumeces fasciatus*); six turtles (all eastern box turtles, *Terrapene c. carolina*); thirty-five frogs and toads, including the wood frog, green frog, pickerel frog, leopard frog, and American toad; and two salamanders (both marbled salamanders) for a total of sixty-seven individual reptiles and amphibians. Past years had produced 49, 85, 63, 50, and 59 individuals, respectively, for 1989 through 1993 (42). Another observation was numerous spotted salamander larvae in a shallow water depression. For our part, Sean and I found a box turtle, worm snake, and five-lined skink, all spotted by Sean.

Both resident and migratory fish are found in the fresh tidal portions of the Patuxent River. Common resident species include the chain pickerel (*Esox niger*), largemouth bass (*Micropterus salmoides*), bluegill (*Lepomis macrochirus*), pumpkinseed (*Lepomis gibbosus*), brown bullhead (*Ameirus nebulosus*), white catfish (*A. catus*), and carp (*Cyprinus carpio*). Yellow perch (*Perca flavescens*) and white perch (*Morone americana*) migrate up the Patuxent each spring to spawning grounds in fresh or nearly fresh tidal waters. After spawning, they move back into the lower part of the river or into the Chesapeake Bay. The American shad (*Alosa sapidissima*), alewife (*Alosa pseudoharengus*), blueback herring (*A. aestivalis*), and striped bass (*Morone saxatilis*) are anadromous -- the adults move into the Chesapeake Bay from the ocean, eventually traveling up the Patuxent (as well as other fresh tidal rivers and streams) to spawn from late winter to late spring, and then return to the sea. Each spring, the marshy banks of the Patuxent River at the Maryland Route 4 bridge are lined with numerous eager fishermen delighted that the migrations have begun.

Personnel from the Jug Bay Wetlands Sanctuary have sampled fish populations in the Sanctuary over the last ten years (43). A total of forty species have been netted. Of this total, nineteen species occur in both tidal and nontidal habitats; eleven species occur only in tidal habitats; ten species occur only in nontidal habitats. The most commonly caught species in the tidal areas over the ten year period were mummichog (*Fundulus heteroclitus*), inland

126

silversides (*Menidia beryllina*), alewife (*Alosa pseudoharengus*), banded killifish (*F. diaphanus*), white perch (*Morone americanus*), spottail shiner (*Notropis hudsonius*), bay anchovy (*Anchoa mitchilli*), tessellated darter (*Etheostoma olmstedi*), golden shiner (*Notemigonus chrysoleucas*), bluegill (*Lepomis macrochirus*), and eastern mosquitofish (*Gambusia holbrooki*). The mummichog is particularly common in the tidal guts and associated marshes.

Another intern, Bill Rodney, sampled fish populations at the Jug Bay Wetland Sanctuary in 1990, concentrating on the mummichog (43). Using a "mark-recapture" technique, he marked more than 1,200 mummichogs. To quote Bill: "Many a night have I closed my eyes to sleep only to see the silhouettes of hundreds [of mummichogs] swimming across my inner eyelids, their little tails swaying in unison." He referred to this phenomenon as "Mummichog madness" and estimated the population in his study area to exceed 60,000 individuals!

* * *

Optimistically, you are now eager for a freshwater wetland trip, a trip perhaps with many unforgettable experiences. My advice is to make your trip goal-oriented -- look specifically for phenomena like those I presented in this Chapter. With proper planning and a little effort, you will not be disappointed. Remember each trip brings something new, even for veterans. And before long, you will find that the more you learn about wetlands, the more you realize you really don't know.

For a more detailed account on the freshwater marshes, I suggest you read Milton Weller's *Freshwater Marshes: Ecology and Wildlife Management* (45) or *The Ecology of Tidal Freshwater Marshes of the United States East Coast: A Community Profile* by William Odum (46). Two informative publications addressing Maryland's wetlands are *Field Guide to Nontidal Wetlands Identification* (47) by Ralph Tiner and *Wetlands of Maryland* (25) by Ralph Tiner and David Burke.

THREE

BRACKISH MARSHES
IN DORCHESTER
AND SOMERSET COUNTIES

*So, here, we have four forces -- the sinking
land, the salty baywater, the silt-bearing river,
and soil-building plant life. These forces are
waging a slow war against each other, two
trying to make it an area of water, and two
trying to build more land.*
-- A.H. Bonwill, 1941

I do not recall my first trip to Dorchester County, Maryland, although it had to occur sometime in the early 1970s, shortly after I started working in the tidal wetlands program for the Maryland Department of Natural Resources.[1] Surely, I was impressed with its wetlands at the outset, considering their extent -- approximately 121,400 acres or 32.7 percent of the total county area and 39.5 percent of the remaining wetland acreage in Maryland, the most for any county (1). These extensive wetlands, most of which are tidal, sustain an abundance of waterfowl, and they support the most muskrats (*Ondatra zibethcus*), bald eagles, and perhaps otter (*Lutra canadensis*) and mink (*Mustela vison*) in the State. Somerset County, with 58,000 acres of wetlands or 27.0 percent of the total county area and 18.9 percent of the existing wetland acreage in the State, ranks second in total acreage. The Somerset

---

[1]Although my *Journal* indicates that I visited the Blackwater National Wildlife Refuge on September 13, 1971, this appears to have been a rather uneventful visit. Given that I started working for the State almost three months to the day earlier, I suspect that I had at least one prior visit that was not recorded.

129

County wetlands (again mostly tidal) are likewise very important from a wildlife perspective.

As a young fur trapper in New Jersey in the late 1950s and early 1960s, I had heard about the extensive Chesapeake Bay tidal marshes and the numerous muskrats they produced. I longed for the day I could trap those areas or the similarly extensive marshes along the Delaware Bay in New Jersey. Being only a teenager, my travels were limited and my trapping was mostly confined to nontidal streams. The closest I got to the big muskrat catches associated with the Delaware Bay's tidal marshes were the fresh tidal marshes of Big Timber Creek, only a few miles from Camden, New Jersey. Therefore, it has always been exciting for me to explore the Dorchester County marshes, especially the extensive stands of the Olney three-square (*Scirpus americanus*) and narrow-leaf cattail (*Typha angustifolia*), two plants readily consumed by the muskrat.[2] In fact, it is extremely difficult to enter an Olney three-square or narrow-leaf cattail marsh in Dorchester County without seeing ample evidence of muskrats -- surface trails (runs), tunnels (burrows), trenches (canals), tracks, feeding platforms (feedbeds or rafts), and houses (lodges), or in trapping jargon, beds. And it is not uncommon to spot a muskrat at times during the day, despite their more characteristic nocturnal activities. According to F. R. Smith (2), the peak activity of the Virginia or coastal muskrat (*Ondatra zibethicus macrodon*) occurs between sunset and dusk. During dark, cloudy, or rainy weather, activity outside their tunnels increases throughout the day. On the other hand, V. T. Harris (3) indicated that the muskrat is more nocturnal and rarely observed on the marsh during the day.

The prime location for the brackish marshes and their abundant wildlife, of course, is in the more southern part of Dorchester County in the Blackwater River-Fishing Bay area, where the watersheds of the Blackwater, Transquaking, and Chicamacomico Rivers alone support 57,329 acres of

---

[2]As indicated in Chapter One, the scientific names for the Olney three-square was historically *Scirpus olneyi*; that for the common three-square was *Scirpus americanus*. The accepted scientific name for the Olney three-square is now *Scirpus americanus*; that for the common three-square is *Scirpus pungens*. Confusing to say the least!

estuarine emergent wetlands (4). Collectively, these three watersheds comprise U.S. Geological Survey Hydrologic Unit 2060007. This area includes the Blackwater National Wildlife Refuge and various units of the Fishing Bay Wildlife Management Area, including those on the extensive marshy peninsula at Elliott Island west of the Nanticoke River drainage. These public areas can be readily visited, and an expansive view of the marshes can be seen from Maple Dam Road, which slices through the heart of the area.[3] Access can also be gained by boat from a public boat ramp on the Blackwater River at Shorters Wharf. Another expansive view can be obtained by traveling south from Vienna along Elliott Island Road.

This Chapter is devoted to the marsh types in Dorchester and Somerset Counties and their origin, some geomorphologically interesting linear features that are present, the dramatic changes that have occurred in some of these extensive marshes, and selected wildlife inhabiting them. I also describe some initial reports of animals and plants found in the area.

*   *   *

The earliest detailed study of Maryland's wetlands, including its tidal wetlands, was apparently conducted around 1908 by the Maryland Conservation Commission (1,5). As far as I can determine, however, the first attempt to specifically classify and inventory the tidal marshes of Maryland's Eastern Shore was done in the early 1950s (6,7). Nicholson and Van Deusen described six types: Type I (Cattail-Aquatic), Type II (Three-square-Cattail), Type III (Three-square), Type IV (Mixed Brackish Marsh), Type V (Needlerush-Saltmeadow), and Type VI (Saltmarsh).

Type I (Cattail-Aquatic) marshes, which are almost entirely fresh, occur along the upper portions of the Choptank, Nanticoke, and Wicomico Rivers, and at the heads of small streams and rivers at the upper part of the Chesapeake Bay. Although cattail species (*Typha angustifolia* and *T. latifolia*) cover many areas, arrow-arum (*Peltandra virginica*), pickerelweed

---

[3]Some maps designate this as Shorters Wharf Road.

131

(*Pontederia cordata*), wild rice (*Zizania aquatica*), and a number of other freshwater species also commonly occur. Type I marshes also occur on the Pocomoke River just below Hickory Point. (See Chapters One and Five for more discussion on wetland areas along the Choptank River and Pocomoke River, respectively, that could be classified under Type I, as well as Type II, marshes.)

Type II (Three-square-Cattail) marshes are similar to Type I; they are located along rivers that have a tidal fluctuation of from one to three feet. Water is slightly brackish and generally covers the soil for up to six inches at high tide. Nearly all species associated with Type I can be found also in Type II (e.g., arrow-arum, pickerelweed, and wild rice), as well as those more characteristic of brackish areas, such as Olney three-square, smooth cordgrass (*Spartina alterniflora*), giant cordgrass (*S. cynosuroides*), and saltmeadow cordgrass (*S. patens*).

In Type III (Three-square) marshes, Olney three-square blankets almost the entire area. Small beds of cattail occur; giant cordgrass is found in narrow bands along larger streams. Saltgrass (*Distichlis spicata*), needlerush (*Juncus romoerianus*), saltmarsh bulrush (*Scirpus robustus*), smooth cordgrass, and saltmeadow cordgrass are of minor importance. The marsh floor is low and the soil is nearly always wet; salinity increases toward the lower part of the river. Type III marshes, which comprise 25,845 acres, are restricted to the middle and upper part of the Blackwater River and its tributary streams.

Type IV (Mixed Brackish) marshes are intermediate between Type III (Three-square) and V (Needlerush-Saltmeadow) marshes. Needlerush, Olney three-square, smooth cordgrass, and saltmeadow cordgrass are the principal species. The soil is relatively dry and is irregularly flooded by tides. Needlerush and saltmeadow cordgrass are the chief cover on drier areas; Olney three-square occupies intermediate, relatively moist zones. There are 37,738 acres of Type IV marshes, nearly all located in Dorchester, Somerset, and Wicomico Counties (6).

Type V (Needlerush-Saltmeadow) marshes are covered almost entirely with pure stands of needlerush and saltmeadow cordgrass. The marsh

132

floor is generally firm and remains relatively dry for the most part, being flooded only irregularly by tidal waters. Dorchester and Somerset Counties have the most extensive areas of this marsh type, although it is also found in Queen Anne's, Talbot, and Wicomico Counties.

The smooth cordgrass dominates Type VI (Saltmarsh) marshes, which are found along the coastal bays (Chincoteague, Assawoman, and Sinepuxent) in Worcester County.

The Nicholson and Van Deusen classification system is accurate and very useful, particularly for management and planning purposes. However, until recently most subsequent classifications and inventories of Maryland's wetlands (1,8) followed a 1956 U.S. Fish and Wildlife Service classification commonly known as Circular 39 (10), which itself was a modified version of the an earlier classification system by Martin and his coauthors (9). Nationally, Circular 39 described twenty wetland types, a few of which are represented by the tidal marshes of Dorchester and Somerset Counties, for example, Type 16 (Saltmeadows) and Type 17 (Irregularly Flooded Saltmarshes).

During 1971 and 1972, the Maryland Department of Natural Resources produced a set of over 2,000 photomaps delineating the inland boundary of tidal wetlands. These maps were refined between 1975 and 1978 to delineate the various types of tidal wetlands occurring in the State based upon their vegetation. In total, thirty-five floristic vegetation types were characterized, described, and identified on the wetland maps (5). More recently, however, Maryland's wetlands have been mapped as part of the National Wetlands Inventory, which follows the *Classification of Wetlands and Deepwater Habitats of the United States* (11); likewise, they have been described in *Wetlands of Maryland* (4), which follows that classification.

In 1982, I developed a geomorphological classification of Maryland's tidal wetlands, which included fifteen wetland types that were separated by physical setting, physiognomic type, and drainage pattern (Table III). I subsequently revised this classification to include water source, hydrodynamics, and salinity based upon comments received from Dr. Mark Brinson of Eastern Carolina University during the 1990s. A number of these

TABLE III. GEOMORPHOLOGICAL CLASSIFICATION OF MARYLAND'S TIDAL WETLANDS.[1]

Type	Physiognomy	Physical Setting	Drainage Pattern	Water Source	Hydrodynamics	Salinity[2]	Tidewater Extent: Examples[3]
Delta Wetland	Marsh and/ or swamp	At estuarine headwaters where relatively high gradient streams deposit heavy sediment loads into receiving waters	Distributary system	Lateral flow by tides and also periodically by river discharge	Bidirectional tides (regularly flooded) but also some nontidal unidirectional stream discharge	Fresh	Mostly in the upper Chesapeake Bay and on the Western Shore: Gunpowder River (Baltimore County), Otter Point Creek (Harford County), Port Tobacco River (Charles County), Northeast River and Principio Creek (Cecil County)
Draw Wetland	Marsh and/or swamp	At small draws having intermittent or perennial feeder streams	Generally only one main stream or gut with little branching; sometimes no guts	Lateral flow by tides	Bidirectional (regularly flooded)	Fresh to polyhaline	Statewide: Severn River and South River (Anne Arundel County); Wye River (Queen Anne's County)
Strip Wetland (mineral base)[4] a. <10 feet b. 10-20 feet c. >20 feet	Marsh	At upland/open water interfaces of Chesapeake Bay/major tributaries, or along perennial feeder streams	Usually no streams or guts; overland or unchannelized flow only	Lateral flow by tides	Bidirectional (regularly flooded)	Fresh to euhaline	Statewide: Severn River and South River (Anne Arundel County), Mill Creek (Calvert County), St. Martin's River (Worcester County)

134

Strip Wetland (peat/sod base)[3] a. <10 feet b. 10-20 feet c. >20 feet	Marsh	At upland/open water interfaces of Chesapeake Bay/major tributaries, or along perennial feeder streams	Usually no streams or guts; overland or unchannelized flow only	Lateral flow by tides	Bidirectional (regularly flooded)	Mesohaline to euhaline	Statewide: Lecompte's Creek (Dorchester County), St. Martin's River (Worcester County)
Estuarine Stream Wetland	Marsh and/or swamp	Along small subestuaries	Usually one meandering stream with few to numerous guts	Lateral flow by tides	Bidirectional (regularly flooded)	Fresh to euhaline	Statewide: Back Creek and Larch Creek (Anne Arundel County), Kings Creek (Caroline County), Waterworks Creek (Worcester County)
Estuarine River Wetland	Marsh and/or swamp	Along large subestuaries	Meandering river with meandering streams and guts; some with extensive mosquito ditching	Lateral flow by tides	Bidirectional (regularly flooded)	Fresh to mesohaline	Statewide except for coastal drainage in Worcester County; most common on the lower Eastern Shore: Nanticoke River (Dorchester and Wicomico Counties), Patuxent River (Anne Arundel, Prince George's, Charles, and Calvert Counties)
Spit Marsh Wetland[4]	Marsh	Landward of Chesapeake Bay spits at mouth of small subestuaries; also along its larger subestuaries at the mouths of their tributaries	Usually no streams or guts; overland or unchannelized flow only	Lateral flow by tides	Bidirectional (regularly flooded)	Fresh to polyhaline	Statewide, but mostly in the upper Chesapeake Bay area: Chesapeake Bay at Flag Ponds (Calvert County), Lloyd Creek (Kent County)

135

Type	Physiognomy	Physical Setting	Drainage Pattern	Water Source	Hydrodynamics	Salinity[3]	Tidewater Extent: Examples[4]
Baymouth Barrier Wetland[1]	Marsh and/or swamp	On Chesapeake Bay proper and its major larger subestuaries where there has been complete spit closure of small tributaries due to littoral drift	Usually only one stream or gut breaches the baymouth barrier (i.e., closed spit); the stream or gut may divide depending upon the amount of marsh/swamp formed landward of the baymouth barrier	Lateral flow from influent stream and sometimes by spring and storm tides	Unidirectional for the most part, although some bidirectional irregular flooding via spring and storm tides. The significance of the latter is contingent upon the elevation of the baymouth barrier and the nature and size of the tidal stream or gut (i.e., some streams/guts are intermittent)	Usually fresh to oligohaline; in the lower parts of the Chesapeake Bay, some may be mesohaline if a significant tidal connection is present.	Statewide, except for Worcester County: Chesapeake Bay at Big Marsh (Kent County), Sassafras River at Ches-Haven (Cecil County), Patuxent River at Douglas Point (Charles County)
Low Headland Wetland	Marsh and/or swamp	Along exposed shorelines where peninsulas project into the open water	Usually no stream or guts; overwash berms frequently around the periphery; periodic overland flow	Lateral flow by tides	Bidirectional (irregularly flooded by spring and storm tides)	Oligohaline to polyhaline	Chesapeake Bay and its larger subestuaries: Eastern Bay at Bennett Point (Talbot County), Chesapeake Bay at Swan Point (Kent County), Chesapeake Bay at Bodkin Point (Anne Arundel County)

Island Wetland	Marsh	Open water; usually associated with eroding shorelines	Frequently no streams or guts or they have been blocked by overwash berms	Lateral flow by tides	Bidirectional (irregularly flooded by spring and storm tides)	Oligohaline to euhaline	Mostly on the Eastern Shore including Worcester County: South Marsh Island in Chesapeake Bay (Somerset County), Hog Island in Prospect Bay (Queen Anne's County), Tizzard Island in Johnson Bay (Worcester County)
Bay Broad Wetland	Marsh	Associated with large coastal bays and subestuary mouths	Abundant meandering streams and guts; some with extensive mosquito ditching	Lateral flow by tides	Bidirectional (both regularly and irregularly flooding)	Mesohaline and polyhaline	Lower Eastern Shore exclusive of Worcester County: Fishing Bay-Elliott Island area (Dorchester County), Deal Island Wildlife Management Area (Somerset County)
Linear Wetland	Marsh	Associated with relict sand ridges (perhaps beach ridges) on large islands in the Chesapeake Bay, as well as the mainland	One main linear stream usually with spurred smaller guts	Lateral flow by tides	Bidirectional (both regularly and irregularly flooding)	Mesohaline and polyhaline	Lower Eastern Shore exclusive of Worcester County: Smith Island and Janes Island (Somerset County), Middle Hopper's Island (Dorchester County)
Back Barrier Island Wetland	Marsh	On the landward side of barrier islands	Truncated dendritic with guts wide relative to their lengths; some with mosquito ditches	Lateral flow by tides	Bidirectional (both regularly and irregularly flooding)	Euhaline	Worcester County: Assawoman Bay and Sinepuxent Bay

Type	Physiognomy	Physical Setting	Drainage Pattern	Water Source	Hydrodynamics	Salinity[2]	Tidewater Extent; Examples[3]
Barrier Island Broad Wetland	Marsh	On the mainland landward of barrier island bays; marsh usually scarped at the bayward edge due to erosion	Dendritic or meandering; frequent mosquito ditches	Lateral flow by tides	Bidirectional (both regularly and irregularly flooding)	Euhaline	Worcester County: Chincoteague Bay, Assawoman Bay, and Sinepuxent Bay
Man-made Wetland	Marsh and/or swamp	Usually associated with dikes, road fills, and spoil islands; sometimes these wetlands are designed and created	Variable depending on conditions	Variable depending on conditions	Variable depending on conditions	Variable depending on conditions	Potentially statewide: Hambleton Island (Talbot County), Barren Island (Dorchester County)

1. This classification system was originally developed in 1982 (12). It is modified here based upon comments received from Dr. Mark Brinson, East Carolina University, in 1992 and 1999. These types could be further divided by floristic vegetation types. The approach is very similar to Brinson' s "A Hydrogeomorphic Classification for Wetlands" (13).

2. Salinity classification follows "Classification of Wetlands and Deepwater Habitats of the United States." (11)

3. As used here, "statewide" refers to the tidewater portion of Maryland only. Salinity, however, is an additional factor in determining the geographic distribution of the various wetland types.

4. Marsh strips wider than adjacent waters and having streams or guts, should be considered Estuarine Stream Wetlands.

5. Marsh strips wider than adjacent waters and having streams or guts, should be considered Estuarine Stream Wetlands.

6. Spit Marsh Wetlands include those with single spits and those associated with a series of spits interspersed with marshes. However, the marshes in such complex spits are usually nontidal.

7. Baymouth Barrier Wetlands have formed after closure of small subestuaries due to littoral drift; they are in various stages of succession. Some support entirely marsh and/or swamp; others also have open water areas.

138

-- Estuarine River Wetland, Estuarine Creek Wetland, Island Wetland, Bay Broad Wetland, Baymouth Barrier Wetland, and Linear Wetland -- occur in Dorchester and Somerset Counties. This geomorphologically-based wetland classification is functionally oriented and is somewhat similar to the hydrogeomorphic classification of wetlands more recently developed by Dr. Brinson (13). The wetland types in this classification can be further divided by floristic vegetation types like those listed above (5,6,7).

All of these publications address, to varying degrees, the types of brackish marshes in Dorchester and Somerset Counties and serve as excellent background material for understanding the nature and extent of coastal marshes on the Eastern Shore.

THE ORIGIN OF THE MARSHES

During my early visits to the Eastern Shore, particularly the Blackwater area, it soon became apparent that things were drastically changing in the brackish marshes of Dorchester and Somerset Counties. I noted loblolly pine (*Pinus taeda*) 'islands' in the marshes that were being encroached upon by marsh plants.[4] Live trees were located in the center of the 'islands,' but dead trees rimmed the periphery and in situ tree stumps studded the surrounding marshes. Tree stumps were also located within estuarine clays, which were situated below contemporaneous marsh peats exposed at bay-front scarps and along tidal guts or ditches (Figures 29, 30, and 31). In addition, outcropped marsh peat was found seaward of transgressing overwash berms associated with Baymouth Barrier Wetlands. This was all strong field evidence of sea level change -- either that sea level was rising or that the land was sinking, or both, but I hadn't a clue as to why.

Then I came upon a 1969 Maryland Department of State Planning report called *Tidal Flooding and Conversion of Lands Adjacent to Tidal*

---

[4]I presented field evidence of this marsh transgression into the pines at the Blackwater National Wildlife Refuge on November 5, 1983 to a group of students. We sampled the soils and vegetation along a short transect running from the brackish marsh into the upland pines along the Little Blackwater River near the hiking trail and elevated walkway over the marsh.

Figure 29. Loblolly pine (*Pinus taeda*) islands being invaded by brackish tidal marsh due to sea level rise. Blackwater National Wildlife Refuge, Dorchester County, Maryland. Note dead standing trees around the periphery of the island. Tree stumps in the marsh are obscured by the thick vegetation. (Photo by the author)

Marsh on the Eastern Shore of Maryland by Robert M. August (14), which indicated that the conversion to tidal marsh was considerably more prevalent in Somerset and Dorchester Counties, but was believed to be occurring throughout the Eastern Shore where expanses of land less than five feet above tide existed and where sufficient buffering was not present. This sounded convincing, but my thoughts on this were particularly reinforced when I read *The Plant Life of Maryland* (15), which indicated that:

> "Geologic evidence shows that the Eastern Shore is at present undergoing a slow subsidence, the end effect of which will be to offset the upbuilding of marshes, if not to actually increase the areas of marshland, causing them to encroach on the Upland. At two localities on the inner edge of the extensive marshes of Dorchester County the writer saw unmistakable evidence of the encroachment of

140

the Fresh Marsh upon forest of *Pinus taeda*. These localities are where the Upland behind them is very flat for many miles...The evidences of the encroachment of the Marsh are the occurrence of remains of *Pinus taeda* at considerable distance beyond the present forest and the occurrence of half dead trees well outside the line of the present shore. The Marsh plants, on the other hand, are to be found in the outermost zone of the Pine forest in undiminished abundance and vigor. The evidence of the vegetation was confirmed by learning at one of the localities that a plantation (Guinea Neck) had existed before the war in a place where there is now only a very small island not already occupied by Marsh vegetation."

Then somewhere around 1975, I obtained a copy of a Master's Thesis by R.G. Darmody involving a reconnaissance survey of the tidal marsh soils of Maryland (16). A related publication by Darmody and J.E. Foss (17) on the

Figure 30. Remains of loblolly pine (*Pinus taeda*) forest that has succeeded to brackish tidal marsh. Blackwater National Wildlife Refuge, Dorchester County, Maryland. Note the numerous tree stumps in the marsh-open water area. (Photo by the author)

141

Figure 31. In situ tree stump capped by marsh peat along the Annemessex Canal, Somerset County, Maryland. (Photo by the author)

142

soil-landscape relationship of the tidal marshes of Maryland was also published in 1979. In these publications, the authors presented a physiographic classification of the tidal marshes of Maryland. Three tidal marsh types were described: Coastal, Estuarine, and Submerged Upland. The Coastal Type marshes have formed along the Atlantic Coast behind barrier islands where tidal and storm derived sediments have been deposited. (See Chapter Four for a discussion of the expansive Coastal Type marshes that have developed.) Estuarine Type marshes are the result of recent accumulation of sediments deposited in stream channels and estuarine meanders, along rivers like the Nanticoke, Choptank, and Wicomico. (See Chapter One for some discussion of the Choptank marshes; Chapter Six for the Nanticoke.) The Submerged Upland Type, which is the most abundant and formed as rising sea level inundated low lying upland, occurs mostly in Dorchester and Somerset Counties. This type was also acknowledged by Stevenson and his coauthors (18). It differs from the Estuarine Type in having a thin veneer of sediment over the recently submerged upland soil profile. This is the landscape setting described above with the marshes invading the loblolly pine areas in Dorchester and Somerset Counties. The dead pines and the in situ tree stumps are direct evidence of the submergence of the upland.

ON SOME INTERESTING LINEAR LANDSCAPE FEATURES

When I first started traversing Maryland's coastal marshes in 1971, I was fortunate to have an ample supply of high altitude aerial photographs along with me. They were invaluable aids, not only for locating projects on the ground, but for interpreting landscape features, something that has fascinated me since my graduate school days at the University of Pennsylvania. Without them, certain landforms and vegetative patterns would have most certainly gone unnoticed by me. One such landform, a series of low linear sandy ridges, perhaps relict beach ridges, are commonly associated with the brackish tidal marshes in Somerset County and southwestern Dorchester

County.[5] I was intrigued by these interesting landscape features. Consequently, I inquired about them and their origin with a coastal geologist, Randy Kerhin, from the Maryland Geological Survey. I had worked with Randy on some joint tidal permit-related projects and accompanied him on a few coastal geology field trips earlier. My interest soon also became his interest, and before long we were on Janes Island in Somerset County investigating some of these features.

Although we did not study these landscape features in detail, Randy produced a report in 1974 called *Linear Distribution of the High Marsh Vegetation Communities of the Lower Eastern Shore and its Geological Significance* (19), and I spent considerable time reviewing high altitude aerial photographs depicting them and visiting many. These landscape features are frequently associated with the Linear Wetland type, under my "Geomorphological Classification of Maryland's Tidal Wetlands" (Table III). This wetland type occurs only on the lower Eastern Shore (exclusive of Worcester County) on large islands and on the mainland. It generally has one main linear tidal gut from which diverges very short, frequently spur-like, lateral guts. Some good examples can be found on Janes Island and Smith Island in Somerset County and Middle Hoopers Island in Dorchester County.

In his report, Kerhin included a series of these low linear sandy ridges and inferred ridges on a map covering the area between Middle Hoopers Island and Maryland-Virginia line. He noted two distinct trends in the ridge systems for the Tangier Sound area. On the east side of Tangier Sound (e.g., on Janes and Deal Islands), the linear trend is in a northeast-southwest direction; on the west side of the sound (particularly for Smith, South Marsh, and Bloodsworth Islands), the linear trend is northwest-southeast (Figures 32 and 33). Cultural features, especially county roads, also frequently follow these sandy ridges.

---

[5]Another good example of aerial photographs having aided me in my field studies of Maryland's wetlands was the discovery of some bogs and the Cypress Creek Swamp and Savanna in Anne Arundel County in the late 1970s (see Chapter Eight). Likewise, my early discoveries around that time associated with the Delmarva potholes (Delmarva bays) in Queen Anne's and Caroline Counties resulted from the use of U.S. Department of Agriculture published county soil surveys and their included aerial photographs (see Chapter Seven).

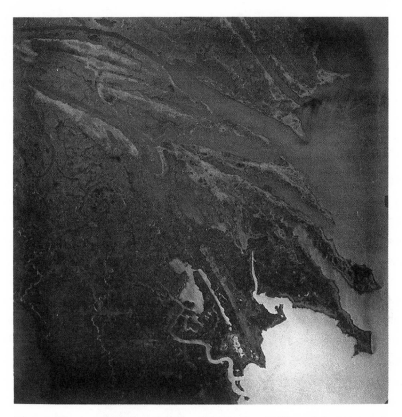

Figure 32. A computer-scanned printout of a 1985 aerial photograph showing the linear ridges on Smith Island at the Martin National Wildlife Refuge, Somerset County, Maryland. The ridges are mostly dominated by high marsh vegetation. Twitch Cove is in the lower right corner and Bull Point is the second peninsula from the bottom on the right.

Kerhin's report included the following description of the vegetation of these landscape features on Janes Island, which was compiled by me specifically for his report:

"Most of the linear structures at Janes Island appear to be vegetated by either high marsh or upland (very low upland). The high marsh is dominated by the *Spartina patens-Distichlis spicata*

145

vegetation type as well as that type mixed with shrubs, such as *Iva frutescens* and *Baccharis halimifolia*. The upland sites are vegetated by either trees (deciduous and some coniferous) with shrub (e.g., *Myrica cerifera*, *Baccharis halimifolia*) and herbaceous (e.g., *Panicum virgatum*, *Spartina patens*) understories. These linear landforms occur within larger low marsh masses dominated principally by *Spartina alterniflora* and low and intermediate marshes dominated by *Juncus roemerianus*."

I have also found similar vegetation types on the low linear sandy ridges on Smith Island and on those immediately northeast of Janes Island. Low and intermediate marshes in these two areas are also vegetatively similar to those on Janes Island.

Although we did some bucket augering through the sandy ridges, which suggested that they dipped under the adjacent marsh sediments, additional studies would have to be conducted to determine the potential role of the ridges in marsh formation on Janes Island, as well as the other Eastern Shore areas supporting these landscape features. Three questions that need to be answered in this regard are: What is the origin of these landscape features? What is their relationship to the formation of the tidal marshes? How do these ridges relate to the Pleistocene and Holocene history of the area? [6]

MARSH LOSSES IN THE BLACKWATER AREA

In the late 1970s, a task force comprised of representatives of the Maryland Department of Natural Resources, U.S. Fish and Wildlife Service, and the University of Maryland, and the Maryland legislative scientific advisor, was established to investigate the substantial conversion of marsh to open water at the Blackwater National Wildlife Refuge in Dorchester County.

---

[6]See Chapter Seven for a discussion of some other interesting landscape features on the Eastern Shore, the Delmarva potholes, which have been shown to be 16,000-21,000 years old. Chapter Seven also discusses some potential Carolina bays in Somerset County, most of which now support brackish marshes.

Figure 33. Linear ridges at Wallace Creek off the Honga River, Dorchester County, Maryland. Many of these ridges are dominated by loblolly pine (*Pinus taeda*); others by high marsh.

The marsh loss problem was documented by Refuge records, as well as personal observations of hunters, trappers, and Refuge personnel. An unpublished preliminary report (20), for example, suggested that the Refuge had lost about 2,100 acres to open water in forty-five years (1933-1978), although a subsequent report discussed below almost triples this marsh loss estimate. The reason for this conversion was unknown at the time, although a number of hypotheses were discussed in the report as possible causes of the losses. These included: impacts related to wildlife (muskrats, nutria, Canada geese, and snow geese); subsidence; and increased runoff and subsequent impoundment of water due to the presence of Maple Dam Road.

147

As a member of the task force while working for the Maryland Department of Natural Resources and a part-time graduate student at the University of Maryland, I gave this marsh loss problem considerable thought, with two objectives in mind: (1) to help resolve the problem and (2) to conduct ecological research relating thereto for a doctoral dissertation project. To aid in this effort and preliminary to my anticipated doctoral research, I compiled an extensive two-volume report on the dominant plant involved, the Olney three-square, including an annotated bibliography containing 180 references and a synthesis of selected references (21,22). This information was very useful in understanding the ecology of the Olney three-square and in evaluating the marsh loss problem at the Refuge.

After reviewing the literature on the Olney three-square and visiting the Dorchester County marshes on numerous occasions, my tentative thoughts on the marsh loss (22) were stated as follows:

> "...my own intuitive feeling after reviewing the literature on *Scirpus olneyi* and observing the site is that the problem probably relates to heavy use of the vegetation by muskrats (e.g., for food and house construction), geese (e.g., for food), and man (e.g., by burning) in conjunction with higher than normal water levels due to either impoundment, sea level rise, or possible subsidence. My hypothesis is that, while *S. olneyi* can normally keep up with sea level rise, it can not do so under heavy cropping (i.e., grazing, rooting, and burning). In fact, these conditions are essentially similar to a common method of wetland vegetation control wherein emergent plants similar to *S. olneyi* (e.g., *Typha latifolia*) are cut and flooded, sometimes repeatedly (23). Death usually occurs with complete submersion of the cut stems, but growth is also reduced by flooding when cut stems are exposed. Thus, over time, such cropping in conjunction with increased water levels could slowly produce the same result."

Initially, as I recall, there was substantial controversy over the causes of the marsh loss, particularly over the role of muskrats, geese, and annual

148

prescribed burning, all of which consume marsh vegetation. This was surely understandable considering that various Refuge management practices relating thereto were being potentially implicated. The controversy persisted and investigations were conducted by the University of Maryland's Horn Point Environmental Laboratories in 1979-1981. These studies, which included experiments, observations, and monitoring activities, culminated in a report called "Investigations of Marsh Losses at Blackwater Refuge" (24).

In contrast to the earlier estimates by Roby in 1974 (20), the University of Maryland report (24) indicated that the Refuge lost 5,700 acres between 1938 and 1979, two thirds of which occurred between 1938 and 1957. The losses were greatest around the confluence of the Blackwater and Little Blackwater Rivers in the center of the Refuge; they were the least in areas below (downstream from) Maple Dam Road, which crosses the Refuge at its lower end. Much smaller losses were also shown for some comparison areas, including Elliott Island. (See Chapter Six for some discussion of marsh losses along the lower Nanticoke River.)

The following potential causes were addressed in the University of Maryland report: lower marsh plant primary production; grazing by Canada geese, snow geese, muskrats, and nutria; annual prescribed marsh burning; salinity; herbicides; impoundment effects due to Maple Dam Road; and rising water levels.

The results of the of the University of Maryland studies indicated the following regarding possible causes. Plants in surviving marsh stands were just as productive as those in areas with no marsh loss, which ruled out differential primary productivity of Olney three-square as a factor. Little evidence was found to implicate grazing by geese, muskrats, and nutria as a primary cause of the marsh losses. On the other hand, certain observations indicated that muskrat and geese activities might accelerate or exacerbate localized marsh losses.

Historically, the muskrat, nutria, and goose populations have been high at the Blackwater National Wildlife Refuge. The following data on muskrat, nutria, Canada geese, and snow geese, which were compiled from Blackwater National Wildlife Refuge records, were available to me as a

149

member of the task force mentioned above. Unfortunately, I have been unable to obtain more recent data on muskrat and nutria populations from the Maryland Department of Natural Resources and the Blackwater National Wildlife Refuge despite its apparent existence and repeated requests. Likewise, I have received only incomplete waterfowl data through the Department. Because of its incomplete nature, however, the waterfowl data is not presented here.

In 1933, the muskrat population was estimated at 19,000 at the Refuge. By 1936, it reached 70,000; by 1938, 80,000. Then it dropped to 65,000 in 1939 and by 1941 was only 32,000. By 1948, it had dropped to 15,000. It was only 8,000 in 1959. Between 1960 and 1971, the muskrat population was below 8,000; between 1972 and 1975, it steadily increased from 8,545 to 11,600. The estimated population was 10,500 in 1977.

The first nutria activity in the area was reported in 1952, and two nutria were estimated to occur in the Refuge in 1953. Population estimates then rose to 200 in 1960, 655 by 1969, 2,075 in 1970, 4,500 in 1972, and 7,800 in 1973. They stabilized through 1976 but dropped from 7,800 in 1976 to 325 in 1977 following a very cold winter with resultant heavy mortality.

The peak Canada goose population at the Refuge was estimated at 200 in 1939. It rose to 1,000 in 1941, 6,000 in 1943, 20,000 in 1949, 60,000 in 1953, 100,000 in 1962, and 105,000 in 1963. Between 1964 and 1973, the goose population exceeded 100,000 only once (1966) and was only 80,000 in 1973.

The peak snow goose population at the Refuge was estimated at 12 in 1950, 175 in 1954, 268 in 1964, 950 in 1965, 1,500 in 1966, and 2,500 in 1967. Then it varied substantially between 1968 and 1971 (600-1,800). In 1972, the total was 2,100, and in 1973 it was 1,500. I should point out that the Blackwater snow geese population has been traditionally made up of lesser snow geese that typically winter along the Gulf Coast. In recent years, large numbers of greater snow geese have left the coastal saltmarshes and now feed in agricultural fields on the Delmarva Peninsula (Matt Perry, personal communication; 25).

150

Given the high historical herbivore populations leading up to the date of the University of Maryland investigations, it is readily understandable, from my perspective, how herbivores could have impacted the marshland, or at least exacerbated the problem. Muskrats, for example, characteristically establish trenches (canals) and surface trails (leads or runs); these were found to persist at Blackwater over the monitoring period on the Refuge (24). Furthermore, Olney three-square and cattails are generally considered two of the muskrat's favorite foods in the area (2,3,26,27), and all but the former author (Smith) mentioned the problem of "eatouts" at the Blackwater National Wildlife Refuge with resultant marsh deterioration. The impacts of muskrat "eatouts" on the Blackwater National Wildlife Refuge was also discussed by Meanley (28). Muskrat food studies in Maryland support this contention. At the Deal Island Wildlife Management Area in Somerset County, for example, narrow-leaf cattail and Olney three-square made up 58.5% and 17.4%, respectively, of the muskrat's diet (29).

Although Canada geese and snow geese did not appear to have a significant visual impact on the intact marshes during the University of Maryland's monitoring period, they did feed on tender Olney three-square shoots at restoration sites, thus interfering with those efforts. Stewart (30) also pointed out that the rootstalks and stems of the common three-square and Olney three-square are taken in large quantities by Canada geese in the Fresh Estuarine Bay Marshes and Brackish Estuarine Bay Marshes, both types of which comprise the bulk of the marshes where the wetland losses are occurring. Snow geese in particular are known to root out marsh rhizomes (31,32,33), and I have observed this myself at the Refuge. On the other hand, Stewart (30) indicated that snow geese feed to a large extent on the rootstalks of the smooth cordgrass.

Annual marsh burning was not implicated in the marsh losses; rather, it was deemed possibly beneficial to marsh accretion. The effect of salinity changes on the Olney three-square was found too difficult to assess due to the lack of long term data. The three common herbicides (atrazine, linuron, and trifluralin) commonly used by farmers in the Blackwater River watershed were not encountered in detectable concentrations in the water columns or

151

suspended material in the Blackwater or Little Blackwater River tributaries; nor were they found in sediment cores taken in deteriorated marsh areas. Furthermore, no evidence of long-term impoundment of water upstream of Maple Dam Road was detected. Since the losses typically began with the break-up of the interiors of the marshes, as opposed to the edges, shoreline erosion was also ruled out as the cause (24).

In contrast with the potential causes discussed above, the University of Maryland report (24) suggested that recent apparent rise in sea level in the Chesapeake Bay Region, acting in concert with a lack of sediment accretion on the marsh surface (as confirmed by a sediment budget for the Refuge), was the primary mechanism for the gradual conversion of marsh to open water on the Blackwater National Wildlife Refuge. This was not surprising to me, given the substantial vegetative field evidence of sea level rise in the Region, as well as elsewhere along much of the East Coast of the United States. (See Chapter Four for additional discussion of sea level rise associated with the coastal bays on the Delmarva Peninsula.)

This marsh loss problem has also been discussed by Stevenson and his coauthors (34,35,36), who emphasize sea level rise in conjunction with reduced sedimentation as the primary causes for the conversion of marsh to open water. For example, between 1940 and 1980 apparent sea level rise in the Blackwater area was 3.2 millimeters per year, whereas sediment accretion was only 2.6 millimeters per year (34). The problem has also been acknowledged by others (4,37).

In summary, the marsh losses on the Blackwater National Wildlife Refuge appear to have resulted from natural causes, primarily rising sea levels that are not being effectively offset by sediment accretion. However, the losses may have been locally accelerated or exacerbated by the activities of muskrats and geese, and perhaps nutria. In fact, in more recent years the significance of the nutria in exacerbating this vexing problem seems to be gaining favor (Carlo Brunori and Glenn Therres, personal communication). An article, "Declaring war on pesky nutria" appeared in the November 12, 1998 issue of *The Sun*. A joint pilot proposal ("Marsh Restoration: Nutria Control in Maryland") from the Federal and State government, as well as the private sector, to control nutria was developed in 1998. This proposal acknowledged erosion, land subsidence, sea-level rise, and non-indigenous species (the nutria) to be the principle causes. The joint goal of the proposal is to develop methods and strategies to reduce nutria populations in the Chesapeake Bay wetlands to the point where they are unable to maintain sustainable populations, to restore marsh habitats, and to promote public understanding of the importance of preserving Maryland's wetlands. In addition, on June 30, 1998, the Refuge Manager at the Blackwater National Wildlife Refuge announced that an environmental assessment for the Refuge's fire management program was available for public review. Long-term evaluation of the effects of fire exclusion, as well as prescribed fire application in 1, 3, and 10-year intervals, on the Refuge vegetation and wildlife is planned. As I indicated earlier, I had suggested in 1979 that the impacts of sea-level rise or subsidence would be exacerbated by heavy cropping, such as grazing, rooting, and burning, with a loss of marsh vegetation due to conditions that are very similar to those resulting from the control of some undesirable wetland plants.

Interestingly, according to Brook Meanley (28), Fran Uhler, a U.S. Fish and Wildlife Service biologist who had made extensive studies of the Blackwater area in the early 1930s, felt that the marshlands had changed little in the last forty-five years (as of 1978). And Meanley went on to say that the "Blackwater country will probably change very little in the next 45 years." I have always admired and respected these two veteran field biologists, and viewed them as giants in the field, with encyclopedic knowledge. I guess this is just an example that no matter how good you are (and they were damn good), you too can be wrong, for as indicated above the marsh loss problem has been well-documented.

MORE ON THE WILDLIFE

In any treatment of the tidal marshes of Dorchester and Somerset Counties, I would be patently negligent not to include a discussion of waterfowl and other wildlife that make this area so unique, including the bald eagle, muskrat, otter, and mink. Various marsh birds, shorebirds, and wading

153

birds are also characteristic of the marshes, mudflats, and shallow waters in the area; they are not, however, discussed in this Chapter.

Waterfowl

In 1962, the U.S. Fish and Wildlife Service published a Special Scientific Report by Robert E. Stewart called "Waterfowl Populations of the Upper Chesapeake Region," which presents information on the distribution, ecology, and harvest of the area's waterfowl. To my knowledge, this is the most comprehensive report produced to date on the waterfowl populations of the Maryland portion of the Chesapeake Bay, its tributaries, and the Worcester County coastal bays, although there have been substantial changes in the waterfowl populations since then. Likewise, the foods utilized by some species have changed -- the whistling swans, for example, now feed more commonly on waste grain in agricultural fields and the Canvasbacks have switched from submerged aquatic vascular plants (the so-called grasses) to Baltic clams (*Macoma baltica*) (25,38,39; Larry Heinman, personal communication).[7] The report discusses thirteen major waterfowl habitats, including these ten types of marshes and bays:

Coastal Embayed Marshes	Coastal Bays
Salt Estuarine Bay Marshes	Salt Estuarine Bays
Brackish Estuarine Bay Marshes	Brackish Estuarine Bays
Fresh Estuarine Bay Marshes	Slightly Brackish Estuarine Bays
Estuarine River Marshes	Fresh Estuarine Bays

The latter four marsh types occur in Dorchester County. Of these four types, all but the Fresh Estuarine Bay Marshes occur in Somerset County. Brackish Estuarine Bays and Salt Estuarine Bays are the most abundant bay types in the two-county area; the Fresh Estuarine Bays and Slightly Brackish Estuarine Bays are not found in the area. The Coastal Embayed Marshes and

---

[7]The geographic extent of the report also extends somewhat into Virginia.

Coastal Bays are restricted to Worcester County, Maryland and adjacent Virginia. Of the remaining three types not shown above, two (Wooded Bottomland and Interior Impoundments) occur more inland; the third (Ocean Littoral Zone) occurs only on the ocean side of the Delmarva Peninsula.

The waterfowl populations are discussed under fifteen biogeographic sections. Three of these, the Choptank River, Blackwater-Nanticoke, and Lower Eastern Shore Sections, include areas of Dorchester and Somerset Counties. A brief summary of the waterfowl populations documented in the U.S. Fish and Wildlife Service report for these three Sections and their waterfowl habitats in Dorchester and Somerset Counties follows.

As mentioned in the report, the Upper Chesapeake Region has historically been one of the more important areas in North America for migratory and wintering waterfowl, including ducks, geese, swans and American coot. In fact, the Upper Chesapeake Region waterfowl population averaged about 4% of the entire continental population and 23% of the Atlantic population between 1953 and 1958. During that period, 42% of the population present in the area was comprised of diving ducks. Others in order of abundance were dabblers (29%), geese (18%), swans (4%), coots (3%), oldsquaws, scoters, and mergansers (2%), and unidentified ducks (2%). More than 50% of the average wintering population was comprised of the canvasback, Canada goose, black duck, and scaup, but the whistling swan, mallard, pintail, American wigeon, redhead, and ruddy duck were also important.

The Brackish Estuarine Bays were considered the most important habitat for waterfowl as a whole. Nevertheless, Fresh Estuarine Bays, Brackish Estuarine Bay Marshes, and Estuarine River Marshes also attracted large numbers of waterfowl. Although the greatest concentrations of transient and wintering waterfowl were present along the Chester River, Eastern Bay, and Choptank River Sections, the Blackwater-Nanticoke Section, which contains extensive Fresh and Brackish Estuarine Marshes, also had large numbers of waterfowl.

The Choptank River Section was considered one of the more important waterfowl areas in the Upper Chesapeake Region. During the late

1950s, January inventory data indicated waterfowl populations ranging from 40,000 to 195,600, with an average of 117,100. Species like the Canada goose, black duck, whistling swan, American wigeon, as well as various species of diving ducks, frequently used the estuarine bays. On the other hand, most dabbling ducks preferred the Estuarine River Marshes, and black ducks bred in the estuarine marshes associated with estuarine bays.

An outstanding feature of the Blackwater-Nanticoke Section is the vast expanse of Fresh and Brackish Estuarine marshes. Four major types of waterfowl habitat occur in the Blackwater-Nanticoke Section: Fresh Estuarine Bay Marsh, Brackish Estuarine Bay Marsh, Estuarine River Marsh, and Brackish Estuarine Bay. The largest area supporting Fresh Estuarine Bay Marshes is along the upper part of the Blackwater River. A large area of contiguous Brackish Estuarine Bay Marshes surrounds and drains into the upper part of Fishing Bay and the upper part of the estuarine bay area of the Nanticoke River from Ragged Point north to Chapter Point. The Estuarine River Marshes occur in two areas, the major one being further north on the Nanticoke River to the village of Riverton; the smaller area is along the upper portion of the Transquaking River and its tributary, the Chicamacomico River. The Brackish Estuarine Bays are located in the upper part of Fishing Bay and the upper part of the estuarine bay of the Nanticoke River.

This important waterfowl area had wintering populations for the late 1950s ranging from a low of 22,400 to a high of 234,500 with an average of 126,500. Canada geese, mallards, black ducks, American wigeons, and canvasbacks were the most important species present. The geese concentrated in the Fresh Estuarine Bay Marshes, but ranged into agricultural fields; they also fed and roosted in shoal areas of the Brackish Estuarine Bays. Black ducks occurred mostly in the Brackish Estuarine Bay Marshes, where they also bred. The American wigeons were found regularly in the Fresh and Brackish Estuarine Bay Marshes; on the other hand, canvasbacks and other diving ducks were generally restricted to the Brackish Estuarine Bays.

Salt Estuarine Bays and Salt Estuarine Bay Marshes are the main waterfowl habitats of the Lower Eastern Shore Section. The extensive Salt Estuarine Bay Marshes in this Section, which occur on the mainland as well as on the offshore islands, constitute the only large areas of this type of marsh in the entire Upper Chesapeake Region. There are also two fairly large areas of Brackish Estuarine Bay Marshes and numerous Brackish Estuarine River Marshes along tidal streams that enter the interior, the largest of which are along the Wicomico and Pocomoke Rivers.

The January inventory data for the late 1950s indicated a wintering waterfowl population for the Lower Eastern Shore Section of from 16,600 to 106,800, with an average of 63,600. During the winter, the predominant species were the Canada goose, black duck, pintail, and American wigeon.

*   *   *

Species-specific information was also given by Stewart. Three of the species inventoried -- the Canada goose, black duck, and pintail -- are discussed further below.

January inventories for the late 1950s showed wintering populations of Canada geese for the Upper Chesapeake Region ranging from 95,000 to 269,000, with an average of 189,000, which represents about 18% of the Continental population and about 45% of the Atlantic population. Approximately 16% of the Upper Chesapeake Region population occurred in the Fresh and Brackish Estuarine Bay Marshes of the Blackwater-Nanticoke Section; about 9% occurred in the Salt Estuarine Bay Marshes of the Lower Eastern Shore Section.

The black duck was the next most widely distributed waterfowl species in the Upper Chesapeake Region year-round, ranging from 49,500 to 229,500, with an average of 129,700 in the winters during the 1950s, which represented about 19% of the continental population and 28% of the Atlantic population. Stewart and Robbins (40) indicated that outstanding wintering and transient concentration areas include the Chester River, Eastern Bay, Blackwater National Wildlife Refuge, and marshes along the Nanticoke River between Savannah Lake and Elliott Island. Stewart (30) pointed out that fairly large numbers of black ducks were noted in the Estuarine Bay Marshes of the Blackwater-Nanticoke and Lower Eastern Shore Sections.

The extensive Brackish Estuarine Bay Marshes of the Blackwater-Nanticoke Section had one of the largest black duck breeding populations, and fairly large breeding populations were also associated with the Salt Estuarine Bay Marshes of the Lower Eastern Shore Section. For example, in 1956 Robert E. Stewart found 53 pairs of black ducks in a 1,000 acre area (5.3 pairs per 100 acres) of Brackish Estuarine Bay Marsh within the Blackwater-Nanticoke Section (30). Data from the *Atlas of Breeding Birds of Maryland and the District of Columbia* indicate that the black duck still breeds in Maryland, but probably in reduced numbers (41).

The pintail was fairly common locally, particularly on the Eastern Shore. Wintering populations ranged from 13,900 in 1958 to 66,700 in 1953, with an average of about 49,600. This was about 1% of the continental population and 15% of the Atlantic population. The largest congregations were in the brackish estuaries and agricultural fields of the Chester River Section. However, large numbers of pintails were also noted in the extensive Estuarine Bay Marshes and Estuarine River Marshes of the Blackwater-Nanticoke and Lower Eastern Shore Sections. Winter survey data from the late 1950s showed that an average of 47% of the Upper Chesapeake pintail population was in these two Sections. Overall, more than 75% of the pintails occurred in the Chester River, Blackwater-Nanticoke, and Lower Eastern Shore Sections. However, the pintail is not known to nest in the State (40,41).

*   *   *

Major changes have occurred in the Chesapeake Bay Region since the publication of that U.S. Fish and Wildlife Service's report, and much smaller waterfowl populations now exist. Aerial Bay-wide surveys conducted annually in January by the U.S. Fish and Wildlife Service and the States of Maryland and Virginia indicate, for example, major declines in most ducks since the 1950s. Of the dabbling ducks, the black duck, pintail, gadwall, and American wigeon, in particular, have had substantial declines. For a forty-five year period (1950-1994), aerial surveys indicated a low of 33,046, a high of 282,029, and an average of 78,748 black ducks in the Chesapeake Bay Region

(25). Similarly, for that same period, aerial surveys indicated a low of 400, a high of 78,211, and an average of 14,169 pintails in the Chesapeake Bay Region. On the other hand, buffleheads have increased in numbers, and swans, mallards, scaup, and sea ducks have been stable. Populations increases in mallards since 1985 have been attributed to the large releases of captive-reared ducks in Maryland (25,42).

*   *   *

Although Canada and snow goose populations increased during the 1950s-1980s due to their increased use of agricultural fields for feeding, there was a subsequent decline, and Maryland's wintering populations have continued to decrease (41,43). For a forty-five year period (1950-1994), for example, aerial surveys indicated a low of 87,100, a high of 701,470, and an average of 390,075 Canada geese in the Chesapeake Bay Region (25). On the other hand, the marshes of the Lower Eastern Shore, particularly near the Blackwater National Wildlife Refuge, evidently support one of the main concentrations of breeding Canada geese in the State (41).

Bald Eagle

On November 17, 1973 I led a field trip to Dorchester County for the Graduate School, U.S. Department of Agriculture. We visited the Blackwater National Wildlife Refuge and recorded twenty-nine bird species, including six ducks (the black, bufflehead, mallard, pintail, shoveler, and gadwall), three geese (lesser snow, blue, and Canada), and the bald eagle.[8] Of the six eagles we saw, two were adults. We had a great view of a couple of eagles out on the flats beyond the observation tower. I believe it was on this trip that I hastily announced that one eagle was a male! What a birding blunder. When a

---

[8]Actually, the blue goose is just a color phase of the snow goose. Although both the lesser and greater snow geese have some blue individuals, the lesser typically has more blue phase birds and is the more common species found at the Blackwater National Wildlife Refuge (Matt Perry, personal communication).

159

veteran birder looked amazingly at me, I quickly realized my dumb mistake --
the female eagle is, of course, just as colorful, with white head and all, as a
male. In fact, they are identical in coloration, although the female is slightly
larger (Glenn Therres, personal communication). So much for blundering
haste.

I have always enjoyed seeing the eagles at Blackwater, given their
relative abundance and my limited sightings of eagles while growing up in
South Jersey. Shortly after moving to Maryland, I noted that, according to
Birds of Maryland and the District of Columbia (40), the bald eagle was
relatively common in the tidewater areas of Maryland, with nest records from
a number of counties, including Dorchester and Somerset. So I was always on
the watch for eagles while on my field trips. This particular trip in 1973 was
the first of many on which I annually brought my wetland ecology classes to
Dorchester County in November to examine its expansive marshes and
observe its abundant waterfowl, especially at Blackwater. The waterfowl were
always a big attraction on these field trips; the eagles, of course, were the
icing on the cake.

A year earlier, I had inquired with Jackson M. Abbott about the
nesting distribution of the bald eagle in tidewater Maryland so that this
information could be considered when assessing the potential environmental
impacts associated with proposed tidal wetland permit applications received
by the Department of Natural Resources. Abbott had led a longtime effort
sponsored by the Audubon Naturalist Society to annually survey the nesting
bald eagles in the Chesapeake Bay Region, starting in 1957 (44).

On June 10, 1972, Jackson Abbott thoughtfully responded in a letter
which included a series of annotated maps showing active and inactive nests
as of 1971. As one might expect, the highest concentration of nests was in
Dorchester county; the second highest was along the Potomac River.
Furthermore, Abbott's 1975 survey produced thirteen nests for Dorchester
County, with the second highest Maryland county, St. Mary's, having only six
(45). The total for the entire Chesapeake Bay Region was seventy-five, forty-
two of which were in Maryland, so Dorchester County supported 31% of
Maryland's tidewater nests and 11.4% of the entire Chesapeake Bay Region's

nests in 1975. As pointed out by Abbott, a pair of eagles had built four nests in Dorchester County's Moneystump Swamp for over sixty years, one of which, the original known nest for the site, was more than sixty years old in 1979. Abbott gave a good review of his and predecessor's efforts to monitor the bald eagle in "Bald Eagles in the Chesapeake Bay Region" (44). In addition, he documented forty-five and twenty fledglings in 1977 for Maryland and Virginia, respectively.

Annually, since 1977, the Maryland Department of Natural Resources has surveyed the bald eagle nesting population in Maryland (Glenn Therres, personal communication). The twenty-two years of data show a steady increase in the occupied nests from 41 in 1977 to 86 in 1987, to 128 in 1991, to 201 in 1996, and to a very encouraging 232 in 1998. This trend was also acknowledged by Glenn Therres of the Maryland Department of Natural Resources in his article on the bald eagle in the *Atlas of the Breeding Birds of Maryland and the District of Columbia* for the years 1983-1987 (46). In 1998, Dorchester County had 56 (24.1%) and Somerset County had 10 (4.3%) of the 232 occupied nests in Maryland.

In leading trips to Dorchester County over an eighteen year period up to 1990, I don't think I missed seeing at least one eagle, sometimes quite close on a perch or winging low overhead, on more than a couple of occasions. For example, besides the 1973 sighting mentioned above, my *Journal* entry for November 6, 1982 indicates that I had my "closest and greatest view of bald eagle ever..." when we observed an adult fifty yards away on an osprey nesting platform at the Blackwater National Wildlife Refuge. Then on November 5, 1983, my class viewed four bald eagles (one mature) from the observation tower at the Refuge, and on November 17, 1984, we saw three bald eagles (two mature) at the Refuge, as well as a third mature bird along Maple Dam Road. On November 2, 1985, we spotted a mature bald eagle through a scope from the visitor center, and on November 7, 1987, we observed four eagles on the surface of the marsh from the observation tower and an adult eagle perched about one hundred yards from the automobile drive. Although I was not with my class at the time, I spotted a bald eagle along the dike at the Refuge on August 18, 1989. My class and I once again had some great views of eagles at the Refuge on November 3, 1990.

Additional field trips have produced bald eagle sightings for other areas of the Eastern Shore, such as along the Choptank and Pocomoke Rivers and at the Eastern Neck National Wildlife Refuge. I have similarly observed eagles on the Western Shore along the Patapsco, Patuxent, and Potomac Rivers, including, on occasions, from my office only three blocks from the U. S. Capitol Building in Washington, DC!

The Muskrat and its Role in Biological Community Structuring

Besides waterfowl, perhaps the most common animal that comes to mind with most outdoor people familiar with the Dorchester County marshes is a mammal -- the muskrat. Two muskrat subspecies occur in Maryland (47). The Virginia or coastal muskrat, *Ondatra zibethicus macrodon*, which was originally described by C. Hart Merriam in 1897 from Lake Drummond, Virginia (2), inhabits the coastal marshes and waterways of the Eastern Shore. The other subspecies, *Ondatra z. zibethicus*, is found in the Appalachian Region of Western Maryland. Muskrats inhabiting the central Piedmont Plateau area of Maryland are apparently intergrades of these two subspecies.

The muskrat has been well-studied in Maryland, particularly on the Eastern Shore (e.g., see references 2,3,26,27,29,47,48,49). These studies included information on its taxonomy, geographic distribution, populations, activities, feeding habits, reproduction, sex ratios, weight, color phases, and habitats. Natural mortality due to storms, predation, and diseases, as well as population impacts associated with increased salinity, were also addressed. Much of this information was subsequently reviewed and incorporated into the annotated bibliography (Volume I) on the Olney three-square and its companion synthesis report (Volume II) cited earlier (21,22).

From those two volumes, I also developed my doctoral research proposal, which was to address, in part, the importance of biological versus physical community structuring within stands of the Olney three-square.

162

Therefore, the remainder of my discussion on the muskrat in Dorchester County will concentrate on it's role as a biological community structuring agent.

Over the years while visiting the Dorchester County marshes, I had noted that stands of Olney three-square supported large populations of muskrats. In fact, marshes on the Eastern Shore dominated by the Olney three-square and cattails support the largest muskrat populations in Maryland (2,27,28,29).[9] The muskrat population data presented earlier for the marshes at the Blackwater National Wildlife Refuge reinforces this contention. The importance of the Olney three-square to muskrats has also been reported elsewhere, particularly for Louisiana (50,51,52,53,54,55). Furthermore, it was clear to me at the time that, while certain stands of Olney three-square were monotypic or near-monotypic, others were much more diverse, supporting a variety of vascular plant species. Stands with greater species richness tended to have openings in the three-square resulting from muskrat activity, such as "eatouts" around muskrat houses and adjacent to feedbeds; openings also resulted from muskrat runs and canals. It was not uncommon to find plants like perennial saltmarsh aster (*Aster tenuifolius*), saltmarsh camphorweed (*Pluchea purpurascens*), yellow flatsedge (*Cyperus flavescens*), spikerush (*Eleocharis* sp.), saltgrass (*Distichlis spicata*), and saltmeadow cordgrass (*Spartina patens*) in these openings. Competition for space between Olney three-square and its potential associated plant competitors appeared reduced because of the presence of the muskrat, which selectively fed on the three-square, thereby allowing the co-existence of Olney three-square and its associated plant species. Following this idea, I hypothesized that the muskrat served as a biological community structuring agent (specifically, a keystone species) by allowing for greater plant species richness and vegetative spatial heterogeneity due to its disturbance activities.

As it turns out, I did not complete the graduate program requirements at the University of Maryland. Consequently, I never experimentally tested my

---

[9]Muskrat studies began in the late 1930s to obtain a better fur market. The war effort accelerated these studies as the United States government attempted to find furs with good insulating properties for servicemen in northern climates (Matt Perry, personal communication).

idea about the interaction of the muskrat and the Olney three-square. Nevertheless, the muskrat's role in structuring marsh communities has been espoused by others. Erik Kiviat (56), for example, indicated that clearings around muskrat houses supported a mosaic of varied developmental plant communities at moderate densities and that low muskrat densities may result in extensive, nearly pure stands of cattail and bulrush. In Michigan, a marsh dominated by cattail (*Typha* sp.) and broad-fruited bur-reed (*Sparganium eurycarpum*) also supported twenty-four other plant species (57). The vegetation of the muskrat mounds (houses) themselves was very different from the surrounding marsh. They provided an elevated, drier habitat that supported a rarer group of marsh species. Likewise, in Louisiana J.A. Nyman, R.H. Chabreck, and N.W. Kinler (58) found that species richness was positively related to the frequency of muskrats. They also stated that muskrats feeding in areas dominated by Olney three-square feed primarily on the dominant vegetation and may increase the opportunities for subdominant and minor species, thereby increasing species richness. Strong spatial heterogeneity, attributable to muskrats, was also noted for two Iowa glacial marshes (59). For a brackish marsh in Dorchester County near Elliott Island, Bruce F. Leon (60) examined the role of disturbance and competition in relation to vegetation patterns. Among other findings, he pointed out that a number of vascular plants, including annuals and perennials, rapidly colonize muskrat trenches, which lends additional credence to my hypothesis about the role of the muskrat in biological community structuring.

Similar examples of biological community structuring due to grazing have been reported involving rabbits (61,62); both studies indicated that, with the exclusion of rabbits, marked declines in plant species richness occurred. On the other hand, too much grazing pressure can decrease species richness and, at times, even exclude vegetation due to overgrazing. A pertinent example of this is excessive grazing by an overabundance of muskrats, which can ultimately result in major "eatouts" followed by crashes in the muskrat populations. Likewise, intensive herbivory can result in the invasion of aggressive, less palatable plants resistant to grazing and thereby decrease plant species richness.

Another major biological community structuring agent, of course, is the beaver, which due to its impoundment construction habit, serves as a major agent for modifying hydrology and thereby increasing spatial heterogeneity and landscape diversity within and along many floodplains (63). (See Chapter Ten for some examples of this.)

The Otter and Mink

After the bald eagle, I suppose the next most significant animal that impressed me when I started exploring Maryland's coastal wetlands was the otter. We had but few otters back in my fur trapping days in South Jersey, and those that we did have occurred further south along the tidal marshes and tributary streams of Delaware Bay, locations not readily accessible to me as teenager. When I moved to Maryland, otter sign along Chesapeake Bay and the Worcester County bays seemed to be everywhere. And as pointed out by John L. Paradiso (64) in *Mammals of Maryland*, Maryland's Eastern Shore supports a large otter population. In fact, Paradiso mentions that even John James Audubon and John Bachman (65) and Elliott Coues (66) considered otters common on the Eastern Shore.

Dorchester County led in otter harvest between 1950-1970 with seventy-five otter or 16.9% of the State total (67). A number of other Eastern Shore counties, such as Queen Anne's, Caroline, and Talbot, were also quite high in otter harvest, as was St. Mary's on the Western Shore. Most of the otter sign examined by Brook Meanley in the Blackwater area occurred along the saltmarsh meadows near tidal guts (28). He noted marsh trails that led from one tidal gut to another, along which were strewn fish scales and crustacean fragments resulting from their feeding activities. In the Chesapeake Bay Region, I have observed otter sign, droppings in particular, along the coastal bays in Worcester County, along the Chester, Choptank, Nanticoke, and Pocomoke River marshes, and in Big Marsh in Kent County. I have likewise observed otter sign at a number of localities on the Western Shore, particularly in St. Mary's County. My impression is that the otter population is substantial in the Chesapeake Bay Region.

165

I have found little published information about the distribution and extent of the mink population in Maryland. However, Paradiso (64) indicated that "Maryland does not rank high in wild mink production...[but]...In areas where muskrat abound, such as the muskrat marshes of the Delmarva Peninsula, mink may feed extensively on them." Mink predation on muskrats has also been documented in New York (68,69) and Michigan (70). Mink, as well as raccoon and red fox, are known to break into muskrat houses, where they may also be searching for resident meadow voles (*Microtus pennsylvanicus*) and rice rats (*Oryzomys palustris*) (28,71).

On November 6, 1982, I observed mink tracks along the Blackwater River at Maple Dam Road. Mink are known to occur on Bloodsworth Island in Dorchester County (72), and I recall a reference to mink in a Department of Natural Resources' wetland inventory conducted in the 1960s, which was associated with *Wetlands in Maryland* (1). Specifically, a Dorchester County wetland unit for Bloodsworth Island mentioned a large mink population. In this regard, Paradiso (64) cited a specimen taken from Bloodsworth Island. On the Western Shore, I have found mink tracks along the Piscataway Creek in Prince George's County. I have also seen mink tracks along Severn Run in Anne Arundel County on a number of occasions, and on April 13, 1996 a mink came within about ten feet of me along Severn Run as I relaxed in a portable hammock while recording wildlife observations (see Chapter Ten). That was only my third mink sighting ever, the other two being in New Jersey and Michigan.

A FEW FIRSTS FOR THE REGION

On May 4, 1956, Robert E. Stewart and Don P. Fankhauser located a gadwall nest with seven eggs about six miles northeast of Elliott in a Brackish Bay Marsh between Fishing Bay and the Nanticoke River. This represented the first record for gadwall nesting in Dorchester County. At the time, the only other breeding records for the gadwall were from northwestern Somerset County (73). Likewise, what may have been the first gadwall breeding record for Chesapeake Bay islands was recorded from Smith Island in Somerset County by Henry T. Armistead on June 20, 1975 (74). Two females where observed -- one with two downy young, the other with fourteen. Armistead also discovered the first coot nests in Maryland, on August 16, 1970, then the first for green-winged teal on June 5, 1971 -- both again in Somerset County, at the Deal Island Wildlife Management Area (75,76). A female teal was flushed from a saltmeadow cordgrass area along a dike; the nest contained five eggs, which were partially concealed by the tops of the grass. The first evidence of blue-winged teal nesting in Maryland was reported in the journal *Auk* for the Blackwater area by Oliver L. Austin, Jr. in 1932 (77). The events surrounding this first, as well as related searches for the blue-winged teal along the Blackwater River near Shorters Landing, are discussed by Brooke Meanley in his book, *Blackwater* (28).

On June 4, 1977 Henry Armistead again had another first -- this time the first breeding record for the American oystercatcher for the Maryland portion of the Chesapeake Bay, when he located a nest on Barren Island in Dorchester County (78). At the time, he also established the first breeding record for the herring gull in Dorchester County. The oyster- catcher and gull nests were only eleven paces from one another. Likewise, the first record of the black skimmer for Dorchester County was established by Armistead along Maple Dam Road in the Blackwater National Wildlife Refuge on June 21, 1976, when a flock of seven skimmers flew across the road (79). And the Wilson's phalarope was observed for the first time in Somerset County and the sixth time on the Eastern Shore on August 24, 1968 -- by who else but Henry Armistead!(80)

A new subspecies of the swamp sparrow, *Melospiza georgiana nigrescens*, was originally described from the Nanticoke River marsh near Vienna in 1951 based upon specimens collected there in the summer of 1950 by G. Bond and Robert Stewart (81). According to Brook Meanley (82), Neil Hotchkiss, another veteran U.S. Fish and Wildlife Service biologist, had heard several swamp sparrows along the river bank in 1946 and suspected this was unusual since the sparrows were considered south of their normal breeding range at the time. Hotchkiss then informed Stewart and Chandler S. Robbins, who visited the area and confirmed his suspicion. Until recently, this

167

subspecies was thought to be limited to a few sites along the Chesapeake Bay; its range on the Coastal Plain, however, has been found to be more extensive than previously thought (41).

An article in *The Sun* on July 17, 1998 mentioned the discovery of what might have been the first nesting colony of brown pelicans in the Maryland portion of the Chesapeake Bay. The colony is located at Spring Island, a small island south of Bloodsworth Island in Dorchester County.

SOME PERSONAL PLANT FIRSTS

Most hardcore field naturalists are listers of some sort, and their records tend to document when they first encountered new species for their various life lists. From the outset back in New Jersey as a youngster, I was no exception -- along with compiling my *Jersey Journal* and eventually my *Maryland Journal*, I have kept life lists for everything from ferns to trees and insects to mammals.

I have always said every trip into the field brings something new -- frequently, in my case, vascular plants for addition to my separate life lists for ferns and fern allies, wildflowers, grasses, sedges, rushes, shrubs, vines, and trees. A few of my personal firsts for Dorchester and Somerset Counties are given below.

On May 22, 1972, I found my first saltmeadow rush (*Juncus gerardii*) on the high saltmarsh at Crisfield in Somerset County. This more northern rush occurs along the coast as far south as Virginia. My initial encounter with its close relative, the black needlerush (*J. roemerianus*) apparently occurred on October 21, 1971 at Bloodsworth Island when I visited the site with other Department of Natural Resources' wetland personnel to "ground truth" some draft tidal wetland maps. On that same day, I also found an endangered plant in Maryland, the short-bearded plumegrass (*Erianthus brevibarbis*). In their *Herbaceous Plants of Maryland*, Brown and Brown (83) considered this species rare, and mentioned its occurrence in Somerset County; Robert R. Tatnall (84), in his *Flora of Delaware and the Eastern Shore*, listed it as infrequent. It was not included by Gilman (85) in her treatment of the grasses of the Tidewater-Piedmont Region of northern Virginia and Maryland. Currently, the Maryland Natural Heritage Program considers this species to be highly State rare and endangered. A few years later, on September 3, 1976, I found for the first time its more common congener, the giant plumegrass (*E. giganteus*), in a roadside ditch along Drawbridge Road in Dorchester County.

On June 28, 1972, I collected an interesting succulent brackish marsh sedge that I hadn't seen before, the long-bract sedge (*Carex extensa*), on Rock and Dames Quarter Creeks in Somerset County and again at Windsor Creek in Wicomico County on August 11, 1972. I was curious about this new sedge and checked upon its known distribution. According to *Gray's Manual of Botany* (86), this species is found only locally in coastal areas of New York and Virginia, and it was not listed for the Delmarva Peninsula by Tatnall (84). However, herbaria searches by my colleague, Dick Wheeler, and I uncovered collections from southern Dorchester County by Neil Hotchkiss in 1961 and from Somerset County southwest of Dames Quarter by Fran Uhler in 1948 (87). I have also found it in the Bishops Head area in southern Dorchester County.

An interesting first for me at the Blackwater National Wildlife Refuge was the prairie cordgrass (*Spartina pectinata*), which I found on fairly high ground at the marsh/pine woods interface on November 7, 1987. According to Brown and Brown (83), this more mid-western prairie grass is found infrequently in Maryland on the Coastal Plain and Piedmont. Tatnall considered it infrequent on the Delmarva Peninsula, and Gilman (85) cited it from the Potomac River, but indicated that it was more frequent toward the coast. I have observed it also on the Potomac at Great Falls in an open prairie-like island setting.

One of my favorite brackish tidal marsh plants is the elongated lobelia (*Lobelia elongata*), a beautiful blue gem that I first encountered on August 3, 1976 on Chicamacomico Creek at Drawbridge Road. It was number 774 on my wildflower life list. I subsequently found a number of elongated lobelias at Blackwater along the Little Blackwater River opposite Seward on August 18, 1989. I have also found this colorful species in the brackish marshes of the Pocomoke River below Hickory Point. It was considered rare on the Delmarva by Tatnall (84) and is listed as a watch list species by the Maryland Natural Heritage Program.

Dorchester County also produced a couple of bird firsts for me, namely the surf and white-winged scoters and the boat-tailed grackle, all on October 21, 1971 at Bloodsworth Island, the same day that I found the plumed beardgrass and black needlerush mentioned above.[10] Both scoters are considered common in the mid-lower Eastern Shore bay area during the winter (40). The boat-tailed grackle, a rather large bird compared to the more widely distributed common grackle, is fairly common in coastal areas of Worcester County, but also frequents the Dorchester and Somerset County brackish marshes (40,82). The female boat-tailed grackle is much smaller than the male and brownish in color.

*   *   *

One last thing about firsts: You tend not to forget them if they are rare or otherwise significant species, or perhaps were the first species you encountered in a particular habitat type or geographic area of interest.

In a formal sense, my botanizing started in the early 1960s, during my pre-college days, while driving a small truck for a confectionery (88).[11] More than once on my routes through South Jersey, the panel truck I was driving came to a sudden screeching halt and I promptly exited to examine a small patch of red, white, pink, purple, blue, orange, or yellow. Most of these flowers, of course, were roadside ruderals -- plants of the fields and wood edges like Queen Anne's-lace, chickory, bouncing-bet, butter-and-eggs, pokeweed, and teasel. This act of abruptly stopping in the middle of the road and jumping out to examine what probably appeared to them as nothing special, was undoubtedly strange to many a country youngster.

---

[10]These were numbers 209, 210, and 211 on my bird life lists.

[11]I started college in 1965, after a seven year hiatus from high school and during which I worked a number of blue collar jobs.

170

These trips along my South Jersey routes were quite significant for me from a natural history perspective. Out of them, grew a strong interest in identifying plants. This resulted in some significant firsts for me. One species I found, the devils-shoestring (*Tephrosia virginiana*), was my first New Jersey Pine Barren flower; another, the pickerelweed (*Pontederia cordata*), was my first wetland plant. I will never forget those two species. Likewise, I will never forget the first wildflower I identified with a field guide. It was the yellow troutlily (*Erythronium umbilicatum*), which I found while trout fishing along Raccoon Creek in South Jersey on April 21, 1962. (Trout lilies while trout fishing -- how appropriate!) Every troutlily that I have seen since brings back memories of that wonderful spring day, as I knelt there along the creek, despite the strong urge to continue wetting my flyline, and identified the plant with Dr. Edgar T. Wheery's *Wild Flower Guide* (89). Yes, it is hard to forget those significant firsts.

FOUR

THE SALTMARSHES OF MARYLAND'S COASTAL BAYS

It's not a good deal.
It's not a bad deal.
It's just a deal!
-- EPA EMPLOYEE
U.S. vs. Tull, et.al.

ONE summer day back in the early 1970s, I stood in awe scanning a vast sea of green, a lush meadow of smooth cordgrass swaying with the onshore breeze sweeping in over Sinepuxent Bay. Assateague Island emerged low out of the Atlantic Ocean less than a mile to the east. A moderate surf ran up and over this severely eroded northern end of the island. To the northwest and just out of sight lay West Ocean City opposite the Ocean City Inlet. Near the inlet, a few small craft rolled gently against the low Ocean City skyline immediately to the north. To the south, lay the open bay bordered on the west by more saltmarshes and on the east, by Assateague, a barrier island that runs south for about thirty-four miles to its hooked spit, Fishing Point, in Virginia. South beyond my view, the Sinepuxent opened into a bigger bay, Chincoteague, with its own extensive saltmarshes (Figure 2).

Despite the sharp glare of the sun reflecting from the mirror-like bay, I readily observed the surf breaking on Assateague and overtopping its low compact sands. To my left and well out in the marsh, three small forest-covered islands contrasted sharply with the flowing grassy sward, emerging like miniature mountains in an otherwise flat marshy terrain.[1] The marsh was a sight to behold, and like a child just discovering his new back yard, I had all day to explore it.

I had traveled to Worcester County and the Mystic Harbor Marsh that day to conduct an initial inspection of the site. I was reviewing a developer's application to the State of Maryland to excavate a canal through wetlands and uplands to provide mooring facilities for a major new residential development on the mainland adjacent to the marsh. My goal was to evaluate the ecological significance of the wetlands and to assess the potential impact of the proposed development on it.

So off I trudged, knee deep at times in marsh mud, a salt-ladened marsh mud, smelling so reminiscent of my early childhood days, when my family lived in a house on stilts over a New Jersey saltmarsh. Even as a child back then, it was quite apparent that the South Jersey saltmarshes swarmed with wildlife. In the summer, armies of fiddler crabs scampered across the mud at low tide, sometimes relentlessly pursued by hungry clapper rails (or simply marsh hens to me and my family), while statuesque herons and egrets with spear-like beaks stood motionless in the shallows, more patiently awaiting the approach of passing mummichogs. Come winter, hundreds of black ducks moved onto the marshes in search of prolific saltmarsh snails and black brant swept perilously low over the marshes, alighting in the adjacent bays to feast on lush eelgrass and sea lettuce.

It was soon apparent that summer day on the Mystic Harbor Marsh that it had just as much, if not more, wildlife than the South Jersey marshlands -- it truly teemed with life. The main tidal gut and its tributaries, which I was ultimately to learn imported inorganic nutrients for the growth of the cordgrasses and exported cordgrass detritus so important as a primary energy source for the estuarine food web, literally crawled with eastern mud nassas (*Nassarius obsoletus*) and swarmed with amphipods (*Orchestia grillus*), grass shrimp (*Palaemonetes* spp.), and blue crabs (*Callinectes*

---

[1]Interestingly, the islands appear to be very old unconfined spoil disposal areas that have long since revegetated. The more highly elevated and unvegetated sandy areas in the centers of these spoil sites was evidence of this. They now look quite natural.

sapidus), mummichogs (*Fundulus heteroclitus*), silversides (*Menidia menidia*), bay anchovies (*Anchoa mitchilli*), and spot (*Leiostomus zanthurus*). As they moved up the secondary tidal guts and adjacent mosquito ditches, the mummichogs, silversides, and bay anchovies were particularly prime targets for stalking by great blue herons and snowy egrets (Figure 34).[2]

Figure 34. Snowy egret in a saltmarsh. (Photo by the author)

---

[2]Tidal guts are naturally occurring streams found in tidal wetlands; they are frequently dendritically arranged. Mosquito ditches are lineal man-made channels, generally only 2-3 feet wide, that are excavated in wetlands to help control mosquitoes by eliminating potential breeding areas. They are not without controversy in relation to their effectiveness in eliminating mosquitoes and their environmental impacts on the wetlands.

Marsh fiddlers (*Uca pugnax*) swarmed the marsh at low tide seeking algae and detritus. Dense compact clumps of filter-feeding ribbed mussels (*Modiolus demissus*) clung with SuperGlue tenacity by byssal threads to the base of smooth cordgrasses (*Spartina alterniflora*) lining the gut banks. While numerous sharp-pointed gulf periwinkles (*Littorina irrorata*) grazed on benthic algae and detritus on the mud below the smooth cordgrasses, others grazed well up their tall stems, especially along the more frequently flooded banks of the tidal guts. Locally, at slightly higher elevations in the marsh dominated by saltgrass, a much smaller, blunt-tipped snail, the saltmarsh snail (*Melampus bidentatus*), similarly grazed algae and detritus from the muddy substrate and grass stems.

In a wrack line, I noted a couple of the finely sculptured empty shells of the diamondback terrapin (*Malaclemys t. terrapin*), a beautiful reptile that periodically entered the marsh by tidal guts in search of fiddlers, gulf periwinkles, and saltmarsh snails, and to lay its eggs in the sandy overwash berms and upland islands (Figure 35) During the day, the fiddlers, blue crabs, mussels, periwinkles, and snails were sought after from the landward side of the guts by clappers, willets, and glossy ibises; at night, by raccoons (*Procyon lotor*) and otters (*Lutra canadensis*). Tracks of raccoons and rice rats (*Oryzomys palustris*) were common, as were the three-pronged imprints of herons, egrets, and clappers. An occasional white-tailed deer (*Odocoileus virginianus*) visited the marsh, as evidenced by tracks near its edge. There were also insects like plant hoppers feeding on the marsh grasses, which were in turn preyed upon by spiders. The insects and spiders were then eaten by seaside sparrows, sharp-tailed sparrows, and long-billed marsh wrens.

Initially, the upper marsh surrounding the upland islands, dominated by saltgrass (*Distichlis spicata*) with scattered halophytic groundsel bushes (*Baccharis halimifolia*) and marsh elders (*Iva frutescens*), seemed biologically less active than the smooth cordgrass marsh. Close inspection while kneeling, however, revealed hordes of saltmarsh snails and the numerous runs, feedbeds, and droppings of the prolific meadow vole (*Microtus pennsylvanicus*). Eastern cottontail rabbits (*Sylvilagus floridanus*) apparently frequented the high marsh area and upland hummocks, as indicated by an abundance of round, tan droppings. And near the upland edge, where the marsh was slightly fresher due to groundwater seepage, the runs, droppings, and feedbeds of muskrats were noted. Noisy nesting red-winged blackbirds scolded me from the shrubs, as did an occasional raucous boat-tailed grackle.

Figure 35. Diamondback terrapin (*Malaclemys t. terrapin*) depositing its eggs on a saltmarsh overwash berm. (Photo by the author)

Out in the tall cordgrasses emanated the incessantly bubbling rattle of fidgety marsh wrens and the periodic *cac, cac, cac, cac, cac* of clappers (Figure 36); infrequently overhead came the noisy rattle of a belted kingfisher. At one point, I observed a kingfisher drop below the cordgrass horizon, undoubtedly to nab an unwary mummichog or silverside. Occasionally, a seaside sparrow would rise above the cordgrass, only to quickly drop again out of sight a few feet away. Yes, this marsh was teeming with life -- life of all sorts, in almost unbelievable abundance. But it was life in peril, for if the Mystic Harbor development went on as planned, the impacts would be substantial. The proposal was to dredge 2,000 feet of a the large natural tidal gut to a width of ninety feet and depth of five feet below mean low water, and to similarly excavate into adjacent upland for a length of 5,500 feet. The spoil

Figure 36. The rail of the saltmarshes, the clapper, which is more commonly heard than seen.

material from the dredging and excavation was to be deposited in the wetlands. The direct impact of these efforts would have been the loss of twenty-two acres of ecologically valuable saltmarsh. Based upon the poor water quality associated with existing canal systems excavated in Delaware and Florida coastal areas and flushing models done at this site by the developer's consultants, it was also concluded that severe water quality impacts would occur to the remaining marsh, as well as in Sinepuxent Bay. Basically, the project would have been an ecological disaster.

I was not disenchanted on my initial visit to the Mystic Harbor Marsh; nor was I disappointed during the visits that followed that fall and winter, when Harold Cassell and I collected additional field data on select dominant invertebrates in the marsh to further assess its inherent natural values. We found very large populations of the marsh invertebrates. Furthermore, field studies by the developers own consultant indicated that the saltmarsh cordgrass was very productive with a mean standing crop of 3.12 tons/acre for samples taken in the areas to be destroyed. This plant material, especially on regularly flooded marshes like this one, is eventually moved into the tidal guts and open bays where it serves as the base for significant detrital food webs, including various invertebrates and forage fish eventually leading to important recreational and commercial fish and shellfish like sea trout (*Cynoscion nebulosus*), summer flounder (*Paralichthys dentatus*), bluefish (*Pomatomous saltatrix*), striped bass (*Morone saxatilis*), northern kingfish (*Menticirrhus saxatilis*), black drum (*Pogonias cromis*), and blue crab (*Callinectes sapidus*). In the end -- after substantial field work, considerable testimony at a public hearing, and a detailed written report documenting the site's ecological significance and opposing the proposal based on its adverse environmental impact upon the wetlands -- the development was restricted to the uplands.

What I learned from those Mystic Harbor Marsh visits and from similar field work conducted in other Worcester County saltmarshes, including field work for another major development proposal for the nearby Snug Harbor Marsh, will provide the foundation for the rest of this Chapter. I will also draw upon my numerous experiences associated with Assateague Island, Chincoteague Island, and the Chincoteague Bay wetlands to the south. Most of these experiences came about while I was working for the State; others resulted from eighteen years of leading overnight field trips down the Delmarva Peninsula for the Graduate School, U.S. Department of Agriculture

179

(see Chapter One). Still others surfaced while, as an Environmental Protection Agency employee, I conducted field studies associated with wetland litigation.

In *Wetlands of Maryland*, Tiner and Burke (1) also briefly describe the saltmarshes in Worcester County. In addition, an instructive overview for Virginia's coastal wetlands is found in *Coastal Wetlands of Virginia* (2). A suggested reading for Assateague is *The Flora and Ecology of Assateague Island* (3).

ON THEIR FASCINATING ORIGIN

During the height of the Wisconsin glaciation over 15,000 years ago, much of northern North America was covered by thick ice, so thick that over expansive areas the land actually sank in response to its weight. With such vast amounts of water tied up in the glaciers, the coastline along North America substantially retreated exposing much of the continental shelf. Sea level was 300-400 feet lower than it is today. The shoreline of Maryland and Virginia was some one hundred miles or so to the east. With the warming climate and melting of the glaciers 12,000-15,000 years ago, the sea rose at a rate initially too high for barrier island and saltmarsh formation, flooding much of the continental shelf. However, 5,000-6,000 years ago the rate of sea rise slowed substantially, eventually reaching the present rate of about one foot per century along the mid-Atlantic coast (4,5).[3] At some point in the process, sandy sediments moving along the shoreline formed broad beach deposits that were reworked by the waves. With sea level fairly stabilized, the formation of barrier islands and shallow landward lagoons commenced, and with subsequent sedimentary in-filling, many of these lagoons ultimately became saltmarshes. The rate at which the sea rose was the limiting factor in saltmarsh accretion. As long as the rate of sea level rise exceeded the accretion of mineral sediment and organic matter accumulation, marsh grasses did not

---

[3]However, the global sea level rise has been reported by others to be only about one millimeter per year (Randy Kerhin, Maryland Geological Survey, personal communication), or 3.94 inches per century. For sea level rise and marsh vertical accretion rates in the Chesapeake Bay Area, see Chapter Three.

become established, or those that did were restricted to the immediate interface between the land and the water. On the other hand, once the rate of mineral and organic matter accumulation kept pace with the rising sea, the marsh grasses encroached onto the intertidal flats that had developed in the lagoons. Over time and with continued accretion, they eventually transgressed the low adjacent upland to the west. Marshes developed this way are classified as Submerging Coastal under a marsh classification based on accretionary relationships (6). These are also the Coastal Type marsh proposed by Robert G. Darmody in his *Reconnaissance Survey of the Tidal Marsh Soils of Maryland* in 1975 (7). They are different geomorphologically than the marshes along the Chesapeake Bay, which were discussed in Chapter Three.

Although the Delmarva's Wachapreague lagoon in Virginia and its barrier islands have existed for at least 5,500 years (8) and Holocene back-barrier sediments have been found nine miles offshore of northern Assateague, the rate of submergence in the Wachapreague area did not decelerate appreciably until between 2,500 and 350 years ago, at which time the marsh formed (9,10). Consequently, it has been suggested that the modern barrier system of the southern Delmarva Peninsula has a minimum age of 3,800 years. The saltmarshes on the mainland side of the southern Delmarva back bays started developing about 1,400 years ago, although much of the marshland apparently formed during the present century (11).

The barrier system along the Delmarva Peninsula's coast is currently retrograding (moving upward and landward in time and space) and in the process rolling over saltmarshes on the backsides of the barrier and backfilling lagoons. Evidence that this has been occurring for some time can be found in the way of outcropped marsh peat and remnant tree stumps in the surf at Assateague and elsewhere on the Delmarva Peninsula.[4] These peats were once part of productive saltmarshes that originated on the backside of the barriers in the protected depositional lagoons; the trees once grew on the western side of these islands, well protected from ocean salt spray. An extreme example of

---

[4]This chapter discusses mostly the Maryland and Virginia part of the Delmarva Peninsula. A very informative review of barrier island and saltmarsh ontogeny for Delaware is given in *A Guide to the Geology of Delaware's Coastal Environments* (12).

Figure 37. A computer-scanned printout of a 1985 aerial photograph showing the southern end of Ocean City, Maryland, the northern end of Assateague Island, parts of Assawoman and Sinepuxent Bays, and the Mystic Harbor Marsh on the mainland side of Sinepuxent Bay (lower left). Note the extreme migration of the northern end of Assateague Island (due to the interruption of littoral drift resulting from the jetties at the inlet) and its sparse vegetation. The Route 50 bridge is at the top of the photograph.

this migration is the northern tip of Assateague, which is eroding and moving so fast that, without interference by man, it could someday be welded to the mainland at West Ocean City or the Mystic Harbor Marsh (Figure 37). Iron-ically, it was the interference of man in constructing the jetties at the Ocean

182

City Inlet that precipitated the most severe erosion and migration of the northern end of the island in the first place. Much of the sand normally carried by longshore currents along the coast to replenish the naturally receding Assateague is now trapped by the jetties.

The dynamic nature of Assateague is also seen in the form of overwash areas, remnant flood-tide deltas (now extensive Back Barrier Island Wetlands) associated with earlier inlets, and a series of paleospits toward the southern end of the island.

Detailed paleontological investigations have shown that Chincoteague Island, which is located west of Assateague, could not have formed more than 2,000 years ago. Thus, Chincoteague is a maximum of 2,000 years old and possibly younger in its current location (13). Sometime within the past 2,000 years, Assateague Island accreted southwestward cutting off Chincoteague Island as an active barrier from the sea. This occurred through a series of spit accretions, as reflected in the present geomorphology of the southern Assateague/Chincoteague complex. High altitude aerial photographs and satellite imagery readily show the remnant paleospits in the form of Morris Island, Piney Island, Lighthouse Ridge, and Assateague Point. Fishing Point, the youngest spit and the southernmost five miles of Assateague Island, is a recurved spit that has formed since 1859. In this fashion, Assateague Island has migrated southwesterly capturing Chincoteague Island in a geologic sense, and in so doing undoubtedly also destroyed any evidence of even earlier spits to the northeast. As a result, Chincoteague is no longer an actively retreating barrier. Today, if one drives from the town of Chincoteague to the Chincoteague Wildlife Refuge (actually on Assateague Island) and further to the Assateague National Seashore, physical evidence of the paleospits can be readily observed. Piney Island is crossed just before the marsh at Assateague Channel. After crossing the channel, the road slices through remnant (currently forested) dunes of the Lighthouse Ridge paleospit. The spit associated with Assateague Point forms the northern shore of Toms Cove, with Fishing Point to the south. Vast marshes exist at the southern end of Chincoteague Bay west of Chincoteague Island and Wallops Island. These are the very saltmarshes that are traversed by the only road to Chincoteague as it drops down from an older Pleistocene shoreline on the mainland to cross this great expanse. While traveling the road to Chincoteague, one can readily get a feel for the general extent of the saltmarshes, since they seem to stretch far and wide. However, it is the few small roadside parking areas that serve as access points to the marsh that more adventurous readers may seek. Starting out from these areas, one can literally get a feel for the wetlands on foot.

THEIR EXTENT

Figures vary as to the acreage of the saltmarshes on the Delmarva Peninsula's coastal bays, even within Maryland. For example, *Wetlands in Maryland* (14) listed 685 acres of coastal saltmeadows and 12,314 acres of regularly flooded saltmarshes for a total of 12,999 acres of saltmarshes for Worcester County. In 1982, McCormick and Somes tabulated a total of 4,205 acres of three types of saline high marshes and 9,544 acres of two types of saline low marshes, for a grand total of 13,749 acres for Worcester County (15). On the other hand, Tiner and Burke (1995) gave a total of 18,954 acres for a number of estuarine wetland types for Worcester County. Much of the discrepancy between Tiner and Burke and the other two authors no doubt relates to the more broadly inclusive estuarine category used by Tiner and Burke consistent with the *Classification of Wetlands and Deepwater Habitats of the United States* (16). These acreages are mostly associated with Assawoman Bay, Isle of Wight Bay, Sinepuxent Bay, and Chincoteague Bay in Maryland. There are also saltmarshes in the coastal bays in Delaware and Virginia. For the area from Cape Henlopen south to the State line, *An Atlas of Delaware's Wetlands and Estuarine Resources* (17) gives 3,229 acres of a wetland zone dominated by the smooth cordgrass. On the other hand, for the entire ocean side of Accomack County, Virginia, Silberhorn and Harris (18) reported 46,452 acres of saltmarsh, 40,600 acres of which were dominated by the smooth cordgrass. There is a similar inventory for Northampton County further down the Delmarva (19).

In addition to the expansive marsh area at the southern end of Chincoteague Bay associated with Chincoteague and Wallops Islands, Chincoteague Bay supports two types of saltmarshes from a geomorphological perspective. The main difference between these two wetland types results from their locations relative to the bay itself. Those on the east side of the bay, Back Barrier Island Wetlands, occur immediately behind Assateague Island; those on the west side, Barrier Island Broad Wetlands, abut the mainland. (See Chapter Three for a geomorphological classification of Maryland's tidal wetlands.) Being on the backside of the Assateague Island, Back Barrier Island Wetlands are generally shallow and young, except for certain large areas that have resulted from the closure of preexisting inlets, many of which have been documented for Assateague (20). Once these inlets closed, the floodtide deltas associated with them soon shoaled up and smooth cordgrasses invaded, forming rather large fan-like saltmarshes. The drainage patterns in these Back Barrier Island Wetlands are characteristically truncated, appearing as short, broad guts that quickly narrow to the east, apparently the result of island migration and drainage disruption. On the other hand, the Barrier Island Broad Wetlands on the western side of the bay have deeper sediments; they are generally higher and older marshes, only parts of which are flooded by the daily tides through dendritic systems of tidal guts. It is not uncommon for much of the mainland marshlands to be scarped and undermined at its interface with Chincoteague Bay. The Snug Harbor Marsh on Sinepuxent Bay is a good example of a Barrier Island Broad Wetland dominated by a short growth form of the smooth cordgrass, which is not flooded by every tide. The Mystic Harbor Marsh, also on Sinepuxent Bay, is an exception; being a much younger wetland in close proximity to the Ocean City Inlet, it is well-flooded and dominated by a taller growth form of the smooth cordgrass.

THE SUBTLETY: TAKING A CLOSER LOOK

The evolution of the saltmarshes associated with Delmarva's coastal barriers and the mainland has been quite dynamic and continues to this day. At first glance the wetlands may seem rather static, stationary in time and place, but closer study reveals otherwise. For example, Assateague Island continues to roll up and over its back barrier environments, evidence of which can be observed on aerial photographs (overwash areas) and on the ground in the form of alternating subsurface layers of sand and marsh peat in the Back Barrier Island Wetlands. I have visited a number of these flat overwash areas, and have also examined the alternating subsurface layers under the saltmarshes on the backsides of both Assateague and Wallops Island using soil augers. Furthermore, shallow lagoonal areas immediately behind the island and near the mainland continue to shoal up, allowing invasion by smooth cordgrass. Once while on a site inspection in a remnant marsh area behind Fenwick Island, for example, I was initially befuddled while attempting to interpret an aerial photograph taken from an altitude of about 6,000 feet. By the surrounding development, it was clear that I knew where I was on the ground and on the photograph. Yet, I was totally perplexed by the relative amounts of adjacent open water and saltmarsh. Conditions on the ground appeared clearly inconsistent with what the photograph showed. Then it dawned on me what had happened. In less than two years since the aerial photograph was taken, the area had shoaled up and become entirely vegetated by smooth cordgrass.

Over the years, I have noted similar occurrences when comparing aerial photographs to ground conditions, but none as dramatic as this. During the early, well-flooded intertidal marsh phase, the tall form of the smooth cordgrass dominates. The quintessential example of this might be the Mystic Harbor Marsh. Other excellent examples, for which ground access is readily obtained, are the smooth cordgrass marshes at the northern end of Toms Cove on Assateague and the southeastern end of Chincoteague Island along Assateague Channel.

I have taken students to the Toms Cove site regularly over a number of years, and on low spring tides even walked well out onto the intertidal flats dominated by a large armored polychaete, the plumed worm (*Diopatra cuprea*), and onto an adjacent productive oyster bar replete with estuarine invertebrates. Because of the twice daily flooding at the site, the smooth cordgrass is very lush and supports numerous gulf periwinkles. Over time, of course, the cordgrass traps more sediment, and eventually if the sediment load and organic buildup keep up with sea level rise, the surface of the marsh remains at about mean sea level. The Snug Harbor Marsh and much of the expansive marsh area between Chincoteague Island and the mainland are good examples of this late stage of saltmarsh development. At even higher elevations, the marshes are generally dominated by saltmeadow cordgrass and/or saltgrass and are commonly referred to as saltmeadows.

On the mainland side of Maryland's coastal bays, the saltmarshes are generally eroding at their exposed eastern fronts, particularly by storms that strike at low tides. Under such conditions, the waves release their full energy on the exposed bay-front scarps, as opposed to gradually while rolling up and over the marsh surface on normal or higher tides. The severely undermined scarp can be readily observed at low tide -- a one foot or so thick layer of peat hangs precipitously. This peat readily caves in from its own weight as additional fine lagoonal deposits are eroded from under it. On the other hand, on the landward side of the wetland, the vegetation slowly encroaches over the gently sloping upland in a sort of retrogressive succession, where upland becomes wetland. The lateral extent and rate of this transgression is contingent upon the rate of sea level rise and the slope of the land. So like the barrier island itself, the saltmarsh system tends to move as a unit upward and landward in time and space. Things are changing on the marsh, changing ever so subtly, but changing nevertheless. As two New England researchers, Miller and Egler (21), remarked in 1950, "The present mosaic [on the saltmarsh] may be thought of as a momentary expression, different in the past and destined to be different in the future and yet as typical as would be a photograph of moving clouds." But to the observant and discriminating eye the evidence is there, for sure.

THE PREDICTABILITY OF THE PATTERNS
AND PROCESSES

There is a certain predictability about saltmarshes. This can be largely attributed to the tides, which in our area flood at least parts of the marshes with saline water twice during a twenty-four hour period. As suggested earlier, the tidal guts that penetrate these saltmarshes import inorganic nutrients for the growth of the cordgrasses and export cordgrass detritus so important as a primary energy source for the estuarine food web (Figure 38). This availability of inorganic nutrients, particularly nitrogen, is reflected to a

187

large extent in the highly productive tall growth form of the smooth cordgrass that lines the tidal guts and sometimes entire wetlands, such as with the Mystic Harbor Marsh and the similarly well-flooded marsh at Toms Cove.

Figure 38. Assortment of animals and macroscopic algae seined from the shallows of Sinepuxent Bay, which represent only part of the estuarine food web. Animals evident in the photograph include the horseshoe crab (*Limulus polyphemus*), summer flounder (*Paralichthys dentatus*), black sea bass (*Centropristis striata*), silver perch (*Bairdella chrysura*), and blue crab (*Callinectes sapidus*). (Photo by the author)

With less frequent tidal flooding back from the tidal guts at slightly higher parts of the saltmarsh, a shorter, generally non-flowering, growth form of the smooth cordgrass dominates. At intermediate levels, there are intermediate heights.Although various theories pertaining to the origin of these growth forms exist, including those relating to nitrogen availability, iron concentration, salinity levels, and the extent of soil oxygenation, most correspond in some fashion to the frequency and extent of tidal flooding. One can, therefore, predict twice daily flooding in the presence of tall smooth cordgrass; less frequent flooding with the short smooth cordgrass; and even

188

less flooding in the higher saltmeadows.[5] The two Worcester County saltmarshes that I have most frequently visited over the years represent quite a study in contrast, something that could have been readily predicted at the outset of my investigations. Let me explain using four of the most common and obvious invertebrates found on these marshes.

The marsh fiddler, the gulf periwinkle, the ribbed mussel, the salt-marsh snail -- What do they all have in common? Well, obviously they are invertebrates. But there is more to it than that. They also occur in very high numbers in the saltmarshes, but mostly in the regularly flooded low marsh dominated by the tall smooth cordgrass. As already suggested, this too is quite predictable, and at times the fiddlers are so thick one can not help but step on them, the periwinkles so dense that the cordgrasses bend, and the mussels so clustered that they resemble dark, miniature riprap protecting the tidal guts and exposed bay front peats.

During the fall and winter of 1972-1973, Harold Cassell and I sampled the dominant macroinvertebrates in the Mystic Harbor and Snug Harbor Marshes (24). On the Mystic Harbor Marsh, the periwinkle and mussel were associated with the tall smooth cordgrass in about 98% and 44% of our samples, respectively. Based upon sixty-two quadrats randomly placed over the marsh, we found from 0-144 periwinkles/m^2 with a mean of 44.4 periwinkles, very high densities indeed. For seventy quadrats, we recorded from 0-10 mussels/m^2 with a mean of 2.2 mussels. In both instances, densities were highest near the tidal guts, although the ribbed mussels were also abundant along the bay front. We did not sample for the fiddler crabs, but armies of marsh fiddlers swarmed over the regularly flooded marsh surface at

---

[5]These growth forms all involve the same species, *Spartina alterniflora*. Rather than continually referring to the tall growth form of the smooth cordgrass and the short growth form of the smooth cordgrass, for readability I will just call them tall smooth cordgrass and short smooth cordgrass, respectively. The intermediate form is simply transitional; therefore, there is no exact height breaks between the three growth forms. See Tiner for suggested heights of the three growth forms (22). Keep in mind, however, that the heights within the growth forms, particularly the tall growth form, vary along the coast. For example, the tall growth form in the Southeast is generally much taller than that in Maryland, and can reach up to ten feet (23).

low tide.[6] With high tides, the fiddlers retreated into their burrows as the periwinkles scaled the tall smooth cordgrass stems, both with predictable rhythms that have been repeated experimentally in labs. For the mussel, this was a time of activity, as it opened to filter minute planktonic life and detritus from the overlying estuarine waters.

Given the minimal tidal flooding at the Snug Harbor Marsh, a sharp contrast exists between it and the Mystic Harbor Marsh. Most of the Snug Harbor Marsh is dominated by the short smooth cordgrass, with the tall smooth cordgrass growing only sparsely along the tidal guts. Smaller areas dominated by either saltgrass, saltmeadow cordgrass, or hightide bush exist near the upland edge. As one might predict, very few gulf periwinkles exist at Snug Harbor. In fact, Harold and I found only one periwinkle in sixty-nine randomly placed one meter square plots. Likewise, the ribbed mussel was only found in the short smooth cordgrass, and as expected at low densities: 0-6 mussels/m^2 with a mean of 0.86 mussels for thirty-six quadrats. Again, although the marsh fiddler was not sampled, it was basically restricted to the muddy banks of the main tidal gut entering the marsh.

Harold and I also sampled the saltmarsh snail populations at the Mystic Harbor and Snug Harbor Marshes. At Mystic Harbor we found fairly high densities -- a range of 19-109 snails/m^2 with a mean of 29.7 snails for ten quadrats. In contrast to the gulf periwinkle and ribbed mussel and quite predictably as I have learned, this snail is limited to the higher marsh, either the short smooth cordgrass areas or the saltmeadows, which at Mystic Harbor are represented by a saltgrass community.

At the Snug Harbor Marsh, the saltmarsh snail was found in 100.0, 53.8, 90.9, and 91.7 percent of the samples taken in the saltgrass, hightide bush-mixed, saltmeadow cordgrass-mixed, and short smooth cordgrass vegetation types. Not surprisingly, extremely high densities of the saltmarsh snail were encountered: 1-467 snails/m^2 with a mean of 217.3 snails for

---

[6]The marsh fiddler (*Uca pugnax*) is more commonly found on intertidal muddy or clayey substrates along tidal guts and in regularly flooded marsh. Another fiddler, the sand fiddler (*U. pugilator*) is more commonly found on somewhat open intertidal areas with sandy substrates along creek banks (23,25,26,27,28).

thirteen quadrats in the saltgrass type; 0-157 snails/m^2 with a mean of 23.8 snails for thirteen quadrats in the hightide bush-mixed type; 0-146 snails/m^2 with a mean of 54.3 snails for eleven quadrats in the saltmeadow cordgrass-mixed type; and 0-835 snails/m^2 with a mean of 210.5 snails for thirty-six quadrats in the short smooth cordgrass type.

Perhaps by now you realize the ecological significance of these saltmarsh invertebrates. If not, let me explain. Their huge populations alone should give you a good hint. They constitute a substantial anount of biomass on these marshes -- biomass so important to the associated vertebrates, particularly the birds and mammals that rely on them for food. Thus, these invertebrates are a major part of an important trophic level leading to higher trophic levels through the saltmarsh detrital-based food web. They are also significant for the herbivore-carnivore food web on the marsh. Black ducks, for example, rely heavily on saltmarsh snails during the winter; clapper rails, willets, and glossy ibises consume fiddlers, blue crabs, mussels, periwinkles, and saltmarsh snails; diamondback terrapins feed on fiddlers, gulf periwinkles, and saltmarsh snails.

*   *   *

In saltmarshes, not only the daily activities but also life cycles of many invertebrates are synchronized with tidal cycles. An excellent example of this is the life cycle of the saltmarsh snail. Three cycles of aggregation, copulation, and egg-laying occur at semilunar intervals; hatching and settlement also show such synchronization (29). Specifically, all three of these cycles correspond with a spring tide. Likewise, two weeks later for hatching, then two weeks later again veliger larvae settle on the marsh as spat -- at the base of the cordgrass stems. Thus, interruption of the tidal cycle by structures like dikes or bulkheads would be catastrophic to local populations of invertebrates whose life cycles are linked to it.

As stated earlier, all of these invertebrates are important in the estuarine food web, but one, the ribbed mussel, is considered even more important from another perspective. It has been demonstrated that filtering by the ribbed mussel plays a major role in the biogeochemical cycling of

191

phosphorous (30). A mussel population in the Georgia saltmarshes removed 5.4 mg P/m^2 of particulate phosphorous and 0.07 mg P/m^2 of phosphate daily, of which only 0.78 mg P/m^2 was required as food and 4.7 mg P/m^2 was deposited as pseudofeces. The major effect this Georgia mussel population had on the estuary was in the removal of particulate phosphorous from sea water and its deposition in the saltmarsh. Thus, the ribbed mussel was deemed more important as biogeochemical agent than as energy consumer. One benefit of this activity is that the phosphorous is retained in the marshes, thereby furnishing raw materials to deposit feeders that can regenerate the phosphate.

A related pattern associated with saltmarsh invertebrates involves three univalves: the eastern mud nassa, gulf periwinkle, and saltmarsh snail. Being all grazers/detritivores, there is a strong potential for interspecific competition for food and space. Their varying habitat preferences, however, tend to keep these potential competitors safely apart. The eastern mud nassa, for example, is pretty much restricted to the shallow intertidal flats and tidal guts, sometimes occurring in extremely high densities, which can be readily observed at low tide. Since they are often covered with mud and relatively immobile, they can be easily overlooked except when large numbers converge to scavenge on, say, a dead blue crab or fish (Figure 39). These snails are seldom found further up the gradient in the adjacent tall smooth cordgrass marsh, which is the domain of gulf periwinkle; even further up, of course, is found the saltmarsh snail. Seldom have I seen periwinkles intermixed with saltmarsh snails, and when I have there was but little overlap; I have never seen all three together on the saltmarsh. In this way, although space and food are partitioned over an elevation gradient of only a foot or so, interspecific competition is minimized.

Consistent with the tidal flooding are various predictive patterns and processes involving the plants. First of all, the plants in tidal saltmarshes are very productive, which was initially documented for the Georgia saltmarshes in the 1950s and 1960s by researchers like the Teals and Odums. It is this very productivity and its significance to the estuarine food web that helped precipitate the various coastal wetland protection efforts in the East, including the enactment of Maryland's Tidal Wetland Act in 1970. Thanks to the rich

192

estuarine waters and the energy subsidy of the tides, these ecosystems compare well, in terms of biomass .production, with some of the more productive cultivated systems in the world, including sugar cane and culti-

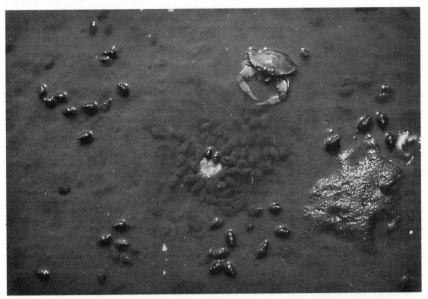

Figure 39. Numerous mud nassas (*Nassarius obsoletus*) converging on a dead crab or fish. These gastropods occur abundantly in the shallow estuarine flats and tidal guts. (Photo by the author)

vated rice. Closer to home, a productivity study of the Chincoteague Bay saltmarshes demonstrated a live standing crop (biomass) of smooth cordgrass ranging from 1.50 to 2.48 tons/acre (31). In general, the significance of these productive species and others for estuarine detrital food webs has been well-established. However, in the case of many Chincoteague Bay marshes, which are dominated by the irregularly flooded short smooth cordgrass, many of the dead plants remain on the marsh surface to decompose in place or to be eventually removed only by spring and storm tides. Therefore, the full significance of the cordgrasses to the estuarine detrital food web of Chincoteague Bay remains to be clarified. On the other hand, regularly flooded marshes like those at Mystic Harbor and Toms Cove surely must contribute substantial detrital material to the estuary.

Interspecific patterns of vegetation on Maryland's coastal saltmarshes are also patently obvious. First off I should note, as anyone who has spent a modicum of time on saltmarshes no doubt already knows, that despite their high primary productivity, saltmarshes tend to have rather low plant species diversity (richness) in terms of vascular plants. Generally, only a few species dominate: the tall smooth cordgrass in regularly flooded zones; the short smooth cordgrass at slightly higher elevations; and saltmeadow cordgrass (*Spartina patens*) and saltgrass in the higher meadow areas. Local patches of glassworts -- dwarf glasswort (*Salicornia biglovii*), slender glasswort (*S. europaea*), and Virginia glasswort (*S. virginica*) -- and scattered sea lavenders (*Limonium carolinianum*), marsh fleabanes (*Pluchea purpurascens*), annual saltmarsh asters (*Aster subulatus*), and perennial saltmarsh asters (*A. tenuifolius*) commonly occur mixed with the short smooth cordgrasses. Shrubs like marsh elder and hightide bush are generally found on small hummocks, such as mosquito ditch spoil piles, or near the upland edge. Sometimes present are herbs like orach (*Atriplex patula*), saltmarsh sabatia (*Sabatia stellaris*), seaside gerardia (*Agalinus maritima*), and saltmarsh foxtail grass (*Setaria geniculata*), which typically occur on higher ground near the edge of the marsh or on hummocks (Figure 40). Where substantial ground water seepage occurs along the upland edge, the common three-square (*Scirpus pungens*) can be found in a rather distinct narrow band on mineral soil. In some locations small patches of the common reed (*Phragmites australis*) are invading the marshes from the upland; the edge of the marsh and adjacent upland also commonly support switchgrass (*Panicum virgatum*). Locally in the area, particularly on the backside of Assateague, are some relatively large stands of a basically southern species, the needlerush (*Juncus romoerianus*). Its northern relative, the blackrush (*J. gerardii*), is similarly found, but in the higher marsh. In fact, in *The Coastal Wetlands of Maryland*, McCormick and Somes (15) list only thirty-six species for Assateague Island saltmarshes based upon their review of *The Flora and Ecology of Assateague Island* (3). Thus, the Delmarva's saltmarshes are floristically poor, particularly when compared to the brackish tidal and fresh tidal marshes of the Chesapeake Bay and its tributaries. However, the most floristically rich part of the Delmarva's saltmarshes is near their transitional upland edges where,

194

due to ground water input and freshwater runoff, a greater variety of species can exist along with some of the more halophytic ones. Nevertheless, a devoted dilettante can quickly get a good grasp on the naturally low numbers

Figure 40. Saltmarsh sabatia (*Sabatia stellaris*), an attractive flower occurring in the higher areas of the saltmarsh. (Photo by the author)

of species occurring on these highly productive wetland ecosystems. Another useful source for the plants of Assateague Island (Maryland and Virginia) is the 1986 flora by Dr. Steven Hill, which includes 562 taxa, although only a small percentage of these plants occur in the saltmarshes (32). Likewise, 488 species were found in a floristic study of Wallops Island and the Wallops mainland in Virginia (33).

OF TRAGEDIES AND TRIUMPHS

In the early 1970s when Harold Cassell and I were busy documenting the ecological values of the Mystic Harbor and Snug Harbor Marshes, I inevitably had to traverse these sites with the various representatives of developers -- attorneys, planners, and sometimes just plain old lackeys. One hot summer day was one such trip. I don't remember all of the details, but there is certainly one thing I will never forget. No, it was not an interesting natural phenomenon or anything like that, although I did receive my share of them from those splendid sites. In fact, what I did that day some may consider downright devilish, but for me it was pure pleasure and payback. You see there was this rather annoying lackey who more or less had been repeatedly tracking all of my activities on the marsh from a remote setting in the upland overlooking the entire saltmarsh. On a previous day, in fact, while checking up on me by small boat, he got caught unexpectedly on a receding tide and I could hear him banging around for what seemed like hours, the noise apparently coming from the oars striking the side of the boat as he laboriously struggled to move through the shallow water and mud. It distinctly contrasted with the pleasant natural sounds emanating from the marsh, but it was a pleasure to hear just the same if you follow my reasoning. On this devilish day, however, the fellow chose to follow me on foot. But to my benefit, there was an extra high tide. As the fateful fellow followed me along taking numerous notes on my activities, I strategically led him to a mosquito ditch. With the deep flooding that overtopped the ditch, of course, he was not aware of its presence. Need I say more? I rather nonchalantly stepped over the flooded ditch trying hard not to exaggerate my stride. He followed unknowingly and was soon up to his waist in water and mud. Of course I helped him out, that was the least I could do! He got the real feel of the wet land, and as I recall, he never trailed me again.

So much for a minor personal triumph, so much for the little things in the tricky business of wetland regulation that sometimes are rewarding in their own small way. The real triumphs came, however, when our hard work paid off on the Mystic Harbor Marsh and Snug Harbor Marsh wetland cases,

196

and times like when we finally convinced our own Wildlife Administration not to impound an expansive area of saltmarsh on the E.A. Vaughn Wildlife Management Area on Chincoteague Bay. Yes, ironically, my own Department of Natural Resources was the culprit, and the wildlife personnel involved sincerely believed they would be doing the right thing for the environment -- meaning, in this instance, the right thing to attract waterfowl. Except for some mosquito ditching, this site was pristine. So it was a grand feeling indeed when the project was dropped in the early 1970s.

At this point some readers may be a little confused by my elation over the rejected waterfowl impoundment proposal. What's wrong with attracting waterfowl? Here's *my* answer. It is true that such shallow impoundments can have many benefits to wildlife, especially waterfowl. And indeed, many of our existing National Wildlife Refuges and State Wildlife Management Areas are extremely important in this regard. Furthermore, they are of exceptional value from an educational perspective. Thousands of people visit these areas each year to observe and enjoy the abundant wildlife. They learn about the significance of wildlife to society and the importance of wetlands. All of this education and information transfer benefits wetlands in the long run in terms of increasing public awareness to the natural functions and values of wetlands and how they benefit society. It also engenders support for wetland conservation. The problem comes, however, when such impoundments result in the destruction of wetlands or other ecologically valuable habitats. In the E.A. Vaughn case, a substantial acreage of saltmarsh cordgrass would have been destroyed with a loss of detritus to the estuarine food web so important to the fishery and shellfishery resources mentioned in the beginning of this Chapter. Furthermore, habitat for one group of critters -- the marsh invertebrates (e.g., the marsh fiddler, gulf periwinkle, and saltmarsh snail) and the marsh birds (e.g., the clapper, willet, savanna sparrow, and seaside sparrow) -- would have been replaced for another group, basically waterfowl in this instance. Such species-specific management may enhance conditions for particular wildlife species, but frequently is detrimental to the non-target species. And, of course, other wetland values could also be lost, such as rare or uncommon plant species due to the inundation, and nursery grounds for estuarine and marine fishes. Nevertheless, this problem is not necessarily

197

insurmountable -- the solution is to construct the shallow impoundments in environmentally acceptable areas.

*   *   *

By early 1970s, however, it was way too late for Fenwick Island (Ocean City) and much of the mainland saltmarsh on Isle of Wight Bay at the Ocean Pines development. Hundreds of acres of saltmarsh and productive shallows in Assawoman and Isle of Wight Bays were already lost. I will never forget my first trip there. It was with Jim Casey, a Department of Natural Resources' fisheries biologist, who agreed to give me an introduction to the Ocean City area by boat. We toured the cut and fill canal developments on both sides of the bays, and at one point docked at a new bulkhead on Fenwick Island that seemed to run forever into Assawoman Bay enclosing a huge marshy and open water area. Two large hydraulic dredges stood poised for the onslaught. All of the fill material for the huge area landward of the bulkhead was to be dredged material from the bottom of Assawoman Bay. Sadly, the bay soon received a double dose -- the loss of productive estuarine benthic communities by dredging and the loss of similar communities and saltmarshes by filling. And it had already been approved by the State Board of Public Works! Needless to say, I was indeed flabbergasted and appalled. Rumor had it back then that these extensive cut and fill activities, which involved insignificant recompense to the State but substantial benefits to the developers as a result of the exorbitant monetary value the Ocean City real estate created, were largely what precipitated the enactment of the Maryland's Tidal Wetland Act of 1970. I can not say for sure that this is true, but I could certainly understand it if it were (Figure 41). A couple of questions come to mind: What was the real benefit to Maryland's citizens by allowing such use of State bottoms? Should the State have enacted a moratorium on filling of saltmarshes until the law was proposed and regulations were in place?

Then there was the infamous golf course proposal on the mainland opposite Ocean City. An entire peninsula was at stake, but the Department of Natural Resource's authority only pertained to the tidal saltmarshes that surrounded much of it. The developer proposed to encroach along the irregular upland-saltmarsh interface to make the site more conducive to a golf course layout. From the developers perspective, one particular area of marsh jutted obtrusively into the upland with undesirable implications for the proposed golf course. Specifically, one hole would have to be relocated if the

Figure 41. Aerial view of the massive cut and fill development along the mainland opposite of Ocean City, Maryland in 1974. Similar wetland and shallow water destruction occurred on the Ocean City side of Assawoman Bay. (Photo by the author)

marshy inland projection was to be left intact. As the agency's technical person evaluating the site, I naturally opposed such destruction with the backing of my supervisor. Discouragingly though, on a site visit to take "another look" with the Secretary of Natural Resources himself, my position was promptly overturned. That hole was forever after in the tidal wetland program referred to as Secretary C...'s Hole, if you follow my thought. I can not remember exactly why now, but fortunately the project never got far off the ground. Maybe it was stopped by the Federal government; or perhaps by a failing economy. For a number of years, some sheet metal shacks associated with the proposed golf course sat desolately exposed near the point, rattled by the persistent winds sweeping in off of Isle of White Bay. So we had another

199

triumph -- a triumph that was especially welcomed, since there is absolutely no sound reason why golf courses need to be constructed in wetlands.

*　　*　　*

Years later, between 1981 and 1986, I spent considerable field time in the saltmarshes and fresh nontidal swales on Chincoteague Island. By then I was working for the U.S. Environmental Protection Agency and visited Chincoteague as a member of a team of mostly Federal technical personnel investigating a number of alleged fill violations by a local developer. Many trips were made to these sites and intensive field work was conducted, which eventually resulted in four different civil actions and four trials at Norfolk, Virginia (U.S. America vs. Tull, et. al.). I learned a lot from these efforts, not only about the wetland sites, but also the geomorphology and natural developmental history of Chincoteague Island and the southern end of Assateague, as described earlier. Weeks of field work went into the various efforts, for my part mostly aerial photointerpretation and augering through the fill areas to further confirm the presence and extent of buried marsh already interpreted indirectly through the photographs. The technique, which I called peat analysis, was ultimately refined and published in *Wetlands* (34). The idea is to core through the fill to locate the buried marsh peat. In this part of the country, the presence of peat alone is predictive of wetlands, because peat only develops under persistent saturated soil conditions. From adjacent undisturbed marshes, I also made a reference collection of roots and rhizomes, which were identified to the species level by examining the above ground plant parts with the roots and rhizomes attached. This method works well because rhizomes in particular have species-specific diagnostic anatomical and morphological features associated with them. Using the reference collection to identify species found in the subsurface peat samples, I found that the species extracted from below the fill corresponded well with the species interpreted indirectly from aerial photographs taken before the filling. So developing this technique was a good example of applied science, forensic ecology if you will.

Being a success also made this forensic approach a personal triumph, as was our winning all four cases in the District Court, in which I participated as an expert witness, and successfully challenging the defense's appeal at the Fourth Circuit Court level in Richmond. Never, never will I forget the first trial in Norfolk in which I spent eleven hours on the stand in one day alone in direct testimony and cross examination. It was not until I left the witness stand late that night, somewhere after eleven o'clock, that I realized my gums actually ached, something I subsequently found to be rather characteristic of me during trials. I can say for sure that this reaction was not a nervous one, for I frequently tested myself while on the witness stand by simply holding a pencil or pen steady in the presence of the defense attorney to demonstrate that fact to myself as well as to him. Apparently, there was just an unknowing tension that built up inside of me. That night in leaving the courtroom, the U.S. Attorney thoughtfully referred to my drawn out performance as a tour de force. I am not so sure he was correct, but regardless it was quite a compliment. Although I did not fully appreciate why at the time, the personal triumph was the hidden joy of the head to head battle of wits with the defense attorney and the challenge of maintaining my professionalism and objectivity while on the stand. And most of all, as an expert witness, sustaining a non-advocacy demeanor. Over the years, I have learned that not all technical people like this role; the pressure is just too much for them, and understandably so. It takes a certain type of person to accept this challenge and withstand the pressure -- trying pressure from the defense attorney's attack on one's credentials, techniques, and technical findings, and at times one's demeanor and credibility. An essentially ineffable challenge, a challenge one has to really experience to appreciate.

Because the government won at Norfolk and Richmond, I was on a high for some time. The programmatic joy of winning all of these cases, however, subsided rather abruptly when the case reached the Supreme Court only to be remanded to the District Court on a technicality for a new trial. Ultimately, in the summer of 1988, a drawn out seven years since the litigation started and only a couple of days before a fifth trial, the U.S. Attorney involved agreed to a settlement. In the words of EPA's Region III representative: "It's not a good deal. It's not a bad deal. It's just a deal!"

Some deal. From my perspective it was a poor choice, a poor settlement -- an opinion that I stated freely and repeatedly, when challenged, to the U.S. Attorney and Department of Justice attorney involved. Much to their dismay and despite substantial pressure -- excessively uncalled for pressure in my opinion -- I held my ground against the proposed settlement, which for all practical purposes resulted in my being intellectually ostracized from the team.[7] So much for my tour de force. Because of my comments at that point, I suppose in their eyes I was some sort of dispensable enfant terrible! As I understand it, things soon got back to normal on Chincoteague after the settlement, back once again to the old ways with the resumption of wetland destruction, despite comments to the contrary to the U.S. Attorney by one of the residing District Court judges.

This scenario is not the exception. All too often much wetland litigation gets extremely drawn out, and it is not uncommon to have discouraging reversals on appeals, or lopsided settlements not always truly in the government's favor, despite bureaucratic rationalization to the contrary. Under such unfortunate circumstances, the tragedies surely exceed the triumphs.

---

[7] I have always tried to be honest and fair with others, as well as objective, but have never been known to be shy when it comes to academic and technical debate, if in fact I have something to contribute.

FIVE

THE PICTURESQUE POCOMOKE

On Tuesday morning leaving Mr. Waples, within a mile of the entrance of the swamp I met with an old man who usually conducts strangers into the swamp...The old man went with me and in about a mile from his house we began to enter one of the most frightful labyrinths you can imagine...on Wednesday I went across the swamp about 7 miles without meeting with one extraordinary vegetable excepting the Bartonia...In this part of the swamp there are bears not unfrequently met with as many as 7 having been caught not many months back.
-- THOMAS NUTTALL, 1809

ALTHOUGH for some reason I failed to document it in my *Journal*, I will never forget my first venture into the Pocomoke Swamp. It occurred sometime in the early 1970s just above Porter's Crossing. At the time, I worked for the Maryland Department of Natural Resources and was field checking some delineations of private wetlands on the State's tidal wetland maps at the request of a landowner. With the large folded map in hand, I ventured into the swamp perpendicular to the floodplain seeking to find the river as a landmark from which I could check the accuracy of the tidal wetlands delineated on the map. I was taking an inordinate amount of time to reach the river; getting somewhat nervous about my orientation, I decided to turn around and go back to the upland area from where I had started. Needless to say, I knew I was in trouble when in a short time I located the river! It was not that I was unfamiliar with the benefits of the compass; I just didn't bring mine along this trip. Knowing the direction of the river flow and the southern orientation of the sun in the early afternoon, I soon was on a straight westerly course back to the upland, albeit a mile or so downstream. Once reoriented, I pursued the effort again with considerable success. However, on my forty subsequent trips

203

to the Pocomoke over the next twenty-five or so years, I have always remembered to take my compass.

That initial Pocomoke trip was a great experience for me and I soon grew to appreciate what I now consider the "wilderness" nature of many swamps. Inevitably, the Pocomoke has changed over the years and it is far from the pristine condition it exhibited when Giovanni da Verrazzano (1524), Bartholomew Gilbert (1603) and Captain John Smith (1608) sailed the shores of the Chesapeake Bay (1,2). Starting back in the 17th century with tobacco farming on the surrounding lands (3), there has been a succession of industries (for example, farming, bog iron, timber, and commercial fisheries) through the 17th, 18th, and 19th centuries that has variously impacted the river and swamp. However, in the southern portion of the swamp at least, little evidence of the impacts remains today except in the form of defunct landings (now partly reclaimed by the forest), remnant pilings (4), and large bald cypress (*Taxodium distichum*) and Atlantic white cedar (*Chamaecyparis thyoides*) stumps. This area of the swamp has maintained much of its original grandeur or has regained it through revegetation, although, locally, two exotic vines, the Japanese honeysuckle (*Lonicera japonica*) and the Japanese virgin's-bower (*Clematis terniflora*), grow abundantly from the bases of trees along the river. And although the swamp has been lumbered over its entire extent (5,6,7,8), certain areas along the Pocomoke River, particularly below Pocomoke City, no doubt appear quite similar to what Captain John Smith saw when he sailed up the river.[1]

The same cannot be said about the part of the swamp above Porter's Crossing. While still an interesting and ecologically important area, the evidence of man's encroachment is much more obvious -- a prime example being the channelization and agricultural drainage above Porter's Crossing, evidence of which can be seen at any river crossing. As indicated by Goodwin

---

[1]For a colorful historical account of the Pocomoke River see the *Rivers of the Eastern Shore* by Hulbert Footner (9). In addition, after this Chapter was prepared for publication, I received a copy of *The Pocomoke: History and Natural History of Maryland's Most Scenic River* from its author, John V. Dennis. This recently produced book, which is undated, gives an overview of the history and natural history of the watershed.

and Niering (10), little of the original swamp north of Maryland Route 50 remains, and as pointed out by Beaven and Oosting (7), the upper part in southern Sussex County, Delaware (between Gumboro and Selbyville) seems to have once been occupied by a swamp of considerable extent. According to Bill Thomas (11), the Federal government initiated projects using unemployed people to drain the Great Cypress Swamp. A twenty-foot-wide canal, fed by ditches, which was completed in 1936, connected the headwaters of the Pocomoke River with the Indian River, resulting in a dry swamp.

Much of the area north of Route 50 in Delaware was once known as the Great Cypress Swamp or Burnt Swamp. Two major fires occurred in this area over the last 200 years (12), wreaking havoc on the swamp. A terrible fire apparently occurred in 1782, which supposedly could be seen seventy miles away in Philadelphia. According to Stalter, an anonymous writer in 1797 (13) indicated: "In short, it appeared as if the last fatal conflagration of this globe was begun." The second major fire occurred after a severe drought in 1931 (7,12). Fire swept the whole area and burned persistently for six months, locally destroying most of the peat accumulation and all of the trees; over 3,000 acres were destroyed. Apparently, there is some disagreement as to year and duration of the second conflagration. Both Dennis (14,15) and Thomas (11) cited the year 1930 and a duration of eight rather than six months, and articles in the Baltimore Sun on May 3 and 4, 1930 mention the drought and devastating forest fires on the Eastern Shore. Regardless, the fire wreaked havoc on the Great Cypress Swamp, destroying standing timber, peat, and embedded logs. Thomas also pointed out that residents in towns as far away as Wilmington could smell the burning swamp.

Cypress were also heavily harvested in the swamp during the 18th century for shingle-making (14,15) and according to Higgins (16), by 1850 "...hardly a decent-sized cypress was left standing in the whole swamp." However, it was not until 1844 that the bald cypress began to be cut and sawed at Pocomoke City (then known as Newtown). Sawmills apparently sprang up everywhere (9). Shortly before the Civil War, the cypress shingle industry was revitalized with the mining of buried cypress logs from the Great Cypress Swamp (14,15). Dennis, Thomas, and Higgins all gave accounts of

205

this industry (11,14,15,17). Higgins states: "Tons of soggy peat were scooped from above tree-trunks. Oxen foundered and wheezed, chains pulled taut, men cursed, and the logs were dragged out to where crosscut saws could be used."

The first detailed account of the Great Cypress Swamp was apparently written in 1797 by the anonymous author cited above and republished in the 1949 issue of Delaware History (14,15). That author reported huge bald cypress trees with trunks four to eight feet in diameter and knees that reached eight to ten feet high. This is not the only account of such stately specimens -- in 1881, the noted Wilmington botanist, William M. Canby, mentioned a huge bald cypress stump, nine feet in diameter in southern Delaware, probably from the Great Cypress Swamp (18). [For comparison, the current Maryland State champion bald cypress is about 5.5 feet in diameter (19)]. With stately trees like that, one ponders the original grandeur of the swamp. William Bartram, for example, in his travels through the south (20,21) was very impressed by the bald cypress, colorfully pointing out: "Its majestic stature is surprising; and on approaching it, we are struck with a kind of awe, at beholding the stateliness of the trunk, lifting its cumbrous top toward the skies; and casting a wide shade upon the ground, as a dark intervening cloud, which, for a time excludes the rays of the sun."

Certainly, anyone who has seen the stately cypress at Four Holes Swamp or along the Congaree River in South Carolina can relate to Bartram's emotional description. Likewise, the Great Cypress Swamp must have been impressive, not only in its virgin state before the 1782 conflagration and subsequent logging during the 1800s, but also well into the early 1900s. As indicated by William S. Taber (22,23,24), Delaware once boasted of "...vast areas of cedar and cypress swamps where the trees stood so thick that semi-darkness prevailed beneath the canopy of their matted crowns and sphagnum moss grew luxuriantly over their roots."

Another interesting account of the Great Cypress Swamp was given by the English printer and botanist, Thomas Nuttall in 1809. He spent two days in the swamp describing his experience in a June 16, 1809 letter to Dr. Benjamin Smith Barton of Philadelphia. During his visit to the swamp, Nuttall found, among other things, two interesting plants, the redbay (*Persea borbonia*) and the sweetleaf (*Symplocos tinctoria*). Thanks to Dr. Alfred E. Schuyler, I had the opportunity to examine Nuttall's redbay voucher specimen, as well as Nuttall's classic 1818 flora, *The Genera of North American Plants and a Catalogue of the Species of the Year 1817* (25), in 1992 at the Academy of Natural Sciences of Philadelphia. Nuttall's collections from his trip were sent to Dr. Barton, who had financially sponsored Nuttall's field work between 1809 and 1811 (26). Of the redbay, Nuttall noted: "I have met with this plant as far north as the Great Cypress Swamp, in Sussex County, Delaware, but only rare." The following is an excerpt from Nuttall's colorful letter, which was published in its entirety by Robert R. Tatnall (27) in *Bartonia*:

> "On Tuesday morning leaving Mr. Waples, within a mile of the entrance of the swamp I met with an old man who usually conducts strangers into the swamp...The old man went with me and in about a mile from his house we began to enter one of the most frightful labyrinths you can imagine[.] It was filled with tall tangling shrubs thickly matted together almost impervious to the light...It was very wet; knee deep in sphagnum if you stept off the bridges of wooden causeways. There were some open places called savannahs, but were literally ponds at this time of the year, but are dry in summer...on the edges of these ponds grew the cupressus disticha [the bald cypress, *Taxodium distichum*]...on Wednesday I went across the swamp about 7 miles without meeting with one extraordinary vegetable excepting the Bartonia...In this part of the swamp there are bears not unfrequently met with as many as 7 having been caught not many months back."

A much shorter account of Nuttall's trip to the swamp was given by Francis W. Pennell in *Bartonia* (26) in his detailed "Travels and Scientific Collections of Thomas Nuttall." Thomas (11) and Dennis (15) also referenced Nuttall's trip.

Obviously, at this point the reader is probably intrigued not only by Nuttall's colorful 1809 description of the swamp, but also by his reference to seven black bears! Actually, in the 1797 account of the Great Cypress Swamp cited above (12,14,15), the anonymous author indicated that black bears were plentiful in the swamp in his day, supposedly so plentiful that thirty could be killed in the swamp in a day with little trouble! According to Dennis (15), the last black bear was seen in the Great Cypress Swamp in 1906.

In his account of extinct wild animals of tidewater Maryland, William B. Marye (28) recorded not only the black bear (*Ursus americanus*), but also the elk (*Cervus canadensis*), beaver (*Castor canadensis*), panther (eastern cougar, *Felis concolor*), bison (*Bison bison*) and bobcat (*Lynx rufus*), mostly from the southern portion of the Eastern Shore. However, David Lee (personal communication) has pointed out that there is no indication that the elk occurred as far south as the Pocomoke watershed. Mansueti (8) specifically listed the black bear, eastern cougar, timber wolf (gray wolf, *Canis lupus*) and the beaver as being present in the Pocomoke forests during colonial days, indicating their likely extirpation by 1800; he obviously was not aware of Nuttall's trip. Mansueti felt that the bobcat may still exist in certain parts of the swamp. In addition to the possibility of the bobcat, Mansueti listed twenty-seven other mammals for the Pocomoke. Interestingly, Mansueti (1) mentioned various unauthenticated 1949 reports from Worcester County, Maryland residents that a cougar was loose in the forests. According to Larson (29), in 1949 many people reported sighting a "mountain lion" near Salisbury the same year. As Larson indicated: "This may have been one of two cougar cubs which were released by a U.S. serviceman in the Pocomoke River area." Likewise, in a December 9, 1994 letter to me, Bill Grogan referenced the reported sighting by an elderly couple in 1980 near Selbyville, Delaware of a large black cat with a tail as long as its body. He examined some plaster casts of its footprints, which apparently were quite large.

David Lee (30) also addressed Maryland's extinct mammals, pointing out that the cougar once probably occurred throughout the State and that gray wolves were once very common in Maryland, and that maybe the red wolf (*C.*

niger) was indigenous to the lower Coastal Plain.[2] Support for this contention has been presented by Kathy Fisher, a local historian at Furnace Town. While reviewing an earlier draft of this material, she pointed out that Henry Norwood in his "A Voyage to Virginia in 1649" in *Forces: Collection of Historical Tracts* refers to wolves eating swans and fowl which he and his stranded sailors had killed for food on a barrier island in an area near the present day Fenwick (32). Norwood's journey was overland from the barrier island down the Pocomoke River and the Eastern Shore of Virginia to Jamestown; his brief account of the trip addresses the flora and fauna, as well as the cultural aspects, that he encountered.

Lee also commented on extinct birds. In reference to the ivory-billed woodpecker (*Campephilus principalis*), he suggested that perhaps this large, now possibly extinct, woodpecker never occurred in Maryland, even though Audubon (1831-1842) stated it was found in the State. Of course, the ivory-billed woodpecker was historically a denizen of the deep southern bottomland hardwood forests and it is interesting to note that our next largest woodpecker, the pileated, is quite abundant in the Pocomoke Swamp today.

Interestingly, Lee mentioned that cypress trees now growing on the Pocomoke River undoubtedly provided roosting sites for flocks of the now extinct Carolina parakeet (*Conuropsis carolinensis*). Again, there may be something to this since a Mr. Edward Derrick killed several Carolina Parakeets while gunning for soras on the Potomac River in September, 1865. Apparently, other parties on the marsh that day also shot numerous parakeets (33,34,35). In citing Smith and Palmer, Kirkwood claimed that the Carolina parakeet was originally well known in tidewater Maryland. However, in reviewing the history of the Carolina parakeet, McKinley (36) argued that even from the pioneer days there is little evidence for it occurring in the middle Atlantic states, despite claims to the contrary by such notables as John J. Audubon and Alexander Wilson! According to McKinley: "There is no

---

[2]Lee's paper, as well as a number of other papers on plants and animals referenced in this Chapter, are found in a publication edited by Norden, Forester, and Fenwick in 1984 on threatened and endangered plants and animals of Maryland (31).

evidence whatsoever for the Carolina Parakeet in Delaware...Reports for Maryland are few and generally unsatisfactory."

Again, the materials presented above tend to make one wonder just what frequented those deep dense swamps along the Pocomoke in the 1700-1800s when huge, four to nine foot diameter, bald cypress trees loomed high overhead. Interestingly, even John Muir may have made it into the Great Cypress Swamp in 1898 while on a botanical trip to Sussex County, Delaware with William M. Canby and the famous Harvard botanist, Dr. Charles S. Sargent. I first noted this possibility while paging through Robert R. Tatnall's 1946 book, *Flora of Delaware and the Eastern Shore* to assemble species information pertinent to the Pocomoke (37). Under his description of the box huckleberry (*Gaylussacia brachycera*), Tatnall wrote:

> "...it was learned that William M. Canby had collected it ('shores of Indian River') in Sussex County, Delaware, May 1870...and that this station, in pine woods 1 ½ mi. e. of Millsboro, had been visited by Commons in 1875, 1876, 1877. It was again lost, for in the autumn of 1898 Canby undertook to show it to his friends, Dr. C. S. Sargent and John Muir, and they 'passed a long day hunting for it without success in southern Delaware. He (Canby) was, I remember, a good deal chagrined at his failure to show us the plant and we always teased him about it' (unpublished letter, C. S. Sargent to H. M. Canby, June 8, 1920)." (See Chapter Eight for a similar experience I had in trying to relocate the box huckleberry in Anne Arundel County, Maryland.)

I immediately wondered, could this be *the* John Muir and sent off a request to Dr. Arthur Tucker of Delaware State University in search of the answer and hopefully the whereabouts of Sargent's letter. In the meantime, I reviewed a 1954 book in my library on Muir (*The Wilderness World of John Muir*, edited by Edwin Way Teale), which soon produced the answer -- Muir was a friend of Sargent's and had been traveling with Sargent in the South around 1897 (38). My thoughts were further confirmed when I heard back from Dr. Tucker, who sent me a copy of Sargent's letter and indicated that William M. Canby was quite good friends with John Muir. At the time, Muir was 60 years old. I find this experience rather fascinating, since Muir, of course, is most famous for his 1,000 mile walk to the Gulf, his work in the American West -- in the High Sierra, its stately trees, its glaciers and Yosemite, and Glacier Bay in Alaska -- and, of course, his wilderness ethic in general. Other than for his trip to the Gulf, I suppose few people realize he botanized the East Coast as well. No doubt his interests here were similar -- in experiencing wilderness areas and in botanizing with his friends. While the box huckleberry certainly is not large, it supposedly is quite old due to its clonal nature, and if anything on the Delmarva represented "wilderness" at the time, certainly the Pocomoke Swamp was it. Whether Muir, Canby, and Sargent went on to the Great Cypress Swamp that day, I suppose I will never know for sure; however, I don't see how Muir could have resisted the opportunity, given his strong interest in virgin forests and wilderness. Canby was very familiar with the Delmarva flora and although I have yet to come across anything that directly indicates that he botanized the Pocomoke drainage (written materials have him at a number of areas on the southern Delmarva Peninsula, particularly around Salisbury), he surely must have at least been to the Great Cypress Swamp, and perhaps shared it with Muir at some point.

ON THE WILDERNESS ASPECT

There is a certain mystique about swamps. Anyone who has spent a fair amount of field time in them surely realizes this -- whether they have been in the tenebrous depths of the densely vegetated Atlantic white cedar swamps in the New Jersey Pine Barrens, meandered through the deep river swamps of the South, or simply rambled through an average red maple swamp in the Northeast on a misty spring morning. Some of the mystery no doubt relates historically to the initial awe and ignorance associated with such places. After all, even John James Audubon mentioned "...those sultry days which rendered the atmosphere of the Louisiana swamps pregnant with baneful effluvia..."

(39) and in reference to a swamp in his 1862 essay "Walking" (40,41), Henry David Thoreau himself once stated:

> "I was surveying for a man the other day a single straight line one hundred and thirty-two rods long, through a swamp, at whose entrance might have been written the words which Dante read over the entrance to the infernal regions, -- 'Leave all hope, ye that enter,'-- that is, of ever getting out again; where at one time I saw my employer actually up to his neck and swimming for his life in his property, though it was still winter."

And certainly their remoteness and somewhat troublesome terrain add to this wilderness mystique. To quote A. H. Wright (42,43) on the fascinating Okefenokee Swamp:

> "June 13, 1912. Minnie Island Bay. Left boat west of Minnie Lake and started directly northeast at 12:15 p.m. Cut a trail through the thicket of tangled vines and briers. Found a bear sign on cypress. Found a little slash pine. Tender growths of 'gallberry'(*Ilex glabra*), 'hurray bushes' (*Leucothoe racemosa* and *Lyonia nitida*) and bay (*Magnolia virginiana*). After a period, the pack became unwieldy and Bishop began the brush work (machete). Cahn came next with compass. After a mile or so we hewed to due west. At 3 p.m. it looked rainy and Bryant climbed a bay and announced himself 'befuddled.' In other words we were lost. We cut boughs and camped on the swamp itself at the base of an immense dead pine. While we were cooking, a pair of pileated woodpeckers stopped nearby. Next we heard the cypress-bay warbler, the Swainson's warbler on our back trail. We were eating at 5:48 p.m. in the worst tangle I ever was in. Can not conceive of a wilder place in the U.S.A. than this spot where we are encamped. Yellow flies (horseflies) by day and mosquitoes by night. If we get out of this spot we can stand anything..."

212

As pointed out by Brooke Meanley (43), Wright's experience in the Okefenokee could be duplicated in some of our own swamps in the tidewater region of Maryland and Virginia, including the Pocomoke Swamp. This is certainly still applicable to some parts of the Pocomoke, particularly below Pocomoke City. According to Meanley (44), floating in a canoe through the cypress wilderness south of Pocomoke City, except for the absence of Spanish moss, reminds one of the Santee in South Carolina or the Ogeeche in Georgia.

Before reading Meanley's views on this, I had my own ideas on the "wilderness" aspects of the Pocomoke Swamp, particularly the area known as Hickory Point Swamp. I had visited the area almost annually for about fifteen years with my wetland plant identification classes for the Graduate School, U.S. Department of Agriculture. We usually had short penetrations into Hickory Point Swamp and sometimes the interesting downstream fresh tidal marsh, but for some time I had been anticipating traversing the entire width of the swamp. Considering that I was going to be in the area for a workshop on the Pocomoke River on October 23-24, 1992, I decided to arrive a day ahead of time to get that "wilderness" experience and make use of it in my presentation at the workshop.

The swamp is an interesting area, and given the curvilinear nature of its upland edge (Carolina bay-like), it no doubt owes its origin to a prehistoric meander in the river, evidence of which shows up clearly on aerial photographs and topographic maps (Figure 42).

Always looking for company on such trips and not having been in the field with him for years, I contacted my second cousin and fellow field botanist, Frank Hirst, about joining me. Frank, having anticipated crossing the swamp himself someday, promptly agreed. Our experience during this venture is described below based upon the October 22, 1992 entry in my *Journal*.

We entered the swamp at a parking area for hunters at the second gate near the northeast end of a farm field along the dirt road at the end of Hickory Point Road. Our compass heading was almost due east as we moved down the slope to the swamp about 9:30 am. Initially, we hit a thick understory of shrubs (*Ilex laevigata, Rhododendron viscosum, Clethra alnifolia, Vaccinium corymbosum*), much Virginia chain fern (*Woodwardia virginica*)

213

Figure 42. Aerial photograph (date unknown) of an area along the lower Pocomoke River in Worcester County, Maryland showing its fresh to slightly brackish tidal marsh and the extensive Hickory Point Swamp. Because the original photograph was a color infrared taken early in the year prior to leafout, the tidal marsh and swamp show up quite well due to their wetness. Note in particular the curvilinear edge of the swamp, which shows up dramatically where it abuts dry land. The author has led three all-day field adventures across the Hickory Point Swamp.

and an overstory of red maple (*Acer rubrum*) and sweetbay (*Magnolia virginiana*), as well as some scattered loblolly pine (*Pinus taeda*) and pond pine (*P. serotina*). The latter pine is a Maryland Natural Heritage Program watchlist species. (For an explanation of the rarity categories of the Maryland Natural Heritage Program, see Table I in Chapter Two.) According to Frank, it has shorter, rounded cones and low, almost prickless, umbos, which seemed to hold up well in the field. We frequently noted scattered Atlantic white cedars and some small cedar stands. One cedar was 22.2 inches in diameter at breast height. In this section, the laurel-leaf greenbrier (*Smilax laurifolia*) was very abundant and in places it almost formed a subcanopy on the lower trees.

Eventually, we moved into a red maple area that was quite open and different from the dense, jungle-like vegetation we had been traversing. This was very interesting, in that it was so open we could see perhaps 300 feet in one direction lateral to our direction of travel. In contrast with the jungle-like section that had much Virginia chain fern, this area had cinnamon fern (*Osmunda cinnamomea*). Frank quickly spotted a sapling redbay, which is currently on the State's threatened list; we then found many more, some being about 20-25 feet high. In this area, the redbay was quite abundant. At this point in our adventure, we were perhaps a third of the way across the swamp.

We next found a 26.4 inch diameter Atlantic white cedar and saw a pair of pileated woodpeckers that were making quite a racket. Then we traversed some small areas of floating mats, which presented a waterbed effect. At times, we expected to perhaps break through the mat and had to periodically retreat. These floating mats were generally in openings between tree bases. In places, the floating mat situation was fairly common and where it occurred, sphagnum moss was the dominant ground cover. We also measured some good size loblolly pines, one being 27.5 inches in diameter.

About two-thirds of the way across the swamp, we came into another interesting section dominated by swamp tupelo (*Nyssa sylvatica* var. *biflora*) with obvious, rather dramatically buttressed bases. The stand, being fairly open in terms of understory and monotypic in nature, was reminiscent of some gum swamps I have seen in North Carolina. It was also difficult to traverse due to a floating mat effect. Immediately after the gum swamp, we came across a nice size area of Atlantic white cedar (a stand) with good size trees, mostly in the 14-20 inch diameter range, although some were larger and one was 26.3 inches in diameter. These trees also had impressive crowns. Later we came across two large cedars that I promptly dubbed the "twin towers" since

215

they were side by side (about four feet apart), one of which was 23.8 inches in diameter and the other 24.6 inches in diameter. However, while one had a lower bole with numerous dead branches, the other had none on the lower bole, a sharp contrast. No other cedars were found around these excellent specimens. Frank and I agreed that the trees in the stand just mentioned and in some of the smaller concentrations we came across were the largest either of us had seen in Maryland, including those in the Nassawango Creek Nature Preserve.

Somewhere after leaving the largest area of cedars, we found a log on which to break for lunch. Admittedly, I for one was getting somewhat uncomfortably chilly. Having gone through to my knees a couple of times and repeatedly hitting wet spots even in the "drier" sections just introduced new cold water. Despite going through a few times himself, Frank seemed to stay a little drier because of his apparent waterproof boots.

After lunch, we came across a couple of mountain laurel (*Kalmia latifolia*) well out in the swamp and sensed that we were getting near the upland edge. And as we approached the eastern edge of the swamp, we noted many more mountain laurels, as well as patches of net-veined chain fern (*Woodwardia areolata*) and a jungle-like area with laurel-leaf greenbrier once again. The last couple of hundred feet were difficult to cross due to the small open areas of water between the clumps of vegetation (tree or shrub bases) that we relied on for footing along with logs. We even spotted a hedge hyssop (*Gratiola virginiana*) and some water willow (*Decodon verticillatus*) before moving up the steeply sloped upland into deciduous forest. Frank pointed out a lady fern (*Athyrium filix-femina*) at the base of the upland slope and I noted indian pipe (*Monotropa uniflora*) up the slope. There were also very large mountain laurels at the edge, a phenomenon we have noticed elsewhere along the edge of the Pocomoke River swamp.

As it turns out, we came out of the swamp around 2:15 p.m., about 1,000 feet south of our designated goal, which was a forested area between two fields on the 7.5 minute quadrangle map (Pocomoke City, Md.-Va., 1968). Our exit point was about a couple of hundred feet south of a new irrigation pond with adjacent high spoil piles.

216

Before long, we were crossing a small drainage where it enters the swamp after paralleling Hickory Point Road. This finger of the swamp had a dense understory of lizard's-tail (*Saururus cernuus*), as did another small draw nearby and to the south of Hickory Point Road. Interestingly, we noted no lizard's-tail while crossing the main swamp, except for a few scattered plants near the eastern edge. We then hoofed it down the macadam road to Frank's truck, botanizing a little along the way.

We spent about five delightful, albeit somewhat uncomfortable, hours in the swamp, having crossed a 1.1 mile wide section. It was much warmer out of the swamp and in the sun. With our wet feet and the shade and moist air in the swamp, you would not have known it was in the 60s. Although the redbay was the only rare plant we encountered, the cedars were impressive and encouraging and the vegetation mix was unexpected -- overgrown areas with much laurel-leaf greenbrier, open understory red maple, open understory buttressed swamp tupelo, and a good-size Atlantic white cedar stand. It was a great experience, a wetland "wilderness" experience for this part of the country.

Enthralled by the area, I crossed the Hickory Point Swamp again (in four hours) on August 27, 1993, this time with Wilbur Rittenhouse, Dawn Biggs, and Kathy McCarthy, and once again saw some rather large Atlantic white cedar. Frank Hirst was unable to attend.

To me, swamps like the Pocomoke Swamp, the Great Dismal Swamp, and those in isolated barrier island swales, such as the large forested swale behind the high paleodune system (Lighthouse Ridge) on the southern tip of Assateague Island and the forested swales at Seashore State Park near Virginia Beach, convey a feeling of wetland "wilderness" when a person is in them, despite the sometimes close proximity to other humans. And despite his boding advice presented earlier, Henry David Thoreau took a strong liking to swamps. To again quote from Thoreau's "Walking" (40):

"Hope and the future for me are not in lawns and cultivated fields, not in towns and cities, but in the impervious and quaking swamps. When, formerly, I have analyzed my partiality for some

217

farm which I had contemplated purchasing, I have frequently found that I was attracted solely by a few square rods of impermeable and unfathomable bog,--a natural sink in one corner of it. That was the jewel that dazzled me. I derive more of my subsistence from the swamps which surround my native town than from the cultivated gardens in the village...Why not put my house, my parlor, behind this plot, instead of behind that meager assemblage of curiosities, that poor apology for a Nature and Art, which I call my front-yard?...Bring your sills up to the very edge of the swamp, then, (though it may not be the best place for a dry cellar) so that there be no access on that side to citizens. Front yards are not made to walk in, but, at most, through, and you could go in the back way.

"Yes, you may think me perverse, if it were proposed to me to dwell in the neighborhood of the most beautiful garden that ever human art contrived, or else of a dismal swamp, I should certainly decide for the swamp..."

Thoreau goes on to say:

"...When I would recreate myself, I seek the darkest wood, the thickest and most interminable, and, to the citizen, most dismal swamp. I enter a swamp as a sacred place, -- a *sanctum sanctorum*...A town is saved, not more by the righteous men in it than by the woods and swamps that surround it..."

Much of the grandeur of swamps is also vividly depicted in such popular books as Bill Thomas's *The Swamp* (11) and John V. Dennis's *The Great Cypress Swamps* (15). Both authors colorfully described the Great Cypress Swamp, devoting a chapter to it; Dennis also discussed other areas of the Pocomoke, including the Nassawango Swamp. And of all the rivers of the Chesapeake Bay drainage, the Pocomoke looms large as a unique, mysterious, and beautiful waterway (8). Beaven and Oosting (7) considered it an almost impenetrable wilderness, remarking that parts of the swamp have

218

not been drained and have seldom been entered since lumbering ceased many years ago. It was called Maryland's swamp wilderness by John Taylor (45), who also felt that the swamp retained much of its primitive splendor. As far as I am concerned, these words still hold today for the reach of the Pocomoke below Porter's Crossing. A trip there would be well worth the effort -- but if you enter the swamp, be sure to bring your compass! Although a canoe trip will be quite productive, I also recommend you get into the swamp on foot, which usually means slogging around all wet and muddy, a great experience indeed.

I often pondered two things about the Pocomoke Swamp: Why it is still relatively natural in the tidewater section and why there is such a paucity of natural history information on the area? My research on the Pocomoke shed some light on both. Obviously, there is a direct relationship between wilderness and isolation, and to the extent that the Pocomoke represents "wilderness" it appears that its isolation, down the Delmarva Peninsula far from the major centers of activity in the 17th, 18th, and 19th centuries, played a big part. For example, steamboats did not regularly ply between Pocomoke River wharves and the outside world until 1868. Prior to that, one traveled to Baltimore, generally allowing two weeks for a round trip by schooner (9). Although it is true that much of the upper swamp (above Porter's Crossing) has been drained for agriculture, little of the swamp has been filled as was the case with many swamps during the early history of this country when wetlands were considered a menace and a hindrance to land development, going back to the days of the Swamp Land Acts of 1849, 1850, and 1860 (46). Of the two largest communities along the river, Snow Hill was founded at the head of navigation during the late 17th century (settled in the 1640s and chartered in 1686) and Pocomoke City (by that name) was not chartered until 1878, although beginning in the 17th century there were settlements and a town at that location known in order as Steven's Crossing, Warehouse Landing, Meeting House Landing, and Newtown (Kathy Fisher, personal communication; 3,47). Developmental pressures really have not been that strong along the Pocomoke and beyond these communities little in the way of human intrusion is evident. In fact, this tranquil tea-colored river seems to be one with the swamp -- it is essentially bankless as it intermingles with the trees and shrubs. Even the southernmost reach of the Pocomoke has sort of a "wilderness" aspect to it, given the extensive fresh and brackish tidal marshes, the few small water-based communities, and the scattered private residences along it.

In my view, the relative isolation of the area has also resulted in the paucity of information available for the Pocomoke River drainage. Let me explain. In 1987, an interesting set of publications on botanical explorations and discoveries in colonial Maryland, variously authored by James L. Reveal, George F. Frick, C. Rose Broome, and Melvin L. Brown, were published in the journal *Huntia* (48,49,50,51,52,53). The authors particularly concentrated on the botanical collections by the Reverend Hugh Jones, Maryland's first naturalist, who lived in the colony between 1696 and 1702, by Dr. David Krieg, a ship's surgeon and naturalist who botanized in Maryland during the summer of 1698, and by William Vernon, another botanist who visited Maryland in the summer of 1698. Some smaller collections by others were also examined. The work of Vernon and Krieg in Maryland was also briefly referenced by F. W. Pennell in 1942 (54). Apparently, these colonial naturalists and botanists collected only on the Coastal Plain in Maryland -- specifically, in modern-day Anne Arundel, Calvert, Prince George's, and St. Mary's Counties on the Western Shore and in Talbot and Dorchester Counties on the Eastern Shore (49). Certainly, no mention was made by the authors of any work in the Pocomoke region, although they alluded to the Pocomoke Swamp in their attempt to conceptually reconstruct generic habitat types that were present in colonial Maryland. Obviously, access to the Pocomoke's wetlands, other than perhaps by boat, was very limited at the time.

Because of its isolation, I suspect that the area remained botanically remote through the 18th and most of the 19th centuries. In 1738, however, two Englishmen, Peter Collinson and Lord Petre underwrote a 1,100 mile trip by the Philadelphia botanist, John Bartram, through Delaware, Maryland, and Virginia to Williamsburg (55). Given the remoteness of the Delmarva Peninsula, it is highly likely that Bartram took a route around the upper part of the Chesapeake Bay bypassing the lower Peninsula. However, according to R.H. True (56), Bartram "...set out in the fall of 1737 *apparently going down* [emphasis mine] through Delaware and the Eastern Shore sections of Maryland and Virginia, thence up the James River by way of Williamsburg to the mountains, turning northward through the Shenandoah Valley." This assumes, of course, that Bartram was able to obtain access across the mouth of the Chesapeake Bay by boat. There is no evidence, however, that he visited the Pocomoke's wetlands.

Historically, there have been numerous collectors who botanized in Philadelphia and surrounding areas. Pennell (54,57) listed many botanists, such as John and William Bartram, Thomas Nuttall, Peter Kalm, Andre Michaux, the Reverend Henry Muhlenberg, Benjamin Smith Barton, and Constantine Samuel Rafinesque, some of whom collected on the Delmarva (e.g., Nuttall and Rafinesque). In this regard, A.O. Tucker and N. H. Dill (58) excerpt an interesting account by Rafinesque of his first sojourn in Delaware, taken from Refinesque's 1836 *Life of Travels* (59), in which Rafinesque mentions his 1804 trip into the "Dismal Swamp" (meaning the Great Cypress Swamp) where he found, among other species, the sweetleaf. For the area covered by the Philadelphia Botanical Club's Local Herbarium at the Academy of Natural Sciences of Philadelphia (covering all of southern New Jersey, Pennsylvania southeast of the Blue Ridge and east of the Susquehanna River, New Castle County, Delaware, and the northeastern-most of Maryland), Pennell cited over 100 collectors. In his book, *Flora of Delaware and the Eastern Shore*, Robert R. Tatnall listed forty-six botanical collectors during the period between 1809 and 1945 (37,60). How many of these botanized the Pocomoke and to what extent? It is difficult to say for sure, but I suspect not many, other than for perhaps those that botanized the Great Cypress Swamp area in Delaware. My reasoning for this claim is presented below.

As pointed out by the Wilmington botanist, William M. Canby, in 1864 (61): "The peninsula lying between Delaware and Chesapeake Bays has been almost a *terra incognita* to botanists..." Canby went on to mention that he, accompanied at times with friends, made short visits to a few places in Sussex County, Delaware and Somerset and Worcester Counties, Maryland in 1863. According to F.W. Pennell (57), Canby collected extensively in Delaware and as indicated by J.N. Rose (62), his knowledge of the plants of the Maryland's Eastern Shore was very great. In fact, based upon an examination of Robert R. Tatnall's 1946 book, it appears as though Canby collected on the Delmarva just about as much as anyone, if not more, until Tatnall himself. Tatnall acknowledged Canby's Delmarva Peninsula plants, although he felt that "...Canby's Peninsula trips were limited, except in the immediate vicinity of Wilmington, to some half-dozen localities accessible by rail, and from which exploration of the surrounding country could be made by means of 'horse-and-buggy.'" Yet Canby's name frequently surfaces in Tatnall's book in association with cited specimens. Interestingly though, I found none that mentions the Pocomoke Swamp, although I can't help but feel that he botanized the area, if only the Great Cypress Swamp. Repeatedly, there are citations for Salisbury; and there are others as well -- for Millsboro in Sussex County, Delaware (the Indian River site mentioned above), Princess Anne in Somerset County, Maryland and Cape Charles City in Northampton County, Virginia to name a few. Canby himself mentioned botanizing in Worcester County *east* of Snow Hill and at Public Landing, as well as his work in Sussex County (18,61). Yet, there is not one reference to the Pocomoke in Canby's works as far as I can determine.

What about Robert R. Tatnall's forty-five other collectors? Well, many of them (e.g., Edward Tatnall) confined most to their activities to the Wilmington and New Castle County areas. On the other hand, some collectors listed by Tatnall apparently visited the Pocomoke's wetlands.

Besides Robert R. Tatnall, collectors that botanized the Pocomoke (according to collections cited in Tatnall) include Thomas Nuttall (see above), Albert Commons in 1874, 1875, and 1876, Rodney H. True in 1926 and 1928, Augustine V. P. Smith in 1939, W. S. Taber in 1941, W. R. Haden in 1927, and Elizabeth C. Earle in 1939. Most of the collection sites were from Gumboro, Delaware or other areas in the vicinity of the Great Cypress Swamp; except for Smith, none of these collections were for the Pocomoke in Maryland and Smith's work involved mostly drained mill ponds (63,64,65). Commons' collections at the Great Cypress Swamp were discussed at length by Tucker and Dill (66) and will not be repeated here, other than to point out that Commons did collect two very rare species from the Gumboro area, the pine barrens boneset (*Eupatorium resinosum*) and Knieskern's beakrush (*Rhynchospora knieskernii*), in 1874 and 1875. Robert R. Tatnall, of course, cited a number of his own collections (sometimes in conjunction with Smith) for the Pocomoke area in Maryland, so he apparently knew it well. In his commentary, Tatnall referenced the work the Reverend John P. Otis and Charles S. Williamson on the Delmarva. Otis in his 1914 "Notes from the 'Eastern Shore'" (67), however, mentioned only the Nanticoke marshes in the vicinity of Sharptown, Maryland and Williamson (68) described a trip to central and southern Delaware seeking a good location for the so-called "Symposium of 1909" but made no mention of the Pocomoke. (The "Symposium," by the way, was held on July 4-9, "...[with] there being at no time more than five and on the first and last days only two botanists present [!]") On a May 23, 1912 meeting of the Philadelphia Botanical Club, Williamson (69) also reported on a trip to Millsboro earlier in the month; again with no mention of the Pocomoke.

In 1945, Harold N. Moldenke (70) reported on numerous collections around the Snow Hill area, some of which were from the Pocomoke Swamp, although many involve upland and/or cultivated species. He also reported on Delaware, including Sussex County collections (71). It is difficult to say whether and how frequently he visited the swamp since many of the collections he cited were from other collectors. Even in George R. Proctor's accounts on Maryland *Isoetes* (72,73), he did not reference the Pocomoke. On the other hand, Tidestrom mentioned the swamp cottonwood (*Populus heterophylla*) and the Atlantic white cedar for the Pocomoke area in his 1913 paper in *Rhodora* (21). Although he did not specifically reference the Pocomoke in his "Peninsula Delmarva," John K. Small (74) mentioned his 1920 trip from the northern end of Delaware to Cape Charles with Edgar T. Wherry, George K. Small, and John W. Small; they were looking mostly for prickly pear, but may have visited the Pocomoke Swamp. Dr. Wherry visited the swamp on May 4, 1947 along with Robert Tatnall and George R. Proctor to see the dwarf trillium, *Trillium pusillum* var. *virginianum*, in relation to its discovery in the swamp by George F. Beaven (75). Having been in the field with him on a number of occasions and knowing how much he got around, my guess is that Wherry botanized the Pocomoke a number of times over his long productive career. Of course, Beaven himself botanized the Pocomoke (6,7), but for some reason this was not acknowledged by Robert R. Tatnall other than for citing Beaven in his "Bibliography of Botany of the Peninsula." Forrest Shreve and his coauthors, who were also mentioned by Tatnall, touched on the Pocomoke Swamp in their book (5), as well as the Pocomoke's fresh tidal marshes opposite Rehobeth, Maryland; he apparently visited both areas. Although he presented little in the way of commentary, Paul J. Redmond (2) published a flora of Worcester County, which included plant citations for the Pocomoke; obviously, he spent time in the area during his field work in 1930-32. Among many other things, Merritt L. Fernald was well known for his visits to southeastern Virginia, including the lower Delmarva Peninsula (76), yet I have come across nothing from him on the Pocomoke.

Although I have not done an exhaustive study of the issue, it appears to me that few botanists collected and reported on the Pocomoke (at least for the Maryland section) up until the time of Robert R. Tatnall, a notable exception being the work of Beaven (6,7). And even as late as 1932 when Redmond published his flora of Worcester County, no flora existed for the region. One possible exception to this is Rafinesque's lost early 19th century manuscript, *Florula Delawarica, or a Catalogue of the Plants Found in the State of Delaware* cited by Robert R. Tatnall (37). A.O. Tucker and N. H. Dill attempted to reconstruct Rafinesque's flora based upon known literature and ancillary sources (58).

Why is there such a paucity of floras? Well, as Canby said, it was *terra incognita* in the old days and again this isolation undoubtedly kept many away. Just scan Tatnall's list of cited collections sometime and see how much field work was done along the Wicomico River (particularly around Salisbury) and along the Nanticoke compared to the Pocomoke -- by rough count, I get forty-five and forty-two citations, respectively, for the Wicomico and Nanticoke compared to twenty-seven for the Pocomoke and vicinity. In discussing this in 1992 with Dr. Alfred E. Schuyler of The Academy of

Natural Sciences of Philadelphia, he too noted the historical concentration of botanical work around Salisbury and on the Nanticoke, particularly in Canby's days. Roland M. Harper's papers (77,78) lend support to this idea. In 1907 he argued that the Coastal Plain of Delaware, Maryland and Virginia appeared to lack many of the species commonly found in New Jersey and the southern pine-barrens, although he indicated that some of them would probably be reported when those areas were more thoroughly explored. In 1909 Harper went on to claim that the flora of eastern United States where either loblolly pine or shortleaf pine (*Pinus echinata*) occurs most abundantly, is uninteresting and consists of comparatively few, widely distributed species (78). Consequently, according to Harper, these regions were not much frequented by botanists and not often described in botanical literature. At the time, the Pine Barrens of New Jersey and those of the southeastern states had been celebrated botanizing grounds for a century or more, but corresponding regions between Delaware and Roanoke Rivers reportedly supported very few typical pine-barren, or other species, that were not considered more common elsewhere. Apparently, as of 1909, comparatively little had been published about this region (outside of Dismal Swamp and vicinity) by botanists. In fact, Harper indicated that for the Delmarva Peninsula, which he considered somewhat more accessible at the time, there seemed to be less than a dozen "local floras." Moreover, citing Nathaniel L. Britton (79), Harper mentions only two floras for Delaware in the vicinity of Wilmington and two for Maryland in the vicinity of Baltimore.

Undoubtedly, Harper's contentions must have discouraged many botanists from visiting the area. Harper himself, who was famous for botanizing from the windows of trains (His 1909 paper was entitled "Car-window notes on the vegetation of the Delmarva Peninsula and southern Virginia."), went the whole length of the Delmarva by train on July 18, 1908, eventually crossing the mouth of the Chesapeake on a steamer. Although he listed a number of species observed, one of which was the bald cypress (at two places in Somerset County, perhaps one being the Pocomoke River) and mentioned a navigable stream at Pocomoke, he did not acknowledge the Pocomoke River by name. However, about ten years later (1917 and 1918),

Harper again visited the Delmarva while conducting a preliminary forest census of the area (80). From that effort, Harper divided the Delmarva Peninsula into five broad forest regions, one of which he called the Pocomoke region. He alluded to the southern affinity of the Pocomoke region and, among other trees, referenced the bald cypress and Atlantic white cedar. Harper also stated that the Pocomoke region had considerable virgin growth, especially along swamps, and mentioned some sandy bogs a few miles southwest of Snow Hill.

Although Harper's earlier contentions about the Delmarva were indubitably convincing to many, he did not fool Merritt Lyndon Fernald who challenged him rather colorfully in *Rhodora* in 1937 (76):

> "The watching of vegetation from a moving train is and long has been a regular diversion of field-botanists but it is Harper who has so far developed the art as to draw considerable deductions from observations thus swiftly made without verifying specimens. A milder form of the sport is botanizing without slowing down from a speeding automobile, 'rumble-seat botany' as Dr. Lincoln Constance calls it. A slower period gave us the 'horse-and-buggy' glimpser. Like more up-to-date methods, even 'horse-and-buggy' identifying was subject to possible error...But 'horse-and-buggy' and rumble-seat botanizing, without slowing down to collect specimens, as well as botanizing from the express train are all obsolescent."

Besides his distaste for Harper's technique (another turn-of-the-century botanist, John W. Harshberger, used a similar approach in New Jersey by the way), the implication from Fernald was that perhaps Harper was wrong about the Delmarva Peninsula and certainly Fernald collected his share of plants in coastal Virginia, including the lower Delmarva Peninsula in Virginia (37,76).

As indicated above, I attribute this lack of botanical interest in the Pocomoke's wetlands to their relative isolation to a large extent, and the materials that I have presented would tend to support that argument.

226

Furthermore, this statement does not apply only to the swamp, which may explain why such contemporaneous rarities like the sensitive joint-vetch (*Aeschenomene virginica*), small waterwort (*Elatine minima*), mat-forming water-hyssop (*Bacopa innominata*), mudwort (*Limosella subulata*), pygmy-weed (*Crassula aquatica*),and spongy lophotocarpus (*Sagittaria calycina*) historically have not been reported from the Pocomoke's fresh to slightly brackish tidal wetlands, whereas some of these species have been reported from the Wicomico and Nanticoke Rivers (Maryland Department of Natural Resources, Maryland Natural Heritage Program data, including records from a number of herbaria; 37). Other rarities, such as Nuttall's micranthemum (*Micranthemum micranthemoides*), American elatine (*Elatine americana*), Parker's pipewort (*Eriocaulon parkeri*), and Long's bittercress (*Cardamine longii*) historically have been reported but once or, at the most, only a couple of times from the Pocomoke watershed. Nor is this argument unique to the Pocomoke -- a prime second example being the Delmarva potholes, at least a few of which occur in the Pocomoke River watershed (e.g., the Dividing Creek Ponds in Worcester County; Kathy McCarthy, personal communication). Apparently, little was known and essentially nothing published specifically on these interesting isolated wetlands until the mid-1970s when Wayne Klockner and I started visiting these sites and pointed out their uniqueness from a natural history perspective (81,82), although Frank Hirst started botanizing them around 1971-72 (personal communication) and referenced them in *Bartonia* (83), and a number of more detailed studies have followed (84). In fact, even the term Delmarva bay is relatively recent; Klockner and I referred to these depressional wetlands as potholes, the appellation I still prefer. (For more on the potholes, see Chapter Seven.) Even more surprisingly, the same can be said of the Pocomoke -- there has been no modern botanical treatment of the swamp, the last ones being Beaven and Oosting's 1939 vegetation study (7) and Redmond's Worcester County flora (2) to the extent that it peripherally touches on the Pocomoke. The only botanical treatment of the Pocomoke's tidal marshes of which I am aware is that of Shreve and his coauthors (5), who discussed its fresh tidal marshes opposite Rehobeth along with similar marshes occurring on the Nanticoke at

227

Vienna and the Choptank near Dover Bridge. They also very briefly discussed the Pocomoke Swamp. Tatnall's 1946 book (37) is the last comprehensive treatment of the Delmarva flora, other than for the wildflower guide for the Delmarva and the Eastern Shore by Claude E. Phillips in 1978 (60). This is not to say that there have not been contemporaneous field workers in the Pocomoke area, and a few State-wide treatments for Maryland have been published (85,86,87,88,89); however, little information specific to the Pocomoke's wetlands has been subsequently published. Perhaps that is why in recent years collectors (83,90,91,92) have come up with such good finds in the way of rare, threatened, and endangered plants. In fact, most of the more contemporaneous interest in relation to Delmarva's flora seems to center around rare, threatened, and endangered species through the Maryland, Delaware, and Virginia State Natural Heritage Programs and individual efforts (93,94,95). Although I produced my own atlas of vascular plant distribution maps for tidewater Maryland (96), which included nine stations for the Pocomoke watershed, and have subsequently conducted another thirty-two trips to the area since compiling the atlas, most of my interests have also centered around rare, threatened, and endangered species.

THE POCOMOKE TODAY

Figures vary as to the correct length of the Pocomoke River -- forty-five miles, fifty-four miles, fifty-five miles to cite a few. The exact length does not really matter, however, for what's important is the fact that the river and much of its original grandeur still remains today. If we did not before, we now realize the significance of the river and its wetlands, and in the last twenty years or so a number of natural area reports addressing the river have been completed (82,97,98,99,100). Its grandeur was aptly pointed out by Romeo Manuseti in 1953 (8): "The Pocomoke River, of all the rivers of the Chesapeake Bay drainage, looms large as a unique, mysterious, and beautiful waterway." And certainly the information I have presented earlier on the Pocomoke's relative isolation and "wilderness" aspect supports Mansueti's view. If there is a central theme to all these reports and opinions in relation to

228

the Pocomoke, surely it must be the Pocomoke's uniqueness. The significance of the Pocomoke is also acknowledged in a few "guides to interesting places" (3,101) and some publications for the general public (45,102). There have also been a few wetland inventories covering the area to varying degrees (10,103,104,105,106). Little has changed in the way of natural values along the Pocomoke since the publication of these documents and the Pocomoke's splendor was once again publicly acknowledged just a few years ago in Chesapeake Bay Magazine with the publication of "The Last Undiscovered River" (107).

But there is more to the Pocomoke than its uniqueness, mystery and beauty -- there are also interesting phytogeographic considerations and the watershed certainly has its share of rare, threatened, and endangered plants and animals, as well as other uncommon or interesting species. My own interests in the Pocomoke centers around its phytogeography and rare and otherwise uncommon plants and animals, as well as its isolation and uniqueness. Thus, the bulk of what follows will concentrate on those aspects. Although my intent below is not to do an exhaustive inventory of the biota of the Pocomoke River and its wetlands and surrounding uplands, I have gathered a fair amount of information on the Pocomoke, particularly its phytogeographic characteristics, rare, threatened, and endangered plants and animals, and other uncommon or interesting species, including breeding bird populations. However, it seems appropriate to begin with a general discussion of the Pocomoke's wetlands, including their vegetation and pertinent wetland inventories.

Wetland Types and Extent

The first major wetland inventory covering the area (103) did not cite figures for the Pocomoke as such but did show 11,643 acres of wooded swamp for Worcester County, most of which would have been for the Pocomoke Swamp. The next major Maryland wetland inventory was conducted by McCormick and Somes (104) for coastal (basically tidal) wetlands; they presented acreages by watersheds, including the Pocomoke's.

However, the Pocomoke watershed was broadly defined based upon the U.S. Geological Cataloging Unit 02060009 (1980 map), which includes all of Somerset County south of Dames Quarter, as well as the immediate Pocomoke drainage. A total of 53,246 acres of coastal wetlands were given for the watershed; 4,152 and 2,884 acres, respectively, were given for bald cypress and red maple/ash wetland types, with the remainder falling under various marsh types. Again, a large part of bald cypress and red maple/ash acreages would have come from the Pocomoke itself, although the inventory only covered the tidal portion. The most recent figures for the immediate Pocomoke drainage are those that were compiled specifically for me through the help of the National Wetlands Inventory in St. Petersburg, Florida; these figures are based upon a subset of Unit 02060009, which includes the area of the Pocomoke watershed above the Pocomoke Sound near Shelltown, Maryland.

According to the U.S. Fish and Wildlife Service's National Wetland Inventory (NWI), the Pocomoke Watershed is 324,128 acres in extent (Table IV). Wetlands comprise 19.6% of that or about 63,422 acres. Under this classification system, wetlands are placed into five broad categories or systems: Palustrine, Estuarine, Riverine, Lacustrine, and Marine. Although the Marine System is not found along the Pocomoke, the other four are present, with data available for 123 attributes (essentially mapping units or types). Table IV lists fifteen broad wetland types under which the 123 attributes can be grouped. For purposes of this paper, the more significant types are the Estuarine intertidal emergent (the brackish tidal marshes; 2,384.4 acres), the Estuarine scrub/shrub (essentially brackish shrub swamps; 91.9 acres), the Palustrine emergent (fresh tidal and non-tidal marshes; 1,396.0 acres), the Palustrine scrub/shrub (essentially fresh tidal and non-tidal shrub swamps; 1,255.8 acres), and the Palustrine forested (fresh tidal and non-tidal forested swamps; 55,726.4 acres). About 260,706 acres (80.4%) of the watershed is considered upland.

The best description of the vegetation of the Pocomoke Swamp is that presented by Beaven (6) and Beaven and Oosting (7). Except for the Great Cypress Swamp area, which Beaven and Oosting referred to as the Burnt Swamp because of the severe destruction caused by the fire in 1931, their

TABLE IV
POCOMOKE WATERSHED ACREAGE SUMMARY*

Attribute (wetland type)		Acres
E1OW	(Estuarine subtidal open water)	593.3
E1UW	(Estuarine subtidal unconsolidated bottom)	3.9
E2EM	(Estuarine intertidal emergent)	2,384.4
E2FL	(Estuarine intertidal flats)	21.6
E2SS	(Estuarine intertidal scrub/shrub)	91.9
L1OW	(Lacustrine limnetic open water)	188.2
PEM	(Palustrine emergent)	1,396.0
PFL	(Palustrine flats)	2.5
PFO	(Palustrine forested)	55,726.4
POW	(Palustrine open water)	406.3
PSS	(Palustrine scrub/shrub)	1,255.8
PUB	(Palustrine unconsolidated bottom)	3.8
R1EM	(Riverine tidal emergent)	195.6
R1OW	(Riverine tidal open water)	1,126.4
R2OW	(Riverine lower perennial)	26.3
Total Wetlands		63,422.4
Uplands		260,705.6
Total Watershed		324,128.0

* Source: National Wetland Inventory, U.S. Fish and Wildlife Service, St. Petersburg, FL (1983).

description of the swamp remains quite accurate today. They included five community types: Swamp Forest, Forest Stream Border, Fresh Water Marsh, Upland Border, and Burned Area (the Burnt Swamp). Because these descriptions are still accurate, I have elaborated on them only briefly below; more detailed accounts of these types can be found in the original works.

According to Beaven and Oosting, the swamp is about thirty miles long and one-half to two miles wide, the bulk of which falls under their Swamp Forest category. They listed 284 plant taxa for the Pocomoke Swamp; by comparison, Musselman and his coauthors (108) recorded 341 taxa for the Great Dismal Swamp in southeastern Virginia, although the latter swamp is much larger. As might be expected, the Swamp Forest category is dominated by the bald cypress and swamp tupelo, particularly near the river, although a number of other trees, such as red maple and green ash (*Fraxinus pennsylvanica*), are also common. The Atlantic white cedar tends to be scattered on the main stem of the Pocomoke, occurring mostly in nontidal portions of the swamp towards the upland border and on tributaries. Representative vascular plants for the Pocomoke Swamp are also presented in a number of tables in *Wetlands of Maryland* (106).

Figure 43. The well-flooded zone of spatterdock (*Nuphar luteum*) along Nassawango Creek, Worcester County, Maryland. Of all the emergent wetland plants in the Chesapeake Bay Region, spatterdock grows in the deepest water. (Photo by the author)

Throughout most of the length of the Pocomoke River and many of its tributaries, no marsh exists between the river and the swamp. However, from about Porter's Crossing to Pocomoke City, an intermittent marshy strip (the Forest Stream Border) occurs, which is dominated by spatterdock (*Nuphar luteum*) (Figure 43). In some areas, particularly near the mouths of tributaries and at small "coves" below Porter's Crossing, the third type, Fresh Water Marsh, can be seen; it supports plants such as spatterdock,

232

pickerelweed (*Pontederia cordata*), arrow-arrum (*Peltandra virginica*) and goldenclub (*Orontium aquaticum*). Beaven and Oosting's next type, the Upland Border, refers to transitional vegetation between the swamp and the adjacent uplands; it supports a larger mix of trees, particularly oaks (*Quercus* spp.). In all of these types, a variety of shrubs, woody vines, and herbaceous plants are also present and in some parts of the swamp I have found the woody plants quite diverse. The area known as the Burnt Swamp has now become revegetated, mostly by the red maple and sweet gum (Frank Hirst, personal communication), although it has been substantially reduced in size due to the drainage cited earlier. On October 2, 1993, Wilbur Rittenhouse and I visited the Burnt Swamp, spending three hours hiking through it. As I indicated in a letter to Wilbur: "We also found sweetleaf growing abundantly, in the Burnt Swamp, as well as Walter's green briar (*Smilax walteri*), both of which are Delaware Natural Heritage Program S2 species (very rare status). But it was just the mystique of the area -- the one-time vast swamp, filled with huge cypress and black bears, John Nuttall's rambles through it in 1809, its great conflagrations -- and a certain excitement in just being there that intrigued me the most."[3]

One particular area in the Pocomoke Watershed, The Nature Conservancy's Nassawango Creek Preserve, which includes uplands as well as wetlands, deserves special mention. A brief description of the Preserve in 1984 was given by Steve Hamblin (109). As of 1994, the Preserve included 3,300 acres (Wayne Klockner, personal communication). While working for the Maryland Field Office of The Nature Conservancy in 1983, Jim Stasz (110) compiled a vascular plant list for the Preserve that contains 604 taxa, including 28 ferns and fern allies, 8 gymnosperms, 179 monocots (58 grasses, 56 sedges, 13 orchids, and 52 miscellaneous monocots), and 389 dicots. From my perspective, two particularly interesting areas on the Preserve are an approximate twenty-acre cedar swamp in the non-tidal portion and a botanically rich area at Wango, including an impressive old millpond. The twenty-acre cedar swamp is probably the largest contiguous stand of Atlantic

---

[3]The sweetleaf and red-berried (Walter's) greenbrier are no longer on Delaware's rare species list.

white cedar in Maryland and is one of fifty-eight present and historic stands of Atlantic white cedar for the Delmarva Peninsula by Dill and his coauthors (23,24), who also listed 117 plant taxa directly associated with stands of Atlantic white cedar on the Delmarva. Their list contains 11 trees, 22 shrubs, 5 vines, and 77 herbs, including 7 ferns, 4 grasses, 2 rushes, 11 sedges, 5 composites, 2 orchids, and 7 carnivorous plants. The Hickory Point Cedar Swamp is another of the authors' fifty-eight Atlantic white cedar swamp sites; they cited personal communication with a forester, Grant Powell, who described the harvesting of eight or nine million board feet of cedar over a three to four year period in the 1950s at an approximate 1,100 acre site in an oxbow of the Pocomoke River now owned by the State of Maryland, which is obviously the Hickory Point Cedar Swamp.

Beaven and Oosting did not consider the tidal marsh south of the Pocomoke Swamp. Shreve and his coauthors (5) examined the fresh tidal marshes along the Pocomoke River opposite Rehobeth, but discussed the fresh tidal system only generically, having considered the Pocomoke along with the Nanticoke at Vienna and the Choptank near Dover Bridge. For the same general area, tidal wetland map WO-141, prepared in conjunction with *The Coastal Wetlands of Maryland* (104), shows mapping units comprised of combinations of five fresh marsh types -- smartweed/rice cutgrass, pickerelweed/arrow-arum, cattail, swamp rose mallow, and big cordgrass, the latter occurring mostly on natural levees along tidal guts. Combinations of similar vegetation types occur downstream to and below Cedar Hall Wharf, but brackish marsh types also appear with greater frequency as the Pocomoke Sound is approached. A description of some of these wetlands based upon my own field work is given below.

I am much less familiar with the tidal marshes of the Pocomoke than I am the swamp. My first trip into the marshes was by boat with Frank Hirst during a family camping trip at Shad Landing in 1982. We obtained access to the area via Cedar Hall Wharf and traveled upstream to explore the large fresh tidal marsh west of the Hickory Point Swamp. Although I did not record much in my *Journal* that day, we found the shoreline sedge (*Carex hyalinolepis*), a species considered highly State rare and endangered by the Maryland Department of Natural Resources. Nevertheless, I was impressed

234

with the area and visited it a number of times over the years with some of my Graduate School, U.S. Department of Agriculture classes in three different areas: the slightly brackish marsh at Cedar Hall Wharf, the large fresh tidal

Figure 44. Smooth orange milkweed (*Asclepias lanceolata*) -- a State of Maryland watchlist species. This was a new species for the author when he first encountered it in the fresh to slightly brackish tidal marsh on the Pocomoke River below the Hickory Point Swamp, Worcester County, Maryland in 1983. (Photo by Jack DeForest)

marsh west of Hickory Point Swamp, and a small fresh tidal marsh along Hickory Point Road. The following brief description of the fresh tidal marsh west of Hickory Point Swamp is taken from my July 9, 1983 *Journal* entry. On this 1983 visit, the marsh appeared lush and diverse, with plants such as scythe-fruited arrowhead (*Sagittaria falcata*), mock bishop's-weed (*Ptilimnium capillaceum*), water parsnip (*Sium suave*), sweetflag (*Acorus calamus*), tall meadow-rue (*Thalictrum polygamum*), swamp rose (*Rosa palustris*), narrow-leaf cattail (*Typha angustifolia*), bedstraw (*Galium* sp.), jewelweed (*Impatiens capensis*), many of which were flowering. I pointed out some of largest clumps of tussock sedge (*Carex stricta*) I have ever seen. As we crashed through the tangle of marsh vegetation, we periodically stopped to

235

view the scene. It was impressive. At one point, I spotted an orange flower in the distance and the thought of smooth orange milkweed (*Asclepias lanceolata*), a species that eluded me for years, flashed through my mind. And sure enough, it was that showy wetland plant with crimson petals and an orange corona. The leaves were lance-shaped, oppositely arranged, and folded somewhat length-wise to the sky (Figure 44).

Figure 45. Large attractive marsh pink (*Sabatia dodecandra*) -- a State watchlist species. (Photo by the author)

Access to this marsh can be obtained via Hickory Point Road, and then by walking an obscure dirt road to its northwestern terminus near the edge of the swamp and hiking west through the strip of swamp vegetation to the marsh, but the hike will not be easy. A more convenient, albeit small, area to view some fresh tidal marsh is the small marsh along Hickory Point Road. While with my class on July 29, 1989, for example, I noted smooth orange milkweed, large marsh pink (*Sabatia dodecandra*), cardinal flower (*Lobelia cardinalis*), and scythe-fruited arrowhead, all flowering, in this interesting freshwater marsh (Figures 45 and 46). The first two are State watchlist

Figure 46. The beautiful cardinal flower *(Lobelia cardinalis)*. (Photo by the author)

species. I have been to this site a number of times over the years and it is quite reliable in producing these plants.

The slightly brackish marsh at Cedar Hall Wharf has a typical band of the giant cordgrass (*Spartina cynosuroides*) on the "levee" fronting the river, along with some scattered smooth cordgrass (*S. alterniflora*) and some dense eastern lilaeopsis (*Lilaeopsis chinensis*) in the wetter fringe and the American geramander (*Teucrium canadense*) on the drier side. Beyond the giant cordgrass, the substrate becomes much softer and a large mixture of plants occurs, including the swamp rose mallow (*Hibiscus moscheutos*), seashore mallow (*Kosteletskya virginica*), small spikerush (*Eleocharis parvula*), saltmarsh bulrush (*Scirpus robustus*), New England bulrush (*S. cylindricus*), narrow-leaf cattail, saltmarsh loosestrife (*Lythrum lineare*), broad-leaf arrowhead (*Sagittaria latifolia*), scythe-fruited arrowhead, annual saltmarsh fleabane (*Pluchea purpurascens*), water pimpernel (*Samolus parviflorus*), mock bishop's-weed, and common three-square (*Scirpus pungens*) (Figure 47). Although I subsequently expressed some doubt because I was unable to find it flowering, I reported the possibility of the mudwort occurring mixed with the eastern lilaeopsis at this site in 1986 and 1987. This site may also be too brackish for the mudwort. The New England bulrush and the mudwort are considered State rare and highly State rare and endangered, respectively, by the Maryland Department of Natural Resources.

There are also a number of noteworthy old millponds in the Pocomoke drainage that deserve mention. Two of these, Willards Pond (Newhope Pond) and Powellville Pond (Atkins Pond), were mentioned by Smith in his 1938 study of four drained millponds on the Eastern Shore (63). Smith reported the bald cypress from both Willards and Powellville Ponds, as well as many plants typical of the Pocomoke Swamp, including the horse sugar or sweetleaf and Pursh's amphicarpum (*Amphicarpum purshii*). Shreve and his coauthors (5) also mentioned Willards Pond, citing the presence of a pure stand of bald cypress. Although Powellville Pond still exists, Willards Pond has apparently been destroyed. They referred to this millpond as Newhope Pond and indicated that it was near Willards and crossed by the Baltimore, Chesapeake and Atlantic Railway. Wilbur Rittenhouse and I found what we considered to be the site of Willards Pond on October 2, 1993. Much of the site has been cleared but one area below the old railroad embankment still supported 80-90 foot tall bald cypress trees with buttressed bases, as well as red maple, sweet gum and black gum. The soils were substantially oxidized

Figure 47. A common brackish tidal plant, the saltmarsh mallow (*Kosteletskya virginica*). (Photo by the author)

around the bald cypress and extremely dry. Plants such as the japanese honeysuckle, pokeweed (*Phytolacca americana*) and blackberry (*Rubus* sp.) were invading the low, dry peat. Some sweetleaf was nearby.

Another interesting drained millpond is near Wango, an account for which is given later. I have also explored a small drained millpond near Porter's Crossing. Drained millponds are some of the best sites to find rare, threatened, and endangered plant species. This no doubt relates to the fact that drained ponds represent secondary successional settings -- settings conducive to invasion by a number of shade intolerant species that are not present, or present in less numbers, under forest canopies.

Phytogeographic Considerations[4]

Dr. John K. Small may have been the first botanist to discuss the interesting phytogeographic aspects of the Pocomoke Swamp, although he did not mention the swamp by name. In 1920, he and Edgar T. Wherry, George K. Small, and John W. Small made a short reconnaissance on the Delmarva Peninsula from the northern end of Delaware to Cape Charles. In 1929 in his "Peninsula Delmarva" he discussed this trip indicating that:

> "Floristic phenomena are abundant in Delmarva. However, in that land of intermediate position between the North and the South, the plentiful thickets of the evergreen calico-bush (*Kalmia latifolia*), on the one hand, reminded one of mountains, while, on the other, the cypress-swamps occupied by the deciduous-leaved *Taxodium distichum*, were much more reminiscent of Florida." (74)

Small considered the Delmarva to be the "...frontier or near frontier, so to speak, for some typically southern species of flowering plants." He considered eleven southern species, including the bald cypress, Spanish moss (*Tillandsia usneoides*) and Canby's bulrush (*Scirpus etuberculatus*), to occur no further north than the Delmarva. He also listed twenty-one southern species with their northern limits in New Jersey, such as the red-berried greenbrier, fringed yelloweyed-grass (*Xyris fimbriata*), and Canby's lobelia (*Lobelia canbyi*). Today, one can visit the Pocomoke Swamp and readily see the stately bald cypress and find some of the largest mountain laurel (calico-bush) one could expect to find anywhere, especially at and near the upland edge of the swamp.

The southern affinity of the bald cypress and a number of other species, such as redbay, sweetleaf, water oak (*Quercus nigra*), cross-vine

---

4Zoogeographic considerations for the lower Delmarva have been addressed by David Lee (111), particularly in reference to the star-nosed mole (*Condylura cristata*). Lee also mentioned a number of other lower Delmarva Pleistocene relicts, such as the narrow-mouthed toad (*Gastrophryne carolinensis*) and red-bellied water snake (*Nerodia e. erythrogaster*).

(*Bignonia capreolata*) and laurel-leaf greenbrier has been acknowledged by others, specifically in relation to the Pocomoke Swamp (112,113). The same can be said of a number of other plant species, including, the red-berried greenbrier, resurrection fern (*Polypodium polypodioides*) and swamp tupelo. The Pocomoke represents, in fact, an extension of the deep swamps of the South. And going back in geologic time and under the then different climatic conditions, the bald cypress was much more abundant in the area. Huge fossil stumps having been reported, for example, from the Washington, Baltimore, and Philadelphia areas (14,114). In this regard, a photograph of now destroyed ancient (estimated to be 35,000 years old) cypress stumps exposed in northeastern Anne Arundel County, Maryland, appeared on the cover of the January/June, 1992 issue of *The Maryland Naturalist*. And on March 25, 1997 *The Sun* reported on the unearthing of huge bald cypress stumps during excavations for the new NFL football stadium in Baltimore. For years there has been an issue as to whether the few bald cypress trees reported from Cape May County, New Jersey and around Newark, New Jersey were natural occurrences. In 1965, however, John M. Bernard concluded the Cape May trees were originally planted and that the Newark site probably no longer existed and therefore that "...there is no evidence at the present time that the bald cypress is a part of the native New Jersey flora." Thus, the Delmarva Peninsula populations are probably the northernmost extant natural bald cypress trees.

In their study of the Pocomoke Swamp, Beaven (6) and Beaven and Oosting (7) addressed in detail the phytogeographic relationships of the Pocomoke Swamp, pointing out its southern affinity. Based upon their survey, 159 species (57% of the flora) are wide ranging species occurring from Canada to Florida, 111 species (40%) range largely southward of the Pocomoke, and only 9 species (3.2%) range largely northward. Of the 9 northern species, 7 are near their southern limit; of the 111 southern species, 40 are near their northern limit. Southern species from the Pocomoke listed by these authors include such plants as the crossvine, red-berried greenbrier, and dwarf trillium. They also pointed out that most species found in the Pocomoke Swamp are likewise found in the Great Dismal Swamp in southeastern Virginia, and that many also occur in the Okefenokee Swamp

(Georgia-Florida). They indicated that the dominant trees, abundant associates, and understory plants are essentially identical to the Great Dismal Swamp, but mentioned the absence of the giant cane (*Arundinaria gigantea*) and the presence of fewer evergreen shrubs in the Pocomoke. Robert R. Tatnall (37) also addressed the southern affinity of a number of Delmarva species, some of which occur on the Pocomoke. He specifically pointed out, for example, that the sweetleaf does not occur north of lower Sussex County, Delaware and that the cross-vine has not been found north of Worcester County, Maryland, citing the northern-most site near Snow Hill.

Interestingly, the Smithsonian Institution report, *Natural Areas of the Chesapeake Bay Region: Ecological Priorities* (99,100) lists the Spanish moss for the Pocomoke Swamp, although the Maryland Natural Heritage Program considers it extirpated from the State. In this regard, E. Spencer Wise (116) in "Early Records of *Tillandsia usneoides* L. on the Eastern Shore of Virginia" mentioned two historical accounts of the Spanish moss occurring abundantly on the Delmarva Peninsula extending into present day Maryland. In fact, the Spanish moss was the first flowering plant to be described from Maryland (by the English naturalist, John Ray in 1688) (48,49,50). And in a May 21, 1807 letter from Drummond Town, Virginia (now Accomack, Virginia) addressed to his mentor, Benjamin Smith Barton of Philadelphia, Peter Custis mentioned range extension notes on Spanish moss, indicating that it may grow as far north as Maryland (117). Wise (116) claimed, however, that its current northernmost limit is the Cape Henry area of the City of Virginia Beach and Tatnall (37) considered it limited on the Delmarva to the southern half of Northampton County, Virginia. Meanley (44) cited its presence on the lower Delmarva at Eastville, Virginia. This leads one to ponder whether the Spanish moss occurred historically in the lower Pocomoke Swamp. It certainly would fit in well!

Rare, Threatened, and Endangered Plants and Animals

I knew the Pocomoke's wetlands and surrounding uplands were unique in many ways, particularly phytogeographically, but it was not until a trip there on July 8, 1983 that the Pocomoke area's abundance of rare,

242

threatened, and endangered plant species became so evident to me. On this trip, my oldest son Mike and I met Wayne Klockner, Frank Hirst, Johnny Warren, and Joe Fehrer at Wango off the Nassawango River in Wicomico County, Maryland to advise The Nature Conservancy on how to deal with a common reed (*Phragmites australis*) problem along a transmission line right-of-way that crossed a botanically interesting wetland area supporting a number of rare vascular plants, such as the pitcher plant (*Sarracenia purpurea*), pink bog-button (*Sclerolepis uniflora*), tall swamp panicgrass (*Panicum scabriusculum*), and the spatulate-leaf sundew (*Drosera intermedia*).[5] After walking the site, we concluded that it would be best to just periodically mow the reedgrass, as opposed to applying herbicides, to keep it from migrating into boggy areas. We also found Florida yellow flax (*Linum floridanum*), tubercled spikerush (*Eleocharis tuberculosa*), and Canby's bulrush, the latter, according to Frank Hirst, being found only at a couple sites for Delmarva Peninsula.[6]

Next we ventured down a small dirt road to an old mill pond that was substantially filled with vegetation, including many shrubs and trees, such as smooth alder (*Alnus serrulata*) and red maple, that we assumed would eventually choke out the more desirable bog vegetation. The area was filled with rare plants, such as the pitcher plant, round-leaf sundew (*Drosera rotundifolia*, currently a watchlist species), spatulate-leaf sundew, pink bog-button, and tall swamp panic-grass, as well as other more common species. This was a great site, especially one large, two to three acre, open boggy area toward the back of the pond. There were also interesting plants downstream, albeit substantial invasion by woody plants, an undesirable outcome vegetatively, was nearly complete. We located the knotted spikerush

---

[5]The pitcher plant is currently considered State rare and threatened; the pink bog-button and tall swamp panicum, highly State rare and endangered; the spatulate sundew is no longer on the State list.

[6]This and the example below are good examples of how rights-of-way across certain type soils can result in the development of quite diverse herbaceous plant communities, many of which support rare vascular plants. Appropriate maintenance of such rights-of-way, however, to control woody plant invasion is imperative for the continued existence of these rare plants. (See Chapter Eight for some additional rare plant sites along rights-of-way.)

243

(*Eleocharis equisetoides*) and vegetative growth of the purple bladderwort (*Utricularia purpurea*). Because of the rare plants, the group was very concerned about walking in bog and we tried to walk single file through it. A management decision was made to go into the bog during the winter to cut out the invading shrubs and trees in the open area and to let the remainder of the site, with a few local exceptions supporting knotted spikerush, further succeed to forest. The entire pond could have been flooded for vegetative control, but it was felt that this might destroy the rare species. This threat from invading woody plants was subsequently studied by Kristen C. Gounaris and Irwind Forseth, who reported in 1998 that winter removal of invasive trees and shrubs was an effective method for maintaining biodiversity in the bog area (118).

After leaving The Nature Conservancy site, Wayne took Mike and me to see a neat transmission line right-of-way area along Mt. Olive Church Road, about two miles northwest of Colbourne. Here we saw the rare and beautiful red milkweed (*Asclepias rubra*), another new species for me and the only recorded locality for it in Maryland. Two orchids, the grass-pink (*Calopogon pulchellus*) and crested yellow orchid (*Platanthera cristata*), were also located. Tall nutrush (*Scleria triglomerata*) was found nearby.

Many of the plants found on this trip were not only new to me; they were also rare plants. At the time at least, the Maryland Natural Heritage Program considered the Florida yellow flax to be no longer extant in the State; tall swamp panicgrass, pink bog-button, Canby's bulrush, knotted spikerush, red milkweed, and grass-pink to be highly State rare and endangered; the pitcher plant, purple bladderwort, and crested yellow orchid to be State rare (or highly State rare) and threatened; the tall nutrush to be State rare/highly State rare; and the round-leaf sundew and resurrection fern to be watchlist species. In addition, Frank Hirst has indicated that another watchlist species, the rose pogonia (*Pogonia ophioglossoides*), was also quite abundant at the mill pond.

This was really an interesting trip botanically. The impressive list of rare, threatened, and endangered plants speaks for itself. And an even more thorough list of rare, threatened, and endangered vascular plants in the Nas-

244

TABLE V
RARE, THREATENED AND ENDANGERED SPECIES
OF THE NASSAWANGO WATERSHED[1]

Scientific Name	Common Name	State Rank[2]
Animals		
Gastrophryne carolinensis	eastern narrow-mouthed toad	E
Incisalia irus	frosted elfin	E
Limnothlypis swainsonii	Swainson's warbler	E
Pituophis m. melanoleucus	northern pine snake	SH
Podilymbus podiceps	pied-billed grebe	S2
Rana virgatipes	carpenter frog	I
Satyrium kingi	King's hairstreak	T
Plants		
Agalinis setacea	thread-leaved gerardia	E
Aristida lanosa	woolly three-awn	E
Aristida virgata	wire grass	E
Asclepias rubra	red milkweed	E
Azolla caroliniana	mosquito fern	S1
Boltonia asteroides	aster-like boltonia	E
Calopogon tuberosus	grass-pink	E
Cardamine longii	Long's bittercress	E
Carex barrattii	Barratt's sedge	T
Carex joorii	cyperus-swamp sedge	T
Carex glaucescens	southern waxy sedge	E
Carex venusta	dark green sedge	E
Centrosema virginianum	spurred butterfly-pea	S2
Crotalaria rotundifolia	rabbit-bells	E
Cyperus retrofractus	rough cyperus	S2
Desmodium laevigatum	smooth tick-trefoil	E
Desmodium lineatum	linear-leaved tick-trefoil	E
Desmodium rigidum	rigid tick-trefoil	E
Desmodium strictum	stiff tick-trefoil	E
Elatine americana	American waterwort	E
Eleocharis equisetoides	knotted spikerush	E
Eleocharis tortilis	twisted spikerush	S2
Elephantopus tomentosus	tabaccoweed	X

245

Eragrostis refracta	meadow lovegrass	T
Erianthus contortus	bent-awn plumegrass	E
Eriocaulon compressum	flattened pipewort	S1
Eriocaulon parkeri	Parker's pipewort	T
Eupatorium leucolepis	white-bracted boneset	E
Fuirena pumila	smooth fuirena	E
Galactia volubilis	downy milk pea	E
Gymnopogon brevifolius	broad-leaved beardgrass	E
Helianthemum bicknellii	hoary frostweed	X
Hypericum denticulatum	coppery St. John's-wort	E
Hypericum gymnanthum	clasping-leaved St. John's-wort	X
Iris prismatica	slender blue flag	E
Iris verna	dwarf iris	E
Leptoloma cognatum	fall witchgrass	E
Lespedeza stuevei	downy bush clover	E
Linum floridanium	Florida yellow flax	X
Linum intercursum	sandplain flax	E
Lobelia canbyi	Canby's lobelia	E
Ludwigia hirtella	hairy ludwigia	E
Lupinus perennis	wild lupine	T
Lygodium palmatum	climbing fern	T
Mecardonia acuminata	erect water-hyssop	E
Micranthemum micranthemoides	Nuttall's micranthemum	X
Nymphoides cordata	floating-heart	E
Oldenlandia uniflora	clustered bluets	S2
Panicum commonsianum	Common's panicgrass	S2
Panicum oligosanthes	few-flowered panicgrass	E
Panicum scabriusculum	tall swamp panicgrass	E
Polygala cruciata	cross-leaved milkwort	T
Polygonum robustius	stout smartweed	X
Potamogeton pusillus	slender pondweed	S1
Prenanthes autumnalis	slender rattlesnake-root	E
Pycnanthemum setosum	awned mountain-mint	T
Rhynchosia tomentosa	rhynchosia	E
Rhynchospora inundata	drowned hornedrush	E
Rhynchospora microcephala	tiny-headed beakrush	X
Rhynchospora rariflora	few-flowered beakrush	X
Rhynchospora scirpoides	long-beaked baldrush	T
Rhynchospora torreyana	Torrey's beakrush	E
Sacciolepis striata	sacciolepis	E

246

Sagittaria engelmanniana	Engelmann's arrowhead	T
Sarracenia purpurea	northern pitcher-plant	T
Scirpus etuberculatus	Canby's bulrush	E
Scleria minor	slender nutrush	E
Scleria nitida	shining nutrush	E
Scleria reticularis	reticulated nutrush	S2
Scleria triglomerata	tall nutrush	S1/S2
Sclerolepis uniflora	pink bog-button	E
Sisyrinchium arenicola	sand blue-eyed-grass	X
Smilax pseudochina	halberd-leaf greenbrier	E
Solidago speciosa	showy goldenrod	E
Spiranthes odorata	sweet-scented lady's-tresses	X
Sporobolus clandestinus	rough rushgrass	E
Symplocos tinctoria	sweetleaf	S2
Thelypteris simulata	bog fern	T
Triadenum tubulosum	large marsh St. John's-wort	S1
Trichostema setaceum	narrow-leaf bluecurls	S1
Trillium pusillum virginianum	dwarf trillium	T
Triglochin striatum	three-ribbed arrow-grass	E
Utricularia fibrosa	fibrous bladderwort	E
Utricularia inflata	swollen bladderwort	E
Utricularia purpurea	purple bladderwort	T
Wolffia punctata	dotted water-meal	S2
Xyris fimbriata	fringed yelloweyed-grass	E
Xyris smalliana	Small's yelloweyed-grass	E

Footnotes for Table V.
[1] Source: Maryland Field Office, The Nature Conservancy (May 8, 1992).
This list does not include watchlist species, such as the rose pogonia (*Pogonia ophioglossoides*), papillose nutrush (*Scleria pauciflora*), seaside alder (*Alnus maritima*), and red-berried greenbrier (*Smilax walteri*), which are also in the watershed..
[2] See Table I in Chapter Two for an explanation of the Ranks/Statuses, which are determined by the Maryland Department of Natural Resources.

sawango watershed is presented in Table V based upon data from The Nature Conservancy. A total of eighty-eight plant species are listed, including fifty endangered, ten endangered-extirpated, fourteen threatened, ten State rare, and four highly State rare species. This is an impressive list. It also includes two birds (the Swainson's warbler and pied-billed grebe), two amphibians (the carpenter frog and the eastern narrow-mouthed toad), one reptile (the northern pine snake), and two insects (the frosted elfin and King's hairstreak).

247

Even more incredible, the Maryland Department of Natural Resources lists (Table VI) a total if 114 current and historical rare, threatened, and endangered vascular plant species for the entire Pocomoke watershed in Maryland (the Nassawango watershed, of course, is within the larger Pocomoke watershed). Of these, sixty-seven plant species are listed as endangered, eleven as endangered-extirpated, seventeen as threatened, eleven as State rare, and seven as highly State rare. In addition, twenty animals are listed, including eleven birds (e.g., the bald eagle and pied-billed grebe), two amphibians (e.g., the carpenter frog), one reptile (the northern pine snake), one fish (the spotfin killifish), and four insects (e.g., the frosted elfin and palamedes swallowtail).

As indicated in the preface, the status of what is considered rare, threatened, or endangered by State Natural Heritage Programs and individuals collecting distributional data may change due to new knowledge that results from herbaria research and particularly new field investigations. Not uncommonly, no sooner is a rarity status published then additional data surfaces, such as a new county or state record, or another study concludes differently. A good example of this can be found in Reveal and Broome (93) for Long's bittercress. The authors concluded that: "It is probable that the species is now extirpated from Maryland." Yet the following year, Reveal and Broome (94) modified their statement to: "*Cardamine longii* Fernald, Long's bitter-cress, has not been found in Maryland since the type was gathered in 1941." Actually, it was found on the Nassawango Creek on July 31, 1982 by Frank Hirst and Jim Stasz (83) and is listed as endangered for both the Nassawango and the Pocomoke watersheds (see Tables V and VI). And on July 13, 1990, I observed this bittercress along Nassawango Creek while on a canoe trip with a group of students. I give this example simply to demonstrate a point -- that such lists are dynamic due to new knowledge that results from herbarium research and particularly new field investigations. In fact, the Nassawango and Pocomoke watershed lists in Tables V and VI, perhaps any lists produced for that matter, are potentially subject to challenge. They simply represent the data as it is currently entered into existing databases. For the latest official rarity status of the species listed, one should always check with the appropriate State Natural Heritage Program. An expla-

TABLE VI
CURRENT AND HISTORICAL RARE, THREATENED, AND ENDANGERED SPECIES OF THE POCOMOKE WATERSHED, MARYLAND[3]

Scientific Name	Common Name	State Status[2]
Animals		
Ambystoma t. tigrinum	eastern tiger salamander	E
Botaurus lentiginosus	American bittern	I
Circus cyaneus	northern harrier	S2
Falco peregrinus[4]	peregrine falcon	E
Fundulus luciae	spotfin killifish	S2
Gastrophyrne carolinensis	eastern narrow-mouthed toad	E
Haliaeetus leucocephalus[3]	bald eagle	E
Incisalia irus	frosted elfin	E
Ixobrychus exilis	least bittern	I
Laterallus jamaicensis	black rail	I
Limnothlypis swainsonii	Swainson's warbler	E
Mitoura hesseli	Hessel's hairstreak	X
Papilio palamedes	palamedes swallowtail	SU
Pituophis m. melanoleucus	northern pine snake	SR
Podilymbus podiceps	pied-billed grebe	S2
Porzana carolina	sora	S1
Rana virgatipes	carpenter frog	I
Satyrium kingi	King's hairstreak	T
Sterna antillarum	least tern	T
Plants		
Aeschynomene virginica[3]	sensitive joint-vetch	E
Agalinis setacea	thread-leaved gerardia	E
Amelanchier obovalis	coastal juneberry	E
Aristida lanosa	woolly three-awn	E
Aristida virgata	wire grass	E
Asclepias rubra	red milkweed	E
Azolla caroliniana	mosquito fern	S1
Bidens coronata	tickseed sunflower	S2/S
Bidens discoidea	swamp beggar-ticks	S2/3
Bidens mitis	small-fruit begger-ticks	E
Boltonia asteroides	aster-like boltonia	E
Calopogon tuberosus	grass-pink	E
Cardamine longii	Long's bittercress	E

249

Carex barrattii	Barratt's sedge	T
Carex gigantea	giant sedge	E
Carex glaucescens	southern waxy sedge	E
Carex hyalinolepis	shoreline sedge	T
Carex joorii	cyperus-swamp sedge	T
Carex louisianica	Louisiana sedge	E
Carex venusta	dark green sedge	E
Carex vesicaria	inflated sedge	T
Centrosema virginianum	spurred butterfly-pea	S2
Crotalaria rotundifolia	rabbit-bells	E
Cyperus retrofractus	rough cyperus	S2
Desmodium laevigatum	smooth tick-trefoil	E
Desmodium lineatum	linear-leaved tick-trefoil	E
Desmodium rigidum	rigid tick-trefoil	E
Desmodium strictum	stiff tick-trefoil	E
Dryopteris celsa	log fern	T
Elatine americana	American waterwort	E
Eleocharis albida	white spikerush	E
Eleocharis equisetoides	knotted spikerush	E
Eleocharis tortilis	twisted spikerush	S2
Elephantopus tomentosus	tobaccoweed	X
Eragrostis refracta	meadow lovegrass	T
Erianthus contortus	bent-awn plumegrass	E
Eriocaulon compressum	flattened pipewort	S2
Eriocaulon parkeri	Parker's pipewort	T
Eupatorium leucolepis	white-bracted boneset	E
Fraxinus profunda	pumpkin ash	S2/3
Fuirena pumila	smooth fuirena	E
Galactia volubilis	downy milk pea	E
Gymnopogon brevifolius	broad-leaved beardgrass	E
Helianthemum bicknellii	hoary frostweed	X
Hottonia inflata	featherfoil	E
Hypericum denticulatum	coppery St. John's-wort	E
Hypericum gymnanthum	clasping-leaved St. John's-wort	E
Iris prismatica	slender blue flag	E
Iris verna	dwarf iris	E
Leersia hexandra	club-headed cutgrass	E
Leersia lenticularis	catchfly-grass	X
Leptoloma cognatum	fall witchgrass	E
Lespedeza stuevei	downy bushclover	E
Limonium nashii	Nash's sea lavender	SU
Linum floridanum	Florida yellow flax	X
Linum intercursum	sandplain flax	E

Lobelia canbyi	Canby's lobelia	E
Ludwigia glandulosa	cylindric-fruit seedbox	E
Ludwigia hirtella	hairy ludwigia	E
Lupinus perennis	wild lupine	T
Lygodium palmatum	climbing fern	T
Mecardonia acuminata	erect water-hyssop	E
Micranthemum micranthemoides	Nuttall's micranthemum	X
Myriophyllum humile	low water-milfoil	E
Nymphoides cordata	floating-heart	E
Oldenlandia uniflora	clustered bluets	S2
Oxydendrum arboreum	sourwood	E
Panicum commonsianum	Commons' panicgrass	S2
Panicum oligosanthes	few-flowered panicgrass	E
Panicum scabriusculum	tall swamp panicgrass	E
Persea borbonia	red bay	E
Polygala cruciata	cross-leaved milkwort	T
Polygonum robustius	stout smartweed	X
Potamogeton pusillus	slender pondweed	S1
Prenanthes autumnalis	slender rattlesnake-root	E
Pycnanthemum setosum	awned mountain-mint	T
Ranunculus flabellaris	yellow water-crowfoot	E
Rhynchosia tomentosa	rhynchosia	E
Rhynchospora filifolia	thread-leaved beakrush	E
Rhynchospora glomerata	clustered beakrush	E
Rhynchospora inundata	drowned hornedrush	E
Rhynchospora microcephala	tiny-headed beakrush	X
Rhynchospora pallida	pale beakrush	X
Rhynchospora rariflora	few-flowered beakrush	X
Rhynchospora scirpoides	long-beaked baldrush	T
Rhynchospora torreyana	Torrey's beakrush	E
Sacciolepis striata	sacciolepis	E
Sagittaria engelmanniana	Engelmann's arrowhead	T
Sarracenia purpurea	nothern pitcher plant	T
Scirpus etuberculatus	Canby's bulrush	E
Scleria minor	slender nutrush	E
Scleria nitida	shining nutrush	E
Scleria reticularis	reticulated nutrush	S2
Scleria triglomerata	tall nutrush	S1/2
Sclerolepis uniflora	pink bog-button	E
Sisyrinchium arenicola	sand blue-eyed-grass	X
Smilax pseudochina	halberd-leaf greenbrier	E
Solidago speciosa	showy goldenrod	E
Spiranthes odorata	sweet-scented lady's-tresses	X

251

Sporobolus clandestinus	rough rushgrass	E
Symplocos tinctoria	sweetleaf	S2
Tephrosia spicata	hoary pea	E
Thelypteris simulata	bog fern	T
Triadenum tubulosum	large marsh St. John's-wort	S1
Trichostema setaceum	narrow-leaf bluecurls	S1
Triglochin striatum	three-ribbed arrow-grass	E
Trillium pusillum virginianum	dwarf trillium	T
Utricularia fibrosa	fibrous bladderwort	E
Utricularia inflata	swollen bladderwort	E
Utricularia purpurea	purple bladderwort	T
Wolffia papulifera	water-meal	S2
Wolffia punctata	dotted water-meal	S2
Xyris fimbriata	fringed yelloweyed-grass	E
Xyris smalliana	Small's yelloweyed-grass	E

Footnotes for Table VI.

1 Source: Maryland Department of Natural Resources (Maryland Natural Heritage Program, October 16, 1992). The Pocomoke watershed for purposes of this Table is cataloging unit 02060009 (Hydrologic Unit Map of the United States, 1980), which includes all of Somerset County south of Dames Quarter, as well as the immediate Pocomoke watershed as otherwise defined in this Chapter. Thus, certain species, for example the sensitive joint-vetch and black rail, have not been historically reported, to my knowledge, in the immediate Pocomoke watershed. This list does not include Watchlist species, such as the rose pogonia (*Pogonia ophioglossoides*), papillose nutrush (*Scleria pauciflora*), seaside alder (*Anus maritima*), short-bristled hornedrush (*Rhynchospora corniculata*), and red-berried greenbrier (*Smilax walteri*). The little blue heron is also on the watchlist.

[2] See Table I in Chapter Two for an explanation of the Ranks/Statuses, which are determined by the Maryland Department of Natural Resources.

[3] This species is listed as threatened by the U.S. Fish and Wildlife Service.

[4] This species is listed as endangered by the U.S. Fish and Wildlife Service.

nation of the rarity status categories used by the States of Maryland and Delaware can be found in Tables I and II, respectively, in Chapter Two.

Another excellent example of how new State records can come about is what in my opinion is the utterly amazing 1990 discovery by Frank Hirst and Ron Wilson of the unique curly grass fern (*Schizaea pusilla*) in a small bog in a dense Atlantic white cedar swamp west of Milton, Delaware in Sussex County (Hirst, personal communication; 90). This well-known fern (at least in botanical circles) was thought to occur no further south than the New Jersey Pine Barrens until Hirst and Wilson's discovery. This is perhaps the botanical find of the 20th Century for the Mid-Atlantic Coastal Plain. A second good example is Canby's dropwort (*Oxypolis canbyi*), which until its discovery in a Delmarva pothole in Queen Anne's County, Maryland in 1982, had not been found on the Delmarva Peninsula since 1894 when it was collected by William Canby at Ellendale in Sussex County, Delaware (119). A third example is the catchfly grass (*Leersia lenticularis*), which was found by Joan Maloof on September 9, 1994 at Whiton Crossing, where it was last collected by A. V. Smith and R. R. Tatnall in 1938 -- fifty-six years earlier!

A number of other field workers have also addressed the rare, threatened, and endangered (or other uncommon) plants along the Pocomoke and its tributaries either indirectly through regional treatments or in reference to specific species. In their regional paper on the Atlantic white cedar, Dill, and his coauthors (23) listed sixteen plant taxa occurring on the Delmarva that are variously noted as rare or endangered on Maryland, Delaware, and Virginia lists. Six of these species, the redbay (*Persea borbonia* var. *palustris*), Parker's pipewort, flattened pipewort (*E. compressum*), slender blue flag (*Iris prismatica*), northern pitcher plant (*Sarracenia purpurea* spp. *purpurea*), and bog fern (*Thelypteris simulata*), occur in the Pocomoke watershed and are currently listed by the Maryland Natural Heritage Program as either rare, threatened, or endangered (Table VI). A seventh, the seaside alder (*Alnus maritima*) is a watchlist species. Reveal and Broome (93,94) listed a few other species that occur or potentially could occur in the Pocomoke drainage in addition to Long's watercress, namely the seaside alder (*Alnus maritima*), Nuttall's micranthemum, and yellow water-crowfoot (*Ranunculus flabellaris*); Riefner and Hill (95) cited the smooth orange milkweed, Pursh's amphicarpum (*Amphicarpum purshii*), and subulate arrowhead (*Sagittaria subulata*) to name a few. Reveal and Broome also indicated that the State threatened dwarf trillium was originally collected by George F. Beaven along Pilchard Creek near Pocomoke City.[7] Edgar T.

---

[7] This species was listed by Beaven (6) as *Trillium sessile*.

Wherry visited this site along with Robert R. Tatnall and George R. Proctor on May 4, 1947 and acknowledged this range extension in a note in *Bartonia* in 1949. This taxon, which is apparently much more abundant in southeastern Virginia (personal observations), is found at a limited number of stations in the Pocomoke drainage. Clyde F. Reed (85) and Donnell E. Redman (89) in their treatments of Maryland ferns and fern-allies, cited a few rare or otherwise uncommon ferns for the Pocomoke drainage, such as the resurrection fern, the log fern (*Dryopteris celsa*), and the bog fern (*Thelypteris simulata*). According to A. C. Skorepa and Arnold Norden (120), the Pocomoke Drainage also supports some rare lichens; they reported a recent collection of *Ramalina stenospora* on bald cypress in a mill pond and *Usnea trichodea* growing on bald cypress, both in Worcester County.

There is no doubt in my mind that field workers will continue to come up with more interesting botanical finds in the Pocomoke drainage, eventually resulting in some State rarity status changes, new county records, rediscoveries of plants now known only from historical records, and even some new State records. So, is anyone ready for some field work? If so, you may want to try some of the drained millponds and utility rights-of-way in the watershed, or perhaps venture into the expansive Hickory Point Swamp. However, even the openings associated with roadsides produce good finds. For example, on August 17, 1990 while botanizing in the Pocomoke area with Wilbur Rittenhouse, Lucretia Krantz, and some students, I located the highly State rare and endangered erect water-hyssop (*Mecardonia acuminata*) growing in a roadside ditch along Nassawango Road (Maryland Route 354) in Worcester County. At Whiton and Porters Crossings, look for the recently rediscovered endangered-extirpated catchfly grass (*Leersia lenticularis*), the giant sedge (*Carex gigantea*, highly State rare and endangered), cypress swamp sedge (*C. joorii*, State rare and threatened), the hop-like sedge (*C. lupuliformis*, a watchlist species), and a tree of somewhat limited distribution in Maryland, the swamp cottonwood (*Populus heterophylla*). Although it is probably not limited to those areas in Maryland, I have seen the swamp cottonwood only in the Pocomoke Swamp and the Zekiah Swamp (Charles County). Tidestrom (121) cited a specimen northeast of Pocomoke City and considered the species rare. Tatnall (37), however, suggested it was frequent

254

on the Coastal Plain. At the Hickory Point Swamp, look for the rare southern twayblade (*Listera australis*), the State endangered red-berried greenbrier, and the State threatened redbay; on July 19, 1986, I found red-berried greenbrier and redbay growing there along with the more common laurel-leaf greenbrier (*S. laurifolia*). On July 29, 1989, I also located the red-berried greenbrier along Nassawango Creek at Route 354. The uncommon seaside alder (*Alnus maritima*) can similarly be readily observed at this site at the interface of the swamp and the spatterdock stand. As opposed to other members of the genus that flower in the spring, the seaside alder flowers in the fall. This phenomena was first reported by William M. Canby in fall of 1863 (61). In upland open areas, watch for the highly State rare and threatened wild lupine (*Lupinus perennis*) or the beautiful, albeit not rare, butterfly pea (*Clitoria mariana*). Both species can be found in the Nassawango Creek Preserve; I have also seen the butterfly pea at the Shad Landing Unit of the Pocomoke River State Park.

Another good bet to botanize for rarities is the Pocomoke's fresh tidal marsh. Frank Hirst and I discussed this possibility back in 1993 and anticipated directing more attention to this portion of the Pocomoke, particularly the interesting Hickory Point Swamp and the fresh tidal marsh just west of it. I opined that the marsh in particular, as well as areas further up the river, would likely yield some rarities -- maybe even the sensitive joint-vetch, Nuttall's micranthemum, American waterwort, small waterwort, mat-forming water-hyssop, mudwort, pygmy-weed (*Crassula aquatica*), Parker's pipewort, Long's bittercress, and spongy lophotocarpus. Following up on this hunch, Gene Cooley, Janet McKegg, Doug Sampson, and I visited the tidal marsh below Hickory Point Swamp on October 8, 1993, looking principally for intertidal aquatic plants. As it turns out, we did not find any even though we examined much of the shoreline along the river, and I now suspect that the area does not support such species. Perhaps they occur further upstream or along some of the tributaries or tidal guts. However, we did find a number of interesting rare plants in the marsh that day, including the sacciolepis (*Sacciolepis striata*, a highly State rare and endangered species) and southern wild rice (*Zizaniopsis miliacea*), which was not on the State list at the time since, until our discovery, the Maryland Natural Heritage Program did not think it occurred in Maryland.[8] It is now listed as highly State rare and endangered. Both are great finds, particularly the latter. The sacciolepis was also found at the Hickory Point Swamp on August 28, 1993, as well as along the shoreline in Somerset County on October 22, 1993. And on August 24, 1994, Gene Cooley, Joan Maloof, Mat Cimino, and I found the sacciolepis growing robustly adjacent to the Shad Landing marina, twelve years after I first found it there in 1984 (see below).[9]

As I indicated earlier, some of the species mentioned in the preceding paragraph have either not been historically reported from the Pocomoke's fresh to slightly brackish tidal wetlands or have been reported but once or only a couple of times, which may be due to the Pocomoke's isolation and resultant paucity of field work. Interestingly, in discussing this with Dr. Alfred E. Schuyler in 1993, it became apparent that the possibility of some interesting aquatics having been overlooked along the lower Pocomoke had already passed his mind. Although Tatnall (37) listed some of these species for the Delmarva, there is no direct indication that they were collected from the fresh tidal marshes along the Pocomoke. Some rare species occurring in fresh tidal wetlands have been reported, however, for the Pocomoke River, particularly in more recent times. I previously mentioned that Frank Hirst and Jim Stasz (83) and I have independently found Long's bittercress on the Nassawango Creek, and that species and Parker's pipewort have also been reported for the Pocomoke watershed (Tables V and VI; Gene Cooley, personal observation in 1988). Gene Cooley also found the American waterwort along the Pocomoke River in 1988 (personal communication) and Gene, Joan Maloof, Mat Cimino, and I likewise found it on August 24, 1994, at Mataponi Landing. Long's watercress and American waterwort are both ranked as highly State rare and endangered by the State of Maryland; Parker's pipewort is considered State rare and threatened. On September 6, 1982, I located the

---

[8]The southern wild rice is listed for Maryland in *Gray's Manual of Botany* (122). This appears, however, to have been based upon a wild rice voucher specimen in the U.S. National Herbarium that was misidentified as southern wild rice, but was later correctly annotated by E.E. Terrel in 1983.

[9]For more discussion of fresh tidal marshes see chapter Two.

highly State rare and endangered sacciolepis in the intertidal zone at Shad Landing, which was a new State record for Maryland, and on June 19, 1984, I also found a quillwort on a small tidal stream in the swamp at Milborn Landing. Although this keyed out to the Tuckerman's quillwort (*Isoetes tuckermanii*), only one manual covering Maryland reports this species from the State (123), and Don Redman (personal communication) indicates that this species is restricted to limestone and glacial swamps in the north. Both *I. riparia* and *I. englemannii* are, however, on the State's watchlist. It is interesting to note that a new species of quillwort (*I. hyemalis*) was recently described (124) from southeastern United States (Virginia, South Carolina, and North Carolina), primarily from the Coastal Plain with a few populations in the Piedmont. The authors indicate that *I. hyemalis* herbarium specimens have been previously identified as *I. riparia* and *I. engelmannii*, among others, particularly the latter. They also mention a partial resemblance of the megaspores of *I. hyemalis* to those of the Tuckerman's quillwort. Unfortunately, I did not collect a specimen that could be compared with their published description of the new quillwort.

My library research has turned up substantial information on the birdlife along the Pocomoke and some interesting and useful information on its reptiles, amphibians, and fish. However, little information has surfaced on insects; nor did I concentrate on that group. Most of the information is on rare, threatened, and endangered animals and other uncommon or interesting species.

In his "Aquatic Zoogeography of Maryland," Dave Lee (125) included forty-one native and ten introduced fish species for the Pocomoke River based upon a list of Maryland fish published in *Chesapeake Science* (126). One of these, the spotted killifish (*Fundulus luciae*) is considered State rare by the Maryland Department of Natural Resources. This species was also listed by Lee and his coauthors (127) as a species of special concern that inhabits brackish waters. In 1994, a doctoral dissertation was produced on the fishes of the Delmarva Peninsula by S. P. McIninch (128). He lists 35 fish species from the Pocomoke River Watershed (Table VII) and indicates that little historical information on freshwater species exists for the drainage.

257

TABLE VII
FRESHWATER FISHES OF THE
POCOMOKE RIVER WATERSHED[1]

Scientific Name	Common Name
Lampetra aepyptera[3]	least book lamprey
Anguilla rostrata	American eel
Alosa aestivalis	blueback herring
A. pseudoharengus	alewife
Dorosoma cepedianum	gizzard shad
Cyprinella analostana[3]	satinfin shiner
Cyprinus carpio[2]	common carp
Notemigonus chrysoleucas	golden shiner
Notropis procne	swallowtail shiner
Erimyzon oblongus	creek chubsucker
Ameiurus catus	white catfish
A. natalis	yellow catfish
A. nebulosus	brown bullhead
Noturus gyrinus	tadpole madtom
N. insignis[3]	margined madtom
Esox a. americanus	redfin pickerel
E. niger	chain pickerel
Umbra pygmaea	eastern mudminnow
Aphredoderus sayanus	pirate perch
Fundulus diaphanus	banded killifish
F. heteroclitus	mummichog
Gambusia holbrooki	eastern mosquitofish
Morone americana	white perch
M. saxatilis	striped bass
Acantharchus pomotis[4]	mud sunfish
Enneacanthus gloriosus	bluespotted sunfish
E. obesus	banded sunfish
Lepomis auritus	redbreast sunfish
L. gibbosus	pumpkinseed
L. macrochirus[2]	bluegill
Micropterus salmoides[2]	largemouth bass
Pomoxis nigromaculatus[2]	black crappie
Etheostoma fusiforme	swamp darter
E. olmstedi	tessellated darter
Perca flavescens	yellow perch

Footnotes for Table VII.

Three of these have been considered relict, but McIninch considers them semi-relict on the Pocomoke since other Coastal Plain populations exist (Steve McIninch, personal communication). One species, the mud sunfish (*Acantharchus pomotis*), is considered State rare by the Maryland Department of Natural Resources. Mansueti (8) in his "Brief Natural History of the Pocomoke River, Maryland" also addressed the Pocomoke's fish, listing a number of species and giving some 1950 landing values for licensed commercial fishermen.

Three insects, all butterflies, are listed on the rare, threatened, and endangered species list for the Pocomoke watershed by the Maryland Department of Natural Resources: the frosted elfin (*Incisalia irus*), Hessel's hairstreak (*Mitoura hesseli*), and King's hairstreak (*Satyrium kingi*). A fourth, the palamedes swallowtail (*Papilio palamedes*) is considered possibly rare (Table VI). In reference to the palamedes butterfly, John H. Fales (130) indicated that a weak colony has been found in recent years on the lower Eastern Shore near Big Cypress Swamp, Worcester County. He considered it of special concern and in need of monitoring. This site is probably the Hickory Point Swamp, since Dennis (15) reported seeing a palamedes butterfly there and pointed out that the swamp contains the northernmost known breeding colony. Jim McCann of the Maryland Natural Heritage Program indicated to me in 1998 that he had noted the palamedes at Hickory Point Swamp sometime in the late 1990s.

TABLE VIII
REPTILES AND AMPHIBIANS IN THE POCOMOKE WATERSHED[1]

Scientific Name	Common Name
Ambystoma opacum	marbled salamander
Ambystoma t. tigrinum	eastern tiger salamander
Hemidactylium scutatum	four-toed salamander
Plethodon c. cinereus	red-backed salamander
Pseudotriton m. montanus	eastern mud salamander
Scaphiopus holbrooki	eastern spadefoot toad
Bufo a. americanus	American toad
Bufo woodhousei fowleri	Fowler's toad
Acris c. crepitans	northern cricket frog
Hyla cinerea	green treefrog
Hyla chrysoscelis	southern gray treefrog
Hyla versicolor	gray treefrog
Pseudacris c. crucifer	spring peeper
Pseudacris triseriata kalmi	New Jersey chorus frog
Gastrophryne carolinensis	eastern narrow-mouthed toad
Rana catesbeiana	bullfrog
Rana virgatipes	carpenter frog
Rana clamitans melanota	green frog
Rana utricularia	southern leopard frog
Rana palustris	pickerel frog
Rana s. sylvatica	wood frog
Sceloporus undulatus hyacinthinus	northern fence swift
Leiolopisma laterale	ground skink
Eumeces faciatus	five-lined skink
Eumeces laticeps	broadhead skink
Carphophis a. amoenus	eastern worm snake
Diadophis punctatus edwardsi	ringneck snake[2]
Heterodon platyrhinos	eastern hognose snake
Opheodrys aestivus	rough green snake
Coluber c. constrictor	northern black racer
Elaphe o. obsoleta	black rat snake
Pituophis m. melanoleucus	northern pine snake[3]
Lampropeltis g. getulus	eastern kingsnake
Lampropeltis t. triangulum/elapsoides	"Coastal Plain" milk snake[4]
Nerodia e. erythrogaster	red-bellied water snake
Nerodia s. sipedon	northern water snake
Storeria d. dekayi	northern brown snake
Storeria o. occipitomaculata	northern red-bellied snake

Virginia v. valeriae	eastern earth snake
Thamnophis s. sauritus	eastern ribbon snake
Thamnophis s. sirtalis	eastern garter snake
Agkistrodon c. contortrix mokasen	copperhead[5]
Sternotherus odoratus	stinkpot
Kinosternon s. subrubrum	eastern mud turtle
Chelydra s. serpentina	common snapping turtle
Clemmys guttata	spotted turtle
Terrapene c. carolina	eastern box turtle
Malaclemys t. terrapin	northern diamondback terrapin
Chrysemys p. picta	eastern painted turtle
Chrysemys rubriventris	red-bellied turtle

Footnotes for Table VIII.

1 Source: Harris (130) and Conant and Collins (131). Common and scientific names follow Conant and Collins (131).

[2] Ringneck Snakes from this area represent intergrades between northern and southern subspecies (130).

[3] Presence of Pine Snake in this area requires confirmation.

[4] The distinctive milk snakes from this area are considered to be intergrades between the eastern milk snake and the scarlet kingsnake (130,131). However, Grogan and Forester (132) suggest that the mid-Atlantic Coastal Plain milk snake population should be recognized as the subspecies *Lampropeltis t. temporalis*, since true intergradation of *L t. elapsoides* with *L. t. triangulum* may occur only at the extreme northern and western portions of the form's range along the Fall Line.

[5] Copperheads from this area represent intergrades between northern and southern subspecies (131).

According to *Distributional Survey (Amphibia/Reptilia): Maryland and the District of Columbia* (131), five species of salamanders (e.g., the marbled salamander, *Ambystoma opacum,* and the four-toed salamander, *Hemidactylium scutatum*), fifteen species of frogs and toads (e.g., the carpenter frog, *Rana virgatipes,* and the eastern narrow-mouthed toad, *Gastrophryne carolinensis*), four species of lizards (e.g., the ground skink, *Leiolopisma laterale,* and the broadheaded skink, *Eumeces laticeps*), fifteen species of snakes (e.g., the red-bellied water snake, *Nerodia e. erythrogaster,* and the northern pine snake, *Pituophis m. melanoleucus*), and ten species of turtles (e.g., the eastern mud turtle, *Kinosternon s. subrubrum,* and the spotted turtle, *Clemmys guttata*) occur in the Pocomoke watershed (Table

VIII). Some of these are rarities (Tables V and VI). According to Robert H. McCauley (134), the red-bellied water snake is known in Maryland by herpetologists only from two localities along the Pocomoke River, but he suggested that it occurs elsewhere on the Eastern Shore and possibly in Southern Maryland. McCauley pointed out that in Worcester County people frequently refer to the "copper-bellied moccasin" and in Wicomico County to "copper-bellies," implying that they may be referring to the red-bellied water snake. McCauley further indicated that: "Undoubtedly it occurs along the entire length of the Pocomoke River, but may be difficult to collect because of the thick, nearly impenetrable cypress swamps which border it." In a December 17, 1994 letter to me, Brooke Meanley indicated that he collected a red-bellied water snake along the Pocomoke on April 2, 1950. In his distributional survey, Harris (131) included it only for the Pocomoke and Dorchester County. However, the red-bellied water snake is not considered rare, threatened, or endangered by the State of Maryland. The copperhead (*Agkistrodon contortrix mokasen*) was reported from the Pocomoke drainage by Harris, apparently based upon a McCauley record for Snow Hill. In the early 1970s, I was told of a copperhead find on State property along the Pocomoke by a State forester. Another rare snake, the scarlet snake (*Cemophora coccinea*), which is a State watchlist species, was found at Shad Landing State Park by Mark Mengele, a park ranger, in 1975, which was a new Worcester County record (135). Prior to this sighting, the scarlet snake was reported southeast of the Choptank River only from one Wicomico County site (131). A second scarlet snake was found in the Pocomoke drainage by Michael J. Geiger on May 25, 1991 at Millville off Old Stagecoach Road north of Maryland Route 12 (136).

In my own travels around the area, I have encountered some of these species. For example, as reported in my *Journal*, my first encounter with a four-toed salamander occurred on September 6, 1982 at Shad Landing. At the time, my son Mike and I were rambling through the area in search of reptiles and amphibians. We had caught some musk turtles (*Sternotherus odoratus*) along Corkers Creek Canal and were searching for ringneck snakes (*Diadophis punctatus edwardsi*) and pine swifts (*Sceloporus undulatus hyacinthinus*) under loose bark and under logs. We located some four-toed

262

salamanders in a hilly area behind section "B" where they occurred under moist logs and bark. They made very little movement and were frequently coiled like a snake. All three diagnostic characteristics -- a white belly with black specks, the tail/body constriction, and four toes on the hind feet -- were quite evident. The tail also was slightly orange colored.

The four-toed salamander was a pretty good find. Herbert S. Harris in *Distributional Survey (Amphibia/Reptilia): Maryland and the District of Columbia* (131) shows two collections for it along the Pocomoke, and one was discovered in 1986 near the junction of Twilley Bridge Road and Fooks Road (Pocomoke drainage), which was only the second Wicomico County record for it (136). The upland habitat Mike and I found it in is apparently either not typical of the species or just not typically acknowledged. According to Conant (137), it is usually associated with sphagnum moss, especially in areas adjacent to woods and in boggy woodland ponds. However, Conant does indicate that it is terrestrial as an adult like woodland salamanders. Harris (131) also indicates that it occurs in association with sphagnum where the females deposit eggs usually during March. There is substantial sphagnum in the adjacent Pocomoke Swamp.

While on a second trip to Shad Landing on August 13-17, 1982, Mike and I located a number of reptiles and amphibians, including a northern dusky salamander (*Desmognathus f. fuscus*). Based upon Harris (131), the northern dusky salamander is a new county record, since the nearest station he gave for it is in Wicomico County near the Nanticoke River.

Dare I mention further at this point the northern pine snake? Why not! As John E. Cooper asked in his 1970 paper (138), after driving home his position in reference to the debate over the Maryland distribution (or lack thereof in his view, and the view of most Maryland herpetologists) of the pine-woods treefrog: "...*Pituophis m. melanoleucus* anyone?" In other words, after having dispensed with the pine-woods tree frog argument, Cooper was asking if anyone wanted to debate the distribution of the northern pine snake. Herpetologists seem to have good debates on distributions! And many, perhaps rightfully so, are what I call doubters when it comes to new discoveries and distributions that run contrary to existing data and experience. I will address this issue below as it relates to the Delmarva.

263

I only have a few examples to discuss and I will start with the northern pine snake. According to H. A. Kelly, A. W. Davis, and H. C. Robertson (139) in *Snakes of Maryland*: "The pine snake appears only in the pine and sandy regions of our Eastern Shore..." They cited a specimen reported by Dr. R. V. Truitt that was collected in Worcester County and one taken near Centreville in Queen Anne's County in 1930. Robert H. McCauley (134) in his *Reptiles of Maryland and the District of Columbia* also referenced the Centreville specimen, stating that he saw the specimen and that the record might be correct but he did not accept it because it was not collected by Dr. Kelly or Mr. Robertson. McCauley likewise addressed the Truitt reference indicating that Truitt informed him that: "This snake was taken in rather dense growth of pine, approximately twenty-five years of age...about one-half of a mile from the Pocomoke River and about three-fourths of a mile from Snow Hill, Maryland." In reference to yet another report on a pine snake, in 1936 near Ocean City (Isle of Wight), Maryland, McCauley noted that Walter Connell, an entomologist, had identified this specimen as a pine snake by comparing it with a photograph illustration in a natural history book. In McCauley's opinion, there was no reason to doubt Connell's identification, and except for the lack of a specimen, the record was deemed sound. However, in a series of errata to *Snakes of Maryland* published in the *Bulletin of the Maryland Herpetological Society* in 1966 (138), John E. Cooper rejected the Queen Anne's County and Truitt specimens indicating that the northern pine snake, opining that it was probably not part of the State's fauna. Another reference to the northern pine snake is given by David S. Lee (141), who indicated that a Mr. Irving Hampe spotted what he thought was a pine snake swimming in Sinepuxent Bay in 1969.

As pointed out by William L. Grogan (142), whether or not the northern pine snake is indigenous to Maryland has been debated for some time. Grogan considered the above referenced specimens and others, including that of a Shad Landing State Park ranger, Wes Fortney, who informed Grogan that he had seen pine snakes in the vicinity of the park. He did not necessarily reject its presence in Maryland, nor did the Committee on Rare and Endangered Amphibians and Reptiles of Maryland, Maryland Herpetological

Society (143). In fact, in a letter to me in 1994, Grogan suggested that, based upon separate accounts from Kitt Hechscher and Mike Geiger in 1966 and 1993, a relict population of pine snakes may exist on the west side of the Nanticoke River in Delaware just above the Maryland/Delaware line. On the other hand, John E. Cooper (140) rejected the anecdotal accounts from Snow Hill and Isle of Wight due to the absence of specimens. Interestingly, in addressing this debate, Herbert S. Harris (131) concluded that: "I would like to see a legimate [sic] Maryland specimen of *P. m. melanoleucus* before adding this species to the official list of Maryland herpetofauna, but have tentatively listed it on the basis of Dr. Truitt's record and the recent sightings." The Truitt citation is apparently the basis of the Maryland Department of Natural Resource's listing the northern pine snake for the Pocomoke watershed (Table VI). I must admit that some of the areas in the New Jersey Pine Barrens where I have seen the northern pine snake somewhat resemble the Pocomoke uplands, except for the presence of pitch versus loblolly pine.

The debate over the northern pine snake is interesting and provocative to say the least, and I for one am not proposing that it should be added at this point to the Maryland herpetofauna. However, we should keep an open mind about this and I would not be surprised if diligent searching does not some day produce some specimens. Certainly, the Pocomoke drainage with its sandy pineland uplands would be a good bet. After all, there have been a number of rather surprising new records in recent years on the Delmarva Peninsula, a prime example being the barking tree frog (*Hyla gratiosa*). Formerly thought to occur only south of the Chesapeake Bay, this treefrog is now known to occur on the Delmarva Peninsula. Collections have been made from a site in Caroline County, Maryland in 1982 (145) and in New Castle County, Delaware in 1987 (146). Jim White (personal communication) indicates that four additional populations have been more recently found in Maryland and Delaware. In addition, Frank Hirst (personal communication) also mentioned its presence near Bennett Bog in Cape May County, New Jersey.

Another good example is the carpenter frog. To quote Roger Conant: "Ever since its discovery in Delaware in 1936, it has been virtually a foregone conclusion that the carpenter frog (*Rana virgatipes*) eventually would turn up on the Eastern Shore of Maryland (147,148). But eleven years of intermittent collecting have been required to find it." Conant found the carpenter frog near the edge of the Blackwater National Wildlife Refuge in Dorchester County. He also reported it from the Great Cypress Swamp (Burnt Swamp) in Delaware. Brook Meanley collected a carpenter frog in the Pocomoke Swamp just below the Maryland line on June 12, 1948 (149). In a December 17, 1994 letter to me, Meanley also mentions collecting carpenter frogs on April 20, 1950 and at other times on the Pocomoke. Clyde F. Reed (150) reviewed the distribution of the carpenter frog in Maryland considering it only from Dorchester County, but subsequently collected it in Worcester County (151). Herbert S. Harris (131) indicated that this frog is: "Known at present only on the southern part of the Eastern Shore..."

In 1976 Nick Carter and Harley Spier (152), then I, independently reported it from the upper Eastern Shore in some Caroline County potholes (Delmarva bays), which represented about a forty mile range extension for this species on the Delmarva Peninsula. As pointed out earlier, little was known about these interesting wetlands until after Wayne Klockner and I published on them (81,82). Considering how thorough professional and avocational herpetologists can be in their field work, these Delmarva potholes represent a rather striking example of how certain habitats have been overlooked.

The same can be said for the plants. Although Klockner and I examined only a few of these interesting wetlands, many rare plant species have since been reported from the Delmarva potholes. The significant discoveries of the Canby's dropwort (*Oxypolis canbyi*) in a Delmarva pothole in Maryland and the curly grass fern (*Schizaea pusilla*) in a Delaware Atlantic white cedar swamp are excellent examples of how plants can be overlooked for nearly a century in the case of the former and throughout the history of botanical collecting on the Delmarva for the latter. Another good example of this is the pondspice (*Litsea aestivalis*), which Frank Hirst added to Maryland's flora when he found it in Wicomico County, Maryland in 1985 (90); North Carolina is the closest state with a known extant station! In 1974, Frank Hirst also added Harper's fimbristylis (*Fimbristylis perpusilla*) to the Maryland flora, finding it in a Delmarva pothole at Goldsboro (83). Prior to

266

this find and one in 1980 by Steven Leonard in South Carolina (153), this species was for many years thought to be a Georgia endemic! Another first by Hirst (90) is the Atamasco lily (*Zephyranthes atamasco*), which prior to his finding it near Snow Hill, Maryland, had apparently never been reported north of the mouth of the Chesapeake Bay. Again, I give these simply as examples of how plants and animals can be easily overlooked. If the northern pine snake is, in fact, a part of the Delmarva's fauna, the Pocomoke watershed is again a good bet, in my opinion. Really now, who would have ever guessed that the curly grass fern, Harper's fimbristylis, pondlice, and barking tree frog would have turned up on the Delmarva? And what about the rediscovery of Canby's dropwort, after being sought unsuccessfully for so many years? And the catchfly grass at Whiton Crossing?

Birds of the Pocomoke Area

I would be remiss if I did not address the birds of the Pocomoke, and discussing them last has no particular significance in terms of importance or interest on my part. To the contrary, there is certainly an interesting group of species present, including many warblers, and the Pocomoke is one of our better birding areas during spring migration. See, for example, Carl W. Carlson's hints on birding (154,155) for both the North Pocomoke Swamp (an area just south of the Delaware line) and the South Pocomoke Swamp (an area in and around the Pocomoke River State Park). Carlson colorfully referred to the "...magnificent warbler-woods of the North Pocomoke Swamp... [where] ...you may expect 20 or more species of warblers, with side dressings of orioles, tanagers, thrushes and woodpeckers." Carlson further remarked that: "The richness of the bird life here in spring migration always astonishes me. It is not just the variety of species, but also the great numbers of individuals..." He also spoke favorably of the South Pocomoke Swamp. Robert E. Stewart and Chandler S. Robbins (112) considered the Pocomoke River Valley to be a concentration point for migrating passerine birds. As noted by Brooke Meanley (43), swamps typically support substantial bird populations. He referenced a breeding bird census conducted by Paul Springer and Robert Stewart on a nineteen acre tract in the Pocomoke Swamp just

267

south of the Maryland-Delaware line. In that census, Springer and Stewart found a population density of 363 birds per 100 acres, with 36 species present. The nesting species, ordered by their relative abundance, were

Figure 48. The colorful prothonotary warbler (left), a summer resident commonly seen and heard while canoeing the Pocomoke River. The Swainson's warbler (right), a rare and endangered warbler in Maryland found along the Pocomoke River and known to nest in the Hickory Point Swamp and near the Maryland/Delaware border.

American red-start, prothonotary warbler, white-eyed vireo, hooded warbler, parula warbler, red-eyed vireo, black and white warbler, Louisiana water-thrush, Kentucky warbler, tufted titmouse, Swainson's warbler, yellow-throated warbler, Maryland yellow-throat, yellow-throated vireo, cardinal, crested flycatcher, Acadian flycatcher, Carolina chickadee, worm-eating warbler, scarlet tanager, Carolina wren, red-shouldered hawk, barred owl,

268

yellow-billed cuckoo, ruby-throated hummingbird, yellow-shafted flicker, pileated woodpecker, red-bellied woodpecker, hairy woodpecker, downy woodpecker, eastern wood pewee, American crow, blue jay, blue-gray gnatcatcher, pine warbler, and cowbird (Figure 48). Notice the large number of warblers -- twelve species breeding!

In a 1949 issue of the *Atlantic Naturalist* (44), Meanley went on to say: "It is doubtful if a greater number of different nesting warblers can be found elsewhere on the Atlantic Coastal Plain. No less than fourteen species were noted by Bill Pruitt and the writer [meaning Meanley] during a camping trip last June." In another issue of the *Atlantic Naturalist*, Meanley also mentions, apparently for the same trip, that "Fifteen species [of warblers] were seen, and *in every case they were feeding young* [emphasis his] (156). These were all observed near Selbyville, Delaware, but actually in Maryland about a quarter of a mile below the state line. And in a recent avian inventory of the Great Cypress Swamp by Christopher Heckscher and Cherie Wilson, sixty-four species of birds were discovered during the nesting season, twelve of which were warblers (157). The Delaware Natural Heritage Program considers ten of the sixty-four species to be of high conservation concern.

Scanning "The Season" in Maryland Birdlife (variously authored by R. F. Ringler or C. S. Robbins depending upon the year) will give one a good idea of the diversity of warblers along the Pocomoke. Here are a few examples for the years 1948-1987, some of which simply represent migrants passing through the area:

1948: Eighteen yellow-throated warblers along the northern Pocomoke on April 1.

1953: Swainson's warbler feeding young out of nest near Milburn Landing on June 2.

1970: Brewster's warbler reported from Pocomoke Swamp near Whaleysville.

1973: Sixty yellow-throated warblers and 135 ovenbirds in the Pocomoke Swamp below Shad Landing on May 5.

1976: Six worm-eating warblers at Shad Landing State Park on April 11; golden-winged warbler on April 25 at Whaleysville.

1981: Estimated 200 prothonotary warblers during canoe trip between Whiton Crossing and Porter's Crossing on April 18.

1982: Blue-winged warbler in Nassawango area that remained through June 8; five ovenbird nests in the Nassawango area.

1987: Swainson's warbler in Hickory Point Swamp on May 10; Canada warbler at Shad Landing on May 30; northern parula at Nassawango on October 12; orange-crowned warbler near Pocomoke City, November 7-8.

One of the more elusive of these warblers, the Swainson's was first procured by the Reverend John Bachman on the banks of the Edisto River, just south of Charleston, South Carolina in 1832. He presented the specimen to his friend, John James Audubon, who described and named it after the English ornithologist, William Swainson (158).[10] The first Delmarva record was a sighting by Joseph M. Cadbury in 1942 near Willards, Maryland (160,161). Stewart and Robbins (160) also saw two pairs of Swainson's warblers and collected an adult male in the Pocomoke Swamp about five miles southwest of Pocomoke City, no doubt the Hickory Point Swamp. The second nesting record for this species in Maryland was reported by Edward Fleisher and Leonard Worley on June 20, 1954 near Pocomoke City (162). As indicated by Meanley (161,163), the principal nesting areas are an area just below the Delaware line near Willards, Maryland and Selbyville, Delaware and another below Pocomoke City, again apparently the Hickory Point Swamp. According to Chandler S. Robbins and D. Daniel Boone (164), no more than ten nesting pairs of Swainson's warblers per year have ever been found in Maryland. A brief status of the Swainson's warbler in the Delaware portion of the North Pocomoke Swamp is also presented by David Shoch in 1991 (165). Unfortunately, this elusive warbler may be disappearing from the Great Cypress Swamp area since only one territorial male was found by Christopher Heckscher and Cherie Wilson during an avian inventory conducted in 1996. On the other hand, Jim McCann of the Maryland Natural Heritage Program indicated to me in 1998 that he noted at least three breeding

---

[10]See also "Audubon's Firsts" by J. d'Arcy Norwood (159) in the *Atlantic Naturalist.*

pairs, and perhaps a fourth, along the upland-swamp interface on the Hickory Point Swamp in the summer of 1998.

Brooke Meanley (166) considered the Swainson's song one of the finest of all the warblers and he certainly should know, for while studying it in the Great Dismal Swamp in Virginia on June 2, 1966 he recorded an amazing 1,168 songs between 4:27 a.m and 5:00 p.m., when it ceased singing! He also published a *Natural History of the Swainson's Warbler* in 1971 (167). Audubon was a good friend of both Bachman and Swainson (39) and would certainly be most impressed with Meanley's experience and knowledge of this interesting warbler, were he alive today.

Table IX is a list of the breeding birds in the Pocomoke River watershed, which by definition includes both wetlands and uplands. This list is based upon information derived from the Maryland and District of Columbia Breeding Bird Atlas Project during a five year period (1983-1987) (168). A total of 109 species is shown for the entire watershed. Seventeen species are warblers, although two of these, the blue-winged warbler and the black-throated green warbler, appear as only two breeding records and the Swainson's warbler only three. To mention a few other groups, there are also three vireos, five flycatchers, three goatsuckers, six woodpeckers, four owls, and four raptors, although one owl, the barn owl, has only three breeding records. The data in the survey are divided into six blocks, each with four quarter-blocks, based upon U.S. Geological Survey 7.5 minute quadrangle maps. A few examples of some block data for different parts of the watershed for warblers will give an idea of the diversity of breeding birds in selected areas of the watershed. One block in the Whaleysville quadrangle produced a total of eighty-seven breeding species, sixteen of which were warblers (the northern parula, yellow warbler, yellow-throated warbler, pine warbler, prairie warbler, black-and-white warbler, American redstart, prothonotary warbler, worm-eating warbler, Swainson's warbler, ovenbird, Louisiana waterthrush, Kentucky warbler, common yellowthroat, hooded warbler, and yellow-breasted chat). A block in the Wango quadrangle produced a slightly different list of sixteen warblers -- the blue-winged warbler, northern parula warbler,

271

TABLE IX
BREEDING BIRDS OF THE POCOMOKE RIVER WATERSHED[4]

green heron	white-breasted nuthatch
Canada goose	brown-headed nuthatch
wood duck	brown creeper
hooded merganser[2]	Carolina wren
black duck	house wren
mallard	marsh wren
black vulture	blue-gray gnatcatcher
turkey vulture	eastern bluebird
broad-winged hawk	wood thrush
red-shouldered hawk	American robin
red-tailed hawk	gray catbird
Cooper's hawk	mockingbird
American kestrel	brown thrasher
wild turkey	cedar waxwing
ring-necked pheasant[2]	starling
bobwhite	white-eyed vireo
Virginia rail	yellow-throated vireo
king rail	red-eyed vireo
killdeer	blue-winged warbler[3]
American woodcock	northern parula warbler
rock dove	black-throated green warbler[3]
mourning dove	yellow warbler
yellow-billed cuckoo	yellow-throated warbler
black-billed cuckoo	pine warbler
eastern screech owl	prairie warbler
great horned owl	black-and-white warbler
barred owl	American redstart
barn owl[4]	prothonotary warbler
common nighthawk	worm-eating warbler
whip-poor-will	Swainson's warbler[4]
chuck-will's-widow	ovenbird
chimney swift	Louisiana waterthrush
ruby-throated hummingbird	Kentucky warbler
belted kingfisher	common yellowthroat
red-headed woodpecker	hooded warbler
red-bellied woodpecker	yellow-breasted chat
downy woodpecker	summer tanager
hairy woodpecker	scarlet tanager
northern flicker	northern cardinal
pileated woodpecker	blue grosbeak

eastern wood pewee	indigo bunting
Acadian flycatcher	rufous-sided towhee
eastern phoebe	chipping sparrow
great crested flycatcher	grasshopper sparrow
eastern kingbird	field sparrow
horned lark	song sparrow
purple martin	red-winged blackbird
rough-winged swallow	eastern meadowlark
barn swallow	common grackle
tree swallow	brown-headed cowbird
blue jay	orchard oriole
American crow	northern oriole
fish crow	American goldfinch
Carolina chickadee	house sparrow
tufted titmouse	

Footnotes for Table IX.

1 Source: *Atlas of the Breeding Bird of Maryland and the District of Columbia* (Robbins and Blom, 1996).The table is based upon data collected between 1983 and 1987.

[2] Only one breeding record.

[3] Only two breeding records.

[4] Only three breeding records.

black-throated green warbler, yellow-throated warbler, pine warbler, prairie warbler, black-and-white warbler, American redstart, prothonotary warbler, worm-eating warbler, ovenbird, Louisiana waterthrush, Kentucky warbler, common yellowthroat, hooded warbler, and yellow-breasted chat. In fact, many of the blocks for various quadrangles show thirteen to fifteen breeding warbler species. For example, selected additional blocks contained the following numbers of breeding warbler species for the following quadrangles: Whaleysville (14), Wango (15), Dividing Creek (13, 14, 14, 14), Snow Hill (13, 14, 14), Public Landing (14), Kingston (13), and Pocomoke City (14). (In some instances, the number of breeding warblers for more than one block per quadrangle are shown in parentheses.) Considering these data, a lot can be said for Carlson's colorful reference to the "...magnificent warbler-woods..." and the "wilderness" nature of the area. Some observations on the parula and prairie warblers at the Hickory Point Swamp, based upon a trip I led into the area on June 10, 1997, are also presented by Kitt Heckscher in *The Maryland Naturalist* (169).

Another interesting breeding bird for Maryland from my perspective is the cedar waxwing, which, much to my surprise, was reported twelve times (from the Whaleysville, Dividing Creek, Salisbury, Snow Hill, Public Landing, Kingston, Girdletree and Pocomoke City quadrangles) during the five year period cited above. The first Worcester County nest record for this species was reported by D. Daniel Boone while on a camping trip at Shad Landing in 1980 (170).

Although the bald eagle was not reported in the survey, Robbins and Boone (164) included three nesting sites for it in the Pocomoke Watershed (near Snow Hill, Hickory Point Swamp, and Pocomoke Sound) and on October 23, 1992 while on a boat on the Pocomoke River I spotted two apparently different adult bald eagles below and one above Pocomoke City. A couple of eagles were also spotted at the Hickory Point Swamp on the June 10, 1997 trip mentioned above. (See Chapter Nine for a description of that trip.)

A POSTSCRIPT OF SORTS

It is truly unfortunate that in the summer of 1997 numerous dead and dying fish were found in the Pocomoke River near Shelltown, Maryland, which prompted State and local officials to close a part of the River. Similar fish kills were subsequently found in other Eastern Shore rivers and in the Rappahannock River in Virginia. A one-celled organism, a dinoflagellate named *Pfiesteria piscicida*, was soon considered the causal agent. Some researchers suggested that excessive nutrient loading was involved and various newspapers implicated runoff from chicken waste and manure as the main source of nutrients supporting the dinoflagellate. The contention that copper rather than nutrients was the culprit behind the disease was presented by Ritchie Shoemaker, a Pocomoke City medical doctor heavily involved in the controversy. An entire issue of *The Maryland Medical Journal* (May 1998; Volume 47, number 3) was devoted to the problem and Dr. Shoemaker wrote a book, *Pfiesteria: Crossing Dark Water,* on his experience with it (171).

Although I have my subjective suspicions, I have no firm scientific opinion as to what is behind the problem, since water quality and public health are really not my field. I will say, however, that on June 10, 1997 five other biologists and I ate an early lunch along the muddy riverbank just above Hickory Point, then spent the entire day mucking our way across a mile-wide stretch of the Hickory Point Swamp getting quite wet and muddy. To my knowledge, all of us are still alive and kicking with no health problems we can relate to our venture. I do not mean to be brash by this statement, for I accept the fact that at least the lower part of the river has, or at least has had, a serious water quality problem. My point is that I do not feel that it is the river and swamp that are the problem. Rather the river (and the swamp?) are perhaps the victims, victims of something man-induced, that is no doubt exacerbating natural environmental stresses associated with these estuarine waters. So from my perspective, the Pocomoke is still a wonderful system, in part a picturesque wilderness system so redolent of some rivers and swamps of the deep South.

275

SIX

THE NIFTY NANTICOKE

At Long Point, about fifteen miles above its mouth, the Nanticoke suddenly narrows to about half a mile, but still for many a long mile above that it continues to swing widely back and forth through the salt marshes. On the east there is nothing but marsh; on the west side fast land comes down to the river at the outside of each swing. Even on the fast land few houses are to be seen. It always was a lonely land and is so still.
-- HULBERT FOOTNER, 1944, *Rivers of the Eastern Shore*

RIGHT up front, I should confess that I have not spent much time on the nifty Nanticoke. In fact, my *Maryland Journal* indicates only about fifteen trips along the Nanticoke and its tributaries, most of which were to botanize its rich wetlands and uplands. I also annually visited the Nanticoke at Sharptown for a number of years during overnight field trips down the Delmarva with my wetland ecology classes from the Graduate School, U.S. Department of Agriculture. (See Chapter One for a swamp visit at Sharptown.) Some of these excursions involved an informal botanical group. (Trips by this group to other areas are presented in Chapter Nine.) There were also, no doubt, a number of additional trips that I did not document in writing. So all told, I suspect twenty-five or so field trips would cover it. Although few in number, the quality of some of those excursions were superior, and my botanical colleagues and I shared some great experiences. I discuss some of our more interesting trips to the Nanticoke watershed in this Chapter, which will be supplemented at times with other technical information. First, however, I will present some background information on this great natural resource.

THE WATERSHED AND ITS SIGNIFICANCE

The Nanticoke River drains over 718,000 acres of wetlands, forests, and farmland in Maryland and Delaware, and supports two major tributaries -- Marshyhope Creek and Broad Creek (1). The Maryland portion of the Nanticoke Watershed alone supports 16,419 acres of estuarine wetlands, 29,886 acres of palustrine wetlands, and 346 acres of riverine wetlands, for a total of 46,651 acres (2). In fact, the expansive tidal marshes in the Maryland portion of the watershed account for much of the watershed's total wetland acreage, which is approximately 80,000 acres (1).

Vast estuarine marshes exist from the mouth of the river at Clay Island upstream to a few miles above Vienna. Of particular interest are the expansive marshes of the Elliott Island Peninsula. (Figure 49; see also Chapter Three). Above Long Point, the estuarine marshes are associated with impressive river meanders that are strikingly depicted on topographic maps and aerial photographs. From just below its confluence with Marshyhope Creek north to the limit of the tides, the Nanticoke supports tidal mixed forested wetlands dominated by deciduous and evergreen trees. Beyond the tidal limits, the remaining wetlands are mostly non-tidal mixed forested (2). Indeed, these are impressive wetlands, which has led the Chesapeake Bay Foundation to conclude that, "The wetlands of the Nanticoke watershed include some of the most significant wetlands of the Delmarva Peninsula and the Chesapeake Bay region."

Given its interest in protecting this valuable resource, the Foundation produced the *Nanticoke River Watershed: Natural and Cultural Resource Atlas* in 1996. The stated purpose of the atlas was "...to assist residents, business owners, teachers, planners, and elected officials in developing an understanding of the Nanticoke and an ability to view the watershed as a whole, instead of as a series of independent political jurisdictions." The atlas, which includes information on land use, agriculture, wetlands, submerged

278

aquatic vegetation, wildlife habitat, aquatic habitat, cultural resources, and water quality, gives a good overview of the watershed and its resources. See also Robert A. Hedeen's *A Naturalist on the Nanticoke* for an overview of the Nanticoke and some of its estuarine animals (3) and Carl W. Carlson's a brief overview of some of the birds found in the Nanticoke River below Vienna in the *Atlantic Naturalist* (4).

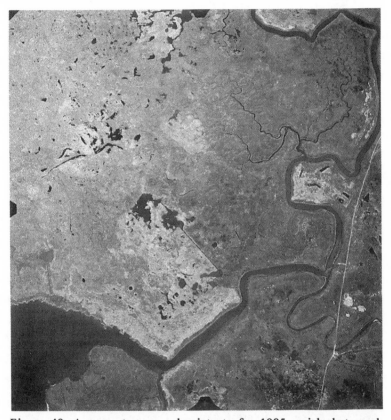

Figure 49. A computer-scanned printout of a 1985 aerial photograph showing part of the Elliott Island marsh along Elliott Island Road, Dorchester County, Maryland. Note the numerous small open water depressions in the marsh, which attract waterfowl and wading birds. The larger creek is Island Creek; its smaller tributary is Pokata Creek.

279

The significance of Nanticoke has also been acknowledged by The Nature Conservancy in their Campaign for the Chesapeake Rivers -- a four year program initiated in 1994 to raise $10,000,000 in private and public support (5). The effort focused on the "...[the Chesapeake Bay's] outstanding tributaries -- those still in pristine condition with the best chance for sustaining a rich natural diversity and exceptional water quality." I remember, in this regard, attending a meeting at the Maryland Department of Natural Resources on September 9, 1993 to brainstorm the Nanticoke's significant natural features and assist The Nature Conservancy in the development of a strategic plan that would direct their conservation efforts on the Nanticoke. I supported then, and certainly continue to support, efforts to protect this valuable resource. It is a wonderful system, an irreplaceable natural resource. Its loss or severe degradation would be unforgivable by future generations. Unfortunately, the lower part of the river, like the Blackwater area, has lost a considerable amount of its wetlands (1,6,7) because of sea level rise and land subsidence. For more on the marsh loss problem in the Blackwater-Fishing Bay-Elliott Island area, see Chapter three.)

SELECT FIELD EXCURSIONS

On June 18-20, 1984 I attended a joint botanical foray sponsored by the Northeastern Section Botanical Society of America, Torrey Botanical Club, and Philadelphia Botanical Club. This was my first trip with the Philadelphia Botanical Club since 1971. Over the years since leaving New Jersey, I had pursued a number of outdoor and natural history activities, both professionally and as an avocation, but by this point in my career, my botanizing had reached an all-time low. These three days of field trips, however, rekindled my interest somewhat in the Coastal Plain flora and I have maintained a moderate interest ever since.[1] I co-led one of the trips, to

---

[1] Interestingly, this trip took me away during my wedding anniversary, not an uncommon event I have found over the years due to botanical trips – the most extreme one being my 25th wedding anniversary when I was doing botanical field work in Jackson Hole, Wyoming for EPA from June 18-21, 1991!

Assateague, with Ernie Schuyler and Liz Higgins. The following day we had a trip to Nassawango Creek led by Jim Stasz. Our last trip, however, was to various areas in the Nanticoke River watershed. On the latter trip, I met for the first time two professors from Delaware State University, Norm Dill and Art Tucker, as well as two of their students, Rob Naczi and Nan Seyfried, the four field trip leaders. We saw two extremely rare plants in Delaware -- the box huckleberry (*Galylussacia brachycera*) at two sites along a tributary of the Nanticoke and the floating heart (*Nymphoides cordata*) at Trussum Pond. A very rare plant, the New Jersey tea (*Ceanothus americanus*), was also noted along the roadside in transit.[2]

In the afternoon, Dan Boone from the Maryland Natural Heritage Program led the group to an interesting relict sand dune area along the Nanticoke River below Sharptown where we found the attractive butterfly pea (*Clitoria mariana*), as well as pale hickory (*Carya pallida*), a watchlist species in Maryland. These relict dune areas, and similar ones along Marshyhope Creek, support a number of rare plants. They were apparently known and botanized by some of the early botanists in the region, such as J.P. Otis, who mentions them in an article in the 1914 issue of *Bartonia* (8). Otis was apparently also familiar with and botanized a number of old millponds in the Nanticoke drainage, since he states:

> "Along most of the course of the Nanticoke are marshes, locally called 'cripples', back of which in numerous localities are dense swamps. Through this border of marsh and swamps run a number of creeks; these in former years were thickly studded with sawmills, mostly now gone and in some cases the ponds changed into quaking bogs, much like the savannas of Southern New Jersey."

Many plants listed in Otis' article for the Nanticoke watershed, such as the pitcher plant (*Sarracenia purpurea*), pink bog-button (*Sclerolepis uniflora*), clustered beakrush (*Rhynchospora glomerata*), flattened pipewort

---

[2]"Extremely rare" and "very rare" are rarity designations used by the Delaware Natural Heritage Program. See Table II in Chapter Two for a more detailed explanation.

(*Eriocaulon compressum*), seven-angled pipewort (*E. aquaticum*), velvety tick-trefoil (*Desmodium viridiflorum*), stiff tick-trefoil (*D. strictum*), and downy bushclover (*Lespedeza stuevei*), are currently considered rare in Maryland and Delaware.

*   *   *

Another impressive Coastal Plain area we visited was near Vienna, Maryland and Chicone Creek, a tributary of the Nanticoke. Here we examined a floristically rich mesophytic forest not typical of the Coastal Plain in Maryland, which supported trees like the red oak (*Quercus rubra*), tulip poplar (*Lireodendron tulipifera*), American beech (*Fagus grandifolia*), and flowering dogwood (*Cornus florida*). Many of the associated herbaceous species, such as pale indian-plantain (*Cacalia atriplicifolia*), bloodroot (*Sanguinaria canadensis*), wild coffee (*Triosteum perfoliatum*), sicklepod (*Arabis canadensis*), lopseed (*Phryma leptostachya*), wild comfrey (*Cynoglossum virginianum*), and may-apple (*Podophyllum petatum*), were likewise plants generally found at mesic sites -- commonly the rich forests of the Piedmont Physiographic Province. According to The Nature Conservancy, over thirty plant species known from Dorchester County only occur at this area.

Bill McAvoy of the Delaware Natural Heritage Program has shown me similar mesophytic vegetation adjacent to Huckleberry Pond in Delaware. Another excellent example is the Ivytown Woods near Easton, Maryland. The site is located southeast of Easton and opposite Frazier Neck along a tributary of the Choptank River. According to Bill, who has been searching for such sites by following up on some of the earlier work of the botanist, Elizabeth Earle, the mesic forest covers approximately fifty-five acres, including a relatively flat area and the slopes of a rather steep ravine. Bill has produced a rather impressive list of mesic, typically Piedmont, species for the site, including plants like northern maiden-hair fern (*Adiantum pedatum*), ginseng (*Panax quiquefolius*), bugbane (*Cimicifuga racemosa*), round-lobed hepatica (*Hepatica americana*), and showy orchid (*Galearis spectabilis*). The orchid grows quite abundantly there. According to Bill, the Christmas fern and may-apple are reliable common indicators of such sites. The site supports numerous beech trees, as well as some tulip poplars, red oaks, and slippery elms (*Ulmus rubra*).

*   *   *

July 28, 1984, saw me once again in the field with Art Tucker, Norm Dill, Rob Nasci, Nan Seyfried, and Ernie Schuyler -- this time botanizing principally the fresh intertidal zone and Atlantic white cedar swamps in the Nanticoke drainage in Delaware. Our first site was on Broad Creek at White River Estates; the second on Broad Creek at Phillip's Landing. We found small waterwort (*Elatine minima*), an extremely rare species in Delaware, at Broad Creek on a sandy spit and overwash berm, rather than along the general shoreline, which was apparently too turbulent given the narrow intertidal zone and landward steeply sloping bank. I immediately predicted that we would find more of these plants and perhaps other rarities at similar locations downstream where tributaries entered Broad Creek. We found this to be true at the only other intertidal site we visited, Phillips Landing, where we again found small waterwort, as well as Long's bitter-cress (*Cardamine longii*), another extremely rare species in Delaware. A third extremely rare species, the purple bladderwort (*Utricularia purpurea*), was found washed up on shore.

Two other very rare species in Delaware were found at or near Phillips Landing -- a prince's-pine (*Chimaphila umbellata* var. *cisatlantica*) in an oak woods and eight yellow-crested orchids (*Platanthera cristata*) along a dirt road (Figure 50). Collin's sedge (*Carex collinsii*), a Delaware watchlist species, and red-berried greenbrier (*Smilax walteri*) were located in an adjacent deciduous swamp. We also found a toad, the eastern spadefoot (*Scaphiopus h. holbrooki*), number seventy-six on my reptile/amphibian life list.

At another site near White River Estates, Rob Nasci showed us five spikerushes, two of which, the three-ribbed spikerush (*Eleocharis tricostata*) and the black-fruited spikerush (*E. melanocarpa*), are extremely rare and very rare, respectively, in Delaware. I also added a new bird to my life list, the summer tanager, number 294.

Our last stop was to Ellis Pond, where we found another extremely rare plant -- the showy purple passion-flower (*Passiflora incarnata*). Although we did not observe them, this old pond site also supports at least two other rarities, knotted spikerush (*Eleocharis equisetoides*, very rare) and Canby's bulrush (*Scirpus etuberculatus*, extremely rare). Many of the plant species found on this trip were new to me.

*   *   *

One of my better trips to the Nanticoke River watershed occurred six years later, when on September 21, 1990, a number of folks from my informal botanical group traveled to Galestown Pond in search of plant rarities. Some

of the regulars, for example, Yvette Ogle and Wilbur Rittenhouse participated, as did some new-comers, like Dave Williams and Joan Maloof. We had about eight people all told, and three canoes. And from beginning to end, nobody was disappointed. In terms of rarities, the pond far exceeded our expectations. We found, for example, Robbin's spikerush (*Eleocharis robbinsii*), water clubrush (*Scirpus subterminalis*), and sessile-leaf water-horehound (*Lycopus amplectens*) (all highly State rare and endangered), long-beak baldrush (*Rhynchospora scirpoides*, State rare and threatened), seven-angled pipewort (*Eriocaulon aquaticum*, endangered-extirpated in Maryland), and green spikerush (*Eleocharis olivacea*, a watchlist species). An impressive sight was a large stand of flowering golden-club (*Orontium aquaticum*), the largest I have seen outside of the New Jersey Pine Barrens in the mid-Atlantic states.

Figure 50. Crested yellow orchid (*Plananthera cristata*), a rare swamp species.

And a friend of Yvette's interested in edible plants, offered us some fresh-cut cattail stems. I tried one. The experience apparently reminded me of a passage in Edwin Way Teales's *A Walk Through the Year*, for I made a marginal note to that effect in my *Journal* in reference to cattail pollen pancakes, which Teale mentioned on page 98 (9).[3]

Before leaving the pond to botanize the stream below the spillway, we had a sudden and rather nasty experience -- an experience I suppose none of us will ever forget. It occurred at the upper end of the pond after our three canoes wormed their way up a narrow creek dense with overhanging shrubbery, including an uncomfortably prickly plant, the swamp rose (*Rosa palustris*). When the vegetation over the stream became too thick to penetrate further with the canoes, Wilbur left his canoe to explore the swamp. Yvette and I followed, and I almost immediately felt a sting on my shoulder. On first glance, I thought it was yellow spider (A golden garden spider, *Argiope aurantia*) from our lunch site was still fresh in my mind.), but quickly realized it was a yellow jacket. It took but a few seconds for the truth to sink in. With yellow jackets buzzing all around me I yelled: "Lets get the hell out of here!" By the time I got into the boat, I was stung at least three times -- twice on the arm and once on the leg. As I was busily swatting them off, one yellow jacket got under my glasses, whereupon I almost lost my balance while trying to prevent being stung on my face or eye. Then a colleague, Joe DaVia, suddenly toppled his canoe, dumping both him and another fellow into the creek. This evoked substantial laughter even as we hectically fought off the yellow jackets while turning our canoes around in the narrow creek. Finally, we got our canoes out of further danger. Despite the confusion, I was the only one that got stung. But as I wrote in my *Journal*, "I'm sure we won't forget this one!"

On the stream below the spillway, which led to the Nanticoke River, we encountered another pipewort, an intertidal species, Parker's pipewort (*Eriocaulon parkeri*, State rare and threatened species).

*   *   *

Because of our success at Galestown Pond in 1990 and our interest in exploring the downstream area more thoroughly, we visited the area again

---

[3]Mixed with batter, Teale considered these a delicacy.

285

a year later, on August 17, 1991. Yvette Ogle and Wilbur Rittenhouse, as well as another group veteran, Gene Cooley, and four other folks attended. As I wrote in my *Journal*: "One of the best botanical days ever in the field for me in Maryland, perhaps best ever anywhere in terms of rarities." The thousands of trips I have had into the field since the early 1960s speaks to the significance of this statement.

First, we canoed the pond, where we noted hundreds, if not thousands, of rosettes of either the grass-leaf arrowhead (*Sagittaria graminifolia*, a State watchlist species) or Eaton's arrowhead (*S. eatonii*) in a couple of feet of water. We also saw many areas supporting highly State rare and endangered Robbin's spikerush. Other rarities included the highly State rare and endangered smooth fuirena (*Fuirena pumila*), water clubrush, pink bog-button, reversed bladderwort (*Utricularia resupinata*), and larger floating-heart (*Nymphoides aquatica*); the State rare and threatened long-beaked baldrush; and a watchlist species, the green spikerush.

A small floating mat we visited was replete with rarities, including all of those above except the floating-heart. Here we added the seven-angled pipewort, an endangered-extirpated species in Maryland. Again, we had a great view of the large goldenclub stand, which was reminiscent of Dr. Plitt's description for Lake Waterford in Anne Arundel County, where numerous plants occurred in the early 1900s. (See Chapter Eight for more on Dr. Plitt's finds.) An unidentified rushfoil (*Crotonopsis* sp.), one of which is a watchlist species, was found in an upland sandy area during lunch. Adding to our excitement before leaving the pond, was a small flock of those aristocrats of the bird world -- cedar waxwings.

Downstream the tide was low, ideal conditions under which to seek out fresh intertidal rarities. We once again found State rare and threatened Parker's pipewort, and almost immediately heard the *quenk, quenk, quenk* of a green tree frog (*Hyla cinerea*) emanating from the swamp. Then we located some small waterwort (highly State rare and endangered), the grass-leaf arrowhead (a State watchlist species) or Eaton's arrowhead, and another watchlist species, the seaside alder (*Alnus maritima*). This area looked potentially good for other rare plants like the mudwort (*Limosella australis*),

286

and we noted an unidentified "scoph-like" plant (not flowering) with opposite, elliptic to roundish leaves. It was growing in dense patches submerged on a sand-gravel bar. In retrospect, I have often wondered whether it may have been a long-lost rarity, Nuttall's micranthemum (*Micranthemum micranthemoides*), which has not been reported in Maryland for many years. Interestingly, the micranthemum was reported from "...the edge of a pond near Galestown in Dorchester County..." by A. V. Smith in 1939 in an issue of *Rhodora* (10). This may have been Galestown Pond.

*   *   *

On May 14, 1993, I once again traveled to the Eastern Shore. My purpose was two-fold. First, to examine areas along the upper Pocomoke River for a publication I was preparing on the Pocomoke, which subsequently was incorporated into this book (Chapter Five). Secondly, to preview some sites in Dorchester and Wicomico Counties for a field trip I was to lead the following Sunday for the Maryland Native Plant Society. Since my field trip sites were to be in the Nanticoke drainage, I spent considerable time there. At Marshyhope Creek near Eldorado, Maryland, I found the eastern sedge (*Carex atlantica*); at Chicone Creek near Vienna, the seaside alder, both watchlist species. A highly State rare and endangered species, the stiff tick-trefoil, was spotted along a dirt road northeast of Chicone Creek. I also checked the forested swamp astride Route 313 opposite Sharptown, where I located both the red-berried greenbrier (a watchlist species) and laurel-leaf greenbrier (*Smilax laurifolia*) (Figure 51). Below Sharptown, along a dirt road on the southeast side of the river, I found some attractive wild pink (*Silene caroliniana* var. *pensylvanica*). In an open field further downstream, I encountered that paragon of variability, the ipecac spurge (*Euphorbia ipecacuanhae*) manifesting what else but extreme variability -- narrow-leaf green plants and broad-leaf green plants, narrow-leaf maroon plants and broad-leaf maroon plants, all juxtaposed.

As it turns out, my field trip with the Maryland Native Plant Society on May 16 went very well. We visited many of the sites I had inspected

287

earlier, saw similar plants, and added a new site, an Atlantic white cedar swamp, that was familiar to some trip attendees from the Department of Natural Resources. We again located red-berried greenbrier and laurel-leaf greenbrier. Although not uncommon, an interesting plant in the sandy upland

Figure 51. Laurel-leaf greenbrier (*Smilax laurifolia*), a fairly common woody vine in the Eastern Shore swamps. (Photo by the author)

was the anise-flavored goldenrod, whose apt scientific name is *Solidago odora*.[4] Don't be fooled by it, however, for one form of it does not smell or taste like licorice. You may have guessed it by now -- Its equally apt scientific name is *Solidago odora* form *inodora*!

We also traveled into Delaware to see the extremely rare box huckleberry near White River Estates. A second species given extremely rare status in Delaware, the blue lupine (*Lupinus perennis*), was also observed.

---

[4]The anise-flavored goldenrod has been officially designated the State herb of Delaware, the only such designation in the United States (11).

*   *   *

It was a full moon when I left my residence at Shipley's Choice on October 1, 1993 anticipating an exciting day botanizing in the field. I met Gene Cooley and Kathy McCarthy near the Bay Bridge and we were soon heading east, then southeast for the LeCompte Wildlife Management Area in Dorchester County where we met Bill Perry. Bill had generously offered to take us by boat to some wetlands on the nifty Nanticoke below Vienna. I was looking forward to this trip since we would be exploring a section of the river supporting expansive estuarine marshes. In fact, just upstream, where Route 50 crosses the Nanticoke, I had frequently viewed these slightly brackish tidal marshes while driving to the lower Eastern Shore and Worcester County. These were generally brief stops along the roadside to scan or sometimes enter the marshes -- the same marshes where Brooke Meanley, a veteran U.S. Fish and Wildlife Service biologist, had pursued king rails nesting at the bases of swamp rose mallow (*Hibiscus moscheutos*) in 1965 and where Neil Hotchkiss, another long-time Fish and Wildlife Service biologist, heard several swamp sparrows along the river bank in 1946, an event that eventually led to the naming of a new subspecies of swamp sparrow (12,13). (See Chapter Three for more details.)

One evening back in the 1970s while on a trip to Elliott Island in quest of the elusive black rail, my colleagues and I also listened for this tiny bird in the marshes just north of Route 50 opposite Vienna. The presence of the black rail at Elliott Island is well known in ornithological circles and according to The Nature Conservancy, Savanna Lake supports the largest population in the mid-Atlantic region (Figure 52). Meanley specifically suggests the vicinity of Pokata Creek along the road leading to the village of Elliott. In fact, he presents a rather colorful account of his capture of a black rail that walked between his legs around midnight while he, Robert E. Steward, and John S. Webb were stalking a calling bird. Our evening rail trip was not successful, however, for all we heard below Savanna Lake and opposite Vienna were buzzing mosquitoes and persistent long-billed marsh wrens well into the night.

289

So when we launched the boat at a ramp in Vienna that October, I was excited to say the least, hoping for interesting birds as well as plants. Perhaps the pines would produce a brown-headed nuthatch; the oaks, a sum-

Figure 52. The black rail, an elusive marsh bird that breeds along the Nanticoke River in the Elliott Island area.

mer tanager; the switchgrass meadows, a Henslow's sparrow; the marsh, a least bittern -- all of which are known to occur in the area (Figures 53 and 54)

Mud flats were exposed along the shore, accentuated by the low spring tide. It was a clear cool day with a medium breeze. Soon, however, a brisk wind smarted our faces as we sped off in the boat for the our first site, Igam Gut, on the Wicomico County side of the Nanticoke River. The giant cordgrass (*Spartina cynosuroides*) stood out like rows of sentinels on the natural river-bank levees, seaward of which was a narrow intermittent band of the smooth cordgrass. The smooth cordgrass, which is so abundant in the saltmarshes of Worcester County and the highly brackish marshes of the Chesapeake Bay and its tributaries, seems to "retreat" to the streambank edges in these fresh to slightly brackish marshes. Although it can persist under fresh conditions, the smooth cordgrass appears to be outcompeted by the plethora of other species that occur along the fresher reaches of the

Figure 53. The brown-headed nuthatch. Watch for this nuthatch amongst the pines in Dorchester and Somerset Counties, Maryland.

Chesapeake and its tributaries. Therefore, the smooth cordgrass is sub-stantially restricted to the deeper seaward edge of the fresh to slightly brackish tidal marshes where competition with other vascular plants is apparently reduced or absent due to the water depths.

Except for the addition of exposed mudflats, the vegetation pattern along Igam Gut was similar -- smooth cordgrass seaward of giant cordgrass rooted in the low natural levees. In some areas, however, the giant cordgrass formed large stands beyond the levees, although a more diverse array of plants

Figure 54. The least bittern, a rare marsh bird that breeds in the Chesapeake Bay Region's fresh tidal marshes .

was more typical in the hinterland of the expansive slightly brackish tidal marsh.

When Bill cut the motor, the pleasant honking of Canada geese filled the autumn air. Nevertheless, our thoughts soon turned to plants and we noted low mats of the small spikerush (*Eleocharis parvula*) in the mud flats. As we snaked up the gut, Gene spotted a red-bellied turtle (*Chrysemys rubriventris*), then some others. Diatom blooms blazed golden-brown on flats and exposed stream banks. We soon stirred up a green heron, which was repeatedly flushed along the meandering gut.

At one point, we disembarked to examine the brackish marsh. Besides the giant cordgrass, smooth cordgrass, and small spikerush, we found rice cutgrass (*Leersia oryzoides*), marsh elder (*Iva frutescens*), saltmarsh bulrush (*Scirpus robustus*), arrow-arum (*Peltandra virginica*), Walter's millet (*Echinocloa walteri*), dotted smartweed (*Polygonum punctatum*), saltmarsh mallow (*Kosteletzkya virginica*), smooth beggar-ticks (*Bidens laevis*), perennial saltmarsh aster (*Aster tenuifolia*), creeping spikerush (*Eleocharis ambigens*, a watchlist species), tidemarsh waterhemp (*Amaranthus cannabinus*), swamp rose mallow (*Hibiscus moscheutos*), common three-square (*Scirpus pungens*), slender flatsedge (*Cyperus filicinus*), chufa (*C. esculentus*), and camphorweed (*Pluchea purpurascens*). We also spotted a belted kingfisher on a small, remnant dock.

Our second landing occurred where the gut meandered against an upland forest. The shoreline was quite firm and sandy here, so we explored for rare aquatics, finding none. I noted inkberry (*Ilex glabra*), swamp chestnut oak (*Quercus michauxii*), water oak (*Q. nigra*), Spanish oak (*Q. falcata*), and slender spikegrass (*Chasmanthium laxum*) in the woodland. Meadow spike-moss (*Selaginella apoda*) grew in a wet spot at the edge of the woods.

Leaving Bill behind with the main boat, we took what he referred to as a "ganoe" (a small boat shaped like a canoe but squared off in the back for a small motor) and motored slowly up the gut, which supported a submerged aquatic plant, the coontail (*Ceratophyllum demersum*). The creek quickly shallowed, however, which found us poling with the paddles as we drifted upstream on the incoming tide, while simultaneously maneuvering to avoid

293

mud flats and eating our lunches. We quickly discovered a vegetation shift in the marsh to wildrice (*Zizania aquatica*) and other fresh to slightly brackish species. Then there was a bit of excitement as Gene adroitly nabbed a dragonfly perched in a stupor on a sweetflag plant.

Our upstream excursion ended where a road crosses Igam Gut. We again disembarked to examine the vegetation above the road. About this time, Gene became really excited over the butterflies, and caught a few with his net, as well as some additional dragonflies. Besides the monarchs (*Danaus plexippus*), the buckeye (*Precis lavinia*), painted lady (*Vanessa* sp.), little yellow (*Eurema lisa*), pearl crescent (*Phyciodes tharos*), and gray hairstreak (*Strymon melinus*), were spotted. At one point, Gene jumped from the gut bank to the "ganoe" and immediately to the other bank in quick succession, then dashed after and netted what he at first thought was a new lifer for him, a great purple hairstreak (*Atlides halesus*). On closer inspection, however, it proved to be just another gray hairstreak, much to his dismay.

Soon after the flurry of excitement over the butterflies, we were once again poling in the "ganoe," this time heading downstream. By 2:10 p.m. we were speeding up the Nanticoke for Mill Creek, a tributary on the Dorchester County side of the river. According to Gene and Kathy, a highly State rare and endangered species, the marsh wild senna (*Chamaecrista fasciculata* var. *macrosperma*) and a State rare species, the spongy lophotocarpus (*Sagittaria calycina*), has been historically reported from this area. Before going up the creek, however, we examined some dense riverbank vegetation just south of Mill Creek, which turned out to be the shoreline sedge (*Carex hyalinolepis*), a highly State rare and threatened species. Gene pointed out a dagger moth larvae (Family Noctuidae) at this spot.

While moving up Mill Creek, we repeatedly jumped a number of wood ducks -- first two, then another, then six more -- getting very close to some. We also stirred up some mallards that just swam ahead of us, perhaps some of the captive-reared types, which have been released in Maryland in great numbers for a number of years (14).

Since so little time was spent on Mill Creek, we did not seriously pursue the marsh wild senna and spongy lophotocarpus; the tide was too high to see the latter anyway. Thus, before long we were back at the boat ramp and off to Lecompte. I got home at 6:30 p.m., red faced with windblown warmth. Despite the long day, I keyed out three of the plants (the shoreline sedge, chufa, and creeping spikerush), realizing that I should get the jump on them given the trip scheduled for the following day with Wilbur Rittenhouse to the Pocomoke watershed in Maryland and Delaware, which would produce many more plants to identify.

* * *

My last major trip to botanize in the Nanticoke watershed was with Bill McAvoy on August 8, 1996. Our plans involved stopping along North Tar Road off Route 392 and east of Hurlock in search of a plant that Frank Hirst and Ron Wilson discovered the previous year, another first for them for Maryland. The plant, Fernald's tick-trefoil (*Desmodium fernaldii*), was previously thought to occur no further north than southeastern Virginia. It is named for the famous Harvard botanist, Merritt Lyndon Fernald, an idol of mine, whose book I have now patiently carried with me into the field since the early 1960s. We also anticipated visiting the Boy Scout camp along the Nanticoke south of Hurlock in search of the indian side-oats (*Chasmanthium latifolium*), which had been found in the area by Rob Nasci years ago. Our third planned stop was to Dorchester Pond, the largest Delmarva pothole (Delmarva bay) in Maryland. (See Chapter Seven for more on the Delmarva potholes.)

We initiated our search for Fernald's tick-trefoil around 10:15 a.m., along the roadside as we slowly drove down North Tar Road. We spotted it around 10:25, but not after finding both velvety tick-trefoil (*Desmodium viridiflorum*, highly State rare to State rare) and smooth tick-trefoil (*D. laevigatum*, highly State rare and endangered), all three of which were new species for me. We also found the poison oak (*Toxicodendron quercifolia*) and creeping bush clover (*Lepedeza repens*). All but the poison oak were flowering. Pineweed (*Hypericum gentianoides*), a small plant in the St. John's-wort family, was also flowering.

Upon entering the Boy Scout camp south of Hurlock, Bill pointed out another new species for me, southern goat's-rue (*Tephrosia spicata*, highly State rare and endangered), along the sandy roadside. However, since our goal was to rediscover indian side-oats, we searched the swamp, based upon Rob Nasci's site description, which proved fruitless. In all honesty, I did not think we would find it considering I have found it in Virginia and elsewhere in the Southeast mainly on firmer ground along river levees in the Piedmont or inner Coastal Plain. I suspect Rob may have found it near Eldorado along Route 14 by the bridge over Marshyhope Creek. We noted some Virginia dayflower (*Commelina virginica*, a watchlist species), cardinal flower, and southern white cedar (*Chamaecyparis thyoides*, a watchlist species), the former two flowering. The swamp, which was dominated by green ash (*Fraxinus pennsylvanica*) and red maple (*Acer rubrum*) was exceptionally sinky between tree and shrub clumps. Water willow (*Decodon verticillatus*) was flowering in the understory and wild rice occurred sporadically near the river in canopy openings. We were out of the swamp and heading for Maryland's largest pothole, Dorchester Pond, by 12:30 p.m.

Neither of us had been to Dorchester Pond before this trip. We hiked down a dirt road to access the site, which is southwest of Rhodesdale. While walking down the road, we noted smooth tick-trefoil, panicled tick-trefoil (*Desmodium paniculatum*) (or perhaps a related hybrid according to Bill), and stiff tick-trefoil (highly State rare and endangered). Then we angled towards what appeared to be an open bay area well beyond the forest edge. After struggling through some dense common greenbrier, we dropped down into the bay, which at that spot was dry and vegetated with sapling sweet gums (*Liquidambar styraciflua*). Soon, however, we were walking in standing water where we noted scattered maidencane (*Panicum hemitomon*, a watchlist species). As the water got deeper, perhaps a foot or so, we entered a zone of even smaller red maples, sporting, interestingly enough, mostly red leaves. I pondered whether the maples, and maybe the sweet gums, were stunted. Beyond the maples, it was basically all open water other than for a dense band of maidencane from which we had a great view of the open ponded portion. Obviously, with our record July rains, the pothole was completely full.

296

Therefore, the typical drawdown rarities were not evident. Despite this, we observe small swollen bladderwort (*Utricularia radiata*, a watchlist species), twigrush (*Cladium mariscoides*, a watchlist species), Virginia meadowbeauty (*Rhexia virginica*), white waterlily (*Nymphaea odorata*), and a yellow-eyed-grass, perhaps Small's yellow-eyed-grass (*Xyris smalliana*, highly State rare and endangered). We were out of the pond by 2:00 p.m. and botanized the same dirt road back to my car where I noted hairy hawkweed (*Hieracium gronovii*) and frostweed (*Helianthemum* sp.).

Bill had to leave early on this trip so we headed back, only briefly scanning the roadside for potential rarities, noting none. We reached the "park and ride" at the junction of Routes 50 and 404 at 3:25 p.m., whereupon Bill departed for Elkton, I for Millersville.

In a note to me on August 12, Bill submitted a list of his collections for our August 8 trip. Species that I had not already listed included the whorled mountain mint (*Pycnanthemum verticillatum*, highly State rare and endangered) from the upland at Dorchester Pond and the field sandbur (*Cenchrus longispinus*) along North Tar Road.

*   *   *

The trips described above represent some of my better ventures into the Nanticoke River watershed. Yet I would be the first to admit that I have substantially neglected this area in my field activities over the years. I know from what little literature there is on the area and from discussions with others in the field that there is much more to see and experience -- for this watershed is surely a natural history paradise. Places like Dorchester Pond and other potholes, Galestown Pond and similar old mill ponds, the fresh intertidal marshes on the upper Nanticoke and its tributaries, the vast brackish marshes of the lower Nanticoke and Elliott Island, the mesic woods, and the xeric dunes are treasures just waiting to be explored. I hope to spend more field time there in the future and would suggest you do too. Surely, we will not be disappointed.

297

POSTSCRIPT

When this book was about to go to press in the spring of 1999, I happened to attend a presentation by Doug Samson on The Nature Conservancy's Nanticoke River Bioreserve Strategic Plan (The Nature Conservancy, July, 1998). I subsequently reviewed a copy of the plan forwarded to me by Doug. As I suspected all along, the watershed has substantial biodiversity. The Maryland and Delaware Natural Heritage Programs have documented almost 200 plants and almost 70 animals that are rare, threatened or endangered in the watershed. Twenty of these plants, for example, the sensitive joint-vetch (*Aeschynomone virginica*), rose coreopsis (*Coreopsis rosea*), box huckleberry (*Gaylussacia brachycera*), Canby's dropwort (*Oxypolis canbyi*), awned meadowbeauty (*Rhexia aristosa*), and Canby's bulrush (*Scirpus etuberculatus*), are globally rare. Six of the animals, for example, the peregrine falcon (*Falco peregrinus*), King's hairstreak (*Satyrium kingi*), and Atlantic sturgeon (*Acipenser oxyrhynchus*), are globally rare.

Ecologically significant community types recognized from a *rarity perspective* included fresh intertidal wetlands, Coastal Plain ponds (Delmarva potholes), xeric dunes, and Atlantic white cedar swamps. The significance of riverine wetlands, rich woods, and open-canopy herbaceous wetlands (for example, Coastal Plain bogs), was also acknowledged.

Many of the highest ranking threats to these conservation targets related to the dominant land use in the watershed -- agriculture. Of the seven target communities listed, freshwater intertidal wetlands were judged to be under the greatest stress, due mostly to nutrient and sediment runoff from agricultural fields. The report also concluded that Coastal Plain ponds have been historically impacted by ditching (drainage), and that they continue to be threatened by groundwater withdraws for crop irrigation. Both Coastal Plain ponds and xeric dune communities were considered threatened by forestry practices. Threats to the four other target community types, however, were deemed minor or non-existent.

298

SEVEN

OUR DEPRESSIONAL GEMS: DELMARVA POTHOLES

And last, in his majesty comes man, who if he does not like the marsh, will dig ditches and drain it off. In a year he will be turning a furrow there, sowing his domesticated crop, the obedient grain; he will drive out every animal and plant that does not bow down to him.
-- DONALD CULROSS PEATTIE,
An Almanac for Moderns

POTHOLES, whale wallows, Maryland basins, Carolina bays, Delmarva bays, coastal plain ponds, vernal ponds -- whatever you choose to call them -- make no doubt about it, these depressions astride the spine of the Delmarva Peninsula are different from any other wetlands on the Delmarva, and they are very important ecologically. Up front, however, I should state that my preferred name for these interesting depressions is potholes -- the name I originally applied to them in 1976. Therefore, it will be used in the remainder of this Chapter. My justification follows.

The name "whale wallow," while colorful, is technically in-appropriate, and "Maryland basins" gives no indication that these features are wetlands, at least the interiors. Nor am I convinced that these depressions are of the same origin as the Carolina bays to the south, since many are more circular or irregular than elliptical and they generally are much smaller. In fact, the potholes are reported to have appreciable range of size, shape, and orientation (1), which can also be confirmed from the soil survey map sheets for Caroline, Kent, and Queen Anne's County, Maryland. In addition,

299

Carolina bays range in size from a few to several thousand acres (2). The largest pothole in Maryland, Dorchester Pond, is only about seventeen acres (3); the largest in Delaware, Huckleberry Pond, is about twenty-five to thirty acres (Bill McAvoy, personal communication). (For some discussion on Dorchester Pond and Huckleberry Pond, see Chapters Six and Nine, respectively.) Furthermore, intuitively, the potholes just seem so different from the Carolina bays that I have read about and seen in the South, and they are probably of a different origin. I also feel that the name Carolina bay itself is geographically inappropriate for the Delmarva Peninsula.[1] Moreover, to most people the term bay -- although in this instance the word "bay" refers to a few trees that occur in these wetlands, specifically sweet bay, red bay, and loblolly bay -- implies open water, particularly estuarine water in this region. There are, however, depressions on the Delmarva Peninsula, namely in Somerset County, Maryland and in Virginia that appear to be true Carolina bays. These will be discussed further later.

I should report, however, that in reviewing a draft of this Chapter, Mark H. Stolt, who has examined geomorphological and soil aspects of these Delmarva wetlands in detail, suggested a greater range of size -- commonly fifteen to twenty acres, with the largest in the central part of the Delmarva being perhaps fifty acres, and those in Somerset County, Maryland much larger. He also pointed out that the bays in the Carolinas are odd shapes or circular, rather than always elliptical, and that they are not always large. Furthermore, he feels that they are *not* different in origin from those on the Delmarva, so please keep that in mind as you read this Chapter. From my perspective, however, the large depressions discussed later for Somerset County and those that have been found in the Virginia portion of the Delmarva are quite different from those astride the spine of the Delmarva in Maryland and Delaware, which may explain in part our different views on their size and origin. Therefore, as you read this Chapter, it is very important to keep in mind my concept of a Delmarva pothole, which is different from the larger wetland depressions, generally hundreds of acres, that are found on the

---

[1] For a comprehensive bibliography of Carolina bays and a list of various theories on their origin, see T. E. Ross (4).

Delmarva in Somerset County and in Virginia and appear similar to the Carolina bays in the Southeast.

Calling these wetlands Delmarva bays presents a similar problem, since they too could be confused with the estuarine bays along the coast, and the potholes support only one bay tree, the sweet bay. Nor do I visualize these wetlands as ponds, since they are only intermittently wet and generally filled rim to rim with vegetation seasonally during low water. Moreover, many are forested or permanently vegetated with perennials like Walter's sedge. And given their geographic separation and absence of glaciation on the Delmarva Peninsula, I do not feel these wetlands will be confused with the well-known prairie potholes of the upper mid-west. Nor by calling them potholes, do I mean to imply that they are of similar origin as the prairie potholes. Rather, they are Delmarva potholes, not at all related to the prairie potholes. My second choice would be to use the term "vernal pond."

*　　*　　*

Rather amazingly, it has only been in the last fifteen years or so that researchers have begun to seriously study these areas. Little was known and published about them until the mid-1970s when Wayne Klockner and I started visiting these sites and pointed out their uniqueness from a natural history perspective (5,6,7). I should also note in this regard that Frank Hirst started botanizing these wetlands around 1971-1972 (personal communication) and referenced them in an article in *Bartonia* in 1983 (8). This aspect of the Delmarva potholes will be discussed more later.

Following our presentation on uncommon wetlands in the Coastal Plain of Maryland at a 1981 Towson University symposium, substantial interest developed in the potholes. Consequently, they have been studied floristically and vegetatively in more detail. Considerable interest has surfaced in their amphibian populations, and soil and hydrological investigations have also been conducted. Some of this information is presented below.

I first visited these interesting wetlands in 1976 while representing the Maryland Department of Natural Resources on an interagency State/Federal team to classify inland wetlands on the Delmarva Peninsula. At

301

one, I found, to my surprise, a carpenter frog (*Rana virgatipes*). That same year, I published an article on the carpenter frog in the *Bulletin of the Maryland Herpetological Society*, pointing out that my observation extended its distribution about forty miles north of its previously known Delmarva range (5). Subsequent to my observation, however, I learned that Nick Carter and Harley Speir had collected the carpenter frog in one of the potholes about four miles further northeast of my site (9). The carpenter frog also occurs, of course, further north in the New Jersey Pine Barrens.

In my article, I also indicated that these wetlands are: "...apparently little known, but ecologically interesting natural areas in and around the Maryland-Delaware border...These areas are essentially isolated 'potholes' some of which are glade-like in nature and others which are dominated by trees and/or shrubs." Because of their interesting nature and obvious potential uniqueness, Klockner and I conducted a floristic study of six of the Maryland potholes in 1976-1977. We also examined eight other sites less intensively, although plant lists were not compiled.

ON THEIR ORIGIN

The first person to scrutinize the origin of the Delmarva potholes may have been W. C. Rasmunssen in 1958 (10). Rasmunssen critically examined twenty hypotheses relating to the origin of what he called bays and basins. He proposed a compound origin of the bays and basins in Delaware, which he called the "Water table-sinkhole-lacustrine-aeolian" theory. Starting with a basin phase (steps 1-3) and leading to a bay phase (steps 4-6) the following sequence was suggested:

1. Initial slight depression concentrates runoff.
2. Percolating waters clean sands beneath the depression by taking suspended clays and colloids (and some solute) to the basin floor, or to the nearest stream, deepening the basin preferentially over the rims, as a sinkhole.
3. Development of a water table pond.
4. Wind generates waves that round the shoreline of the pond.

5. Waves elongate the bay in the direction of prevailing wind, as an oriented ellipse.

6. Continued sinking permits the capture of one basin by another through drainage.

Rasmunssen also described a geomorphic cycle for erosion in sandy flat lands in which the basin phase is youth and early maturity, the bay phase is late maturity, and the drainage of the bays by incursion of streams, is old age. If Rasmunssen was correct, this information would likely be applicable to the potholes in Maryland, since they are part of the area of major pothole concentration on the Delmarva Peninsula.

Rasmunssen's sinkhole theory, as well as similar theories of others for the origin of the Carolina bays to the south, were considered by M. H. Stolt and M. C. Rabenhorst during their study of the Delmarva potholes in the mid-1980s (1,11). As an alternative, however, Stolt and Rabenhorst, who considered these depressional wetlands Carolina bays, postulated the following origin of the Delmarva potholes. Two types of depressions (blowouts and interdunal swales) based on the sediments in the basin were suggested to have evolved through a series of steps, possibly over thousands of years before attaining their present morphology. In their words:

"The first step involved either the trapping of precipitation, or the establishment of a water table at the surface of the depression, forming a wetland. Next, a rough rim of sandy material was formed by vegetation growing around the wetland which trapped blowing sand. The third step involved currents or waves, created by strong winds, working the sands around the depression similar to the process in beach formation. This causes the depression to become preferentially oriented and the sandy rim to become regular in shape. Last, loessal sediments [2] were deposited on the depression and sub-

---

[2]However, Stolt has pointed out that only the potholes (he calls them Carolina bays) on the Delmarva Peninsula have the loess materials, since there is no loess source for those to the south (personal communication).

303

sequently eroded off the rims into the basins, leaving an ellptical depression with a sandy rim, similar to those bays found today."

Given the glade type potholes, I always suspected that these depressional wetlands were quite old. The study by Stolt and Rabenhorst appears to bear this out. For example, radiocarbon dates they obtained in buried organic-rich horizons found under the rims of many potholes indicate that the rims began forming between 15,000 and 20,000 years ago.[3]

Stolt and Rebenhorst's hydrologic observations showed a substantial difference between the depressional type containing fine textured sediments and the type with more coarse materials (Stolt, personal communication).

THE POTHOLE TYPES

From our field investigations at the six sites (Table X), we considered the undrained potholes on the Delmarva Peninsula to be of three types based upon the vegetation present: glades, shrub swamps, and forested swamps, with more than one vegetation type sometimes occurring in a given depression. We considered the glade and forested wetlands to be the least and most abundant types, respectively.

For historical purposes, I have retained our original descriptions of the three types of potholes, which are based upon, for the most part, the six sites we examined. However, the reader should keep in mind that a number of subsequent studies of these Delmarva potholes, which will be discussed in part below, have further characterized these interesting wetlands. Where appropriate, information from site visits to these six potholes on July 29, 1998 and November 7, 1998 is also incorporated.

The glade potholes are open areas surrounded by forests where undesturbed (Figure 55). Most of the glades are variously dominated by the giant plumegrass (*Erianthus giganteus*), Walter's sedge (*Carex walteriana*),

---

[3]Stolt and Rabenhorst also characterized and classified the soils of the Delmarva potholes (12).

TABLE X
LOCATION OF SIX POTHOLE SITES SAMPLED BY SIPPLE
AND KLOCKNER IN 1976-1977

Site one. About 500 feet north of Coolspring Branch of Tidy Island Creek and 500 feet west of Marvel Road near Mt. Zion in Caroline County.

Site two. On the west side of Templeville Road, about one mile north of Mt. Zion in Caroline County.

Site three. Along a southeastern dirt road extension of Jones Road, about one mile north of Hollingsworth Crossroads in Caroline County.

Site four. At the same general location as site three, but about 1000 feet to the southeast.

Site five. On the south side of Busicks Church Road, about one quarter of a mile northeast of Maryland Route 302 in Queen Anne's County.

Site six. Near Carson Corner in Queen Anne's County.

and twigrush (*Cladium mariscoides*). Sphagnum moss also forms a dense groundcover beneath these angiosperms. Surface water levels vary from a foot or so in depth in early spring to zero in late summer and fall when only a damp or dry substrate exists. Sites one and six, both of which are a few acres in extent, exemplify this type. Although totals of sixteen and twenty vascular plant taxa were found within sites one and six, respectively, the giant plumegrass and Walter's sedge (and to a lesser extent twig-rush) clearly dominate. The other species are infrequent, although isolated clumps of persimmon (*Diospyros virginiana*) occur at site six. Some glades, on the other hand, are almost entirely vegetated by smartweeds (*Polygonum* sp.).

Although we reported the giant plumegrass from these sites, we may have been off on our estimates of its abundance. I can not say for sure now. However, on my July 29, 1998 site visit to all of these potholes, I found the maidencane (*Panicum hemitomon*) in numbers one, four, five, and six (only abundantly in six), but little or no evidence of the giant plumegrass. Maidencane has also been reported as abundant in some potholes (8).Either we originally mistook the maidencane for the plumegrass in potholes one, four, and six, or the vegetation has changed. Such changes may be characteristic or common, however, since Frank Hirst's records for four Delmarva potholes over about a ten year period indicate dramatic year by year vegetation changes.[4]

Figure 55. The author with a small group of Environmental Protection Agency personnel examining a glade type Delmarva pothole in Caroline County, Maryland in the early fall of 1997. Note its open nature, and the absence of standing water by this time of the year due to evapotranspiration

[4]Hirst prefers to call these wetlands coastal plain ponds. The sites for which he has kept records are not the ones Klockner and I studied.

The shrub swamps are dominated by buttonbush (*Cephalanthus occidentalis*) (Figure 56) and/or water willow (*Decodon verticillatus*). Some of these sites have up to a few feet of standing water in spring, but only damp substrate by late summer or fall. This natural drawdown results in dense annual plant invasion and seasonal dominance in openings in some shrub swamps. Sites two and three, both of which are less than an acre in extent, are

Figure 56. The buttonbush (*Cephalanthus occidentalis*) is frequently the dominant shrub in potholes on the Delmarva Peninsula.

examples of this type. Site two is dominated by buttonbush and water willow, with scattered specimens of persimmon. Site three is dominated by buttonbush. Both sites, however, have seasonally dominant herbaceous vegetation in more open areas, for example, smartweeds, warty panic grass (*Panicum verrucosum*), devil's beggar-ticks (*Bidens frondosa*), teal lovegrass (*Eragrostis hypnoides*), and rice cutgrass (*Leersia oryzoides*), as a result of water level changes. A total of sixteen and eleven vascular plant species were found, respectively, within these sites.

The wooded swamps were not examined seasonally during our study. Those visited were dominated by red maple (*Acer rubrum*), sweet gum

307

(*Liquidambar styraciflua*), and/or oaks, such as the pin oak (*Quercus palustris*) and willow oak (*Q. phellos*). They have little in the way of herbaceous understory, although ericaceous shrubs are sometimes common.

Some of the potholes support a mixture of glade and shrub swamp vegetation, for example, site four. This site is a few acres in extent with spring water levels in the shrub swamp and open water areas one to a few feet deep; spring water level in the glade area appears less than one foot. Buttonbush dominates the shrub swamp area and Walter's sedge and giant plumegrass dominate the glade area. Much of the pothole is open water without emergent vegetation in spring, but with patchy annual vegetation in late summer and fall, such as slender fimbry (*Fimbristylis autumnalis*) and long-beaked baldrush (*Rhynchospora scirpoides*). The vegetation of this site has changed substantially since the late 1970s (see below).

Site five, about an acre in size, is different from the others examined perhaps due to its location adjacent to Busicks Church Road. Much of the site is dominated by globe-fruit seedbox (*Ludwigia sphaerocarpa*). Although two other sites (two and six) contain this species sparsely, no other site has it as a dominant. Other dominants throughout much of this site include smartweed and comb-leaf mermaid-weed (*Proserpinaca pectinata*). Water willow and lizards tail (*Saururus cernuus*) are locally abundant around its periphery. The site has a few feet of water in the spring but the substrate is damp or even dry in late summer and fall. During high water in the spring, open water areas occur without emergent vegetation. On July 29, 1998, I did not find the globe-fruit seedbox and found very little lizards tail at this site. On the other hand, woolgrass (*Scirpus cyperinus*) was very abundant, but was not found during 1976-1977.

VEGETATION STUDIES

Personnel from the Maryland Natural Heritage Program investigated six potholes in 1987-1988 to classify them and determine the structure of their plant communities (3). Five of these potholes (Bridgetown Pond, Persimmon Preserve, Jackson Lane, and two at Baltimore Corner) were in Caroline County; the sixth (Dorchester Pond) was in Dorchester County.

Collectively, five community types were identified in the ground layer based upon presence and cover data using vegetation ordination techniques. Swamp sweetbells (*Leucothoe racemosa*) dominated the most frequent community type, which was restricted to the forest perimeter; it had an overstory dominated by red maple and/or sweet gum. The Virginia meadowbeauty (*Rhexia virginica*) and warty panic grass communities were restricted to the innermost zone of potholes. The maidencane community only occurred as a narrow band near or adjacent to the perimeter of the forest. The Walter's sedge community existed as an inter-lying zone near or contiguous with forested perimeter and as the sole non-perimeter community. The swamp sweetbells, maidencane, and Walter's sedge communities, which were restricted to the drier end of the gradient, had lower species diversities and annual cover differences compared to the Virginia meadowbeauty and warty panic grass communities found in the inner-most zones of the potholes.

ECOLOGICAL SIGNIFICANCE

As best I can tell, no one studied these wetlands botanically until the independent field work by Frank Hirst in 1971-1972 and Klockner and me in 1976-1977. They were not mentioned by Forest Shreve and his co-authors in *The Plant Life of Maryland* in 1910 (13) or by Robert R. Tatnall in the *Flora of Delaware and the Eastern Shore* in 1946 (14), or any other botanical or ecological publications with which Klockner and I were familiar at the time. In reviewing a draft of this Chapter, however, Bill McAvoy indicated that Tatnall listed several pothole-associated plant collections made by Albert Commons from the Townsend area in New Castle County, Delaware. McAvoy also indicated that the Townsend area contains hundreds of potholes. Based upon these collections, he suggests that Tatnall described them as bogs. However, under a section on Coastal Plains in Tatnall's 1946 book, all I could find was the following statement, "Sphagnous bogs in many places harbor acid-loving rarities." Nevertheless, It appears that Commons visited at least the potholes in New Castle County. Similarly, the Delmarva potholes were not studied faunistically until more recent years. The lack of floristic and faunistic field work in these areas was amazing to us in the late 1970s, given that the

309

potholes had a number of uncommon phenomena associated with them. It is even more amazing now, considering all of the subsequent interest, the significant discoveries, and their estimated number (1,500-2,500).[6]

Klockner and I expressed our amazement over the lack of field work on these interesting sites in our 1981 presentation on them and some other uncommon wetlands in Maryland's Coastal Plain at the Towson University threatened and endangered species symposium mentioned earlier (7). In presenting a five-point argument on their ecological significance below, I will also address information that has surfaced from subsequent studies.

First Point

Klockner and I considered the potholes to be restricted to parts of only five counties (Caroline, Kent, and Queen Anne's Counties in Maryland and Kent and New Castle Counties in Delaware). The U.S. Geological Survey 7.5 minute quadrangle maps for Sudlersville, MD-DE (1953) and Goldsboro, MD (1944) depict about twenty-two and forty-five intermittent ponds and permanent water ponds, respectively, for the region in which the potholes occur. One area of the Goldsboro quadrangle, within a one to two mile radius of Mount Zion, Maryland shows thirty-five such features. Even higher densities are shown on soil survey map sheets (15). We estimated that the total number of potholes in Caroline and Queen Anne's County alone exceeded 500. Stolt and Rabenhorst (1) considered the greatest concentrations to be in Queen Anne's, Caroline, Kent, and Talbot Counties, Maryland and in Kent County, Delaware, and estimated 1,500-2,500 potholes in this larger area.

These wetlands have been subsequently shown to occur also in Dorchester, Talbot, Wicomico, and Worcester Counties in Maryland, Sussex County, Delaware, and the Virginia part of the Delmarva, and some

---

[6]One of the reasons these depressional wetlands were not studied earlier is perhaps because there large extent was not recognized until aerial views of the landscape made their uniqueness very obvious (Mark H. Stolt, personal communication). I suspect this is true, although local folks probably hunted for deer and waterfowl in them long before the availability of aerial photographs.

researchers consider them equivalent to Carolina bays and thus to occur from southern New Jersey to Florida (1,3,10,16,17,18,19,20). What appears perhaps to be similar depressions also occur on Long Island (21). I have visited Dorchester pond, but have not visited any potholes in Wicomico County. I suspect, however, that the reference to Carolina bays in Wicomico County really refers to what I am calling potholes, not true Carolina bays (22).

Although as indicated earlier, I do not consider these depressional wetlands astride the spine of the Delmarva Peninsula to be Carolina bays, I have noticed three rather large elliptical landforms, all oriented northwest-southeast, in Somerset County, Maryland. These large depressional areas resemble (and perhaps are comparable in origin to) Carolina bays of the Southeast. I first spotted one of them on an aerial photograph in the late 1970s but never followed up on it with a site visit. Then in writing this Chapter twenty years or so later, I examined the Somerset County soil survey map sheets for similar elliptical landforms, and sure enough found two more (23). Two of these bays are about one mile in diameter; the other is about one-half a mile. All of these, which are evident on Somerset County soil survey map sheets 26, 30 and 43/48, are not only elliptically shaped like Carolina bays, but they likewise have the same northwest-southeast orientation. They all also have very evident curvilinear rims, but the rims are on their northwestern ends. In most instances, the rims of Carolina bays are most pronounced on their southeastern margins (20). However, D.J. Bliley and D.E. Pettry indicated that high rims associated with Carolina bays they examined in the Virginia part of the Delmarva Peninsula were not located consistently in any single bay quadrant, which again lends support for my find (24). Other than that situation, the landscape pattern is remarkably similar to Carolina bays of the South.

On July 24, 1998, I visited two of these potential Carolina bay sites that were reasonably accessible. One, which is located at Manokin (map sheet 26), is about 648 acres in extent. Route 361 bifurcates it (Figure 57). About one half of this site is forested and one half is comprised of cultivated fields or old fields and a county landfill. The curvilinear rim, being in soybean and old field vegetation to a large extent, is quite evident, although part of it has been excavated and supports an elongated pond. According to the soil survey,

311

Figure 57. A computer-scanned printout of a 1985 aerial photograph showing part of a large elliptical depression (upper right), apparently a Carolina bay, near Manokin in Somerset County, Maryland. Much of this depression has been cleared and drained for agriculture, although substantial forested swamp still exists. Note also the farmed or otherwise cleared curvilinear upland rim. Maryland Route 361 bifurcates the site.

the rim supports upland soils (Sassafras, Matapeake, Mattapex, and Lakeland-Galestown); the forested area supports hydric soils (Fallsington, Othello, and Portsmouth). The forested area has been extensively ditched and the ditches are very old. Much of the area, which is now dominated by red maple, has rather old moss-covered agricultural furrows, evidence of past tillage. Although the interior of the area, being quite large, does not seem like a depression, it is clearly depressional compared to the rim. In addition, it still

312

supports a number of wetland plants, including a State rare and threatened species, the crested yellow orchid (*Platanthera cristata*). The tillage, of course, may have affected it, or it could have filled with wind-blown materials, as has been suggested for the Maryland potholes (1,11).

The second site, which is at Rumbley (map sheet 30), is about 450 acres in extent (Figure 58). Again, a curvilinear rim is quite evident since small houses and lawns at Rumbley and another village area on Mine Island sit on its convex surface. A small cemetery lends further evidence to its elevation relative to the interior basin. The interior area supports brackish tidal marsh dominated by needlerush (*Juncus romoerianus*), smooth cordgrass (*Spartina alterniflora*), saltmeadow cordgrass (*S. patens*), and saltgrass (*Distichlis spicata*). Goose Creek, a tributary of Tangier Sound, penetrates it from the northwest. The photographic evidence is not as convincing for this site, since, if it was originally a Carolina bay, much of the surficial evidence has been obscured by the transgressing brackish marsh. Actually, there may be twin Carolina bays at this location, since an apparent curvilinear rim exists immediately to the north.

The third potential Carolina bay site, which is located near Andy's Point and Parsonville (map sheets 43/48), is about 162 acres in extent. It has a rim-like curvilinear landform on its northwestern end, but like the Rumbley site, much of this site has been masked by the transgressing brackish marsh. I have not visited this site.

In terms of size and vegetation, these sites are all very different from the potholes. They are also much lower in elevation (Mark H. Holt, personal communication). Whether they are in fact Carolina bays is speculative at this point. A definitive answer would likely come only from detailed subsurface soil investigations. This would not likely, however, resolve the issue as to whether they have formed by a different process than the smaller depressions, the Delmarva potholes, to the north.

About a week after I visited the potential Carolina bays in Somerset County and drafted the above account, I mentioned these sites to Wayne Tyndall of the Maryland Natural Heritage Program. He alluded to some similar large areas considered to be Carolina bays on the Virginia part of the

313

Figure 58. A computer-scanned printout of a 1985 aerial photograph of a large elliptical depression (lower right), apparently a Carolina bay, at Rumbley in Somerset County, Maryland. Because of the low elevation, this depression has succeeded to saltmarsh. Note a possible twin depression in the upper right side of the photograph. The town of Rumbley is approximately in the center of the photograph.

Delmarva Peninsula and sent me the two related publications (24,25). These publications strongly support my suspicion that the Somerset County sites are indeed Carolina bays. First of all, the authors reported some Carolina bays in Virginia up to almost one mile in diameter. Furthermore, some of their largest bays were located in tidal marsh, and most had ridges that resembled sections

314

of rims that had been breached by tidal marsh. Thus many of these bays did not have complete rims. Likewise, the setting of the Virginia tidal bays suggested that the marshes were gradually covering and destroying the bays, which is to be expected considering the transgressive nature of the coastal marshes on the Delmarva (see Chapters Three and Four).

Consequently, it appears that some of the Carolina bays in Virginia are similar to the Rumbley and Parsonville bays that I located in Somerset County. In fact, the rims of the bays in Virginia found in association with the tidal marshes commonly supported roads, buildings, and cemeteries. The authors pointed out that in more elevated areas, lack of natural drainage was rectified in cultivated areas by internal ditching and excavating through the rims to outlets. They also mentioned that mechanized cultivation appears to be gradually leveling the rims and filling the bay centers. Thus, the descriptions presented by these authors closely resemble the three landscape features described above for Somerset County that resemble Carolina bays.

Second Point

Many of the glade types appear to be natural "grasslands" within the oak-hickory-pine forest potential natural vegetation of A. W. Kuchler (26). One glade near site three and four, for example, is a circular "grassland" depression about 500 feet in diameter surrounded by dense forested swamp. According to Gene Cooley, who called the potholes Carolina bays, the glade type potholes are one of eight natural grassland communities found in Maryland, the others being eastern shore xeric sand woodlands, serpentine areas, Great Falls area of the Potomac River, greenstone glades, limestone glades, shale barrens, and mountain peatlands (27).

Third Point

Klockner and I originally suggested that the glades had been in existence for a long time, and that there was little evidence of long-term invasion by woody plants. Likewise, we saw no surficial evidence, such as

315

dead trees, that these sites were once swamp forests. Nor did we find evidence of buried tree trunks in these areas.

I revisited these glade sites on July 29, 1998 to assess the extent of woody plant invasion, but my observations can not be considered conclusive. For example, although the oldfield that was adjacent to pothole number six is now in young forest, the pothole itself remains very open and glade-like with what *might* be essentially the same extent of tree invasion that existed in the late 1970s. What appears to be the remains of pothole number one, which was also an open glade in the late 1970s, is now forested in young red maple and sweetgum with an understory of Walter's sedge and maidencane, but this vegetative change obviously relates to the associated clearing and drainage. Pothole number four, which we considered a mixed type, no longer has perennial glade vegetation and most of the buttonbush has died; herbaceous annuals are invading. It appears as though high water levels have impacted this pothole, so, if anything, this site has lost woody plants. Nevertheless, another glade-like pothole near Lentz Road in the Baltimore Corner Preserve, which we visited but did not floristically study, seems to remain as open as it was in the late 1970s. And as indicated above, many potholes apparently existed for 15,000-20,000 years (1), although not necessarily with the same vegetation.

On the other hand, successional changes to woody plants in some potholes have been reported based upon aerial photographic interpretation. For example, although Dorchester Pond's herbaceous cover decreased by only five percent between 1938 and 1980, decreases ranging from twenty-eight to eighty-three percent were documented for five other potholes during the same period (3,28).

I suspect that flooding, either annual or during very wet years, is the main factor in keeping out the woody species, with the deeper potholes having the least invasion, such as with Dorchester Pond. Support for this idea is that many of the smaller, shallower potholes are entirely forested, since less stress is present due to the ponding. Of course, too much ponding can also destroy the herbaceous vegetation, but in the long run, it would likely recover quicker considering the rhizomatous nature of many of the dominant species. With the dense stands of Walter's sedge, allelopathy may also be a factor. And

316

historically, fire may have played an important role. Perhaps certain potholes are more susceptible to change than others, particularly those that have ditching impacts. In fact, the smaller and shallower potholes are especially susceptible to drainage, and many have already been converted to agricultural land. Some of the larger ones, however, have withstood drainage attempts as evidenced by remnant ditches. The drier peripheries around potholes and surrounding upland forests are particularly susceptible to clearing. A prime example of this is the destruction of the forested swamp and upland forest surrounding a large glade, our site one, in 1977. As already suggested, this site is hardly recognizable today.

Fourth Point

Ecologically, these sites are "islands." Consequently, they may also have other interesting ecological or biogeographical phenomena, such as disjunct populations, endemics, and ecotypes, associated with them. I have already alluded to the carpenter frog (*Rana virgatipes*), a State rare and local species on the Delmarva Peninsula, which I have found in eleven of these potholes. Furthermore, it occurs in them abundantly. For example, Wayne Klockner and I caught twelve carpenter frogs and heard numerous others at one large glade in less than an hour on June 1, 1979. It no doubt occurs disjunctly in many, if not all, of these acidic wetlands, at least those in Maryland. And we predicted that some potholes might support the State rare and endangered eastern tiger salamander (*Ambystoma t. tigrinum*), which subsequently has been confirmed. Considering the potential for amphibian use of these temporarily ponded and isolated wetlands, it has always amazed me that little was known about the potholes when Klockner and I first explored them. The discoveries of the carpenter frog and the tiger salamander are prime examples of this.

The presence of persimmon in some of the well-flooded potholes may be an example of ecotypic variation in this species since it is generally an upland plant in this part of the United States. M. L. Fernald (29), for example, indicates that it occurs in "Dry areas, old fields and clearings..."

317

Fifth Point

Klockner and I compiled a list of sixty taxa for the six sites we inventoried over the two year period. However, the two glade types supported only twenty-six and twenty-seven taxa respectively. In my tentative description of these sites (6), I indicated that: "...for the present at least the *glades* should not be considered floristically diverse, individually or collectively [emphasis added]. A collective total of only 27 vascular plant taxa were found (probably due to the abundance of the glade dominants). In addition, none of the vascular plant species found is considered rare or unique." As it turns out, this statement was somewhat premature. Numerous rare species have been found in the Delmarva potholes since our studies, and we did not even realize that some species we found were rare. To a large extent, however, this is understandable considering that our field work took place over twenty years ago and at the time there was not much published material available on rare, threatened, or endangered plants of the Delmarva Peninsula. Furthermore, the Maryland Natural Heritage Program did not even exist. Moreover, it was not until the publication of *Rare and Endangered Vascular Plant Species in Maryland* by Broome and her co-authors that we had anything to go by other than our own experience with species distributions in the Coastal Plain, since the Maryland Natural Heritage Program was not established until 1979 (30). The Program's first list of rare, threatened, and endangered plants and animals was not published until 1984. In addition, none of the plants we found in the potholes were on Broome's list. And it is true that many glades have rather uniform (low diversity) perennial vegetation, commonly Walter's sedge.

As indicated earlier, we discussed these sites, along with some other interesting wetlands in Maryland, at a threatened and endangered plants and animals symposium at Towson University in 1981 and published paper in its proceedings in 1984 (7). In publishing the article, however, we did not mention a lack of rarities. In fact, two of our species, the coppery St. John's-wort (*Hypericum denticulatum*) and long-beaked baldrush, are rare and currently considered endangered and threatened, respectively, by the Maryland Natural Heritage Program. A third, the twigrush, is on the Program's watch-

318

TABLE XI
RARE PLANTS REPORTED FROM MARYLAND POTHOLES *

Scientific Name	Common name
Boltonia asteroides	aster-like boltonia
Carex bullata	button sedge
Eleocharis melanocarpa	black-fruited spikerush
Eleocharis quadrangulata	square-stem spikerush
Eleocharis robbinsii	Robbin's spikerush
Fimbristylis perpusilla	Harper's fimbry
Hottonia inflata	featherfoil
Hypericum adpressum	creeping St. John's-wort
Hypericum denticulatum	coppery St. John's-wort
Leersia hexandra	club-headed cutgrass
Lobelia canbyi	Cany's lobelia
Muhlenbergia torreyana	Torrey's dropseed
Oldenlandia uniflora	clustered bluets
Paspalum dissectum	Walter's paspalum
Ranunculus flabellaris	yellow water-crowfoot
Rhynchospora filifolia	thread-leaved beakrush
Sagittaria engelmanniana	Engelmann's arrowhead
Scleria reticularis	reticulated nutrush
Sclerolepis uniflora	pink bog-button
Utricularia purpurea	purple bladderwort

* Source: Frank Hirst, D. Daniel Boone, and
George Fenwick in 1982.

list. A fourth species at one pothole, which was listed only as an umbelliferous plant, turned out to be exceptionally rare; it will be discussed further later. When we published our article in the proceedings, we added a list of twenty taxa compiled from extensive field work conducted in 1982 in Maryland potholes by Frank Hirst, D. Daniel Boone, and George Fenwick, all of which were considered rare, threatened, or endangered plants in Maryland by the Maryland Natural Heritage Program (Table XI). Rare plant species have continued to surface with additional field work on the Delmarva Peninsula. As of April 1998, for example, Bill McAvoy of the Delaware Natural Heritage Program had compiled a list of sixty-one rare vascular plant

319

TABLE XII
LIST OF VASCULAR PLANTS
IN POTHOLES ON THE
DELMARVA PENINSULA AS OF 1998*

Scientific Name	Common Name
Amphicarpon purshii	blue maiden-cane
Asclepias lanceolata	smooth orange milkweed
Bidens discoidea	swamp beggar-ticks
Boltonia asteroides	aster-like boltonia
Carex barrattii	Barrett's sedge
Carex bullata	button sedge
Carex gigantea	giant sedge
Carex joorii	cypress-swamp sedge
Carex lupuliformis	false hop sedge
C. typhina	cattail sedge
C. vesicaria	inflated sedge
Centella erecta	coinleaf
Coelorachis rugosa	wrinkled jointgrass
Coreopsis rosea	pink tickseed
Dichanthelium wrightianum	Wright's witchgrass
Echinodorus parvulus	burhead
Eleocharis melanocarpa	black-fruited spikerush
Eleocharis robbinsii	Robbin's spikerush
Eleocharis tricostata	three-ribbed spikerush
Eragrostis hypnoides	teal lovegrass
Eriocaulon compressum	flattened pipewort
Fimbristylis perpusilla	Harper's fimbry
Glyceria acutiflora	short-scaled manna grass
Hottonia inflata	featherfoil
Hypericum adpressum	creeping St. John's-wort
Hypericum denticulatum	coppery St. John's-wort
Leersia hexandra	club-headed cutgrass
Iris prismatica	slender blue flag
Juncus elliottii	bog rush
Lachnanthes caroliana	Carolina redroot
Litsea aestivalis	pondspice
Lobelia boykinii	Boykin's lobelia
Lobelia canbyi	Canby's lobelia
Muhlenbergia torreyana	Torrey's dropseed
*Nymphoides aquatica***	larger floating-heart
Nymphoides cordata	floating-heart

320

*Oldenlandia uniflora***	clustered bluets
Oxypolis canbyi	Canby's dropwort
Panicum hemitomon	maiden-cane
Panicum hirstii	Hirst's panic grass
Paspalum dissectum	Walter's paspalum
Polygala cruciata	crossed-leaved milkwort
Polygala cymosa	tall pine-barren milkwort
Polygala ramosa	low pine-barren milkwort
Ranunculus flabellaris	yellow water-crowfoot
Rhexia aristosa	awned meadowbeauty
Rhynchospora c. cephalantha	capitate beakrush
Rhynchospora c. microcephala	tiny-headed beakrush
Rhynchospora corniculata	short-bristled hornedrush
Rhynchospora filifolia	thread-leaved beakrush
Rhynchospora harperi	Harper's beakrush
Rhynchospora inundata	drowned hornedrush
Rhynchospora nitens	short-beaked baldrush
Rhynchospora scirpoides	long-beaked baldrush
Sabatia difformis	two-formed pink
Sagittaria engelmanniana	Engelmann's arrowhead
Saccharum coarctatum	short-bearded plumegrass
Scleria reticularis	reticulated nutrush
Sclerolepis uniflora	pink bog-button
Trachelospermum difforme	climbing dogbane
Utricularia inflata	swollen bladderwort
Utricularia purpurea	purple bladderwort
Xyris smalliana	Small's yelloweyed-grass

* This list was originally compiled by Bill McAvoy, Delaware Natural Heritage Program, with assistance from Karen Bennett, Information Manager for the Delaware Natural Heritage Program and Lynn Davidson, Information Manager for the Maryland Natural Heritage Program, with review and comment by Frank Hirst and Ron Wilson. The original list, which was presented by families, is here alphabetized by genera and species.
* *Rare species not shown on the original list, but included on the December 31, 1996 Maryland Natural Heritage Program list.

2 1

taxa associated with the potholes of the Delmarva Peninsula.[6] This represents forty-five percent of the 135 vascular taxa collectively found in the potholes. Twenty of these rarities are sedges; eleven are grasses (Table XII). One, a shrub called pondspice (*Litsea aestivalis*), was not found in Maryland until 1985 when Frank Hirst located it in a Wicomico County pothole (31); until then, North Carolina was the closest known state with an extant population. Another, Canby's dropwort (*Oxypolis canbyi*), was found at one of our study sites (site six) in 1982 and was reported in an issue of *Bartonia* in 1984 by D.D. Boone, G.H. Fenwick, and Frank Hirst (32). Their find represents a rediscovery of a plant that had not been found on the Delmarva Peninsula since 1894. This species is not only rare on the Delmarva, it is also Federally endangered. Interestingly, I received a phone call from one of the authors prior to the publication of their *Bartonia* article who, without mentioning Canby's dropwort, inquired about the reference to an unidentified umbelliferous plant in my original paper from that same pothole (6). As I recall now, the umbellifer was not flowering, so I did not attempt to determine its identity, and for some reason unknown to me now, the unidentified umbellifer was not listed in the publication by Klockner and me in 1984.[7] Had we had seen the long-lost Canby's dropwort without realizing it? Probably so.

Although as a group, the potholes support a substantial number of rare plants, adjacent or nearby potholes apparently do not always contain the same rare species. For example, one pothole that we did not floristically examine at Baltimore Corner, which was in the same vicinity of our mixed type pothole (glade and shrub swamp), supports purple bladderwort (*Utricularia purpurea*), aster-like boltonia (*Boltonia asteroides*), Walter's paspalum (*Paspalum dissectum*), and reticulated nutrush (*Scleria reticularis*).All four of these are rare species in Maryland; the aster-like boltonia and Walter's paspalum are also endangered and the purple

---

[6]McAvoy prefers the term coastal plain ponds for these unique wetlands (personal communication). This information was presented at a workshop on Delmarva bays conducted as part of a Conservation of Biological Diversity Conference held at Annapolis, Maryland on May 10-13, 1998.

[7]I suspect we deleted it because we identified it only to the family level.

bladderwort is threatened.[8] Only the reticulated nutrush occurs at any of our six sites, that being site four at Baltimore Corner.

Another impressive thing about the potholes on the Delmarva Peninsula is that they support a rich array of amphibians. Amy and Jim White, for example, of the Delaware Nature Society have compiled a list of twenty-eight species of amphibians that occur in aquatic habitats on the Delmarva Peninsula, including Piedmont freshwater marshes, mill ponds, freshwater impoundments, Piedmont streams, Coastal Plain streams, cedar swamps, cypress swamps, rivers, Coastal Plain freshwater marshes, and potholes.[9] Collectively, the potholes support the highest number of species, nineteen, an impressive sixty-eight percent. Fourteen of these are frogs or toads and five are salamanders (Table XIII). One species, the barking tree frog (*Hyla gratiosa*), which is a rarity in Maryland and Delaware, was not found in Maryland until 1982 when it was located in Caroline County (33), then in New Castle County, Delaware in 1987 (34). The potholes at The Nature Conservancy's Golts Pond Preserve in Caroline County support the barking tree frog (35). It was formerly thought to occur only south of the Chesapeake Bay, although Frank Hirst (personal communication) also mentioned its presence near Bennett Bog in Cape May County, New Jersey. In addition, Jim White (personal communication) indicates that four additional populations have been found more recently in Maryland and Delaware.

Surprisingly, the carpenter frog, which is rare in both states, was not listed by the Whites for the Delmarva potholes, although they agree that it may occur in some (personal communication). As I have already pointed out, it is abundant in a number of Maryland potholes.

I have often wondered why the potholes support so many rare plants and animals compared to other wetland types on the Delmarva Peninsula. I broached this phenomenon during a workshop on Delmarva bays at a bio-

---

[8]Source: Maryland Natural Heritage Program database.

[9]The Whites used the name Delmarva bays for these wetlands. This information was presented at a workshop on Delmarva bays conducted as part of a Conservation of Biological Diversity Conference held at Annapolis, Maryland on May 10-13, 1998.

TABLE XIII
AMPHIBIANS KNOWN TO OCCUR IN THE
POTHOLES OF THE DELMARVA PENINSULA

Scientific Name	Common Name
Acris c. crepitans	northern cricket frog
Ambystoma maculatum	spotted salamander
Ambystoma opacum	marbled salamander
Ambystoma t. tigrinum	eastern tiger salamander
Bufo woodhousei fowleri	Fowler's toad
Hemidactylium scutatum	four-toed salamander
Hyla chrysoscelis	Cope's gray treefrog
Hyla gratiosa	barking treefrog
Hyla versicolor	gray treefrog
Notophthalmus v. viridescens	red-spotted newt
Pseudacris c. crucifer	northern spring peeper
Pseudacris triseriata kalmi	New Jersey chorus frog
Rana catesbeiana	bullfrog
Rana clamitans melanota	green frog
Rana palustris	pickerel frog
Rana sylvatica	wood frog**
Rana u. utricularia	southern leopard frog
Rana virgatipes	carpenter frog
Scaphiopus h. holbrooki	eastern spadefoot

* The list was compiled by Amy and Jim White of the Delaware Nature Society in 1997.
** Personal communication, Amy and Jim White.

diversity conference in Annapolis, Maryland in 1998, seeking an explanation independent of my own thoughts. I received little response. So I have nothing to add but my own views. I feel that the richness principally relates to the spatial and temporal heterogeneity associated with these wetlands. For one thing, there is a variety of sizes and types: glades, shrub swamps, forested swamps, and mixed glades/shrubs. They also function like "islands" due to their isolated nature, which, as I pointed out above, has resulted in some instances in adjacent or nearby potholes having different rare plant species. And perhaps most importantly, they are only seasonally wet. The contrast at any given pothole between winter/spring and summer/fall is typically quite dramatic hydrologically.[10] My experience has been that people unfamiliar with the ecology of these wetlands are astonished by the hydrological contrast between these seasons. Using the glade type (particularly the glades with more open centers) as an example, the impression one gets in the winter/spring is that of a shallow pond with peripheral emergent herbaceous vegetation surrounded by a forested swamp. With leaf out and evapotranspiration, however, the water table soon drops. Consequently, the same pothole in the summer/fall has merely moist soil (sometimes dry) and emergent perennial or annual vegetation surrounded by forested swamp. Under such conditions the potholes not only support perennial emergents, but also submerged aquatics and floating leaved plants, as well as annuals that invade during the natural summer and fall drawdown. The species diversity data found in the vegetation study by Tyndall and his coauthors discussed above seems to also support this idea (3). Likewise, the high plant species diversity in shallow Coastal Plain ponds found on Long Island has been attributed to their natural heterogeneity, particularly their long-term water level fluctuations and the spatial patchiness and temporal variability of nutrients (21).

The seasonal hydrological nature of the potholes also makes them ideal for breeding amphibian populations, given the absence of fish that could prey on their eggs and larvae. Many of these species, certain salamanders for example, only breed in these areas. Most of their life cycles occur in the adjacent sandy uplands, generally under ground or under fallen logs and other vegetative debris. In this regard, it is an overall complex of potholes and adjacent upland forested areas that is important for maintaining viable populations of these animals.

---

[10]In 1987-1988, groundwater-surface water investigations were conducted in some potholes at Delaware's Blackbird State Park (36). Two major conclusions resulted. First, no single water table profile for a given time can adequately represent the range of groundwater flow conditions and groundwater interactions with the surface water. Secondly, the hydrology and chemistry of shallow seasonal ponds are strongly influenced by the adjacent groundwater flow system.

ON THEIR PROTECTION

Because of the unique nature of these wetlands, Klockner and I recommended in our symposium paper that some of them be acquired, preferably where representative examples of each type occurred in a matrix of upland forest. One such area, which encompassed a number of potholes, was in the general location of sites three and four near Baltimore Corner. As it turns out, these very potholes soon became protected when Mr. and Mrs. Thomas H. Eaton donated the land for what is now known as the Baltimore Corner Preserve to The Nature Conservancy in 1982 (37). The protection of similar areas soon followed: Persimmon Pond (1983), Pristine Pines (1983), Jackson Lane/Eaton's Pond (1985), Dorchester Pond (1986), and Wetiquin Pond/Doris Ranch Rend, Virginia Palmer (1988) Preserves.

The reader should keep in mind, however, that these interesting wetlands are fragile systems subject to adverse impacts from frequent visitation. Therefore, they are only open to scientific research with prior permission from The Nature Conservancy.

EIGHT

THE WILDS OF ANNE ARUNDEL

In the swamp [Glen Burnie Bog], *hundreds of Pitcher plants were still found in bloom, notwithstanding the depletion that is constantly going on.*
-- Charles C. Plitt, 1900

In the late 1880s, a number of Baltimore residents led by George Smith, a local teacher, formed the Baltimore Botany Club. This group eventually became incorporated in the Maryland Academy of Sciences, although most of the older members dropped out of the organization by the turn of the century. One of the younger members was Dr. Charles C. Plitt. Dr. Plitt was born in Baltimore on May 6, 1869, and died there on October 13, 1933. He was a graduate of the Baltimore City College (a high school) and went on to receive a degree of Graduate in Pharmacognosy from the Maryland College of Pharmacy in 1891. He taught in the public school system, including City College, and also taught part-time at the Maryland College of Pharmacy, which eventually became a part of the University of Maryland, where he was an associate professor of botany and materia medica.[1] In 1921, Dr. Plitt received the degree of Doctor of Science from the University of Maryland. He ultimately resigned from City College to work full time at the University of Maryland (2,3).

Dr. Plitt had been a botanical collector for some time, starting in the 1890s. His earlier excursions were usually alone or with a friend, Charles

---

[1] According to Stedman's Medical Dictionary, materia medica is: that aspect of medical science concerned with the origin and preparation of drugs, their doses, and their mode of administration; any agent used therapeutically (1).

Weber, Jr. Since he was in charge of teaching the University's extension normal classes in botany for public school teachers, these excursions gradually grew to regular Saturday afternoon "tramps" to botanize and instruct a group of educators, many of which were from the public school system (2,3). According to a May 1, 1984, article in *The Sun*, Dr. Plitt kept a detailed journal on these tramps, of which there were 3,153 between 1899 and 1922.

Actually, Dr. Plitt assembled a series of documents numbered 1-29, plus a series of Notes to Tramps (see below). In this Chapter, I refer collectively to these twenty-nine volumes and his Notes to Tramps as his journal (Figure 59). On average, over the twenty-three year period there were 2.4 trips per week. However, botany was not the only thing that Dr. Plitt studied on these trips and discussed in his journal. He frequently mentioned animals, particularly birds. For example, on March 24, 1900, Dr. Plitt spotted bluebirds in the woods along "Annapolis Rd" after leaving Sawmill Pond, and on March 14, 1903, he indicates that "There were...a great many [bluebirds] and they were generally in the fields." At times, he met and spoke with local people (e.g., a blacksmith). He also mentioned housing conditions, and in one entry even discussed the upcoming Bryan-McKinley presidential race.

These weekly botanical excursions took Dr. Plitt and his botanical students and friends through more than 400 square miles of Maryland's countryside around Baltimore (4).[2] Although most of these trips were to places like Loch Raven, Towson, Ellicott City, Curtis Bay, Glen Burnie, Waterford, and Round Bay, there were also distant trips to places like The Falls of the Potomac, Ocean City (Maryland), and the New Jersey coast and Pine Barrens. Many of the more local sites were visited more than once a year and repeatedly year after year. Some sites were even visited in the winter. Consequently, Dr. Plitt documented the changes that had occurred over the twenty-three year period that the records were kept.

This turn-of-the-century botanist frequently came into Anne Arundel County from Baltimore by train, particularly when he was visiting areas

---

[2]Rather than repeatedly refer to "Dr. Plitt and his botanical students and friends," I will simply refer to "Dr. Plitt" in the rest of this chapter.

between Baltimore and Annapolis, exiting the train at stations at Glen Burnie, Marley, Elvaton, Earleigh Heights, Robinson, and Round Bay. From Elvaton, for example, he would hike to Lake Waterford; from Robinson or Earleigh Heights to the Benfield area and Severn Run. On the other hand, in his May 16, 1908 journal entry, Dr. Plitt mentions that the Benfield area was also approached from the "...new Naval Academy Junction Station" via the "B.W.

Figure 59. Partial replication of Dr. Charles C. Plitt's ornate cover for his journal volumes.

& A. trolley line." In this instance, he passed through Sappington in going to Benfield. On July 13, 1901, he also indicated that he took the "electric car" as far as Brooklyn, then walked to Glen Burnie. At times, however, he even traveled into the County by steamer, the *Petrel*, to either the Stony Creek Wharf or Rock Creek Wharf. From all of these stations or wharves, he often walked for miles to his favorite botanical sites, including the Lake Waterford area.

Having lived and botanized in Anne Arundel County for a number of years, Dr. Plitt's tramps into the "wilds of Anne Arundel" have particularly caught my interest. Therefore, those interesting tramps and my own adventures while on the trail of Dr. Plitt are the subject of much of this

Chapter, particularly in relation to what plants he did and did not find.[3] A discussion of some additional botanically interesting sites, most of which Dr. Plitt evidently did not visit, comprises the remainder.

ON THE TRAIL OF DR. CHARLES C. PLITT

In 1998, I was able to obtain access to a photocopy of Dr. Plitt's journal through the courtesy of the Maryland Department of Natural Resources. After reviewing it for five days, I was greatly enlightened. I have uncovered a number of entries that changed my ideas on the extent of Dr. Plitt's field activities and the plants he found in Anne Arundel County. Yet, I still ponder what I may have missed while struggling with his handwritten entries. Fortunately, the Department anticipates typing Dr. Plitt's journal, which will make it more easily accessible and readable in the future. I am confident, therefore, that additional interesting facts will surface.

Many of Dr. Plitt's journal entries were very detailed, at least until the last few years. Being a journal keeper myself since 1955, I can appreciate his dogged devotion to maintain this effort. His journal is indubitably an invaluable source of information on what sites looked like in the early 1900s. The botanical community in particular should be very thankful for Dr. Plitt's endeavors.

I initially encountered some confusion in reviewing the photocopy of Dr. Plitt's journal in Annapolis. The Maryland Department of Natural Resources has more than one document produced by Dr. Plitt. One is a series of volumes with title pages marked "Tramps" and numbered from 1-29. These run from March 4, 1899 to April 29, 1905, and are obviously part of Dr. Plitt's journal. A second document has no title page. It includes a 16-page index, 43-page plant list, several blank pages, a page on lichens, a page with a poem, and starting on page 49 and running to page 285, a section called Notes to Tramps. The first journal entry on page 49 is March 19, 1904; the

---

[3]My own field experiences, including those while on the trail of Dr. Plitt, are documented in my *Journal*.

last on page 285 is September 1, 1906. This document is continued on legal size paper (pages 1-501) starting with an entry on September 4, 1906 and ending with an entry on November 5, 1922, which ends the Notes to Tramps. Thus, there is overlap and both documents sometimes give substantially different accounts of the same visits; sometimes a given visit is not included in both. The overlap period is for about one year (between March 19, 1904 and April 29, 1905). I first encountered this overlap while considering materials from 1905 -- specifically, the April 1 entry, which in itself is rather ironic, considering that is April Fool's Day! This overlap initially left me in a quandary, since it appeared as though I was dealing with a second document other than Plitt's journal, especially since the Tramps volumes ended in 1905 and Plitt's journal was supposed to run to 1922. On my fifth day in Annapolis, I solved the problem, when I encountered for the first time the only page in the second document that has the heading Notes to Tramps. This is a critical page in understanding the relationship between the two documents and the overlap. It appears that Dr. Plitt started making some additional notes to accompany his Tramps volumes as of March 19, 1904, but discontinued the Tramps volumes after April 29, 1905 (the overlap period). After that, his Notes to Tramps constituted the remainder of his journal. There are also some additional smaller documents in Annapolis, such as a volume on mosses and two volumes on plants found near Baltimore, which include 1,147 taxa.

Some of Dr. Plitt's journal entries were published in a number of issues of *Wild Flower* in 1954-1956 by G. R. Fessenden (4,5,6). Fessenden indicated in a footnote that: "Very much condensed extracts from Dr. Plitt's notes, particularly after the first year, will be continued through three or four issues of *Wild Flower*...." In this regard, Fessenden's condensed treatments can be misleading. I determined this problem when I examined the photocopy of Dr. Plitt's journal. Although Fessenden's condensation does not appear to have affected the species listed, it has resulted in potential confusion in some instances regarding the exact route traveled by Dr. Plitt and the sequence of visits, and therefore the location of some species he referenced. Three good examples of this are the September 6, 1899, March 28, 1903, and May 2,

1903 journal entries. Moreover, the extracts are written as if they were verbatim material, which could be misleading to the uninformed.

Sawmill Pond and the Glen Burnie Bog

Although I had been exploring the wetlands of Anne Arundel County since I arrived in Maryland in 1971, I did not become familiar with Dr. Plitt's journal until 1989 when Gene Cooley of the Maryland Natural Heritage Program sent me the extracts from it that were published by G. R. Fessenden (4,5,6). I was so excited by these fascinating accounts that Gene and I visited one of the sites, Sawmill Pond, on August 11, 1989 in search of the elusive Glen Burnie Bog. The Glen Burnie Bog was no doubt the same site described by C.E. Waters in 1905 (7), by Forrest Shreve and his coauthors in 1910 (8), and A.V.P. Smith in 1938 (9).[4] A few years prior to the trip with Gene, I had located what I thought might be the general location of the Glen Burnie Bog on Anne Arundel Soil Survey map sheet number 4, which showed what appeared to be a drained pond along Sawmill Creek (10). However, I never got around to visiting the area until the August trip. Although we waded almost waist deep through much of the now shallow marshy pond that day, we found no evidence of the bog. Two additional trips to the drained millpond by me on August 19 and 26, 1989, further confirmed in my mind that the bog, assuming it was in fact associated with the millpond, no longer exists.

In comparing the three publications cited above, it is obvious that they all refer to Sawmill Creek and particularly the Sawmill Pond area.[5] Smith, for example, indicated that the bog "...is situated on the right bank of

---

[4]See Shreve, et al's Plate XVI, Figure 1 for a photograph of the bog. Smith discussed the Glen Burnie Bog under a general discussion of other sites, referring to it as "Glenburnie Bog."

[5]Sawmill Creek is a tributary of Furnace Branch of the Patapsco River. Sawmill Pond is also called Wagner's Pond (11). The pond is not shown on the 1969 Curtis Bay, MD 4.5 minute quadrangle map; it is shown, however, as Wagner's Pond on an undated "Map of Anne Arundel County Showing the Maryland Coordinate System" (Williams & Heintz Map Corporation, Washington, DC). Although Dr. Plitt referred to this as Saw Mill Pond, he sometimes called it the Sarracenia Pond (e.g., see his December 27, 1899, January 6, 1900, and March 10, 1900 journal entries).

Furnace Creek, and is just upstream from an existing millpond," and Dr. Plitt repeatedly referred to Saw Mill Branch and Saw Mill Pond when discussing bog type plants.

In studying Dr. Plitt's journal and the Fessenden extracts taken from it, it is not clear when the Glen Burnie Bog was destroyed. The September 6, 1899 entry references a conversation Dr. Plitt had with Mr. Wagner, the apparent owner, who indicated that they hoped to "...raise the level...[of the pond] by damming up at its mouth." The June 30, 1900 journal entry indicates that Mr. Wagner "...had reclaimed quite a large marshy area...." Dr. Plitt also quotes Wagner: "Yes, me and my sons cut all of those woods [along the edge of the pond] down." On the other hand, numerous subsequent journal entries (for example, between October 15, 1907 and May 21, 1919) give no indication of a problem with Sawmill Pond and the Glen Burnie Bog.[6] Furthermore, Fessenden adds a footnote to the May 29, 1920 journal entry, which indicates that: "The dam which had recently been built at the outlet of the pond was evidently responsible for this flooding that later caused the Pitcher Plant to disappear and nearly eliminate the *Marsilea*."[7] If Fessenden's footnote is correct, there was either a small natural pond or man-made pond associated with the bog, which was expanded as a result of the dam, and this inundation eliminated the bog. The footnote is given in reference to what Dr. Plitt called "...a very interesting place, a newly formed swamp in which trees were gradually dying." A close read of Dr. Plitt's May 29, 1920 journal entry (as opposed to Fessenden's extract of it) suggests that this swamp with dead trees was far upstream from the pond, perhaps even near where the railroad tracks crossed Sawmill Creek, since they are mentioned. Furthermore, Dr. Plitt went "...to the *Sarracenia* locality and found still a number of plants, not as many, however, as from former occasions." He also found some sundews.

---

[6]During visits to this site, it is repeatedly referred to as Glenburnie, Saw Mill Pond, or just the pond [at Glenburnie]. Although it is obvious that the bog was present, I found no mention in Plitt's Journal to a Glenburnie Bog.

[7]The photocopy of Dr. Plitt's journal shows underlining of most of the scientific plant names, but also some common names. I am not sure whether this underlining was done by Dr. Plitt on the original journal or by a subsequent reviewer on the original or a photocopy. Regardless, I have italicized the scientific names given by Dr. Plitt in any quoted material.

Figure 60. The northern pitcher-plant (*Sarracenia purpurea*). This State rare
insectivorous plant was much more abundant in Anne Arundel County, Maryland in
Dr. Plitt's days, although even then it was restricted to a few bog habitats.

Near the dam he "...found still a little *Marsilea*." These statements, with words like "former occasions" and "still," seem to imply change, but I am not convinced that the bog was destroyed in 1920. In fact, on May 28, 1921, Dr. Plitt once again visited the "*Sarracenia* locality near Glenburnie," indicating that, "[I] set out at once for the pond...I got the material I wanted..." Thus, it appears as though the Glen Burnie Bog persisted at least until 1921 and probably later (Figure 60).

In its heyday, the Glen Burnie Bog must have been a botanical gem, perhaps not unlike another Anne Arundel County bog, which was apparently unknown to Dr. Plitt, the extant Arden Bog on the Gumbottom Branch of Plum Creek off the Severn River. Their descriptions seem fairly similar geomorphologically, hydrologically, and floristically. In 1910, Shreve and others described the Glen Burnie Bog as an area less than an acre in extent that was slowly drained by a nearby stream and derived its water from springs on the adjacent banks. There was ample sphagnum and several of the vascular plants present, at that time at least, had not been found elsewhere in the State. Associated with the sphagnum were the pitcher-plant (*Sarracenia purpurea*), round-leaf sundew (*Drosera rotundifolia*), spatulate-leaf sundew (*D. intermedia*), bog clubmoss, ten-angle pipewort (*Eriocaulon decangulare*), Carolina yelloweyed-grass (*Xyris caroliniana*), Virginia meadow- beauty (*Rhexia virginica*), common bladderwort (*Utricularia macrorhiza*), tawny cottongrass (*Eriophorum virginicum*), and leatherleaf (*Chamaedaphne calyculata*).[8] The margin of the bog had a shrub zone supporting dominantly sweet pepperbush (*Clethra alnifolia*), smooth alder (*Alnus serrulata*), and water willow (*Decodon verticillatus*), but also lesser numbers of swamp azalea (*Rhododendron viscosum*), poison sumac (*Toxicodendron vernix*), and sweetbay (*Magnolia virginiana*); peripheral to that was a forested area dominated by red maple (*Acer rubrum*), black gum (*Nyssa sylvatica* var. *sylvatica*), and loblolly pine (*Pinus taeda*).

---

[8] Although listed as *Lycopodium inundatum* (the northern bog clubmoss) , this species was probably the southern bog clubmoss (*L. appressum*) mentioned by Waters in 1905, since the northern bog clubmoss is a similar more northern species (6).

335

On May 30, 1900, Dr. Plitt visited Glen Burnie. He wrote:

"Reaching G [Glen Burnie] we walked along our usual path to the branch [either Saw Mill Creek or Furnace Branch]....In the swamp, hundreds of Pitcher Plants were still found in bloom, notwithstanding the depletion that is constantly going on. This locality is known to a great many (hundreds of) people, botanists, and others, who each year visit the place to get one or more specimens. Still the plant seems to hold its own and even is increasing...We reached the pond, here we found our first *Nymphaea odorata*....On the shore we found *Viola lanceolata* growing with *V. primulifolia*....Leaving the pond we went in the direction of the old furnace but stopped to examine the *Pogonia* spot....containing at least 25 plants..."

The white waterlily (*Nymphaea odorata*) and water shield (*Brasenia schreberi*) were found in an adjacent shallow pond, which as indicated above, was either a natural pond or a shallow man-made one.[9] On August 5, 1899, Dr. Plitt also mentioned the flattened pipewort (*Eriocaulon compressum*).

Some additional species listed by Waters (7) for the more open part of the bog included the crested yellow orchid (*Platanthera cristata*) and southern bog clubmoss. He also mentioned Virginia chain fern (*Woodwardia virginica*), red-berried greenbrier (*Smilax walteri*), and white-fringed orchid (*Platanthera blephariglottis*) for the wet woods. European water fern (*Marsilea quadrifolia*) was reported to have been introduced six or eight years earlier. The highly State rare and endangered New Jersey rush (*Juncus caesariensis*) has also been reported from the Glen Burnie Bog (9). This was apparently based upon a collection there on August 19, 1905 by M.A. Chrysler. However, it was not reported by Waters (7) or Shreve and his coauthors (8), and has apparently never been reported from elsewhere in the County, according to the Maryland Natural Heritage Program. In fact, this rare

---

[9]On the August 11, 1989 trip, Gene Cooley and I found some white waterlilies in Saw Mill Pond.

plant was thought to be extinct in the State until its discovery in the Piney Branch Bog in Charles County in 1989 (12) (See Chapter Ten for information on this bog.) In addition, Plitt reported the horned bladderwort (*Utricularia cornuta*) at the pond on July 13, 1901, the white fringed orchid at the head of the pond on July 13, 1904, and the fly poison (*Amianthium muscitoxicum*) in the Sawmill Pond area on June 6, 1903, June 20, 1903, and May 26, 1906.

*   *   *

One last point on Sawmill Pond. On March 14, 1998, while searching for climbing fern (*Lygodium palmatum*) and swamp pink (*Helonias bullata*) along Furnace Creek, I found the remains of a quite old, rather substantial earth dam (perhaps twenty-five feet high and fifteen feet wide at the top) only 500 feet or so downstream from Sawmill Pond. Furnace Creek cuts through it near the middle, and the dam protrudes onto the floodplain from each upland slope. There is a second higher notch in the dam, perhaps an old spillway location on the east side of the creek. Upstream of the dam, it is meadow-like, with scattered shrubs and some trees, almost up to Sawmill Pond. Plants present include tearthumb (*Polygonum* sp.), jewelweed (*Impatiens capensis*), Japanese honeysuckle (*Lonicera japonica*), goldenrod (*Solidago* sp.), blackberry (*Rubus* sp.), elderberry (*Sambucus canadensis*), northern arrowwood (*Viburnum recognitum*), skunk cabbage (*Symplocarpus foetidus*), dock (*Rumex* sp.), and others, including a few large red maples along the stream bank, one of which measured 31.7 inches diameter. Sediments were easily penetrated with a probe to at least four feet. Could this have been the dam for the original Sawmill Pond? And therefore, was it the existing dam that backed up the water resulting in the demise of the Glen Burnie Bog? Or, was this dam once associated with a larger Sawmill Pond? The dam is now forested with large oaks and other trees and shrubs, including the mountain laurel (*Kalmia latifolia*). One southern red oak (*Quercus falcata*) measured 21.1 inches in diameter.

337

The Dwarf Iris and the Wild Lupine

The sandy uplands in the vicinity of the Glen Burnie Bog similarly supported some interesting, and now rare, plants. For example, on an April 22, 1899 trip to Glen Burnie by train, Dr. Plitt indicated that while walking a woods path to the bog he found the dwarf iris (*Iris verna*) and wild lupine (*Lupinus perennis*) almost everywhere (Figure 61). He again reported this iris from the area on May 1, 1906. The lupine is also reported for the Glen Burnie area by Dr. Plitt on May 1, 1906, May 10, 1910 (in profusion), May 21, 1918, and May 29, 1920. Downy goldenrod (*Solidago puberula*) was noted on a September 6, 1902 trip to Glen Burnie. I have tried unsuccessfully to relocate these species while walking the upland periphery of Sawmill Pond. I was also unsuccessful in searching for his more common species, such as the sweetfern (*Comptonia peregrina*), bluecurls (*Trichostema dichotomum*), and golden aster (*Chrysopsis mariana*), which were reported for either April or September of 1899. This is to be expected considering the amount of commercial development that now exists around much of the pond. On my August 26, 1989 trip, however, I did locate a small, relatively undisturbed upland area on the slope adjacent to the northwest side of the remnant pond, which supported dwarf chestnut (*Castanea pumila*), small Solomon's-seal (*Polygonatum biflorum*), and bracken fern (*Pteridium aquilinum*), and no doubt existed in Dr. Plitt's days.

On April 29, 1922, Dr. Plitt noted fifty flowering dwarf iris between Lake Waterford and Elvaton. He also found it in the Marley area on May 3, 1904 and May 5, 1905. The lupine was reported while in transit between Elvaton and Lake Waterford on June 6, 1905 and again on April 29, 1922. The lupine was also observed by Dr. Plitt in the Marley area on May 12, 1900 (immense patches) and May 5, 1905. On May 16, 1908, he reported an "immense patch" between the Naval Academy Junction Station and Benfield; on May 15, 1909, he referenced "...large beds of Lupine..." between the Naval Academy Junction Station and Sappington. Apparently, the lupine was much more common in the County in Dr. Plitt's days, for he cites a 1899 trip to Curtis Bay where: "Great patches of *Lupinus perennis* were frequently seen."

338

Figure 61. The dwarf iris (*Iris verna*), wild lupine (*Lupinus perennis*), and swamp pink (*Helonias bullata*) -- three rare plants in Maryland that appear to have been of particular interest to Dr. Charles C. Plitt when he botanized his "wilds of Anne Arundel" during the turn-of-the-century.

339

There is an extant population of the dwarf iris at Solley, which is the only known site for it on Maryland's Upper Coastal Plain (13). I visited the Solley site on April 24, 1998 and found over 500 flowering stems along a transmission line on the east side of Solley Road. I also found twenty-two flowering stems on the west side of Solley Road, again along the transmission line. This is the only site that I have found the dwarf iris on the Western Shore, except for one location at Waldorf in Charles County, again in 1998.

Until 1998, I searched for the wild lupine in northern Anne Arundel County without any luck. Then in a February 16, 1998 letter to me, Colby Rucker mentioned a sighting of the lupine by Dave Williams about twenty years ago. This site is listed in Rucker's Anne Arundel County flora as "Picture Spring Branch: Nevamar sand pit," which, according to Rucker, is near the junction of Route 175 and Telegraph Road in Odenton (11). On June 21, 1998, I attempted to relocate this site to no avail, but in the process searched along some transmission line rights-of-way in the general area. At the end of my search, I located some lupine -- by rough count, 134 fruiting stems along one side of the right-of-way, as well as some on the opposite side. Since the Maryland Natural Heritage Program reports only one extant population of this species for Anne Arundel County, along a transmission right-of-way near Odenton, this is probably the same location.

The Swamp Pink

If there was any one plant that caught the attention of Dr. Plitt in his wilds of Anne Arundel, perhaps it was the swamp pink (Figure 61). His two main sites in the County for this now State rare and endangered plant were at Stony Run near Elkridge and along Marley Creek, both tributaries of the Patapsco River. The Stony Run site has an extant population of swamp pink that was rediscovered by Wayne Klockner and Mike Barnett in 1984; it had more than 1,000 plants in 1989 (14). I have searched a number of times but never found this site or the several small sub-populations that have been reported from the headwaters of Stony Run. Conversely, the Marley Creek site in Glen Burnie was apparently destroyed years ago. The site was evidently a

340

forested swamp between the North Arundel Hospital and Elvaton Road, the remnants of which are adjacent to the Southgate Apartments.[10] It was mentioned by Dr. Plitt in a number of journal entries and in the Baltimore Botany Club's April 29, 1905 journal entry (3). On his May 3, 1904 visit, Dr. Plitt "...counted 322 when seeing so many before me. I became confused and gave it up; there were no doubt more than 400 plants in bloom, perhaps more than 500." In 1991 and again in 1993, I tried to relocate this Marley Creek site after Gene Cooley gave me a detailed March 12, 1990 map of it drawn by Colby Rucker. The remnant site, currently a red maple-smooth alder swamp, was severely impacted by runoff. In my April 24, 1993 *Journal* entry I wrote:

"Decided to pursue the *Helonias bullata* (swamp pink) that Plitt referenced on his trip to Marley Station on Baltimore-Annapolis Railroad Line. Tried a number of places with no luck finding the swamp pink. First went to Southgate area to follow up on Colby Rucker's map that Gene Cooley gave me showing what Colby felt was the swamp pink site. This site is along Hospital Drive near North Arundel Hospital and at the Southgate Apartments. The stream is part of Marley Creek. It is a red maple-smooth alder (*Acer rubrum-Alnus serrulata*) swamp. Also much skunk cabbage (*Symplocarpus foetidus*) and common catbrier (*Smilax rotundifolia*); some sweet pepperbush (*Clethra alnifolia*). Tussock sedge (*Carex stricta*) flowering; also being grazed...

"If *Helonias bullata* was once at this site, I could easily understand why it isn't now. The floodplain was a mess, a debris-strewn mess -- extremely heavy sediment load, obvious evidence of extensive flooding, toys, styrofoam cups, bottles, cans, a shopping cart, and even a couch. Also some filling along edge with construction debris and stumps and other plant debris.

---

[10]The Maryland Natural Heritage Program reports four extant populations of the swamp pink in Anne Arundel County. These are the same locations for the extant populations discussed in this Chapter. Apparently, the Stony Run population is comprised of four sub-populations.

341

"Upstream of Hospital Drive on the same stream was also a red maple-smooth alder swamp with skunk cabbage, common catbrier, and much sweet pepperbush. More open areas had wood reed (*Cinna arundinacea*). Much further upstream at another tributary of the stream that flows behind the North Arundel Hospital and Southgate, was an extremely perturbed system. Rampant runoff had deeply incised it -- to six feet! Extreme undercutting, with bank slumping, trees falling over, and even a four foot waterfall at one point. Debris almost sickening -- at one point in a ten foot radius circle I counted 65 cans, bottles, styrofoam cups, etc. How can we continue to do this to our streams? So much development and runoff. Terrible. Did note flowering sessile-leaf merrybells (*Uvularia sessilifolia*) on high, now isolated and drying (due to the stream degradation in a geomorphological sense), floodplain. [For another account of this site see my September 30, 1994 *Journal* entry.]

"Next I went to yet another Southgate area tributary to the same stream, but east of Oakwood Drive. This tributary was again dominated by red maple in the canopy, but it also had some black gum (*Nyssa sylvatica*), some common catbrier and dense sweet pepperbush. Much tapering fern (*Dryopteris noveboracensis*), which was up about 9 inches; sessile-leaf merrybells were flowering. In a depression along an old sewer right-of-way that had shallow water, I found a mature spotted turtle (*Clemmys guttata*). Also heard goldfinches overhead and spotted a brown thrasher in uplands. Along upland trail, I got flowering trailing arbutus (*Epigaea repens*). At the upper end of this tributary, above Elvaton Road, it looks pretty good, but still no swamp pink."

Interestingly, in the early 1970s before I bought my first house in Maryland, I lived in two apartment complexes, one of which, the Southgate Apartments, was adjacent to this site. At that time, there was somewhat of a respite in my botanical field activities. Although I frequented the swampy area along Marley Creek and the adjacent upland and recollect the swamp as being

342

rather undisturbed, I had no idea that it was a historic swamp pink site, which may still have had some plants at the time. Indeed, this was a potentially important opportunity missed.

A third swamp pink site known to Dr. Plitt was along Stony Creek in Pasadena. Although a number of his journal entries mention coming into the County via steamer, the *Petrel*, to wharves either at Stony or Rock Creeks, they indicate that he continued elsewhere, often to Waterford, with no mention of the swamp pink along Stony Creek. To my surprise though, Dr. Plitt's May 1, 1906 journal entry mentions finding the swamp pink on a "...rivulet running to head of [Stony] creek."

*   *   *

I continued my pursuit of the swamp pink with trips in the mid-1990s to the main stems and some tributaries of Severn Run, Cattail Creek, Old Man Creek, Stony Creek, Stony Run, Marley Creek, and Lake Waterford, as well as Sawmill Creek above Route I-97. (As indicated earlier, Dr. Plitt reported the swamp pink from three of these streams -- Stony Run, Stony Creek, and Marley Creek.) During the early 1990s, for example, I systematically searched for the swamp pink, as well as the climbing fern, but found neither along the Lake Waterford tributaries above Route 10. My luck changed in the spring of 1993 when I walked the section of the stream between Route 10 and Lake Waterford. As I recorded it in my April 30, 1993 *Journal* entry:

"Well, I finally did it. I found one of the two main species I've been looking for, *Lygodium palmatum* (climbing fern) and *Helonias bullata* (swamp pink), about half way to Lake Waterford, on the left side of the floodplain going downstream. Plitt had reported both, somewhere between the Marley Station and Lake Waterford [see below]. Initially, the floodplain had a small (about 5' wide) stream with adjacent marshy openings in an otherwise forested swamp with numerous shrubs. Periodically, I noted non-flowering turks-cap lilies (*Lilium superbum*). Soon the stream was more

343

braided and open (a marsh/shrub swamp complex with numerous dead standing trees), apparently the result of water backing up from the old "dam" downstream. Much of the open area had bur-reed (*Sparganium* sp.), water starwort (*Callitriche heterophylla*), and skunk cabbage (*Symplocarpus foetidus*). I wore my low rubber boots since it was a little cool in the morning, but soon went over them. Fortunately, it soon warmed up (in the 70s) and was a nice sunny day. For the most part, I tried to stay near the edge of the swamp in saturated to shallowly flooded areas, assuming they might be optimal for the swamp pink versus the deeper open areas. At one point as I struggled along, I looked up and lo and behold there it was -- a swamp pink standing out above the skunk cabbage staring me in the face. My immediate reaction to myself was: 'Damn! Damn! There it is! I'll be damned!' Then I looked in another direction and only 20' from me was another one. I inspected the general area pretty thoroughly, doubling back and forth a few times and recorded a total of six clones (?), five of which had a flowering scape. Because of the dense skunk cabbage, however, I could have missed some other plants, particularly non-flowering ones." (For more on the climbing fern, see the next section.)

I found the swamp pink in a red maple-black gum swamp just upstream from Lake Waterford on the north side of the floodplain, adjacent to what I have described in the past as an apparent old lake bed or otherwise impounded area behind the existing lake. This impounded area has the remnants of a low "dam" and is currently mostly a shrub swamp/marsh complex with scattered standing dead trees. The most abundant and characteristic herb in the immediate vicinity of the swamp pink was the skunk cabbage. The plants were in an area perhaps a tenth of an acre in extent and there was one flowering scape per cluster of plants. The flowering specimens had mature, greenish-brown, flaccid leaves; the adjacent ramets had clusters of younger, bright-green, erect leaves. I collected data on the general plant community composition, as well as information on what I assumed were

344

individual swamp pink clones. An article on my find was published in *The Maryland Naturalist* in 1993 (15).

I originally thought that Dr. Plitt had reported the swamp pink somewhere between Elvaton and Lake Waterford, which is where I found it. As it turns out, however, in re-reading Dr. Plitt's May 2, 1903 journal entry extracted by Fessenden (5), I concluded that the site he described for the swamp pink was in the Marley Creek drainage rather than above Lake Waterford. In addition, none of Dr. Plitt's other entries for Lake Waterford mention the swamp pink at or near that location. Thus, what I at first thought was a re-discovery, was apparently a new site for the swamp pink in Maryland, heretofore unknown to the botanical community.

After an initial failure, I observed the swamp pink on Stony Creek on May 12, 1994 during a day of botanizing with Yvette Ogle.[11] As I wrote in my *Journal*:

> "...thanks to Yvette's memory we located the Stony Creek *Helonias bullata* site off of Solley Road. It was the same site I checked a few weeks back, but I only went a short distance upstream, spending most of my time downstream from Solley Road. The area upstream eventually opens up somewhat and parallels a new housing development. We only walked a small section but it had many large swamp pink plants. I counted 25 plants along the stream on hummocks and off the stream in swampy depressions, but only about 6 had fruiting scapes. The site was dominated by red maple [*Acer rubrum*] in the canopy, with substantial amounts of sweet pepperbush [*Clethra alnifolia*] and common catbrier [*Smilax rotundifolia*] in the thick woody understory; cinnamon fern [*Osmunda cinnamomea*] and net-veined chain fern [*Woodwardia areolata*] were very abundant in the herbaceous layer. We also noted pitch pine [*Pinus rigida*], swamp azalea [*Rhododendron viscosum*],

---

[11]This site was found by Nancy Kelly in 1988 (11). However, like my Cypress Creek site discussed below, which had its own array of rare plants, this would be a rediscovery, since Dr. Plitt was aware of it at least as of 1906.

sweetbay [*Magnolia virginiana*], spicebush [*Lindera benzoin*], and skunk cabbage [*Symplocarpus foetidus*] but not until about where we stopped. Thus, the swamp pink was not necessarily associated with skunk cabbage and the site was much thicker with shrubs as opposed to the Lake Waterford site. Some plants had scapes about two feet tall, some had clustered scapes (2-3), and all the plants looked very healthy. The site looks good despite the development. A great site.

"We assumed that there were many more swamp pinks downstream, but given that they were done flowering, we decided to wait until next year to walk through to Solley Road. Besides, our main goal today was to find some lupine. Interestingly, a road in the development is called Helonias Court! Seeing that earlier, we obviously knew we were at the correct area. Near the edge of the upland but in upland we found wild sarsaparilla [*Aralia nudicaulis*]; in the upland, [we also found some] flowering pink ladyslipper [*Cypripedium acaule*]."

I inspected this site again on April 24, 1998. In general, the stream appeared to be receiving more runoff with overbank flooding than when I was first there. However, the swamp pink was still present and one particular swale off of Pine Ridge Road looked good, with robust fruiting plants.

On March 14, 1998, I searched for the swamp pink and climbing fern along the Furnace Creek floodplain from Sawmill Pond down nearly to Crain Highway. I was surprised to see the good condition of the backwater red maple swamps along the creek. Given the habitat, I could readily envision the presence of both of these species. Therefore, I thoroughly scanned the swampy areas for last years rosettes of swamp pink and on the stream levee and drier floodplain for the climbing fern, but found neither. I did, however, locate the old dam site that I mentioned earlier. I searched this area again for the swamp pink on April 30, 1998, still with no luck.

There is one last point that I would like to make about the swamp pink sites cited by Dr. Plitt. In at least four journal entries covering the Stony

Run or Marley Creek sites (May 12, 1900, April 30, 1904, May 3, 1904, and April 30, 1907), Dr. Plitt mentioned substantial numbers of sessile-leaf merrybells (*Uvularia sessilifolia*) and Canada mayflowers (*Maianthemum canadense*). I find this potentially important in that a number of the streams that I have walked in search of the swamp pink, such as the Marley Creek, Sawmill Creek, and Stony Creek, have these species or at least the sessile-leaf merrybell. The merrybell was also found at my Lake Waterford swamp pink population. In reality, these two species occur on a little higher ground than the swamp pink does, but they may still have some indicator value of potential nearby swamp pink sites.

The Climbing Fern

Another species that seemed to be of special interest to Dr. Plitt and his companions was the climbing fern (Figure 62). On November 22, 1902, Dr. Plitt wrote:

"F.H. [Forest Home] and Robinson's dam...we came to the road leading to the dam. Just before coming to this road we made one of the best finds we have ever made and that is a new locality for *Lygodium palmatum*....hundreds of the beautiful climbing plants! Here, surely, the plant was growing at its best."

On April 29, 1905, after visiting Lake Waterford and passing through Elvaton, Dr. Plitt proceeded to Forest Home on Marley Creek.[12] He states: "Just before reaching this old country seat [meaning Forest Home], I passed through the *Lygodium palmatum*-The Climbing Fern district" (3). On another excursion (May 2, 1903) with Mr. Weber to Marley, Forest Home, and Glen Burnie, Dr. Plitt reports: "We took the early train, arrived at Marley

---

[12]This excursion was with the Baltimore Botany Club (3). According to Haven Kolb (personal communication), the Baltimore Botany Club kept its own journals documenting its trips, of which Dr. Plitt had written only one, an account of this April 29, 1905 trip.

[and] proceeded to our *Lygodium* place...[then] to the pond to our other *Lygodium* spot."

According to the March 12, 1990 map drawn by Colby Rucker, Forest Home was located on the southeast side of Marley Creek and east of Oakwood Drive. After discussing Forest Home with Haven Kolb on January, 27, 1998, what should have been evident to me in examining Rucker's map is that Forest Home was a residence, not a geographic location. I had initially assumed that there was a typographical error and that Dr. Plitt meant "county seat," which is incorrect, since Annapolis is the only county seat that Anne Arundel County has had in its history. A good clue that I missed was the "extinct" farm road shown by Rucker, which led to Forest Home. Rucker (11) refers to Forest Home as "A farm of 700 acres on the south side of Marley Creek Branch owned by the Robinsons." He goes on to say that it included an old grist mill. Rucker's map shows a drained millpond east of Forest Home and adjacent to Route 100. I can relate to Rucker's millpond location based upon my own visits to the site in the early 1970s when I lived in the Southgate Apartments. It was a somewhat open wetland meadow with scattered shrubs grading into a shrub swamp upstream. In this regard, the 1878 *Atlas of Fifteen Miles Around Baltimore Including Anne Arundel County Maryland* (16) shows a private road, two ponds, and an "old mill" in the area of the southeast side of Marley Creek associated with the property of a Mrs. A. Robinson. The private road appears to be the "extinct farm road" shown by Rucker. Apparently, the site

Figure 62. The rare and strange-looking climbing fern (*Lygodium palmatum*).

of Forest Home was destroyed with the construction of the Southgate Community. Again, I was a little too late, for had I been aware of Dr. Plitt's journal and the potential presence of climbing fern when I lived in the Southgate Apartments in the early 1970s, perhaps I would have found it, since all of the houses in Southgate were not built at the time.

Apparently, the two sites mentioned by Dr. Pitt were both at or near Forest Home. I have often wondered whether one of these sites could have been along Marley Creek below the pond, which in modern times would apparently be below Route 100. I searched for the climbing fern there on August 9, 1991 and again on March 13, 1998 with Judy Broersma-Cole, both times to no avail. I have also examined the Marley Creek tributaries above Route 100 (on April 24, 1993 and March 16, 1998), without success. I suspect that the climbing fern no longer exists in the area considering the extensive residential development present and the deplorable condition of Marley Creek and its tributaries from stormwater runoff.

*   *   *

In his March 14, 1903 journal entry, Dr. Plitt reported that he observed a nice patch of *Lygodium palmatum* near a spring on the north side of the Severn River (not Severn Run) at the property of a Mr. Leimbach. This is the same site on the Severn where Dr. Plitt observed some Atlantic or southern white cedars (*Chamaecyparis thyoides*), which is discussed later in this Chapter.

On March 28, 1903, Dr. Plitt and Mr. Weber walked from Robinson Station (at Robinson Road) to Benfield. Along the roadside at the Butler Estate, which was apparently along Forked Creek, on the northeast side of the Severn River, they found a "nice patch" of the climbing fern. They also visited a currently well-known site for the climbing fern at Severn Run. A "fine colony" was located just a short distance beyond the old mill on the right side of the stream.

Many local botanists are familiar with the Severn Run climbing fern population. I have found it growing abundantly on the main stem and also

349

quite dense in places below an old pond site on the first northeastern tributary above Dicus Mill Road. I have often wondered whether the climbing fern may have been introduced at this old pond site. On a slope immediately downstream, the fern is quite abundant near a small remnant brick structure. Possibly it moved downstream to the mainstem from here. On the other hand, I have not found it, despite considerable searching, along any tributaries above Lake Waterford, along Marley Creek, or along Sawmill Creek.

In his book on the ferns and fern-allies of Maryland, Delaware, and the District of Columbia, Clyde Reed (17) maps four sites for Anne Arundel County, all in the northern part, one of which is Severn Run. The Maryland Natural Heritage Program cites only three extant stations for this species in Anne Arundel County -- Severn Run, a tributary of the Severn River at Ben Oaks, and Indian Creek. I tried to locate the Ben Oaks site on March 14, 1998 and found no evidence of climbing fern below Benfield Road down to tidewater, nor upstream to the large stormwater earthdam. However, after receiving a more detailed site location from Jennifer Meininger, I located a very small population of the plants on the northeast side of the tributary below the earthdam on May 13, 1998. A sewer line right-of-way runs down the floodplain. Perhaps during construction, the fern population was reduced in extent.

The Goldenclub

When Dr. Plitt visited Lake Waterford, he seemingly always inspected a broad marshy area at the head of the millpond before proceeding on to his box huckleberry (*Gaylussacia brachycera*) site downstream near the limit of tidewater. He first visited the headwaters of the Magothy River and the Lake Waterford area on September 13, 1902. From two accounts of visits (Dr. Plitt's July 2, 1904 journal entry and his April 29, 1905 entry for the Baltimore Botany Club), it sounds as though the wetland area associated with the old millpond supported some acidophiles. For example, on the 1905 visit Dr. Plitt found a profusion of sundews and observed over an acre of marsh thickly covered with the goldenclub (*Orontium aquaticum*). Moreover,

350

according to his 1904 journal entry, it was one of the largest patches of goldenclub he had ever seen. Although the goldenclub is not a rare plant in Maryland, its presence is predictive of a quality aquatic environment.

On August 25, 1989 my youngest son Sean and I searched the shoreline of Lake Waterford for some of the plants mentioned by Dr. Plitt. Although we did not find any sundews, at one cove on the south shore and near the back of the lake we saw a couple of goldenclubs (quite the contrast with the acre observed by Dr. Plitt) and blunt manna grass (*Glyceria obtusa*), marsh St. John's-wort (*Triadenum virginicum*), Virginia chain fern, and leatherleaf (*Chamaedaphne calyculata*), as well as some sphagnum. At the nearby pond edge was the humped bladderwort (*Utricularia gibba*). I was also quite surprised to find the remains of some sort of old low stone dam or bridge mentioned earlier. The structure had clearly impounded a large area of the upstream floodplain years ago. Tree stumps were evident and the old pond site had by then succeeded to a marsh with invading shrubs and trees. Our trip is also described in a September 29, 1989 letter from me to Gene Cooley. At the time, I asked myself: Could this be the real pond Dr. Plitt spoke of rather than the contemporaneous one downstream? Perhaps this was where he found the goldenclub and sundew growing so abundantly.

The Box Huckleberry

Dr. Plitt generally approached his box huckleberry site from the upland on the southern side of the Magothy River below Lake Waterford (i.e., Magothy Beach Park). For example, according to his April 29, 1905 entry for the Baltimore Botany Club (3), after crossing "...the bridge at the mouth of the pond...[he] turned in to the left and proceeded [east] to the spot...." This neat huckleberry was quite easily located "...very close to a little side ravine, an off-shoot of the main ravine." Dr. Plitt mentioned that pines were slowly encroaching upon a large field south of the river. In his July 2, 1904 journal entry, he remarks that he and Mr. Sollers found quite a lot of box huckleberry. Although Rucker (11) and Stieber (18,19) both report this species also from Magothy Park Beach (four anonymous collections between 1921 and 1961), this is the only known extant site for this species in Maryland. Unfortunately, in recent years it has been steadily decreasing.

I first saw the box huckleberry here probably sometime in the mid-1970s, and Gene Cooley and I located it again on August 11, 1989. I do not recall seeing many plants in 1989, and nothing like the dense stands I have seen in Delaware. Sometime back in the late 1980s I was given some Critical Area site data for this locality dated June, 1987 that was compiled by the Maryland Natural Heritage Program. An accompanying site map showed fifteen scattered individuals, as well as a one square meter patch. The plants were delineated on the slope down gradient from a large mature stand of pines on the flat, and a nearby side ravine was depicted. The setting is very similar to what Dr. Plitt described, except that the pines were by now (mid-1970s) mature.

I visited this site a few more times since 1989, one of the more recent being on January 4, 1998 with Keith Underwood and Phil Sheridan. Sadly, after considerable searching, we finally found it -- only three plants, one of which was depauperate and dying! Since it took a while to find the first specimen, I was beginning to think I was in the same awkward position that the turn-of-the-century Delaware botanist, William M. Canby, was in the autumn of 1898. Canby tried to show a box huckleberry site on the Indian River in Delaware to his friends, the famous Harvard botanist, Dr. C. S. Sargent, and John Muir (*The* John Muir!), but to no avail despite a long day hunting for it. According to Dr. Sargent (June 8, 1920 letter to H.M. Canby), Canby was a good deal chagrined at his failure to show them the plant and they always teased him about it. See Chapter Five for more elaborate explanation of this; also the original explanation in R.R. Tatnall's book, *Flora of Delaware and the Eastern Shore* (20).

I suspect the drastic decrease in the box huckleberry at this site has to do with its dense understory, mostly sweet pepperbush (*Clethra alnifolia*) and common greenbrier (*Smilax rotundifolia*), which are competing with the huckleberry for light, much to its detriment. The Maryland Natural Heritage Program materials suggested this fate too. Indeed, this *is* sad, for we appear destined to add this species to the extirpated list for Maryland. Fortunately, an intergovenmental effort to save and propagate this rare plant by culturing tissue from cuttings has begun, with the goal of managing the area and reestablishing a viable populations. On February 12, 1999, the Maryland Natural Heritage Program also conducted a thorough search of the area between Old Annapolis Road and Catherine Avenue for additional plants, but none were found. Thus, as of that date, the population was down to only two plants.

The Sweet Pine Sap

When Dr. Plitt botanized in the Benfield and Severn Run areas, he regularly visited his favorite sweet pine sap site. On April 19, 1919, for example, he mentioned sweet pine sap: "...in great profusion. I soon detected the odor and Mr. [Burner ?] found the plant, after which we found [it] everywhere. There were 1000s of plants and of course 1000s of flowers."

According to Wayne Tyndall (21), two areas in Anne Arundel County were popular among botanists seeking this plant in the 1920s and 1930s -- Conway Station and Benfield. Tyndall examined a number of herbarium specimens of the sweet pine sap. Three collections (not by Plitt) in 1938, 1939, and 1941 indicated either "Benfield" or "near Benfield" on their labels. Dr. Plitt's site was evidently at Benfield. I unsuccessfully attempted to relocate this species in the Benfield area on April 24, 1998, although I did locate what was undoubtedly the remnant concrete road mentioned on one of the herbarium labels. This old road is partly covered with dirt and is located north of Severn Run and immediately east of Veterans Highway; it parallels Veterans Highway. This species is highly State rare and endangered in Maryland.

SOME SURPRISES

In examining Dr. Plitt's detailed journal, I soon realized that I was in for many surprises. Five that really stood out for me are presented below. I

353

suspect additional interesting facts will surface with a more thorough review of the journal.

The Cedar Swamps

I had initially assumed that Dr. Plitt and his friends were not familiar with the southern white cedar swamps on Cypress Creek. Here is why: The Plitt journal extracts (5) mentioned his visit to Round Bay on July 29, 1899, where he recorded the yellow-fringed orchid (*Platanthera ciliaris*) and tawny cottongrass (*Eriophorum virginicum*) at "the swamp." However, there was no mention of any southern white cedar. In addition, a number of his journal entries mentioned stops at Round Bay and visits to a swamp where he found leatherleaf, large cranberry (*Vaccinium macrocarpon*), pitcher-plants, sundews, red-berried greenbrier, and rose pogonia (*Pogonia ophioglossoides*). But again there was no mention of Cypress Creek or the Magothy River or southern white cedars (only, at times, the "Cypress swamp").[13]

As it turns out, I was wrong on my assumption about Dr. Plitt, which was my first big surprise. For on my third day examining the Plitt journal I came across references to Cypress Creek. On May 28, 1904, Dr. Plitt indicated that:

"To-day, I visited the Cypress swamp near Round Bay exploring it. I was pleased to find it much larger than I at first expected and that there are still many of the interesting [southern white cedar] trees growing there. What I had all along called the Cypress swamp is merely the head of...the best part, by far, is down further, near the creek...an arm of the Magothy river...My first surprise, on reaching it, was the finding of the cranberry, *Vaccinium macrocarpon*, Ait. It is here in all its glory, great patches. Here too,

---

[13]By cypress, Plitt was referring to the southern white cedar or Atlantic white cedar, *Chamaecyparis thyoides*. This cedar has been called by alternate names like falsecypress, false-cypress, and white cypress.

I found, what I am sure will prove to be *Pogonia ophioglossoides* Nutt. Here too, is the Pitcher Plant and *Nymphaea*."

On June 25, 1904, Dr. Plitt indicated that he went:

"To Round Bay and the swamp at the head of the creek, a branch of the Magothy...As we passed the swamp, I stopped to examine the *Smilax walteri* that had formed fruit. After a little trouble I found the large sphagnum swamp at the head of the creek. I found that my suspicion that *Pogonia ophioglossoides* and the cranberry grow here were correct. Both were in bloom. Of the former, there were hundreds of the plants in bloom, and of the latter immense patches. *Habenaria* is here too, but it is not in bloom." (He also reported inkberry, *Ilex glabra*.)

Dr. Plitt once again visited Cypress Creek (he called it Magothy Creek in this instance) on July 23, 1904. He visited the "cranberry bog" and again found the rose pogonia, and was "...pleased to find *Habenaria ciliaris*, 16 specimens were counted. No doubt there are many more, for the plant is just beginning to flower and is therefore hard to see." The white-fringed orchid was "very plentiful" and flowering. On an adjacent hillside, he found butterfly pea (*Clitoria mariana*) and mentions that in the "...beautiful swampy region at the head of the creek..." he found red-berried greenbrier. On a June 24, 1907 trip, Dr. Plitt wrote:

"My first intentions were to visit the *Pogonia* place near the Magothy and then later go to the hotel...I took the route along the shore, then through the woods to railroad, then over to the cranberry swamp, and back to the hotel. Over 70 plants were found...Everybody that went to the bay were delighted for the *Pogonia* were in full bloom, also the cranberries, and we found *Itea*."

355

Finally, in a June 19, 1909 journal entry, Dr. Plitt actually mentioned Cypress Creek. He says:

"Arrived at R.B. [Round Bay] we proceeded through the woods to the hotel grounds. After depositing our packages we made a short trip around stopping at the pond in the rear of the dancing pavilion and then later to the little settlement. At the pond we got water lilies and sundew and cranberry...After dinner we paid a visit to Cypress Creek and here we got *Pogonia* in full bloom and sphagnum in fruit...We proceeded through the swamp to the headwaters of the creek. Many changes are taking place here, bungalow and shacks are being erected and all natural beauty is being destroyed."

So it is quite clear to me that Dr. Plitt was very familiar with the southern white cedar swamps on Cypress Creek.

Fresh Pond

The second surprise relates to Fresh Pond. Historically, this site was well known to the botanical community because of Angel's Bog. Therefore, I suspected that Dr. Plitt visited it, but there was no evidence of this in the Plitt extracts (4,5,6). However, Dr. Plitt's journal refers to a number of visits to Fresh Pond and various acidophiles with no mention of the name Angel's Bog as such. No doubt that name is of more recent origin.

It appears that Dr. Plitt first visited Fresh Pond and what is now called Angel's Bog on September 23, 1905. He wrote:

"A trip to Fresh Pond, a beautiful sheet of water not far from Bodkin Creek, in fact, the source of one of its tributaries....no trouble finding the lake, as a view of it can be had from the road...The scenery here was indeed beautiful. The pond is enclosed by beautiful wooded hills. As soon as I reached the pond I descended to its shore.

356

Here I found the Cranberry in profusion, also *Cassandra* [leatherleaf], and the Pitcher Plant."

He also visited Fresh Pond at least four more times (February 17, 1906, June 9, 1906, September 26, 1906, and June 6, 1914). On the February 17, 1906 trip to Fresh Pond, he states:

> "To-day I went at once to the little pond near the road. *Sarracenia* is found here in quantity not only along the edge of the pond but also along the stream. From the pond, I proceeded along the left bank of the stream to the creek and then along it to Main Cr."

On June 9, 1906, Dr. Plitt took a trip to Fresh Pond:

> "...hoping to find *Arethusa* but in this I was disappointed. Cranberries were in full bloom. After visiting the pond I proceeded along the right bank of its outlet to the second pond. On trip found *Pogonia ophioglossoides*..."

On September 26, 1908, Dr. Plitt traveled to Fresh Pond mainly to get cranberries, but the ground was so wet due to the rain, he did not enter the swamp. But on June 6, 1914, he went to Lake Shore and Fresh Pond finding, "*Sarracenia* was in profusion & so too *Drosera*."

From the above accounts, there appears to have been at least one other pond in the area besides Fresh Pond that supported pitcher-plants in Plitt's days.

I do not recall why now, but for some reason I never checked the two small ponds mentioned above when I was initially searching for bogs in the County in the late 1970s. Perhaps I did not notice them on the Gibson Island 7.5 minute quadrangle map, which shows a small pond up a tributary of Main Creek, the same body of water that the stream from Fresh Pond flows into after entering Mathias Cove. The map also shows a tiny pond on the tributary

357

leaving Fresh Pond.[14] However, in 1998 when I started updating the status of the extant bogs for this Chapter, I noticed the two ponds on the maps. I visited the pond on the tributary of Main Creek with Judy Broersma-Cole on March 13, 1998 in anticipation of finding a bog, assuming the pond still existed. Sure enough, the old pond had succeeded, for the most part, to a mat of herbaceous vegetation and a smooth alder (*Alnus serrulata*) swamp; there was a small area of shallow open waters. What appeared to be a remnant wooden sluiceway was just downstream. Even under the winter conditions, we detected a number of bog plants. On the spot, we named this site the Main Creek Bog. This bog is described in more detail later in this Chapter.

On March 16, 1998, I checked what I believe is the location of the "second pond" and the "little pond" mentioned by Dr. Plitt. They appear to refer to the same site, which is only about 300 feet upstream from tidewater located where a dirt road approaches the stream from each side of the floodplain at an apparent old dam site or road crossing. The pond has succeeded to a red maple swamp with numerous shrubs supported by a firm floating mat over at least four feet of sediments.

A White Pine Stand

The third surprise was Dr. Plitt's reference to a large stand of white pines (*Pinus strobus*). On August 31, 1904, he mentioned that: "On my way [to Curtis Bay] made a nice little discovery on the left side of the road, a short distance beyond the road leading to the post-office I found a grove of White Pine....Quite a number of very large trees were observed." However, on February 25, 1905, Dr. Plitt "...was surprised on reaching the White Pine forest to find so many of the trees cut down and split up into cord wood." One tree was 2.5 feet at the base and calculated to be seventy-five years old.

---

[14]Apparently, the Gibson Island quadrangle map was a special edition produced by the Army Map Service. It was copied from the Maryland, 1:31,680, AMS, Sheet III SW, 1944. The original map was based upon 1942 aerial photography. Both of these ponds are also shown on an undated "Map of Anne Arundel County Showing the Maryland Coordinate System" (Williams & Heintz Map Corporation, Washington, DC.).

He spoke with a local man who referenced more white pines on the Severn below Annapolis and in Prince Georges County.

On Searching for Rarities

The fourth surprise was that Dr. Plitt mentioned searching for a rare plant on October 31, 1903, in this instance the box huckleberry. Obviously, certain species were no doubt rare even back then. But if they were rare then, what are they now? I guess this just stood out for me, given that Dr. Plitt was dealing with "the wilds of Anne Arundel" at the time, and so much has been lost since.

On Spreading and Introducing Rarities

The fifth, and perhaps the biggest, surprise for me was not what Dr. Plitt found; it was what he was spreading around while botanizing! I was amazed to read that Dr. Plitt spread rare native plants and introduced species not native to the Coastal Plain in Maryland. I found reference to at least seven species for which he spread seeds, bulbs, or transplants: the fringed gentian (*Gentianopsis crinita*), swamp pink, arethusa (*Arethusa bulbosa*), wild calla (*Calla palustris*), climbing fern, sweet pine sap (*Monotropsis odorata*), and Venus' fly trap (*Dionaea muscipula*). Imagine that, even the Venus' fly trap! He frequently went back to these plantings to see how well they were doing. Seeds of the fringed gentian were spread while on a trip to Glen Burnie and Marley; seeds of the swamp pink were spread at Sawmill Pond and between Marley and Forest Home; bulbs of the arethusa were planted at Lake Waterford; rhizomes of wild calla were planted at Lake Waterford and Stony Creek; transplants of climbing fern were apparently made at Furnace Branch; transplants of sweet pine sap were made at Brooklyn; transplants of Venus' fly trap were made at Bent Oaks, Bear Creek off the Severn, and Cypress

Creek.[15] Given the above, a lingering question in my mind is: Considering that the one small area below Lake Waterford is the only known site for the box huckleberry in Maryland, could Dr. Plitt, or some other botanical enthusiast back then, have planted it there? Maybe a more thorough search of the Plitt journal will shed some light on this.

SOME ASSUMPTIONS

Despite his twenty-three years of tramping the region, Dr. Plitt and his followers apparently were either not familiar with or did not botanize a number of extant Anne Arundel County bog sites and southern white cedar swamps. Partial support for this assumption is the fact that the bog sites are quite far from the Baltimore-Annapolis Railroad Line on which these botanical enthusiasts frequently traveled into the County, albeit they frequently walked substantial distances after detraining. Furthermore, it was not until the early 1920s that the first automobile was acquired by a member of the group (2). The only sites that were fairly close to the Baltimore-Annapolis railroad line were Sawmill Pond, the Marley-Forest Home area, and the southern white cedar swamp on Cypress Creek. Nevertheless, there are at least two exceptions to this contention since Dr. Plitt did visit Fresh Pond (Angel's Bog) and a site on the Severn River (somewhere between the Earleigh Heights Station and Severn Run), where on March 14, 1903 he saw "...a number of cypress trees" at the property of a Mr. Leimbach. On April 1, 1905, Dr. Plitt mentioned seeing cypress trees near Bear Creek, also off the Severn. He even listed *Chamaecyparis sphaeroides* (*Chamaecyparis thyoides*, the southern white cedar). In his July 25, 1903 journal entry, Dr. Plitt also mentioned "Mr. B's" property being on Bear Creek. This is probably the Butler Estate, that is alluded to in Dr. Plitt's March 28, 1903 journal entry.

---

[15] I can find no reference to a Bear Creek off the Severn River in this locality on any maps accessible to me. However, Fork Branch was also mentioned along with Bear Creek by Dr. Plitt in his July 25, 1903 Journal entry. This appears to be Forked Creek, which is shown on the northeast side of the Severn River on modern maps. Bent Oaks is the correct spelling and it may refer to the contemporaneous location called Ben Oaks.

(In his journal, Dr. Plitt frequently used only last name initials of people he knew.) Forked Creek still supports southern white cedars. There is also a Cedar Neck and a Cedar Creek shown on an 1878 map in the *Atlas of Fifteen Miles Around Baltimore Including Anne Arundel County Maryland* (16). Cedar Neck (modern day Linstead-on-the Severn) lies between Cedar Creek (modern day Yantz Creek) and Sullivan Cove, both of which support cedar today. Yet I found no evidence in his journal that Dr. Plitt was to either of these locations. Although Dr. Plitt described a trip to Eagle Hill in his September 28, 1912 entry, he evidently was not aware of Eagle Hill Bog, a nearby wetland off the southeastern-most fork of Blackhole Creek.

EXTANT CEDAR SWAMPS AND BOGS IN ANNE ARUNDEL COUNTY

One day during my tenure with the Department of Natural Resources, someone asked me what I knew about Angel's Bog, which is located off of Mountain Road at Fresh Pond. I was quite embarrassed, for I new nothing, not even that it existed. I had been working in the Maryland tidal wetland program for about five years, but my responsibilities at that time took me only to tidal wetlands. Consequently, I soon found myself checking on its location and visiting Angel's Bog. About that time (1976), Wayne Klockner and George Robbins, while participating in a natural area inventory for the Department, discovered Eagle Hill Bog. I soon visited that site too, as well as another fairly well-known site, at least in botanical circles, the Round Bay Bog on Deep Ditch Branch of Maynedier Creek, a tributary of the Severn River. After visiting these sites and noting their interesting plants -- including eye-catching pitcher-plants, sundews, and orchids -- the idea that there may be additional undiscovered bogs surfaced. With this thought in mind, I started scanning the Department's high altitude aerial photographs for potential bog sites in Anne Arundel County.

A number of potential sites, appearing as partially to nearly filled in ponds, surfaced, all in the Magothy River drainage. Two of them, both on Gray's Creek off Sillery Bay, turned out to be bogs, which I subsequently named North Gray's Bog and South Gray's Bog. Therefore, during 1976-1977, I floristically examined these five bogs. Three of them (Eagle Hill, South Gray's, and North Gray's) had not been documented in the literature prior to studies by Wayne Klockner and me on the County's bogs and southern white cedar swamps (22,23,24,25). Subsequent to our field work, other researchers have studied the vegetation of these interesting sites. For example, a detailed phytosociological investigation of the Cypress Creek Cedar Swamp and Savanna and five of the bogs (North Gray's Bog, South Gray's Bog, Eagle Hill Bog, Angel's Bog, and Round Bay Bog) using cluster analysis soon followed (26,27). Four of these bogs (Angel's Bog, Eagle Hill Bog, South Gray's Bog, and North Gray's Bog) originated in remnant ponds, perhaps ice ponds or millponds; Round Bay Bog appears to have resulted from the establishment and maintenance of a transmission right-of-way through an otherwise forested swamp.

Besides these sites, there are three more recently discovered bogs in the County. One of these, Main Creek Bog, is a remnant pond; the other two, Blackhole Creek Bog and Arden Bog seem, as best that I can tell, to be natural openings. Main Creek Bog and Blackhole Creek Bog occur in the Magothy River drainage; Arden Bog in the Severn River drainage. There are also some additional southern white cedar locations -- one on the Magothy and a number on the Severn. The general location of all of these bogs and two areas on Cypress Creek supporting southern white cedars is shown in Figure 2.

*　　*　　*

The remainder of this Chapter is devoted to this handful of botanically interesting Anne Arundel County cedar swamps and bogs. I will first discuss the southern white cedar sites, then move on to the various bogs. Many of the vascular plants found at these sites are rare and some are legally threatened or endangered in Maryland. The descriptions of these sites are for the most part based upon earlier accounts cited above from the late 1970s and early 1980s. However, I revisited all of these sites in 1998, and unless otherwise indicated, they remain similar floristically to my earlier descriptions.

362

One might question whether these sites should be classified as fens rather than bogs. In this regard, bogs and fens are peatlands, which is true for all of these sites, including the southern white cedar swamps. One classification suggests bogs have a water pH below 4.2 and a calcium concentration below 2 mg/l (28,29). This water chemistry is also reflected in the different floras associated with bogs and fens. Data from five of the Anne Arundel County bogs (30,31; Dennis Whigham, personal communication) indicate that they are chemically similar, and that they probably should be classified as bogs, or at the most very weak fens. On the other hand, the southern white cedar swamps, at least the ones that interface with estuarine waters, are perhaps fens. Cypress Creek Swamp and Savanna, for example, has a much higher pH and levels of calcium and magnesium than the bogs, which is to be expected since it is adjacent to the estuary. Therefore, it probably should be considered a sea-level fen, similar to the ones discovered on the Delmarva Peninsula a few years ago by Delaware and Virginia Natural Heritage Program personnel.

Cypress Creek! An intriguing name for Anne Arundel County, intriguing indeed since, historically, the County never had native populations of bald cypress. Despite this fact, I know of one bald cypress tree growing in a natural setting between the upland and fresh tidal marsh on the Magothy River below Catherine Avenue. I suspect this came in somehow by chance -- perhaps a bird, perhaps water -- or was planted. It is actually a tree that fell over, from which a lower branch has sprouted up like a normal tree. Bald cypress has been found in fossil deposits, however, in Anne Arundel County and Baltimore City (32,33). In fact, a photograph of now destroyed ancient (estimated to be 35,000 years old) cypress stumps exposed in northeastern Anne Arundel County, Maryland, appeared on the cover of the January/June, 1992 issue of *The Maryland Naturalist*. Similarly, *The Sun* on March 25, 1997 reported on the unearthing of bald cypress stumps during the construction of Baltimore's new National Football League stadium. (See Chapter Five for more on the bald cypress.)

As indicated earlier, the southern white cedar is sometimes referred to by the alternate names of falsecypress, false-cypress, and white cypress.

Given this and considering the historically known and extant stands of cedar associated with Cypress Creek, it appears as though most if not all of the headwaters area of Cypress Creek (and perhaps all of its tributaries) were once dominated by this species. I base this deduction largely on the contemporaneous presence of the cedar at the Cypress Creek Swamp and Savanna and the Cypress Creek Cedar Swamp. The latter site has the densest stand of cedar that I am aware of in Maryland. Furthermore, on the northwestern side of Cypress Creek, about three-tenths of a mile southwest of its large northwestern branch, there is a smaller tributary that clearly supported a large cedar swamp at one time. Wayne Klockner showed me this swamp on August 15, 1978. I do not know the origin of the name, but he called it Bonnie's Bog. On that brief visit to the lower end of the site, I noted that the site contained many large dead southern white cedar trees, but only a few live ones. It also supported, among other species, the pitcher-plant, round-leaf sundew, and leatherleaf.[16] The site was just upstream from the fresh to slightly brackish tidal marsh.

On January 29, 1998, after a twenty year hiatus, I attempted to relocate Bonnie's Bog with Keith Underwood and Phil Sheridan. What a surprise -- it was still there! It supported many more trees than my memory from 1978 suggested -- at least forty fairly large ones by quick count, and dead ones all the way up to Dill Road. However, this time there were no sundews or pitcher-plants, and we found but one leatherleaf plant. Undeniably though, this was a large cedar swamp at one time. And it is still in pretty good condition. So I can visualize many southern white cedars on the various tributaries of Cypress Creek a century or two ago prior to their demise perhaps by logging, no doubt even on the large northwestern branch, which once had a series of dams, the remnants of which can still be seen. These dams may have been for millponds or ice ponds, and the cedars were probably harvested or killed by flooding in the 1800s.[17]

---

[16] As indicated earlier, Dr. Plitt was familiar with the cedar swamps on Cypress Creek and reported on the presence of pitcher-plants.

[17] Ice ponds were apparently constructed in part at least to harvest ice. In fact, Dr. Plitt cited an example of ice harvest for Sawmill Pond in his January 6, 1900 journal entry.

Equally amazing is the fact that the botanical community was basically unaware of the cedars, or at least did not report on them in the literature, except for Michael T. Stieber who listed the southern white cedar in his flora of Anne Arundel County (based upon collections by Neil Hotchkiss and Francis Uhler at Cypress Creek on October 24, 1951 and by E.P. Killip on the north fork of Cypress Creek on May 27, 1953) and, of course, Dr. Plitt (18,19).[18] For example, Brown and Brown (34) considered the southern white cedar uncommon in Maryland and to occur only on the Eastern Shore. The Browns were apparently not initially familiar with Stieber's flora of Anne Arundel County, or else they just overlooked it. They did not acknowledge it in their *Woody Plants of Maryland* (34); they did, however, list it in *Herbaceous Plants of Maryland* (35). Nor were they familiar with Plitt's journal. Otherwise, they would have known of the southern white cedar in Anne Arundel County.

The southern white cedar was once abundant within the predominantly deciduous tidal swamps along the major Eastern Shore rivers (8). At the present, this species occurs as scattered individuals or loose aggregations within this range. (See Chapter Five and Nine for accounts of some impressive southern white cedar stands in the Hickory Point Swamp on the Pocomoke River.)

I have also seen this species at one other location on the Magothy River (Cockey Creek) and at several other areas on the Severn River. Where observed in these locations, the southern white cedar normally occurs only as scattered trees within a deciduous swamp or along a brackish marsh and deciduous swamp interface. The Cockey Creek site also supports the largest area of giant cane (*Arundinaria gigantea*) that I have observed on the Western Shore, although it occurs mostly in the adjacent upland.

More recently, a small group of researchers has demonstrated an interest in preserving these remaining southern white cedar sites and restoring some of the lost or degraded ones; an intensive survey has been conducted (36). The seven sites inventoried are Arlington Echo, Carrollton Manor,

---

[18] However, there is no evidence in his flora that Michael Stieber visited the Cypress Creek cedar areas.

Forked Creek, Lakeland, and Sullivan Cove on the Severn River; Cockey Creek and Cypress Creek on the Magothy. According to them, the western shore cedar populations consist of 1,214 trees measuring over 1.2 meters tall, 1,895 seedlings and saplings less than 1.2 meters tall, and 827 dead trees. Seedling recruitment was highest at Sullivan Cove on the Severn with 1,475 seedlings. Their efforts have also been presented in an October 13, 1997 article in *The Sun*. With the aid of volunteers, they plan to harvest seeds and take root cuttings for spring plantings. They also anticipate studying the archives to determine where, based upon records, the most heavily logged sites occur. Their ultimate goal is to restore these areas.

The Cypress Creek Swamp and Savanna

On November 10, 1977, I visited an area on Cypress Creek that showed up on 1971 aerial photographs as a small meadow just above a deltaic tidal marsh. I soon discovered what I subsequently called the Cypress Creek Swamp and Savanna. I could hardly believe my eyes upon entering the savanna. It was like the New Jersey Pine Barrens in miniature; like I was standing in a Pine Barren savanna scanning the site with its scattered young southern white cedars in a matrix of grasses, sedges, and cranberries surrounded peripherally by a band of taller cedars, then followed in turn by a red maple-sweetbay-black gum deciduous swamp. All of this stood in stark contrast to the oaks and pines just upslope. And here it all sat, essentially forgotten by the botanical community since the days of Charles C. Plitt -- forgotten that is, until that auspicious autumn day.[19]

I just stood for awhile in admiration and almost disbelief. Despite its small size, it was a grand site for sure. An intense one-year floristic examination followed through which we determined that the site supported a diverse acidophilic flora. A total of forty-seven, thirty-nine, and forty-two

---

[19]Three exceptions to this statement mentioned earlier involved Neil Hotchkiss and Francis Uhler who collected the southern white cedar at Cypress Creek on October 24, 1951 and E.P. Killip who collected the southern white cedar on the north fork of Cypress Creek on May 27, 1953.

vascular plant taxa were recorded within the three zones described: savanna, southern white cedar swamp, and deciduous swamp. The acidophiles included the white-fringed orchid, yellow-fringed orchid, rose pogonia, spatulate-leaf sundew, twig-rush (*Cladium mariscoides*), pine-barrens rush (*Juncus abortivus*), white beakrush (*Rhynchospora alba*), large cranberry, marsh St. John's-wort, green spikerush (*Eleocharis olivacea*), yellow flatsedge (*Cyperus flavescens*), inkberry, small-leaf panic grass (*Panicum ensifolium*), and bladderwort . The Maryland Natural Heritage Program (13) also lists beaked spikerush, coast sedge, and fibrous bladderwort for this site.

Through probing the soils, we also noted that the peat covering the majority of the site was quite thick, mostly about five to six feet, but one station had an eight foot layer! Clearly, this savanna and swamp existed at the site for some time. Even many small cedars bore cones. There was no evidence of aggressive invasion of the savanna or swamp zones by the dominant plants in the surrounding deciduous zone. In fact, numerous cedar seedlings were found throughout the savanna. There were two relatively small patches of the common reed (*Phragmites australis*), a commonly aggressive invader in wetlands, one at each end of the savanna. Despite the presence of the common reed, Wayne Klockner and I considered the site vegetatively unique in Maryland.

The above description of the Cypress Creek Swamp and Savanna is the way it was in 1978; regretfully, that is not the way it is today. After our initial field work at the Cypress Creek Swamp and Savanna, I did not visit the site again until June 26, 1982 and then again on June 25, 1983. Apparently, the site was fine, for I mentioned nothing in my *Journal* entries for these dates other than the presence of flowering rose pogonia, which is itself a good sign. I next visited the site in 1986 and then once more in 1987, both in the summer; there was still no reference to a problem. I recall, however, that someone suggested to me back in the late 1980s that the site was changing vegetatively, namely that the cedars were dying.

I first noted this change on July 9, 1988 when I visited the site with a small group of students from one of my wetland plant identification classes. Here is what I recorded in my *Journal* that day for the site:

"Disappointed with Cypress Creek Savanna -- almost all cedars [*Chamaecyparis thyoides*] appear dead, and no evidence of *Drosera* [sundews], *Sarracenia* [pitcher-plants], *Eleocharis flavescens* [pale spikerush], orchids, and other interesting plants I found ten years ago. [...The savanna has continued to change, although some cedar still persists. Sea level rise may be a factor. Since I never found it growing naturally at either the Cypress Creek Savanna or Cedar Swamp, my mention of the pitcher-plant would refer to one of two things: Either its presence in the Cypress Creek Savanna after it was planted there by a Virginia horticulturist or the natural population of it that Wayne Klockner and I observed on another branch of Cypress Creek in the late 1970s.]"[20]

Then on June 10, 1992 I indicated the following:

"At Cypress Creek Savanna found quite a changed ecosystem. Many of the fresh tidal marsh plants have now displaced the bog species....Did see some acidophiles....Many small cedars [*Chamaecyparis thyoides*] have died; didn't see any sundews or orchids."

Similarly, on June 18, 1993, I wrote:

"The Cypress Creek Savanna has changed substantially since Wayne Klockner and I studied the site in the 1970s. Much of the Atlantic white cedar [*Chamaecyparis thyoides*] is dead, particularly the smaller trees. This site appears dominated by *Cladium mariscoides* [twig-rush], a plant found in bogs, but also in fresh tidal marshes adjacent to Maryland's fresh-slightly brackish tidal rivers. It

---

20 Unfortunately, the Virginia horticulturalist has been planting various insectivorous plants in the Anne Arundel County bogs for a number of years. This is very undesirable from a native plant distribution perspective and could cause substantial confusion about natural distributions in the future. Fortunately, however, someone has been pulling many of them out!

wasn't as abundant here in the 1970s. The two reedgrass patches (*Phragmites australis*) have spread. No signs of the spatulate-leaf sundew (*Drosera intermedia*) or orchids. On the other hand, *Sagittaria falcata* (coastal arrowhead) is fairly common in the savanna, particularly in the lower end, but it is well into the site; prior [in the 1970s], it was only in the slightly brackish marsh. The tidal marsh itself appears to be breaking up at the lower end, resembling, in a small way, the marsh break up that a summer intern of ours, Vic Pyle, and I have seen in the Louisiana Delta area."

On an encouraging note, I visited the Cypress Creek Swamp and Savanna on August 13, 1998 and found, much to my surprise, the yellow fringed orchid, but only one specimen. However, I also found a white beakrush, some scattered pine-barrens rush and large cranberry, and substantial twig-rush. The common reed, on the other hand, seems to have increased in extent.

The Cypress Creek Cedar Swamp

I first visited the Cypress Creek Cedar Swamp in 1980. This site, which is located just upstream and on the southwest side of Governor Ritchie Highway, is about three acres in extent with the densest area of southern white cedars occurring about 400 feet southwest of Governor Ritchie Highway. It is drained by a small stream that passes under the highway prior to entering Cypress Creek. The surrounding terrain has slight to moderate slopes and for the most part is forested. Although this site is physically separated from Cypress Creek Swamp and Savanna, it undoubtedly was once connected to it prior to highway construction.

The eastern-most portion of this swamp (about 1.5 acres) is dominated by southern white cedar. It contains from 200-300 cedar trees,[21]

---

[21]Based upon the southern white cedar inventory mentioned earlier, an aggregate total of 359 living trees over 1.2 meters in height are given for the Cypress Creek Swamp and Savanna *and* the Cypress Creek Cedar Swamp (36).

many of which are one foot or more in diameter. The substrate is hummocky. Highbush blueberry (*Vaccinium corymbosum*), sweet pepperbush, and swamp azalea are the dominant shrubs; cinnamon fern is the dominant herbaceous plant. Although the western-most part (about 1.5 acres) of the swamp has many cedars, it is dominated by deciduous trees, especially the red maple. Sweetbay and black gum are also present. The site also supports northern long sedge and red-berried greenbrier, a watch list species in Maryland that was also reported from here by Dr. Plitt. A tentative flora of thirty-four species has been compiled.

Angel's Bog

Angel's Bog is located almost adjacent to the north side of Mountain Road at Fresh Pond. The bog exists as a floating mat of vegetation with a maximum width of over 150 feet at the southern end of the pond where a small stream enters (Figure 63). Fresh Pond is about 130 acres in size (37), but the bog covers only about 2.2 acres. Nevertheless, it is larger than all of the other known Anne Arundel County bogs, and, with the possible exception of Blackhole Creek Bog near Blackhole Creek, it supports the largest area of leatherleaf in the County. Slopes adjacent to the pond are relatively steep and forested, at least in the bog area.

Angel's Bog resembles a true southern bog more than any of the other bogs in the County except possibly for Arden Bog. Other than for the abundance of water willow, it is also similar in appearance to many of the bogs in the New Jersey Pine Barrens. Although no one species appears to dominate, large areas of water willow, leatherleaf, and large cranberry occur. Sphagnum moss is also abundant. There are numerous tree stumps and small red maples scattered throughout the bog. At the northeast end of Fresh Pond down to near its outlet at Mathias Cove (a tributary of Main Creek), there is a large area dominated by red maples, which probably was once also bog-like.

The site has the most diverse flora of any of the bogs in Anne Arundel County -- at least fifty-two species of vascular plants. Many of these, such as leatherleaf, large cranberry, twig-rush, silvery sedge (*Carex* canescens), Canadian St. John's-wort (*Hypericum canadense*), marsh St. John's-wort, long-tubercle spikerush (*Rhynchospora tuberculosa*), blunt

Figure 63. The author with a small group of Environmental Protection Agency personnel at Angel's Bog in 1992. (Photo by Rod Frederick)

manna grass, pine-barrens rush, white beakrush, spatulate-leaf sundew, and round-leaf sundew, are typically found in bogs.

Although the pitcher-plant has also been reported from the site, Wayne Klockner and I did not find any pitcher-plants during our original field work in the Angel's Bog. We subsequently found some in 1979, but these were planted there by a Virginia horticulturist. In a December 8, 1977 letter to me, Clyde Reed indicated that his thesis at Loyola College dealt with the pitcher-plants in Fresh Pond. In 1968, he took the Ecological Society of America on a foray to Fresh Pond, implying in his letter that he saw pitcher-plants then too. Furthermore, Dr. Plitt reported pitcher-plants in profusion at Fresh Pond on September 23, 1905 and June 6, 1914.

371

Considering the large maple area towards the outlet of Fresh Pond and the presence of numerous small red maples, the bog may ultimately succeed to a red maple swamp.

Unfortunately, local residents elevated the water level of Fresh Pond probably in 1994 or at least by the spring of 1995. On March 11, 1995 I noted this without realizing its consequences at the time. The consequences soon became quite apparent, however, as indicated in my June 22, 1995 *Journal* entry given below:

"Everything went well except for the Angel's Bog site, which was suffering from high water levels. Many of the peripheral shrubs have died and most of the open meadow areas are now inundated with a foot of water. Substantial water is also at the base of the leatherleaf, *Chamaedaphne calyculata*. Although bladderwort (*Utricularia* sp.), some twig-rush (*Cladium mariscoides*), and a few cranberries (*Vaccinium macrocarpon*) were flowering, there was substantially more cranberry last year, and we found no *Xyris* [yelloweyed-grass], *Eriocaulon* [pipewort], *Drosera intermedia* [spatulate-leaf sundew], or *Carex canescens* [hoary sedge]. Obviously, this site is really suffering. The only benefit of the flooding is that the invasive red maple appear to be hurting a little (some dead branches). I had noted this spring that someone had done some makeshift work on the old 'dam'. Perhaps this is why the water levels are so high. Another possibility is that beaver have moved into the area. In the long run, this *may* be a benefit if it knocks back the woody plants, particularly the red maple, but for now the high water appears to have eliminated a number of desirable herbaceous bog plants, perhaps even *Drosera rotundifolia* [round-leaf sundew] and *Sarracenia purpurea* [pitcher-plant] at the other end of the pond."

On July 25, 1995, I again visited Angel's Bog to determine the height of the water at the dam. There was a make-shift concrete structure that was about sixteen inches in elevation and upstream of the old spillway. All I could

372

see in the area was open water and water willow. I scanned the upstream area supporting the small red maples with my binoculars. Some maples appeared dead; others had brown leaves. The water level was about fourteen inches above the elevation of the old spillway. Then on August 4, 1995, I met Kathy McCarthy of the Maryland Natural Heritage Program to check on the bog again. In my *Journal* I wrote:

"The site doesn't look quite as bad as it did earlier in the year (see June 22, 1995 entry). Either more of the open meadow mats have floated up in response to the increased water level, or the water level has dropped. (Actually, it has dropped some, perhaps 8 inches since June.) A number of plants were observed flowering on the mats, including *Eleocharis olivacea* [bright-green spikerush] (abundant), *Rhynchospora alba* [white beakrush] (common), *Xyris* sp. (yelloweyed-grass) (infrequent), *Cladium mariscoides* [twig-rush] (common), *Juncus abortivus* [pine-barrens rush] (infrequent), *Utricularia gibba* [humped bladderwort] (abundant), *Glyceria obtusa* [blunt manna grass] (frequent), *Juncus canadensis* [Canada rush] (infrequent), and *Drosera intermedia* [spatulate-leaf sundew] (a few plants on one section of floating mat). The *Chamaedaphne calyculata* [leatherleaf] has now died in part. (In June it appeared okay.) Will it continue to die, or has it peaked? The dead shrubs are mostly *Clethra alnifolia* [sweet pepperbush] and *Vaccinium corymbosum* [highbush blueberry], although many of the red maples [*Acer rubrum*] and sweetbay magnolias [*Magnolia virginiana*] are showing stress (dead branches in both and non-green leaves in the former). Much of the *Vaccinium macrocarpon* [large cranberry] is dead, but some of it is alive and has fruited. The *Utricularia gibba* is extremely abundant and has even moved into the inner shrub zone where the shrubs have died allowing for sunlight penetration.

"Assuming that there's a good seed bank (and there probably is), this flooding may be a benefit if they keep it high through winter and knock back the woodies, especially the red maple, then drop it or

373

at least permanently stabilize the water level. One big unknown, however, is the status of the leatherleaf. Hopefully, it will not continue to die back.

"We also hiked up to near the dam, discovering that most of the maple swamp appears to have been impacted. This, of course, could be a real plus, creating open areas for more bog vegetation establishment."

Ever since I first saw the vegetation damage at Angel's Bog in 1995, a nagging thought has been with me: Will this site go the way of the famous Glen Burnie Bog? Remember its unfortunate fate, as documented by Dr. Plitt in the early 1920s? The dam at Sawmill Pond was raised around 1920 and the resultant elevated water levels in the millpond apparently eventually caused the demise of that bog. Angel's Bog, however, seemed to be holding its own on my last 1995 visit.

I checked on Angel's Bog again twice in 1998. On my first trip on June 5, 1998 I indicated that:

"Angel's Bog looks really bad, with many trees/shrubs dead around the periphery of the floating mat. The water willow (*Decodon verticillatus*) has invaded much of the peripheral swamp now that the canopy is open. It seems to also be displacing the leatherleaf. I did find *Chamaedaphne calyculata* (leatherleaf), *Cladium mariscoides* (twig-rush), *Carex canescens* (silvery sedge), *Vaccinium macrocarpon* (large cranberry), *Utricularia gibba* (humped bladderwort), *Nymphaea odorata* (white waterlily), *Juncus canadensis* (Canada rush), and *Dulichium arundinaceum* (three-way sedge)..."

My next visit was on October 10, 1998. To my surprise the makeshift dam was removed. It apparently had been removed a day or two after my June visit through the auspices of the Maryland Department of the Environment. Needless to say I was delighted to see the restoration, and utterly elated by the

374

early response of the vegetation. As indicated in my *Journal* entry for that visit and in a December 9, 1998 letter to the Maryland Department of the Environment thanking them for their effort, many of the bog plants appeared on the rebound and there may have been some long-term benefits is knocking back the common, more invasive, woody plants like red maple.

Eagle Hill Bog

Eagle Hill Bog is located above the headwaters of the southeasternmost fork of Blackhole Creek, a tributary of the Magothy River, about two tenths of a mile west of Eagle Hill Road. It is predominantly a floating mat of vegetation that has encroached over a small (one acre) remnant pond. Two small streams enter the site. Its watershed is almost entirely forested. Surrounding slopes are relatively steep. A small earth dam capable of impounding water at the mouth of the bog is still effective, but no evident water control structure or culverts exist. If structures ever existed, they now lie buried in sediments or were otherwise destroyed long ago. During late winter and spring, the mat of vegetation is frequently covered with a foot or so of water.

This wetland is meadow-like in appearance with woody plants being essentially confined to its periphery and headwater areas. Various herbaceous plants dominate the main body of the bog. In August, the bog has an overall whitish aspect due to the presence of white beakrush, whereas in September, it turns a light brown color as that species fruits. Around the periphery and in the headwater area, the bog is dominated by leatherleaf and large cranberry. The vascular flora of the bog does not appear to be very diverse -- only twenty species. I suspect that a more intensive survey will produce some additional species. Typical bog plants found at the site include leatherleaf, spatulate-leaf sundew, three-way sedge (*Dulichium arundinaceum*), pine-barrens rush, Virginia meadowbeauty, white beakrush, and large cranberry. The giant cane occurs along the periphery of the bog and near the old earth dam.

South Gray's Bog

South Gray's Bog is located a short distance above the headwaters of Gray's Creek off of Sillery Bay, a tributary of the Magothy River. It is about two tenths of a mile northwest of North Shore Road. This two acre bog occurs at the mouth of a remnant pond site. A mat of vegetation is developing over the open water, but it is still quite clumpy and difficult to traverse. The remainder of the remnant pond is forested swamp. One stream enters the pond from the surrounding, entirely forested, watershed. Surrounding slopes are slight to moderate. Because of the numerous tree stumps and scattered shrubs, South Gray's Bog has a shrub swamp appearance. Water willow in particular is very abundant. However, in open areas, the site has an overall surface color appearance similar to that of Eagle Hill Bog in August and September because of the presence of white beakrush.

Floristically, the bog is not very diverse. A tentative survey produced only twenty-three vascular plants. Typical bog plants found at the site include leatherleaf, spatulate-leaf sundew, three-way sedge, pine-barrens rush, Virginia meadowbeauty, Canadian St. John's-wort, white beakrush, and large cranberry. The sundew is quite abundant in the bog. Red maple and other woody plants are invading this site from upstream, and the bog was probably larger in the past. The giant cane is encroaching slightly on the bog from the shore.

A red maple swamp, dominated in the understory by giant cane, occurs downstream; skunk cabbage is absent. Sweetbay forms the subcanopy. There are also some pitch pines (*Pinus rigida*) and black gums, as well as sweet pepperbush. It appears to be a unique vegetation type for Maryland. This is probably because the giant cane is uncommon in Maryland, it being restricted to a few places on the Western Shore and one location (a ten acre hardwood swamp) on Marshyhope Creek in Dorchester County discovered by Bill McAvoy of the Delaware Natural Heritage Program in 1997. A somewhat similar area occurs on a tributary of Cockey Creek.

On June 5, 1998 I added a new species for South Gray's Bog, the coast sedge. I visited it again on March 13, 1998 with Judy Broersma-Cole.

376

The site appears basically the same as it did in the late 1970s except for one thing: We found a number of transplanted crimson pitcher-plants (*Sarracenia leucophylla*), probably by that same Virginia horticulturalist. Fortunately, at least ten of these non-native plants had already been pulled out!

North Gray's Bog

North Gray's Bog is found upstream from the north fork of Gray's Creek off Sillery Bay and adjacent to a dirt road which crosses the earthen dam. It is more or less an incipient bog with floating mats in early stages of development supporting only a few dominant species. Many dead trees occur upstream interspersed with small live sweetbays. Dominant shrubs include leatherleaf and water willow; the pine-barrens rush dominates the herbaceous layer. The white water lily is common in open water areas. Based upon an initial visit to this site in 1977 and a follow up in 1980, I listed twenty-five species of vascular plants; besides the leatherleaf, other acidophiles included spatulate-leaf sundew, three-way sedge, green spikerush, marsh St. John's-wort, white beakrush, yellow-eyed grass, and bladderwort. The Maryland Natural Heritage Program also lists coast sedge and tawny cottongrass for this site.

Regretfully, this site has been substantially degraded. According to the Maryland Natural Heritage Program (13), "...the greatest threat to the rare species has been fluctuating water levels, especially high water levels due to periodic habitation by beaver and partial blockage of the dam overflow pipe." As a result, "...large portions of the rare species communities have died back." Judy Broersma-Cole and I visited the site on March 13, 1998 and indeed found the water level 1.5-2.0 feet higher than when I remembered it back in the late 1970s. However, there was no recent evidence of beaver activity. It appears as though the culvert can not handle the water flow, since water was overtopping the low road dam and flooding the adjacent ball field. The non-metal pipe culvert appeared rather modern; perhaps it is a new one that was placed too high. There was no evidence of the floating mats of pine-barrens rush or the leatherleaf and water willow, except for one small patch of the latter. The sweetbays are now all dead, and their hummocky bases, as well as the bases of shrubs, which once supported bog plants, are inundated. The general appearance is that of a recently flooded pond with numerous dead trees. This site could probably be restored over time, however, by lowering the water level by about two feet.

Blackhole Creek Bog

The Blackhole Creek Bog occurs upstream of where three intermittent headwater streams converge before flowing into Blackhole Creek off the Magothy River (see the Gibson Island, Maryland 7.5 quadrangle map). It was discovered by Judy Broersma-Cole in the winter of 1979. Judy informed me of this bog many years ago, but I did not attempt to locate it until 1994. I was unsuccessful on that trip, but finally saw it on January 31, 1998 with Judy and Keith Underwood. I again visited the site on July 17, 1998.

The bog is dominated by the leatherleaf, but there is also substantial inflated sedge (*Carex vesicaria*), a highly State rare endangered species that, according to the Maryland Natural Heritage Program, is found only at one other Anne Arundel County site. The bog appears to be a natural opening, basically a floating mat with one very small area of open water. Only a few herbaceous species occur in the bog proper, perhaps due to the abundance of leatherleaf and sedges. The surrounding floodplain supports a forested swamp dominated by red maple and sweetbay.

The origin of this bog is unknown, but given the surrounding upland forest, one possibility is that a deep peat burn into the pre-existing forested wetland during a severe drought resulted in an open water area within the swamp. Following this scenario the open water was then invaded by the leatherleaf. I have seen such depressional sites dominated by leatherleaf in the New Jersey Pine Barrens (historically, a fire induced ecosystem), where they are locally referred to as spongs (pronounced "spung" as in "rung"). According to Judy Broersma-Cole, a recently discovered 10-foot thick clay lens under the bog may also be a factor in maintaining the open nature of the site (personal communication).

While at Towson University, Judy conducted a floristic study of this site (38). She reported twenty-two vascular plant species for the bog itself, including the following acidophiles: leatherleaf, inflated sedge, silvery sedge, eastern sedge (*C. atlantica*), Barrett's sedge (*C. barrettii*), three-way sedge, blunt manna grass, Virginia chain fern, and hidden-fruit bladderwort. Other than for the bladderwort, no carnivorous plants were found. The surrounding swamp forest supported twenty-three species, including the red-berried greenbrier, a watchlist species. All of these plants except the leatherleaf were identified for the site in 1985 by Dan Boone, who at the time was in the Maryland Natural Heritage Program (February 3, 1998 letter to me from Judy Broersma-Cole). They are given as an appendix to Judy's 1984 report. An additional herb, *Bartonia* sp., was added in 1998.

Main Creek Bog

As indicated above, Judy Broserma-Cole and I found this site on March 13, 1998. I visited it again on June 5, 1998 and October 8, 1998. This site has a floating mat, which supports bog species, and a contiguous smooth alder swamp. Based upon these trips, I recorded the following acidophiles: Virginia meadowbeauty, spatulate-leaf sundew, small-leaf panic grass, green spikerush, leatherleaf, pine-barrens rush, marsh St. John's-wort, Canadian St. John's-wort, white beakrush, white waterlily, three-way sedge, yellow-eyed grass, bladderwort, and blunt manna grass. Twenty-one non-bog species were also found for a total tentative flora of thirty-five species.

Round Bay Bog

Round Bay Bog occurs along Deep Ditch Branch of Maynedier Creek off of Round Bay, a tributary of the Severn River. Although the site extends both northeast and southeast of River Road, the only bog vegetation is found along the transmission line right-of-way upstream of River Road. Acreage

379

estimates of eighty acres (39) and 140 acres (37) have been given for this site. The substantial acreage discrepancy undoubtedly relates to how the authors defined the boundaries of the site. The majority of the area referred to as Round Bay Bog is nontidal forested wetland located along a floodplain of a small creek system. It has a diverse but mostly forested watershed. The stream valley has a somewhat springy substrate and is apparently underlain by considerable sediments. To a large extent, the name Round Bay Bog is a misnomer, because more than ninety-nine percent of the site is dominated by deciduous swamp vegetation. Although I have not systematically sampled the deciduous swamp site, it appears to be dominated by red maple and sweetbay; cursory examination suggests that it has a diverse vascular flora. One species of greenbrier, the halberd-leaf greenbrier, is high State rare and endangered in Maryland.

The description of the Round Bay Bog that follows relates principally to a 75 by 850 foot gas line right-of-way area, that is, the bog proper. This area is dominated to a large extent by the large cranberry and sphagnum moss. There is also a large stand of Virginia chain fern; although it is not considered rare, I have observed this species only infrequently on the Western Shore. A tentative flora of thirty-nine vascular plant species has been compiled. Besides the large cranberry and Virginia chain fern, other acidophiles include the rose pogonia, Canadian St. John's-wort, marsh St. John's-wort, pine-barrens rush, white beakrush, and loose-head beakrush (*Rhynchospora chalarocephala*). In addition, on June 26, 1982, I visited this site and found a number of individual nothern pitcher-plants, as well as spatulate-leaf sundews. Both species were apparently introduced to the site, again by a Virginia horticulturist. Apparently, the thread-leaf sundew (*Drosera filiformis*) was also planted there around that time.

Geologically, the larger system, of which the bog is but a small part, developed over the years on floodplain alluvial and colluvial deposits between the adjacent side-slopes. Perhaps the filling for River Road also helped create the bog, at least the lower end above the road. The bog proper, however, is the direct result of construction of the transmission line right-of-way. In fact, if the right-of-way is not managed to maintain the existing open vegetation, it

380

will probably revert to the original deciduous swamp in a relatively short period. This is evinced by the presence of deciduous tree saplings, particularly red maple in the right-of-way.

I revisited this site on July 17, 1998 with Judy and Robert Cole and Dave Walbeck of the Maryland Department of the Environment. Overall, the site still looks quite viable, although there is much more woody plant cover than when I was there in 1982. The site still supports a diverse flora, and about eighty-seven percent of the species recorded in the early 1980s were again observed. Acidophiles present included rose pogonia, large cranberry, inflated sedge, bog fern (*Thelypteris simulata*), pine-barrens rush, white beakrush, loose-head beakrush, and Virginia chain fern. The round-leaf sundew, spatulate-leaf sundew, and four species of pitcher-plants were also found, including the northern pitcher-plant, yellow pitcher-plant (*Sarracenia flava*), sweet pitcher-plant (*S. rubra*), and crimson pitcher-plant. However, all six of these insectivorous plants have apparently been introduced at the site.

Arden Bog

Arden Bog is located on the Gumbottom Branch of Plum Creek off the Severn River. It is part of a freshwater wetland complex referred to as the Gumbottom Wetland by the Maryland Natural Heritage Program. I was not familiar with the Arden Bog when I worked for the Maryland Department of Natural Resources during the 1970s; nor was anyone else in a botanical sense as far as I know. Had it been in the Magothy system, I probably would have found it through my aerial photographic scanning efforts that resulted in the rediscovery of the Cypress Creek Swamp and Savanna and the discovery of South Gray's Bog and North Gray's Bog. It was discovered by Kathy McCarthy and Judy Modlin of the Maryland Natural Heritage Program on June 1, 1988. Having been the person to rediscover the Cypress Creek Swamp and Savanna, I can readily relate to their excitement and elation at the time. In fact, until I did the research for this Chapter, I assumed I was the first botanically inclined person to discover the Cypress Creek Swamp and

381

Savanna. As I indicated earlier, however, Dr. Plitt and his friends visited it in the early 1900s. Likewise, Neil Hotchkiss and Fran Uhler collected southern white cedar on Cypress Creek in 1951; E.P. Killip collected it there in 1953.

Arden Bog appears to be a natural opening. The Maryland Natural Heritage Program (13) suggests that the bog may have originated as an oxbow of the stream that flows through it.

I did not visit the Arden Bog until Keith Underwood and Phil Sheridan showed it to me on January 4, 1998. It is a great site, supporting the most northern pitcher-plants that I have seen in Maryland other than some areas in the Nanticoke and Pocomoke drainages. The only other Anne Arundel County sites that I am familiar with that historically had numerous northern pitcher-plants (at least in Dr. Plitt's days) were the Glen Burnie Bog, Fresh Pond (Angel's Bog), and perhaps Cypress Creek. For example, on May 30, 1900, Dr. Plitt stated: "In the swamp [Glen Burnie Bog], hundreds of Pitcher-plants were still found in bloom, notwithstanding the depletion that is constantly going on." On May 17, 1902, he indicated that: "*Sarracenia* was to-day in all its glory. Hundreds of flowers were seen [at Glen Burnie Bog]." Similarly, on September 23, 1905 and June 6, 1914, he found pitcher-plants in profusion at Fresh Pond.

Based upon three site visits in 1998, I have compiled a tentative vascular flora of thirty-three species, including the following acidophiles: the northern pitcher-plant, round-leaf sundew, leatherleaf, coast sedge, humped bladderwort, tawny cottongrass, large cranberry, pine-barrens rush, white beakrush, small-leaf panic grass, and yellow-fringed orchid. The Maryland Natural Heritage Program (13) also listed the button sedge and twining bartonia, and the spatulate-leaf sundew has also been reported in a January 6, 1997 letter from Phil Sheridan to William Mouldan.

Whereas most of the bog looks quite healthy, the eastern end has been adversely impacted by a storm drain. According to Keith Underwood and Phil Sheridan, the effect has been an undesirable successional shift to a shrub swamp in that area and the death of various bog plants. Based upon my site visits, I confirmed in my mind that serious impacts have occurred. I noted, for example, dead large cranberry plants and what appeared to be stressed

382

leatherleaf. Fortunately, in 1998 the County removed this storm drain in order to protect the site.

A PLEASURE AND A PLEA

Anyone with a botanical interest who has visited some of these Anne Arundel County cedar swamps and bog sites will surely appreciate their ecological significance. There are but a few of them, some of which are unique. They are replete with rare vascular plants, including many that are State threatened or endangered. In fact, most of the species mentioned in this Chapter are considered rare in Maryland. True, the region is no longer "the wilds of Anne Arundel" as Dr. Plitt experienced it. Nevertheless, these interesting sites, albeit limited in number, represent the wilds of the County in their own way, an impressive botanical way, given that they support many rare, threatened, and endangered plants.

Indeed, it has been quite a pleasure to have experienced and studied these ecologically significant sites. Local and State governments should immediately institute a truly effective effort, perhaps acquisition, including appropriate buffer areas, to preserve their natural integrity. Indeed, I am convinced that society should demand it.

NINE

SELECT EXCURSIONS OF
AN INFORMAL BOTANICAL GROUP

In full daylight now, though the sky remained overcast, we waded
out knee-deep into the marshes, among the coarse grasses that
rose above the level of our eyes, trying to walk on the wobbling
hummocks. The trick of tramping in cold water is to get your feet
as wet as possible right away, so that you no longer spoil your
enjoyment by trying to keep dry. Away with that instinct! Let your
boots fill with water at the start; it makes you free to go where you
please.
-- LOUIS J. HALLE, JR., *Spring In Washington*

AS indicated in Chapter One, when I taught my wetland classes at the
Graduate School, U.S. Department of Agriculture, I met many people who had
similar natural history interests. Certain individuals kept in touch with me in
various capacities, which eventually led to some springtime field excursions
in the late 1980s and well into the 1990s. My *Maryland Journal* indicates
that the first such excursion, which was with Gene Cooley of the Maryland
Natural Heritage Program and Dwight Fielder of the Department of the Navy,
was on June 14, 1987. Although over twelve years have passed since that trip,
I still recall the experience well. It was a great trip to a wonderful stream --
Severn Run in Anne Arundel County -- and one of my favorites, at least then.
In hip waders, we rather arduously worked our way downstream from Route
3 through the swampy floodplain forest to the tidal delta, which supported a

nifty fresh tidal marsh.[1] We also found a rare and threatened species in Maryland, the leatherleaf, atypically growing on a small hummock surrounded by marsh vegetation in a backwater area of the stream. It typically occurs in bogs. (See Chapter Eight for some bog sites on the Western Shore supporting the leatherleaf.)

That first field excursion was a landmark for me. It sparked a desire to seek out rare, threatened, and endangered plants -- a desire that has stuck with me ever since. It also stimulated the formation of an informal botanical group, which took many similar trips over the years, trips frequently along floodplains on the Western Shore.

As I recalled that first botanical field excursion with Gene and Dwight and the others that followed while writing this Chapter, one thing stood out -- change. Everything changed -- me, Gene, Dwight, our group, the nature of the excursions, and even Severn Run. I stopped teaching for the Graduate School in 1990 and a few years later started at the Northern Virginia Community College and the Institute for Wetland & Environmental Education & Research, and eventually Johns Hopkins University. Gene now works for the State of California; Dwight moved on to the Bureau of Indian Affairs, then the Bureau of Land Management. The excursions, which started mostly with ex-students of mine, evolved to other folks -- assuming they had similar interests and were willing to really rough it, sometimes getting quite wet and muddy up to the waist. Eventually, my companions were mostly people from the Maryland or Delaware Natural Heritage Programs, who organized and led some of the trips. Besides Gene and Dwight, the regular participants included Yvette Ogle, Wilbur Rittenhouse, and Kathy McCarthy. Others participants recorded in my *Journal* less frequently included Diane Eckles, Joe DaVia, Don McLean, Wayne Tyndall, Steve Hambalek, Chris Swarth, Bob Maestro, Jim Turek, Curtis Bohlen, Bernie Raftery, Dave Williams, Wayne Longbottom, Joan Maloof, Paul Spitzer, Bob Zepp, Joe Hautzenroder, J. Gill, Doug Samson, Dawn Biggs, Bill McAvoy, Kitt Heckscher, Dave Shock, Jan Reese, Frank Hirst, Gwyne Thunhorst, Jessie Harris, Janet McKegg, Mat

---

[1] My first trip to the Severn River delta marsh below Route 3 occurred on September 18, 1983, when I waded waist deep in the lower part of Severn Run before entering the large marsh.

Cimino, Avery Dalton, Hal White, Mary Kilbourne, Scott Smith, Drew Dyer, Barbara Medina, Ed Pendleton, Richard Smith, and Jonathan McKnight.

Severn Run? Well, it still flows, but not without pains -- substantial growing pains due to excessive stormwater runoff that is downcutting its channel and laterally slicing into its banks. The floodplain seems fine, but the channel is definitely out of kilter with the amount of runoff it is receiving. Too bad for a stream that I, soon after arriving in Maryland, compared favorably to my favorite Coastal Plain stream in South Jersey -- what I called its stream of streams before its sad demise -- Big Lebanon Run near Turnersville.

According to my *Journal*, I led over forty field excursions with the informal botanical group after that first trip to Severn Run in the spring of 1987. We had some great experiences in the Coastal Plain, not only along streams, but also to ponds, bogs, swamps, tidal wetlands, and various upland sites. Six of these trips, as recorded in my *Journal*, are presented chronologically below. Most of the material is taken verbatim, including the scientific names of the plants and animals. Since I added supplemental explanatory material to many of my *Journal* entries when they were printed, that too is again included, as it was then, in brackets. Therefore, there has been only minor editing, including the addition of common names as necessary. However, all State rarity rankings have been updated to conform with the most recent official State heritage program lists available to me. Therefore, the updated rarity rankings will not always be consistent with the wording in the original text, which has been retained.

SELECT BOTANICAL EXCURSIONS

July 26, 1991 [Great and Little Bohemia Creeks, Cecil County, MD]

Trip with Gene Cooley and Wayne Tyndall of Maryland Natural Heritage Program to Great Bohemia and Little Bohemia Creeks in Cecil County, Maryland. Pretty good trip. Main goal was to try solving *Scirpus fluviatilis-S. cylindricus* [river bulrush-New England bulrush] problem. Ernie

Schuyler feels that *S. cylindricus* is the main fresh to slightly brackish leafy bulrush in tidewater Maryland; *S. fluviatilis* not in Maryland or rare (only in larger river systems like Potomac and Delaware). [This contention was conveyed to me by the Maryland Natural Heritage Program personnel; I had not consulted with Dr. Schuyler specifically on it.] My atlas data show thirty or so sites for *S. fluviatilis* and none for *S. cylindricus* (1). At the time, I didn't know of *S. cylindricus*, it not being in *Gray's Manual of Botany* (2), but in subsequent years I have found a few of what works out in *Gray's* to be *S. maritimus* var. *fernaldii* (and also fits description of *S. cylindricus*). As it turns out, we found a few scattered *S. cylindricus* flowering or fruiting. Most of the flowering (actually fruiting) specimens were from *S. fluviatilis*, so we think the numerous non-flowering stems were the latter (large areas of it). At Little Bohemia Creek we got:

Scirpus cylindricus [New England bulrush]
S. fluviatilis [river bulrush]
Zizania aquatica [wildrice]
Pontederia cordata [pickerelweed]
Acorus calamus [sweetflag]
Amaranthus cannabinus [water hemp]
Hibiscus moscheutos [swamp rose mallow]
Typha angustifolia [narrow-leaf cattail]
T. X *glauca* (?) [blue cattail]
Peltandra virginica [arrow-arum]
Cuscuta sp. [dodder]
Nuphar luteum [spatterdock]
Scirpus pungens [common three-square]
Hypericum mutilum [dwarf St. John's-wort]
Iris versicolor [large blue flag]
Impatiens capensis [jewelweed]
Polygonum punctatum [dotted smartweed]
Phragmites australis [common reed]
Rudbeckia laciniata [tall coneflower]

Scirpus validus var. *creber* [soft-stemmed bulrush]
Lobelia cardinalis [cardinal flower]
Myriophyllum spicatum [Eurasian water-milfoil]
Potamogeton crispus [curly pondweed]
Asclepias incarnata [swamp milkweed]

We also saw a glossy ibis flying over the marsh, a cormorant on a piling, a number of melanistic (brownish) tiger swallowtails [*Papilio glaucus*], a marsh wrens nest in *Scirpus fluviatilis* (and made of it), Japanese beetles [*Popillia japonica*] eating flowers of *Hibiscus moscheutos* and leaves of *Peltandra virginica*, and a beaver [*Castor canadensis*] scent mound. [According to Alexander B. Klots, as many as 50% of the female tiger swallowtails are dark brown in ground color, the remainder being yellow like the males; in the north, as well as in the extreme south, the brown form is less common to non-existent (3).]

In addition, we observed the most impressive area of hemlock (*Tsuga canadensis*) I've seen on Coastal Plain -- many trees all along upper end of N-NW facing slope. [In an August 1, 1991 letter to Gene Cooley summarizing our trip, I indicated the following regarding the hemlock: "...the *Tsuga canadensis* stand was impressive. I was amazed at its extent along the southern shoreline (northern exposure) of Little Bohemia Creek. The trees extended for quite a distance and at one point while scanning the slope from about 200 feet offshore with my wide angle, 8 x 40, binoculars I had absolutely nothing but hemlocks in sight as if I were viewing a mountain slope. I realize that hemlock is known to occur on the Coastal Plain, but this is the largest area of it that I've ever come across." See my December 1, 1989 *Journal* entry for more on Coastal Plain hemlocks and the Helen Creek hemlock stand in Calvert County.] At Great Bohemia Creek we found:

Nelumbo lutea [American lotus, State rare] (big stand in coves on north side)
Sagittaria subulata [subulate arrowhead, a watchlist species] (gravelly-sandy substrate)
Limosella subulata [mudwort, State rare and endangered] (neat blunt tips and

not partitioned like *Sagittaria subulata*) [It was flowering.]

Bidens mariana [=*Bidens bidentoides mariana*, Maryland bur-marigold, a watchlist species] (new to me)

Eleocharis quadrangulata [square-stem spikerush] (grows in clumps versus rhizomatous more or less single-stemmed *Scirpus pungens*; although the clumps of square-stem spikerush are probably also connected by rhizomes)

Eryngium aquaticum [rattlesnake master]

Pluchea purpurascens (var. *succulenta* ?) [saltmarsh camphorweed]

Hibiscus moscheutos [swamp rose mallow]

Typha angustifolia [narrow-leaf cattail]

Peltandra virginica [arrow-arum]

Rumex verticillatus [water dock]

Pontederia cordata [pickerelweed]

Asclepias incarnata [swamp milkweed]

Polygonum punctatum [dotted smartweed]

Wayne claims there's a large stand of *Elatine* [waterwort] exposed at low tide on Little Bohemia Creek (spring high tide had it covered today). Also noted lots of *Spartina cynosuroides* [giant cordgrass] farther down on Great Bohemia Creek.

October 2, 1993 [Pocomoke River at the Great Cypress Swamp (Burnt Swamp) and a sea-level fen, both in Sussex County, Delaware]

Trip with Wilbur Rittenhouse to explore the Burnt Swamp in the upper Pocomoke drainage in Delaware, relocate the old millpond at Willards, Maryland, and visit one of the so-called sea-level fens in coastal Delaware off Rehoboth Bay. Left home at 6:00 a.m. sharp. Mild out, partly cloudy, a few rain drops on windshield. Crossed the Bay Bridge at 6:30 noting beautiful bright red sky in the east in contrast with the dark forested shoreline along the bay and a few scattered clouds. Venus shining brightly across the bay at two o'clock (three o'clock being the horizon). At 6:35 (Kent Narrows), the sky turns to orange. Looks like a nice day ahead. Now heading east on Route 404

(6:48 a.m.), the sky at the horizon is a light purple, with an abrupt change to dull orange above, then a dirty yellow, light blue, and finally a rich blue overhead.

Met Wilbur at the "Shellstop" at the junction of Routes 404 and 309 at 7:00 a.m. From there, we continued east and eventually south to check for the site of the now destroyed Newhope Pond (Willards Pond) at Willards, Maryland. This was an unplanned stop, a spur of the moment thought on my part, I having unsuccessfully searched for the pond site earlier in the year (see May 14, 1993 *Journal* entry). I subsequently determined [from *The Plant Life of Maryland* (4)] that the now defunct railroad running through Willards crossed the millpond, which is discussed in my June 1, 1993 letter to Gene Cooley of the Maryland Natural Heritage Program.

Prior to entering Maryland, we found the tall flat-topped white aster (*Aster umbellatus*) [extremely rare status in Delaware]. It was growing in the open roadside adjacent to a forested area just north of Delaware County Road 468 on the west side of Route 13 in Sussex County, Delaware.

At Willards, Wilbur and I walked down the old railroad bed from an adjacent ballfield and into a remnant swamp, the apparent old bed of the millpond. We found numerous bald cypress (*Taxodium distichum*), mostly 80-90 feet tall trees and quite buttressed. Obviously, they once grew in very saturated soils or shallow standing water. The peat had badly oxidized around the trees due to artificial drainage (a large main-stem ditch off Burnt Mill Branch and at least one good size secondary ditch). The soils in the drained swamp (apparent old pond bottom) were hardly moist let alone saturated; probing with my hand (I forgot my soil probe), it was quite organic but essentially dry for the most part. This area, which is just south of the old railroad embankment, also had red maple (*Acer rubrum*), black gum (*Nyssa sylvatica*) and sweet gum (*Liquidambar styraciflua*), with an abundant understory of Japanese honeysuckle (*Lonicera japonica*), pokeweed (*Phytolacca americana*) and a tall blackberry (*Rubus* sp.). Also much jewelweed (*Impatiens capensis*). It, as well as the remainder of the site described below, would make an excellent area for an advanced wetland delineation class, given the remnant hydric soils, remnant wetland trees,

391

invasion by drier understory, and the absence of hydrology due to drainage. Some other species present in this part included black cherry (*Prunus serotina*), poison-ivy (*Toxicodendron radicans*), northern arrow-wood (*Viburnum recognitum*), Virginia willow (*Itea virginica*), net-veined chain fern (*Woodwardia areolata*), sweet pepperbush (*Clethra alnifolia*), and Walter's St. John's-wort (*Triadenum walteri*).

We next crossed the smaller ditch and checked an area that had only a few live cypress but some large stumps, as well as much red maple and again ample pokeweed, blackberry and Japanese honeysuckle. East of that area is the large main-stem ditch, which had marsh vegetation in it and standing water. We didn't cross this ditch, opting instead to follow the ditch south in hope of locating the remains of the dam site for the old millpond, which we never could locate and something that really bothered me. Perhaps it was obliterated with the channelization; even as far back as 1938 when Smith described the pond it had already been drained (twenty-three years earlier) and was apparently entirely vegetated. See "The ecological relations and plant successions in four drained millponds of the Eastern Shore of Maryland" by Augustine V.P. Smith, 1938 (5).

At this point, we decided to start back towards the car to head on for the Burnt Swamp, our main goal for the day. However, on the way back we followed the drained swamp southeast of the first area we entered. This area was likewise quite dry yet peaty and was similarly invaded by the blackberry, pokeweed and Japanese honeysuckle. Yet it had a few wetland plants, including stout wood-reedgrass (*Cinna arundinacea*), royal fern (*Osmunda regalis* var. *spectabilis*), and again spotted touch-me-not. And then I spotted it -- my first sweetleaf (*Symplocos tinctoria*, State rare) in Maryland. I had always heard that sweetleaf was abundant in the Pocomoke drainage up in Delaware and knew of its occurrence in Maryland, but just hadn't come across it. It was a first for Wilbur in Maryland too. At one point (only a few hundred feet from Route 346), we counted at least twelve clumps, 8-15 feet tall, all within sight of where we were standing. Then we spotted a few swamp cottonwoods (*Populus heterophylla*). This area was between the main and small ditch at the southern end of the site. We also noted a few scattered

392

plants further north. Somewhere in this area we came upon a couple of rather large old cypress stumps, one of which measured 168.7 centimeters (66.4 inches) diameter at two feet off the ground.

Our next stop was a scheduled one, one that I had been anticipating for some time -- the Burnt Swamp or Great Cypress Swamp in Delaware. It wasn't that I expected a lot of rare plants; quite the contrary, I doubted that we would find many, if any, rarities. It was just the mystique of the area -- the one-time vast swamp, filled with huge cypress and black bears, John Nuttall's ramblings through it in 1809, its great conflagration [see my Pocomoke paper] -- and a certain excitement in just being there. Yes, I was looking forward to it, no matter how thick it was. [See Chapter Five for more on the Pocomoke Swamp.]

We entered the Burnt Swamp from Route 54, which bisects it between Gumboro and Selbyville. At 11:05 a.m., we sliced into the swamp on a seventeen degrees west of north heading at a road pull-off where a dirt road angles northeast from Route 54 in the part of the swamp owned by Delaware Wildlands, Inc. Our plan was to walk pretty far into the swamp, then arrow to the right for a while, and eventually head back towards the macadam road east of the car, more or less a rectangular route. We no sooner got into the swamp and there it was again, more sweetleaf and more sweetleaf. It was all over the place, but in the drier areas only. So my thoughts quickly turned to Thomas Nuttall and his exploits in the swamp, including his finding of the redbay (*Persea borbonia*), which incidentally we didn't find. But I musingly asked myself: Were we walking where he rambled? Possibly, but I doubt it. In 1809 Nuttall described the swamp as being seven miles wide (6); along Route 54 it is now only 2.2 miles wide by my car odometer. It's been subsequently ditched and a major conflagration reeked havoc in the area in 1930.

In this drier part of the swamp, besides the sweetleaf we found inkberry (*Ilex glabra*, which was quite abundant), smooth holly (*I. laevigata*), American holly (*I. opaca*), cinnamon fern (*Osmunda cinnamomea*), sweetbay (*Magnolia virginiana*), common catbrier (*Smilax rotundifolia*), glaucous greenbrier (*S. glauca*), water oak (*Quercus nigra*), bracken fern (*Pteridium aquilinum*), Virginia chain fern (*Woodwardia virginica*), highbush blueberry (*Vaccinium corymbosum*), red maple (*Acer rubrum*), swamp azalea (*Rhododendron viscosum*), sweet pepperbush (*Clethra alnifolia*), teaberry (*Gaultheria procumbens*), muscadine (*Vitis rotundifolia*), black gum (*Nyssa sylvatica*), loblolly pine (*Pinus taeda*), sassafras (*Sassafras albidum*), and sweetgum (*Liquidambar styraciflua*).

We soon broke through the shrubs into a open forested area that obviously was much wetter earlier in the year, certainly in the winter and spring if not early summer, given the water marks, water-stained leaves, and wetter herbaceous vegetation, including large areas of sphagnum. This area was again dominated by small red maples, mostly 3-6 inches diameter breast height and had an abundance of Virginia chain fern. We debated for a while whether some of the pines were pond pines (*Pinus serotina*), but the cones weren't right; perhaps it was just loblolly. There was a marked absence of sweetleaf in this wetter area. Then at 11:40 a.m., we hit a 4-foot wide, 2.5-foot deep ditch following essentially our heading at seventeen degrees west of north; its double spoil banks were quite overgrown with vegetation, including one pretty large dead oak (57.7 centimeters or 22.7 inches dbh). Consequently, the ditch was quite old. However, within five minutes we were back into an open area, which was again dominated by small red maples; it had scattered loblolly pines and lots of Virginia chain fern. Wilbur spotted a smooth holly (*Ilex laevigata*) with its large red berries, absence of cilia on the sepals and more ovate and shiny leaves than common winterberry (*Ilex verticillata*). Heard a red-bellied woodpecker.

By 11:50 a.m., we were back into an area with sweetleaf, supporting abundant shrubby growth, particularly sweet pepperbush. It was a higher area containing mostly loblolly pine and red maple, but also beech (*Fagus grandifolia*), flowering dogwood (*Cornus florida*), tulip poplar (*Liriodendron tulipifera*), sassafras (*Sassafras albidum*), oblong-leaf service-berry (*Amelanchier canadensis*), and New York fern (*Thelypteris noveboracensis*). A couple of the sweetleaf trees were about twenty feet tall.

We stopped for lunch on a ditch bank at 12:25 p.m. Heard a crow while eating. As I sat there, I noticed the numerous bristles on a catbrier stem

394

and became suspicious. Looking up, the leaves, half hidden about twenty feet above our heads, appeared to be of the red-berried catbrier (*Smilax walteri*). I tried to shinny a narrow red maple to get access, but was only half way up when Wilbur managed to pull the plant part way down and close enough for us to verify that it was indeed *S. walteri*. Now I have a feel for the bristly stem; I'll watch for it. According to Fernald, *Smilax rotundifolia* [common catbrier] has less, plus broad-based, prickles and green angular stems; *S. walteri* [Walter's catbrier] has many subulate prickles and duller more round stems (2). While observing the catbrier, we also noted the large broken off top of a tree hanging precariously over our heads!

After lunch, we walked down the logging road along the ditch heading forty-seven degrees east of north. Noted a few large, 35-40 feet high, sweetleaf trees; one was 13.1 centimeters (5.2 inches) diameter breast height. They had a water oak type bark. We also found some maleberry (*Lyonia ligustrina*) along the logging road and there was much sweet pepperbush, New York fern, and slender spikegrass (*Chasmanthium laxum*). At 1:00 p.m., we headed back out, south-southwest on the logging road, which as we had anticipated came out to where we had parked our car. Heard a chickadee along the road and some sort of tree frog, perhaps just a spring peeper [*Hyla c. crucifer*]. We were out of the swamp by 1:25 p.m.

We next drove up Route 54 a thousand feet or so and around the bend, parked, and were off again into the swamp, this time heading ten degrees south of west on the opposite side of Route 54. Red maple again dominated the canopy (small trees, although some were 12-14 inches dbh); lots of open water and spring-ponded areas currently only saturated and very spongy to walk, supporting much sphagnum. Scattered Virginia chain fern; swamp sweetbells (*Leucothoe racemosa*) dominates the shrub layer. Some sweetgum, loblolly pine, black gum, and sweet pepperbush. One very wet area had water willow (*Decodon verticillatus*). Also some possum haw viburnum (*Viburnum nudum*). Sweetleaf present on drier areas. Drier areas were dominated by sweet pepperbush in the shrub layer and some fairly large red maples in the canopy. One maple was 54.3 centimeters (21.4 inches) dbh. There were many sweetgum seedlings less than one foot high, but no red maple seedlings. We again made a loop down, then to the right, and eventually back north to Route 54. On a ditch running fourteen degrees east of north, we saw a large dead oak about 100 feet from Route 54 that was 62.7 centimeters (24.7 inches) dbh. Given the size of the tree, the ditch had to be quite old, as its appearance would indicate. It was about seven feet wide and two feet deep. We were out of the swamp at 2:05 p.m. [See Chapter Five for more on the Great Cypress Swamp.]

Our next stop was to the sea-level fen site at Philips Branch off Hopkins Branch which is a tributary of Herring Creek in Sussex County, Delaware; this is off Delaware Road 302 at Pine Water Neck. Wilbur had been to this site before and assumed we would come across some interesting plants. As it turns out, it was a great botanical site and we found numerous rare plants, some of which I collected to key out and for voucher specimens.

We first searched for some Walter's catbrier [red-berried catbrier] in the swampy area near the roads to no avail. Soon, however, we walked down a dirt road until an opening beyond the swamp was apparent. We moved down the slope and into the forested swamp edge, then the shrubs, but before we broke out fully into the open I spotted some Parker's pipewort, *Eriocaulon parkeri* (very rare status). Then the rare plants just poured in one after another. There were so many to consider, particularly plants in Cyperaceae, that I didn't know which one to check next.

My full list for the site with their rarity status where appropriate includes: meadow spike-moss (*Selaginella apoda*), tall beakrush (*Rhynchospora macrostachya*), loose-head beakrush (*Rhynchospora chalarocephala*), beakrush (*Rhynchospora* sp.), dwarf umbrella-sedge (*Fuirena pumila*, a watchlist species), Hairy umbrella-sedge (*Fuirena squarrosa*, a watchlist species), New York aster (*Aster novi-belgii*), Robbins' spikerush (*Eleocharis robbinsii*, a watchlist species), bright-green spikerush (*Eleocharis olivacea*), twigrush (*Cladium mariscoides*), Canada rush (*Juncus canadensis*), brown-fruit rush (*Juncus pelocarpus*, a watchlist species), burreed (*Sparganium* sp.), cardinal flower (*Lobelia cardinalis*), nodding ladies-tresses (*Spiranthes cernua*), rice cutgrass (*Leersia oryzoides*), common reed (*Phragmites australis*), white water lily (*Nymphaea odorata*), marsh seedbox (*Ludwigia palustris*), Engelmann arrowhead (*Sagittaria enngelmanniana*, very rare status), skullcap (*Scutellaria* sp.), marsh St. John's-wort (*Triadenum virginicum*), many-flower penny-wort (*Hydrocotyle umbellata*), bugleweed (*Lycopus* sp.), Canadian St. John's-wort (*Hypericum canadense*), water willow (*Decodon verticillatus*), Virginia meadowbeauty (*Rhexia virginica*), twisted yelloweyed-grass (*Xyris torta*), pickerelweed (*Pontederia cordata*), long-beak baldrush (*Psilocarya scirpoides*, very rare status), two-flowered bladderwort (*Utricularia biflora*, very rare status), bearded sedge (*Carex comosa*), bedstraw (*Galium* sp.), swamp rose (*Rosa palustris*), bay forget-me-not (*Myosotis laxa*, a watchlist species), seaside alder (*Alnus maritima*, a watchlist species), climbing hempweed (*Mikania scandens*), dotted smartweed (*Polygonum punctatum*), Atlantic manna grass (*Glyceria obtusa*), and smooth beggar-ticks (*Bidens laevis*). We initially thought the meadowbeauty may have been *Rhexia aristosa*, but finally concluded that it was not. This was quite a sinky, floating mat area but we got around much of it fairly well, despite some messy breakthroughs.

Given that we were running out of time, we didn't investigate the entire open area and I kept imagining pitcher plants showing up, but they didn't. We got back to the upland at 4:50 p.m. via a plank walkway into the wetland that ended at some sort of trap or cage that contained a small snapping turtle. Scattered metal wood duck boxes were also present. We followed the dirt road to a sign-post pointing the way to a nature trail (apparently this is some sort of camp) and a small elevated walkway over another part of the wetland. Wilbur spotted some laurel-leaf greenbrier (*Smilax laurifolia*); I checked a patch of the smooth beggar-ticks. There were also some cardinal flowers and white turtleheads (*Chelone glabra*) flowering along the walkway. Otter [*Lutra canadensis*] droppings filled with fish scales were abundant on the walkway. We then headed back the dirt road for the car, reaching it at 5:10 p.m.

We were quite muddy, I having sunk to the knees and Wilbur to the waist. I changed my socks and footwear and keyed out the smooth beggar-ticks while Wilbur made a more complete change of clothes. By 5:17 p.m. we were heading into the setting sun. We reached my car at the "Shellstop" at

6:25 p.m. and I was home at 7:20 with a smile on my face. It was a great day, a great trip. In total, we found twelve rare plants and one watchlist species for Delaware from the sea-level fen area, to say nothing for our relocating the millpond site at Willards and our adventure into the Burnt Swamp.[2] I suspect areas similar to this sea-level fen are found in Worcester County, Maryland; something to check out next year.

August 4, 1994 [Cherry Walk Fen and Huckleberry Pond in Sussex County, Delaware]

Botanical trip to Sussex County, Delaware with Wilbur Rittenhouse (Adkins Arboretum), Bill McAvoy, Avery Dalton, and Kitt Heckscher of the Delaware Natural Heritage Program (DNHP), and Hal White (University of Delaware). Last year when I met Bill at the Adkins Arboretum during our computer plant key workshop, he had promised to show me a sea-level fen. Wilbur, of course, was interested too and is always willing to get out in the field. Avery, Kitt, and Hal were interested in odonates at the sites we visited, which included the Cherry Walk Fen on Angola Neck and Huckleberry Pond west of the Prime Hook National Wildlife Refuge.

I met Wilbur, along with the always pleasant songs of some bobwhites, at the Adkins Arboretum at 9 a.m. sharp. We met Bill and the others on Angola Neck around 10:30. After a short drive and a hike through a xeric upland forest, we entered the fen, having first traversed some pretty thick swamp vegetation. It was an impressive site. Bill first pointed out *Bartonia paniculata* (very rare), a new species for me, my having seen only *B. virginica* in the New Jersey Pine Barrens in the 1960s. And by the time we hit the edge of the open fen, rare plants were everywhere. From one spot alone, we easily spotted ten or so. Amazing! We next moved around the periphery at the shrub-herbaceous interface adding more species, Bill pointing out the rarities, particularly a number of yelloweyed-grasses (*Xyris* spp.), bladderworts (*Utricularia* spp.), and beak-rushes (*Rhynchospora* spp.). At

[2]As noted earlier, this is an example of how the rarity status has changed since 1993. I've corrected the statuses given parenthetically, but the original written text has been retained.

one point while trying to examine a beak-rush, I dropped my *Gray's Manual* half into the water, once again ripping open the binding; only a quick retrieval saved it. Eventually, we moved out into the herbaceous area of the fen to find, among other plants, the rare *Eleocharis equisetoides* (very rare) and the strange *E. rostellata* (extremely rare), with its long arching stalks that, like water willow (*Decodon verticillatus*), readily root at their tips. These stalks were easily 4-5 feet long, yet some plants were erect and fertile, albeit generally substantially shorter. Our full list for the site is given below (nomenclature and rarity status follow the DNHP):

Acer rubrum (red maple)
Alnus maritima (seaside alder)   S3*
Andropogon glomeratus (bushy bluestem)
Bartonia paniculata (twining bartonia)   S2
Bidens mitis (tickseed sunflower)   S3
Calopogon tuberosus (tuberous grass-pink)   S1
Carex canescens (silvery sedge)
C. howei (Howe's sedge)
Cladium mariscoides (twigrush)
Clethra alnifolia (sweet pepperbush)
Diospyros virginiana (persimmon)
Drosera intermedia (spatulate-leaf sundew)
D. rotundifolia (round-leaf sundew)   S2
Eleocharis equisetoides (horse-tail spikerush)   S2
E. rostellata (beaked spikerush)   S1
E. tuberculosa (long-tubercle spikerush)
Eriocaulon compressum (flattened pipewort)   S2
E. decangulare (ten-angled pipewort)   S1
Eupatorium leucolepis (white-bract thoroughwort)
Fuirena squarrosa (hairy umbrella-sedge)   S3
Gaylussacia frondosa (dangleberry)
Glyceria obtusa (blunt manna grass)
Hypericum canadense (Canadian St. John's-wort)

Ilex glabra (inkberry)

I. laevigata (smooth winterberry)

Iris prismatica (slender blue flag)   S3

Juncus canadensis (Canadian rush)

J. pelocarpus (brown-fruited rush)   S3

Lycopodium appressum (southern bog clubmoss)

Lycopus amplectens (sessile-leaf bugleweed)   S2

Lyonia ligustrina (maleberry)

Myrica cerifera (wax myrtle)

Nymphaea odorata (white waterlily)

Osmunda cinnamomea (cinnamon fern)

O. regalis (royal fern)

Panicum (Dichanthelium) lucidum (cypress witchgrass)

Phragmites australis (common reed)

Pinus serotina (pond pine)

Pogonia ophioglossoides (rose pogonia)   S2

Polygala cruciata (cross-leaf milkwort)   S2

Pyrus arbutifolia (red chokeberry)

Rhexia virginica (Virginia meadowbeauty)

Rhododendron viscosum (swamp white azalea)

Rhynchospora alba (white beakrush)

R. fusca (brown beakrush)   S2

R. gracilenta (slender beakrush)   S3

Sagittaria latifolia (broad-leaf arrowhead)

Scirpus americanus (= S. *olneyi*) (Olney three-square)

S. pungens (common three-square)

Selaginella apoda (meadow spikemoss)

Spiraea tomentosa (steeple-bush)

Triadenum sp. (St. John's-wort)

Utricularia biflora (two-flowered bladderwort)   S2

U. fibrosa (fibrous bladderwort)   S2

U. gibba (humped bladderwort)

U. juncea (southern bladderwort)   S2

U. purpurea (purple bladderwort)   S2
U. vulgaris (common bladderwort)
Vaccinium corymbosum (common highbush blueberry)
Vernonia noveboracensis (New York ironweed)
Xyris difformis var. *difformis* (common yelloweyed-grass)
X. fimbriata (fringed yelloweyed-grass)   S1
X. smalliana (Small's yelloweyed-grass)   S2
X. torta (twisted yelloweyed-grass)

*   S1 = extremely rare
       S2 = very rare
       S3 = watchlist species
       [See Table II in Chapter Two for an explanation of the rarity
       categories for Delaware.]

Unfortunately, we missed square-stem spikerush (*Eleocharis quadrangulata*) and Robbin's spikerush (*E. robbinsii*, a watchlist species), both of which are present at the site; seeing them along with horse-tail spikerush (*E. equisetoides*, very rare) on the same day at the same site would have been great from my perspective, especially considering that *E. quadrangulata* is my favorite spikerush and the other two are particularly interesting finds (Figure 64). Likewise, the two orchids were done flowering. Although it is no longer tracked by the DNHP, my best plant for the day was white-bract thoroughwort (*Eupatorium leucolepis*), another species I hadn't seen since my Pine Barren days. None of the bladderworts were new for me, but I hadn't seen most of them, exclusive of two-flowered bladderwort (*Utricularia biflora)* and purple bladderwort (*U. purpurea*), in years, and really didn't recognize them as to species. I did, however, get three new species: twining bartonia (*Bartonia paniculata*), slender beakrush (*Rhynchospora gracilenta*), and Small's yelloweyed-grass (*Xyris smalliana*), and reacquainted myself with a number that I had only seen once or twice before. In total, we found twenty-five out of the thirty-eight rare plants that are known from the site. What a site! It was quite impressive, even more so than

401

Figure 64. The author's favorite spikerush, the square-stem spikerush (*Eleocharis quadrangulata*). This species superficially resembles the common three-square (*Scirpus pungens*).

402

the sea-level fen that Wilbur and I visited last year on Philips Branch (see October 2, 1993 *Journal* entry).

The fen also reminded me of the smaller but similarly located (in relation to brackish tidewater) Cypress Creek Swamp and Savanna off of the Magothy River in Anne Arundel County, Maryland. That site, which I had discovered back in 1977 (7), had a number of similar species until more recent years, for example, spatulate-leaf sundew (*Drosera intermedia*), tickseed sunflower (*Bidens mitis*), twigrush (*Cladium mariscoides*), Nuttall's small reed-grass (*Calamagrostis cinnoides*), marsh St. John's-wort (*Triadenum virginicum*), white waterlily (*Nymphaea odorata*), rose pogonia (*Pogonia ophioglossoides*), Virginia meadowbeauty (*Rhexia virginica*), white beakrush (*Rhynchospora alba*), and bladderwort (*Utricularia* sp.). It also had some different plants, for example, large cranberry (*Vaccinium macrocarpon*), pine-barrens rush (*Juncus abortivus*), southern white cedar (*Chamaecyparis thyoides*), white-fringed orchid (*Habenaria blephariglottis*), and yellow-fringed orchid (*H. ciliaris*). Unfortunately, the adjacent slightly brackish marsh vegetation has invaded the Cypress Creek Savanna over the years, apparently due to sea level rise. The Atlantic white cedars are mostly dead, particularly the smaller ones; the only noticeable bog plants left are remnant cranberries and the Atlantic white cedars.[3] Two patches of the bane of the marshes, the common reed (*Phragmites australis*), have also expanded further into parts of the site at both ends. [See Chapter Eight for more on the Cypress Creek Swamp and Savanna.]

My first thought about these Delaware fens when I saw them was their potential susceptibility to sea level rise/salinity changes and resultant brackish marsh plant invasion, as well as aggressive invasion by *Phragmites australis*. Although there is not much that can be done about the former situation short of water level manipulation (control structures), the common reed should be controlled if its spread is documented.

We left the fen quite wet and muddy, having broken through the surface in several places and sinking to well above the knees, essentially to the

---

[3] I am happy to report, however, that I did find a few additional bog plants at the site on August 13, 1998, including the beautiful yellow fringed orchid.

buttocks. We wondered: Did the old-timers wade right in like this, or was that just not their style (more genteel) in those days? While hiking out of the area, Bill spotted common wintergreen (*Chimaphila umbellata* var. *cisatlantica*, very rare) and pale hickory (*Carya pallida*). Along the roadside during lunch, I noted a number of native edge or forest herbaceous species, including rattlebox (*Crotalaria sagittalis*), frostweed (*Helianthemum canadense*), pinweed (*Lechea* sp.), and that paragon of variability, ipecac spurge (*Euphorbia ipecacuanhae*), among others. The roadside looked excellent for rare Pine Barren type plants, such as wild lupine (*Lupinus perennis*).

During our visit to the fen, Hal, Avery, and Kitt collected some odonates, including a dragonfly that apparently hadn't been collected on the Delmarva since the early 1900s. [A complete list of the odonates noted on this trip is given below.] I also found some northern cricket frogs (*Acris c. crepitans*); Kitt, a ribbon snake (*Thamnophis s. sauritus*). I tried to feed a 3-inch praying mantis to a golden garden spider (*Argiope aurantia*); the spider made an initial quick approach only to slow down and just touch the mantis a couple of times with a leg. I don't know the outcome, having left after about two minutes of observation, the plethora of rare plants pulling me away. However, the golden garden spider didn't attack and embalm immediately as they generally do when tossed grasshoppers.

[Perhaps this colorful account of an encounter between a praying mantis and what probably was a golden garden spider, which was given in *Exploring the Insect World with Edwin Way Teale* (8), will suggest the fate of my spider:

"One windy day in mid-September I was walking along a creek when I stumbled upon a singular death struggle among the bushes. A praying mantis, its wings widespread, was imprisoned in the silver web of a black and orange spider. The gusts, catching the outspread wings of the mantis, were billowing out the web and threatening to break it. In a frenzy of excitement the spider danced along the swaying threads, running back and forth across the web. The forelimbs of the mantis were free and each time the spider rushed close, in an effort to throw deadly loops of thread over its prize, the mantis lashed out with its scythe-like legs.

"Thread by thread the web gave way under the pounding of the gusts and the struggles of the mantis. For fifteen minutes the silent duel continued. Then it ended with dramatic suddenness. The spider ran a fraction of an inch too close. The spiked forelegs snapped shut over its body. This effort broke the remaining threads and the mantis dropped to the ground with the spider in its grasp. The last I saw of it, the victor was carefully cleaning its legs of the sticky silk, before it dined on its foe."

In the same book, Teale also mentions another mantis-spider encounter, which, like me, he induced by presenting a mantis with a black widow spider. According to Teale, the mantis soon nabbed the spider and started devouring it, but soon dropped the spider "...in what seemed to be disgust."]

Our next stop was Huckleberry Pond. Before visiting the pond, we traversed a rich woods area that had been hard hit by last years ice storm. Numerous tree branches were broken off; sprouting of secondary branches gave them a strange physiognomy, almost as though they had huge clusters of mistletoe or air plants, a tropical appearance. We found Huckleberry Pond, a Delmarva bay, quite inundated, at least with two feet of standing water with water marks on trees being about another two feet higher. Hardly any plants were emersed -- just the tips of some Robbin's spikerush (*Eleocharis robbinsii*, a watchlist species). We saw a few uprooted Carolina redroot (*Lachnanthes caroliniana*, extremely rare) and found some of last years square-stem spikerush (*Eleocharis quadrangulata*). Due to the high water, however, we didn't get to see pink coreopsis (*Coreopsis rosea*), creeping St. John's-wort (*Hypericum adpressum*), Wright's witchgrass (*Panicum wrightianum*), Walter's paspalum (*Paspalum dissectum*), and reticulated nutrush (*Scleria reticularis*), all of which are rare plants known to occur here; they all would have been new species for me. And I certainly would like to have seen wrinkled jointgrass (*Coelorachis rugosa*), another species I left back in the Pine Barrens. [I finally got to see this species again, over three decades later, on September 17, 1998 while teaching a grass, sedge, and rush course with some colleagues at Moncks Corner, South Carolina.] This too is obviously a great site with sixteen rare plant species known to be present. Nevertheless, our trip here was not wasted given that Hal, Avery, and Kitt again collected some odonates and we got to experience what is perhaps the most significant physical factor keeping open (i.e., glade-like) many Delmarva bays -- the deep water that periodically kills young woody plants such as red maples and sweetgums, and even stresses larger trees as we witnessed today by the discolored leaves of the few scattered sweetgums in the open bay area. I always suspected that water (and perhaps fire) to be the main factor. Inundation likewise appears to be the case with some of the Anne Arundel County bog sites, especially Eagle Hill Bog, where invading red maple seedlings don't persist, apparently due to periodic deep flooding.

We also observed numerous tadpoles rising to the water surface to gulp air and whirligig beetles zipping around on the surface. Once again I noted how persimmon (*Diospyros virginiana*) seems to do so well in these well-flooded bay systems, whereas in this part of the country it usually occurs on quite dry sites. I've always suspected the Delmarva bay persimmons, which don't appear to get very big and, in fact, may be old stunted trees, are manifesting ecotypic variation. Bill and I discussed these possibilities. [For more on the Delmarva potholes see Chapter Seven.]

After leaving Huckleberry Pond, we again traversed the rich woods dominated by tulip poplar (*Liriodendron tulipifera*), sweetgum (*Liquidambar styraciflua*), and flowering dogwood (*Cornus florida*), this time stopping to examine its understory, which regretfully is being overrun by japanese honeysuckle (*Lonicera japonica*). I spotted a few other invasive plants as well, such as pokeweed (*Phytolacca americana*) and fireweed (*Erechtites hieraciifolia*). In spite of the disturbance, we still found swamp Jack-in-the-pulpit (*Arisaema triphyllum*), bugbane (*Cimicifuga racemosa*), enchanter's nightshade (*Circaea lutetiana*), bloodroot (*Sanguinaria canadensis*), Canada moonseed (*Menispermum canadense*), mayapple (*Podophyllum peltatum*), bedstraw (*Galium* sp.), Virginia knotweed (*Polygonum virginianum*), lopseed

(*Phryma leptostachya*), and yellow passion flower (*Passiflora lutea*, very rare), a nice assemblage.

We finished up around 4 p.m. and Wilbur and I headed back to Adkins Arboretum, where upon exiting our vehicle we were again greeted by the song of a bobwhite. It was another great trip. We were well prepared for it thanks to Bill who had furnished plant lists for both sites and was quite familiar with the species on site. I question, though, whether these sites are really fens, technically.

Later in the day, I verified the identity of some plants I had collected, including *Xyris smalliana, Eriocaulon compressum* var. *compressum, Panicum lucidum, Rhynchospora fusca*, and *R. gracilenta*. There was one species that I could not identify: a one-foot long straggling forb with smooth entire, almost coriaceous, opposite dark green leaves and axillary flowers that were either not yet open or aborted. I collected it in the inundated shrubby vegetation around the periphery of the fen.

[During our field trip, Kitt Heckscher compiled the following list of odonates from Cherry Walk Fen and Huckleberry Pond:

<u>Cherry Walk Fen</u>

Dragonflies

Libellula incesta	slatey skimmer	S5
L. needhami	Needham's skimmer	S5
Tramea carolina	violet-masked glider	S4
T. lacerata	black-mantled glider	S3
Celithemis eponina	Halloween pennant	S4
Erythrodiplax berenice	seaside dragonlet	S5
Pachydiplax longipennis	blue dasher	S5
Erythemis simplicicollis	eastern pondhawk	S5
Sympetrum vicinum	yellow-legged meadowfly	S4
S. ambiguum	blue-faced meadowfly	S1

Damselflies

Lestes spp.	spreadwings	
Argia bipunctulata	seepage dancer	S1
Ischnura posita	fragile forktail	S5
I. ramburii	Rambur's forktail	S5
Nannothemis bella	elfin skimmer	S1

Huckleberry Pond

Dragonflies

Tramea carolina	violet-masked glider	S4
Pachydiplax longipennis	blue dasher	S5
Perithemis tenera	eastern amberwing	S5
Anax junius	common green darner	S5
Celithemis eponina	Halloween pennant	S4
Sympetrum ambiguum	blue-faced meadowfly	S1

Damselflies

Ischnura posita	fragile forktail	S5
Enallagma civile	familiar bluet	S5

Nomenclature and rarity status follow the Delaware Natural Heritage Program. See Table II in Chapter Two for an explanation of the rarity categories. Three of these species, *Sympetrum ambiguum*, *Argia bipunctulata*, and *Nannothemis bella*, are considered extremely rare in Delaware.]

August 21, 1994 [Little Patuxent Oxbow, Anne Arundel County, Maryland]

According to Edwin W. Teale (8), somewhere in his writings William Beebe commented: "There is one joy of reading, another of painting, and

408

another of writing, but none to compare with the thrill which comes to one who, loving Nature in all her moods, is about to start on a voyage of discovery." And so it was today as Steve Hambalek, Bernie Raftery, Wilbur Rittenhouse, Dawn Biggs, and I hiked up and over the high ridge surrounding the Little Patuxent Oxbow near Laurel, Maryland. (The Little Patuxent Oxbow, which has been called the jewel of natural areas in Anne Arundel County, is apparently the largest natural impoundment in Maryland.) Upon reaching the oxbow and immediately flushing about ten wood ducks, we stood there for a few minutes pondering just how long ago the old meander originated. It was a great view from the toe of the sloping uplands -- an expansive area, for the most part seemingly covered by water shield (*Brasenia schreberi*), although there were scattered buttonbushes (*Cephalanthus occidentalis*) throughout and large patches of emergent plants in the distance. From here, we followed the periphery of the oxbow to and beyond a few swales that entered the oxbow from the south and west, eventually reaching the neck of the meander and locating the Little Patuxent River. By this point, we had already eaten lunch and had noted a pileated woodpecker, green heron, and yellow-billed cuckoo. I listed the following plants from either the edge of the oxbow, the adjacent wet forested swales, the sloping seep areas, or the neck area of the oxbow:

Brasenia schreberi [water shield]
Nuphar luteum [spatterdock]
Nymphaea odorata [white waterlily]
Cuscuta gronovii [love dodder]
Triadenum virginicum [marsh St. John's-wort]
Asclepias incarnata [swamp milkweed]
Bidens sp. [beggar-ticks]
Lobelia cardinalis [cardinal flower]
Scutellaria lateriflora [mad dog scullcap]
Lysimachia terrestris [swamp loosestrife]
Carex comosa [bearded sedge]
C. stricta [tussock sedge]

C. folliculata [northern long sedge]

C. festucacea (?) [fescue sedge]

C. lurida [sallow sedge]

Toxicodendron vernix [poison sumac]

Cinna arundinacea [stout wood-reedgrass]

Eleocharis obtusa [blunt spikerush]

Sparganium sp. [burreed]

Polygonum sagittatum [arrow-leaf tearthumb]

P. arifolium [halberd-leaf tearthumb]

Dulichium arundinaceum [three-way sedge]

Sagittaria latifolia var. *latifolia* [duck-potato]

S. latifolia var. *pubescens* [hairy duck-potato]

Leersia oryzoides [rice cutgrass]

Ilex verticillata [common winterberry]

Leucothoe racemosa [swamp sweetbells]

Osmunda cinnamomea [cinnamon fern]

O. regalis var. *spectabilis* [royal fern]

Thelypteris thelypteroides [New York fern]

Athyrium filix-femina [northern lady fern]

Laportea canadensis [Canadian wood-nettle]

Boehmeria cylindrica [small-spike false-nettle]

Pilea pumila [Canada clearweed]

Impatiens capensis [jewelweed]

I. pallida [pale touch-me-not]

Galium sp. [madder]

Rotala ramosior ? [toothcup]

Chionanthus virgincus [white fringe tree]

Saururus cernuus [lizard's-tail]

Aronia prunifolia (= *Pyrus floribunda*) [purple chokeberry]

Utricularia biflora [two-flower bladderwort]

Lindera benzoin [spicebush]

Calamagrostis canadensis [blue-joint reedgrass]

After reaching the Little Patuxent River, I realized we had seen a few plants more typical of the Piedmont, such as *Laportea canadensis* and *Impatiens pallida*. As I have noted in the past, this phenomenon is typical of the Patuxent River (and the Potomac as well), since it penetrates far into the Piedmont, the source of these plants. We also found a cache of mud turtle shells (*Kinosternon subrubrum subrubrum*), three in all, at the base of an eight inch diameter tree on the upland slope about 40 feet from the edge of the oxbow.

At one point, we came across a large ditch, an apparent attempt to drain some of the old agricultural area, much of which has now succeeded to forest cover with remnant earlier successional species, such as multiflora rose (*Rosa multiflora*), in abundance. The ditch supported a number of plants including *Lobelia cardinalis*, *Mimulus ringens*, *Penthorum sedoides*, *Panicum stipulatum* (= *P. rigidulum*), and *Helenium nudiflorum* (= *H. flexuosum*, a Maryland Natural Heritage Program watchlist species), among others.

Around 1 p.m., we headed back towards where, earlier in the day, we had initially encountered the oxbow. Our intent, however, was to first investigate the large marshy area south of the meander (oxbow) neck. After struggling through dense oldfield vegetation and passing through the forested area supporting, much to our dismay, the dense understory of multiflora rose, we eventually located the marsh. At this point, we had two choices: Should we arrow across the expansive wetland with its dense emergent vegetation and substantial, water shield-filled, open water area? Or should we struggle around the periphery of the oxbow, a much longer route? We opted to give the marshy oxbow a try knowing all too well that it could eventually get pretty deep and that we might have to turn back, which would be quite arduous after having already traversed much of the deep marsh once. We chanced it, starting across at 1:37 p.m. After pushing though the cattail and other emergent vegetation, we were soon well into the water shield, about waist deep, and struggling to say the least as the stringy water shield plants substantially impeded our leg movements, clinging to us like slender underwater ropes. I've never seen so much water shield, anywhere. Between

411

its tangled masses of leaf petioles, an abundance of coontail (*Ceratophyllum demersum*), and hidden submerged logs, it was quite a task crossing that wetland. Yet this didn't draw my attention from the numerous aquatic insects in and above the water. Dragonfly exuviae were quite abundant and at one point I even spotted a large predaceous diving beetle (*Dytiscus* sp.) scurrying across the water shield pads. (These large beetles generally hang down head first from the surface receiving air through their posterior end. Thus, not having gills, they can readily leave the water and will, of course, even fly off to another wet site when a backwater area dries out.) When pursued today, however, this one promptly entered the water, whereupon I then noted a water measurer (*Hydrometra* sp.) scooting readily along the surface, seemingly effortlessly.

A sort of debate started at 1:57. Should we continue or not? Consequently, being in the lead and perhaps the only one at this point willing, I volunteered to check the depths further out and signal the rest to continue, assuming I thought we could make it. I sensed that the others had reservations, given that one or two of them had already gone in above their waists. Around 2 p.m., I informed them that I would keep going, although by now the water was over my armpits as I held my vest high over my head. Therefore, I suggested that they should take the alternate peripheral route. They took my advice, but Steve stayed back to keep tabs on me, apparently for safety purposes, although this was never discussed. I continued to push through the water shield, at times gaining access to some "higher" spots in the form of buttonbush (*Cephalanthus occidentalis*) clumps, many of which were dead due to the excessive water depths. Certainly, having gotten this far, with only perhaps 150 feet to go, I didn't want to turn back, initially assuming I could always swim a hundred feet or so. But as I continued to sink and struggle with the water shield stems tangling my legs and feet, for the first time, I started seriously doubting whether I could make it across. How could I swim through this mass of vegetation using only one arm while holding my vest, which was burdened with my *Gray's Manual of Botany*, binoculars, and other items, over my head and out of the water? If it weren't for the dense clinging water shield, I could have successfully gone on; likewise, if I didn't

412

have my vest, I'm sure I would have made it. But struggling while wrapped in dense water shield while up to my armpits and somewhat sinking in bottom mud just wouldn't do it. I finally gave up at 2:10, reluctantly. I had no choice but to struggle back through it all once again (something I didn't look forward to for more than one reason) to get the hell out of there, and a struggle it was. Disappointed, I finally caught up with the others about 2:20. Twenty minutes later we were out of the marsh and once again traversing the steep forested slope south of the oxbow, albeit at a slower pace. We then hiked up the new road, quite wet and muddy, to our two cars.

Well, from my perspective it was an great field trip exploring that expansive and interesting oxbow. And our failed attempt at crossing it in the afternoon surely added to the fun, excitement, and adventure. Although we didn't locate *Cuscuta polygonorum* (a MNHP endangered species), we found many plants of *Utricularia biflora* (MNHP endangered species), usually in clusters throughout much of the deep marsh area dominated by water shield. We also found what appeared to be *Rotala ramosior* (at one time considered rare by the MNHP), but because it was not flowering or fruiting we couldn't confirm it.

September 16, 1994 [Pocomoke River, Worcester County, Maryland]

Gene Cooley, Joan Maloof, and I were botanizing today -- once again along the Pocomoke in Worcester County, but this time in quest of the catchfly grass, *Leersia lenticularis* (Figure 65), a Maryland Natural Heritage Program endangered-extirpated species. (I was originally supposed to teach a Compositae course at the Northern Virginia Community College, but it was canceled due to insufficient interest.) I met Gene at the McDonalds near Cape St. Claire and by about 9:15 a.m. we were heading for the Pocomoke after buying some paddles and other equipment and picking up the canoe at Sandy Point State Park. We met Joan at Whiton Crossing and were on the river, heading upstream, by 11:15.

Joan and Mat Cimino have been doing field work on the Pocomoke for the Maryland Natural Heritage Program this year, and at Gene's prompting

Joan checked the Whiton Crossing site on September 9 where *L. lenticularis* was last collected by A. V. Smith and R. R. Tatnall, in 1938. And to Joan's surprise, she found it -- fifty-six years later -- a thousand feet or so upstream and perhaps two hundred feet east of the channelized river.

So here Gene and I, guided by Joan, where eagerly heading upstream to see a plant that neither of us had ever seen and, most incredibly, no one had seen in Maryland for fifty-six years prior to Joan's recent discovery. In all appearance, it was to be a clear but humid day, full of mosquitoes, but we couldn't care less -- we were eager for an encounter with *L. lenticularis*. After tying up the canoe and crossing the man-made levee (spoil bank), we were soon in the wetter part of the swamp and encountering a number of interesting plants, such as hop-like sedge (*Carex lupuliformis*, a watchlist species), giant sedge (*C. gigantea*, a highly State rare and endangered species), and Walter's catbrier (*Smilax walteri*, a watchlist species). For a while, we debated over whether or not we had *C. gigantea*, eventually concluding that we did, particularly after finding some obvious *C. lupuliformis*. Besides its different shaped achenes, *C. lupuliformis* spikes are so much broader and larger overall. Then at 12:30, Gene spotted it, one specimen of *L.*

Figure 65. The rare catch-fly grass (*Leersia lenticularis*), a plant that until fairly recently, had not been seen on the Delmarva Peninsula since 1938 when it was collected by A. V. Smith and R. R. Tatnall along the Pocomoke River. In 1994, however, it was rediscovered by Joan Maloof after a fifty-six year hiatus!

lenticularis, which saw us immediately on our knees examining the plant. Boy, did it stand out -- so much more robust, both the leaves and spikelets, than the rice cutgrass (*L. oryzoides*) and the groups of spikelets (spike-like clusters of spikelets stacked upon one another somewhat like slanted oblong

414

poker chips) were so diagnostic. The spike-like clusters also somewhat reminded me of the orchard grass, *Dactylis glomerata*.[4]

We then searched for more catchfly grass, finding many plants as we meandered through much of the area. They seemed to be associated with areas that earlier in the year held either standing water or had well saturated soils; some areas were still saturated. These areas contained various sedges, such as *C. lupuliformis, C. gigantea,* and blunt broom sedge (*C. tribuloides*), as well as a white flowered smartweed (*Polygonum* sp.) that we didn't key out. While searching for the catchfly grass, we also found cypress-swamp sedge (*C. joorii)*, a State rare and threatened species. While Joan and I keyed out *C. joorii,* making sure it wasn't southern waxy sedge (*C. glaucescens*), Gene caught an Appalachian eyed brown (*Satyrodes appalachia*).

We ate lunch on the man-made levee, where, as expected, we noted an abundance of pawpaw (*Asimina triloba*), as well as some cross-vine (*Bignonia capreolata*). In the swamp, we also found many bald cypress (*Taxodium distichum*) and swamp cottonwood (*Populus heterophylla*) saplings, Joan making the point that the bald cypress may be on its way back in the area. And Joan and I each independently located one specimen of short-bristled hornedrush (*Rhynchospora corniculata,* a watchlist species) and we noted a few overcup oak (*Quercus lyrata,* a watchlist species) and swamp chestnut oak (*Q. michauxii*). During lunch, Gene pressed some plants, including *L. lenticularis, C. lupuliformis, C. joorii,* and *C. gigantea.*

After lunch, we decided to check the western side of the river for the catchfly grass, but the original river channel was just beyond the man-made channel and levee, so we didn't attempt to cross it. However, I did walk the swampy area between the man-made channel and the old meandering channel down to the bridge at Whiton Crossing, while Joan and Gene hiked back to the boat and motored down to meet me. Although I found no catchfly grass on the west side, I did see ample *C. lupuliformis* and *C. gigantea,* as well as

---

4 In an October 17, 1994 letter to me, Bill McAvoy indicated that he was of the opinion that what we identified as *Carex lupuliformis* was actually the hop sedge, *C. lupulina.* See also Chapter Five in this regard.

substantial marsh dewflower (*Murdannia keisak*), an invasive aquatic that I first reported for the Eastern Shore in 1971, on the Wicomico River three miles south of Salisbury (9). I beat Gene and Joan down to the bridge and, therefore, decided to check for the catchfly grass in the swamp east of the river but north of the road. Sure enough, I found it in similar swamp habitat as that upstream and associated with similar plants.

When Gene and Joan caught up with me, we continued downstream intent on exploring the unchannelized section of the river about one mile from Porters Crossing. As we moved downstream with Gene navigating, he pursued a large dragonfly that was outrunning us, while I at the bow held the insect net. Then Gene spotted the same or another large dragonfly perched on a branch high above the boat. As he stood up from the stern, I passed him the net just in time to nab the dragonfly, a dragon hunter (*Hagenius brevistylus*).

Before reaching the unchannelized section, we opted to again search for *Leersia lenticularis* on the east side of the river beyond the levee. As I stepped out of the canoe onto what appeared to be firm sloping ground, I immediately sunk to my ankle; in instinctively reacting, I pulled back with an audible sound of mud sucking at my foot. Needless to say, I took the blunt of a few remarks and laughs at that point. Soon I confidently made firm ground and pulled up the canoe only to abruptly slip on the muddy slope and land on my butt, with additional laughter -- energetic laughter. (I should mention that Gene and Joan had their own moment of excitement earlier in my absence, unfortunately. While getting to the boat after I had departed from them upstream of the bridge, Joan leaned against a dead tree bole that promptly fell releasing a bunch of bumblebees in the process, a couple of which stung them.) We were soon into the swamp, however, and before long I spotted a couple of flowering stems of *L. lenticularis*. So by now I started thinking that perhaps this plant is much more abundant along the Pocomoke where habitat is conducive to it, at least this year. After locating these specimens, but no others, we circled back to the river, subsequently splitting up -- Gene and Joan going upstream, me downstream -- all trying to find the canoe. They found it and picked me up downstream. From here we finally reached the unchannelized section, but soon turned back due to some log obstructions and the time (5:10 p.m.). We were back at Whiton Crossing at 5:30.

While taking out the boat and equipment, I heard two barred owls from different parts of the swamp, as well as a pileated woodpecker. Then one pileated swept low over the road to land in a dead roadside tree; its white underwing patches flashed boldly.

Around 6:15 p.m., Joan headed for home but Gene and I decided to try Porters Crossing in hopes of finding more *Leersia lenticularis*, getting there near dark, at 6:30. I suggested that we try the western side of the river south of the road. As we worked our way into habitat appearing suitable for the catchfly grass (i.e., like that at Whiton Crossing), I remarked to Gene something to the effect that: "My guess is that we will find it here." To his amazement, within a minute of that statement, he spotted some catchfly grass...that I had passed by without noticing. Then, as we continued to meander through the area, these interesting plants, robust specimens, repeatedly appeared. Our remarks went something like this:

"Here's a big one. There's another batch. Look at the size of those plants. Impressive. The leaves are really wide. I got one that's 23 millimeters. I just can't believe all these plants. How have they been missed all of these years?"

They were indeed excellent specimens and, as indicated above, one had a 23 millimeter wide leaf, 3 millimeters greater than the 10-20 millimeter range given by Fernald (2). Gene collected additional specimens, including ditch stonecrop (*Penthorum sedoides*) and overcup oak (*Quercus lyrata*), and we also noted Virginia dayflower (*Commelina virginica*, a watchlist species) and Allegheny monkey-flower (*Mimulus ringens*), as well as substantial patches of *Saururus cernuus*. While Gene was pressing his specimens back at the car, I collected rice cutgrass (*Leersia oryzoides*) and whitegrass (*L. virginica*) to compare them with Gene's *L. lenticularis* specimens. After comparing the three readily differentiated species, I handed them to Gene and

417

pointed out that he and I may be the only people that ever held all three species at one time in Maryland, at least since 1938.

It was dark before we left Porters Crossing, which found me working in the headlights on a grass, a plumegrass (*Erianthus* sp.), which we had collected earlier along Route 354. I eventually gave up, deciding to work on it at home on Sunday. Gene packed away his press and we headed for home, not reaching my car at McDonalds until around 10 p.m. I was home by 10:30. Gene didn't get home until after midnight since he had to go back to the office to return some equipment.

October 14, 1994 [Big Marsh, Kent County, Maryland]

Trip with Gene Cooley and Kathy McCarthy to Big Marsh in Kent County, Maryland. I met Gene and Kathy at the usual place, McDonald's, near Cape St. Claire around 9 a.m. We then traveled to Echo Hill School (a private outdoor education facility) to botanize Big Marsh, a huge nontidal scrub-shrub swamp fronting on the Chesapeake Bay at Howell Point. I was really looking forward to this trip, having last been to the site sometime back in the early 1970s when I worked for the Maryland DNR.

We arrived at the Echo Hill School just after 10 a.m. to cool and cloudy weather. We met with Peter Rice, the school's founder, and examined some aerial photographs of the site. He then took us to the beach area to obtain paddles and life preservers for use once we hiked out to a canoe landing.

Earlier, Gene had mentioned that tufted loosestrife (*Lysimachia thyrsiflora*), American frog's-bit (*Limnobium spongia*), flat-leaf bladderwort (*Utricularia intermedia*), and bulb-bearing water hemlock (*Cicuta bulbifera*) had recently been reported from the swamp, along the boardwalk, as well as near the beach for the latter species. A school naturalist, Brent Steury, reported *L. thyrsiflora* and *C. bulbifera* earlier in the year; Gene and Wayne Tyndall verified them during a site visit on which they also found *L. spongia* and *U. intermedia*. These are all significant species for Maryland: Brown and Brown (10) do not include *L. thyrsiflora* in our flora; this is apparently its

418

first reporting from Maryland. *L. spongia*, a highly State rare and endangered species according to the Maryland Natural Heritage Program, is considered "...rare in Delaware; no certain Maryland record" by Brown and Brown. *U. intermedia* is reported as rare in Delaware and Virginia by Brown and Brown and "...may be expected in Maryland." This is apparently the first reporting of this species in Maryland. *C. bulbifera* is listed by Brown and Brown; it is considered endangered by the Maryland Natural Heritage Program. Historically, the white water crow-foot (*Ranunculus trichophyllus*), a highly State rare and endangered species, has also been reported from the site according to Gene. In addition, Brent Steury also recently found clammyweed (*Polanisia dodecandra*), an endangered-extirpated species according to the Maryland Natural Heritage Program, on the large overwash berm at the bay-front at Howell Point.

As we approached the beach, Gene showed us a *C. bulbifera* plant with its axillary bulblets. We then drove out to the head of a trail leading to the boardwalk. When we first arrived at the school, I had spotted a large chinquapin oak (*Quercus muehlenbergii*), a watchlist species, and we found additional large specimens at the head of the trail. Our first thought was that maybe these trees were planted since this species is not considered a component of Coastal Plain forests in Maryland and they were found near roads and/or buildings. For example, Brown and Brown (11) indicate that chinquapin oak grows on: "Dry, shaly [sic] ridges and calcareous slopes; rare." Later though, we found it on both sides of the swamp on the steeply sloping uplands (see below).

We didn't start walking the boardwalk until around 11 a.m. It soon became evident that the swamp had a diverse flora -- many shrubs and a number of herbaceous plants. The trees were mostly red maple (*Acer rubrum*). While Gene and Kathy were talking to a camp counselor (or teacher) and some grammar school students, I utilized the time to compile a quick list of twenty-nine species along a short stretch of the boardwalk:

Acer rubrum (red maple)
Rosa palustris (swamp rose)

419

Ilex verticillata (common winterberry)
Aronia arbutifolia (red chokeberry)
Clethra alnifolia (sweet pepperbush)
Hibiscus moscheutos (swamp rose mallow)
Vaccinium corymbosum (common highbush blueberry)
Decodon verticillatus (water willow)
Peltandra virginica (arrow-arum)
Nuphar luteum (spatterdock)
Boehmeria cylindrica (small-spike false-nettle)
Cuscuta sp. (dodder)
Bidens sp. (beggar-ticks)
Mikania scandens (hemp vine)
Polygonum arifolium (halberd-leaf tearthumb)
Polygonum sp. (a white-flowered smartweed)
Triadenum virginicum (marsh St. John's-wort)
Lemna minor (lesser duckweed)
Aster sp. (aster)
Eleocharis obtusa (blunt spikerush)
Leersia oryzoides (rice cutgrass)
Rumex verticillatus (swamp dock)
Ludwigia palustris (water purslane)
Osmunda cinnamomea (cinnamon fern)
Thelypteris thelypteroides (marsh fern)
Carex sp. (in Stellulatae) (sedge)
Ceratophyllum demersum (coontail)
Brasenia schreberi (water shield)
Potamogeton sp. (pondweed)

Before developing my list, we had already found, as expected, four rarities along the boardwalk: *Utricularia intermedia** with its unique flat aquatic liverwort-like branches (we also found the aquatic liverwort, *Riccia fluitans*), *Lysimachia thrysiflora* (only vegetative, but Gene and Wayne had seen it in flower earlier in the year), *Limnobium spongia*, and *Cicuta*

420

bulbifera*, all along the two-plank wide boardwalk. It should be noted that the boardwalk was constructed only this year so the disturbance should have nothing to do with the presence of these plants; they obviously were there all along. While Gene was talking to the counselor, I also noted some flocks of grackles and red-winged blackbirds, heard some Canada geese, and spotted a pair of house wrens.

We didn't reach the canoe landing until 12:30 p.m., but were soon in the water and heading downstream in the old man-made channel. Years ago, in the early 1970s when I was with DNR, a peat extraction endeavor was started which resulted in a large area of the swamp being excavated. There was a legal battle over the effort since more than one property owner was involved at Big Marsh and the adjacent land. After mining a large area in the swamp, the contractor started to dredge his way out, down to the Chesapeake Bay, but was stopped, perhaps a thousand feet or so short. Part of the court settlement over the endeavor was to not continue through to the bay and to plug up the channel in two places.

As we traveled down the channel, we encountered these plugs (small earth dams), one being right at the canoe landing. We also noted abundant beaver sign -- cuttings, older dams, many pull-outs and large (up to 2-3 foot wide, 1.5 foot high) scent mounds comprised of mud and vegetation, some canals, and eventually one large lodge. I tried to chop into one of the larger scent mounds; it was quite firm, almost sod-like. We also heard a wood duck. We encountered the second plug around 1:15 p.m. and debated whether to continue on from there due to the sinky substrate just downstream. Normally, that wouldn't bother us, but we were determined today not to get wet because of the chill in the air. With some difficulty, we made it -- only to soon encounter another obstacle, the large thickly vegetated marshy area near the lower end of the wetland.

At this point, we had to make a decision. Given that we had planned to check the overwash berm at the bay-front for rarities, particularly *Polanisia dodecandra* [clammyweed], should we attempt a traverse of the marsh on foot, surely getting quite wet, or should we turn back? Perceptively, Gene suggested a third option of hiking laterally across the marsh to the upland on

421

the northeast side of the swamp, a short distance and seemingly reasonable. Unfortunately, on examination this proved impractical due to the open water-intermittent floating mat area along the edge of the swamp just beyond some "higher ground" along the channel. A fourth option then surfaced. Why not just navigate the canoe through an opening and across the sinky open water-intermittent mat area? This wasn't easy -- but it worked. In climbing out of the canoe, I straddled clump after clump thus taking some weight out of the boat and guiding it while Kathy and Gene pushed with their paddles. Considering that Kathy was seven months pregnant, Gene and I were amazed at her agility and willingness to attempt this maneuver; she certainly didn't hold back. Before crossing, we also examined some red-top panic grass (*Panicum agrostoides*) along the canal and discussed our disappointment that such morphologically different looking species as *P. agrostoides* and *P. stipitatum* are now lumped under one species, *P. rigidulum*. I've often wondered whether the botanist who lumped them really ever saw them in the field.

After reaching the upland and climbing the steep slope to the flat above, we were disappointed to see a large residence across the fields. Not knowing the school's exact property boundary, we thought it best to walk the toe of the slope rather than what obviously may not be their property. It soon became evident, however, that we would have rough going and quite a distance to traverse in reaching the large overwash berm and hopefully some rare plants. The berm was angling well away from us and we were running out of time, since Gene and Kathy had hoped to be back at Annapolis by around 5 p.m. Regretfully, we turned back. All wasn't lost, however, since we found more large chinquapin oak (*Quercus muehlenbergii*) growing on the steep slope supporting an abundance of oyster shell (Indian middens). We checked it out thoroughly, examining the leaves and even finding some acorn cups and working through the key in *Gray's Manual of Botany* (2). The slope also had a basswood (*Tilia* sp.), a number of hackberries (*Celtis occidentalis*), and some remnant red cedars (*Juniperus virginiana*). [See also Chapter Ten for examples of Western Shore sites that support chinquapin oak, American basswood, and other plants more typically found in piedmont and mountainous areas, but occur on the Western Shore also due to calcareous fossil beds exposed along stream bottoms and in ravines.]

The understory woody vegetation was dominated by pawpaw (*Asimina triloba*). Oyster middens are undoubtedly typical of many of the Baymouth Barrier Wetlands, wetlands that I sometimes also call truncated wetlands due to their truncation where they front the Chesapeake Bay or its major tributaries. Historically, such landscape settings had more open water with apparently good connections to adjacent water bodies. Thus, they served as protected coves for Indians with encampments up on the flats. In fact, in the early 1970s when I worked for the DNR, two archaeologists, Steve Wilke (University of Washington) and Gail Robinson (University of Washington) were conducting field work in such Kent County sites, perhaps even Big Marsh, in relation to Indian occupation and their use of native plants and animals. At their request, I sent them a list of potential plant species occurring in the six successional stages that they predicted for such systems (see September 27, 1974 letter with attachment), but I don't recall the outcome of their study. Successionally, such sites start as open water, then succeed to marsh and eventually shrub swamp and at times forested swamp with full closure due to the littoral drift causing spit and eventually overwash berm formation. For more information on this type of wetland and a pertinent tidal wetland geomorphological classification system that I developed see a paper entitled "Tidal Wetlands of Maryland's Eastern Shore and Coastal Bays," which was presented at a Conference on Rare and Endangered Plants and Animals of the Delmarva Peninsula held on June 12, 1982 at Delaware State College in Dover (12). [This classification is also presented in Chapter Three.]

As we maneuvered back to the channel, we closely examined some clearweed, which turned out to be *Pilea fontana* (see October 15, 1994 *Journal* entry). On our return up the canal, we checked out some beaver (*Castor canadensis*) landing areas, where we noted Canadian rush (*Juncus canadensis*), Virginia chain fern (*Woodwardia virginica*), and green spikerush (*Eleocharis olivacea*), a watchlist species, and some otter droppings. At a somewhat "open" area in the swamp, conditions looked good for bog type plants considering the abundance of sphagnum. Kathy found a

423

bulrush that turned out to be weak-stalk bulrush (*Scirpus purshianus*)* In a lineal open area (a tributary stream?), I noted more lesser duckweed (*Lemna minor*) and water shield (*Brasenia schreberi*).

We were back at the canoe landing around 3 p.m. and out of the swamp by 4:05. And as planned, we pretty much stayed dry; only I got wet, simply a little water that twice seeped in as I dragged my right foot too low stretching between vegetative clumps. After leaving the swamp, we noted some more large *Q. muehlenbergii* on the southwest upland slope.

We got back to Annapolis somewhat later than planned, around 5:30 p.m. Although we covered only a small area of the swamp, we saw a number of rarities. And we expect the area will produce more interesting finds on further examination. Obviously, we planned to return next year.

* a new species for me

June 10, 1997 [Pocomoke River at Hickory Point Swamp, Worcester County, Maryland]

Trip to the Pocomoke River to once again (i.e., for the third time) cross the Hickory Point Swamp. I left home around 6:45 a.m., stopped for some donuts, and reached the Jamesway Shopping Center outside of Denton about 8:05 a.m., where Wayne Tyndall and Scott Smith from the Maryland Natural Heritage Program were waiting. We then traveled to the Quality Inn just south of Pocomoke City on Route 13 to meet Bill McAvoy and Kitt Heckscher of the Delaware Natural Heritage Program and Dave Shock, who traveled down from Pennsylvania to join the group. Unfortunately, Frank Hirst, who had also planned to attend, called to cancel out last evening. From here, we drove in two vehicles to the DNR parking area at the end of Hickory Point Road, reaching it about 10:10 a.m. So we had three botanist types (me, Wayne, and Bill), two ornithologists (Kitt and Dave), and a herpetologist (Scott), and were looking forward to an exciting and productive trip across the swamp. I was speculating to myself: Perhaps Bill, Wayne, and I would find some rare plants, although based upon past trips across the swamp I didn't expect too much. My main goal was just to cross it in a different area this time and have a "wilderness" experience. Perhaps Kitt and Dave would spot or hear a Swainson's warbler. And Scott might luck upon a red-bellied water snake (*Nerodia e. erythrogaster*). Maybe we all might encounter an exemplary stand of southern white cedar (*Chamaecyparis thyoides*). No, we didn't spot a Swainson's warbler or a red-bellied water snake, but we saw the cedars, impressive cedars, many of them.

Within a few minutes after reaching the parking area, we were heading north towards the Pocomoke River. Our plan was to hike north to the river, then follow the river upstream to a point where we could slice S-SE into the swamp and in so doing cross about a two mile section running the length of the old river meander, which constitutes the current Hickory Point Swamp. To reach the river, we followed a trail along the edge of the swamp until the upland edge ended and swung west. We then continued east through a one-quarter mile wide swath of swamp to reach the river. On our way to the river, of course, we were scanning the vegetation, and at one spot (about half way between the upland end of the trail and the river) there was a good number of sedges (*Carex intumescens* [bladder sedge], *C. folliculata* [long sedge], *C. stipata* [owlfruit sedge], *C. comosa* [bearded sedge], and *C. laevivaginata* [smooth-sheath sedge], the latter being a new species for me. Nearby was *C. lurida* [sallow sedge]).

At this point, we heard a prothonotary warbler, and just earlier, a pine warbler. Kitt and Dave pointed out the song of a worm-eating warbler. (From this point on, I was generally ahead of Kitt and Dave so I couldn't record what they were hearing or seeing. However, Kitt promised me a list of birds, which will be included at the end of this entry.) We also noted a 20 foot redbay (*Persea borbonia*) and an odd caterpillar that was feeding on water willow (*Decodon verticillatus*).

We reached the river at 11:19 a.m. As expected there was a natural levee covered with *Carex hyalinolepis* [shoreline sedge], giving it an open almost savanna-like appearance. [As far as I know, this part of the Pocomoke River is the only place on the Delmarva Peninsula that supports a bald cypress-shoreline sedge savanna.] Just prior to reaching the levee, Scott noted

425

two adult bald eagles heading downstream. Since the tide was out, we examined the intertidal area and soon located a *Callitriche* sp. [water-starwort] and *Cardamine longii* [Long's bitter-cress]. As we moved upstream, sometimes stumbling over cypress knees in the dense *C. hyalinolepis*, we spotted *Fraxinus profunda* [pumpkin ash] and *Elymus virginicus* [Virginia wild-rye], not yet in flower. We again spotted a grass unfamiliar to all of us, that was in the Aveneae Tribe. Using Radford's *Flora of the Carolinas* (13), Wayne suggested it might be *Trisetum*. [And indeed it was, as I keyed it on 6/11 to *T. pensylvanicum* (= *Sphenopholis pensylvanica*, swamp wedge-scale), another new species for me.] Actually, we saw the *Trisetum* earlier while hiking in; we also spotted some flowering *Danthonia spicata* [poverty-grass] in the upland.

At 12:09 p.m., we stopped to eat lunch on a log along the river after crossing a tricky tidal gut jutting into the swamp. We had a nice view up and down the river and could see a pier apparently associated with the sand and gravel operation upstream along the east bank of the Pocomoke. Directly across the river, I noted a large red-bellied turtle (*Pseudemys rubriventris*) basking on a log.

Our exact location at this point was debatable. Given the distance we had walked upstream, we thought we were somewhere near the northern end of the river meander that encloses the swamp (Somerset County side) just opposite the upland peninsular area between the Hickory Point Swamp to the east and the fresh to slightly brackish tidal marsh to the west. However, with the unobstructed view of the upstream sand and gravel property pier, this didn't seem right. The other option, which didn't seem correct either given the distance we would have had to walk, was that we were further upstream. However, that would have placed the upland directly across from where we were eating, and it was wetland (swamp) on the Somerset County side. So the consensus was that our first option was the correct one. Given that decision, I set a S-SE bearing on my compass to assure that we wouldn't angle back into the upland we had crossed earlier in getting to the swamp. We then sliced back and began a crossing of Hickory Point Swamp at 12:43 p.m., after which we soon found *Smilax walteri* [Walter's catbrier]. Initially, there were also many small seedling and sapling red bays (*Persea borbonia*) and some small to medium size southern white cedars (*Chamaecyparis thyoides*). Then we found a 2.5 inch dbh redbay and four cedars, one of which was 13.0 inches dbh. We also noted *Smilax laurifolia* (bamboo-vine) and continued noting it in the area we had been crossing, which was thick with shrubs.

At 1:27 p.m., we broke out of the shrub zone and found a 19.6 inch dbh *Chamaecyparis thyoides*; at 1:39 p.m., we were in a cedar stand. I soon measured seven cedars at 25.47, 22.64, 24.21, 21.85, 26.89, 26.89, and 24.8 inches dbh, and there were many more. After leaving this stand, which I will call cedar stand number one, we started noting many sweetbay magnolias (*Magnolia virginiana*), whereas earlier we had seen many young redbay (*Persea borbonia*). (Based upon my three trips, the redbay is definitely more abundant towards the western side of the swamp.) There was also substantial bamboo-vine.

At 2:12 p.m., we entered cedar stand number two. This stand was even more open than stand number one. It had a mat of sphagnum mosses with only a few scattered shrubs or saplings, despite an extremely high density of red maple (*Acer rubrum*) seedlings. I measured 20.28, 17.4, 20.94 inch dbh cedars, and there were many cedars greater than 12 inches dbh. This stand was impressive and we speculated over its openness despite the presence of numerous red maple seedlings. What's preventing the maples from taking over? Allelopathy? Mature and sapling maples were quite abundant outside the stand. We also debated whether or not the old tree stumps were the result of a logging operation or from natural death given how low they were. Nearby we confirmed the presence of a pond pine (*Pinus serotina*). Then after traversing some dense vegetation, we once again entered a cedar stand at 2:50 p.m., a very impressive cedar stand, cedar stand number three. It was a large stand indeed with many 12-16 inch dbh trees with an open understory of sphagnum mosses again supporting numerous red maple seedlings, but little in the way of understory forbs. Again there were exceptional trees -- 25.98, 19.49, 25.59, and 25.47 inches dbh. And at one point, I counted seventy-five cedars ranging from about 10-26 inches dbh within a sixty foot radius circle. I, of course, had seen similar stands like these on my earlier crossings further

427

south in the swamp, so I knew what to expect if we found a cedar stand. But I must admit that the stands I encountered in my earlier crossings did not compare in extent and grandeur with cedar stand number three. It was also in this stand that we jumped two fawns.

At 3:35 p.m., we spotted a large cedar (24.01 inches dbh) sitting like a strangler fig, a West Indian tropical plant, on a huge mound that was obviously an old stump. The vegetation was also somewhat thick again and the ground surface very sinky with much open water and many tree/shrub hummocks. Based upon other crossings, this suggested that we might be nearing the southern edge of the swamp. In this area, I made a quick list of plants: *Nyssa biflora* [swamp tupelo], *Acer rubrum* [red maple], *Magnolia virginiana* [sweetbay], *Clethra alnifolia* [sweet pepperbush], *Vaccinium corymbosum* [highbush blueberry], *Rhododendron viscosum* [swamp azalea], *Decodon verticillatus* [water willow], *Smilax rotundifolia* [common catbrier], *Woodwardia areolata* [net-veined chain fern], *Boehmeria cylindrica* [false nettle], *Osmunda cinnamomea* [cinnamon fern], and *Saururus cernuus* [lizard's-tail]. At 3:55, we were slowly traversing this last stretch, jumping from clump to clump, occasionally missing and sinking to the knee or more, sometimes crossing on logs or with the aid of bent saplings or shrubs, all the while with slow progress. I spotted a large swamp tupelo, *Nyssa biflora* (= *N. sylvatica* var. *biflora*). It measured 26.61 inches dbh and had quite a buttressed base. We had also seen a number of swamp tupelos earlier. [This large swamp tupelo could very well be the largest in Maryland since the species is not all that common (I've only noticed it on the Pocomoke, for example, although I suspect it occurs elsewhere on the lower Eastern Shore.) and it is not included in *The Big Tree Champions of Maryland 1990* (14).] I examined some leaves, which were much larger and more acuminate than typical black gum; the bark was also deeply furrowed. About that time, we also found a strange fungus that was comprised of a three to four-inch, hair-like growth, which on immediate examination appeared to be dark fur that was standing on end as if by an electric shock.

About 3:50 p.m., someone spotted the upland slope at the edge of the swamp; we were all on it at 3:59. We were surprised, however, when we broke out into the farm field for we were much further north than anticipated. In fact, we were almost immediately west of the farm house at the end of Bishop Road. Obviously, our crossing had taken us more SE than a S-SE heading, so instead of traversing about two miles of swamp, we crossed about one mile. I suppose this was fortunate given the time. The originally planned two mile transect would likely have meant getting out after dark, which would surely have been problematic.

In heading back to the cars, we crossed three tributary swamps before reaching Hickory Point Road at 4:36 p.m. On the way, we found *Dichanthelium boscii* (Bosc's panic grass) and *Carex digitalis* (slender woodland sedge) in the upland forest. The sedge was a new species for me. *Danthonia spicata* (poverty-grass) was also frequently noted. In addition, I found a one-gallon jug manifesting some amethyst tinting, which indicates its exposure to the sun for a number of years. I saved it for my bottle collection.

We reached our cars at 5:05 p.m. It was a long trek back but I still felt quite energized, which was surprising even to me given the swampy terrain and distance we traversed. We all agreed that it was a great trip and I suspect we will never forget it and those impressive southern white cedar stands. I didn't get home until around 8:30 p.m.

The Maryland Natural Heritage Program ranks *Cardamine longii* and *Persea borbonia* as highly State rare and endangered, *Carex hyalinolepis* as highly State rare and threatened, *Fraxinus profunda* as both State rare and a watch list species, and *Chamaecyparis thyoides*, *Smilax walteri*, and *Pinus serotina* as watchlist species. *Nyssa sylvatica* var. *biflora* is not listed and I wonder if it should be.

Bill McAvoy collected a number of plants on this trip (collection numbers 2415-2455), including two sedge species, *Carex bromoides* (brome-like sedge) and *C. abscondita* (thicket sedge), that would have been new for me had I seen them.

Kitt Heckscher submitted the following list of birds. I have also included a few of his comments.

429

prothonotary warbler

Carolina wren

yellow-throated warbler

pine warbler

downy woodpecker

great crested flycatcher

American crow

white-eyed vireo

blue-gray gnatcatcher

northern cardinal

tufted titmouse

Carolina chickadee

red-eyed vireo

worm-eating warbler

red-shouldered hawk

ovenbird

yellow-billed cuckoo

acadian flycatcher

brown-headed cowbird

common grackle

common yellowthroat

bald eagle

indigo bunting

ruby-throated hummingbird

turkey vulture

northern flicker

northern parula

prairie warbler

white-breasted nuthatch

green heron

wood thrush

blue jay

Kitt states: "Most notable is that Prairie Warblers were found in the swamp interior (often associated with Northern Parula)...This species was *abundant* in areas dominated by gum, red maple, *Magnolia virginiana*, and Atlantic white cedar...a 90-100% closed canopy averaging approximately 15 meters high....This species is usually associated with early successional or scrub-shrub type habitat." He also indicated that, although the northern parula seems to be disappearing from areas in the north Pocomoke watershed, it was abundant in the Hickory Point Swamp (Figure 66). Kitt subsequently published a short article on this trip in *The Maryland Naturalist* that addressed these bird species (15).]

*   *   *

The above field trips represent but a smattering of the botanical group's better trips. Additional trips are discussed in Chapters Five, Six, Eight, and Ten. They can also be found in my *Journal*.

430

Figure 66. Prairie warbler (left) and parula warbler, two of the eight warblers recorded by Kitt Heckscher and Dave Shock during our crossing of the Hickory Point Swamp in 1997.

TEN

SLEEPERS ON THE
LOWER WESTERN SHORE

Of course one must not only see sharply, but read aright what he sees. The facts in the life of Nature that are transpiring about us are like written words that the observer is to arrange into sentences. Or, the writing is in cipher and he must furnish the key.
-- JOHN BURROUGHS, *Locusts and Wild Honey*

SOME of my trips with the informal botanical group were to a few streams on the Western Shore that from the public's perspective I suppose generally take a back seat to the larger, better known systems: the Potomac and Patuxent Rivers. These streams are what I sometimes refer to as the Sleepers -- the many small streams and their floodplains that generally empty into the Potomac or Patuxent, or into the drowned river valleys (subestuaries) we call the Patapsco, Magothy, Severn, South, Rhode, and West Rivers, or directly into the Chesapeake Bay. The few examples I cover in this Chapter are Severn Run, Piscataway Creek, Mattawoman Creek, Zekiah Swamp Run, and St. Mary's River.[1] Their locations are shown in Figure 2. The last four of these streams flow directly into or eventually into the Potomac River; the first, is the main fresh water source for the Severn River. They will be described from

---

1There is no special meaning to the term Sleepers. I simply use it to contrast the smaller streams mentioned with the better known larger ones. One might say they are asleep (to the general public) just waiting to be explored. And at times, I have even fallen asleep along a couple of them while in my portable hammock observing wildlife.

personal experiences documented in my *Maryland Journal*, supplemented at times by published literature and unpublished reports, starting with Severn Run.

SEVERN RUN

Many of my visits to Severn Run involved short, one to two hour, nostalgic birding forays along Dicus Mill Road. I say nostalgic because they always brought back memories of my more serious birding experiences in the 1960s with the Audubon Wildlife Society, a local birding group centered in Audubon, New Jersey. Back then, I frequently led or otherwise attended a number of trips each year to New Jersey or Pennsylvania.

The short trips along Dicus Mill Road, which started in the early 1980s and have continued annually to the present, included observations from the road, along the upstream floodplain, and in the adjacent forested uplands. I was particularly interested in the migrating warblers, although I routinely listed whatever birds I observed or heard. I chose Severn Run for these short trips somewhat for convenience (I live close by), but also because forested floodplains support numerous nesting birds -- birds like the prothonotary warbler, hooded warbler, blue-gray gnatcatcher, tufted titmouse, wood duck, red-shouldered hawk, barred owl, and pileated woodpecker -- in addition to the migrants just passing through. [See, for example, Brooke Meanley's 1950 publication in the *Atlantic Naturalist*, "Birds of the Swamps," for a typical mid-winter list of birds found in our Maryland swamps (1).] For a number of years, I also took a couple of short birding trips each spring to Lake Waterford Park in the Magothy River watershed.

It seems that I was never disappointed on my birding trips to Severn Run. I generally noted between fifteen and twenty species, and at times close to thirty. I can not recall ever being there in the spring without encountering the beautiful hooded warbler and hearing its musical *sweet, sweet, sweet, swe-a-weet*. The same can be said for the *chip-chabur-chip* of the white-eyed vireo, a bird more commonly heard than seen due to its leaf-blending colors, and whose song, once learned, is seemingly never forgotten. And from the uplands would emanate the sharp *teacher, teacher, teacher* of the ovenbird. Other warblers that I commonly heard and sometimes spotted were the yellowthroat, black and white warbler, and parula warbler. Occasionally, I would hear or see a prothonotary warbler, and on May 5, 1985 I got lifer, the golden-winged warbler, number 296. While standing along the roadside, it was not uncommon to hear the overhead chipping of goldfinches as they undulated, woodpecker-like, across the sky, and at least once I had a great view of the spectacular male scarlet tanager in a tulip poplar (*Liriodendron tulipifera*). And given enough time, the *wheeeep* of the great crested flycatcher and the *peter, peter, peter* of the tufted titmouse were guaranteed on every visit.

On April 30, 1983, I had a nice treat along Dicus Mill Road. While observing the fidgety activity of a blue-gray gnatcatcher in the swamp below the road, the bird settled, much to my surprise, into a hidden nest in a crotch of a dead tree. The nest appeared to be made of lichens, and both the male and female birds alternately occupied it. The gnatcatchers seemed to be forming the inner cup, since they did not bring new material; they simply squirmed around in it while sitting. Then they would leave and five minutes later be back again going through the same routine. In the process, I also noticed how the gnatcatcher quickly wags its tail sideways, sort of flicking it one way then the other.

Two years later almost to the day, I again observed a gnatcatcher building a nest along Severn Run, only about one hundred feet from the one I observed in 1983. This time the nest was almost complete and the gnatcatcher was apparently only adding some lining; again many lichens were evident on it.

Another interesting observation of a gnatcatcher occurred on May 4, 1986 during a birding trip along Severn Run. As I watched the gnatcatcher impetuously hopping around, flitting and chatting while catching insects, I saw it capture some worm-like critter (apparently some type of caterpillar) and repeatedly bang the caterpillar against a branch before swallowing it.

Although not on specific birding trips, at least twice now I have seen pileated woodpeckers flying over Maryland Route 3 (now also Interstate 97) at Severn Run. They no doubt inhabit the area. I have also commonly heard, and at times have seen, red-shouldered hawks along Severn Run and its tributaries, in one instance carrying a stick for its nest. An interesting observation of an immature buteo occurred on May 18, 1995, when I was returning home from a plant collecting trip for an upcoming course. While driving down East-West Highway, I spotted the buteo in the grass beside a small sediment pond. I stopped to investigate. Although I was only a hundred feet or so from the hawk, it did not fly when I got out and moved to the rear of my car. The buteo stood there picking at some prey it had captured. However, upon opening my trunk, the squeaky noise frightened the hawk before I could get to my binoculars. Nevertheless, I readily saw its prey when it flew -- a bullfrog with its legs limply hanging, another first for me. This buteo was probably a red-shouldered hawk, since they are common in the area and along the tributaries of Severn Run.

*   *   *

Some of my trips to Severn Run and its tributaries involved extended hikes along the floodplain, generally from Gambrills Road to Dicus Mill Road on the mainstem, although at least one hike occurred between Burns Crossing Road and Gambrills Road. Shorter forays were made along a tributary near the Millersville Post Office down to Severn Run and on to Dicus Mill Road. I have also walked Jabez Branch from Hog Farm Road down to its confluence with Severn Run. These trips, which were sometimes with my sons or friends, tended to produce an abundance of wildlife, particularly reptiles, amphibians, and birds. While moving downstream, for example, it was not uncommon to surprise five-lined skinks (*Eumeces fasciatus*) sunning on fallen trees, pickerel frogs (*Rana palustris*) hidden on the grassy streambank, and wood ducks bucking the current of the shallow stream (Figure 67).

On one such trip along Jabez Branch in 1997, I heard some crashing in the brush on the drier floodplain and a loud squawking as a large bird promptly exited the area. Although I did not observe the bird, it no doubt was a wild turkey, since they are on the increase in Maryland. On July 17, 1998,

436

for example, Judy and Robert Cole, Dave Walbeck, and I observed a few turkeys on a section of the upland right-of-way that crosses Round Bay Bog, another noteworthy site on a tributary of the Severn River. (For a description of Round Bay Bog, see Chapter Eight.)

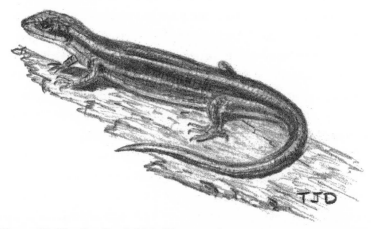

Figure 67. The five-lined skink (*Eumeces fasciatus*), a common lizard in forested swamps and adjacent uplands in the Chesapeake Bay Region.

At other times, I have followed Severn Run down from Veteran's Highway, eventually examining the delta at tidewater. This too is a noteworthy site supporting a large fresh tidal marsh with a nice assortment of marsh plants, including showy cardinal flowers (*Lobelia cardinalis*) and goldenclubs (*Orontium aquaticum*). (See Chapter Nine for a trip to this delta.)

Certain finds were a given on these trips, such as the exotic-looking (palmately-leaved) climbing fern (*Lygodium palmatum*) along the mainstem, as well as raccoon (*Procyon lotor*) tracks and abundant beaver (*Castor canadensis*) sign along the mainstem and many of its tributaries. (See Chapter Eight for more on the rare climbing fern.) And on September 18, 1983, while wading my way downstream in Severn Run below Veteran's Highway, I noted something big, submerged, and swimming ahead of me. At first, I thought it was a large snapper, then an otter (*Lutra canadensis*); finally, I realized it was a beaver. I pursued the beaver as it slipped through the clear shallow water.

After about one hundred feet, the beaver pulled up along the bank under some submerged brush. I actually grabbed the beaver by its tail, but it soon shot away. I caught up with it again about ten feet downstream after waiting a couple of minutes to see if it would surface. Finally, I lost the beaver in deeper water under some heavier brush. (See Chapter Two for more on this irresistible tail-grabbing habit of mine.)

Occasionally, I would spot my favorite turtle -- the spotted (*Clemmys guttata*), always an adult. I emphasize adult, for in all of my trips along the Severn (or anywhere for that matter) and despite the many spotted turtles I have found over the years, I have yet to see a young one (Figure 68). Apparently, spotted turtles are either rather secretive when young or they blend in very well with the wetland vegetation. Not uncommonly, I have also noted mink (*Mustela vison*) tracks along the mainstem.

Some of my trips down Severn Run were in search of a rare plant, the swamp pink (*Helonias bullata*), which to my knowledge has never been reported from the watershed. I have felt for years that some of the smaller clear tributaries might support the swamp pink, although I have yet to find it along the mainstem or any of its tributaries. Consequently, April 26, 1996 found Dwight Fielder, Kathy McCarthy, and I hiking down Severn Run between Burns Crossing Road and Gambrill's Road searching the backwater swamps and small tributaries for the swamp pink.

We searched some of the wetter areas supporting skunk cabbage (*Symplocarpus foetidus*) on this April trip, particularly where small tributaries entered. Although a few places looked favorable for swamp pink, we found none. We had other disappointments as well. The stream was badly downcut and slicing laterally into its banks. There was substantial evidence of debris on the floodplain, vegetation as well as trash, due to excessive flooding from runoff. In addition, many areas with skunk cabbage, a common associate of the swamp pink, appeared too dry for this rare monocot. Downcutting by the stream had apparently lowered the floodplain water table with adverse impacts on the vegetation -- hydrophytes were being supplanted by more mesophytic species. I have seen similar vegetative impacts elsewhere in the county, all associated with extreme downcutting by streams. The underlying cause of this severe perturbation is excessive stormwater runoff from impervious surfaces in the watershed. For example, it has been shown that urban stream degradation typically occurs when the amount of impervious surfaces in a watershed exceeds about 10-15 percent (2,3,4)

In addition, one area of the floodplain had numerous trees broken at

Figure 68. Although not necessarily abundant, the spotted turtle (*Clemmys guttata*) is characteristic of clean woodland streams in the Chesapeake Bay Region.

their boles or blown over. Obviously, it had been hit by a twister or subjected to a bad wind storm. Substantial gypsy moth (*Porthetria dispar*) damage to the upland oaks was also evident. In more recent years, the response of the understory to the canopy loss along Severn Run has been tremendous. Common greenbrier (*Smilax rotundifolia*) and sweet pepperbush (*Clethra alnifolia*), for example, have become extremely dense.

On the more favorable side of things, one small tributary on the south side of Severn Run, which was pristine and had great potential for swamp pink, supported numerous attractive flowering goldenclubs. Among other plants, this tributary also supported the sessile-leaf merrybells (*Uvularia sessilifolia*), net-veined chain fern (*Woodwardia areolata*), cinnamon fern (*Osmunda cinnamomea*), and turks-cap lily (*Lilium superbum*).

Thirteen species of birds -- including the hooded warbler, ovenbird, and white-eyed vireo -- were noted during the hike. Two box turtles (*Terrapene c. carolina*) were found on the floodplain.

439

Over the years, I have repeatedly noticed that the box turtle, a species typically thought of as occurring basically in uplands, is commonly associated with floodplains and sometimes even fresh meadows and marshes. Once during a hot summer in South Jersey, for example, I found a box turtle almost entirely submersed in a well-flooded marsh, and I have repeatedly found box turtles in my fish pond during hot summers. At another time, I accidentally stepped on a box turtle while wading in the shallow water of a small farm pond in Urbana, Maryland. All this suggests that box turtles may regularly visit wetlands and shallow ponds during hot weather and probably hibernate in them during winter, given their soft bottom substrates.

*　　*　　*

Sometimes I visited the Dicus Mill Road area not specifically for birding. I was usually accompanied by one of my sons, Mike or Sean, as well as a minnow bucket and a couple of dip nets. We were seeking reptiles and amphibians, as well as aquatic invertebrates, in the backwater areas astride Severn Run. Our ultimate goal, at least in reference to the invertebrates, was to replenish a small fish pond behind our house. At times, we also kept some of the herps for the pond or aquaria/terraria, although many were eventually released.

The backwater we visited most frequently was located immediately upstream of Dicus Mill Road on the west side of the stream. Despite its small size, this lush marsh supported a rich flora -- arrow-arum (*Peltandra virginica*), broad-leaf arrowhead (*Sagittaria latifolia*), bur-reed (*Sparganium americanum*), spatterdock (*Nuphar luteum*), rice cutgrass (*Leersia oryzoides, arrow-leaf tearthumb (*Polygonum sagittatum*), halberd-leaf tearthumb (*P. arifolium*), blunt manna grass (*Glyceria obtusa*), three-way sedge (*Dulichium arundinaceum*), and tussock sedge (*Carex stricta*), to name a few. The marsh graded into a shrub swamp and eventually a forested swamp upstream, which also had a lineal marshy inclusion, apparently a remnant stream channel.

During the winter and spring, the entire backwater area brimmed with water a foot or so deep. In contrast, the substrate in this area was merely moist

440

in the summer, except for during severe thunderstorms when the swollen stream overtopped its natural levee and flooded it. During this flooding, especially in the spring and early summer, the backwater area teemed with critters. Because of the absence of permanent water, these intermittently wet areas were excellent sites for breeding amphibians, since predatory fish populations for the most part were absent.[2] Therefore, various toads, frogs, and salamanders converged on these breeding sites in late winter and early spring.

The backwater marsh on Severn Run was no exception. On April 27, 1983, for example, my son Mike and I observed a number of mating American toads (*Bufo americanus*) -- individuals calling from hiding spots on micro-hummocks, the bases of dead or fallen trees, patches of early herbaceous vegetation, and shrub clumps; doubles out in the open water, the males mounted on the females. The mating pairs would not separate when dip-netted; nor would they plunge under while still attached or swim away. A few times while we were there one started calling, then a whole chorus of toads erupted. Once or twice I tried to spot a singing single. I finally located one with my binoculars, half hidden in a small hole in the bank under a fallen tree -- with its vocal sack exposed like a balloon. Their eyes appeared golden despite a lack of direct sunlight causing reflection. The males were smaller than females, which is the typical situation in most instances with Bufonidae. Their voice was a long, low-pitched musical trill (*preeeeeeeeee*) with a long "e" sound.

On the same trip that we encountered the toads, we dip-netted numerous, three-quarter inch long, pickerel that still had their egg sacks, resembling inflated bellies. They were hidden in water starwort and evidently were either redfin pickerel (*Esox americanus*) or chain pickerel (*E. niger*) that had been spawned during overbank flooding into the backwater depression. The presence of these young pickerel in the backwater area is a good indication of the function of such habitats as fish spawning and nursery areas, since they accumulate substantial water from overbank flooding during high

---

[2]Mud minnows are characteristic of such sites, however, and as indicated below, I have found them, as well as young pickerel, in this Severn Run backwater.

441

water events. Therefore, spawning pickerel gain access to the backwaters at this time. Apparently, the hatched fish prey heavily on the abundant aquatic invertebrates before moving into the stream itself during periodic summer rainstorms when the entire floodplain is covered with a foot or two of water.

On April 6, 1991, I was again attracted to this backwater by the melodious songs of numerous American toads. Due to the minimal herbaceous vegetation that early in the growing season, the toads had sought cover in the woody buttonbush (*Cephalanthus occidentalis*). Over the years in this same backwater marsh I have found green frogs (*Rana clamitans* var. *melanota*), southern leopard frogs (*R. utricularia*), northern water snakes (*Nerodia s. sipedon*), five-lined skinks, snapping turtles (*Chelydra s. serpentina*), painted turtles (*Chrysemys p. picta*), box turtles, as well as at least one spotted turtle and a rough green snake (*Opheodrys aestivus*). The spotted turtle, which was basking on a clump of tussock sedge during an April visit, made no attempt to flee when I picked it up. Until it moved, the green snake blended in very well as it clung to the lush summer marsh vegetation. A large snapper was spotted during a May visit with its checkered back (scutes) protruding from the shallow water in some buttonbush. I was surprised by the turtle's strength when I grabbed its tail and the turtle braced itself firmly against the surrounding vegetation with its rather long claws. The backwater is also annually replete with tadpoles -- of toads, frogs, and probably salamanders.

Sampling with the dip nets almost always produced tadpoles and mud minnows (*Umbra pygmaea*), sometimes resulted in a captured frog or two, and occasionally bagged a turtle. But it was the invertebrates, along with the tadpoles, that squirmed with every dip of the net. Backswimmers (Family Notonectidae) and water boatman (Family Corixidae) were common, as were crawing water beetles (Family Haliplidae) and some medium-size black beetles. And every so often a water tiger, the larva of the predaceous diving beetle (*Dytiscus* sp.), was netted. These ravenous larvae soon latched onto a tadpole or mud minnow when placed into the minnow bucket, and once while trying to show one to a friend at the Little Patuxent Oxbow in Laurel, it latched into my finger, promptly drawing blood. Other invertebrates encountered include various hemipterans, such as the water-bug (*Belostoma* sp.) with its piercing mouth parts used to suck out the juices of smaller hemipterans like backswimmers as well as small snails, and the water scorpion (*Ranatra fusca*) -- a walkingstick-like critter -- that hangs down from the surface ready to prey on passing insects, tadpoles, and even small fish. There were also plenty of dragonfly larvae, damselfly larvae, and finger-nail clams (Family Sphaeriidae), as well as occasional crayfish (*Cambarus diogenes*) and leeches on the muddy substrate or aquatic vegetation. Water striders *(Gerris* sp.) and fisher spiders (*Dolomedes* sp.), on the other hand, glided around rather effortlessly, supported by the water's surface tension. As indicated above, many of these invertebrates ended up in our small fish pond, which over the years has become essentially a natural aquatic environment.

*   *   *

The plants found in these backwater areas have developed a wide array of adaptations -- such as aerenchyma tissue and shallow roots -- for survival in the anaerobic soil characteristically present. (For more on the adaptations of plants that enable them to survive in this superabundance of water and the resultant anaerobic soil conditions, see Chapter Two.)

*   *   *

Aquatic habitats -- particularly shallow ponds, intermittently wet backwater areas, and slow-moving, warm-water streams -- can also be quite stressful to animals due to the presence of shallow waters, fine inorganic sediments, accumulated decaying organic matter, microbial respiration, and resultant low dissolved oxygen levels and anaerobic soil conditions. These conditions are particularly harsh during the summer. Various environmental gradients also occur laterally in ponds (as the water shallows) and across streams and their adjacent floodplains, including changes in wetness, substrate type, and soil chemistry. Therefore, many animals have to cope with the anaerobic soil conditions, as well as the low dissolved oxygen concentrations in ponds and slow streams, and adjust to the seasonal drying conditions of adjacent wetlands and backwaters. They cope and adjust through physical and behavioral adaptations.

Brown bullheads (*Ameiurus nebulosus*) and mud minnows, for example, are adapted to the high turbidity and low dissolved oxygen levels in backwater areas on the floodplain; in addition, mud minnows apparently aestivate as the backwater areas dry out in summer.

Particularly interesting are the adaptations of sundry aquatic insects. Water scorpions have a posterior air tube to take in oxygen from above the water surface as they hang down headfirst poised to prey on other animals. Water measurers, water striders, and fisher spiders float on the surface without getting wet (i.e., their feet do not break the surface tension). The fisher spider also submerges to prey on tadpoles and small fish. Backswimmers, water boatman, and predaceous diving beetles obtain oxygen while hanging down from the surface, then take it with them in the form of bubbles when they dive like miniature scuba divers. They manage to stay under the water for considerable time because of the diffusion of additional oxygen from the water into the air bubble as the original concentration of oxygen decreases. Carbon dioxide and nitrogen concentrations are also important in this process. A detailed explanation of this phenomenon is given in *Ecology and Field Biology* (5). Water striders, the giant water bug (*Leptocerus americanus*), whirligig beetles (Family Gyrinidae), and predaceous diving beetles can fly away to another ponded area when a shallow pond or backwater dries up. Whirligigs also, by the way, have two sets of eyes, which allows them to see simultaneously above and below the water (Figure 69).

Crayfish retreat into burrows as shallow water areas dry up; many other small animals use these same burrows during low water, which is analogous to the use of alligator holes by smaller animals during droughts in the Florida Everglades. (See Chapter Two for more on this.) Finger-nail clams go dormant in mud when shallow water areas dry up; flatworms form one to many cysts under such conditions, whereas leeches aestivate in the mud.

Tubifex worms (*Tubifex tubifex*) have tubes from which their projecting posterior ends wave vigorously in the overlying water, apparently to circulate it and obtain more oxygen. The frequency of waving increases with decreasing oxygen concentration. On the other hand, being pulmonates, pond snails can simply come to the surface and obtain oxygen from the atmosphere.

For me, appreciating these various plant and animal adaptations has made visiting backwater areas on Severn Run all the more interesting. You

Figure 69. The whirligig (Family Gyrinidae). Watch for groups of these beetles scooting against the current of slow streams and sometimes on the surface of ponds and open floodplain backwaters.

too can achieve such enjoyment. All it takes is a pair of boots, a dip net, and a little time. And it does not have to be on Severn Run. Almost any backwater

445

area, shallow pond, or slow-moving stream will do. Check the bottom substrate, check the aquatic vegetation, check the water column -- the critters will be there, that is guaranteed.

*   *   *

A few years ago, during a trip along Severn Run and one of its tributaries near the Millersville post office, my approach to wildlife observation changed, probably forever, with very productive results. To a large extent, I can thank Lawrence Kilham for my new approach, for it was by reading his book, *On Watching Birds*, the idea largely surfaced (6). Actually, the idea was not entirely new to me for I had tried it infrequently before with mixed success. It is just that Kilham was so convincing of its effectiveness. The trick is simply to sit silently and watch. The wildlife will come to you -- that too is guaranteed.

The idea was rekindled on Easter morning, April 7, 1996. Besides typical Easter activities with my family, my *Journal* indicates that I made a few bird observations behind my house and finished reading A.M. Peterson's *Wild Bird Neighbors* (7), then started on Lew Dietz's *Touch of Wilderness: A Maine Woods Journal* (8). Being springtime, I was evidently eager to once again get into the field, and perhaps do a little birding. As I wrote in my *Journal*: "The urge to get out into the field is creeping up on me. I think this year I may even take Lawrence Kilham's approach and sit quietly along a remote stretch of stream, perhaps Severn Run, or at a beaver pond and note all animal activity that I observe." Six days later found me hiking down a trail to the Severn Run tributary near the Millersville post office. Besides an array of standard field equipment, my field vest had two additions on this trip: A portable hammock and a 1919 copy of John Burroughs' *Field and Study*, for inspiration and potential reading during ebbs in wildlife activity (9).

Earlier, I had parked my car where my hike would terminate at Dicus Mill Road and my wife Geri dropped me off at the upstream starting point at 10:46 a.m. It was a clear day, that was supposed to hit around seventy degrees. Immediately upon reaching the tributary, I spotted a palm warbler

446

flitting around and wagging its tail in some smooth alder bushes (*Alnus serrulata*) just beyond a beaver dam. As I moved closer to the beaver pond, I spotted three male wood ducks. The ducks did not flush -- they just swam away from me, and eventually one flew further back, albeit hardly off the water. With this quick action, I opted to circle the pond, approaching it from a forested hill to the east. By 11:10 I was sitting on a log about forty feet from the pond taking notes. All I heard at this point were a few crows, a titmouse, and some distant gulls, as well as a few northern spring peepers (*Hyla c. crucifer*). A painted turtle was sunning itself on a small log on the far shore.

My hope was to see a beaver and perhaps the woodies again, so there I patiently sat. Now and then I heard a chickadee above the drone of the vehicles on I-97. At 11:28 a.m., I heard some rustling to my right and upslope, perhaps a gray squirrel I thought, then silence. Then the rattle of a belted kingfisher as it flew in from the back of the pond, only to move on out of my sight and perch somewhere on the far shore. It soon swung back and perched again about one hundred feet from me, but within a minute moved to another nearby perch, then another, all the while rattling away and lifting its crest as if scolding something. The peepers and chickadees sang on and on -- *peep, peep, peep* and *febee-feba, febee, febee, febee, febee*. By 11:36, they were silent.

The rest of this adventure is presented below as recorded in the present tense in my *Journal* with only minor editing and interspersed at times with commentary.

11:42 a.m. -- I continue to hear movement off to my right and upslope and note some water moving amongst the flooded out trees below. I can not see what stirred the water, but the ground movement now seems like crawling. And it is; it's an eastern mud turtle [*Kinosternon s. subrubrum*] heading down-slope to the pond. Great view as it moves along, passing only about twenty feet from me. I can only conclude that it has deposited some eggs up in a sandy area on or above the slope, since hibernation would likely have been in the pond, not upslope -- unless it is migrating to new territory. The kingfisher is still intermittently rattling.

11:46 -- I spot it [the kingfisher] dip for something in the water, apparently only water, and perch low on the far shore.

11:49 -- A medium horsefly lands on my leg; a second large non-biting fly (iridescent blue) keeps bothering me, but I "ping" it off. The peepers are at it again.

11:57 -- There in the water. See its light colored (contrasting with the black of the water) appearance, something slowly gliding towards the back of the lake, perhaps a snapper. A closer look with my binoculars suggests that I am correct. Good luck to the woodies if they raise a brood here this year. It is a big snapper. I soon lose it while writing these notes. Obviously, Kilham is correct. Sit and wait, be patient, and the wildlife will come to you. [Kilham (6) seems to be a master at this. And as a favorite of mine, John Burroughs, indicated in *Wake Robin* (10): "One has only to sit in the woods or fields, or by the shore of the river or lake, and nearly everything of interest will come round to him, the birds, the animals, the insects." In this instance, to my delight, it was a mink, on which I will elaborate later. On the other hand, in *Near and Far*, Burroughs considered himself lucky if, in the course of a season, he could pick up two or three facts in natural history that were new to him (11).]

12:06 p.m. -- There, the snapper again. This time a rear view, but it soon turns right and glides toward the back of the pond. All is silent, even the peepers. Only the drone of I-97 vehicles apparent. No sooner said and the peepers sounding off again.

12:13 -- Decide to eat lunch -- an apple, pear, and banana -- and read some of Burroughs.

12:26 -- I hear a red-shouldered hawk upslope to my back, not close. No action on the pond, though I may have missed it while reading.

12:31 -- I decide to move on after an hour and twenty minutes of silent observation, leaving to the tunes of the chickadee and red-shouldered hawk.

After leaving the pond, I circled it, as well as the smaller impounded areas in the drainage upstream, traversed the upland to the west but east of Severn Run, and finally reached Severn Run at 1:19. During this time, I kept

448

notes in my small field notebook. Specifically, I hiked through the scrub pine [*Pinus virginiana*]/old agricultural area of high ground east of Severn Run, getting almost half way through by 1:03. At the back of the pond in another depressional extension, I flushed a pair of woodies from a buttonbush swamp (12:48); earlier (12:37), I had flushed one woody not far from where I had been sitting.

1:34 -- So here I am now in my portable hammock on a steep slope about seven feet above an outside bend of Severn Run ready for more wildlife.

1:42 -- I'm still waiting, waiting for Kilham's wildlife at Severn Run, comfortably ensconced in my hammock. Will it come? All I've heard so far is the distant automobile drone from I-97, a faint *chewink* from a towhee, some goldfinches flying overhead, and some unidentified bird notes. Since, given my position, my eyes would most likely catch any movement on the creek and adjacent floodplain, I decide to read awhile.

1:50 -- I note a small bird flitting around in the trees across the creek; I also keep hearing the unidentified low chips.

1:55 -- I focus in on a small bird moving up a tree trunk, a good find -- a brown creeper. Then I see a white-breasted nuthatch on another tree. I think the chips were from the creeper.

2:00 -- More *chewinks*. Spring peepers in the background. Finally resume reading Burroughs.

2:04 -- I hear a chipping sparrow or pine warbler; more *chewinks*.

2:08 -- *Febee-feba* of a chickadee, repeatedly.

2:10 -- Goldfinches overhead.

2:18 -- Falling asleep while reading; decide to take a nap.

2:33 -- I wake up, perhaps because my legs are a little numb having not been moved for some time. Luckily for me, I soon hear a rustle in the sweet pepperbush [*Clethra alnifolia*] to my left. Then I spot it, what at first I think is a gray squirrel (*Sciurus carolinensis*). But it is not hopping; it is sort of walking or loping along. It stops to look towards me and appears to sniff, then continues along, passing only ten feet to my left. Yes, only ten feet away and passing by is a beautiful mink (Figure 70). Amazing! Oh, how correct Kilham is. The mink was apparently traveling the main floodplain or a small tributary coming in from the side my hammock was on (west) and went up and over the high upland I am on rather than along a small trail below me near the toe of the bank. Was it a short cut? I would have expected the mink to follow the creek trail if it were in transit.

Believe it or not, earlier on the hammock, I was thinking mink. My first and only other mink sighting in the East came as a teenager, along Big Lebanon Run behind Grenloch Lake. And isn't it a coincidence that Severn Run, when I first saw it in the early 1970s, immediately reminded me of that Stream of Streams for South Jersey, Big Lebanon.[3] Well now, that certainly made my day. Will the mink return my way if it was simply on a hunting mission?[4]

2:48 -- Everything's been rather silent for awhile now, sort of anticlimactic noise only (a few bird notes, some squeaking trees) since the mink passed by.

2:53 -- Resumed reading Burroughs.

2:58 -- Titmouse seven feet below me, at toe of slope; sounds a few notes.

3:11 -- A large buteo, probably a red-shouldered hawk, sweeps in silently from behind and to my left and lands in a large tree, in full view, about 100 feet away, but on the floodplain. After it leaves, I hear a red-shouldered hawk, no doubt the one that landed. I've been here now about an hour and a half.

3:16 -- A woodpecker's drumming; I thought I heard downy's notes earlier.

3:27 -- Reading Burroughs. Hear goldfinches overhead.

3:37 -- Not much action, but I hear the *yakking* of a distant flicker. I must be going soon. I told Geri to expect me back by 5:00 p.m. or so, or expect something is wrong, and I am still pretty far up Severn Run. My guess is that toward evening it would be great here for wildlife observation -- perhaps some deer and beaver at least.

---

[3]Sadly, because of various man-induced perturbations, Big Lebanon Run can no longer be called the Stream of Streams for South Jersey.

[4]In total, I have seen three minks in the wild; the third was along the Des Plaines River (forested floodplain) outside of Chicago in 1990.

Figure 70. The mink. In 1996, a mink came within about ten feet of me as I lay in my portable hammock observing wildlife along Severn Run.

3:45 -- I spot the brown creeper again searching the bark of the river birch [*Betula nigra*] across the creek. The sound of the spring peepers is increasing now, much more evident. It has been three hours now that I have been in this hammock; I better move on. But first I'll check the tributary, from where the mink may have come, for tracks. As it turns out, it is not much of a tributary, more or less a swampy swale with a less than one foot wide trickle entering Severn Run. I do find what appear to be some fresh tracks on a sandbar along Severn Run. If they were from the mink (about right size but substrate a little too firm), it was running the creek not the tributary. There are also muskrat, coon, and beaver tracks.

4:12 -- Given what I told Geri, I've been pushing it a little to get out by 5:00 p.m. At a spot where the bank is badly undercut and the trail eroded into, I swing out and around one-handed, while clinging to a stout sapling and end up in Severn Run, up to my waist with my hat floating off. It all happened so fast that I don't know how I lost it. Perhaps I misjudged the sloping bank that I swung towards, for before I could respond to catch myself I was in the water. At first I thought I lost my glasses since I couldn't see well, but I soon realized that my poor sight was due to the water on my glasses. I waded downstream, retrieved my hat, and pulled myself up the bank. Actually, the water wasn't cold, almost refreshing, so after emptying my boots I was on my way.

Later, when I tripped and darn near fell while pushing it on the floodplain, I decided to cool it. Although I slowed down a little, my main goal at this point was to get out. However, I made some additional observations as shown below:

4:27 -- Note fresh fox tracks on floodplain; also fresh raccoon tracks.

4:28 -- Red-backed salamander [*Plethodon c. cinereus*] under white oak [*Quercus alba*] bark on the ground.

4:40 -- Note a spotted turtle [*Clemmys guttata*] at a tributary. Starting to notice *Lygodium palmatum* [climbing fern].

4:51 -- A pair of wood ducks take off from the stream.

452

4:53 -- Otter droppings (all fish scales). Also note, to my surprise and dismay, trail bike tracks on natural levee.

4:56 -- Another woodie takes off.

4:58 -- I reach the big red cliff. [This is a badly eroded bank on the right side of the creek (going upstream) not far from Dicus Mill Road.]

5:08 -- Examine pine bark on fallen tree and find young five-lined skink [*Eumeces fasciatus*]. I put my hand out and it climbs on. I let it run up my arm but lose sight of it and move along.

5:10 -- I note how thickly overgrown the upland trail is due to successional changes since all the oaks died from gypsy moth attack.

5:15 -- Back at my car. While walking down Dicus Mill Road, I feel something on my neck and reach up. It is the skink, which jumps off into grass. I had assumed that it exited a long time ago after it ran up my arm.

This was an interesting experience for me, a somewhat new experience and approach to observing nature. And I noted in my *Journal* that I planned to take this approach more often in the future, generally when I am alone, assuring silence and patience. Following that reasoning, the very next day found me once again in my hammock at Severn Run.

I was up early on that day, around 8:30 a.m. Having walked a lot the previous day and having country line danced late into the evening the previous night, I did not sleep well. I glanced out my bathroom window in full view of a male bluebird in a dogwood. Beautiful! The window was partially open and I could hear the *old sam peabody, peabody, peabody* of a white-throated sparrow, as well as some robins, red-bellied woodpeckers, flickers, and mourning doves. Nuthatches, goldfinches, and house finches were busy at my tube feeder extracting sunflower achenes; juncos were still active in the mulch. A female cardinal flew in, then I heard the *yank, yank* of a white-breasted nuthatch near its nesting box. Given the previous days experience and all of this avian activity behind the house, I once again got the urge, and by 9:30 a.m. I was heading down the trail to the beaver pond.

On arriving at the pond around 9:40 a.m., I had a pretty good view of two woodies swimming through the water at the back of the pond. The peeping of spring peepers and the *preeping* of upland chorus frogs (*Pseudacris triseriata* var. *feriarum*) was in the air, as were the sounds of jays and red-bellied woodpeckers. Again my account of the rest of this trip, as recorded in my *Journal* with only minor editing, follows.

9:47 -- Ensconced in hammock near front of pond on west side near trail; good view of mid-back end of pond.

9:53 -- Spot a wagtail, a palm warbler, in tree 30 feet away, then two more.

9:55 -- As I look up the call notes of the palm warbler [in *Birds of North America* (12)], suddenly I hear splashing and look up to see a Canada goose exiting toward the back of the pond, 150 feet or so away, where I had seen the woodies earlier. Palm warbler notes not given in the book; these birds are giving a sound sort of similar to but higher pitched than a nuthatch's *yanking*.

9:59 -- I scan pond with binoculars and immediately spot another palm warbler in a tree on the far shore, probably 125 feet away. Nothing else.

10:02 -- *Drink-your-teeeee*, repeatedly by a towhee. Crows in distance causing a ruckus; maybe harassing an owl or hawk, since it persists and intensifies.

10:05 -- Hear a red-bellied woodpecker.

10:06 -- Spot a goose about 150 feet out, then a second, both cruising over the pond. Then two male woodies moving further toward the back around shrubs and out of sight. One goose feeding in shallows.

10:12 -- Decide to read some of Burroughs.

10:16 -- A rustle of leaves below me toward the pond (I am about 10 feet upslope of pond), but I see nothing.

10:20 -- Continued *peeping* of spring peepers and *preeping* of chorus frogs.

10:24 -- Geese still hanging tight in shrub zone projecting into pond on west side.

10:27 -- A large bird [a great blue heron] glides in over back of pond but quickly disappears around bend. Note that geese have moved further back and to the far shore.

10:36 -- Lone chorus frog *preeping*. Resume reading Burroughs.

10:50 -- I look up to spot three male woodies crossing the pond, east to west, smoothly, about one foot apart. As they move into the shrubby projection, I note a fourth. They move too far to my left and out of sight into the shrubs and trees.

10:54 -- Another duck, smaller and grayish-black with a rusty brown head glides across, disappears under water, and reappears, only to dive again in shrub area. My first thought is hooded merganser, but I can not recollect a female's colors. Since I lost the duck, I look it up in Robbins. I believe that is what it is.

10:59 -- Kingfisher wings high overhead, rattling and heading downstream.

11:03 -- As I am reading Burroughs, I am startled by the splashing and whistling of three woodies as they leap from the pond and head towards the back end. Did they spot me even though I was still in my hammock? Then I see the smaller duck again, and surely it is a female hooded merganser. The duck soon dives under and I again lose it. Clouds increasing; a little chilly and still breezy.

11:20 -- A noisy jay wings in.

11:48 -- Mourning cloak [*Nymphalis antiopa*] flaps by. Peepers still at it.

11:53 -- Hear a pine warbler across pond in short-leaf pines [*Pinus echinata*].

12 noon -- Decide to pull up stakes and check further up western shore for better view of back end of pond.

12:05 -- Trailing arbutus (*Epigaea repens*) flowering on earth bank (southern exposure) along upland trail near pond. Very pleasant smell up close.

12:30 -- I try downstream from pond for *Helonias bullata* [swamp pink], having not found a good observation point on the west side of the pond near the back end. Skunk cabbage [*Symplocarpus foetidus*] now about a foot high. *Cardamine hirsuta* [hairy bitter-cress] flowering. Cotyledonous leaves of *Impatiens capensis* [jewelweed] out. Area open and quite wet with fair amount of skunk cabbage and small (4 feet wide) stream. Looks good for swamp pink. Maybe that is why a strange, nervous, uneasy feeling has come over me -- I am sort of shaking in the legs and hands while writing this. Could it be the thought of *Helonias*?

12:47 -- I catch a green northern cricket frog [*Acris c. crepitans*].

12:56 -- Spot red-shouldered hawk sweep up the creek with nesting material and land in tree, then another or the same bird. Both silent.

1:09 -- I'm back at the pond area, since the stream has down-cut (gradient change) and does not appear to be conducive to *Helonias*. As I approach the stream to jump across, a one foot long submarine-like object is coursing through the water. At first I think it is a fish as it glides upstream, but soon realize that it is a brown muskrat. I didn't hear a splash, so perhaps it hasn't seen me. It glides by below me, pops up where the stream shallows and goes under a bank. Out it comes again whereupon it swims on the surface to a small beaver dam and goes up and over it. It again ducks under, apparently heading towards the large dam and I see no more of it. I'm impressed with its underwater speed.

1:37 -- Back at my car.

I continued this approach to wildlife observation, going again to Severn Run two more times in 1996 and twice in 1997. I have also applied the approach on some of the other Western Shore's Sleepers. Due to my commitment to writing this book, however, my field activity was perhaps at an all time low in 1998, with minimal use of my hammock for wildlife observation. Bob Frazen (personal communication), retired former wildlife biologist with the USDA-Soil Conservation Service, tells me that this approach to wildlife observation is exactly akin to the procedure used to successfully hunt white-tailed deer (*Odocoileus virginianus*) throughout the Northeast. He states:

> "To be a successful deer hunter year after year, requires a very substantial amount of time afield. Usually a week or more is expired but for a second of shooting time with bow or gun. Diligent immobility and silence are required. Observations of birds, insects, small mammals, and the surrounding plants occupy the great majority of the hunter's time afield. These sightings and interactions often comprise the memories that are the most memorable part of the hunt."

Most of my visits to Piscataway Creek were either field trips that I led for the U.S. Environmental Protection Agency or excursions with the informal botanical group. The field trips for the government involved all-day hikes between Brandywine Road and Windbrook Road; the excursions with my botanical friends were of shorter duration along the stream reach between Windbrook Road and Route 210.

I have conducted various types of field training in wetland ecology, wetland delineation, and plant identification over the years, both in the private sector and for the Federal government. Although this training was always heavily field-oriented, the degree of rigor obviously varied with the type of training and the people participating. Many of the private sector folks, although interested, did not care to rough it, and at times some people would not even get their feet wet. The same can be said for some of the government trips I have led. Likewise, most of the intern or public school groups that have been on my field trips preferred to stay on the trails or boardwalks, since for some it was just simply a day out of the school room and they were nervous about encountering snakes and other strange (to them) critters. On many of my trips with adults, however, the attendees didn't have much choice. Otherwise, they would have been standing on the roadside learning nothing as the rest of the group got very wet and muddy while experiencing the marsh and shallow water. Some of those having little choice were my colleagues from the U.S. Environmental Protection Agency who had chosen to attend knowing all too well the rigorous nature of some of my trips -- specifically, those along floodplains. And despite the all-day hike, the mucking around, and the wading, which I am sure were debilitating and discouraging to some, there was generally plenty to see and experience and the attendees always learned a lot. They regularly thanked me at the end of the trips, sometimes even with applause, and my guess is they will never forget them. If anything, they will certainly serve for good bar-stool-talk with friends.

I regularly lead three field trips a year for my office, one of which is a rigorous spring-time adventure along either the Piscataway Creek or

Mattawoman Creek floodplains. Generally, less than a dozen people attend and we have great trips. Accounts of what we typically experience on these trips are given below for the Piscataway and in the next section for the Mattawoman.

Along the Piscataway, I routinely discuss various geomorphological aspects relating to the stream and its floodplain, including stream order -- a measure of the position of a stream in the hierarchy of tributaries. First-order streams are headwater streams (intermittent or otherwise) without tributaries. When two first-order streams meet, the larger stream formed is called a second-order stream. It would remain a second-order stream, despite any number of additional first-order streams entering it, until it merges with another second-order stream to become a third-order stream. It takes the merger of two third-order streams to make a fourth-order stream, and so on. It should be obvious that there is an inverse relationship between stream order and the number of stream channels. In the United States, for example, there are 1,570,000 first-order streams, 80,000 third-order streams, 950 sixth-order streams, and only one tenth-order stream, the mighty Mississippi (13). The Piscataway is probably a third-order stream.

Stream order also has an effect on the biota present. This is exemplified by a study on the distribution of fish in first through third order stream segments of Clemons Fork, a tributary of Buckhorn Creek in eastern Kentucky (14). First order segments had only one fish species; second order streams had eight species; third order streams had fifteen species. Thus, fish species were added with each increase in stream order, although increases would not likely continue indefinitely since, at some point, habitat diversity would tend to stabilize despite an increase in stream order. Following this reasoning, the Piscataway mainstem should have more species of fish than its smaller tributaries.

I explain that this meandering creek is replete with sand and gravel bars, undercut banks, and deep pools. Low natural sandy levees line its banks. Floodwaters overtopping the levees in the winter and spring inundate depressional backwater areas on the floodplain. Some of these low areas pond water -- shallow intermittent water so important for amphibian breeding. The

458

fine anaerobic sediments in these shallow backwater areas contrast sharply with the coarser, well-oxygenated soils of the natural levees.

The first plants generally noted flowering when walking the natural levees below Brandywine Road in late April or early May are narow-leaf spring beauties (*Claytonia virginica*) and yellow trout-lilies (*Erythronium umbilicatum*) (Figure 71). Gazing skyward one might also note the non-

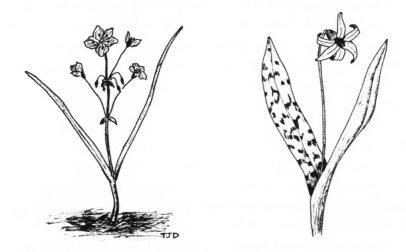

Figure 71. Two spring-blooming wildflowers commonly found along the Sleepers of the Western Shore -- the narrow-leaf spring beauty (*Claytonia virginica*) (left) and the yellow trout-lily (*Erythronium umbilicatum*). The yellow trout-lily was the first wildflower that I identified with a field guide, back in New Jersey in 1962.

showy flowers on the numerous small pawpaw trees (*Asimina triloba*). I generally point out these species and others, and mention the rank smell of the pawpaw leaves and twigs. Then along a short transect over the floodplain, I demonstrate select aspects of wetland delineation -- indicators of wetland hydrology, hydric soils, and hydrophytic vegetation. These three features are

459

typically used to determine the presence, extent, and boundaries of wetlands for technical and legal purposes.

On the south side of the creek just downstream from a pipeline right-of-way below Brandywine Road, stands a rather interesting tree with a major truncated limb protruding from one side. An odd structure like this tells a story -- a story of events that happened to the tree many years ago, and it makes for great interactive discussions as to its origin. We always stop here for an interactive forensic inquiry. In addition, the floodplain supports some rather stately trees. On various trips, for example, I have measured a 44.7 inch diameter swamp chestnut oak (*Quercus michauxii*), a 48.9 inch diameter American beech (*Fagus grandifolia*), and a 50.6 inch diameter tulip poplar (*Liriodendron tulipifera*) -- all considerably large, albeit far from being State champions.

Moving downstream, one encounters substantial beaver sign -- girdled trees, downed trees, pull-outs, tracks, small dams. Raccoon tracks are almost axiomatic, and on a May 1, 1997 trip I noted mink tracks.

About half way down, there is a large man-made pond that has been hydrologically modified by beaver. A very sinky marsh, scattered throughout with dead standing timber, is in the back. Characteristically, the pond and marsh are loaded with beaver sign, and we generally spot some Canada geese and sometimes even wood ducks. Tree and barn swallows seem to be constantly winging their way over the marsh and pond. We typically spot a great blue heron or two, occasionally a green heron, and once a little blue heron. Ineluctably, we always exit the marshy area quite wet and muddy.

Another pond, my favorite beaver pond in the area, which is much closer to Windbrook Drive, always deserves a visit. We wade through it, sometimes up to our waists, while pushing though the thick aquatic vegetation, mostly smartweeds. On a May 1, 1997 trip, we found a goose nest and noted a small great blue heron rookery, about seven nests, along with a few adults. As will be shown later, however, this pond is not always easy to locate.

Most of our trips produce a number of neotropical migrants, like the hooded warbler, blackpole warbler, yellow warbler, parula warbler, ovenbird, redstart, yellowthroat, white-eyed vireo, red-eyed vireo, scarlet tanager, yellow-billed cuckoo, wood thrush, and indigo bunting. We also sometimes observe barred owls and red-shouldered hawks.

Leopard frogs and pickerel frogs are prolific in the area, and the ponds also support bullfrogs (*Rana catesbiana*) and green frogs. We sometimes find northern cricket frogs (*Acris c. crepitans*) and spring peepers along the floodplain and at the ponds. Box turtles can be expected on the floodplain -- one time we found four. On one trip, I caught a large black rat snake (*Elaphe o. obsoletus*) that was firmly ensconced in some low common greenbriers. On another trip, we found two black rat snakes up the same tree. At first I thought we could reach one of the snakes with a long stick but they were too high. I then suggested that if someone was willing to grab a snake, assuming I could climb the tree to shake it out, I would attempt it in order to confirm its identity.

Needless to say, it was not a routine task going for those snakes considering that the poison ivy-covered birch was a good 2.5-3.0 feet diameter. I thought I could climb it, however, because of the exfoliating, somewhat rotted bark and the tree's slightly tilted nature. Following a bear hug technique and by sinking my heals into weak bark, I managed to get up about eight feet. Holding on with one hand and with one good foot anchored well into the bark, and by stretching with a long stick, I was able to reach the snake, which was higher up and out on a narrow limb. However, no matter how much I tried, while struggling to hold on, I could not dislodge the snake from the branch, even when I positioned the stick into a hanging loop of its body. The snake always kept part of its body well wrapped around the limb. Now all the while my right foot was not firmly in place, for the bark on that side had crumbled and flaked off. Fortunately, Daryl Jones supported my right foot with his hands, and I believe others stayed below just in case my grip failed. It was a struggle but when we forced the snake out on the end of the branch, I managed to bend the branch down and someone from below was able to reach the branch with a pole at that point and catch the snake. I backed down and we examined it (Figure 72). As I expected, it was a black rat

461

snake as opposed to a northern black racer, as it had weakly keeled scales on its middorsal region and a loaf-of-bread-like cross section.

It was a rather interesting and challenging feat climbing that large, almost vertical, tree bear-hug style. And in retrospect, it was bold and potentially dangerous on my part (from a possible fall, not from handling the snake). Later, I thought of the possibility of falling backwards if the bark gave

Figure 72. The black rat snake (*Elaphe o. obsoletus*). This common snake is an adept climber found in uplands, including residential areas (backyards, gardens, fields, woodlots). It is frequently also encountered along floodplains in the Chesapeake Bay Region, where it seeks prey like five-lined skinks (*Eumeces fasciatus*), bird eggs and hatchlings, deer mice, and meadow voles.

way and becoming impaled on a broken shrub or beaver cut stump. The poison ivy was not a problem, however, since I do not catch it, and it may even have helped me with my hand and foot grips.

I find black rat snakes commonly on floodplains and sometimes in marshes or swamps. They are good climbers and seek bird eggs and young birds, and no doubt get their share of five-lined skinks and frogs as well.

462

Finding the two black rat snakes was perfect. I had been talking about how they climb dead trees in search of skinks and bird eggs and young, and sure enough, as I was about to examine some loose bark on the large river birch, someone spotted the two snakes in its branches about twenty-five feet up. On the same day that I found the two black rat snakes, I also suggested the possibility of five-lined skinks being found under loose tree bark as I approached a promising dead tree. The bark came off easily enough and there it was -- a small skink!

Instances like this have not been all that uncommon on my trips with groups. Once, for example, while on an historic town tour to the New Jersey Pine Barrens led by my friend Bill Leap, a lady inquired about the carpenter frog (*Rana virgatipes*). I took her across a dirt road and to the edge of a bog and immediately pointed out a carpenter frog. Another time while lecturing in the field on the Chincoteague Bay saltmarshes, I no sooner explained how abundant meadow voles (*Microtus pennsylvanicus*) are on the high marshes, when a vole quickly shot out from under the first batch of rafted saltmarsh cordgrass flotsam I overturned in searching for one. And there have been a number of times on the Eastern Shore that bald eagles flew by not long after I mentioned their potential presence. Maybe I have just been lucky with these predicted finds, although knowledge of the natural history of the animals involved and former experiences and revisited sites does gives one an edge. Nevertheless, such instances seem to some, no doubt, almost as if they were staged.

The Piscataway itself appears to be of good water quality, at least as indicated by its aquatic critters. Freshwater mussels are present. I have also found some rather round, three centimeter long, dragonfly larvae (perhaps the genus *Hagenius*) that superficially resembled large aquatic hemipterans, and even some stonefly nymphs.

*   *   *

Our spring trip along the Piscataway in 1998 stands in sharp contrast with all others, since it was not exactly pleasant. In fact, it was somewhat a fiasco, since near the halfway point one lady badly sprained her ankle and had to be escorted out by two men. This was soon followed by a misunderstanding over instructions I gave to another member of the group about continuing downstream as I independently paralleled them while searching once again for my favorite beaver pond. Unfortunately, they did not budge from the spot where I left them. So this eventually found me waiting downstream as my colleagues held tight upstream. At one point, they apparently even assumed I was injured or lost and sent out some search parties. As explained more thoroughly in my *Journal*, dissention ensued within the group over how to proceed in my absence. The upshot was that we did not reach our cars at Windbrook Road by 4 p.m as originally planned. In fact, the last of us, including me, did not exit the floodplain until 7:30 -- three and a half hours late. In doubling back a couple of times to retrieve all of the folks, I concluded that I had walked equivalent to twice the length of the three mile reach we had intended to walk, not counting all of my meandering on the floodplain. Needless to say, I was indeed tired when it was over -- given the thick brush, the current I had to buck while wading upstream, the ups and downs of creek banks, the logs to climb over, and other obstacles. However, I soon hustled home, showered, and dressed. And 9 p.m. found me reinvigorated and where else but on the dance floor with my wife at our standard Friday country dance hall near Glen Burnie!

*   *   *

A May 13, 1988 trip with the botanical group stands out in particular. Dwight Fielder, Yvette Ogle, and I hiked a two or three mile section of the floodplain below Windbrook Road. Although the floodplain was not that interesting botanically, we found Virginia waterleaf (*Hydrophyllum virginianum*), a first for me on the Coastal Plain, as well as the highly State rare small-flower baby-blue-eyes (*Nemophila aphylla*). We also found two box turtles on the floodplain and saw a prothonotary warbler and a pair of indigo buntings in a swampy area. I suppose most birders associate indigo buntings with hedgerows, wood edges, oldfields, and similar early succes-

TABLE XIV
SPECIES ON NORTH FACING SCARP AND SLOPE
ALONG PISCATAWAY CREEK

Scientific Name	Common Name
*Aquilegia canadensis**	wild columbine
Arabis laevigata	smooth rockcress
Aralia nudicaulis	wild sarsaparilla
Arisaema sp.	Jack-in-the-pulpit
Asimina triloba	pawpaw
Cornus florida	flowering dogwood
Epifagus virginiana	beechdrops
Fagus grandifolia	American beech
Galium aparine	catchweed bedstraw
Galium sp.	bedstraw
Hieracium sp.	hawkweed
*Hydrangea arborescens**	wild hydrangea
Lonicera japonica	Japanese honeysuckle
Nyssa sylvatica	black gum
Osmorhiza claytonii	hairy sweet cicely
Parthenocissus quinquefolia	Virginia creeper
Polygonatum biflorum	small Solomon's-seal
*Polypodium virginianum**	polypody fern
Polystichum acrostichoides	Christmas fern
Quercus rubra	northern red oak
*Saxifraga virginiensis**	Virginia saxifrage
*Sedum ternatum**	woodland stonecrop
Smilacina racemosa	false Solomon's-seal
Smilax rotundifolia	common catbrier
*Staphylea trifolia**	American bladdernut
*Tilia americana**	American basswood
Toxicodendron radicans	poison ivy
Ulmus americana	American elm
Viburnum acerifolium	mapleleaf arrowwood
Viburnum prunifolium	black haw

*These are apparently infrequent or rare on the Coastal Plain.

465

TABLE XV
SPECIES ON 45 DEGREE NORTH FACING SLOPE
ALONG PISCATAWAY CREEK

Scientific Name	Common Name
Arisaema sp.	Jack-in-the-pulpit
Asimina triloba	pawpaw
Cardamine concatenata	cut-leaf toothwort
Celtis occidentalis	hackberry
Euonymous sp.	strawberry-bush
Fagus grandifolia	American beech
Fraxinus sp.	ash
Galium aparine	catchweed bedstraw
Hydrophyllum virginianum	Virginia waterleaf
Juglans nigra	black walnut
Lindera benzoin	spicebush
Liriodendron tulipifera	tulip tree
*Nemophila aphylla**	small-flowered baby-blue-eyes
Osmorhiza claytonii	hairy sweet cicely
Podophyllum peltatum	may-apple
Polystichum acrostichoides	Christmas fern
Quercus rubra	northern red oak
*Sanguinaria canadensis***	bloodroot
Smilacina racemosa	false Solomon's-seal
*Staphylea trifolia***	American bladdernut
*Tilia americana***	American basswood
Ulmus americana	American elm
Urtica dioica	stinging nettle
*Viola striata***	striped cream violet
Vitis sp.	grape

* Highly State rare for Maryland.
** These are apparently infrequent or rare on the Coast.

sional habitats, but over the years I have seen them also in thick, quite wet forested swamps -- two good instances being on this occasion and while on a trip along the Potomac River at Douglas Point.

This trip stands out, however, because of what we encountered near the end of the trip in an American beech-northern red oak forest. Where the creek swung south and undercut a bluff, we found a fossil bed. It was an outcrop of the Aquia Formation loaded with ancient pelecypods and gastropods. While examining it for fossils, we also noted wild stonecrop (*Sedum ternatum*), then early saxifrage (*Saxifraga virginiensis*), then wild hydrangea (*Hydrangea arborescens*), and so on. This north facing scarp and adjacent steep upland slope, had a number of plants not typical of the Coastal Plain, including basswood (*Tilia americana*), polypody fern (*Polypodium virginianum*), wild columbine (*Aquilegia canadensis*), and American bladdernut (*Staphylea trifolia*). Further downstream where the north slope was at forty-five degrees, we found small-flower baby-blue-eyes again, as well as basswood, American bladdernut, pale violet (*Viola striata*), and bloodroot (*Sanguinaria canadensis*). For complete lists of species observed on the scarp and slope, see Tables XIV and XV.

I have been to other areas in Prince George's and Charles Counties, such as Pomonkey Creek, where north facing slopes similarly support plants more typical of physiographic provinces west of the Coastal Plain. I suspect that a more serious examination of such sites, including this one, would produce a number of interesting botanical finds. Another good Coastal Plain location for finding what are normally piedmont and mountainous plants occurs along the Potomac River at Chapman's Landing in Charles County, where deep ravines cut into fossiliferous deposits producing calcareous soils. A description of the Chapman Landing site and a flora has been prepared by Roderick Simmons (15); a comparison of his list with those in Table XIV and Table XV show many similar species.

MATTAWOMAN CREEK

Back in the 1970s, I frequently represented the Maryland Department of Natural Resources at State wetland hearings in tidewater country. At one controversial hearing, a concerned citizen who was challenging the applicant's project on environmental grounds referred to one of the applicant's rebuttal statements as a red heron. Well, with a lot of effort, I held back my laughter and just sort of smiled and chuckled a little, then forced myself to move on to

467

the issue. Obviously, the concerned citizen meant a red herring, since he suggested that the applicant's rebuttal statement was an attempt to distract from the real issue. And I doubt that he even realized his mistake. Obviously, he was not a birder, and perhaps not a fisherman either. So, what does this have to do with Mattawoman Creek? If you have ever fished the Mattawoman, you probably have guessed it by now. Each spring numerous herring (*Alosa pseudoharengus*) migrate upstream to spawn, and whenever I am there in their presence, I think of that applicant, my chuckle, and his red heron.[5]

Thoughts of the Mattawoman also bring to mind the large concentration of ospreys that I observed there in the spring of 1976 near the interface of the fresh tidal marsh and swamp 1,000 feet or so downstream from Route 225. The herring were running and many fishermen were at the Route 225 bridge. At any one time, at least two or three osprey were fishing over the tidal creek and I counted as many as thirteen ospreys perched in trees in the green ash-red maple swamp. My conclusion was that the ospreys were concentrated there to feed on the spawning run. I wrote a small unpublished report on this osprey concentration, attributing it the fish migration. Subsequent correspondence from Jan Reese, who has studied Maryland osprey populations for some time, lends support for my conclusion. Jan frequently finds ospreys fishing near the heads of small tributaries in April, which suggests their nesting is timed to coincide with the abundance of fish.

Although the tidal portion of the Mattawoman is interesting in its own right and I have visited it a few times, my comments here will concentrate principally on a nontidal reach of the creek between Rassmunsen's Crossing and Route 225. (For more on the tidal portion of Mattawoman Creek, see Chapter Two.)

---

[5]Would you believe that at another public hearing, someone referred to riprap (the large rock used for shoreline protection) as riffraff; at yet another, a person pronounced the word Corps in Corps of Engineers as if it were corpse, sounding the letter p! For sure, however, the Corps is far from dead.

*   *   *

Would you like some good birding? Maybe see a prothonotary warbler, our only cavity nesting warbler, or the first American bird species shot and examined by Alexander Wilson, the uncommon, at least for our region, red-headed woodpecker? If so, you might want to try this reach of Mattawoman Creek. In the spring it is loaded with warblers, and spotting a red-headed woodpecker in one of its shallow impounded areas containing dead standing timber is a strong possibility.

I have encountered yellowthroats, redstarts, parula warblers, yellow-rumped warblers, Kentucky warblers, hooded warblers, and prothonotary warblers along the floodplain. The Kentucky was another first for me. And on April 25, 1994, while leading the government folks on a hike down the floodplain, we had a great find -- a pair of nesting prothonotary warblers. The prothonotaries were using an old woodpecker hole about seven feet off the ground in the dead trunk of a river birch angled out of the creek bank. We all had great views and saw both parents enter the hole at different times.

My second sighting of a red-headed woodpecker occurred along Mattawoman Creek just below Route 225 on December 4, 1975.[6] I had an excellent view of the bird and heard its call, as well as the call of two others. I again spotted some red-headed woodpeckers on the Mattawoman on April 26, 1996, this time while leading one of my government field trips. This observation occurred in the beaver impounded area supporting dead standing timber on the upstream side of Route 227 (Bumpy Oak Road) at Rassmunsen's Crossing. On approaching the beaver impounded area, I immediately spotted a red-headed woodpecker, then another. No one in the group other than me had seen a red-headed woodpecker before, so we took in some great views of this beautiful bird for a good ten minutes (Figure 73).

---

[6]My first red-headed woodpecker sighting was in the New Jersey Pine Barrens many years ago. In the east, I have also seen this stunning woodpecker at a beaver pond at Camp A.P. Hill in Virginia and in a pasture near Charles Town, West Virginia.

Figure 73. Red-headed woodpecker, an uncommon bird on the Coastal Plain.

According to the *Atlas of the Breeding Birds of Maryland and the District of Columbia*, the red-headed woodpecker can be found, at least sparingly, in every Maryland County, but it is an uncommon and local breeder (16). It is most widespread in the northeastern part of the Ridge and Valley Province and the northern Piedmont. Its increase on the Western Shore during the past eighteen years has been attributed to, in part, the increase in beaver populations, since flooding by beavers results in an abundance of dead standing timber. Clearly, conditions at the Mattawoman site, where we saw our woodpeckers in 1996, support the view of these authors.

After our great views of the red-headed woodpecker on the 1996 trip, we meandered downstream along the floodplain into the Mattawoman Natural Environmental Area. We repeatedly spooked up great blue herons, birds seemingly out of place in a dense floodplain forest, since they are commonly seen downstream in shallow tidal areas or at beaver ponds. But there was the creek, Mattawoman Creek, and as you may have guessed, it was full of herring. The opportunistic herons were there taking advantage of the situation -- they were feeding on the hundreds of small herring running up the stream. The herons had moved upstream along with the herring. (Actually, I regularly flush herons along this creek when I walk it in April or May -- their squawking is quite characteristic and their white splattered droppings are frequently encountered on gravel bars.)

So now we have not only fisherman and ospreys preying on the herring, but also herons. And guess what else -- otters. Otter predation on fish, of course, is to be expected. The proof of the otter predation here came earlier, in 1992, while leading another spring trip. We noted where otters were bedding down on the stream levee (matted grass), their access route up the streambank, and numerous fish scale-filled scats -- so many that the area stunk badly and at first I thought there was a dead fish present. There was no doubt in my mind that the scales were from herring, given the herring run at the time and the live and dead fish we observed.

Our various hikes produced an abundance of other wildlife, some rare plants, and some rather stately trees. To a large extent this probably has to do with the considerable spatial heterogeneity on the floodplain -- the creek, its

471

natural levees, the backwater forested swamps, higher forested terraces, shrub swamps, and assorted beaver impoundments. Reptiles and amphibians are particularly abundant. Box turtles, painted turtles, snapping turtles, and eastern mud turtles (*Kinosternon s. subrubrum*); black rat snakes, garter snakes (*Thamnophis s. sirtalis*), eastern kingsnakes (*Lampropeltus g. getulus*), and northern water snakes; five-lined skinks; green frogs, leopard frogs, pickerel frogs, and wood frogs (*Rana sylvatica*); spring peepers, northern cricket frogs, upland chorus frogs, and gray tree frogs (*Hyla versicolor*); marbled salamanders (*Ambystoma opacum*) -- I have encountered them all along the Mattawoman, and obviously there are others. One day, for example, just below Route 225 I found three mud turtles -- one in the forested swamp, one in a small marshy area, and the other trying to cross the railroad tracks. The mud turtle in the forested swamp was found while simultaneously discovering a five-lined skink under some loose bark on a fallen tree.

The attractive zebra swallowtail (*Papilio marcellus)*, which has both early and late season forms, is also fairly common. Its presence in the area could have been predicted given the abundance of pawpaw, on whose leaves the larvae feed (Figure 74). There are fresh water mussels and gilled snails (*Campeloma* sp.) in the stream, and examining a few small rocks or woody debris usually produces some caddisfly, mayfly and stonefly larvae -- all indicative of a healthy, well-oxygenated stream.

Speaking of insects, the various beaver impounded areas are just loaded with them, as well as crayfish. In the flooded bottomland at Rassmunsen's Crossing, I have dip-netted crayfish, various aquatic beetles, dragonfly nymphs, damselfly nymphs, waterbug (*Belostoma* sp.), creeping water-bugs (*Pelocoris* sp.), and some small, rather frail-looking, walkingstick-like hemipterans -- water measurers (*Hydrometra martini*).

Another beaver impoundment, this one of considerable size, occurs on the floodplain immediately north of Route 225 and west of Route 224. I visited this area on my third trip to the Mattawoman Creek back on April 6, 1976 when it apparently had been recently flooded due to beaver activity. I traversed much of the main meandering dam. As might be expected, many of the floodplain trees were dying and herbaceous understory plants like halberd-

472

leaf tearthumb and rice cutgrass were already invading. I spent considerable time that day in one marshy area observing a downy woodpecker feeding on grubs extracted from cattail stems. (See Chapter Two for more on this field observation.)

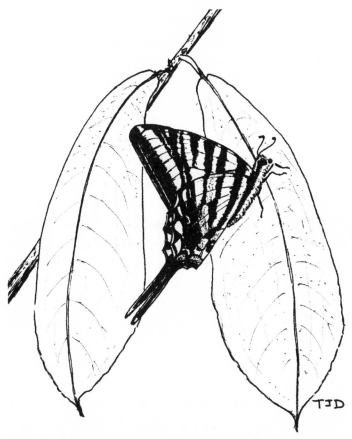

Figure 74. The zebra swallowtail (*Papilio marcellus*) on the pawpaw (*Asimina triloba*), the characteristic food of its larvae.

Over the years, I have followed the successional changes occurring in this impounded area with shifts toward wetter and wetter vegetation, leading to plants like spatterdock and buttonbush. In more recent years, the water has been rather deep, which has resulted in a high interspersion of vegetation and open water, making the site ideal for certain wildlife. Seemingly fearful mallards stand out in its openings, while wood ducks course stealthily about -- about long enough to be focused in with the binoculars, then promptly lost. The *kong-ka-ree* of red-winged blackbirds, the *witchity, witchity, witchity* of yellowthroats, the *peter, peter, peter* of titmice -- they all emanate from this wetland. Scanning with the binoculars always produces one or two great blue herons, unless they are all down by the creek seeking the herring. Belted kingfishers sometimes wing overhead rattling all the way, while barn swallows and tree swallows dip and swerve like toy gliders as they relentlessly pursue flying insects. And nowadays, some nesting geese can also be expected.

One day while intently scanning the beaver pond for birds, I also had a great view of a muskrat swimming across the pond and feeding in four different areas. It stood up to snip off young buttonbush leaves, snipped off some herbaceous leaves (a grass or sedge), and for about ten minutes worked in two different clumps of well-flooded softrush. Every so often, the muskrat would duck under and come up with something to eat, I believe it was the bases of the softrush (*Juncus effusus*) stems.

I suspect that many Marylanders and Delawareans, even serious botanists, have not seen the deciduous holly (*Ilex decidua*), unless they have botanized in the South, where it is fairly common on floodplains.[7] In Maryland, this dioecious species is not all that common -- in fact, it is considered highly State rare and legally threatened. It occurs on Mattawoman Creek, as well as a few other areas on the Coastal Plain, including Zekiah Swamp. Obviously, it is not evergreen like the American holly, otherwise it would not be called the deciduous holly, and those only familiar with the spiny American holly (*I. opaca*) would not likely recognize the deciduous holly, for like our other native hollies, it is unarmed. Physiognomically, it resembles blackhaw (*Viburnum prunifolium*), if that helps, and the female

---

[7] I probably can not say the same for Virginians, however.

474

plants have small red berries. Other than that, this species is a rather nondescript shrub.

There are other rare plants along the nontidal portion of the Mattawoman. Some that I have observed include small-flowered baby-blue-eyes, large-seeded forget-me-not (*Myosotis macrosperma*), and narrow melicgrass (*Melica mutica*), all of which are highly State rare. Also present are some State watchlist species -- Virginia dayflower (*Commelina virginica*), Howe's sedge (*Carex howei*), and flattened sedge (*C. complanata*). In addition, the floodplain supports some rather large trees -- tulip poplars, sweet gums (*Liquidambar styraciflua*), willow oaks (*Quercus phellos*), pin oaks (*Q. palustris*), and swamp chestnut oaks, including a monstrous 15 foot, 7.2 inch circumference swamp chestnut oak. There is also a 3 foot, 7.2 inch circumference American hornbeam (*Carpinus caroliniana*) and a 4.2 inch diameter deciduous holly.[8]

ZEKIAH SWAMP RUN

Zekiah Swamp Run is probably a third order stream, in places braided, that originates at Cedarville State Park and courses southward through the Zekiah Swamp. It eventually flows into Allen's Fresh Run, which in turn flows into the Wicomico River, a major tributary of the Potomac.[9] In 1975, the State of Maryland designated the Wicomico River, including the Zekiah, a wild and scenic river, and in 1981 the Zekiah was designated an area of critical concern by the Department of State Planning (17).

As is the case with most of the Sleepers, little published information exists on Zekiah Swamp Run and Zekiah Swamp despite their significant ecological value. Although it was referred to as the "celebrated" Zekiah Swamp as early as 1910 (19), the Zekiah was only briefly mentioned in

---

[8]Large sweet gums were reported from the Sleepers, specifically Mattawoman Creek and Zekiah Swamp, in the late 1920s (18).

[9]Maryland has two Wicomico Rivers; the other one is on the Eastern Shore of the Chesapeake Bay.

Wetlands in Maryland (20) and *Wetlands of Maryland* (21). The significance of this site has been acknowledged, however, in other government reports. Being relatively undisturbed, this twenty mile long bottomland swamp is considered one of Maryland's largest (about 13,300 acres) and most important nontidal wetland areas (21,22,23). In 1984, the Zekiah was also listed as one of fourteen sites considered uncommon wetlands in the Coastal Plain of Maryland (24). In addition, the Zekiah was acknowledged, particularly for its birds, by John Taylor in his 1954 article in the *Atlantic Naturalist* on the Wicomico River (25).

I first became familiar with the Zekiah in the early 1970s through my colleagues at the Department of Natural Resources who had shown me the site, as well as another tributary of the Wicomico River, Gilbert Swamp Run, or more accurately, what was left of it. (The sad demise of Gilbert Swamp Run is described in Chapter One.) My interest in the Zekiah, however, really did not surface until a few years later when I scanned a copy of the Smithsonian Institution's *Natural Areas of the Chesapeake Bay Region: Ecological Priorities* (26). This report, which was subsequently republished as part of the *Compendium of Natural Features Information* (23), considered and rated 232 natural areas in the Chesapeake Bay Region for preservation on ecological grounds. Of the 232 areas, Zekiah Swamp was ranked number one, which speaks for itself. Among other things, the report mentions the presence of mink, bald eagles, overwintering wood ducks and Wilson's snipe, a heronry, and what was then considered an endemic stonefly, the Zekiah stonefly.[10]   A disjunct population of the swamp cottonwood (*Populus heterophylla*), a species that I had not yet seen at the time, was also mentioned. Obviously, the evaluation suggested that this site was a real gem. And it is.

---

[10] This stonefly (*Allocapnio zekia*) was originally described as a new species. However, it is now considered synonymous with the common stonefly (*Allocapnio wrayi*), a fairly common winter stonefly and slightly variable species (Arnold Nordon, personal communication; 17).

*   *   *

Despite the Zekiah's ecological significance, my visits to the area during and subsequent to my Department of Natural Resources tenure were mostly short forays into the swamp at Route 5, about five miles outside of Waldorf. These trips generally involved various wetland plant identification or wetland delineation classes I was teaching, or sometimes trips with my sons. Route 5 was a convenient spot to access the area, and there was no need to go far upstream or downstream to see a number of plants -- particularly a good array of sedges and oaks. The upstream area was especially diverse because of the backwater flooding resulting from the Route 5 earthen fill causeway, which caused the death of many trees and initiated secondary succession. The result has been an interspersion of dead trees, live trees, shrubs, and herbaceous plants. (See Chapter Two for a more detailed description of this site.) On the other hand, the downstream area was even more inviting, and I had longed for some time to hike deep into its bowels.

That hike deep into the Zekiah came on November 2, 1990, when our botany group met for only the second trip that year. Two regulars, Dwight Fielder and Yvette Ogle, and two newcomers, Bob Maestro and Chris Swarth, participated. All of us were looking forward to the excursion into the heart of one of Maryland's largest bottomland swamps. We were all excited, for sure, but little did we know what we had in store.

We met where Route 6 crosses the Zekiah, left a couple of cars there, and traveled north by car to Route 5 to begin our hike downstream. We knew, of course, that it was a seven mile hike as the crow flies. And we also knew that we, being biologists rather than crows, would meander inadvertently and stop numerous times to examine plants, check animal sign, locate some singing birds, and discuss ecological phenomena. So we expected an all-day hike rambling along the Zekiah's floodplain. We also anticipated perhaps getting wet at times, although not too wet, since the period of overflow and flooding had long passed. Therefore, we assumed that standing water would be non-existent, except for the shallow creek and beaver impounded areas,

477

and that the braided, gravel-bottomed, channels could be easily navigated on foot.

We started downstream from Route 5 at 10:30 a.m., assuming we could readily reach Route 6 by about four o'clock. Over eight hours later -- eight tough hours later -- the last of which was spent in the dark, we reached Route 6! Lucky for us, it was a full moon and the dried stout wood-reedgrass (*Cinna arundinacea*) also showed up well in many places, indicating openness and direction. We had a terrible time of it for the lower one or two miles, the swamp being much wetter, muddier, and thicker there. The evidence of beaver impoundments was obvious even in the dark, as we had to resort to staying in open water and bur-reed areas to avoid thick shrubs and nasty greenbriers that pierced like barbed wire. This presented another problem, however, since we could not see the numerous submerged stumps and logs and were consequently tripping and stumbling often.

I will never forget Bob's early comment when we were probably less than a third of the way: "Hey Bill, are we racing or are we going to have some fun." Little did he realize how far we had to go yet, but Dwight and I knew we had to pick up the pace, and we did. When darkness came, we tried harder to stay close to each other. Once while crossing a flooded tributary, we found ourselves cornered out the end of a swampy peninsula. Dwight hit a hole and went up to the waist and fell over getting wet about to the chest. Right at the end, I tripped over a log and went almost belly down in the swamp. Fortunately for all of us, the day was exceptionally warm, near eighty degrees. We kept hearing cars on the road ahead, but it seemed we could never reach them. Finally, Dwight yelled, "I think I see headlights," and soon we were out.

Admittedly, I was quite worn out at the end of this adventure, given the sinking, stumbling, and wading, and the greenbriers tearing us up. (And I standardly keep in good shape!) Dwight's shirt was somewhat shredded; he retired it. At Route 6, we joked a bit, had a few of Bob's donuts, and also three of Chris' beers, before we drove to the other cars at Route 5. As newcomers to the group, what an experience for Chris and Bob.

During the trip, we saw about ten scattered specimens of short-bristled hornerush (*Rhynchospora corniculata*), a few swamp cottonwoods, a number of overcup oaks (*Quercus lyrata*), and many Virginia dayflowers (all watchlist species). Other plants noted include the white turtlehead (*Chelone glabra*), ditch-stonecrop (*Penthorum sedoides*, a first time for me on the Coastal Plain), and sharp-wing monkey-flower (*Mimulus alatus*). As anticipated, we found a number of other oaks as well -- willow oak, pin oak, swamp chestnut oak, and cherry-bark oak (*Quercus falcata* var. *pogodifolia*).

At one point, about fifteen or twenty wood ducks rose abruptly and headed downstream. Later we spotted one jump up on a log before it flew off. There was substantial beaver sign all along the stream, as well as frequent buck rubs on saplings and ground scrapes. We encountered a large beaver impoundment on the western side of the mainstem somewhere beyond the halfway point. I have subsequently observed this large area from a commercial jet while on a return trip from the South.

Unfortunately, Yvette, with about two miles to go, remembered that she had left her soil probe far upstream. Retracing our steps and searching was impractical, however, considering the distance and approaching darkness. Given those conditions, I would rather search for the fictional needle in a haystack!

While on this trip, I made some additional observations of shallowly rooted trees -- American beech and swamp chestnut oak. This was the first time I came across these species with evident shallow roots, which is of interest to me given that shallow rooting is an indicator of wetland hydrology in such settings, and therefore very useful for wetland delineation.

This was another trip that none of us will ever forget -- a trip into the bowels of a deep swamp with all of its mysteries, a trip of adventure that ended well after dark with well worn out participants.

*   *   *

In 1997, Chris Fleming from the Maryland Natural Heritage Program was kind enough to pass on to me her field reports on a number of areas along Zekiah Swamp Run or its tributaries, including Peartree Hill Swamp, Mud Creek Swamp, Dentsville Bridge Swamp, Jordan Swamp Headwaters Marsh,

TABLE XVI
LIST OF RARE OR UNCOMMON SPECIES FOUND AT ZEKIAH SWAMP*

Scientific Name	Common Name	Status * *
Andropogon ternarius	silvery beardgrass	WL
Carex gigantea	giant sedge	S1&E
C. grayii	Asa Gray's sedge	WL
C. louisianica	Louisiana sedge	S1&E
C. lupuliformis	hop-like sedge	WL
Commelina virginica	Virginia dayflower	WL
Hydrocotyle verticillata	whorled water-pennywort	WL
Ilex decidua	deciduous holly	S1&T
Iris virginica	Virgina blue flag	WL
Ludwigia decurrens	willow primrose	S2
Lycopus rubellus	stalked water-horehound	WL
Quercus lyrata	overcup oak	WL
Polygala curtissii	Curtiss' milkwort	WL
Rhododendron atlanticum	dwarf azalea	WL
Rhynchospora corniculata	short-bristled hornedrush	WL
Sparganium androcladum	branching bur-reed	WL
Utricularia gibba	humped bladderwort	WL

* Source: Maryland Natural Heritage Program.
* * WT refers to watch list species. For and explanation of the other rarity statuses, see Table I in Chapter Two.

Jordan Swamp, Old Mill Branch, Bryantown Swamp, and Bel Alton Runs, based upon field work she conducted in 1995.[11] A summary of the rare and uncommon species found at these sites is given in Table XVI. Two of these species, the giant sedge (*Carex gigantea*) and Louisiana sedge (*C. lousianica*), are considered highly State rare and endangered by the Maryland Natural Heritage Program; one, the deciduous holly, is considered highly State rare and threatened. Another species, the wingstem water-primrose (*Ludwigia decurrens*), which I have not seen in Maryland but have found across the river

---

[11]The Bryantown Swamp is the area at Route 5 that I most frequently visited with my classes.

480

in Woodbridge, Virginia, is listed as State rare. The remaining thirteen species are on the State's watchlist.

*   *   *

Another site worthy of mention is the Piney Branch Bog, which is located where a utility line right-of-way crosses Piney Branch, a tributary of Zekiah Swamp Run. This site was discovered by Phil Sheridan and Bill Scholl in 1989 (27). It supports at least nine rare and uncommon plants, including the northern pitcher plant (*Sarracenia purpurea*), for which few localities are known on the Western Shore, and the only known Maryland population of the New Jersey rush (*Juncus caesariensis*), highly State rare and endangered in the State. I have never seen this rare rush, nor have I been to this site. I hope to botanize it in the summer of 1999.

ST. MARY'S RIVER

Having only explored it a few times, I have little to say about the St. Mary's River. Most of my trips there related to the proposed St. Mary's Recreation Lake Project, which would have inundated a large reach of the floodplain. A Department of the Army permit was required to do the work in compliance with Section 404 of the Clean Water Act. Therefore, as an Environmental Protection Agency technical person, who at the time dealt with controversial cases that reached the Agency's Headquarters level for resolution, I was asked to inspect the site and advise my superiors on its ecological significance. In conjunction with our Region III Office in Philadelphia, I also led a couple of field trips to the site for various managers, including two different Assistant Administrators for the Office of Water. So, in total, I suppose I spent two different full days walking the site on my own and led two long field trips there for my management folks. I also spent half a day there with my youngest son Sean and a friend of his, exploring much of the floodplain and its many beaver impoundments. Actually, the reach I am referring to is near Great Mills, well above the large estuarine portion of St. Mary's River. At most, it is a third order stream.

Immediately, three things come to mind when I think about the St. Mary's River -- its habitat diversity and wildlife, going right up the middle, and a lost soul.

On April 22, 1983, I spent seven hours rambling along a two mile reach of the St. Mary's River floodplain, inspecting it for the Environmental Protection Agency. I have always cherished these kind of visits -- all day explorations assessing landscape and habitat diversity, examining plants, listing birds, checking for herps, recording mammal sign, and making sundry other wildlife observations. What pleasures they brought, especially on beautiful spring days. And guess what -- I got paid for them too!

I was very impressed with the landscape and habitat diversity along this particular floodplain. The forested swamp was a typical overflow area with higher, drier levees; levee sediments were a grayish fine sand, as opposed to the finer sediments in the adjacent backwater areas. The stream was clear but manifested ample evidence of overbank flooding with bent shrubs and assorted natural debris. The forest was dominated by red maple (*Acer rubrum*), sweet gum, river birch, and tulip poplar, although some beech and flowering dogwood were found in drier areas. The floodplain also supported American hornbeam, American holly, sweetbay (*Magnolia virginiana*), spicebush (*Lindera benzoin*), highbush blueberry (*Vaccinium corymbosum*), and various oaks. Much of drier floodplain, especially levees, were covered with exotic Japanese honeysuckles (*Lonicera japonica*) and native spring beauties. As might be expected, the floodplain was wetter towards its edges (from groundwater seepage and shallow ponding) and where small tributaries entered. The floodplain forest also supported some rather large trees, including a forty-four inch diameter red maple and a sixty-six inch diameter southern red oak (*Quercus falcata*) -- monsters indeed.[12]

---

[12]For a more detailed account of the vegetation of the floodplain, including the various beaver impoundments, see my May 10, 1983 *Journal* entry.

In a small narrow backwater area, I noted something splash near shore and suspected a turtle, maybe a spotted turtle considering the location. Therefore, I sat for a while next to a muddy pad from which the critter had apparently dropped. About ten minutes went by before I spotted some bright yellow spots as a submerged turtle moved toward the surface and the mud pad. I nabbed it -- a spotted turtle sure enough -- just before it surfaced.

While waiting for the turtle to show, I was amazed by what appeared, things that would have gone unnoticed had I not been patient. At least thirty caddisflies covered a fifteen foot stretch of the backwater -- some floundering, some appearing listless on the water surface. Were they adults that had died and fallen onto water surface? Or were they metamorphosing larvae that had emerged and were drying somewhat prior to flying off as adults? A diving beetle skipped along erratically under water, then a large water boatman. A water strider periodically inspected the immobile caddisflies and perhaps sucked some juices with its piercing mouthparts. These observations clearly suggest that by walking one misses most wildlife, especially small critters. One needs to stop, wait, and observe closely at times. This approach, of course, was characteristic of the famous American naturalist, John Burroughs (1837-1921), and in more recent years, Lawrence Kilham and Hope Ryden.[13]

Scattered along the floodplain were a number of beaver ponds in different stages of succession, resulting in ample landscape diversity. I spent considerable time in one of the beaver ponds, a large, perhaps ten acre, pond on April 22, 1983 during a seven hour hike along the floodplain. This large pond had substantial open water and marsh, the latter overgrown with bur-reed, spatterdock, pondweed (*Potamogeton* sp.), river bulrush (*Scirpus fluviatilis*), arrow-arum, and broad-leaf cattail (*Typha latifolia*). Button-bushes, swamp roses (*Rosa palustris*), and young red maples, as well as dead standing trees, were scattered about. The marsh eventually turned into a shrub swamp of about equal size. Beaver and muskrat droppings and raccoon tracks

---

[13]See Kilham's *On Watching Birds* (6) and Ryden's *Lily Pond: Four Years with a Family of Beavers* (28).

were abundant. The site looked well-suited for breeding bitterns, rails, red-winged blackbirds, tree swallows, and great crested flycatchers.

I slowly and alertly traversed the beaver impoundment, all the while noting painted turtles, numerous northern cricket frogs, and a musk turtle (*Sternotherus odoratus*). At one point as I waited for a painted turtle to surface, I watched a small water boatmen maneuvering along the sediment surface, alight, then simply disappear. Then a dead mayfly floated by. Shrub bases supported a few muskrat houses and feed beds. Fresh beaver cuttings were evident along with old. Two great blue herons squawked loudly as they angled awkwardly out of the marsh.

Although the site was well-flooded, the water level was only about six inches above my knees, so I could maneuver well in it, especially in its small hard-bottom streams. The numerous dead trees and high interspersion of herbaceous plants and water no doubt accounted for much of its wildlife diversity. This was one of the nicer, more accessible, deep fresh marshes I have ever seen in our area.

Further back in the shrub swamp, I saw two deer that slowly moved off into the brush. While examining the loose bark on standing dead river birches, I spotted a small five-lined skink; then about ten bessybugs (*Popilius disjunctus*) under the bark of a fallen oak (Figure 75). Later, I jumped a third deer at a small ponded area supporting marsh and shrub swamp vegetation here water impounded by a beaver dam had caused the death of the floodplain trees. This too had a

Figure 75. The bessybug (*Popilius disjunctus*), a large shiny black beetle generally found under the bark of dead trees and inside of decaying logs and stumps.

good interspersion of herbaceous plants -- arrow-arum, spatterdock, bur-reed, softrush -- and water with scattered shrubs and trees like smooth alder and river birch. The showy spadices of goldenclubs protruded true to their names, like miniature golden clubs. I flushed a wood duck and jumped yet another deer, then while searching under some loose bark on a standing dead river birch I uncovered a three and one-half foot black rat snake, which no doubt was seeking a meal -- large insects and skinks, or perhaps a southern flying squirrel (*Glaucomys volans*).

Repeatedly during the day, I noted tiger swallowtails (*Papilio glaucus*). At one spot three swallowtails intermittently "dipped" into wet sand (perhaps seeking water) and a fourth alighted on a dried beaver dropping. The latter butterfly would not leave the dropping until I pulled it off. At first I thought it was hurt, but when I sat it down a second time it flew away. About three weeks later, I again spotted numerous tiger swallowtails in the area. At one spot, eight or ten were congregating on white splattered bird droppings. Perhaps the butterflies obtain an essential element from them. Plenty of spring azures (*Celastrina argiolus*) were noted, along with some beautiful early season forms of zebra swallowtails, sporting the bright red spot near the base of their wings.

In all honesty, I think this was the most diverse floodplain I have traversed in Maryland, which can be attributed mostly to the beaver. This account also brings to mind other trips along the St. Mary's River -- trips going right up the middle.

*   *   *

On May 12, 1983, my good friend and colleague, Charlie Rhodes, and I guided a small group of Environmental Protection Agency's Headquarters and Region III folks up the St. Mary's River so they could see the nature of the area and what was at stake if the proposed recreation lake was constructed. This group was comprised of some low-level managers, some technical staff, and one attorney, all of whom were involved in some way with regulatory aspects of the Agency's wetland program. We conducted a reconnaissance of much of the site, did some cursory soil sampling, and pointed out an array of wildlife, mostly birds, as we hiked up the floodplain. Red-eyed vireos, red-bellied woodpeckers, ovenbirds, parula warblers, tufted titmice -- they were all present along the floodplain forest. Red-winged blackbirds were scattered throughout the large marshy beaver impoundment, and we even noted a green heron, solitary sandpiper, and rail, probably a Virginia rail. Red-winged blackbirds were also present in the upstream shrub swamp, along with white-eyed vireos, great crested flycatchers, and tufted titmice. A yellowthroat blurted out loudly at one small beaver meadow on a tributary. A solitary sandpiper was again noted at the upper beaver pond.

We ate lunch at the large old beaver pond while sitting on some downed tree boles near the dam. By lunch, we had only traveled about half the distance upstream that we had intended. So after lunch, it was decision time. Should we circumvent the large, well-flooded, beaver impoundment, all the while fighting our way through some rather thick underbrush, in reaching the upstream area? Or should we save time by trying an alternative route, my suggested route -- going right up the middle? A little coaxing did it. I led off, and one by one they followed, right up the middle, a strung out line of bureaucrats meandering through the marsh/shrub swamp complex, up to their waists in mud and water. Quite a scene. But it was great! I sensed temporary disappointment in some, but in the end they enjoyed the adventure. I am confident that they will never forget or regret the experience. It will stick with them forever -- a great experience for office bureaucrats, some of whom had seldom gotten into the field to inspect first hand and to appreciate the resource they were regulating. I guess it was also rather humorous, from my perspective, watching them struggle!

I took a similar trip in the summer of 1988 with my youngest son, Sean, and his friend, Carl. We spent four hours on the floodplain, traversing forests, swamps, and beaver ponds. I took them up the middle of the large old beaver pond, which still was very wet despite dense herbaceous vegetation in the lower end and shrubs and scattered trees upstream. There were narrow waterways coursing through it and we followed them trying, unsuccessfully at times, not to trip over submerged logs. I am sure the boys, who were only about ten years old at the time, will never forget that trip, including getting wet almost to their armpits and all of the reptiles and amphibians we found -- three box turtles, three five-lined skinks, one wood frog, four green frogs, four toads. Along the transmission line right-of-way, I saw and heard a bluebird and found two vascular plants new to me -- side-beak pencil flower (*Stylos-*

anthes biflora) and Carolina wild petunia (*Ruellia caroliniensis*) -- as well as Curtis' milkwort (*Polygala curtisii*), a State watchlist species.

So the boys and bureaucrats both got really wet and muddy on these trips. I know the boys would have done it again the next day if asked; I am not so sure about the bureaucrats. Yet, I have always said: "To get a good feel for a wetland, you literally have to feel it." Well, they certainly did on those two trips, and no one got lost.

*   *   *

Lost. Well now, that reminds me of a lost soul, at the time the Wetland Coordinator in our Region III office in Philadelphia who, being a friend of mine, I will just call Mr. Unfortunate. Although he was far from an amateur, on this particular day he got a little confused and lost his way, and ultimately was surely embarrassed, given the folks we were escorting.

This particular trip also occurred in 1983, but in the fall. Charlie and I were guiding some high level bureaucrats -- including one of my favorites during my tenure at the Agency, Jo Cooper, the Assistant Administrator for Water, a very down-to-earth lady, and Alan Hirst, the Director of the Office of Federal Activities -- through the site. The project was active and very controversial at the time and major high-level decisions had to be made over whether or not to approve it. We had a pleasant walk along the floodplain up to the large beaver pond area and planned to exit the site by following a transmission line right-of-way that paralleled the floodplain. We were running a bit late and were scheduled to fly the site for a bird's-eye view.

Upon leaving the well-flooded beaver pond, Mr. Unfortunate decided to separate from the group, hike briskly back to the vehicles, and contact the pilot to inform him of our slight delay. In so doing, however, he got lost. He unknowingly traveled in a big circle, and after crossing the river, headed way upstream in the opposite direction. About two hours later, after substantial calling and a long upstream hike along the transmission right-of-way, someone spotted a person rushing along the right-of-way in our direction. We soon concluded it was Mr. Unfortunate, and before long he reluctantly

487

approached us, all sweaty and torn up by blackberries and greenbriers -- and most of all substantially embarrassed. By then, of course, the flight had been canceled.

I doubt that Mr. Unfortunate will ever live that one down. In fact, on his very first day back in Philadelphia, he was guided by numerous directional signs leading to and from the elevator and his office! For the record though, without a compass, any of us could have been Mr. Unfortunate. I'm sure glad I wasn't.

*   *   *

The status of the St. Mary's Recreation Lake? The project sort of stalled and eventually just faded away. Fortunately, the river still runs clean and the floodplain remains replete with wildlife. It's waiting for your visit.

LITERATURE CITED

PREFACE

(1) Sipple, W.S. 1993. Maryland journal: Outdoor and natural history observations and experiences, 1971-1986. Volumes I (p.1-256).

(2) Sipple, W.S. 1993. Maryland journal: Outdoor and natural history observations and experiences, 1987-1992. Volume II (p.257-483).

(3) Sipple, W.S. 1998. Maryland journal: Outdoor and natural history observations and experiences, 1993. Volumes III (p.484-687).

(4) Sipple, W.S. 1998. Maryland journal: Outdoor and natural history observations and experiences, 1994. Volume IV (p. 688-896).

(5) Sipple, W.S. 1998. Maryland journal: Outdoor and natural history observations and experiences, 1995-1996. Volume V (p.897-1,092).

(6) Sipple, W.S. 1998. Maryland journal: Outdoor and natural history observations and experiences, 1997. Volume VI (p.1,093-1,217).

(7) Sipple, W.S. 1992. Jersey journal: Outdoor and natural history observations and experiences, 1955-1971. 341 p.

(8) Sipple, W.S. 1991. Through the eyes of a young naturalist. Gateway Press, Baltimore, MD. 204 p.

(9) Sipple, W.S. 1990. Exploring Maryland's freshwater tidal wetlands. *Atlantic Naturalist* 40: 3-18.

(10) Tiner, R. W., Jr. and David G. Burke. 1995. Wetlands of Maryland. U.S. Fish and Wildlife Service, Ecological Services, Region 5, Hadley, MA and Department of Natural Resources, Annapolis, MD. Cooperative publication. 193 p.

(11) Soil Conservation Service. 1982. National list of scientific plant names. Volume I: List of plant names. U.S. Department of Agriculture. 416 p.

(12) Reed, B.P. 1988. National list of plant species that occur in wetlands: National summary. U.S. Fish and Wildlife Service. Biological Report 88(24). 244 p.

(13) Soil Conservation Service. 1994. Plants: Alphabetical listing of scientific names. U.S. Department of Agriculture. (not paginated)

CHAPTER ONE

(1) Meanley, B. 1975. Birds and marshes of the Chesapeake Bay Country. Tidewater Publishers, Cambridge, MD. 157 p.

(2) Pritchard, D.W. 1967. What is an estuary: Physical viewpoint. *In*: Lauff (editor), Estuaries. American Association for the Advancement of Science. Publication No. 83. p. 3-5.

(3) Shaw, S.P and C. G. Fredine. 1971. Wetlands of the United States: Their extent and their value to waterfowl and other wildlife. U.S. Department of the Interior, Fish and Wildlife Service. Circular 39. 67 p.

(4) Cowardin, L.M., V. Carter, F.C. Golet, and E.T. LaRoe. 1979. Classification of wetlands and deepwater habitats of the United States. U.S. Department of the Interior, Fish and Wildlife Service. FWS/OBS-79/31. 103 p.

(5) Sipple, W.S. 1987. Wetland identification and delineation manual. Volume I: Rational, wetland parameters, and overview of jurisdictional approach. 30 p. Volume II: Field methodology. 40 p.

(6) Sipple, W.S. 1971. The past and present flora and vegetation of the Hackensack Meadows, New Jersey, and suggestions for management. Master's Thesis, University of Pennsylvania, Philadelphia, PA. 165 p.

(7) Sipple, W.S. 1971-1972. The past and present flora and vegetation of the Hackensack Meadows. *Bartonia* 41:4-56.

(8) Laing, H.E. 1940. Respiration of the rhizomes of *Nuphar advena* and *Typha latifolia*. *American Journal of Botany* 27:574-581.

(9) Laing, H.E. 1940. Respiration of the leaves of *Nuphar advena* and *Typha latifolia*. *American Journal of Botany* 27:583-585.

(10) Laing, H.E. 1941. Effect of concentration of oxygen and pressure of water upon growth of rhizomes of semi-submerged water plants. *Botanical Gazette* 102:712-724.

(11) Wass, M.L. and T.D. Wright. 1969. Coastal wetlands of Virginia: An interim report to the Governor and General Assembly. Virginia Institute of Marine Science. Special Report in Applied Marine Science and Ocean Engineering Number 10. 152 p.

(12) Chesapeake Bay Foundation. 1996. Nanticoke River watershed: Natural and cultural resources atlas.

490

(13) Metzgar, R.G. 1973. Wetlands in Maryland. Maryland Department of State Planning. Publication No.157.

(14) Sculthorpe, C.D. 1967. The biology of aquatic vascular plants. St. Martin's Press, New York, NY. 610 p.

(15) Teal, J. and M. Teal. 1969. Life and death of the salt marsh. National Audubon Society and Ballantine Books, Inc., New York, NY. 274 p.

(16) Kraft, J.C. 1971. A guide to the geology of Delaware's coastal environments. University of Delaware, College of Marine Studies, Newark, DE. Publication 2GL039. 220 p.

(17) Elliott, G.K. 1972. The Great Marsh, Lewes, Delaware: The physiography, classification and geologic history of a coastal marsh. University of Delaware, College of Marine Studies, Newark, DE. Technical Report No. 19. 139 p.

(18) Hill, S.R. 1986. An annotated checklist of the vascular flora of Assateague Island (Maryland and Virginia). *Castanea* 51(4):265-305.

(19) Harvill, A.M., Jr. 1967. The vegetation of Assateague Island, Virginia. *Castanea* 32:105-108.

(20) Klotz, L.H. 1986. The vascular flora of Wallops Island and Wallops Mainland, Virginia. *Castanea* 51(4):306-326.

(21) Dolan, R., B. Hayden, and J. Heywood. 1977. Atlas of environmental dynamics: Assateague Island National Seashore. U.S. Department of the Interior, National Park Service. Natural Resource Report No. 11. 40 p.

(22) Goettle, M.S. 1981. Geological development of the southern portion of Assateague Island, Virginia. *Northeastern Geology* 3(3-4):278-282.

(23) Boule, M.E. 1979. The vegetation of Fisherman Island, Virginia. *Castanea* 44:98-108.

CHAPTER TWO

(1) Sipple, W.S. 1990. Exploring Maryland's freshwater tidal wetlands. *Atlantic Naturalist* 40: 3-18.

(2) Sipple, W.S. and W.A. Klockner. 1984. Uncommon wetlands in the Coastal Plain of Maryland. *In*: Norden, Forester, and Fenwick (editors). Threatened and endangered plants and animals of Maryland. Maryland Department of Natural Resources. Natural

Heritage Program Special Publication 84-I. p. 111-138.

(3) Sipple, W.S. 1976. The carpenter frog (*Rana virgatipes*) in Caroline County, Maryland. *Bull. Maryland Herpetological Society* 12:129.

(4) Sipple, W.S. 1982. Tidal wetlands of Maryland's Eastern Shore and coastal bays. Paper presented at Conference on Rare and Endangered Plants and Animals on the Delmarva Peninsula, June 12, 1982 at Delaware State College, Dover, DE. 22 p.

(5) Steury, B.W. 1996. Floristic survey for vascular plants of Cove Point, Calvert County, Maryland. Alice Ferguson Foundation/National Park Service, Accokeek, Maryland. 105 p.

(6) Seton, E.T. 1913. Wild animals at home. Grosset & Dunlap Publishers, New York, NY. 226 p.

(7) McCormick, J. and H. Somes, Jr. 1982. Coastal wetlands of Maryland. Prepared for the Maryland Department of Natural Resources by Jack McCormick & Associates, a subsidiary of Wapora, Inc. 243 p.

(8) Meanley, B. 1975. Birds and marshes of the Chesapeake Bay Country. Tidewater Publishers, Cambridge, MD. 157 p.

(9) Hotchkiss, N. and H.L. Dozier. 1949. Taxonomy and distribution of N. American cat-tails. *American Midland Naturalist* 41:237-254.

(10) Teal, J. and M. Teal. 1969. Life and death of the salt marsh. National Audubon Society and Ballantine Books, Inc., New York, NY. 274 p.

(11) Horton, T. and W.M. Eichbaum. 1991. Turning the tide: Saving the Chesapeake Bay. Island Press, Washington, DC. 324 p.

(12) Kahn, H. 1992. Wetlands as nutrient sinks. *Marsh Notes* 7(1): 1-2.

(13) Baxter, J.C. 1973. Morphological, physical, chemical, and mineralogical characteristics of some tidal marsh soils in the Patuxent Estuary. Master's Thesis, University of Maryland. 92 p.

(14) Scofield, C.S. 1905. The salt water limits of wild rice. U.S. Department of Agriculture, Bureau of Plant Industries. Bulletin No. 72.

(15) Kearns, G. 1995. Migration chronology, habitat preference, and refinement of capture methods for migrant soras (*Parzana carolina*) on Jug Bay, Patuxent River, Maryland. Abstract for Chesapeake National Estuarine Research Reserve -- Maryland research meeting on April 28, 1995.

(16) Thompson, D.Q., R.L. Stuckey, and E.B. Thompson. 1987. Spread, impact, and control of purple loosestrife (*Lythrum salicaria*) in North American wetlands. U.S. Fish and Wildlife Service. Fish and Wildlife Research 2. 55 p.

(17) Stein, B.A. and S.R. Flack (editors). 1996. America's least wanted: Alien species invasions of U.S. ecosystems. The Nature Conservancy, Arlington, VA. 31 p.

(18) Shima, L.J., R.R. Anderson, and V.P. Carter. 1976. The use of aerial color infrared photography in mapping the vegetation of a freshwater marsh. *Chesapeake Science* 17:74-85.

(19) Swarth, C. and M. Damon. 1998. Short-term vegetation changes in a freshwater tidal wetland. Abstract for Conference on Wetland Plant Ecology and Conservation, June 22, 1996, Jug Bay Wetlands Sanctuary, Lothian, MD.

(20) Sipple, W.S. and R.H. Wheeler. 1974. On the presence of three vascular plants, *Melothria pendula*, *Carex extensa*, and *Aneilema keisak*, in Maryland. *Chesapeake Science* 15:173-174.

(21) Anderson, R.R., R.G. Brown, and R.D. Rappleye. 1968. Water quality and plant distribution along the upper Patuxent River, Maryland. 1968. *Chesapeake Science* 9:145-156.

(22) Sipple, W.S. 1978. An atlas of vascular plant species distribution maps for tidewater Maryland. Maryland Department of Natural Resources, Water Resources Administration, Wetlands Permit Section, Annapolis, MD. Wetland Publication No. 1. 280 p.

(23) Damon, M. 1996. What's new with wetland plant research. *Marsh News* 11(2):5.

(24) Tyndall, R.W., B.J. Holt, and G. Lamb. 1996. Scientific Note. *Castanea* 61: 86-89.

(25) Tiner, R. W., Jr. and David G. Burke. 1995. Wetlands of Maryland. U.S. Fish and Wildlife Service, Ecological Services, Region 5, Hadley, MA and Department of Natural Resources, Annapolis, MD. Cooperative publication. 193 p.

(26) Shreve, F., M.A. Chrysler, F.H. Blodgett, and F.W. Besley. 1910. The plant life of Maryland. The Johns Hopkins Press, Baltimore, MD. 533 p.

(27) Garbisch, E. 1994. The result of muskrat feeding on cattails in a tidal freshwater wetland. *Wetland Journal* 6(1):14-15.

(28) Sculthorpe, C.D. 1967. The biology of aquatic vascular plants. St. Martin's Press, New York, NY. 610 p.

493

(29) Johnson, M. 1970. Preliminary report on species composition, chemical composition, biomass, and production of marsh vegetation in the upper Patuxent Estuary, Maryland. *In* Flemer, Hamilton, Keefe, and Mihursky. Final report to Office of Water Resources Research on the effects of thermal loading and water quality on estuarine primary production. University of Maryland, Natural Resources Institute. Reference No. 71-6. p. 164-178.

(30) Flemer, D.A., D.R. Heinle, M. Cole, E. Hughes, B. Zeisel, J. Ustach, and R. Murtagh. 1973. Summary report of marsh production studies for the upper Patuxent River Estuary and Parker Creek, Maryland, during the summer 1973. University of Maryland, Natural Resources Institute. Reference No. 73-123. 30 p.

(31) Meanley, B. 1965. Early-fall food and habitat of the sora in the Patuxent River Marsh, Maryland. *Chesapeake Science* 6:235-237.

(32) Stewart, R.E. and C.J. Robbins. 1958. Birds of Maryland and the District of Columbia. U.S. Department of the Interior, Fish and Wildlife Service. North American Fauna No. 62. 386 p.

(33) Robbins, C.S. and E.A.T. Blom (editors). 1996. Atlas of the breeding birds of Maryland and the District of Columbia. University of Pittsburgh Press, Pittsburgh, PA. 479 p.

(34) Weller, M.W. and C.E. Spatcher. 1965. Role of habitat in the distribution and abundance of marsh birds. Iowa Agriculture and Home Economics Experiment Station. Special Report No. 43. 31 p.

(35) Weller M.W. and L.H. Fredrickson. 1974. Avian ecology of a managed glacial marsh. *The Living Bird* 12:269-291.

(36) Beecher, W.J. 1942. Nesting birds and the vegetation substrate. Chicago Ornithological Society, Chicago, IL. 69 p.

(37) Springer, P.E. and R.E. Stewart. 1948. Twelfth breeding-bird census; tidal marshes. *Audubon Field Notes* 2:223-226.

(38) Dubill, A. 1994. The birdman cometh: Summer ornithology in the wetlands. *Marsh Notes* 9(3):1-2.

(39) Sipple, W.S. 1977. Woodpecker chooses larvae from dead cattail stems. *The Audubon Naturalist News* 3(6):6.

(40) Reynolds, M. 1991. The marsh snail of Jug Bay. *Marsh Notes* 6(3):1-2, 11.

494

(41) Conant, R. 1975. A field guide to reptiles and amphibians of eastern and central North America. Houghton Mifflin Company, Boston, MA. 429 p.

(42) Smithberger, S.I. and C.W. Swarth. 1993. Reptiles and amphibians of the Jug Bay Wetlands Sanctuary. *The Maryland Naturalist* 37(3-4):28-46.

(43) Molines, K. and C. Swarth. 1996. Fish seining for fun & (scientific) profit. *Marsh Notes* 11(1):1,4-5.

(44) Rodney, B. 1990. Mummichogs: Mighty midgets of the marsh. *Marsh Notes* 5(3):1,11.

(45) Weller, M.W. 1981. Freshwater marshes: Ecology and wildlife management. University of Minnesota Press, Minneapolis, MN.

(46) Odum, W.E. 1984. The ecology of tidal freshwater marshes of the United States East Coast: A community profile. U.S. Department of the Interior, Fish and Wildlife Service. FWS/OBS-83/17. 117 p.

(47) Tiner, R. W., Jr. 1988. Field guide to nontidal wetland identification. Maryland Department of Natural Resources, Annapolis, MD and U.S. Fish and Wildlife Service, Newton Corner, MA. Cooperative publication. 283 p.

CHAPTER THREE

(1) Metzgar, R.G. 1973. Wetlands in Maryland. Maryland Department of State Planning. Publication No. 157.

(2) Smith, F.R. 1938. Muskrat investigations in Dorchester County, MD., 1930-34. U.S. Department of Agriculture, Washington, DC. Bulletin No. 474. 24 p.

(3) Harris, V.T. 1951. Muskrats on tidal marshes of Dorchester County. Department of Research and Education, Chesapeake Biological Laboratory, Solomons, MD. Publication No. 91. 36 p.

(4) Tiner, R. W., Jr. and David G. Burke. 1995. Wetlands of Maryland. U.S. Fish and Wildlife Service, Ecological Services, Region 5, Hadley, MA and Department of Natural Resources, Annapolis, MD. Cooperative publication. 193 p.

(5) McCormick, J. and H. Somes, Jr. 1982. Coastal wetlands of Maryland. Prepared for the Maryland Department of Natural Resources by Jack McCormick & Associates, a subsidiary of Wapora, Inc. 243 p.

(6) Nicholson, W.R. 1953. Marsh types found in Maryland. *Maryland Conservationist* 30(2):6-9.

(7) Nicholson, W.R. and R.D. Van Deusen. 1954. Marshes of Maryland. Maryland Game and Inland Fish Commission in cooperation with the Department of Research and Education, Solomons, MD. Resource Study Report No. 6. (not paginated).

(8) Office of River Basin Studies. 1954. Wetlands of Maryland. U.S. Department of the Interior, Fish and Wildlife Service. 15 p.

(9) Martin, A.C., N. Hotchkiss, F.M. Uhler, and W.S. Bourn. 1953. Classification of wetlands of the United States. U.S. Department of the Interior, Fish and Wildlife Service. Special Scientific Report -- Wildlife No. 20.

(10) Shaw, S.P and C. G. Fredine. 1956. Wetlands of the United States: Their extent and their value to waterfowl and other wildlife. U.S. Department of the Interior, Fish and Wildlife Service. Circular 39. 67 p.

(11) Cowardin, L.M., V. Carter, F.C. Golet, and E.T. LaRoe. 1979. Classification of wetlands and deepwater habitats of the United States. U.S. Department of the Interior, Fish and Wildlife Service. FWS/OBS-79/31. 103 p.

(12) Sipple, W.S. 1982. Tidal wetlands of Maryland's Eastern Shore and coastal bays. Paper presented at Conference on Rare and Endangered Plants and Animals on the Delmarva Peninsula, June 12, 1982 at Delaware State College, Dover, DE. 22 p.

(13) Brinson, M.M. 1993. A hydrogeomorphic classification for wetlands. U.S. Army Corps of Engineers, Waterways Experiment Station, Vicksburg, MS. Wetlands Research Program Technical Report WRP-DE-4. 79 p.

(14) August, R.M. 1969. Tidal flooding and conversion of lands adjacent to tidal marsh on the Eastern Shore of Maryland. Maryland Department of State Planning. (16-page unpublished report).

(15) Shreve, F., M.A. Chrysler, F.H. Blodgett, and F.W. Besley. 1910. The plant life of Maryland. The Johns Hopkins Press, Baltimore, Maryland. 533 p.

(16) Darmody, R.G. 1975. Reconnaissance survey of the tidal marsh soils of Maryland. Master's Thesis, University of Maryland, College Park, MD. 181 p.

(17) Darmody, R.G. and J.E. Foss. 1979. Soil-landscape relationships of the tidal marshes of Maryland. *Soil Science Society of America Journal* 43:534-541.

(18) Stevenson, J.C., L.G. Ward, and M.S. Kearney. 1986. Vertical accretion in marshes with varying rates of sea level rise. *In*: Wolfe (editor), Estuarine variability.

Academic Press, Inc. New York, NY. p. 241-259.

(19) Kerhin, R.T. 1974. Armistead distribution of the high marsh vegetation communities of the lower Eastern Shore and its geological significance. *In*: K.N. Weaver (editor), Research and investigation of geology, mineral and water resources of Maryland. Maryland Geological Survey Final Report, NASA, Goddard Space Flight Center. p. 5-1 to 5-14.

(20) Roby, D. 1974. Marsh regression at the Blackwater National Wildlife Refuge. (16-page draft report).

(21) Sipple, W.S. 1978. A review of the biology, ecology, and management of *Scirpus olneyi*. Volume I: An annotated bibliography of selected references. Department of Natural Resources, Water Resources Administration, Wetlands Permit Section, Annapolis, MD. Wetland Publication No. 2. 96 p.

(22) Sipple, W.S. 1979. A review of the biology, ecology, and management of *Scirpus olneyi*. Volume II: A synthesis of selected references. Department of Natural Resources, Water Resources Administration, Wetlands Permit Section, Annapolis, MD. Wetland Publication No. 4. 85 p.

(23) Nelson, N.F. and R.H. Dietz. 1966. Cattail control methods in Utah. Utah State Department of Fish and Game. Publication No. 66-2. 31 p.

(24) Pendleton, E.C. and J.C. Stevenson. 1983. Investigations of marsh losses at Blackwater Refuge. Final Report submitted to U.S. Fish and Wildlife Service, Region 5 and Coastal Resources Division, Tidewater Administration, Maryland Department of Natural Resources. 213 p.

(25) Perry, M.C. and A.S. Deller. 1994. Waterfowl population trends in the Chesapeake Bay area. Proceedings of the 1994 Chesapeake Research Conference. Toward a Sustainable Coastal Watershed: The Chesapeake Experiment. June 1-3, 1994. Norfolk, VA. 490-504.

(26) Dozier, H.L. 1947. Salinity as a factor in Atlantic Coast tidewater muskrat production. *Transactions North American Wildlife Conference* 12:398-420.

(27) Dozier, H.L., M.H. Markley, and L.M. Llewellyn. 1948. Muskrat investigations on the Blackwater National Wildlife Refuge, Maryland, 1941-1945. *Journal of Wildlife Management* 12:177-190.

(28) Meanley, B. 1978. Blackwater. Tidewater Publishers, Cambridge, MD. 148 p.

(29) Willner, G.R., J.A Chapman, and J.R. Goldsberry. 1975. A study and review of muskrat food habits with special reference to Maryland. Maryland Department of Natural Resources, Wildlife Administration. Publication in Wildlife Ecology No. 1. 25 p.

(30) Stewart, R.E. 1962. Waterfowl populations in the upper Chesapeake Bay Region. U.S. Department of the Interior, Fish and Wildlife Service, Bureau of Sport Fisheries and Wildlife. Special Scientific Report -- Wildlife No. 65. 208 p.

(31) Hoffpaur, C.M. 1961. Methods of measuring and determining the effects of marsh fires. *Proceedings Southeastern Association of Game and Fish Comissioners* 15:142-161.

(32) Lynch, J.J., T. O'Neil, and D.W. Lay. 1947. Management significance of damage by geese and muskrats of Gulf Coast marshes. *Journal of Wildlife Management* 11:50-76.

(33) Chamberlain, J.L. 1959. Gulf Coast marsh vegetation as food of wintering waterfowl. *Journal of Wildlife Management* 23:97-102.

(34) Stevenson, J.C., L.G. Ward, M.S. Kearney, and T.E. Jordan. 1985. Sedimentary processes and sea level rise in tidal marsh systems of Chesapeake Bay. *In*: H.A. Groman, D.M. Burke, and J.A. Kusler, Proceedings of the Conference on Wetlands of the Chesapeake, April 9-11, 1985. p. 37-62.

(35) Kearney, M.S. and J.C. Stevenson. 1985. Sea-level rise and marsh vertical accretion rates in Chesapeake Bay. Coastal Zone '85. p. 1,451-1,461.

(36) Stevenson, J.C., L.G. Ward, and M.S. Kearney. 1986. Vertical accretion in marshes with varying rates of sea level rise. *In*: Wolfe (editor), Estuarine variability. Academic Press, Inc. New York, NY. p. 241-259.

(37) Horton, T. and W.M. Eichbaum. 1991. Turning the tide: Saving the Chesapeake Bay. Island Press, Washington, DC. 324 p.

(38) Munro, R.E. 1980. Field feeding by *Cygnus columbianus columbianus* in Maryland. *In*: G.V.T. Mathews and M. Smart (editors), Proceedings Second International Swan Symposium. International Waterfowl Research Bureau, Slimbridge, England. p. 261-272.

(39) Perry, M.C. and F.M. Uhler. 1988. Food habits and distribution of wintering canvasbacks, *Aythya valisneria*, on Chesapeake Bay. *Estuaries* 11(1):57-67.

498

(40) Stewart, R.E. and C.J. Robbins. 1958. Birds of Maryland and the District of Columbia. U.S. Department of the Interior, Fish and Wildlife Service. North American Fauna No. 62. 386 p.

(41) Robbins, C.S. and E.A.T. Blom (editors). 1996. Atlas of the breeding birds of Maryland and the District of Columbia. University of Pittsburgh Press, Pittsburgh, PA. 479 p.

(42) Perry, M.C. 1987. Waterfowl of Chesapeake Bay. *In*: S.K. Majumdar, L.W. Hall, Jr., and H.M. Austin, Contaminant problems and management of living Chesapeake Bay resources. The Pennsylvania Academy of Sciences. p. 94-115.

(43) Hindman, L.J. and F. Ferrigno. 1990. Atlantic flyway goose populations: Status and management. *Transactions North American Wildlife and Natural Resources Conference* 55: 293-311.

(44) Abbott, J.M. 1979. Bald eagles in the Chesapeake Bay Region. *In*: Audubon Naturalist Society: Who we are, what we have done. p. 13-19.

(45) Abbott, J.M. 1975. Bald eagle nest survey 1975. *Atlantic Naturalist* 30 (3): 116-118.

(46) Therres, G.D. 1996. Bald eagle. *In*: Robbins, C.S. and E.A.T. Blom (editors), Atlas of the breeding birds of Maryland and the District of Columbia. University of Pittsburgh Press, Pittsburgh, PA. p. 94-95.

(47) Zucker, E.E. and J.A. Chapman. 1984. Morphological and physiological characteristics of muskrats from three different regions in Maryland, USA. *Z. Saugetierkunde* 49: 90-104.

(48) Dozier, H.L. and R.W. Allen. 1942. Color, sex ratios, and weights of Maryland muskrats. *Journal of Wildlife Management* 6:294-300.

(49) Dozier, H.L. 1944. Color, sex ratios and weights of Maryland muskrats, II. *Journal of Wildlife Management* 8:165-169.

(50) O'Neil, T. 1949. The muskrat in the Louisiana coastal marshes. Louisiana Wildlife and Fish Commission. 159 p.

(51) Allan, P.F. and W.L. Anderson. 1955. More wildlife from our marshes and wetlands. *In*: The yearbook of agriculture. Water. U.S. Department of Agriculture. p. 589-596.

(52) Harris, V.T. 1956. The nutria as a wild fur mammal in Louisiana. *Transactions North American Wildlife Conference* 21:474-485.

(53) Joanen, T. and L.L. Glasgow. 1965. Factors influencing the establishment of widgeongrass stands in Louisiana. *Proceedings Southeastern Association Game and Fish Commissioners* 19:78-92.

(54) Palmisano, A.W. and J.D. Newsom. 1967. Ecological factors affecting occurrence of *Scirpus olneyi* and *Scirpus robustus* in Louisiana coastal marshes. *Proceedings Southeastern Association of Game and Fish Commissioners* 21: 161-172.

(55) Perkins, C.J. 1968. Controlled burning in the management of muskrats and waterfowl in Louisiana coastal marshes. *Proceedings Tall Timbers Fire Ecology Conference* 8:269-280.

(56) Kiviat, E. 1978. The muskrat's role in the marsh ecosystem: A qualitative synthesis. *Bulletin Ecological Society of America* 59(2):124.

(57) Hanna, G.L. and P.C. Kangas. 1984. Effects of muskrat mounds on marsh vegetation diversity. *Bulletin Ecological Society of America* 65(2):246.

(58) Nyman, J.A., R.H. Chabreck, and N.W. Kinler. 1993. Some effects of herbivory and 30 years of weir management on emergent vegetation in brackish marsh. *Wetlands* 13(3):165-175.

(59) Schalles, J.F. 1984. Distribution and biomass of aquatic invertebrates and small vertebrates in two northwest Iowa glacial marshes. *Bulletin Ecological Society of America* 65(2):131.

(60) Leon, B.F. 1978. Disturbance tolerance and competition in brackish marsh plants. Doctoral Dissertation, Princeton University, Princeton, NJ.103 p.

(61)) Tansley, A.G. and R.S. Adamson. 1925. Studies on the vegetation of the English Chalk. III. The chalk grasslands of the Hampshire-Sussex border. *Journal of Ecology* 13:176-223.

(62) Hope-Simpson, J. F. 1940. Studies of the vegetation of the English Chalk. VI. Late stages in succession leading to chalk grassland. *Journal of Ecology* 28:386-402.

(63) Naimen, R.J., J.M. Melillo, and J.E. Hobbie. 1986. Ecosystem alterations of boreal forest streams by beaver (*Castor canadensis*). *Ecology* 67(5):1,254-1,269.

(64) Paradiso, J. L. 1969. Mammals of Maryland. U. S. Department of the Interior, Bureau of Sport Fisheries and Wildlife. North American Fauna 66. 193 p.

(65) Audubon, J.J. and J. Bachman. 1851. The viviparous quadrupeds of North America. Volume 2: 334.

500

(66) Cues, E. 1877. Fur bearing animals: A monograph of North American Mustelidae. Department of the Interior, U.S. Geological Survey of the Territories. Miscellaneous Publication 8. 348 p.

(67) Mowbray, E.E., J.A. Chapman, and J.R. Goldsberry. 1976. Preliminary observations on otter distribution and habitat preferences in Maryland with descriptions of otter field sign. *Transactions Northeast Fish and Wildlife Conference* 33:125-131.

(68) Hamilton, W.J., Jr. 1940. The summer food of minks and raccoons on the Montezuma Marsh, New York. *Journal of Wildlife Management* 4(1):80-84.

(69) Hamilton, W.J., Jr. 1959. Foods of mink in New York. *New York Fish and Game Journal* 6(1):77-85.

(70) Sealander, JA 1943. Winter food habits of mink in southern Michigan. *Journal of Wildlife Management* 7(4):411-417.

(71) Harris, V.T. 1953. Ecological relationships of meadow voles and rice rats in tidal marshes. *Journal of Mammalogy* 34(4):479-487.

(72) McKewen, S.E. and C.R. Brunori. 1980. Environmental assessment of terrestrial flora and fauna for Bloodsworth Island shore bombardment and bombing range. Maryland Department of Natural Resources, Wildlife Administration, Technical Services Division. 33 p.

(73) Stewart, R.E. 1956. Gadwall breeding in Dorchester County. *Maryland Birdlife* 12(3):86.

(74) Armistead, H.T. 1975. Breeding of greater black-backed gull, herring gull, and gadwall at Smith Island, Maryland. *Maryland Birdlife* 31(4):131-134.

(75) Armistead, H.T. 1970. First Maryland breeding of coot at Deal Island. *Maryland Birdlife* 26:79-81.

(76) Armistead, H.T. 1971. First Maryland breeding of green-winged teal. *Maryland Birdlife* 27(3):111-114.

(77) Austin, O.L., Jr. 1932. The breeding of the blue-winged teal in Maryland. *Auk* 49:191-198.

(78) Armistead, H.T. 1977. American oystercatcher and herring gull breed in Dorchester County. *Maryland Birdlife* 33(3):111-112.

(79) Armistead, H.T. 1976. Black skimmers in Dorchester County. *Maryland Birdlife* 32(4):87.

501

(80) Armistead, H.T. 1968. Wilson's phalarope at Fairmount Wildlife Management Area. *Maryland Birdlife* 24(4):108-109.

(81) Bond, G. and R.E. Stewart. 1951. A new swamp sparrow from the Maryland Coastal Plain. *Wilson Bulletin* 63:38-40.

(82) Meanley, B. 1975. Birds and marshes of the Chesapeake Bay Country. Tidewater Publishers, Cambridge, MD. 157 p.

(83) Brown, M. L. and R. G. Brown. 1984. Herbaceous Plants of Maryland. Port City Press, Baltimore, MD. 1,127 p.

(84) Tatnall, R. R. 1946. Flora of Delaware and the Eastern Shore. The Society of Natural History of Delaware. 313 p.

(85) Gilman, E.M. 1957. Grasses of the Tidewater-Piedmont region of Northern Virginia and Maryland. *Castanea* 22(1):1-105.

(86) Fernald, M. L. 1950. Gray's manual of botany. Van Nostrand Reinhold Company, New York, NY. 1,632 p.

(87) Sipple, W.S. and R.H. Wheeler. 1974. On the presence of three vascular plants, *Melothria pendula, Carex extensa*, and *Aneilema keisak*, in Maryland. *Chesapeake Science* 15:173-174.

(88) Sipple, W.S. 1991. Through the eyes of a young naturalist. Gateway Press, Baltimore, MD. 204 p.

(89) Wheery, E.T. 1948. The wild flower guide. Doubleday & Company, Inc. and the American Garden Guild, Inc. 202 p.

CHAPTER FOUR

(1) Tiner, R. W., Jr. and David G. Burke. 1995. Wetlands of Maryland. U.S. Fish and Wildlife Service, Ecological Services, Region 5, Hadley, MA and Department of Natural Resources, Annapolis, MD. Cooperative publication. 193 p.

(2) Wass, M.L. and T.D. Wright. 1969. Coastal wetlands of Virginia: An interim report to the Governor and General Assembly. Virginian Institute of Marine Science. Special Report in Applied Marine Science and Ocean Engineering Number 10. 152 p.

(3) Higgins, E.A.T., R.D. Rappleye, and R.G. Brown. 1971. The flora and ecology of Assateague Island. University of Maryland, Agricultural Experiment Station, College

Park, MD. Bulletin A-172. 70 p.

(4) Dolan, R., B. Hayden, and J. Heywood. 1977. Atlas of environmental dynamics: Assateague Island National Seashore. U.S. Department of the Interior, National Park Service. Natural Resource Report No. 11. 40 p.

(5) Leatherman, S.P. 1988. Barrier island handbook. University of Maryland, Laboratory for Coastal Research. Coastal Publication Series. 92 p.

(6) Stevenson, J.C., L.G. Ward, and M.S.Kearney. 1986. Vertical accretion in marshes with varying rates of sea level rise. *In*: Wolfe (editor), Estuarine variability. Academic Press, Inc. New York, NY. p. 241-259.

(7) Darmody, R.G. 1975. Reconnaissance survey of the tidal marsh soils of Maryland. Master's Thesis, University of Maryland, College Park, MD. 181 p.

(8) Newman, W.S. and C.A. Munsart. 1968. Holocene geology of the Wachapreague Lagoon, Eastern Shore Peninsula, Virginia. *Marine Geology* 6:81-105.

(9) Field, M.E. and D.B. Duane. 1976. Post-Pleistocene history of the United States inner continental shelf: Significance to origin of barrier islands. *Geological Society of America Bulletin* 87: 691-702.

(10) Newman, W.S. and G.A. Rusnak. 1965. Holocene submergence of the Eastern Shore of Virginia. *Science* 148:1,464-1,466.

(11) Shideler, G.L., J.C. Ludwick, G.F. Oertel, and K. Finkelstein. 1984. Quaternary stratigraphic evolution of the southern Delmarva Peninsula coastal zone, Cape Charles, Virginia. *Geological Society of America Bulletin* 95:489-502.

(12) Kraft, J.C. 1971. A guide to the geology of Delaware's coastal environments. University of Delaware, College of Marine Studies, Newark, DE. Publication 2GL039. 220 p.

(13) Goettle, M.S. 1981. Geological development of the southern portion of Assateague Island, Virginia. *Northeastern Geology* 3(3-4):278-282.

(14) Metzgar, R.G. 1973. Wetlands in Maryland. Maryland Department of State Planning. Publication No. 157.

(15) McCormick, J. and H. Somes, Jr. 1982. Coastal wetlands of Maryland. Prepared for the Maryland Department of Natural Resources by Jack McCormick & Associates, a subsidiary of Wapora, Inc. 243 p.

(16) Cowardin, L.M., V. Carter, F.C. Golet, and E.T. LaRoe. 1979. Classification of wetlands and deepwater habitats of the United States. U.S. Department of the Interior,

Fish and Wildlife Service. FWS/OBS-79/31. 103 p.

(17) Daiber, F.C., L.L. Thornton, K.A. Bolster, T.G. Campbell, O.W. Crichton, G.L. Esposito, D.R. Jones, and J.M. Tyrawski. An atlas of Delaware's wetlands and estuarine resources. University of Delaware, College of Marine Studies, Newark, DE. Delaware Coastal Management Program Technical Report Number 2. 528 p.

(18) Siberhorne, G.M. and A.F. Harris. 1977. Accomack County tidal marsh inventory. Virginia Institute of Marine Science. Special Report No. 138 in Applied Marine Science and Ocean Engineering. 106 p.

(19) Moore, K.A. 1977. Northampton County tidal marsh inventory. Virginia Institute of Marine Science. Special Report No. 139 in Applied Marine Science and Ocean Engineering. 123 p.

(20) Truit, R.V. 1967. High winds......high tides: A chronicle of Maryland's coastal hurricanes. University of Maryland, Natural Resources Institute. Education Series No. 77. 35 p.

(21) Miller, W.R. and F.E. Egler. 1950. Vegetation of the Wequetequock-Pawcatuck tide-marshes, Connecticut. *Ecological Monographs*. 20:143-172.

(22) Tiner, R.W. 1993. Field guide to coastal wetland plants of the southeastern United States. University of Amherst Press, Amherst, MA. 328 p.

(23) Teal, J. and M. Teal. 1969. Life and death of the salt marsh. National Audubon Society and Ballantine Books, Inc., New York, NY. 274 p.

(24) Sipple, W.S. and H. Cassell. 1974. Comparative distribution and abundance of three mollusks, *Littorina irrorata*, *Melampus bidentatus*, and *Modiolus demissus*, in relation to vascular plants and tidal inundation in two marshes at Sinepuxent Bay, Maryland. Maryland Department of Natural Resources, Wetlands Section, Annapolis, MD. (22-page unpublished report)

(25) Teal, J.M. 1958. Distribution of fiddler crabs in Georgia salt marshes. *Ecology* 39(2):185-193.

(26) Miller, D.C. 1961. The feeding mechanism of fiddler crabs, with ecological considerations of feeding adaptations. *Zoologica* 46:89-100.

(27) Engel, D.W. 1973. The radiation sensitivities of three species of fiddler crabs (*Uca pugilator*, *U. pugnax*, and *U. minax*). *Chesapeake Science* 14(4):279-280.

(28) Lippson, A.J. and R.L. Lippson. 1984. Life in the Chesapeake Bay. The Johns Hopkins University Press, Baltimore, MD. 229 p.

(29) Russell-Hunter, W.D., M.L. Apley, and R.D. Hunter. 1972. Early life-history of *Melampus* and the significance of semilunar synchrony. *Biological Bulletin* 143 (3):623-656.

(30) Kuensler, E.J. 1961. Phosphorus budget of a mussel population. *Limnology and Oceanography* 6:400-414.

(31) Keefe, C.W. and W.R. Boynton. 1973. Standing crop of salt marshes surrounding Chincoteague Bay, Maryland-Virginia. *Chesapeake Science* 14(2):117-123.

(32) Hill, S.R. 1986. An annotated checklist of the vascular flora of Assateague Island (Maryland and Virginia). *Castanea* 51(4):265-305.

(33) Klotz, L.H. 1986. The vascular flora of Wallops Island and Wallops mainland, Virginia. *Castanea* 51(4):306-326.

(34) Sipple, W.S. 1985. Peat analysis for coastal wetland enforcement cases. *Wetlands* 5:147-154.

CHAPTER FIVE

(1) Mansueti, R. 1950. Extinct and vanishing mammals of Maryland and District of Columbia. *Maryland Naturalist* 20 (1-2):3-48.

(2) Redmond, P. J. 1932. A flora of Worcester County Maryland. Doctoral Dissertation, The Catholic University of America, Washington, DC. Contribution No. 11. 107 p.

(3) Williams, J. P. 1992. Exploring the Chesapeake in small boats. Tidewater Publishers, Centreville, MD. 190 p.

(4) Kensey, C. C. 1967. The Pocomoke River. 18 p. (published by the author).

(5) Shreve, F., M.A. Chrysler, F.H. Blodgett, and F.W. Besley. 1910. The plant life of Maryland. The Johns Hopkins Press, Baltimore, MD. 533 p.

(6) Beaven, G. F. 1936. A study of the flora of the Pocomoke River Swamp on the Eastern Shore of Maryland. Master's Thesis, Duke University. 60 p.

(7) Beaven, G. F. and H. J. Oosting. 1939. Pocomoke swamp: A study of a cypress swamp on the Eastern Shore of Maryland. *Bulletin Torrey Botanical Club* 66(6): 367-389.

(8) Mansueti, R, 1953. A brief natural history of the Pocomoke River, Maryland. Maryland Department of Research and Education, Chesapeake Biological Laboratory,

Solomons, MD. 9 p.

(9) Footner, H. 1944. Rivers of the Eastern Shore: Seventeen Maryland rivers. Farrar & Rinehart, Inc. New York, NY. 375 p.

(10) Goodwin, R. H. and W. A. Niering. 1975. Inland wetlands of the United States. U.S. Department of the Interior, National Park Service. Natural History Theme Studies Number Two. 550 p.

(11) Thomas, B. 1976. The swamp. W. W. Norton & Company, Inc., New York, NY. 223 p.

(12) Stalter, R. 1981. Some ecological observations of *Taxodium distichum* (L.) Richard, in Delaware. *Castanea* 46(2):154-161.

(13) Anonymous. 1797. "Answers to sundry queries relative to the Indian River, or Cypress Swamps, in the Delaware State, in a letter to Thomas McKean, esq. from a citizen of the said state." In *Delaware History* 3(3):123-137, with an introduction by F. M. Jones.

(14) Dennis, J. V. 1986. The bald cypress in the Chesapeake Bay Region. *Atlantic Naturalist* 36:5-7.

(15) Dennis, J. V. 1988. The Great Cypress Swamps. Louisiana State University Press, Baton Rouge, LA. 142 p.

(16) Higgins, A. 1932. The swamp where they mined cypress. *Baltimore Sun*, April 3, 1932.

(17) Higgins, A. 1938. A guide to the first state. Viking Press, New York, NY.

(18) Canby, W. M. 1881. Notes. *Botanical Gazette* 6(9):270-271.

(19) Prenger, R. S. and T. B. Brooks (editors). 1991. The big tree champions of Maryland 1990. Maryland Department of Natural Resources, Forests, Parks, and Wildlife Service, Forestry Division. 119 p.

(20) Bartram, W. 1791. Travels through North and South Carolina, Georgia, East and West Florida, the Cherokee Country, the Extensive Territories of the Muscogulges, or Creek Confederacy, and the Country of the Choctaws. James & Johnson, Philadelphia, PA.

(21) Tidestrom, I. 1913. Notes on the flora of Maryland and Virginia, -- I. *Rhodora* 15(174):101-106.

(22) Taber, W. S. 1937. Delaware trees. State Forestry Department, Dover, DE.

(23) Dill, N. H., A. O. Tucker, N. E. Seyfried, and R. F. C. Naczi. 1987. Atlantic white cedar on the Delmarva Peninsula. *In*: Laderman (editor), Atlantic White Cedar Wetlands. p. 41-55.

(24) Laderman, A. D. (editior). 1987. Atlantic white cedar wetlands. Westview Press, Inc., Boulder, CO. 401 p.

(25) Nuttall, T. 1818. The genera of North American plants and a catalogue of the species to the year 1817. Vol. I & II. Printed for the author by D. Heartt.

(26) Pennell, F. W. 1936. Travels and scientific collections of Thomas Nuttall. *Bartonia* 18:1-51.

(27) Tatnall, R. R. 1940. Nuttall's plant collections in Southern Delaware. *Bartonia* 20:1-6.

(28) Marye, W. B. 1945. Some extinct wild animals of Tidewater. *Maryland Tidewater News* 2(1):1-3.

(29) Larson, J. S. 1966. Panthers in Maryland. *Maryland Conservationist* 18(4).

(30) Lee, D. S. 1984. Maryland's vanished birds and mammals: Reflections of ethics past. *In*: A. Norden, D. Forester, and G. Fenwick (editors), Threatened and endangered plants and animals of Maryland. p. 454-471.

(31) Norden, A. W., D. C. Forester, and G. H. Fenwick (editors). 1984. Threatened and endangered plants and animals of Maryland. Maryland Department of Natural Resources. Natural Heritage Program Special Publication 84-I. 475 p.

(32) Norwood, H. 1844. A voyage to Virginia in 1649. *In*: Peter Force, Collection of Historical Tracts. Vol. 3. Section 1. p. 3-50.

(33) Smith, H. M. and W. Palmer. 1888. Additions to the avifauna of Washington and vicinity. *Auk* 5(1):147-148.

(34) Kirkwood, F. C. 1895. A list of the birds of Maryland. *Transactions of the Maryland Academy of Science* 2:241-382.

(35) Meanley, B. 1987. Maryland's pioneer ornithologists. *Maryland Birdlife* 43(3):63-64.

(36) McKinley, D. 1979. History of the Carolina parakeet in Pennsylvania, New Jersey, Delaware, Maryland and the District of Columbia. *Maryland Birdlife* 35(1):3-10.

(37) Tatnall, R. R. 1946. Flora of Delaware and the Eastern Shore. The Society of Natural History of Delaware. 313 p.

507

(38) Teale, E. W. 1954. The wilderness world of John Muir with an introduction and interpretive comments by Edwin W. Teale. Houghton Mifflin Co., Boston, MA. 495 p.

(39) Audubon, M. R. 1897. Audubon and his journals, with zoological notes by Elliott Cues. Vol. II. Charles Scribner's Sons. 532 p. (Reprinted, 1972, by Peter Smith, Publishers, Inc., Magnolia, MA.).

(40) Thoreau, H. D. 1862. Walking. The Atlantic Monthly (June, 1862). *In*: Lyon (editor) This incomperable lande.

(41) Lyon, T, J. 1989. This incomperable lande: A book of American nature writing. Penguin Books. New York, NY. 495 p.

(42) Wright, A. H. 1932. The habitats and composition of the vegetation of Okefenokee Swamp, Georgia. *Ecological Monographs* 2(2):110-232.

(43) Meanley, B. 1950. Birds of the swamps. *Atlantic Naturalist* 5(3):105-111.

(44) Meanley, B. 1949. Pocomoke, a typical southern swamp in Maryland. *Atlantic Naturalist* 4(4):150-153.

(45) Taylor, J. W. 1965. The Pocomoke, Maryland's swamp wilderness. *Maryland Conservationist* 42(4):8-11.

(46) Shaw, S. P. and C. G. Fredine. 1956. Wetlands of the United States. U. S. Department of the Interior, Fish and Wildlife Service. Circular 39. 67 p.

(47) Murray, Rev. J. 1883. History of Pocomoke City, Formerly New Town, from its Origin to the Present Time. Curry, Clay & Company, Baltimore, MD.

(48) Broome, C. R., G. F. Frick, M. L. Brown, and J. L. Reveal. 1987. 1698 Maryland florula by the London apothecary James Petiver (*ca*. 1663-1718). *Huntia* 7:61-90.

(49) Brown, M. L., J. L. Reveal, C. R. Broome, and G. F. Frick. 1987. Comments on the vegetation of colonial Maryland. *Huntia* 7:247-283.

(50) Frick, G. F., J. L. Reveal, C. R. Broome, and M. L. Brown. 1987. Botanical explorations and discoveries in colonial Maryland, 1688 to 1753. *Huntia* 7:5-59.

(51) Reveal, J. L., C. R. Broome, M. L. Brown, and G. F. Frick. 1987. The identification of pre-1753 polynomials and collections of vascular plants from the British colony of Maryland. *Huntia* 7:91-208.

(52) Reveal, J. L., C. R. Broome, M. L. Brown, and G. F. Frick. 1987. On the identities of Maryland plants mentioned in the first two editions of Linnaeus' Species plantarum. *Huntia* 7:209-245.

508

(53) Reveal, J. L. G. F. Frick, C. R. Broome, and M. L. Brown. 1987. Botanical explorations and discoveries in colonial Maryland: An introduction. *Huntia* 7:1-3.

(54) Pennell, F. W. 1942. Botanical collectors of the Philadelphia local areas. *Bartonia* 21:38-57.

(55) McLean, E. P. 1992. John and William Bartram: Their importance to botany and horticulture. *Bartonia* 57:10-27.

(56) True, R. H. 1931. John Bartram's life and botanical excursions. *Bartonia* Special Issue -- 1931, An account of the two hundredth anniversary of the founding of the first botanic garden in the American colonies by John Bartram. p. 7-19.

(57) Pennell, F. W. 1943. Botanical collectors of the Philadelphia local area (concluded). *Bartonia* 22:10-31.

(58) Tucker, A. O. and N. H. Dill. 1989. Rafinesque's Florula Delawarica. *Bartonia* 55:4-14.

(59) Rafinesque, C. S. 1836. A life of travels and researches in North America and South Europe, or outlines of the life, travels and researches of C. S. Rafinesque, A.M.Ph.D. F. Turner, Philadelphia, PA. 148 p.

(60) Phillips, C. E. 1978. Wildflowers of Delmarva and the Eastern Shore. Delaware Nature Education Society, Hockessin, DE. 305 p.

(61) Canby, W. M. 1864. Notes of botanical visits to the lower part of Delaware and the Eastern Shore of Maryland. *Proceedings Academy of Natural Sciences of Philadelphia* 16:16-19.

(62) Rose, J. N. 1904. William M. Canby. *Botanical Gazette* 37(5):385-388.

(63) Smith, A. V. P. 1938. The ecological relations and plant successions in four drained millponds of the Eastern Shore of Maryland. Doctoral Dissertation. The Catholic University of America, Washington, DC. Biology Series No. 27. 36 p.

(64) Smith, A. V. P. 1939. Some noteworthy plants recently found in the Coastal Plain of Maryland and Delaware. *Rhodora* 41:111-112.

(65) Smith, A. V. P. 1940. Some plants recently found in the Coastal Plain of Maryland. *Rhodora* 42:277-280.

(66) Tucker, A. O. and N. H. Dill. 1993. The collections of Albert Commons on Delmarva, 1861-1901, with attention to August 4-5, 1874 and September 9-10, 1875. *Bartonia* 57, Supplement: 9-15.

(67) Otis, J. P. 1914. Notes from "The Eastern Shore." *Bartonia* 7:17-21.

(68) Williamson, C. S. 1909. Notes on the flora of Central and Southern Delaware. *Torreya* 9(8):160-168.

(69) Williamson, C. S. 1912. (reported on results of May, 18-19, 1912 Millsboro, DE field trip at May 23, 1912 Philadelphia Botanical Club meeting) *Bartonia* 5.

(70) Moldenke, H. N. 1945. A contribution to our knowledge of the wild and cultivated flora of Maryland -- I. *Torreya* 45(3):79-92.

(71) Moldenke, H. N. 1945. A contribution to our knowledge of the wild and cultivated flora of Delaware -- I. *Torreya* 45(4):106-109.

(72) Proctor, G. R. 1949. Notes on *Isoetes* in Maryland. *American Fern Journal* 39(3):86-87.

(73) Proctor, G. R. 1949. *Isoetes riparia* and its variants. *American Fern Journal* 39(4):110-121.

(74) Small, J. K. 1929. Peninsula Delmarva. *Journal of the New York Botanical Garden* 30(351):62-71.

(75) Wherry, E.T. 1949. *Trillium pusillum* in Maryland. *Bartonia* 25:71.

(76) Fernald, M. L. 1937. Local plants of the inner coastal plain of southeastern Virginia. *Rhodora* 39: 465-491.

(77) Harper, R. M. 1907. Centers of distribution of Coastal Plain plants. Presentation at December 11, 1906 meeting of the Torrey Botanical Club. *Science* 25(640):539-540.

(78) Harper, R. M. 1909. Car-window notes on the vegetation of the Delmarva Peninsula and southern Virginia. *Torreya* 9(11): 217-226.

(79) Britton, N. L. 1890. List of local floras. *Annals New York Academy of Sciences* 5:237-300.

(80) Harper, R. M. 1919. A forest reconnaissance of the Delmarva Peninsula. *Journal of Forestry* 17:546-555.

(81) Sipple, W. S. 1976. The carpenter frog (*Rana virgatipes*) in Caroline County, Maryland. *Bulletin of the Maryland Herpetological Society* 12(4):129-130.

(82) Sipple, W. S. and W. A. Klockner. 1984. Uncommon wetlands in the Coastal Plain of Maryland. *In*: Norden, Forester, and Fenwick (editors), Threatened and endangered plants and animals of Maryland. p. 111-138.

(83) Hirst, F. 1983. Field report on the Delmarva flora, I. *Bartonia* 49:59-68.

510

(84) Tyndall, R. W., K. A. McCarthy, J. C. Ludwig, and A. Rome. 1990. Vegetation of six Carolina Bays in Maryland. *Castanea* 55(1):1-21.

(85) Reed, C. F. 1953. The ferns and fern-allies of Maryland and Delaware including the District of Columbia. Reed Herbarium, Baltimore, MD. The Science Press, Lancaster, PA. 286 p.

(86) Reed, C. F. 1964. Orchidaceae of Maryland, Delaware and the District of Columbia. *Castanea* 29 (2):77-109.

(87) Brown, R. G. and M. L. Brown. 1972. Woody Plants of Maryland. Port City Press, Baltimore, MD. 347 p.

(88) Brown, M. L. and R. G. Brown. 1984. Herbaceous Plants of Maryland. Port City Press, Baltimore, MD. 1127 p.

(89) Redman, D. E. 1991. An annotated list of the ferns and fern allies of Maryland and the District of Columbia. *The Maryland Naturalist* 35(1-4):15-24.

(90) Hirst, F. 1990. Three new taxa for the Delmarva Peninsula. *Bartonia* 56:70-71.

(91) Naczi, R. F. C. 1984. Rare sedges discovered and rediscovered in Delaware. *Bartonia* 50:31-35.

(92) Naczi, R. F. C., R. J. Driskill, E. L. Pennell, N. E. Seyfried, A. O. Tucker, and N. H. Dill. 1986. New records of some rare Delmarva sedges. *Bartonia* 52:49-57.

(93) Reveal, J. L. and C. R. Broome. 1981. Minor nomenclatural and distributional notes on Maryland vascular plants with comments on the State's proposed endangered and threatened species. *Castanea* 46(1):50-82.

(94) Reveal, J. L. and C. R. Broome. 1982. Comments on Maryland's proposed endangered and threatened vascular plants. *Castanea* 47:191-200.

(95) Riefner, R. E. and S. R. Hill. 1983. Notes on infrequent and threatened plants of Maryland including new state records. *Castanea* 48(2):117-137.

(96) Sipple, W. S. 1978. An atlas of vascular plant species distribution maps for tidewater Maryland. Department of Natural Resources, Water Resources Administration, Wetlands Permit Section. Wetland Publication No. 1. 280 p.

(97) Maryland Department of State Planning. 1970. A catalogue of natural areas in Maryland. Publication No. 148. 108 p.

(98) Maryland Department of State Planning. Scenic Rivers in Maryland. Publication No. 161. 40 p.

(99) Maryland Department of State Planning and Smithsonian Institution. 1975. Compendium of natural features information. Volumes I and II.

(100) Smithsonian Institution. 1974. Natural areas of the Chesapeake Bay Region: Ecological priorities. Center for Natural Areas Ecology Program.

(101) Lawrence, S. 1984. The Audubon Society field guide to the natural places of the Mid-Atlantic states. Pantheon Books, New York, NY. 341 p.

(102) Bailey, 1977. Canoe trip through a cypress swamp. *Maryland Conservationist* 53(5):8-11.

(103) Metzgar, R. G. 1973. Wetlands in Maryland. Department of State Planning. Publication No. 157.

(104) McCormick, J. and H. A. Somes. 1982. The coastal wetlands of Maryland. Maryland Department of Natural Resources. 241 p.

(105) Tiner, 1987. Mid-Atlantic wetlands, a disappearing natural treasure. U. S. Fish and Wildlife Service and U. S. Environmental Protection Agency. 28 p.

(106) Tiner, R.W. and D.G. Burke. 1995. Wetlands of Maryland. U.S. Fish and Wildlife, Ecological Services, Region 5, Hadley, MA and Maryland Department of Natural Resources, Annapolis, MD. Cooperative publication. 193 p.

(107) Vojtech, P. 1992. The last undiscovered river. *Chesapeake Bay Magazine* 22(7):133-142.

(108) Musselman, L. J., D. L. Nickrent, and G. F. Levy. 1971. A contribution towards a vascular flora of the Great Dismal Swamp. *Rhodora* 79(818):240-268.

(109) Hamblin, S. T. 1984. Nassawango Creek, Maryland: A case study in habitat preservation by The Nature Conservancy. *In:* Norden, Forester, and Fenwick (editors), Threatened and endangered plants and animals of Maryland. p. 472-475.

(110) Stasz, J. 1983. Nassawango Creek Preserve plant list. (19-page unpublished list)

(111) Lee, D. S. 1987. The star-nosed mole on the Delmarva Peninsula: Zoogeographic and systematic problems of a boreal species in the south. *The Maryland Naturalist* 31(2):44-57.

(112) Stewart, R. E. and C. S. Robbins. 1958. Birds of Maryland and the District of Columbia. U. S. Department of the Interior, Bureau of Sport Fisheries and Wildlife. North American Fauna No. 62. 386 p.

512

(113) Paradiso, J. L. 1969. Mammals of Maryland. U. S. Department of the Interior, Bureau of Sport Fisheries and Wildlife. North American Fauna 66. 193 p.

(114) Richards, H. G. 1931. The subway tree -- A record of a Pleistocene cypress swamp in Philadelphia. *Bartonia* 13:1-6.

(115) Bernard, J.M. 1965. The status of *Taxodium distichum* (L.) Richard (bald cypress) in New Jersey. *Bulletin Torrey Botanical Club*. 92:305-307.

(116) Wise, E. S. 1988. Early records of *Tillandsia usneoides* L. on the Eastern Shore of Virginia. *Jeffersonia: A News Letter of Virginia Botany* 19 (1):8-9.

(117) Ewan, J. 1988. Benjamin Smith Barton's influence on Trans-Allegheny Natural History. *Bartonia* 54:28-38.

(118) Gounaris K.C. and I. Forseth. 1998. Secondary succession effects on biodiversity in Adkins Bog, Salisbury, Maryland. Abstract for Conservation of Biological Diversity: A key to the restoration of the Chesapeake Bay ecosystem and beyond, May 10-13, 1998. Annapolis, MD.

(119) Boone, D. D., G. H. Fenwick, and F. Hirst. 1984. The rediscovery of *Oyxpolis canbyi* on the Delmarva Peninsula. *Bartonia* 50:21-22.

(120) Skorepa, A. C. and A. W. Norden. 1984. The rare lichens of Maryland. *In*: Norden, Forester, and Fenwick (editors), Threatened and endangered plants and animals of Maryland. p. 57-73.

(121) Tidestrom, I. 1914. Notes on the flora of Maryland and Virginia, -- II. *Rhodora* 16(192):201-209.

(122) Fernald, M. L. 1950. Gray's manual of botany. Van Nostrand Reinhold Company, New York, NY. 1,632 p.

(123) Gleason, H. and A. Cronquist. 1991. Manual of vascular plants of northeastern United States and adjacent Canada. New York Botanical Garden, Bronx, New York, NY. 910 p.

(124) Brunton, D. F., D. M. Britton, and W. C. Taylor. 1994. *Isoetes hyemalis* sp. nov. (Isoetaceae):A new quillwort from the southeastern United States. *Castanea* 59(1):12-21.

(125) Lee, D. S. 1976. Aquatic zoogeography of Maryland. *Atlantic Naturalist* 31(4):147-158.

(126) Lee, D. S., A. W. Norden, C. R. Gilbert, and R. Franz. 1976. A list of the freshwater fishes of Maryland and Delaware. *Chesapeake Science* 17(3):204-211.

(127) Lee, D. S., A. W. Norden, and C. R. Gilbert. 1984. Endangered, threatened, and extirpated fishes of Maryland. *In*: Norden, Forester, and Fenwick (editors), Threatened and endangered plants and animals of Maryland. p. 287-328.

(128) McIninch, S. P. 1994. The freshwater fishes of the Delmarva Peninsula. Doctoral Dissertation. University of Maryland, Eastern Shore Campus. Princess Anne, MD.

(129) Robbins, C. R., R. M. Bailey, C. E. Bond, J. R. Brooker, E. A. Lachner, R. N. Lea, and W. B. Scott. 1991. Common and scientific names of fishes from the United States and Canada. American Fisheries Society. Special Publication 20. Bethesda, MD.

(130) Fales, J. H. 1984. The status of Maryland's less-common butterflies. *In*: A. Norden, D. Forester, and G. Fenwick (editors), Threatened and endangered plants and animals of Maryland. p. 273-280.

(131) Harris, H. S. 1975. Distributional survey (amphibia/reptilia): Maryland and the District of Columbia. *Bulletin of the Maryland Herpetological Society* 11(3):73-167.

(132) Grogan, W.L. and D.C. Forester. 1998. New records of the milk snake, *Lampropeltis triangulum*, from the Coastal Plain of the Delmarva Peninsula, with comments on the status of *L. t. temporalis*. *The Maryland Naturalist* 42(1-2):5-14.

(133) Conant, R. and J. T. Collins. 1991. A field guide to reptiles and amphibians of eastern and central North America. Houghton Mifflin Co., Boston, MA. 450 p.

(134) McCauley, R. H. 1943. Reptiles of Maryland and the District of Columbia. Hagerstown, MD. 194 p. (published by the author).

(135) Grogan, W. L. 1985. New distribution records for Maryland reptiles and amphibians. *Bulletin of the Maryland Herpetological Society* 21(2):74-75.

(136) Grogan, W. L. 1994. New herpetological distribution records from Maryland's Eastern Shore. *Bulletin of the Maryland Herpetological Society* 30(1):27-32.

(137) Conant, R. 1975. A field guide to reptiles and amphibians of eastern and central North America. Houghton Mifflin Co., Boston, MA. 429 p.

(138) Cooper, J. E. 1970. *Hyla femoralis* in Maryland, revisited. *Bulletin of the Maryland Herpetological Society* 6(1):14-15.

(139) Kelly, H. A., A. W. Davis, and H. C. Robertson. 1936. Snakes of Maryland. The Natural History Society of Maryland. 103 p.

(140) Cooper, J. E. 1966. Errata for Snakes of Maryland by H. A. Kelly, A. W. Davis, and H. C. Robertson, Natural History Society of Maryland, Baltimore, 1936. *Bulletin of the Maryland Herpetological Society* 2(3):1-4.

(141) Lee, D. S. 1972. List of amphibians and reptiles of Assateague Island. *Bulletin of the Maryland Herpetological Society* 8(4):90-95.

(142) Grogan, W. L. 1973. A northern pine snake, *Pituophis m. melanoleucus*, from Maryland. *Bulletin of the Maryland Herpetological Society* 9(2):27-30.

(143) Committee on Rare and Endangered Amphibians and Reptiles of Maryland, Natural History Society of Maryland. 1973. Endangered amphibians and reptiles of Maryland: A special report. *Bulletin of the Maryland Herpetological Society* 9(3): 42-99.

(144) Cooper, J. E. 1960. Distributional survey V of Maryland and the District of Columbia. *Bulletin of the Philadelphia Herpetological Society.* May-June: 18-24.

(145) Anderson, K. and H. G. Dowling. 1982. Geographic distribution: *Hyla gratiosa. Herpetological Review* 13(4):130.

(146) Arndt, R. G. and J. F. White. 1988. Geographic distribution: *Hyla gratiosa. Herpetological Review* 19(1):16.

(147) Conant, R. 1940. *Rana virgatipes* in Delaware. *Herpetologica* 1:176-177.

(148) Conant, R. 1947. The carpenter frog in Maryland. *The Maryland Naturalist* 17(4):72-73.

(149) Meanley, B. 1951. Carpenter frog, *Rana virgatipes*, on the Coastal Plain of Maryland. *Proceeding of the Biological Society of Washington* 64:59.

(150) Reed, C. F. 1957. *Rana virgatipes* in Southern Maryland, with notes upon its range from New Jersey to Georgia. *Herpetologica* 13:137-138.

(151) Reed, C. F. 1957. The carpenter frog in Worcester Co., Maryland. *Herpetologica* 13:276.

(152) Carter, W. R. and F. Speir. 1976. Memorandum to Michael Ports. Appendix C. *In*: Final Environmental Impact Statement for the Upper Choptank River Watershed. U.S. Department of Agriculture, Soil Conservation Service.

(153) Leonard, S. W. 1981. *Fimbristylis perpusilla* Harper in South Carolina. *Castanea* 46:341-342.

(154) Carlson, C. W. 1966. The Ocean City area and North Pocomoke Swamp. *Atlantic Naturalist* 21(2):69-77.

515

(155) Carlson, C. W. 1967. South Pocomoke, Worcester County, Maryland. *Atlantic Naturalist* 22(4):217-223.

(156) Meanley, B. 1949. Nesting warblers of the Pocomoke. *Atlantic Naturalist* 4(3):106.

(157) Heckscher, C. M. and C. L. Wilson. 1996. An avian inventory of the Great Cypress (North Pocomoke) Swamp: Preliminary determination of forest-dependent species composition, relative abundance and implications for conservation. A 70-page unpublished report submitted to the National Biological Service and Delaware Wild Lands, Inc. Delaware Natural Heritage Program, Delaware Division of Fish and Game, Dover, DE.

(158) Meanley, B. 1947. Swainson's warbler. *The Wood Thrush* 3(2):5-6.

(159) Norwood, J. d'Arcy. 1956. Audubon's firsts. *Atlantic Naturalist* 11(5):222-229.

(160) Stewart, R. E. and C. S. Robbins. 1947. Recent observations on Maryland birds. *Auk* 64(2):266-274.

(161) Meanley, B. 1950. Swainson's warbler on Coastal Plain of Maryland. *Wilson Bulletin* 62(2):93-94.

(162) Willis, E. 1954. Summary of Maryland nest records, 1954. *Maryland Birdlife* 10(2-3):34.

(163) Meanley, B. 1975. Birds and marshes of the Chesapeake Bay Country. Tidewater Publishers, Cambridge, MD. 157 p.

(164) Robbins, C. S. and D. D. Boone. 1984. Threatened breeding birds of Maryland. *In*: Norden, Forester and Fenwick (editors), Threatened and endangered plants and animals of Maryland. p. 363-389.

(165) Shock, D. T. 1991. Are there Swainson's Warblers in Delaware's Pocomoke Swamp? *Delmarva Ornithologist* 24:11-15.

(166) Meanley, B. 1969. Swainson warbler in the Dismal Swamp. *Atlantic Naturalist* 24(4):204-205.

(167) Meanley, B. 1971. Natural history of the Swainson's warbler. U. S. Department of the Interior, Bureau of Sport Fisheries and Wildlife. North American Fauna No. 69. 90 p.

(168) Robbins, C.S. and E.A.T. Blom (editors). 1996. Atlas of the breeding birds of Maryland and the District of Columbia. University of Pittsburgh Press, Pittsburgh, PA. 479 p.

(169) Heckscher, C.M. 1998. Notes on the occurrence of the prairie warbler (*Dendroica discolor*) in Hickory Point Swamp, Worcester County, Maryland. *The Maryland Naturalist* 42(1-2):15-16.

(170) Boone, D. D. 1982. A cedar waxwing nest in Worcester County, Maryland. *Maryland Birdlife* 38(1):28.

(171) Shoemaker, R.C. 1998. *Pfiesteria*: Crossing dark water. Gateway Press, Inc., Baltimore, MD. 350 p.

CHAPTER SIX

(1) Chesapeake Bay Foundation. 1996. Nanticoke River Watershed: Natural and cultural resources atlas. Chesapeake Bay Foundation, Annapolis, MD. (not paginated)

(2) Tiner, R. W., Jr. and David G. Burke. 1995. Wetlands of Maryland. U.S. Fish and Wildlife Service, Ecological Services, Region 5, Hadley, MA and Department of Natural Resources, Annapolis, MD. Cooperative publication. 193 p.

(3) Hedeen, R.A. 1982. Naturalist on the Nanticoke: The natural history of a river on Maryland's Eastern Shore. 170 p.

(4) Carlson, C.W. 1966. Elliott Island Marsh, Dorchester County, Maryland. *Atlantic Naturalist* 21(3):125-129.

(5) The Nature Conservancy. 1994. Preserving Maryland's natural heritage. *The Nature Conservancy News* 18(3):1, 5-6.

(6) Horton, T. and W.M. Eichbaum. 1991. Turning the tide: Saving the Chesapeake Bay. Island Press, Washington, DC. 324 p.

(7) Stevenson, J.C., L.G. Ward, M.S. Kearney, and T.E. Jordan. 1985. Sedimentary processes and sea level rise in tidal marsh systems of Chesapeake Bay. *In*: H.A. Groman, D.M. Burke, and J.A. Kusler, Proceedings of the Conference on Wetlands of the Chesapeake, April 9-11, 1985. p. 37-62.

(8) Otis, J. P. 1914. Notes from "The Eastern Shore." *Bartonia* 7:17-21.

(9) Teale, D.W. 1978. A walk through the year. Dodd, Mead & Company, New York, NY. 408 p.

(10) Smith, A. V. P. 1939. Some noteworthy plants recently found in the Coastal Plain of Maryland and Delaware. *Rhodora* 41:111-112.

(11) McAvoy, W.A. 1998. Native plant highlight: Goldenrod. *The Turk's Cap* 1(3):1. (Newsletter of the Delaware Native Plant Society.)

(12) Meanley, B. 1975. Birds and marshes of the Chesapeake Bay Country. Tidewater Publishers, Cambridge, MD. 157 p.

(13) Bond, G. and R.E. Stewart. 1951. A new swamp sparrow from the Maryland Coastal Plain. *Wilson Bulletin* 63:38-40.

(14) Perry, M.C. and A.S. Deller. 1994. Waterfowl population trends in the Chesapeake Bay area. *In*: P. Hill and S. Nelson (editors). Proceedings of a Conference Toward a Sustainable Coastal Watershed: The Chesapeake Experiment, June 1-3, 1994. Chesapeake Research Consortium Publication No. 149. p. 490-504.

CHAPTER SEVEN

(1) Stolt, MH and M.C. Rabenhorst. 1987. Carolina bays on the Eastern Shore of Maryland: II. Distribution and origin. *Soil Science Society of America Journal* 51:399-405.

(2) Richardson, C.J., R. Evans, and D. Carr. 1991. Pocosins: An ecosystem in transition. *In:* C.J. Richardson (editor), Pocosin wetlands. Hutchinson Ross Publishing Company, Stroudsburg, PA. p. 3-19.

(3) Tyndall, R.W., K.A. McCarthy, J.C. Ludwig, and A. Rome. 1990. Vegetation of six Carolina bays in Maryland. *Castanea* 55(1):1-21.

(4) Ross, T.E. 1987. A comprehensive bibliography of the Carolina bays literature. *The Journal of the Elisha Mitchell Scientific Society* 103(1):28-42.

(5) Sipple, W.S. 1976. The carpenter frog (*Rana virgatipes*) in Carolina County, Maryland. *Bulletin of the Maryland Herpetological Society* 12(4):129.

(6) Sipple, W.S. 1977. A tentative description of the vegetation and flora of some unique "pothole" wetlands on the Delmarva Peninsula. Maryland Department of Natural Resources, Wetland Permit Section. (8-page unpublished report)

(7) Sipple, W.S. and W.A. Klockner. 1984. Uncommon wetlands in the Coastal Plain of Maryland. *In*: Norden, Forester, and Fenwick (editors), Threatened and endangered plants and animals of Maryland. p. 111-138.

(8) Hirst, F. 1983. Field report on the Delmarva flora, I. *Bartonia* 49:59-68.

(9) Carter, W. R. and F. Speir. 1976. Memorandum to Michael Ports. Appendix C. *In*: Final Environmental Impact Statement for the Upper Choptank River Watershed. U.S. Department of Agriculture, Soil Conservation Service.

(10) Rasmunssen, W.C. 1958. Geology and hydrology of the "bays" and basins of Delaware. Doctoral Dissertation, Bryn Mawr College, Bryn Mawr, PA. 206 p.

(11) Stolt, M.H. 1986. Distribution, characterization, and origin of Delmarva bays on Maryland's Eastern Shore. Master's Thesis, University of Maryland, College Park, MD. 193 p.

(12) Stolt, M.H. and M.C. Rabenhorst. 1987. Carolina bays on the Eastern Shore of Maryland: I. Soil characterization and classification. *Soil Science Society of America Journal* 51:394-398.

(13) Shreve, F., M.A. Chrysler, F.H. Blodgett, and F.W. Besley. 1910. The plant life of Maryland. The Johns Hopkins Press, Baltimore, Maryland. 533 p.

(14) Tatnall, R. R. 1946. Flora of Delaware and the Eastern Shore. The Society of Natural History of Delaware. 313 p.

(15) Matthews, E.D. 1964. Soil survey of Caroline County, Maryland. U.S. Department of Agriculture, Soil Conservation Service. Series 1959, No. 33. 53 p.

(16) Johnson, D.W. 1942. Origin of the Carolina bays. Columbia University Press, New York, NY.

(17) Melton, F.A. and W. Schriever. 1933. The Carolina 'bays': Are they meteor scars? *Journal of Geology* 41:52-66.

(18) Prouty, W.F. 1952. Carolina bays and their origin. *Geological Society of America Bulletin* 63:167-224.

(19) Savage, H. 1982. The mysterious Carolina bays. University of South Carolina Press, Columbia, SC.

(20) Sharitz, R.R. and J.W. Gibbons. 1982. The ecology of southeastern shrub bogs (pocosins) and Carolina bays: A community profile. U.S. Department of the Interior, Fish and Wildlife Service, Washington, DC. FWS/OBS-82/04. 93 p.

(21) Schneider, R. 1992. Examination of the role of hydrology and geochemistry in maintaining rare plant communities of Coastal Plain ponds. A final report to The Nature Conservancy. (unpublished 51- page report)

(22) Hall, R.L. 1970. Soil survey of Wicomico County, Maryland. U.S. Department of Agriculture, Soil Conservation Service. 90 p.

(23) Matthews, E.D. and R.L. Hall. 1966. Soil survey of Somerset County, Maryland. U.S. Department of Agriculture, Soil Conservation Service. 90 p.

(24) Bliley, D.J. and D.E. Pettry. 1979. Carolina bays on the Eastern Shore of Virginia. *Soil Science Society of America Journal* 45:558-564.

(25) Pettry, D.E., J.H. Scott, Jr., and D.J. Bliley. 1979. Distribution and nature of Carolina bays on the Eastern Shore of Virginia. *Virginia Journal of Science* 30:3-9.

(26) Kuchler, A.W. 1964. Manual to accompany the map Potential Natural Vegetation of the Conterminous United States. American Geographical Society. Special Publication No. 36. 38 p. plus map legend descriptions.

(27) Cooley, G.D. 1997. The natural grasslands of Maryland. *Native News* 5(2): 11-13.

(28) Tyndall, R.W., K.A. McCarthy, J.C. Ludwig, and A. Rome. 1990. Vegetation of six Carolina bays in Maryland. *Castanea* 55(2):133-135.

(29) Fernald, M. L. 1950. Gray's manual of botany. Van Nostrand Reinhold Company, New York, NY. 1,632 p.

(30) Broome, C.R., A.O. Tucker, J.L. Reveal, and N.H. Dill. 1979. Rare and endangered vascular plant species in Maryland. U.S. Department of the Interior, Fish and Wildlife Service. 64 p.

(31) Hirst, F. 1990. Three new taxa for the Delmarva Peninsula. *Bartonia* 56:70-71.

(32) Boone, D. D., G. H. Fenwick, and F. Hirst. 1984. The rediscovery of *Oyxpolis canbyi* on the Delmarva Peninsula. *Bartonia* 50:21-22.

(33) Anderson, K. and H. G. Dowling. 1982. Geographic distribution: *Hyla gratiosa*. *Herpetological Review* 13(4):130.

(34) Arndt, R. G. and J. F. White. 1988. Geographic distribution: *Hyla gratiosa*. *Herpetological Review* 19(1):16.

(35) The Nature Conservancy. 1997. Delmarva bays: Saving an endangered habitat. *The Nature Conservancy News* 21(2):1,3-4.

(36) Phillips, P.J. and R.J. Shedlock. 1993. Hydrology and chemistry of groundwater and seasonal ponds in the Atlantic Coastal Plain in Delaware, USA. *Journal of Hydrology* 141:157-178.

(37) Williams, E. (editor). 1991. Mountains to marshes: The Nature Conservancy preserves in Maryland. The Nature Conservancy, Chevy Chase, MD. 51 p.

CHAPTER EIGHT

(1) Stedman's Medical Dictionary. 1976 (23rd edition). Williams & Wilkins, Baltimore, MD. 1,678 p.

(2) Goldberg, A.R. 1954. Introduction to Extracts from the Journal of Charles C. Plitt, (edited by GR. Fessenden). *Wild Flower* 30(4):83-85.

(3) Kolb, H. 1958. Botanizing in Anne Arundel County fifty years ago. *The Maryland Naturalist* 28(14):19-22.

(4) Fessenden, GR. (editor). 1954. Extracts from the Journal of Charles C. Plitt. *Wild Flower* 30(4):81, 85-90.

(5) Fessenden, GR. (editor). 1955. Extracts from the Journal of Charles C. Plitt. *Wild Flower* 31(1):5-13;31(2):35-39;31(3):48,53-59.

(6) Fessenden, GR. (editor). 1956. Extracts from the Journal of Charles C. Plitt. *Wild Flower* 32(3):44-47.

(7) Waters, C.E. 1905. The flora of a Sphagnum Bog. *Science,* July 7, 1905.

(8) Shreve, F., M.A. Chrysler, F.H. Blodgett, and F.W. Besley. 1910. The plant life of Maryland. The Johns Hopkins Press, Baltimore, MD. 533 p.

(9) Smith, A.V.P. 1938. The ecological relationships and plant successions in four drained millponds of the Eastern Shore of Maryland. Doctoral Dissertation. The Catholic University of America, Washington, D.C. Biology Series No. 27. 36 p.

(10) Kirby, R.M. and E.D. Matthews. 1973. Soil Survey of Anne Arundel County, Maryland. U.S. Department of Agriculture, Soil Conservation Service. 127 p.

(11) Rucker, C. 1992. A survey of the vascular flora of Anne Arundel County, Maryland. (not paginated)

(12) Sheridan, P. 1991. Noteworthy collections. *Castanea* 56(1):71-72.

(13) Maryland Natural Heritage Program. 1997. Ecologically significant areas in Anne Arundel and Prince Georges Counties: Sites newly identified and updated in 1997. Maryland Department of Natural Resources, Annapolis, MD. 97 p.

(14) Thomas, J. 1989. Swamp pink. Maryland Department of Natural Resources, Maryland Natural Heritage Program Bulletin No. 6. 2 p.

(15) Sipple, W.S. 1993. A new site for the swamp pink (*Helonias bullata*) in Maryland. *The Maryland Naturalist* 37(3-4):24-27.

(16) Hopkins, G.M. 1878. Atlas of fifteen miles around Baltimore including Anne Arundel County, Maryland. (Compiled, drawn and published by G.M. Hopkins, C.E. 320 Walnut Street, Philadelphia)

(17) Reed, C.F. 1953. The ferns and fern-allies of Maryland and Delaware including District of Columbia. Reed Herbarium, Baltimore, MD. The Science Press, Lancaster, PA. 286 p.

(18) Stieber, M.T. 1967. An annotated checklist of the vascular flora of Anne Arundel County, Maryland. Master's Thesis, Catholic University of America, Washington, D.C. 70 p.

(19) Stieber, M.T. 1971. The vascular flora of Anne Arundel County, Maryland: An annotated checklist. *Castanea* 36:263-312.

(20) Tatnall, R.R. 1946. Flora of Delaware and the Eastern Shore: An annotated list of the ferns and flowering plants of the peninsula of Delaware, Maryland and Virginia. The Society of Natural History of Delaware. 313 p.

(21) Tyndall, R.W. 1997. Chronology of a lost *Monotropsis odorata*. (2-page unpublished report)

(22) Sipple, W.S. 1977. Revised tentative floras of five Anne Arundel County bogs. Wetlands Permit Section, Water Resources Administration, Department of Natural Resources, Annapolis, MD. (7-page unpublished report).

(23) Sipple, W.S. 1977. A brief report on a recently discovered cedar swamp/savanna area in Anne Arundel County, Maryland. Department of Natural Resources, Water Resources Administration, Wetlands Permit Section, Annapolis, MD. (4-page unpublished report).

(24) Sipple, W.S. and W.A. Klockner. 1980. A unique wetland in Maryland. *Castanea* 45:60-69.

(25) Sipple, W.S. and W.A. Klockner. 1984. Uncommon wetlands in the Coastal Plain of Maryland. *In*: Norden, Forester, and Fenwick (editors), Threatened and endangered plants and animals of Maryland. p. 111-138.

(26) Whigham, D.F. 1981. An ecological comparison of 6 bog sites in Anne Arundel County, Maryland. Department of Natural Resources, Annapolis, MD.

(27) Hull, J.C. and D.F. Whigham. 1987. Vegetation patterns in six bogs and adjacent forested wetlands on the Inner Coastal Plain of Maryland. *In*: Laderman (editor), Atlantic white cedar wetlands. Westview Press, Inc., Boulder, CO. p.143-173.

(28) Larsen, JA 1982. Ecology of the northern bogs and conifer forests. Academic Press, New York, NY. 307 p.

(29) Glaser, P.H. 1987. The ecology of patterned boreal peatlands of northern Minnesota: A community profile. U.S. Department of the Interior, Fish and Wildlife Service. Biological Report 85(7.14).

(30) Whigham, D.F. and C.J. Richardson. 1988. Soil and plant chemistry of an Atlantic white cedar wetland on the Inner Coastal Plain of Maryland. *Canadian Journal of Botany* 66(3):568-576.

(31) Whigham. D.F. 1987. Water quality studies of six bogs on the Inner Coastal Plain in Maryland. *In*: Laderman (editor), Atlantic white cedar wetlands. Westview Press, Inc., Boulder, CO. p. 85-90.

(32) Richards, H. G. 1931. The subway tree -- A record of a Pleistocene cypress swamp in Philadelphia. *Bartonia* 13:1-6.

(33) Dennis, J. V. 1986. The bald cypress in the Chesapeake Bay Region. *Atlantic Naturalist* 36:5-7.

(34) Brown, R.G. and M.L. Brown. 1972. Woody plants of Maryland. Port City Press, Inc., Baltimore, MD. 347 p.

(35) Brown, R.G. and M.L. Brown. 1984. Herbaceous Plants of Maryland. Port City Press, Inc., Baltimore, MD. 1127.

(36) Sheridan, P., K. Underwood, R. Muller, J. Broersma-Cole, R. Cole, and J.R. Kibby. 1999. A census of Atlantic white cedar, *Chamaecyparis thyoides* (L.) B.S.P. on the Western Shore of Maryland. *In*: Shear, T.H. and K.O. Somerville (editors), Alantic white cedar: Ecology and management symposium, August 6-7, 1997. p. 61-65.

(37) Smithsonian Institution. 1974. Natural areas of the Chesapeake Bay Region: Ecological priorities. Center for Natural Areas Ecology Program.

(38) Broersma-Cole, J. 1984. A vegetational survey of Black Hole Creek bog, Anne Arundel County, Maryland. (30-page unpublished report)

(39) Department of State Planning. 1968. A catalog of natural areas in Maryland. Maryland Department of State Planning. Publication No. 148. 108 p.

523

(1) Sipple, W.S. 1978. An atlas of vascular plant species distribution maps for tidewater Maryland. Maryland Department of Natural Resources, Water Resources Administration, Wetland Permit Section, Annapolis, MD. Wetland Publication No. 1. 280 p.

(2) Fernald, M. L. 1950. Gray's manual of botany. Van Nostrand Reinhold Company, New York, NY. 1,632 p.

(3) Klots, A.B. 1951. A field guide to the butterflies. Houghton Mifflin Company, Boston, MA. 349 p.

(4) Shreve, F., M.A. Chrysler, F.H. Blodgett, and F.W. Besley. 1910. The plant life of Maryland. The Johns Hopkins Press, Baltimore, Maryland. 533 p.

(5) Smith, A. V. P. 1938. The ecological relations and plant successions in four drained millponds of the Eastern Shore of Maryland. Doctoral Dissertation. The Catholic University of America, Washington, DC. Biology Series No. 27. 36 p.

(6) Tatnall, R. R. 1940. Nuttall's plant collections in Southern Delaware. *Bartonia* 20:1-6.

(7) Sipple, W.S. and W.A. Klockner. 1980. A unique wetland in Maryland. *Castanea* 45:60-69.

(8) Teale, E.W. 1944. Exploring the insect world. Grosset & Dunlap Publishers, New York, NY. 240 p.

(9) Sipple, W.S. and R.H. Wheeler. 1974. On the presence of three vascular plants, *Melothria pendula*, *Carex extensa*, and *Aneilema keisak*, in Maryland. *Chesapeake Science* 15:173-174.

(10) Brown, M. L. and R. G. Brown. 1984. Herbaceous Plants of Maryland. Port City Press, Baltimore, MD. 1,127 p.

(11) Brown, R. G. and M. L. Brown. 1972. Woody Plants of Maryland. Port City Press, Baltimore, MD. 347 p.

(12) Sipple, W.S. 1982. Tidal wetlands of Maryland's Eastern Shore and coastal bays. Paper presented at Conference on Rare and Endangered Plants and Animals on the Delmarva Peninsula, June 12, 1982 at Delaware State College, Dover. 22 p.

(13) Radford, A.E., H.E. Ahles, and C.R. Bell. 1964. Manual of the vascular flora of the Carolinas. The University of North Carolina Press, Chapel Hill, NC. 1,183 p.

(14) Prenger, R. S. and T. B. Brooks (editors). 1991. The big tree champions of Maryland 1990. Maryland Department of Natural Resources, Forests, Parks, and Wildlife Service, Forestry Division. 119 p.

(15) Heckscher, C.M. 1998. Notes on the occurrence of the prairie warbler (*Dendroica discolor*) in Hickory Point Swamp, Worcester County, Maryland. *The Maryland Naturalist* 42(1-2):15-16.

CHAPTER TEN

(1) Meanley, B. 1950. Birds of the swamps. *Atlantic Naturalist* 5(3):105-111.

(2) Klein, R.D. 1979. Urbanization and stream water quality impairment. *Water Resources Bulletin* 15(4):948-963.

(3) Booth, D.B. and L.E. Reinfelt. 1993. Consequences of urbanization on aquatic systems -- measured effects, degradation thresholds and corrective strategies. *In*: Proceedings of watershed 93 conference, Alexandria, VA. p. 545-550.

(4) Schueler, T.R. 1994. The importance of imperviousness. *Watershed Protection Techniques* 1(1):3-5.

(5) Smith, R.L. 1966. Field biology and ecology. Harper & Row, Publishers, Inc., New York, NY. 686 p.

(6) Kilham, L. 1988. On watching birds. Chelsea Green Publishing Company, Chelsea, VT. 187 p.

(7) Peterson, A.M. 1947. Wild bird neighbors. Wilcox & Follett Company, Chicago, IL. 298 p.

(8) Dietz, L. 1957. Touch of wildness: A Maine woods journal. Holt, Rinehart and Winston, New York, NY. 220 p.

(9) Burroughs, J. 1919. The writings of John Burroughs. Volume XX: Field and study. Houghton Mifflin Company, New York, NY. 337 p.

(10) Burroughs, J. 1871. Wake robin. Hurd and Houghton, New York, NY. (Reprinted in The Complete Writings of John Burroughs, Volume I., Wm. H. Wise, New York, NY. 1924.)

(11) Burroughs, J. 1901. The writings of John Burroughs. Volume XIII: Far and Near. Houghton Mifflin Company, New York, NY. 288 p.

(12) Robbins, C.S., B. Bruun, and H.S. Zim. 1966. A guide to the field identification of birds of North American. Golden Press, New York, NY. 340 p.

(13) Leopold, L.B., M.G. Wolman, and J.P. Miller. 1964. Fluvial processes in geomorphology. W.H. Freeman and Company, San Francisco, CA. 522 p.

(14) Lotrich, V.A. 1973. Growth, production, and community composition of fishes inhabiting a first-, second-, and third-order streams of eastern Kentucky. *Ecological Monographs* 43(3): 377-397.

(15) Simmons, R. 1999. Associated flora of the Chapman shell-marl ravine forest. *Native News* 7(1): 6, 11-15.

(16) Robbins, C.S. and E.A.T. Blom (editors). 1996. Atlas of the breeding birds of Maryland and the District of Columbia. University of Pittsburgh Press, Pittsburgh, PA. 479 p.

(17) Tri-County Council for Southern Maryland and Charles County. 1985. The Zekiah Swamp, Charles County, Maryland: Summary of current information. A report submitted to the Department of Natural Resources, Coastal Resources Division. 66 p.

(18) Trenk, F.B. 1929. Sweet gum in Maryland: "A handbook for growers and users." University of Maryland, State Department of Forestry. 75 p.

(19) Shreve, F., M.A. Chrysler, F.H. Blodgett, and F.W. Besley. 1910. The plant life of Maryland. The Johns Hopkins Press, Baltimore, Maryland. 533 p.

(20) Metzgar, R.G. 1973. Wetlands in Maryland. Maryland Department of State Planning. Publication No. 157.

(21) Tiner, R. W., Jr. and David G. Burke. 1995. Wetlands of Maryland. U.S. Fish and Wildlife Service, Ecological Services, Region 5, Hadley, MA and Department of Natural Resources, Annapolis, MD. Cooperative publication. 193 p.

(22) Maryland Department of State Planning. 1970. Scenic Rivers in Maryland. Publication No. 161. 40 p.

(23) Maryland Department of State Planning and Smithsonian Institution. 1975. Compendium of natural features information. Volumes I and II.

(24) Sipple, W.S. and W.A. Klockner. 1984. Uncommon wetlands in the Coastal Plain of Maryland. *In*: Norden, Forester, and Fenwick (editors). Threatened and endangered plants and animals of Maryland. Maryland Department of Natural Resources. Natural Heritage Program Special Publication 84-I. p. 111-138.

(25) Taylor, J.W. 1954. The Wicomico River. *Atlantic Naturalist* 9(3):133-138.

(26) Smithsonian Institution. 1974. Natural areas of the Chesapeake Bay Region: Ecological priorities. Center for Natural Areas Ecology Program.

(27) Sheridan, P. 1991. Noteworthy collections. *Castanea* 56(1):71-72.

(28) Ryden, H. 1989. Lily pond: Four years with a family of beavers. William Morrow and Company, Inc., New York, NY. 256 p.

INDEX OF PLANT SCIENTIFIC NAMES
AND COMMON NAMES

Note: The numbers given correspond to the pages where either the common name or the scientific name of the taxon is used in the text. In some instances, such as with historic information and quotations, more than one scientific name is used for a taxon, in which case the scientific names are cross-referenced in the index.

Arethusa bulbosa (arethusa) 357, 359
Arisaema triphyllum (Jack-in-the-pulpit) 406
Arisaema sp. (Jack-in-the-pulpit) 465, 466
Aristida lanosa (woolly three-awn) 245, 249
Aristida tuberculosa (sea-beach three-awn) 69
Aristida virgata (wire grass) 249
Aronia arbutifolia (red chokeberry) 400, 420
        (Pyrus arbutifolia)
Aronia prunifolia (purple chokeberry) 410
        (Pyrus floribunda)
Arundinaria gigantea (giant cane) 242, 365, 376
Asclepias incarnata (swamp milkweed) 99, 389, 390, 409
Asclepias lanceolata (smooth orange milkweed) 235, 236, 253, 320
Asclepias rubra (red milkweed) 244, 245, 249
Asimina triloba (pawpaw) 415, 423, 459, 465, 466, 473
Aster novi-belgii (New York aster) 396
Aster subulatus (annual saltmarsh aster) 194
Aster tenuifolius (perennial saltmarsh aster) 163, 194, 293
Aster umbellatus (tall flat-topped white aster) 391
Aster sp. (aster) 420
Athyrium filix-femina (lady fern) 216, 410
Atriplex patula (orach) 194
Azolla caroliniana (mosquito fern) 245, 249
Baccharis halimifolia (hightide bush) 55, 146, 176, 190, 194
Bacopa innominata (mat-forming water-hyssop) 101, 227, 255
Bacopa monnieri (coastal water-hyssop) 69
Bartonia paniculata (twining bartonia) 382, 398, 399, 401
Bartonia virginica (yellow bartonia) 398
Bartonia sp. (bartonia) 379
Betula nigra (river birch) 452, 482, 484
Bidens bidentoides (Maryland bur-marigold) 390
Bidens bidentoides var. mariana (Maryland bur-marigold) 390
        (Bidens mariana)
Bidens coronata (tickseed sunflower) 249
Bidens discoidea (swamp beggar-ticks) 249, 320
Bidens frondosa (devil's beggar-ticks) 307
Bidens laevis (smooth beggar-ticks) 115, 293, 397
Bidens mariana (Maryland bur-marigold) 390
        (Bidens bidentoides var. mariana)

Bidens mitis (small-fruited beggarticks) 249, 399, 403
Bidens sp. (beggarticks) 113, 409, 420
Bignonia capreolata (crossvine) 240, 241, 242, 415
Boehmeria cylindrica (small-spike false nettle) 410, 420, 428
Boltonia asteroides (aster-like boltonia) 245, 249, 319, 320, 322
Borrichia frutescens (sea ox-eye) 55, 65
Brasenia schreberi (watershield) 336, 409, 411, 413, 420, 424
Cacalia atriplicifolia (pale indian-plantain) 282
Calamagrostis canadensis (bluejoint) 410
Calamagrostis cinnoides (Nuttall's small reed-grass) 403
Calla palustris (water arum) 359
Callitriche heterophylla (larger water-starwort) 344, 426, 441
Calopogon pulchellus (grass-pink) 244, 245, 426, 441
         (Calopogon tuberosus)
Calopogon tuberosus (grass-pink) 244, 245, 426, 441
         (Calapogon pulchellus)
Cardamine concatenata (cut-leaf toothwort) 466
Cardamine hirsuta (hairy bittercress) 455
Cardamine longii (Long's bittercress) 227, 245, 248, 249, 253, 255, 256, 283,
426, 429
Carex absconda (thicket sedge) 429
Carex aggregata (glomerate sedge) 85
Carex atlantica (eastern sedge) 286, 379
Carex barrattii (Barratt's sedge) 245, 250, 320, 379
Carex bromoides (brome-like sedge) 429
Carex bullata (button sedge) 319, 320, 382
Carex canescens (silvery sedge) 372, 374, 379, 399
Carex collinsii (Collins' sedge) 283
Carex comosa (bearded sedge) 397, 409, 425
Carex complanata (flattened sedge) 475
Carex digitalis (slender woodland sedge) 429
Carex exilis (coast sedge) 367, 377, 382
Carex extensa (long-bract sedge) 168
Carex festucacea (fescue sedge) 410
Carex folliculata (northern long sedge) 370, 410, 425
Carex gigantea (giant sedge) 249, 254, 320, 414, 415, 480
Carex glaucescens (southern waxy sedge) 245, 250, 415
Carex howei (Howe's sedge) 399, 475
Carex hyalinolepis (shoreline sedge) 101, 234, 250, 294, 295, 425, 426, 429

Carex intumescens (bladder sedge) 425
Carex joorii (cypress-swamp sedge) 245, 250, 254, 320, 415
Carex laevivaginata (smooth-sheath sedge) 425
Carex louisianica (Louisiana sedge) 250, 480
Carex lupuliformis (hop-like sedge) 254, 320, 414, 415, 480
Carex lupulina (hop sedge) 415
Carex lurida (shallow sedge) 410, 425
Carex stipata (stalk-grain sedge) 425
Carex stricta (tussock sedge) xviii, 234, 341, 409, 440
Carex tribuloides (blunt broom sedge) 415
Carex typhina (cat-tail sedge) 320
Carex venusta (dark green sedge) 245, 250
Carex vesicaria (inflated sedge) 250, 320, 378, 379, 381
Carex walteriana (Walter's sedge) 84, 304, 305, 308, 309, 316, 318
Carex sp. (sedge) 420
Carpinus caroliniana (American hornbeam) 475, 482
Carya pallida (pale hickory) 281
Cassandra sp. (leatherleaf) 335, 351, 354, 357, 364, 370, 372, 373, 374, 375, 376, 377, 378, 379, 382, 383, 386
    (Chamaedaphne calyculata)
Castanea pumila (chinquapin) 338
Ceanothus americanus (New Jersey tea) 281
Celtis occidentalis (hackberry) 422, 466
Cenchrus longispinus (field sandbur) 297
Cenchrus tribuloides (dune sandbur) 71
Centella erecta (coinleaf) 320
Centrosema virginianum (spurred butterfly-pea) 101, 245, 250
Cephalanthus occidentalis (common buttonbush) 32, 307, 316, 409, 412, 442, 449, 483
Ceratophyllum demersum (coontail) 293, 412, 420
Chamaecrista fasciculata var. macrosperma (marsh wild senna) 294
Chamaecyparis sphaeroides (Atlantic white cedar) 37, 204, 211, 215, 217, 223, 226, 232, 233, 234, 252, 253, 266, 288, 296, 349, 354, 356, 360, 361, 362, 363, 364, 365, 366, 368, 369, 370, 383, 403, 427, 429, 430
    (Chamaecyparis thyoides)
Chamaecyparis thyoides (Atlantic white cedar) 37, 204, 211, 215, 217, 223, 226, 232, 233, 234, 252, 253, 266, 288, 296, 349, 354, 356, 360, 361, 362, 363, 364, 365, 366, 368, 369, 370, 383, 403, 427, 429, 430
    (Chamaecyparis sphaeroides)

Chamaedaphne calyculata (leatherleaf) 335, 351, 354, 357, 364, 370, 372, 373, 374, 375, 376, 377, 378, 379, 382, 383, 386
  (Cassandra sp.)
Chasmanthium latifolium (indian side-oats) 296
Chasmanthium laxum (slender spikegrass) 293
Chelone glabra (white turtlehead) 397, 479
Chimaphila umbellata ssp. cisatlantica (common wintergreen) 283
Chionanthus virginicus (white fringetree) 410
Chrysopsis mariana (Maryland golden-aster) 338
Cichorium intybus (chicory) 170
Cicuta bulbifera (bulb-bearing water hemlock) 86, 418, 419, 420, 421
Cicuta maculata (spotted water hemlock) 33, 36
Cimicifuga racemosa (black bugbane) 282, 406
Cinna arundinacea (sweet wood-reed) 342, 392, 410, 478
Circaea lutetiana (broad-leaf enchanter's-nightshade) 406
Cladium mariscoides (twigrush) 84, 297, 305, 318, 367, 369, 372, 373, 374, 396, 399, 403
Claytonia virginica (narrow-leaf springbeauty) 459, 482
Clematis terniflora (Japanese virgin's-bower) 204
Clethra alnifolia (sweet-pepperbush) 213, 333, 341, 352, 370, 373, 376, 391, 394, 395, 399, 420, 428, 439, 449
Clitoria mariana (buttterfly pea) 255, 281, 355
Coelorachis rugosa (wrinkled jointgrass) 320, 405
Commelina virginica (Virginia dayflower) 296, 417, 480
Comptonia peregrina (sweet-fern) 338
Conium maculatum (poison-hemlock) 36
Coreopsis rosea (pink tickseed) 298, 320, 405
Cornus florida (flowering dogwood) 282, 394, 406, 465, 482
Crassula aquatica (pygmyweed) 227, 255
Crotalaria rotundifolia (rabbit-bells) 245, 250
Crotonopsis sp. (rushfoil) 286
Cuscuta gronovii (love dodder) 409
Cuscuta polygonorum (smartweed dodder) 413
Cuscuta sp. (dodder) 388, 420
Cynoglossum virginianum (wild comfrey) 282
Cyperus esculentus (chufa) 293, 294
Cyperus filicinus (slender flat sedge) 13, 293
Cyperus flavescens (yellow flat sedge) 163, 367
Cyperus retrofractus (rough cyperus) 245, 250

Echinodorus parvulus (burhead) 320
Elatine americana (American waterwort) 101, 227, 245, 250, 255, 256
Elatine minima (small waterwort) 101, 227, 255, 283, 286
Elatine sp. (waterwort) 390
Eleocharis albida (white spikerush) 250
Eleocharis ambigens (creeping spikerush) 293, 294
      (Eleocharis fallax)
Eleocharis equisetoides (knotted spikerush) 243, 244, 245, 250, 284, 399, 401
Eleocharis fallax (creeping spikerush) 293, 294
      (Eleocharis ambigens)
Eleocharis flavescens (pale spikerush) 368
Eleocharis melanocarpa (black-fruited spikerush) 283, 319, 320
Eleocharis obtusa (blunt spikerush) 410, 420
Eleocharis olivacea (green spikerush) 86, 284, 286, 367, 373, 377, 379, 396, 423
Eleocharis parvula (small spikerush) 13, 64, 65, 238, 293
Eleocharis quadrangulata (square-stem spikerush) 24, 69, 101, 319, 390, 401, 402, 405
Eleocharis robbinsii (Robbins' spikerush) 284, 319, 320, 396, 401, 405
Eleocharis rostellata (beaked spikerush) 367, 399
Eleocharis tortilis (twisted spikerush) 245, 250
Eleocharis tricostata (three-ribbed spikerush) 283
Eleocharis tuberculosa (long-tubercle spikerush) 243, 399
Eleocharis sp. (spikerush) 163
Elephantopus tomentosus (tabaccoweed) 245, 250
Elymus virginicus (Virginia wild rye) 426
Epifagus virginiana (beechdrops) 465
Epigaea repens (trailing-arbutus) 342, 455
Eragrostis hypnoides (teal love grass) 307, 320
Eragrostis refracta (meadow love grass) 246, 250
Erechtites hieraciifolia (fireweed) 406
Erianthus brevibarbis (short-bearded plumegrass) 168, 170, 321
      (Saccharum coarctatum)
Erianthus contortus (bent-awn plumegrass) 246, 250
Erianthus giganteus (giant plumegrass) 84, 169, 304, 305, 308, 418
Eriocaulon aquaticum (seven-angled pipewort) 282, 284, 286
Eriocaulon compressum (flattened pipewort) 246, 250, 253, 282, 320, 336, 399

Eriocaulon compressum var. compressum (flattened pipewort) 407
Eriocaulon decangulare (ten-angled pipewort) 335
Eriocaulon parkeri (Parker's pipewort) 227, 246, 250, 253, 255, 256, 285, 286, 396
Eriocaulon sp. (pipewort) 372
Eriophorum virginicum (tawny cottongrass) 335, 354, 377, 382
Eryngium aquaticum (button snakeroot) 390
Erythronium umbilicatum (yellow trout-lily) 171, 459
Euonymus sp. (strawberry-bush) 466
Eupatorium leucolepis (white-bracted boneset) 246, 250, 399, 401
Eupatorium resinosum (pine-barrens boneset) 223
Euphorbia ipecacuanhae (American-ipecac) 287
Euphorbia polygonifolia (seaside broomspurge) 70
Fagus grandifolia (American beech) 282, 394, 460, 465, 466, 479, 482
Fimbristylis autumnalis (slender fimbristylis) 308
Fimbristylis perpusilla (Harper's fimbristylis) 84, 266, 267, 319, 320
Fraxinus pennsylvanica (green ash) 19, 21, 22, 37, 232, 296, 468
Fraxinus profunda (pumpkin ash) 249, 426
Fraxinus sp. (ash) 466
Fuirena pumila (smooth fuirena) 85, 246, 250, 286, 396
Fuirena squarrosa (hairy umbrella-sedge) 399
Galactia volubilis (downy milk pea) 246, 250
Galearis spectabilis (showy orchis) 282
Galium aparine (catchweed bedstraw) 465, 466
Galium sp. (bedstraw) 83, 235, 397, 406, 410, 465
Gaultheria procumbens (teaberry) 394
Gaylussacia brachycera (box huckleberry) 210, 211, 281, 298, 350, 351, 352
Gaylussacia frondosa (dangleberry) 399
Gentianopsis crinita (fringed gentian) 359
Glyceria acutiflora (short-scaled mannagrass) 320
Glyceria obtusa (blunt mannagrass) 351, 373, 379, 397, 399, 440
Gratiola virginiana (round-fruit hedge-hyssop) 216
Gymnopogon brevifolius (broad-leaved beardgrass) 246, 250
Habenaria blephariglottis (white-fringed orchid) 336, 337, 355, 367, 403
    (Platanthera blephariglottis)
Habenaria ciliaris (yellow-fringed orchid) 354, 355, 367, 369, 382, 403
    (Platanthera ciliaris)
Habenaria cristata (crested yellow orchid) 244, 283, 313, 336
    (Platanthera cristata)

Helenium flexuosum (purple sneezeweed) 411
 (Helenium nudiflorum)
Helenium nudiflorum (purple sneezeweed) 411
 (Helenium flexuosum)
Helianthemum bicknellii (hoary frostweed) 246, 250
Helianthemum sp. (frostweed) 297
Helonias bullata (swamp pink) 337, 339, 340, 341, 342, 343, 344, 345, 346, 359, 438, 455, 456
Hepatica americana (round-lobed hepatica) 282
Hibiscus moscheutos (swamp rose mallow) 13, 92, 97, 117, 123, 234, 238, 289, 293, 294, 388, 389, 390, 420
Hieracium gronovii (hairy hawkweed) 297
Hieracium sp. (hawkweed) 465
Hottonia inflata (featherfoil) 250, 319, 320
Hudsonia tomentosa (sand golden-heather) 69
Hydrangea arborescens (wild hydrangea) 465, 467
Hydrocotyle umbellata (many-flower marsh-pennywort) 397
Hydrocotyle verticillata (whorled marsh-pennywort) 480
Hydrophyllum virginianum (Virginia waterleaf) 464, 466
Hypericum adpressum (creeping St. John's-wort) 319, 320, 405
Hypericum canadense (Canadian St. John's-wort) 376, 379, 380, 397, 399
Hypericum densiflorum (bushy St. John's-wort) 319
Hypericum denticulatum (coppery St. John's-wort) 246, 250, 318, 320
Hypericum gentianoides (pineweed) 69, 295
Hypericum gymnanthum (clasping-leaf St. John's-wort) 246, 250
Hypericum mutilum (dwarf St. John's-wort) 388
Hypericum sp. (St. John's-wort) 83
Ilex decidua (deciduous holly) 474, 475, 480
Ilex glabra (inkberry) 212, 355, 393, 400
Ilex laevigata (smooth winterberry) 213, 393, 394, 300
Ilex opaca (American holly) 293, 393, 474, 482
Ilex verticillata (common winterberry) 394, 410, 420
Impatiens capensis (jewelweed) 15, 97, 122, 235, 337, 388, 391, 392, 410, 411, 455
Impatiens pallida (pale touch-me-not) 410
Iris prismatica (slender blue flag) 246, 250, 253, 320, 400
Iris verna (dwarf iris) 246, 250, 338, 339, 340
Iris versicolor (blue flag) 388
Iris virginica (Virginia blue flag) 480

Limosella australis (mudwort) 101, 227, 238, 255, 286, 389
(Limosella subulata)
Limosella subulata (mudwort) 101, 227, 238, 255, 286, 389
(Limosella australis)
Linaria canadensis (blue toadflax) 69
Linaria vulgaris (butter-and-eggs) 170
Lindera benzoin (spicebush) 346, 410, 466, 482
Linum floridanum (Florida yellow flax) 243, 244, 246, 250
Linum intercursum (sandplain flax) 246, 250
Liqidambar styraciflua (sweet gum) 233, 239, 296, 307, 308, 309, 316, 391,
394, 395, 406, 475, 482
Liriodendron tulipifera (tulip tree) 382, 394, 406, 435, 460, 466, 475, 482
Listera australis (southern twayblade) 255
Litsea aestivalis (pondspice) 266, 267, 320, 322
Lobelia boykinii (Boykin's lobelia) 320
Lobelia canbyi (Canby's lobelia) 240, 246, 251, 319, 320
Lobelia cardinalis (cardinal flower) 99, 236, 237, 294, 389, 396, 397, 409,
411, 437
Lobelia elongata (elongate lobelia) 169
Lonicera japonica (Japanese honeysuckle) 204, 239, 337, 391, 392, 406, 465,
482
Ludwigia decurrens (primrose-willow) 480
Ludwigia glandulosa (cylindrica-fruited seedbox) 251
Ludwigia hirtella (hairy ludwigia) 246, 251
Ludwigia palustris (marsh primrose-willow) 397, 420
Ludwigia sphaerocarpa (globe-fruit primrose-willow) 114, 308
Lupinus perennis (wild lupine) 246, 251, 288, 338, 339, 340, 346

Lycopodium appressum (southern bog club-moss) 335, 336, 400
Lycopodium inundatum (northern bog club-moss) 335
Lycopus amplectens (sessile-leaf water-horehound) 284, 400
Lycopus rubellus (stalked water-horehound) 480
Lycopus virginicus (Virginia water-horehound) 37
Lycopus sp. (water-horehound) 397
Lygodium palmatum (climbing fern) 246, 251, 337, 343, 344, 346, 348, 349,
359, 437, 452
Lyonia ligustrina (maleberry) 400
Lyonia nitida (hurray bush) 212
Lysimachia terrestris (swampcandles) 409

Lysimachia thyrsiflora (tufted loosestrife) 86, 418, 420
Lythrum lineare (saltmarsh loosestrife) 13, 238
Lythrum salicaria (purple loosestrife) 35, 94, 95, 96
Magnolia virginiana (sweetbay) 32, 37, 212, 214, 335, 346, 366, 370, 373, 377, 378, 380, 393, 427, 428, 430, 482
Maianthemum canadense (false lily-of-the-valley) 347
Marsilea quadrifolia (European water-fern) 336
Marsilea sp. (water fern) 333, 335
Mecardonia acuminata (erect water-hyssop) 246, 251, 254
Melica mutica (narrow melicgrass) 475
Menispermum canadense (Canadian moonseed) 406
Micranthemum micranthemoides (Nuttall's micranthemum) 101, 227, 246, 251, 253, 287
Mikania scandens (climbing hempweed) 397, 420
Mimulus alatus (sharp-wing monkey-flower) 479
Mimulus ringens (Allegheny monkey-flower) 411, 417
Mimulus sp. (monkey-flower) 83
Monotropa uniflora (indian pipe) 216
Monotropsis odorata (sweet pinesap) 359
Muhlenbergia torreyana (Torrey's dropseed) 84, 319, 320
Murdannia keisak (marsh dewflower) 98, 100, 416
     (Aneilema keisak)
Myosotis laxa (smaller forget-me-not) 397
Myosotis macrosperma (large-seeded forget-me-not) 85, 475
Myrica cerifera (wax myrtle) 69, 146, 400
Myrica pensylvanica (bayberry) 69
Myriophyllum humile (low water-milfoil) 251
Myriophyllum spicatum (Eurasian water-milfoil) 389
Najas gracillima (thread-like naiad) 101
Nelumbo lutea (American lotus) 97, 98, 99, 389
Nemophila aphylla (small-flowered baby-blue-eyes) 464, 466
Nuphar luteum (spatterdock) 19, 20, 21, 23, 31, 92, 95, 98, 99, 108, 112, 115, 123, 232, 388, 409, 420, 440, 483, 484
Nymphaea odorata (white water-lily) 21, 297, 336, 355, 356, 374, 377, 379, 396, 400, 403, 409
Nymphoides aquatica (larger floating-heart) 286, 320
Nymphoides cordata (floating-heart) 246, 251, 281, 320
Nyssa biflora (swamp tupelo) 32, 215, 217, 232, 240, 428
     (Nyssa sylvatica var. biflora)

Parthenocissus quinquefolia (Virginia creeper) 465
Paspalum dissectum (Walter's paspalum) 319, 321, 322, 405
Passiflora incarnata (purple passion flower) 284
Passiflora lutea (yellow passion flower) 85, 407
Peltandra virginica (arrow-arum) 13, 15, 16, 20, 32, 33, 83, 88, 89, 92, 97, 98, 106, 107, 110, 113, 114, 123, 131, 132, 233, 234, 293, 388, 389, 390, 420, 440, 483, 484
Penthorum sedoides (ditch-stonecrop) 411, 417, 479
Persea borbonia (red bay) 206, 207, 215, 217, 240, 251, 253, 255, 393, 425, 427, 429
Phragmites australis (common reed) 7, 15, 16, 90, 91, 93, 94, 113, 121, 123, 194, 243, 367, 388, 396, 400, 403
Phryma leptostachya (American lopseed) 282, 407
Phytolacca americana (common pokeweed) 170, 239, 391, 392, 406
Pilea fontana (coolwort) 410, 423
Pilea pumila (Canadian clearweed) 37
Pinus echinata (short-leaf pine) 225, 455
Pinus elliottii (slash pine) 212
Pinus rigida (pitch pine) 345, 376
Pinus serotina (pond pine) 214, 394, 400, 427, 429
Pinus strobus (eastern white pine) 358, 359
Pinus taeda (loblolly pine) 68, 139, 140, 141, 147, 214, 215, 335, 394, 395
Pinus virginiana (Virginia pine) 449
Plantago maritima (seaside plantain) 63
Platanthera blephariglottis (white fringed orchid) 336, 337, 355, 367, 403
    (Habenaria blephariglottis)
Platanthera ciliaris (yellow fringed orchid) 354, 355, 367, 369, 382, 403
    (Habenaria ciliaris)
Platanthera cristata (crested yellow orchid) 244, 283, 313, 336
    (Habenaria cristata)
Pluchea purpurascens (saltmarsh camphorweed) 13, 163, 194, 238, 293, 390
Podophyllum peltatum (May-apple) 282, 406, 466
Pogonia ophioglossoides (rose pogonia) 244, 247, 252, 336, 354, 355, 356, 357, 367, 380, 381, 400, 403
Polanisia dodecandra (clammyweed) 86, 419, 421
Polygala cruciata (cross-leaf milkwort) 246, 251, 320, 400
Polygala curtissii (Curtiss' milkwort) 480, 487
Polygala cymosa (tall pine-barrens milkwort) 321
Polygala ramosa (low pine-barrens milkwort) 321

Polygonatum biflorum (small Solomon's-seal) 338, 465
Polygonella articulata (coastal jointweed) 69
Polygonum arifolium (halberd-leaf tearthumb) 13, 33, 110, 122, 410, 420, 440
Polygonum punctatum (dotted smartweed) 115, 122, 293, 388, 390, 397
Polygonum robustius (stout smartweed) 246, 251
Polygonum sagittatum (arrow-leaf tearthumb) 13, 33, 110, 122, 410, 440
Polygonum virginianum (jumpseed) 406
Polygonum sp. (smartweed) 234, 305, 307, 337, 415, 420, 460
Polypodium polypodioides (resurrection fern) 241, 244
Polypodium virginianum (polypody fern) 465, 467
Polystichum acrostichoides (Christmas fern) 282, 465, 466
Pontederia cordata (pickerelweed) 13, 16, 21, 32, 33, 83, 88, 92, 96, 98, 106, 107, 108, 112, 132, 171, 233, 234, 390, 397
Populus heterophylla (swamp cottonwood) 223, 254, 392, 415, 476, 478
Potamogeton crispus (curly pondweed) 389
Potamogeton pusillus (slender pondweed) 246, 251
Potamogeton sp. (pondweed) 420, 483
Prenanthes autumnalis (slender rattlesnake-root) 246, 251
Proserpinaca pectinata (comb-leaf mermaidweed) 308
Prunus serotina (black cherry) 391
Psilocarya scirpoides (long-beaked baldrush) 246, 251, 284, 286, 308, 318, 321, 397
    (Rhynchospora scirpoides)
Pteridium aquilinum (bracken fern) 338, 393
Ptilimnium capillaceum (hair-like mock bishopweed) 13, 235, 238
Pycnanthemum setosum (awned mountain-mint) 246, 251
Pycnanthemum verticillatum (whorled mountain-mint) 297
Pyrus arbutifolia (red chokeberry) 400, 420
    (Aronia arbutifolia)
Pyrus floribunda (purple chokeberry) 410
    (Aronia prunifolia)
Quercus alba (white oak) 452
Quercus falcata (southern red oak) 293, 337, 482
Quercus falcata var. pogodaefolia (cherry-bark oak) 479
Quercus lyrata (overcup oak) 415, 417, 479, 480
Quercus michauxii (swamp chestnut oak) 293, 415, 475, 479
Quercus muehlenbergii (chinquapin oak) 86, 419, 422, 424, 460
Quercus nigra (water oak) 240, 243, 393

Quercus palustris (pin oak) 308, 475, 479
Quercus phellos (willow oak) 308, 475, 479
Quercus rubra (northern red oak) 282, 465, 466
Ranunculus flabellaris (yellow water-crowfoot) 251, 253, 319, 321
Ranunculus trichophyllus (white water-crowfoot) 86, 419
Rhexia aristosa (awned meadowbeauty) 298, 321, 397
Rhexia virginica (Virginia meadowbeauty) 297, 335, 376, 400, 403
Rhododendron atlanticum (dwarf azalea) 480
Rhododendron viscosum (swamp azalea) 213, 335, 345, 370, 394, 400, 428
Rhynchosia tomentosa (rhynchosia) 246, 251
Rhynchospora alba (white beakrush) 367, 369, 373, 375, 376, 377, 379, 381, 382, 400, 403
Rhynchospora cephalantha var. cephalantha (capitate beakrush) 321
Rhynchospora cephalantha var. microcephala (tiny-headed beakrush) 246, 251, 320, 321
        (Rhynchospora microcephala)
Rhynchospora chalarocephala (loose-head beakrush) 380, 396
Rhynchospora corniculata (short-bristled hornedrush) 252, 321, 415, 478, 480
Rhynchospora filifolia (thread-leaf beakrush) 251, 319, 321
Rhynchospora fusca (brown beakrush) 400, 407
Rhynchospora glomerata (clustered beakrush) 251, 281
Rhynchospora gracilenta (slender beakrush) 400, 401, 407
Rhynchospora harperi (Harper's beakrush) 321
Rhynchospora inundata (drowned hornedrush) 246, 251, 321
Rhynchospora knieskernii (Knieskern's beakrush) 223
Rhynchospora macrostachya (tall horned beakrush) 396
Rhynchospora microcephala (tiny-headed beakrush) 246, 251, 320, 321
        (Rhynchospora cephalantha var. microcephala)
Rhynchospora nitens (short-beaked baldrush) 321
Rhynchospora pallida (pale beakrush) 251
Rhynchospora rariflora (few-flowered beakrush) 246, 251
Rhynchospora scirpoides (long-beaked baldrush) 246, 251, 284, 286, 308, 318, 321, 397
        (Psilocarya scirpoides)
Rhynchospora torreyana (Torrey's beakrush) 246, 251
Rhynchospora sp. (beakrush) 396, 398
Riccia fluitans (aquatic liverwort) 33, 34, 420
Romalia stenopora (lichen) 254

Rosa multiflora (multiflora rose) 411
Rosa palustris (swamp rose) 235, 285, 397, 419, 483
Rotala ramosior (tooth-cup) 410, 413
Rubus sp. (blackberry) 239, 337, 391, 392, 488
Rudbeckia laciniata (cut-leaf coneflower) 388
Ruellia caroliniensis (Carolina wild-petunia) 487
Rumex verticillatus (swamp dock) 117, 390, 420
Rumex sp. (dock) 337
Sabatia difformis (two-formed pink) 321
Sabatia dodecandra (large marsh pink) 236
Sabatia stellaris (saltmarsh sabatia) 194, 195
Saccharum coarctatum (short-beard plumegrass) 168, 170, 321
        (Erianthus brevibarbis)
Sacciolepis striata (sacciolepis) 246, 251, 255, 256, 257
Sagittaria calycina (spongy lophotocarpus) 227, 255, 294
Sagittaria eatonii (Eaton's arrowhead) 286
Sagittaria engelmanniana (Engelmann's arrowhead) 247, 251, 319, 321, 397
Sagittaria falcata (scythe-fruited arrowhead) 235, 238
Sagittaria graminea (grass-leaf arrowhead) 286
Sagittaria latifolia (duck-potato) 33, 83, 106, 107, 108, 110, 115, 123, 238,
400, 440
Sagittaria latifolia var. latifolia (duck-potato) 410
Sagittaria latifolia var. pubescens (hairy duck-potatoe) 410
Sagittaria subulata (awl-leaf arrowhead) 101, 253, 389
Salicornia bigelovii (dwarf glasswort) 194
Salicornia europaea (slender glasswort) 48, 55, 65, 194
Salicornia virginica (woody glasswort) 194
Salix nigra (black willow) 63
Sambucus canadensis (American elderberry) 337
Samolus parviflorus (water pimpernel) 238
Sanguinaria canadensis (bloodroot) 282, 406, 466, 467
Saponaria officinalis (bouncing-bet) 170
Sarracenia flava (yellow pitcher-plant) 381
Sarracenia leucophylla (crimson pitcher-plant) 377, 381
Sarracenia purpurea (northern pitcher-plant) 242, 247, 251, 281, 333, 334,
335, 354, 355, 357, 364, 368, 373, 380, 381, 382, 384, 397, 481
Sarracenia purpurea ssp. purpurea (northern pitcher-plant) 253
Sarracenia rubra (sweet pitcher-plant) 381
Sassafras albidum (sassafras) 394

Saururus cernuus (lizard's-tail) 110, 217, 308, 410, 417, 428
Saxifraga virginiensis (Virginia saxifrage) 465, 467
Schizaea pusilla (curly-grass fern) 252, 266, 267
Scirpus americanus (Olney's three-square) 11, 24, 101, 123, 130, 132, 148, 149, 151, 162, 400
     (Scirpus olneyi)
Scirpus americanus (common three-square) 11, 64, 130, 151, 194, 238, 288, 400, 402
     (Scirpus pungens)
Scirpus cylindricus (New England bulrush) 101, 238, 387, 388
     (Scirpus maritimus var. fernaldii)
Scirpus cyperinus (woolgrass) 308
Scirpus etuberculatus (Canby's bulrush) 240, 243, 244, 247, 251, 284, 298
Scirpus fluviatilis (river bulrush) 387, 388, 389, 483
Scirpus maritimus var. fernaldii (New England bulrush) 101, 238, 387, 388
     (Scripus cylindricus)
Scirpus olneyi (Olney's three-square) 11, 24, 101, 123, 130, 132, 148, 149, 151, 162, 400
     (Scirpus americanus)
Scirpus pungens (common three-square) 11, 64, 130, 151, 194, 238, 288, 400, 402
     (Scirpus americanus)
Scirpus purshianus (weak-stalk bulrush) 424
Scirpus robustus (saltmarsh bulrush) 132, 238
Scirpus subterminalis (water clubrush) 284
Scirpus validus var. creber (softstem bulrush) 389
Scirpus sp. (bulrush) 92
Scleria minor (slender nutrush) 247, 251
Scleria nitida (shining nutrush) 247, 251
Scleria pauciflora (papillose nutrush) 247, 252
Scleria reticularis (reticulated nutrush) 247, 251, 319, 321, 322, 405
Scleria triglomerata (tall nutrush) 244, 247, 251
Sclerolepis uniflora (pink bog-button) 242, 244, 247, 251, 281, 319, 321
Scutellaria lateriflora (mad dog skullcap) 409
Scutellaria sp. (skullcap) 397
Sedum ternatum (woodland stonecrop) 465, 467
Selaginella apoda (meadow spike-moss) 293, 396, 400
Sesbania drummondii (Drummond's rattle-bush) 115
Sesuvium maritimum (sea-purslane) 65

Setaria geniculata (saltmarsh foxtail grass) 194
Silene caroliniana var. pensylvanica (wild pink) 287
Sisyrinchium arenicola (sand blue-eyed-grass) 247, 251
Sium suave (water-parsnip) 36, 235
Smilacina racemosa (false Solomon's-seal) 465, 466
Smilax glauca (glaucous greenbrier) 392
Smilax laurifolia (laurel-leaf greenbrier) 215, 216, 217, 241, 255, 287, 288, 397, 427
Smilax pseudochina (halberd-leaf greenbrier) 247, 251
Smilax rotundifolia (common greenbrier) 341, 342, 345, 352, 393, 395, 428, 439, 465, 488
Smilax walteri (red-berried greenbrier) 233, 240, 241, 247, 252, 283, 287, 288, 336, 354, 355, 370, 379, 395, 396, 414, 426
Solidago odora (anise-scented goldenrod) 247, 288
Solidago odora forma inodora (anise-scented golderrod) 288
Solidago puberula (downy goldenrod) 338
Solidago sempervirens (seaside goldenrod) 73, 74
Solidago speciosa (showy goldenrod) 247, 251
Solidago sp. (goldenrod) 337
Sparganium americanum (American bur-reed) 83, 440
Sparganium androcladum (branching bur-reed) 480
Sparganium eurycarpum (broad-fruited bur-reed) 164
Sparganium sp. (bur-reed) 114, 344, 396, 410, 483, 484
Spartina alterniflora (saltmarsh cordgrass) 10, 40, 41, 44, 45, 47, 48, 49, 51, 53, 55, 63, 116, 132, 146, 151, 176, 177, 179, 184, 186, 188, 189, 190, 192, 193, 194, 197, 238, 291, 313
Spartina cynosuroides (giant cordgrass) 115, 132, 234, 238, 290, 291, 390
Spartina patens (saltmeadow cordgrass) 13, 43, 44, 63, 132, 145, 146, 163, 187, 190, 194, 313
Spartina pectinata (prairie cordgrass) 169
Sphenopholis pensylvanica (swamp-oats) 426
        (Trisetum pensylvanicum)
Spiraea tomentosa (steeplebush) 400
Spiranthes cernua (nodding lady's tresses) 396
Spiranthes odorata (sweet-scented lady's tresses) 251
Spirodela polyrrhiza (greater duckweed) 34
Sporobolus clandestinus (rough rushgrass) 247, 252
Staphylea trifolia (American bladdernut) 465, 466, 467
Stylosanthes biflora (side-beak pencil-flower) 486, 487

548

Typha sp. (cattail) 114, 164, 234
Ulmus americana (American elm) 465, 466
Ulmus rubra (slippery elm) 283
Uniola paniculata (sea oats) 72
Urtica dioica (stinging nettle) 466
Usnea trichoda (lichen) 254
Utricularia biflora (two-flowered bladderwort) 397, 400, 401, 410, 413
Utricularia cornuta (horned bladderwort) 337
Utricularia fibrosa (fibrous bladderwort) 247, 252, 367, 400
Utricularia geminiscapa (hidden-fruit bladderwort) 379
Utricularia gibba (humped bladderwort) 351, 373, 374, 382, 400, 480
Utricularia inflata (swollen bladderwort) 247, 252, 321
Utricularia intermedia (flat-leaf bladderwort) 86, 418, 420
Utricularia juncea (rush bladderwort) 400
Utricularia macrorhiza (common bladderwort) 335
Utricularia purpurea (purple bladderwort) 244, 247, 252, 283, 319, 321, 322, 400, 401
Utricularia radiata (small floating bladderwort) 297
Utricularia resupinata (reversed bladderwort) 286
Utricularia vulgaris (common bladderwort) 400
Utricularia sp. (bladderwort) 367, 372, 377, 379, 378, 403
Uvularia sessilifolia (sessile-leaf merrybells) 342, 347, 439
Vaccinium corymbosum (highbush blueberry) 69, 213, 370, 373, 374, 394, 400, 420, 428, 482
Vaccinium macrocarpon (large cranberry) 354, 356, 357, 366, 367, 369, 372, 373, 374, 376, 380, 381, 382, 383, 403
Vernonia noveboracensis (New York ironweed) 400
Viburnum acerifolium (mapleleaf viburnum) 465
Viburnum nudum (possumhaw viburnum) 395
Viburnum prunifolium (black haw) 465, 474
Viburnum recognitum (northern arrow-wood) 32, 69, 391
Viola lanceolata (lance-leaf violet) 336
Viola primulifolia (primrose-leaf violet) 336
Viola striata (striped cream violet) 466, 467
Viola sp. (violet) 466
Vitis rotundifolia (muscadine grape) 394
Wolffia papulifera (water-meal) 352
Wolffia punctata (dotted water-meal) 247, 352
Woodwardia areolata (net-veined chain fern) 216, 345, 391, 428

INDEX OF ANIMAL SCIENTIFIC NAMES AND COMMON NAMES

Note: Page numbers indicate where either the common name or the scientific name of a taxon is used in the text. This is not, however, a complete list of animals cited, since a taxon is listed only if its scientific name occurs in the text. Birds are a good example of this, since scientific names for that group were seldom given. In some instances, such as with historic information and quotations, more than one scientific name is used for a taxon, in which case the scientific names are cross-referenced in the index.

Belostoma sp. (waterbug) 443, 472
Bison bison (American bison) 208
Botaurus lentiginosus (American bittern) 249
Bufo a. americanus (American toad) 124, 126, 260, 441
Bufo woodhousei fowleri (Fowler's toad) 69, 260, 324
Bufo sp. (toad) 486
Callinectes sapidus (blue crab) 57, 58, 174, 179, 188, 191
Cambarus diogenes (chimney crayfish) 123, 443
Campeloma sp. (a gilled snail) 472
Campephilus principalis (ivory-billed woodpecker) 209
Canis lupus (timber wolf) 208
Canis niger (red wolf) 208, 209
Carphophis a. amoenus (eastern worm snake) 126, 260
Castor canadensis (beaver) 84, 88, 208, 389, 423, 437,
    452, 460, 469, 477, 483, 484, 486, 487
Celastrina argiolus (spring azure) 485
Celithemis eponina (Halloween pennant) 408
Cemophora coccinea (scarlet snake) 262
Centropristis striata (black sea bass) 58, 188
Cervus canadensis (elk) 208
Cervus nippon (sika deer) 62, 86
Chelydra s. serpentina (common snapping turtle) 125, 261, 442, 448, 472
Chrysemys p. picta (eastern painted turtle) 125, 261, 442, 447, 472
Chrysemys rubriventris (red-bellied turtle) 125, 261, 293, 426
    (Pseudemys rubriventris)
Cicindela d. dorsalis (northeastern beach tiger bettle) 85
Circus cyaneus (northern harrier) 249
Clemmys guttata (spotted turtle) 125, 261, 438, 439, 452, 483
Cnemidophorus s. sexlineatus (six-lined racerunner) 126
Coluber c. constrictor (northern black racer) 260
Condylura cristata (star-nosed mole) 240
Conuropsis carolinensis (Carolina parakeet) 209
Crasssotrea virginica (American oyster) 56
Cynoscion nebulosus (sea trout) 179
Cynoscion regalis (weakfish) 58
Cyprinella analostana (satinfin shiner) 258
Cyprinus carpio (common carp) 126, 258
Danaus plexippus (monarch) 72, 73, 74, 294
Desmognathus f. fuscus (northern dusky salamander) 263

Littorina irrorata (gulf periwinkle) 41, 42, 43, 46, 55, 116, 176, 186, 189, 190, 191, 192, 197

Lutra canadensis (river otter) 46, 129, 153, 165, 176, 397, 423, 437, 453, 471

Lynx rufus (bobcat) 208

Macoma baltica (Baltic clam) 154

Malaclemys t. terrapin (northern diamonback terrapin) 46, 176, 191, 197

Melampus bidentatus (saltmarsh snail) 43, 46, 47, 116, 174, 176, 177, 190, 191, 192, 197

Melospiza georgiana nigrescens (swamp sparrow) 167

Menidia beryllina (inland silversides) 127

Menidia menidia (Atlantic silversides) 57, 58, 175

Menticirrhus saxatilis (kingfish) 179

Mercenaria mercenaria (hard clam) 56

Micropterus salmoides (largemouth bass) 126, 258

Microtus pennsylvanicus (meadow vole) 47, 166, 176, 462, 463

Mitoura hesseli (Hessel's hairstreak) 249, 259

Modiolus demissus (ribbed mussel) 41, 42, 46, 56, 116, 176, 189, 190, 191, 192

Morone americana (white perch) 126, 258

Morone saxatilis (striped bass) 126, 179, 258

Mustela vison (mink) 116, 129, 153, 165, 166, 438, 450, 451, 452, 460

Myocastor coypus (nutria) 147, 149, 150, 152, 153

Nannothemis bella (elfin skimmer) 408

Nassarius obsoletus (mud nassa) 46, 47, 174, 192, 193

Nereis sp. (polychaete worm) 59

Nerodia e. erythrogaster (red-bellied water snake) 85, 240, 260, 261, 262, 425

Nerodia s. sipedon (northern water snake) 124, 125, 260, 442, 472

Notemigonus chrysoleucas (golden shiner) 127, 258

Notophthalmus v. viridescens (red-spotted newt) 84, 324

Notropis hudsonius (spottail shiner) 127

Notropis procne (swallowtail shiner) 258

Noturus gyrinus (tadpole madtom) 258

Noturus insignis (margined madtom) 258

Nymphalis antiopa (mourning cloak) 455

Ocypode quadrata (ghost crab) 73, 74

Odocoileus virginianus (white-tailed deer) 62, 176, 456, 484

Ondatra zibethicus (muskrat) 65, 83, 85, 86, 88, 116, 117, 452, 474, 483

Ondatra z. macrodon (muskrat) 129, 130, 147, 148, 149, 150, 151, 152, 153

Ondatra z. zibethicus (muskrat) 12, 13, 163, 177

Opheodrys aestivus (rough green snake) 125 , 260, 442
Orhestria grillus (amphipod) 174
Oryzomys palustris (rice rat) 166, 176
Ovalipes ocellatus (lady crab) 75
Oxyloma effusa (amber snail) 123
Pachydiplax longipennis (blue dasher) 407, 408
Pagurus sp. (hermit crab) 60
Palaemonetes sp. (grass shrimp) 57, 58, 174
Papilio glaucus (tiger swallowtail) 389, 485
Papilio marcellus (zebra swallowtail) 472, 473, 485
Papilio palamedes (palamedes swallowtail) 248, 249, 259
Paralichthys dentatus (summer flounder) 58, 179, 188
Pelocoris sp. (creeping water bug) 472
Perca flavescens (yellow perch) 126, 258
Perithemis tenera (eastern amberwing) 408
Peromyscus maniculatus (deer mouse) 462
Pfiesteria piscicida (a dinoflagellate) 274
Phyciodes tharos (pearl crescent) 294
Physa sp. (tadpole snail) 123
Pisidium sp. (pill clam) 123
Pituophis m. melanoleucus (northern pine snake) 245, 247, 248, 249, 260, 261, 263, 264, 265, 267,
Plethodon c. cinereus (red-backed salamander) 260, 452
Podilymbus podiceps (pied-billed grebe) 247, 248, 249
Pogonias cromis (black drum) 179
Pomatromus saltatrix (bluefish) 58, 179
Pomoxis nigromaculatus (black crappie) 258
Popilius disjunctus (bessybug) 484
Popillia japonica (Japanese beetle) 389
Porthetria dispar (gypsy moth) 439, 453
Porzana carolina (sora) 249
Precis lavinia (buckeye) 294
Procyon lotor (raccoon) 46, 86, 88, 176, 437, 452, 460, 483
Pseudacris c. crucifier (northern spring peeper) 84, 124, 260, 324
        (Hyla c. crucifer)
Pseudacris triseriata feriarum (upland chorus frog) 124, 454, 472
Pseudacris triseriata kalmi (New Jersey chorus frog) 260, 324
Pseudemys rubriventris (red-bellied turtle) 125, 261, 293, 426
        (Chrysemys rubriventris)

556

Pseudotriton m. montanus (eastern mud salamander) 260

Rana catesbeiana (bullfrog) 124, 260, 324, 461

Rana clamitans melanota (green frog) 124, 126, 260, 324, 442, 472, 486

Rana palustris (pickerel frog) 124, 126, 260, 324, 436, 461, 472

Rana s. sylvatica (wood frog) 124, 126, 260, 324, 472

Rana u. utricularia (southern leopard frog) 124, 126, 260, 324, 442, 461, 472, 486

Rana virgatipes (carpenter frog) 84, 245, 247, 248, 249, 260, 261, 265, 302, 317, 323, 324, 463

Ranatra fusca (water scorpion) 83, 443, 444

Regina septemvittata (queen snake) 125

Satyrium kingi (King's hairstreak) 245, 247, 249, 259, 298

Satyrodes appalachia (Appalachian eyed brown) 415

Scaphiopus h. holbrooki (eastern spadefoot) 260, 283, 324

Sceloporus undulatus (northern fence swift) 126

Sceloporus undulatus hyacinthinus (northern fence swift) 260, 262

Scincella lateralis (ground skink) 260, 261
         (Leiolopisma laterale)

Sciurus carolinensis (eastern gray squirrel) 449

Selene volmer (lookdown) 75

Sesarme reticulata (purple marsh crab) 42, 43, 44

Sphoeroides maculatus (puffer) 58

Stenotherus odoratus (musk turtle) 125, 261, 262, 484

Sterna antillarum (least tern) 249

Storeria d. dekayi (northern brown snake) 260

Storeria o. occipitomaculata (northern red-bellied snake) 260

Strymon melinus (gray hairstreak) 294

Sylvilagus floridanus (cottontail rabbit) 86, 176

Sympetrum ambiguum (blue-faced meadowfly) 407, 408

Sympetrum vicinum (yellow-legged meadowfly) 407

Terrapene c. carolina (eastern box turtle) 126, 261, 439, 461, 472, 486

Tetragnatha sp. (longjawed spider) 124

Thamnophis s. sauritus (eastern ribbon snake) 125, 261

Thamnophis s. sirtalis (eastern garter snake) 261, 472

Tramea carolina (violet-masked glider) 407, 408

Tramea lacerata (black-mantled glider) 407

Tubifex tubifex (tubifex worm) 445

Uca pugilator (sand fiddler) 174, 190

Uca pugnax (mud fiddler) 41, 42, 43, 45, 46, 116